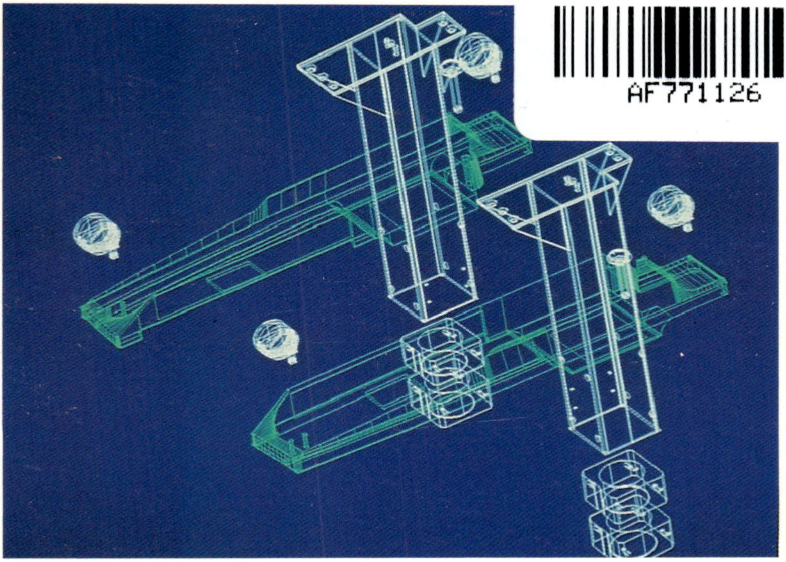

Wire-frame assembly drawing of mechanical part, created on Intergraph Corporation computer graphics system.

Sculptured surface model of automobile fender, with three views of fender cross sections. Created with Intergraph Corporation computer graphics system.

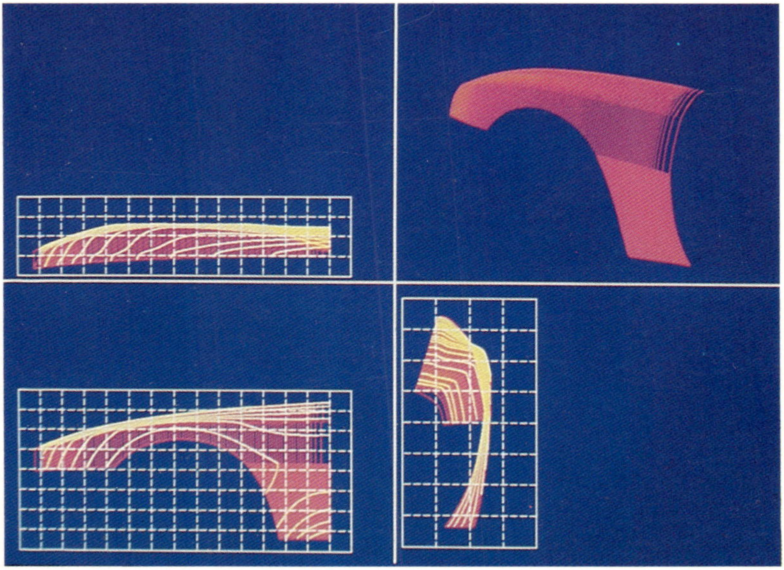

INTERACTIVE MICROCOMPUTER GRAPHICS

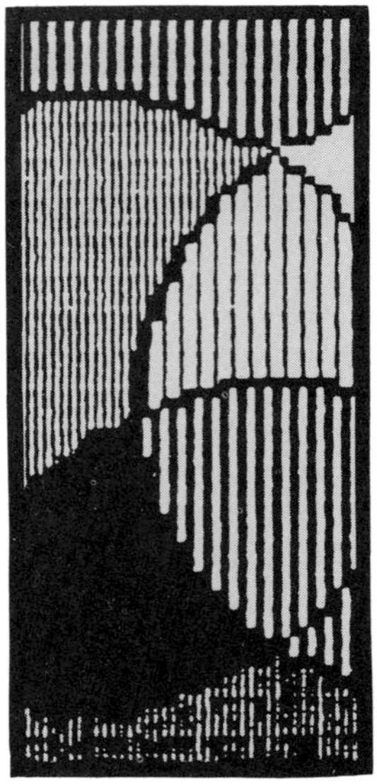

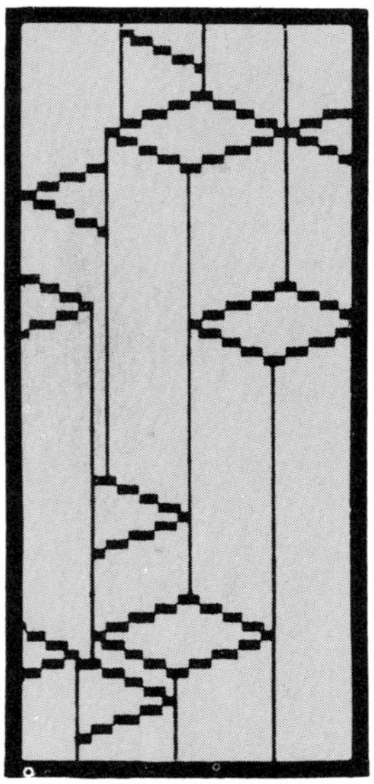

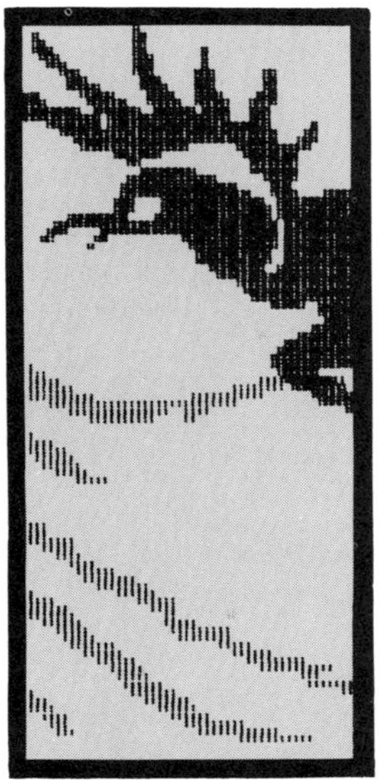

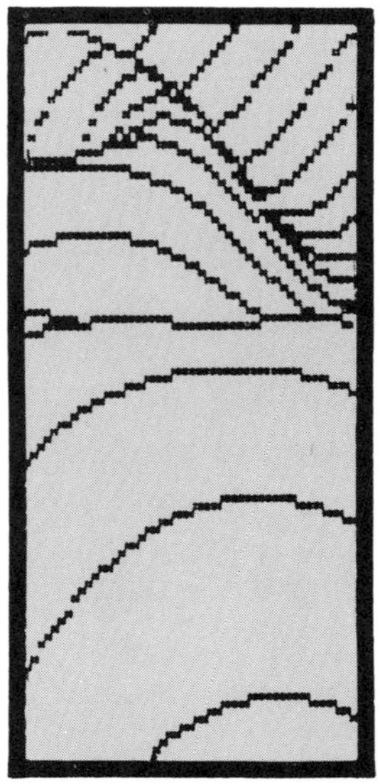

Addison-Wesley Publishing Company
Reading, Massachusetts ■ Menlo Park, California ■ Don Mills, Ontario
Wokingham, England ■ Amsterdam ■ Sydney ■ Singapore
Tokyo ■ Mexico City ■ Bogotá ■ Santiago ■ San Juan

INTERACTIVE MICROCOMPUTER GRAPHICS

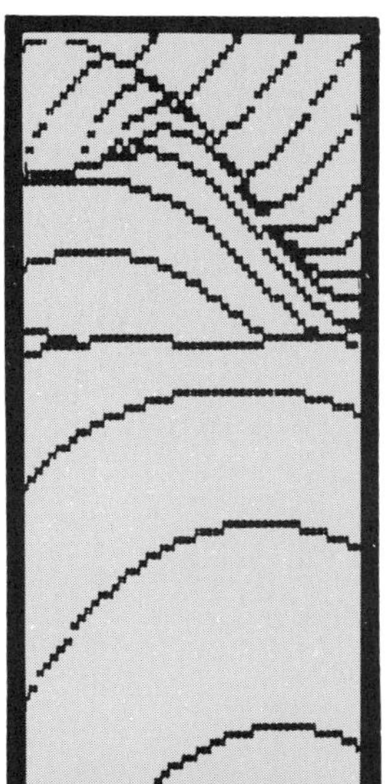

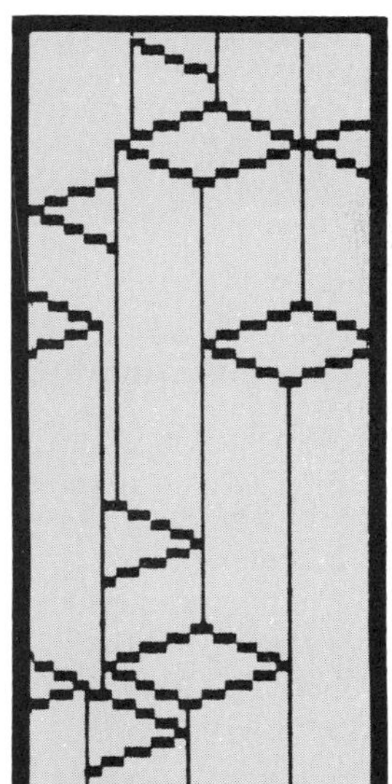

CHAN S. PARK Auburn University

To the memory of my father

Photographs on endpapers used by permission of Intergraph Corporation, Huntsville, Alabama.

Library of Congress Cataloging in Publication Data

Park, Chan S.
Interactive microcomputer graphics.

Includes index.
1. Computer graphics. 2. Interactive computer systems. I. Title.
T385.P37 1985 001.64'43 84-9207
ISBN 0-201-05541-4

ABCDEFGHIJK-DO-898765

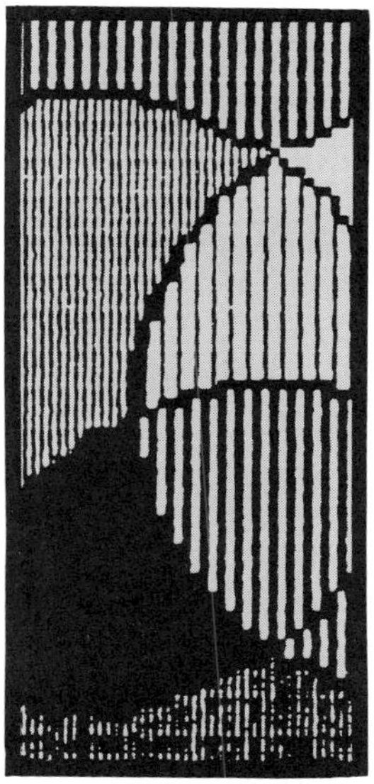

Preface

The area of computer graphics since its inception more than a decade ago has captured the imagination and technical interest of rapidly growing numbers of practicing engineers from many disciplines. In particular, interactive computer graphics has become an increasingly important aspect of computer-assisted management decisions. The enormous potential of computer graphics as an aid for making such decisions has been obvious, but it is only recently that the costs of the necessary equipment have begun to fall to a level at which the technique can be applied in business and engineering disciplines. The number and variety of applications continue to increase, and the growing availability of microcomputers will make the use of graphics increase even more rapidly in the future.

Computer graphics can provide the analyst with several benefits. It reduces the time required to interpret results, simplifies the communication of results to others, and enhances formal reports. Another benefit is that graphic output is much easier to use in decision making than is tabular output. Visual information is presented clearly. Differences between anticipated and actual figures are evident, and discrepancies in data become obvious.

Understanding the practical aspects of computer graphics with regard to both the theory and use of applications represents an essential and ultimate requirement in the development of computer graphics systems. The purpose of this book is to unify the various advances that have been made in the field and to present these in a manner understandable to management and practicing engineers. The uses of computers for graphics purposes in business and industrial applications are many and varied. It is the intent of this book to consider the mathematical components and programming techniques necessary to generate reasonable graphics images on a low-cost microcomputer. The programs provided are written in BASIC for use on the IBM PC; many can be adapted for use with other languages and microcomputers.

No attempt has been made to teach programming in BASIC. We assume that the reader is familiar with the language and has access to the IBM PC BASIC Reference Manual and the Disk Operating System (DOS) Manual (DOS 2.00 or higher version is recommended). The program examples are written to illustrate graphics techniques, not programming techniques. This approach, while appropriate for our purposes here, normally does not lead to the most efficient program. The experienced programmer will find ways to improve the execution time by writing more efficient programs.

The book's organization reflects the author's desire to provide the reader with a thorough understanding of the basic principles and techniques of microcomputer graphics. The reader can progress through a carefully designed sequence of chapters, starting with simple, generally applicable fundamentals and ending with the more complex and more specialized subjects. Toward this end we have arranged the book in four parts:

Part One: *Graphics Characteristics of the IBM PC.* Part One consists of two chapters that explore the capabilities of microcomputers for graphics applications. The IBM PC is used as the basis of discussion for creating computer graphics. We learn best by hands-on experience. Therefore, the graphics application programming is introduced in Chapter 2 in order to prepare readers at the earliest possible moment to write their own simple programs and thus deepen their understanding of the graphics capabilities of microcomputers.

Part Two: *Mathematical Elements for Computer Graphics.* Chapters 3 and 4 introduce the basic two-dimensional and three-dimensional geometrical transformations used in computer graphics. Chapter 5 presents algorithms by removing hidden edges and surfaces of 3-D objects. Our intention is to provide the reader with the mathematical foundation essential to the development of any graphics applications.

Part Three: *User Interface Design.* Part Three serves mainly to show how the basic concepts presented in Part Two can be utilized in the design of simple graphics packages. Because interaction is such a vital part of interactive graphics, we stress good program structures and screen layout designs. Through a sequence of progressive programming examples, we show how picture plotting and input handling can be integrated to achieve such a design.

Part Four: *Graphics Applications in Management Decision Making.* After having explored the various methods that provide us with tools to create graphics displays, we look at applications in greater detail. Three areas of applications are presented: forecasting systems, multiple regression analysis, and risk simulation.

This book may be used as a text for a variety of different introductory computer graphics courses: The only prerequisite is that the student have basic programming experience and have some knowledge of linear algebra. This book is also suitable as a supplementary text in more advanced computer programming courses or as a supplementary text in some engineering graphics and management science courses. Naturally, not all topics of interactive computer graphics are equally relevant to a reader, depending on the reader's interest. The same holds for the use of this book as a text. For computer graphics courses with programming orientation, instructors may concentrate on Chapters 3, 4, and 5. For computer graphics courses with application orientation, instructors may concentrate on Chapters 3, 4, 6, 7, 8, and 9. For management science courses with computer applications, instructors may elect to choose Chapters 11, 12, and 13.

ACKNOWLEDGMENTS

Many individuals contributed to the completion of this book. I am grateful to Alan J. S. Huang for his assistance in developing the computer programs in Parts Three and Four. Special thanks are due Amar Hammouche who developed the assembly language program in Section 2.4. I thank Dr. V. E. Unger for providing resources in support of this project. The expert editorial assistance provided by Mrs. Mary Joan Mykytka is gratefully acknowledged. I wish to extend my thanks to Dr. Gary Whitehouse who first got me interested in microcomputers. Finally my wife, Kim, deserves my special thanks for her continued support and encouragement throughout the project.

Auburn, Alabama **C.S.P.**
January 1985

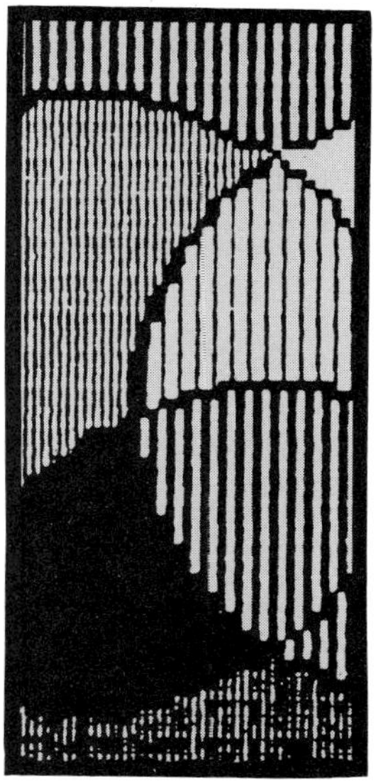

Contents

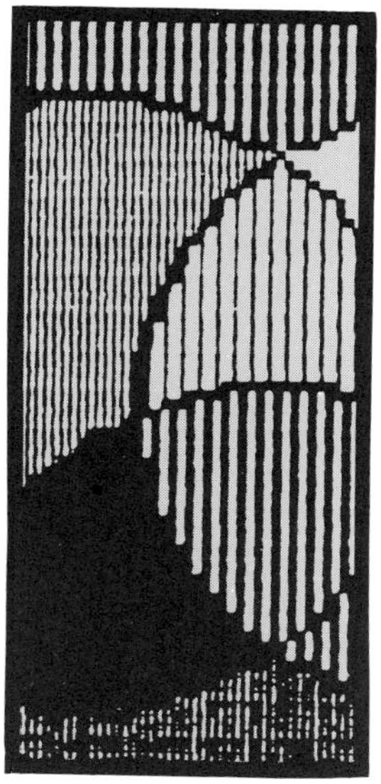

PART ONE
Graphics Characteristics of the IBM PC

The uses of microcomputers for graphics purposes are many and varied. The intent of this book is to present the mathematical components and programming techniques necessary for creating graphics images on a microcomputer. The IBM PC is used as the basis of discussion. In Part One, we will briefly introduce the subject of computer graphics with several examples that are familiar to most of our readers. In general, however, our exposition will be limited to the types of graphics commonly obtainable from a low-cost microcomputer. Then we will present an overview of the hardware characteristics of the IBM PC and its capability as a graphics device. A simple method of creating pictures will be presented through the use of special graphics commands available on the IBM PC. BASIC is chosen as the base language because its rich set of graphics commands allows convenient, straightforward representation of the programming examples. Transforming these control commands to equivalent code in structured languages such as Pascal is not difficult. Since no single set of graphics statements applies to all microcomputer systems, the users of other microcomputer systems may have to identify the corresponding graphics commands available on their system.

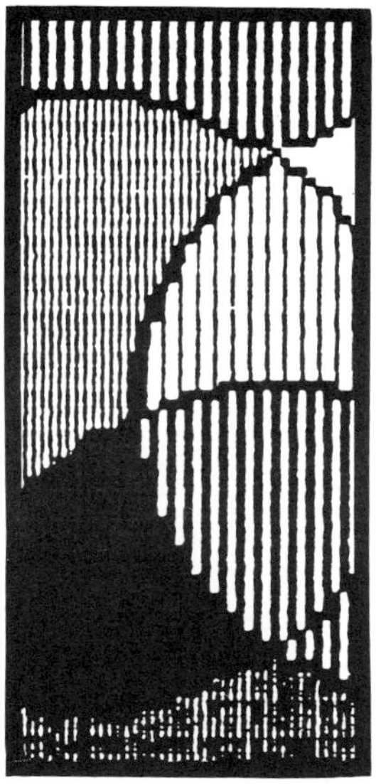

CHAPTER ONE
The Microcomputer and Its Graphics Capabilities

1.1 MICROCOMPUTER GRAPHICS APPLICATIONS

In computer graphics a computer and a graphics device are combined to form a medium by which a user manipulates visual information. The basic reason for using graphics, whether generated by computer or by hand, is that they convey more information to the user. The use of such information can increase productivity and provide more effective problem solving. Conceptual representation of all types of abstract and physical data is enhanced through graphic presentation.

Microcomputer graphics is used extensively in many different areas of industry, business, government, and education. We often classify graphics applications in terms of either visualization function or application area.

1.1.1 CLASSIFICATION BY VISUALIZATION FUNCTION

Burchi [1] breaks down computer graphics applications into the following visualization functions, or services, provided by computer graphics devices:

- Graphics display of computation results as they occur
- Replacement of paper as a drafting medium
- Rapid presentation of large quantities of information
- Observing and influencing change
- Visualization of nonexistent or unbuilt objects for the rapid study of design options

- Enhancement of interpretation or impact of data
- Visual communication between user and machine to replace alphanumeric communication
- Process simulation and verification before committing real resources
- Simulation of real-world scenes
- Graphic representation and observation of simulated theoretical models
- Creation of artistic designs
- Entertainment

In order to accommodate all types of visual functions, graphics devices and software routines come in various styles and packages. If drawings are going to be generated by means of the computer, the type of drawing will dictate the quality of the graphics devices. Computer-aided design or simulation of real-world scenes will require a CRT (Cathode Ray Tube) monitor of higher resolution, or even a complete graphics system. [The term "resolution," when applied to the graphics screen, refers to the number of blocks (called pixels) in the grid used for graphing. More blocks (higher resolution) produce sharper graphics images.] The complete graphics system will typically have a much higher resolution than that found in the many microcomputer monitors being used with small computer systems. Thus the microcomputer applications to such areas are currently limited, but they are growing as technology advances.

1.1.2 CLASSIFICATION BY APPLICATION AREA

Another way to look at graphics applications is in terms of application area. Most graphics applications exploit one or more of the visualization functions or services discussed above.

Scientific and statistical graphics. This group may include graphs and charts that can be used to represent statistical information or other numerical data. Two-dimensional (2-D) or three-dimensional (3-D) graphs of mathematical and economic functions, together with histograms, bar charts, and pie charts, are typical examples (see Fig. 1.1). All are used to present trends and patterns in data in a meaningful fashion to promote the understanding of complex phenomena.

Command and control. Typical examples in this category include those that are providing real-time information about the performance of a manufacturing operation, chemical process, or power distribution system. This type of graphics can improve the display of data recording and the subsequent analysis.

Computer-aided design (CAD). The replacement of paper as a drafting medium is one of the most commonly exploited advantages of a graphics sys-

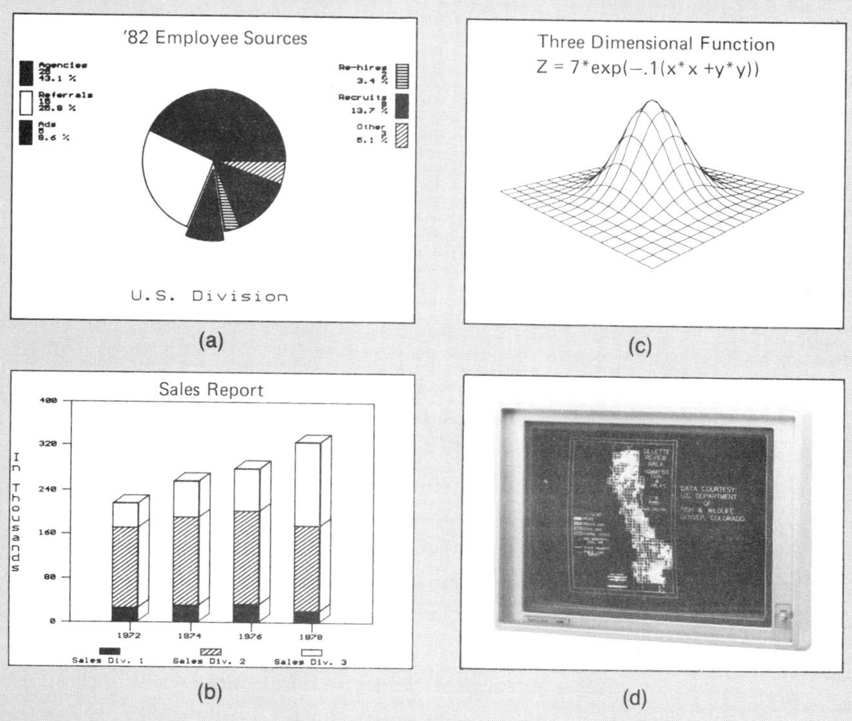

FIGURE 1.1 Scientific and statistical graphics: (a) pie chart, (b) bar chart, (c) 3-D function, and (d) computer mapping. Figures (a), (b), and (c) are obtained from the HP7470 Plotter driven by the IBM PC. Figure (d) is obtained from the Tektronix 4100 Series of computer display terminals. (Courtesy of Tektronix.)

tem. Applications in this category include designing mechanical, electrical, and electronic components, together with systems built up from such components. For example, the computer graphics systems available today are ideally suited to producing electrical schematic diagrams (see Fig. 1.2). Normally, high-performance graphics systems are used in such applications because they offer superior screen resolution.

Topological definition. This category includes program flowcharts, chemical and physical process diagrams, organization charts, electronic schematics, and other similar drawings. Many software packages available for microcomputers support this type of computer graphics for small business.

FIGURE 1.2 Computer-aided design: electronic schematic. (Courtesy of Tektronix.)

Geometric design. This category represents the most challenging segment of computer graphics. Not only does an object have to be represented in 3-D, but it usually has to be rotated to allow the user to observe different views of an object. This is required in applications that display structures (such as a bridge), curved surfaces, or even small mechanical parts. Usually applications in this category require a complete graphics system to support the high-speed display. Thus the microcomputer applications in this area are limited but growing (see Fig. 1.3).

Pictorial communication. Graphics in this category include textual material as well as pictures. News broadcasts using the teletext magazine format are good examples of this. The graphics enhance the readability of the material and highlight certain information. This same technique can be used to prepare technical documentation, especially material to be used in group discussions.

Graphic arts and animation. The microcomputer can be an innovative tool for artists and designers. Csuri [3] provides a survey of computer art, and

Musgrave [6] describes a color system that is used for creative design. Animation is frequently used in computer games (Fig. 1.4). Color graphics and animation are also often used in demonstrating processing operations, product assembly steps, and information routing.

1.2 THE IBM PERSONAL COMPUTER

Our intention is to use the IBM PC (or IBM PC-XT) as the basis of discussion for creating computer graphics. For this reason, it is worthwhile to review the basic hardware configuration needed to generate a graphics image.

1.2.1 COMPONENTS OF IBM PC

The IBM PC has two essential elements, a system unit and a keyboard. The system consists of a variety of optional devices including one or two 5-1/4 inch diskette drives with adapter (these can be housed inside the system unit), a monochrome display unit, a color display unit, a graphics printer, a printer

(a) (b) (c)

FIGURE 1.3 Geometric modeling: (a) This schematic of the body design has been defined as a separate segment, which can be stored in or recalled from local memory. Once it is stored locally, any display can be revised, then redrawn at about 150K mm/sec. (b) Repositioning scaling, or rotating this refresh segment requires only a single command from the host, rather than the usual string of commands. Result: a marked improvement in user interactivity and communications efficiency. (c) By using the local segments capability of the Tektronix 4114, this automobile schematic can be defined as one or more discrete graphic elements to be retained in the terminal's memory and redrawn by a simple command from the host computer. (Photographs courtesy of Tektronix.)

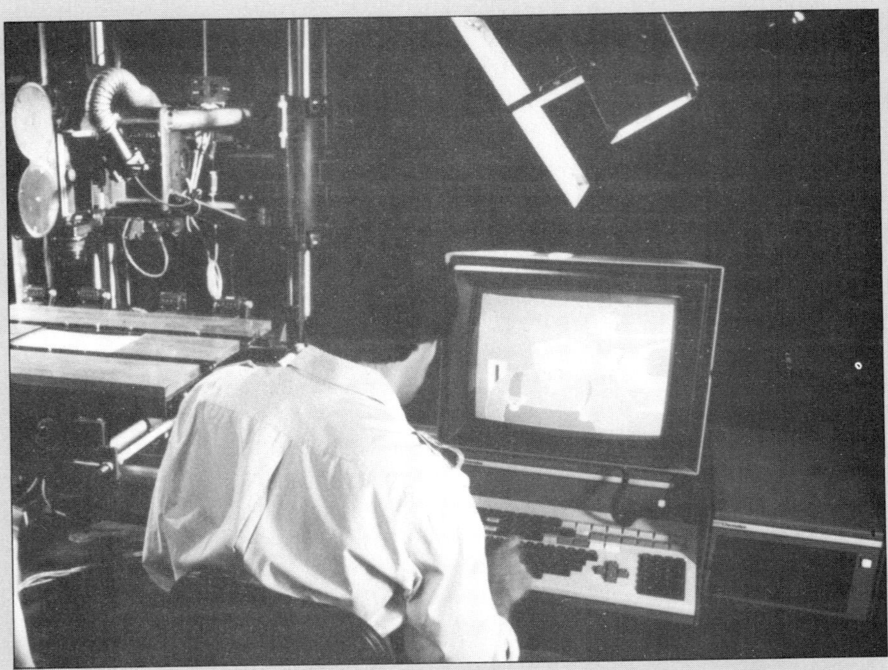

FIGURE 1.4 Graphic art and animation. (Photograph courtesy of Chromatics, Inc.)

adapter, a game control adapter, and storage additions in increments to 256K bytes (1K = 1024 bytes). A block diagram of the system is shown in Fig. 1.5.

System unit. The main computing block is called the system unit. Its board contains the central processing unit (CPU), 40K bytes of read-only memory (ROM) and 64K bytes of random-access memory (RAM). It also contains the electronics needed to drive a small speaker and an external audio cassette tape drive.

The microprocessor device is the 8088, designed by Intel. The 8088 uses 16-bit 8086 chips and can access memory at a speed of 4 MHz. While the 8088 retains all of the 8086's internal 16-bit computing capabilities, it communicates with external devices (such as ROM and RAM) via an 8-bit communications bus. Thus it is more than an 8-bit microprocessor but less than a 16-bit one.

Keyboard. The keyboard is attached to the system unit with a coiled cable. The keyboard features 83 keys and offers commonly used data and word processing functions in a design combining the familiar typewriter and calculator pad layouts. Overlaying the calculator-style ten-key pad are left, right, up, down, and home keys to control the screen's cursor movement. The layout of the keyboard is shown in Fig. 1.6.

Display units and adapters. One of the first choices to make is whether we want a color/graphics display. A different adapter and display unit are required

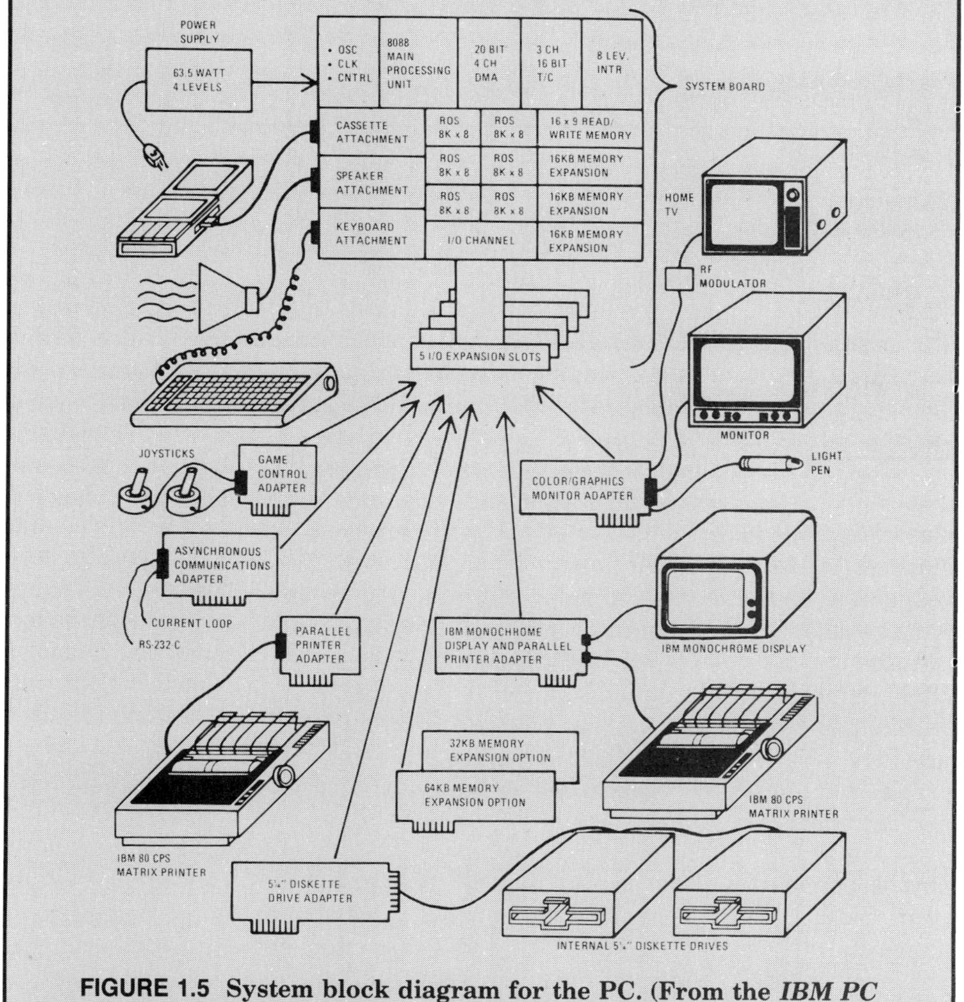

FIGURE 1.5 System block diagram for the PC. (From the *IBM PC Technical Reference Manual*. Used by permission.)

FIGURE 1.6 **Keyboard diagram of the IBM PC. (From the *IBM PC BASIC Reference Manual*. Used by permission.)**

for each. If our needs do not include color (or graphics) display, we can use a monochrome display unit with monochrome/parallel printer adapter. As its name indicates, it combines two functions in one: displaying and printing. The display portion drives a monochrome display unit; the printing portion drives a printer with parallel interface. The IBM monochrome display unit is a high resolution green phosphor display offering the quality usually found on expensive computer systems. The display features an $11\frac{1}{2}$-inch screen with a variety of highlighting choices. The screen displays 25 lines of 80 characters.

The IBM Color Display has a 13-inch CRT screen. It displays up to 16 colors and defines characters on an 8-high by 8-wide matrix. The display unit has the maximum video band width of 14 MHz; the screen is refreshed at 60 Hz with 200 vertical lines of resolution. It is basically a RGB type monitor—that is, red, green, and blue video signals and intensity are independent.

The color/graphics monitor adapter is intended to drive the color display, but also operates at standard television frequencies (15,750 Hz). Thus a variety of industry standard monitors can be attached, including home televisions with a user-supplied radio frequency (RF) modulator. In addition, the adapter provides a light-pen input port. Because of its important role in generating graphics images on the screen, we will discuss how the color/graphics adapter works in detail in a later section.

Graphics printer. The printer is a dot-matrix impact unit with a moving print head. It is connected to the parallel printer adapter (or monochrome display/parallel printer adapter). Up to 80 characters can be printed each second, and the print head can form characters while moving backward as well as forward. Several enhanced printing modes are available to provide normal, compressed, emphasized, double-strike, subscript, superscript, double width, and underline printing. This graphics printer also provides a variety of printer functions, graphics characters, and several bit-image graphics modes. This last feature permits the user to dump the graphics screen contents to the printer. As an option, the user may install the IBM PC Color Printer. It is a 35 to 200 character-per-second (cps) printer, and is capable of two-direction printing in several character sizes. There are three basic types of printing: data processing quality, text quality, and near-letter quality. With the use of control commands, this printer is able to blend a four-band ribbon (yellow, red, blue, and black) to produce seven colors, plus black. The printer also provides a high quality of bit-image graphics, allowing a color graphics screen dump from the color monitor.

The asynchronous communication adapter. The asynchronous communication adapter is the system's window to the serial communications world. Although intended for interfacing to the telephone network via a modem, this adapter can also be used to connect the system directly to a local serial printer terminal, or to a nearby graphics plotter.

Game control adapter. This adapter permits the attachment of user-supplied joysticks or paddles. Two joysticks and up to four paddles can be attached. Far from being mere computer game devices, analog hand controllers have serious applications in the field of graphic data analysis.

1.2.2 COMPONENTS OF IBM PC XT

The IBM PC XT model is basically the IBM PC model with a new, larger power supply and a fixed disk (or hard disk) system. The XT also has a slightly reworked and redesigned system board. The basic design and all of the major circuit chips remain the same. The base design features 128K RAM on the system board. One double-sided floppy disk drive and one 10-megabyte fixed disk drive are installed in the system unit. Also included are the disk and disk adapter cards and the asynchronous adapter, all of which take up three of the eight expansion slots on the XT. (The regular PC has only five slots.) A typical XT configuration is given in Fig. 1.7.

XT System unit. The XT's system board uses 64K RAM chips instead of the 16K chips that were standard on the original PC, allowing 256K memory without an expansion card. The XT allows expansion of the internal memory to 640K, with available memory cards adding as much as 384K RAM. The cassette port on the PC has been dropped for the XT model. A "color trimmer capacitor" has been added for adjusting the RGB (red, green, blue) color output.

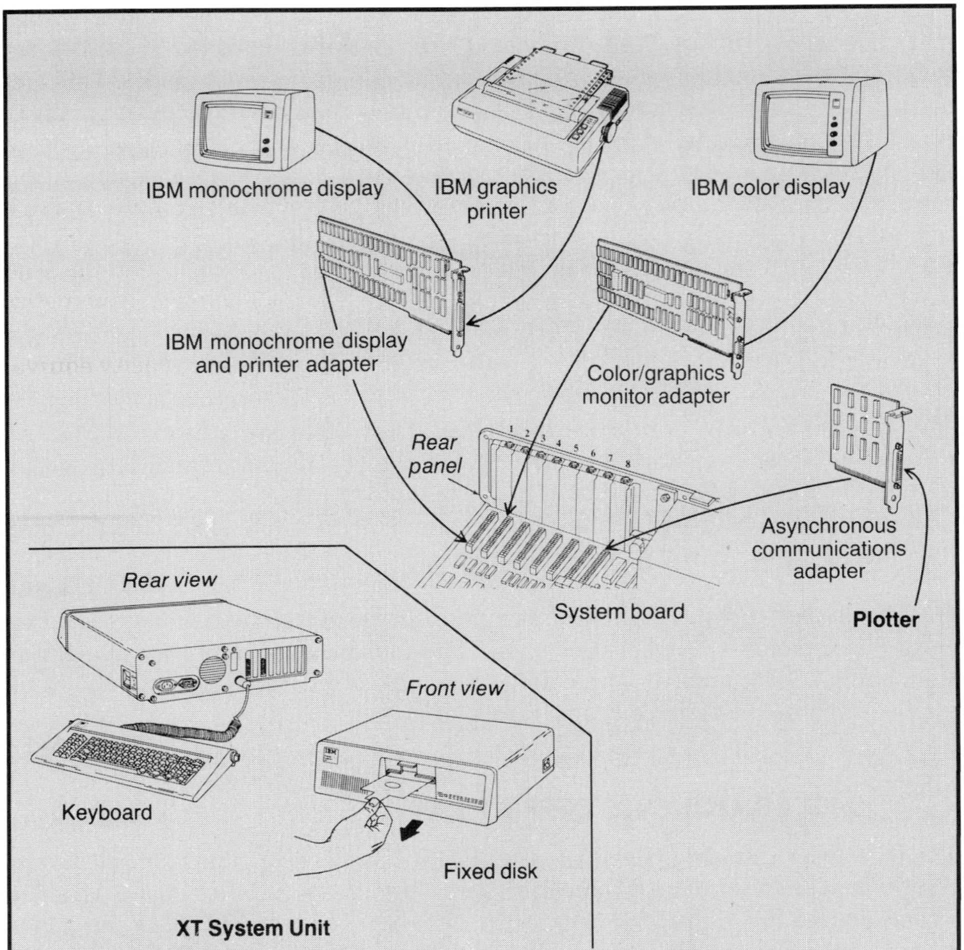

FIGURE 1.7 A typical XT configuration

The power supply on the XT draws 130 watts, more than double the requirements of the PC (63.5 watts). The system board still has 40K ROM, but these circuits have been redesigned to support DOS (Disk Operating System) 2.0 and BASIC 2.0 versions.

The IBM fixed disk system. The XT's fixed disk system is a Winchester-type hard disk system with 10,240,000 bytes of storage. This storage capacity is equivalent to about 5,500 double-spaced typewritten pages. The four surfaces in the hard disks spin at 3600 rpm and are divided into 17 sectors of 512 bytes each, with 306 tracks per surface. The XT has a 90-millisecond average access time for data and a transfer rate of 5 million bits per second.

1.2.3 THE 8087 MATH COPROCESSOR

The 8088 microprocessor used in both the PC and XT was designed to use a companion processor, the Intel 8087 coprocessor. The 8087 is a specialized processor that can do ordinary addition, subtraction, multiplication, and division, as well as more complex operations such as calculating trigonometric functions.

The coprocessor has eight 80-bit registers, which provide a capacity equivalent to the 40 16-bit registers found in the processor. This register space allows

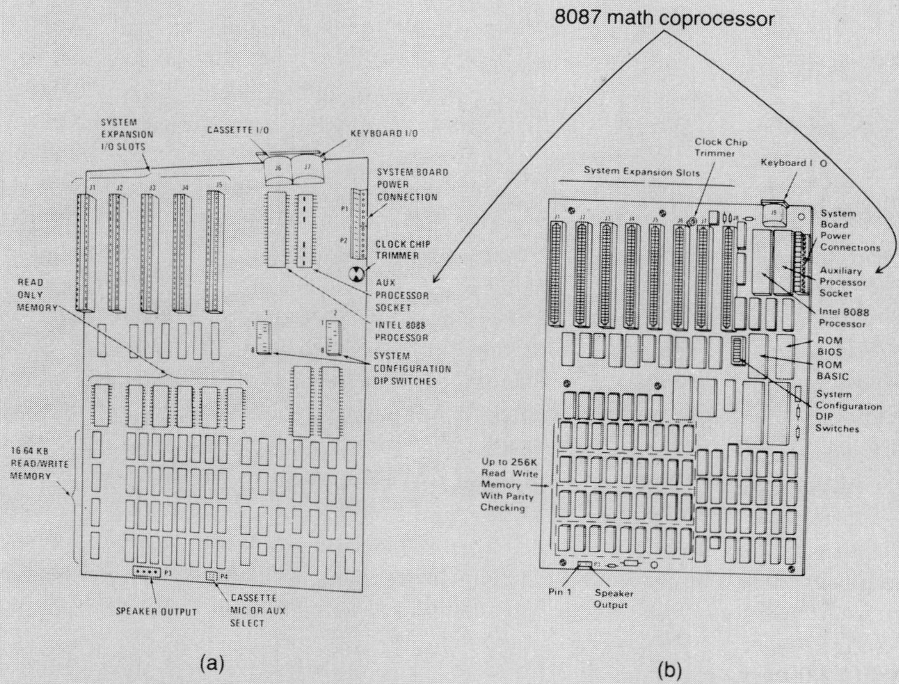

FIGURE 1.8 System board diagram with math coprocessor: (a) PC model and (b) XT model. (From the *IBM PC Technical Reference Manual*. Used by permission.)

TABLE 1.1 Data representation with the 8087

Data type	Bits	Significant digits (decimal)	Approximate range (decimal)
Word integer	16	4	$-32{,}768 \leq X \leq +32{,}767$
Short integer	32	9	$-2 \times 10^9 \leq X \leq +2 \times 10^9$
Long integer	64	18	$-9 \times 10^{18} \leq X \leq +9 \times 10^{18}$
Packed decimal	80	18	$-99\ldots99 \leq X \leq +99\ldots99$ (18 digits)
Short real†	32	6-7	$8.43 \times 10^{-37} \leq \lvert X \rvert \leq 3.37 \times 10^{38}$
Long real†	64	15-16	$4.19 \times 10^{-307} \leq \lvert X \rvert \leq 1.67 \times 10^{308}$
Temporary real	80	19	$3.4 \times 10^{-4932} \leq \lvert X \rvert \leq 1.2 \times 10^{4932}$

†The short and long real data types correspond to the single and double precision data types.
Source: *IBM PC XT Technical Reference Manual.* Used by permission.

constant and temporary results to be held in registers during calculations, thus reducing memory access and improving speed as well as bus availability.

The processor is also designed to allow the 8088 to pass work to the 8087, then to receive results back. However, the 8087 cannot perform control functions for itself or work without the presence of the 8088. The two microprocessors operate synergistically, doing more together than either can do alone. The original PC and XT models are not equipped with the 8087 processor, but they provide a socket in the system board to accommodate it (see Fig. 1.8). The advantage of having the 8087 installed in a PC or XT involves three crucial factors: precision, range, and speed.

Precision. Until the introduction of 16-bit microcomputers, performing complex mathematics on a personal computer was a time-consuming effort. Eight-bit microcomputers were limited in the size of the numbers they could handle, but current 16-bit computers like the PC or XT routinely manipulate numbers up to 32 bits long. These are referred to as double-precision numbers. Seventeen digits of precision are possible, with values ranging from 4.19×10^{-307} to 1.67×10^{308}. These are real numbers since they have a decimal point and a fractional component. (They are also known as floating-point numbers because the decimal point floats around inside the memory location where the number is stored.) Table 1.1 shows representations of large and small numbers in each data type.

Precision is controlled by the size of the mantissa, which holds the most significant digits of a number, regardless of where the decimal point is located. Normally precision is not a problem with integers, but precision is the most important consideration in real number arithmetic because rounding occurs when real numbers cannot be absolutely defined with a limited number of digits. For example, 1 divided by 6 results in the number .166666..., which is accurately represented with an infinite number of digits. Such a number cannot be used easily in calculations. The least significant digit of the number must be rounded so that it can be stored in the limited memory of the computer. The 8087 processor with its 64-bit mantissa is accurate to 1 part in 2^{64}. Such accuracy is seldom needed for a normal computation, but it is important during the intermediate stages of a calculation with a large number of steps involving rounding and truncating operations.

Range. Range determines how large or small a number can be represented. With integers, the range is controlled by the number of bits used. Using 16 bits, the smallest and largest integers we can represent are −32768 and +32767. For real numbers, the range is controlled by the size of the exponent. For the 8087 the exponent is 15 bits long, allowing a wide range of numbers (from 3.4×10^{-4932} to $1.2 \times 10^{+4932}$) to be represented.

Speed. Speed is important for any type of scientific or arithmetic work. In computer graphics, 3-D graphics and animation routines that calculate positional information require extensive arithmetic computation, and will also benefit from the 8087. The 8087 can increase the speed of an 8088 machine language program by a factor of 10 to 1000. Cooke [2] reports that the 8087 far outstrips the 8088 in real number calculations of all kinds.

TABLE 1.2 Minimum hardware configuration

Hardware	Character graphics	Pixel graphics	Plotter graphics
System unit[†]	X	X	X
Keyboard	X	X	X
Monochrome display unit	X		X
Color/graphics display unit		X	
Monochrome/parallel printer adapter	X		X
Color/graphics monitor		X	
IBM graphics printer	X	X	
Printer cable	X	X	
Plotter			X
Asynchronous communication adapter			X
RS 232-C Cable			X

[†]Includes two disk drives, 64K RAM

TABLE 1.3 Character chart with ASCII decimal values

For monochrome display unit

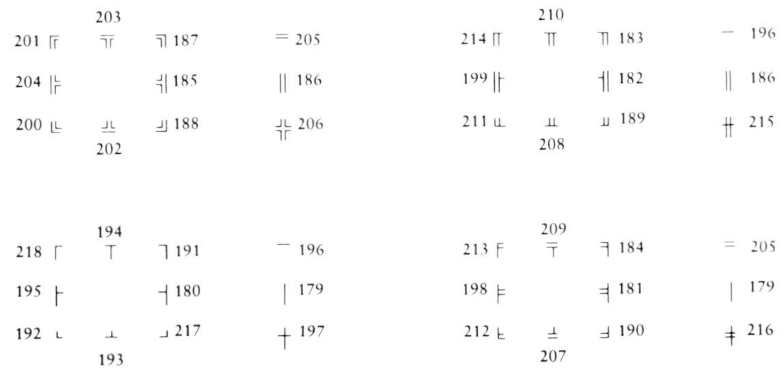

For graphics printer

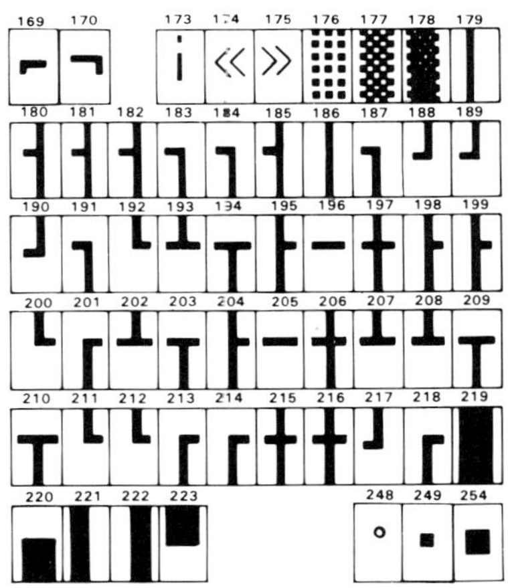

From the *IBM PC Technical Reference Manual.*

1.2.4 METHODS AND HARDWARE REQUIREMENTS TO CREATE GRAPHICS

The IBM PC can be used in three different graphics approaches: character graphics, plotter graphics, and pixel (or raster) graphics. Depending upon the type of graphics desired, the minimum hardware configuration can vary, as shown in Table 1.2.

Character graphics are displays that are made using the extended ASCII (American Standard Code for Information Interchange) character set that the

PC has. There are 128 codes, which have special display forms. About half of these codes are dedicated to characters intended for drawing. In particular, there are full sets of line characters that make it possible to draw single- and double-line boxes, graphs, and charts. With BASIC we can easily access these codes by using a "PRINT CHR$(*n*)" statement, where *n* is the ASCII Code number. A typical set of graphics characters useful in drawing is shown in Table 1.3.

Plotter graphics are obtained by using a special device called a plotter, driven by the PC. Several types of plotters are available that can be connected to the PC, but each plotter has its own graphics language, normally different from the graphics language provided by the PC. For example, the HP-7470 series graphics plotters can be attached to the PC by an RS 232-C cable extending from the PC's asynchronous communication adapter, but the user must use the Hewlett-Packard Graphics Language (HP-GL) to drive the plotters. Most plotter languages are written in BASIC, but their specific graphics commands have different meanings from plotter to plotter.

Pixel graphics takes another approach. The display screen is divided up into a rectangular grid of many small picture elements or dots, called pixels. Each pixel can be on and off. Plotting a point on a screen simply means that we instruct the computer to "turn on" the pixel at the required position. Individual pixels are referenced by coordinates; therefore, we specify the location of a pixel in the form (x, y), where x gives the column number and y gives the row number in the screen grid. On the PC, graphics images are created with pixels, controlled through a memory-mapped display format; each memory location corresponds to a screen location. The PC's memory-mapped screen is linked to an area of the computer's memory that is scanned constantly by the circuitry on the color/graphics adapter to generate the video signal that makes the image appear on the screen. With the memory-mapped screen, we can read and write display data directly, simply by accessing the display memory. This feature provides an easier means of manipulating pictures; therefore, we will use this method throughout the graphics techniques in this book.

Figure 1.9 shows typical graphics output obtained by employing each method.

1.3 CHARACTERISTICS OF THE COLOR/GRAPHICS ADAPTER

The hardware device called the color/graphics adapter activates the PC to manipulate the color graphics image on the screen. This adapter is a single printed circuit card that fits into one of the expansion bus slots in the PC system board. In this section, we will present a brief overview on how the adapter manipulates the display format of the screen and the colors that

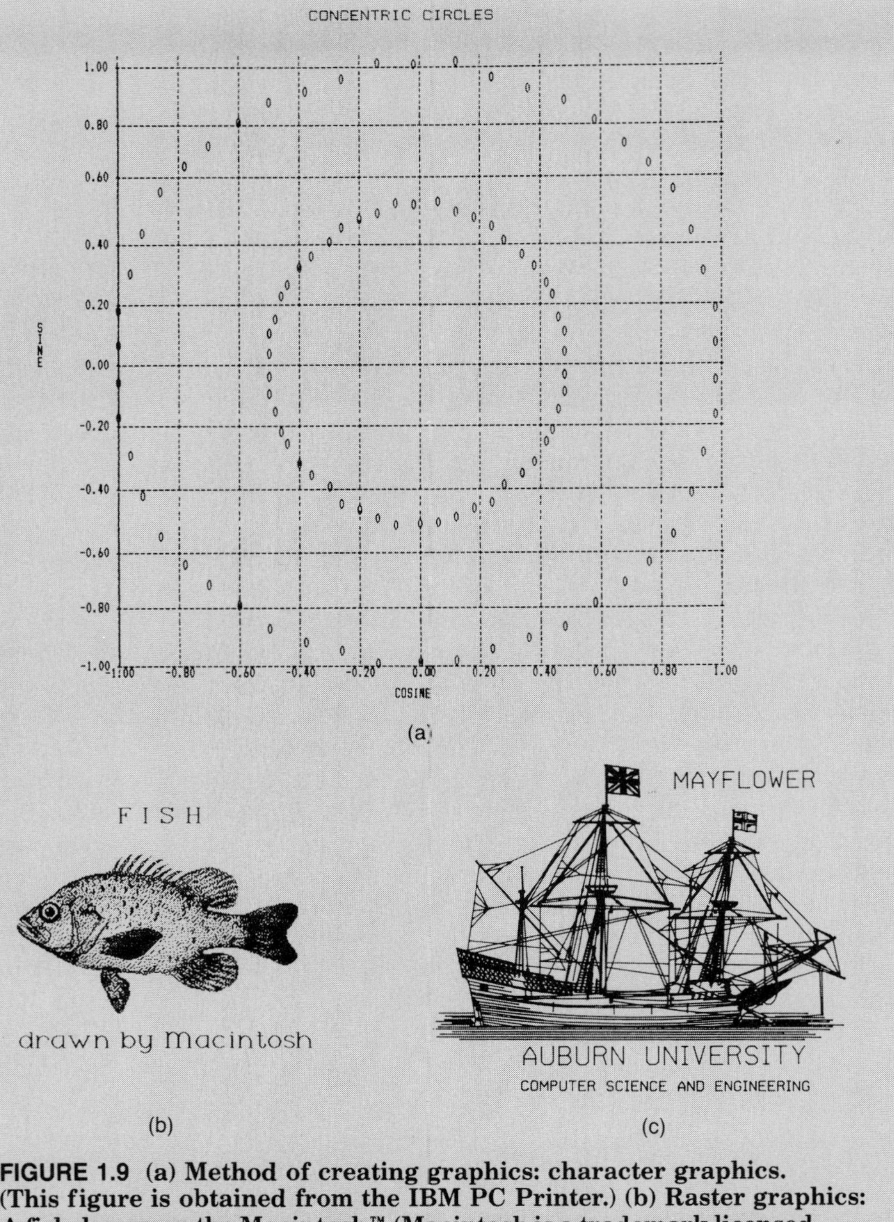

FIGURE 1.9 (a) Method of creating graphics: character graphics. (This figure is obtained from the IBM PC Printer.) (b) Raster graphics: A fish drawn on the Macintosh™ (Macintosh is a trademark licensed to Apple Computer, Inc.). (c) Plotter graphics: A ship plotted by HP7470A PLOTTER

appear. First we will review the system memory map for the 8088, indicating where the PC stores graphics and display data.

1.3.1 MEMORY REQUIREMENT

The graphics output of the IBM PC is really a display of a section of the computer's memory. Therefore, we will begin our consideration of IBM PC graphics with a study of the allocation and use of memory. While we may sometimes make changes in the way memory is used by the computer, standard usage is shown by the memory map in Table 1.4. Each unit of memory (a byte) holds eight bits of information; the location of a byte in memory is called its address. An address and its contents may be identified in decimal or hexadecimal notation (with an "&H" prefix). The PC can have up to 1024K bytes of memory with addresses ranging from 0 to 1024K. (Note the convention of 1K = 1024 in representing computer memory.)

The lowest numbered 64K bytes locations hold the BIOS (Basic-Input-Output-System) routines and the read/write (R/W) memory on the system board. (BIOS routines contain all the fundamental input-output service routines built into the PC. Many of these routines are interrupt service routines implemented as software using the IBM PC Macro Assembler.)

The next 192K bytes are available for add-on memory boards, with which we can expand the R/W memory to 256K bytes. The 384K bytes starting at location 40000 accept additional R/W add-on boards for further expansion.

Following the future expansion area is a block of 16K locations that IBM reserves for future use. (Another reserved 16K block starts at location F0000.) Note that the XT reserves a 128K block. Location B0000 is the start of a 16K block of memory where both the PC and XT store the monochrome screen display data; location B8000 is the start of 16K bytes of memory used by the color/graphics adapter. The chips that contain this memory are actually on the color/graphics adapter. In this sense, the color/graphics adapter acts like a 16K-byte extension of the 8088's main memory.

The 192K bytes starting at location C0000 currently provide ROM expansion or other functions. The 8K bytes starting at location F4000 are available for a user-provided program ROM chip, which we can plug into a spare socket on the system board. Finally, the highest-numbered 40K locations hold the Cassette Basic interpreter and BIOS ROM chips. Note that the XT has a slightly different memory assignment that uses this last segment of the main memory to control the fixed disk.

1.3.2 HARDWARE OVERVIEW

Types of display units supported. The color/graphics adapter supports two types of display devices: direct drive monitors and composite monitors, includ-

TABLE 1.4 System memory map (increments of 16KB).
Source: IBM PC and XT technical reference manuals.

PC model	Memory		XT model
Function	Start address Decimal	Hex	Function
16–64 KB READ/WRITE memory on system board	0 16K 32K 48K	00000 04000 08000 0C000	
Up to 192 KB memory in I/O channel	64K • • • 240K	10000 • • • 3C000	128-256K R/W memory on system board
384 KB future R/W memory expansion in I/O channel	256K • • • 624K	40000 • • • 9C000	384K R/W memory expansion I/O channel
Reserved	640K	A0000	
	656K 672K 688K	A4000 A8000 AC000	

Address	Contents
00000	BIOS interrupt vectors (0H–1FH)
00080	DOS interrupt vectors (20H–3FH)
00100	User interrupt vectors (40H–7FH)
00200	BASIC interrupt vectors (80H–FFH)
00400	BIOS data area
00500	BASIC and DOS data area
00600	62.5 K user raw memory

112 KB Graphics/ display video buffer	Monochrome	704K	B0000	Monochrome	128K reserved
		720K	B4000		
	Color/graphics	736K	B8000	Color/graphics	
		752K	BC000		
192 KB memory expansion area		768K	C0000		192K Read-Only memory expansion and control
		784K	C4000		
		800K	C8000	Fixed disk control	
		816K	CC000		
		832K	D0000		
		848K	D4000		
		864K	D8000		
		880K	DC000		
		896K	E0000		
		912K	E4000		
		928K	E8000		
		944K	EC000		
48 KB base system ROM	Reserved	960K	F0000		64K base system ROM, BIOS, and BASIC
		976K	F4000		
		992K	F8000		
		1008K	FC000		

From the *IBM PC* and *XT Technical Reference Manuals*.

ing television receivers used with an RF modulator. Either type of display can be monochrome or color.

Direct drive monitors, often called the RGB monitors, have three video inputs, one for each of the red, green, and blue electron beam guns. If these inputs are digital so that they are independently on or off, the monitor can display eight colors. Some digital RGB monitors have a fourth input signal that controls the intensity of all three guns, allowing them to display 16 colors. In analog RGB monitors, the intensity of the beam is proportional to the voltage applied to the video inputs. These monitors are much more expensive than digital monitors, but can display practically an infinite number of colors. The color/graphics adapter only generates the binary RGB and intensity signals; it is not intended for use with analog RGB monitors.

Composite monitors accept a combined signal that contains both sync and video information. Television receivers are essentially composite monitors that extract the composite video signal from an RF carrier. They are generally less expensive than RGB monitors, but have poorer resolution.

The major hardware components. The major elements of the color/graphics adapter are the Motorola 6845 CRT controller; a 16K bytes display buffer; a character generator; a mode select register; a color select register; a timing generator; and a composite color generator. A block diagram that illustrates the major data paths connecting these elements is shown in Fig. 1.10.

The IBM PC screen uses a *raster* display consisting of a collection of horizontal lines (rasters) made up of pixels. The 6845 CRT controller provides the electronics needed to drive the raster display. To be specific, the controller provides the basic horizontal and vertical video timing signals and generates the addresses for accessing the display buffer and character generator.

The color/graphics adapter has two basic modes of operation, alphanumeric (text) and graphics. These are controlled by the *mode select register*. In the text mode, the adapter has two display options: 40 column or 80 column. In each option, characters are shown in 25 horizontal lines. In graphics mode, the adapter also has two display options: medium and high resolution. In the medium resolution graphics mode, there are 200 raster lines, each containing 320 pixels (we call it 320 × 200 graphics mode). In the high-resolution mode, there are also 200 raster lines, but each contains 640 pixels (we call it 640 × 200 graphics mode).

The display buffer resides in the processor-address space, starting at address &HB800. It provides 16K bytes of dynamic read/write memory (called random access memory, or RAM) and can be accessed by both the central processing unit (CPU) and the graphics control unit. Data stored in the display buffer is continuously read out, interpreted, and displayed. The basic difference between the text and graphics modes is in how the stored data in this display buffer are interpreted.

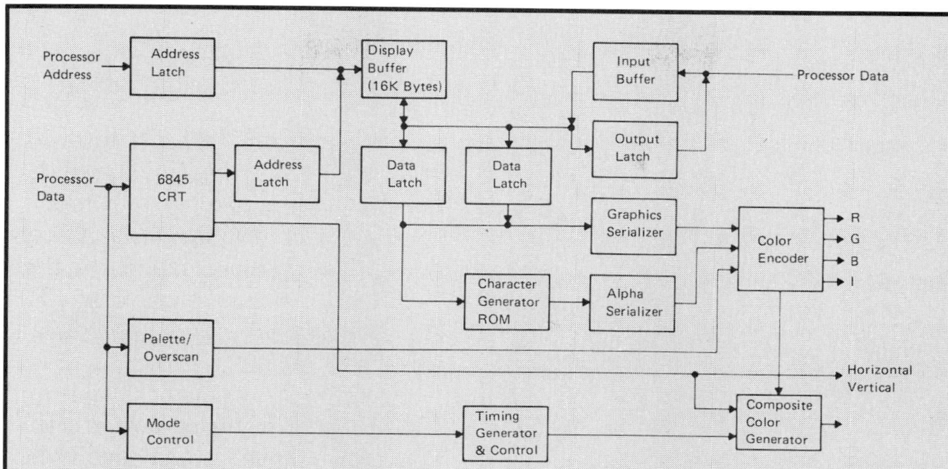

FIGURE 1.10 Color/graphics adapter block diagram. (From the *IBM PC Technical Reference Manual.* Used by permission.)

The character generator consists of 8K bytes of ROM. It contains the patterns used to generate dot matrix characters in text modes. This is a general-purpose character generator with three different character sets, each defining 256 characters. Two sets are for the color/graphics adapter; the other is for the monochrome adapter. Figure 1.11 shows the organization of the character generator. The first 2K contains patterns for the top eight rows of the monochrome 7 × 9 dot character set. The next 2K contains patterns for the bottom eight rows, only the first six of which are used. The third and fourth 2K segments contain patterns for the 5 × 7 single dot characters and the 7 × 7 double dot characters used in color/graphics monitors.

Since the character generator cannot be read from or written to under software control, the adapter goes through a different path to generate characters in graphics mode. Characters in graphics mode are formed by individually programmed pixels. Eight bytes are used to describe each character, which occupies an 8 × 8 pixel region of the display. The PC's ROM BIOS contains a character look-up table that provides the first 128 character codes with the same patterns as those in the character generator. In graphics modes, the BIOS programs read the patterns from the table and turn on the appropriate pixels. To read characters back from the screen memory, the BIOS programs actually match the patterns in the display buffer against those in the character look-up table to determine the character displayed.

The timing generator produces the timing signals used by the 6845 CRT controller and by the dynamic memory. It also resolves the contentions between

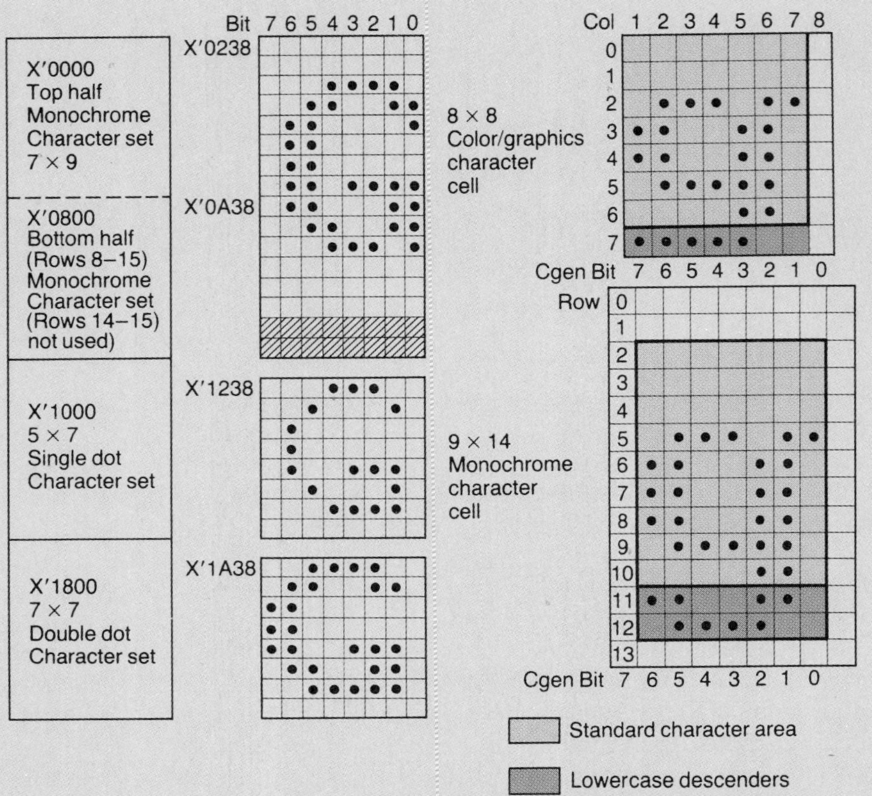

FIGURE 1.11 The character generator: (a) Memory organization and (b) character cell layout. (Reprinted from *PC Technical Journal*, copyright ©1984, Ziff-Davis Publishing Co.)

the central processing unit and the graphic controller for access to the display buffer. In general, the color/graphics adapter processes the data in the following fashion.

Data stored in the display buffer by the CPU are read out two bytes at a time into two 8-bit data latches. From there, the data pass to either a graphics or alpha (text) serializer, which extracts one picture element (pixel) at a time. [For alpha mode, the data first pass to the character generator before reaching the alpha (text) serializer.] From there, the data pass to the color encoder, where they are turned into composite video information for output to the display.

1.3.3 PROGRAMMING THE 6845 CRT CONTROLLER

In addition to the 16K display buffer, the adapter has seven I/O ports that can be programmed to control it (see Table 1.5). We will briefly discuss three of these that are directly relevant to our graphics programming. We use the BIOS

TABLE 1.5 I/O ports for color/graphics adapter

I/O Port Address	Device name	Read/ Write	Active data bits
&H3D4	6845 address register	W	- - - 4 3 2 1 0
&H3D5	6845 data register	R/W	- - - 4 3 2 1 0
&H3D8	Mode select register	W	7 6 5 4 3 2 1 0
&H3D9	Color select register	W	- 5 4 3 2 1 0
&H3DA	Status register	R	- - - - 3 2 1 0
&H3DB	Clear light-pen latch	R/W	- - - - - - - -
&H3DC	Set light-pen latch	R/W	- - - - - - - -

Mode-Register (&H3D8)

Bit 0	High-resolution dot clock (80 character alpha)
1	Graphic select
2	Black and white select
3	Enable video
4	640 graphics select
5	Alpha blink enable

Color Select Register (&H3D9)

Bit 0	Blue	Alpha border/graphics background
1	Green	Alpha border/graphics background
2	Red	Alpha border/graphics background
3	Intensity	Alpha border/graphics background
4	Intensity	Alpha background/medium resolution foreground
5	Medium resolution foreground color select (blue)	

Status Register (&H3DA)

Bit 0	Display inactive
1	Light-pen trigger set
2	Light-pen switch open
3	Vertical sync

From T. V. Hoffmann, "The IBM Color/Graphics Adapter," Reprinted from *PC Technical Journal* 1 (1), 1983. Copyright © 1983, Ziff-Davis Publishing Company. Used by permission.

programs to read or write data from or to these I/O ports. In order to access the BIOS program, we need the IBM Macro Assembler. The I/O ports can also be accessed from BASIC by executing an "OUT" statement to send a byte to a machine output port or an "INP" statement to read a byte from an input port.

The 6845 Address Register is a 5-bit write-only register that is used to select one of the 18 internal data registers of the 6845 CRT Controller by writing the register number to this port. The selected register is then read or written through the 6845 Data Register. Table 1.6 summarizes the values that must be loaded into the 6845 CRT Controller register to control the different modes of operation supported by the adapter. Note that the first ten registers define the character and screen formats. These values must be set to generate the proper timing intervals for the monitor used. The video timing is programmable in terms of character times, which are always eight dot times for the horizontal dimension and vary depending on the programmed number of scan lines per character for the vertical dimension. A complete description of these data registers is provided in [4].

1.3.4 PROGRAMMING THE MODE SELECT REGISTER

The Mode Select Register is a 6-bit write-only register that controls the screen display format. Each bit controls one aspect of the operation of the display electronics; together they establish the basic operation mode for the adapter as follows:

Bit 0: Selects either a 7 or 14 MHz dot clock, which determines both the rate at which dots from the character generator are sent to the screen, and when data is read from the display buffer. A 1 selects 80 × 25 text mode; a 0 selects 40 × 25 text mode.

Bit 1: Selects between text and graphics modes. A 1 selects 320 × 200 graphics mode; a 0 selects text mode.

Bit 2: Selects color or black and white mode. A 1 selects black and white mode; a 0 selects color mode.

Bit 3: Enables the video signal for the displayed area of the screen. A 1 enables the video signal; a 0 disables the video signal. You should disable the video signal when you are changing mode or reprogramming the 6845 CRT Controller.

Bit 4: Enables high-resolution graphics. A 1 selects the 640 × 200 graphics mode in black and white. A 0 disables high-resolution graphics.

Bit 5: Enables blinking in text mode. A 1 enables blinking for characters and restricts the background to eight colors. In this mode, bit 4 of the Color Select Register at I/O address &H3D9 controls the intensity of all background colors. A 0 disables blinking and allows all 16 background colors. This bit has no effect in graphics modes.

TABLE 1.6 The 6845 register description

	Register	Units	R/W	40×25 Alpha	80×25 Alpha	320/640 ×200 Graphics	Maximum programmable value
00	Horizontal total	Char	W	56	113	56	255
01	Horizontal displayed	Char	W	40	80	40	255
02	Horizontal sync position	Char	W	45	90	45	255
03	Horizontal sync width	Char	W	10	10	10	15
04	Vertical total	Char row	W	31	31	127	255
05	Vertical total adjust	Scan line	W	6	6	6	31
06	Vertical displayed	Char row	W	25	25	100	127
07	Vertical sync position	Char row	W	28	28	112	127
08	Interlace mode	—	W	2	2	2	3
09	Max scan line address	Scan line	W	7	7	1	31
10	Cursor start	Scan line	W	6	6	6	127
11	Cursor end	Scan line	W	7	7	7	31
12	Start address (high)	—	W	0	0	0	63
13	Start Address (low)	—	W	0	0	0	255
14	Cursor address (high)	—	R/W	—	—	—	63
15	Cursor address (low)	—	R/W	—	—	—	255
16	Light-pen (high)	—	R	—	—	—	63
17	Light-pen (low)	—	R	—	—	—	255

Note: All values are in decimal.

Several combinations can be used to set the screen mode by varying the bit assignments, but only seven of them are practical. These are summarized in Table 1.7. Mode 1 or 3 is selected by default at power on, depending upon the setting of switches on the system board. The values shown for modes 4, 5, and

TABLE 1.7 Description of mode select register (&H3D8)

BIOS

	Mode description	Bit 5	4	3	2	1	0	Hex	Dec	BASIC statement(s)
0	40 × 25 Alpha B/W	1	0	1	1	0	0	2C	44	SCREEN 0,0: WIDTH 40
1	40 × 25 Alpha color	1	0	1	0	0	0	28	40	SCREEN 0,1: WIDTH 40
2	80 × 25 Alpha B/W	1	0	1	1	0	1	2D	45	SCREEN 0,0: WIDTH 80
3	80 × 25 Alpha color	1	0	1	0	0	1	29	41	SCREEN 0,1: WIDTH 80
4	320 × 200 Graphics color	(1)	0	1	0	1	0	2A	42	SCREEN 1,0
5	320 × 200 Graphics B/W	(1)	0	1	1	1	0	2E	46	SCREEN 1,1
6	640 × 200 Graphics B/W	(0)	1	1	1	1	0	1E	30	SCREEN 2

Note: The meaning of the mode register bits is as follows:

Bit 0 = High resolution
Bit 1 = Graphics
Bit 2 = Black and white
Bit 3 = Enable video
Bit 4 = 640-dot graphics
Bit 5 = Blink enable

6 are those actually written to Mode Select Register by the BIOS routine. The BIOS also saves the current mode register and color register values in segment 0, locations &H465 and &H466, respectively. Thus we can change the screen mode by changing the values in the mode register with the interrupt service provided by the BIOS routine.

For BASIC-oriented readers, we can also access the mode register by using the BASIC statements shown in Table 1.7. The WIDTH command sets the width of the display in columns and the SCREEN command selects the display mode and enables or disables color. In describing these graphics statements we will use the following conventions. (The same conventions will be used for other graphics statements to be described throughout this book.)

- Words in capital letters are keywords and must be entered as shown.
- Words shown in lowercase letters are defined by the user.
- Items in square brackets ([]) are optional.
- All punctuation except square brackets (such as commas, parentheses, semicolons, hyphens, or equal signs) must be included where shown.

Then the SCREEN and WIDTH statements should be entered as:

```
SCREEN mode, burst: WIDTH size
```

where

mode = 0 for text mode
1 for medium resolution
2 for high resolution

burst = 0 disables color for text mode
0 enables color for medium resolution
no effect on high resolution

size = 40 or 80

For example, the BASIC statements, SCREEN 0,1: WIDTH 80 will set the screen for 80-column-text mode in black and white.

1.3.5 Programming the Color Select Register

Before explaining the specific function of the Color Select Register, we will first discuss how the RGB type monitors create colors. Then we describe how the display buffer interacts with the Color Select Register in creating colors on the screen.

IRGB color. The colors are determined by 3 independent bits for each additive primary color — red, green, blue — and a fourth bit, intensity. We call this color composition *IRGB color*. The three primaries can be mixed in eight com-

TABLE 1.8 IRGB colors

Color code number	I	R	G	B	Color name	Composition
0	0	0	0	0	Black	
1	0	0	0	1	Blue	Blue
2	0	0	1	0	Green	Green
3	0	0	1	1	Cyan	Green + blue
4	0	1	0	0	Red	Red
5	0	1	0	1	Magenta	Red + blue
6	0	1	1	0	Brown	Red + green
7	0	1	1	1	White (light gray)	Red + green + blue
8	1	0	0	0	Dark gray	Int
9	1	0	0	1	Light blue	Int + blue
10	1	0	1	0	Light green	Int + green
11	1	0	1	1	Light cyan	Int + green + blue
12	1	1	0	0	Light red	Int + red
13	1	1	0	1	Light magenta	Int + red + blue
14	1	1	1	0	Yellow	Int + red + green
15	1	1	1	1	Intense white	Int + red + green + blue

Bit	3	2	1	0
	I	R	G	B
Decimal Value	8	4	2	1

1 = turn on
0 = turn off

Additive color mixes

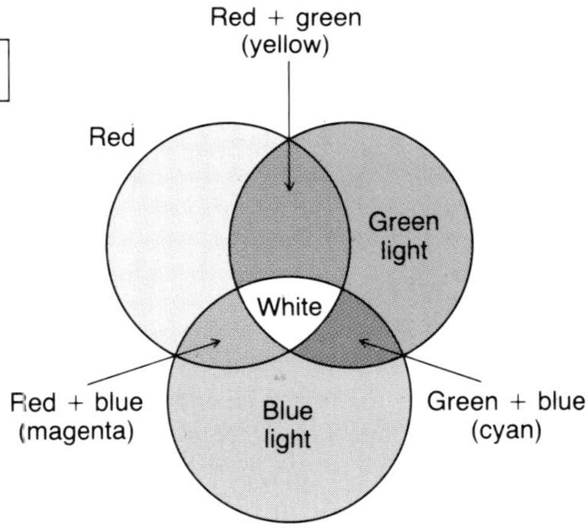

binations to form the basic IRGB colors shown in Table 1.8. Note that the three additive primary colors combine to form white light. In pairs they form the complementary colors cyan, magenta, and yellow. The intensity control gives an additional eight colors, each a brighter version of its nonintensified counterpart. Black is the absence of any light. Table 1.8 also shows all 16 standard

IRGB color compositions available on the PC; note that four bits of memory are required to hold 16 different IRGB colors. Observe also that adding primary colors corresponds to adding their codes. For example, cyan is a mixture of blue and green, and thus has the binary code: 0001 (blue) + 0010 (green) = 0011 (cyan).

Color selection scheme. The display buffer and the Color Select Register are used together to control the entire color settings in either text or graphics mode.

In displaying a character in text mode, we may specify three color parameters: foreground, background, and border. As shown in Fig. 1.12, *foreground* refers to the character itself, *background* refers to the color around the character, and *border* refers to the border of the screen outside the text area. The display buffer determines the foreground color and the background color for the character; the Color Select Register selects the color for the border. One reason computers such as the IBM PC have a border is that they are meant to work with ordinary color televisions, which employ the technique of overscanning.

In 320×200 graphics mode, we may specify two color-related parameters, background and palette. *Background* is the color of pixels we have turned off;

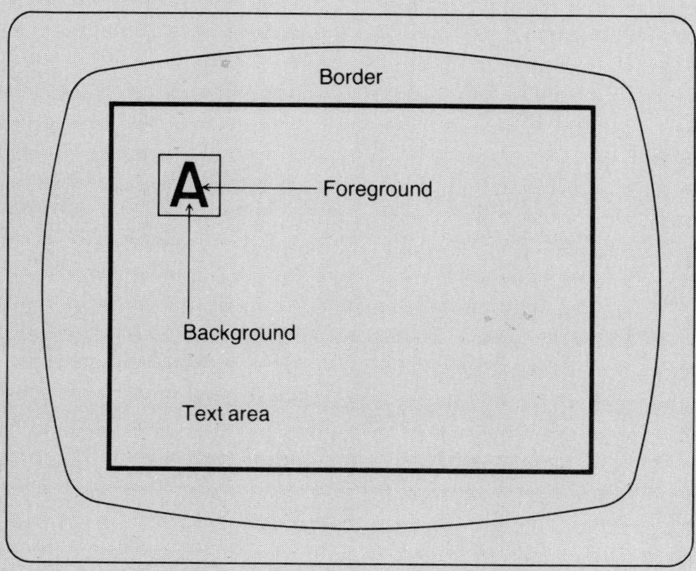

FIGURE 1.12 **Color selection in text mode**

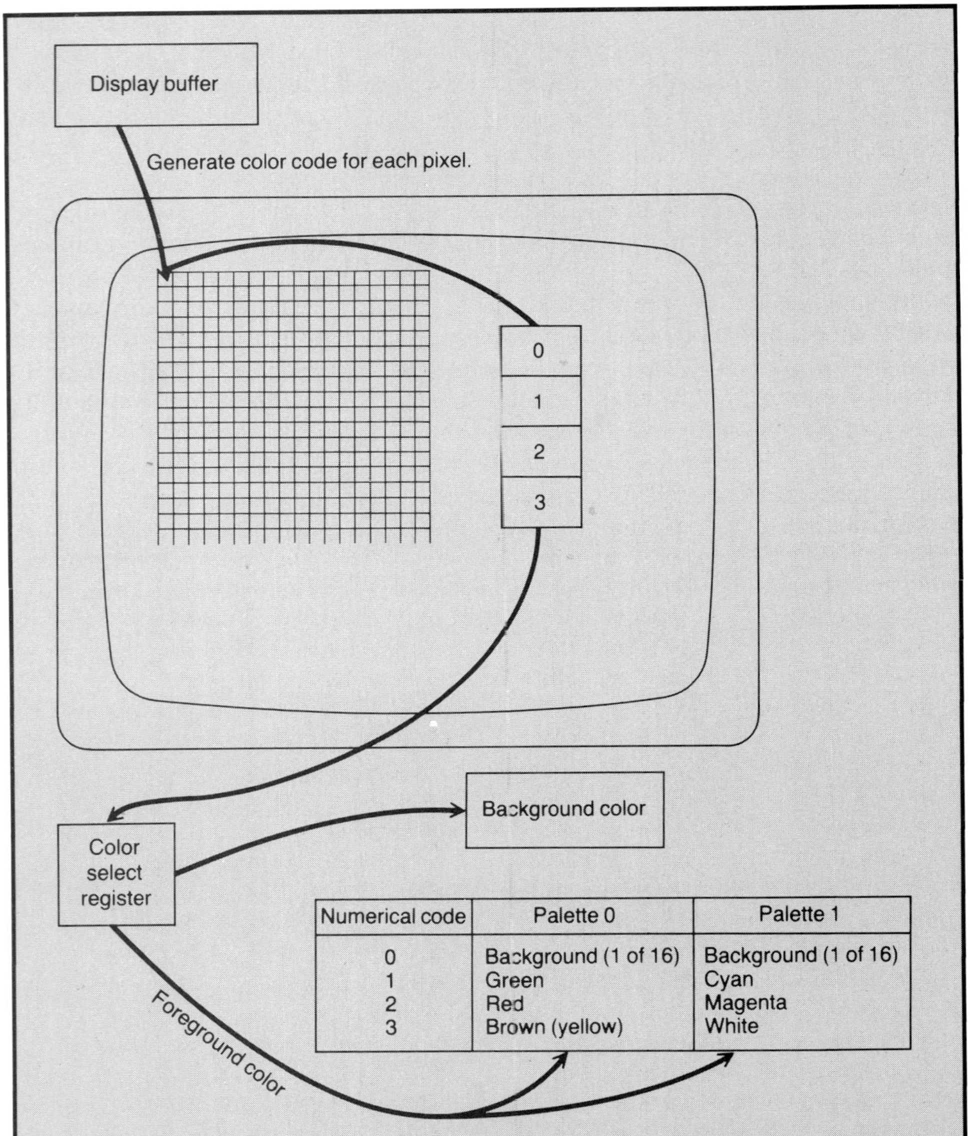

Numerical code	Palette 0	Palette 1
0	Background (1 of 16)	Background (1 of 16)
1	Green	Cyan
2	Red	Magenta
3	Brown (yellow)	White

FIGURE 1.13 Color selection in 320 × 200 mode

palette selects between the two available sets of three colors that work with subsequent pixels to be turned on. Each pixel on the screen is assigned a number from 0 to 3. Figure 1.13 shows how these numerical codes correspond to colors on the screen in these two different palettes. From this table we can see that color number 0 is determined by whatever the background color happens to be, but the other numbers each have two possibilities according to the choice of palette. The display buffer generates a numerical color code (from 0 to 3) for each pixel. The Color Select Register then determines both the background color for the pixels we have turned off and the palette number (between 0 and 1) for the pixels we have turned on.

In 640 × 200 graphics mode, each pixel turned on is allowed to have only one foreground color. The display buffer determines whether or not the pixel should be turned on; then the Color Select Register selects the foreground color for each pixel we have turned on.

Now we will examine how the Color Select Register actually assigns colors in text and graphics modes. (We will present how the display buffer handles color information in Chapter 2). The Color Select Register is a 6-bit write-only

TABLE 1.9 Description of the color select register

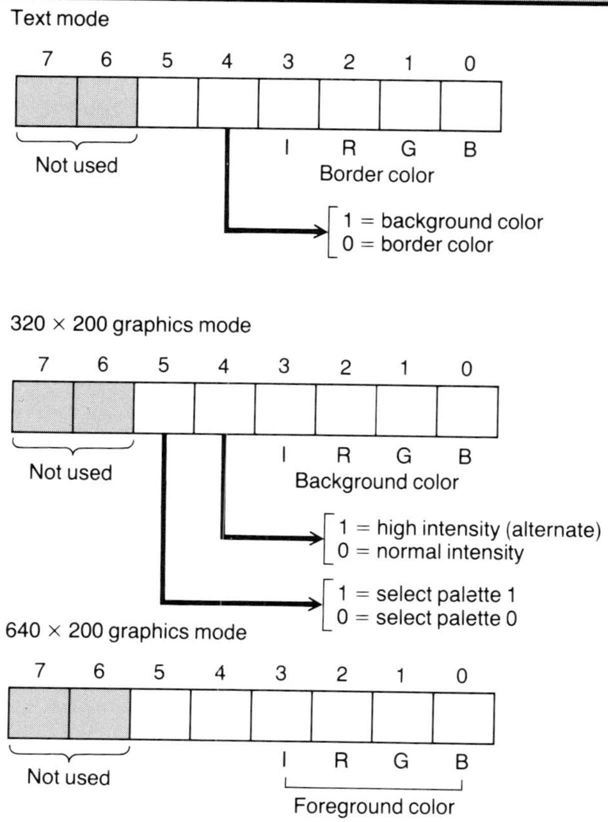

register with an I/O port address of &H3D9 (985 in decimal). It can be written again by using the 8088 I/O Out command. We can also access the register through the OUT statement in BASIC. Table 1.9 defines the values that must be assigned to the Color Select Register to control the color compositions for the different operation modes. Note particularly that, even though the PC made no provision for high-resolution color in BASIC operation mode, we can produce a colored foreground by adding the following statement to the program:

```
OUT &H3D9, n
```

where *n* is a color from 1 to 15 given in Table 1.9. For example, the statement "OUT &H3D9, 2" will provide a green foreground color in high-resolution graphics.

We will conclude this chapter by summarizing the sequence of events in programming the color/graphics adapter.

1. Determine the mode of operation.
2. Reset "video enable" bit in the Mode Select Register.
3. Program 6845 to select mode.
4. Program mode/color select registers, including reenabling video.

1.4 SUMMARY

In this chapter we briefly introduced the subject of computer graphics with several examples. Our expositions were limited, however, to the types of graphics commonly obtainable from a low-cost microcomputer. Then we explored the basic hardware configurations of both the IBM PC and the IBM PC XT that are needed to create a graphics images on the screen. In particular, we presented a brief overview on how the adapter manipulates the display format of the screen and the colors that appear. This hardware overview lays a foundation for the discussions in the next chapter.

REFERENCES

1. Burchi, R. S., "Interactive Graphics Today," *IBM System Journal* **19** (3) 1980.

2. Cooke, W., "Getting Started with an 8087," *PC World* **1** (10) 1983.

3. Csuri, C., "Computer Graphics and Art," *Proceedings of the IEEE* **62** (4) 503–515 1974.

4. Hoffman, T. V., "The IBM Color/Graphics Adapter," *PC Technical Journal* **1** (1) 1983.

5. *IBM Technical Reference Manual—PC XT*, Version 2.02, IBM Corporation, P.O. Box 1328, Boca Raton, Fla. 33432, 1983.

6. Musgrave, J. F., "Experiments in Computer-Aided Graphics Expression," *IBM Systems Journal* **17** (3) 1978.

SURVEY ARTICLES

Machover, C., "A Guide to Sources of Information about Computer Graphics," *IEEE Computer Graphics and Applications* **1**(1), 73–81 1981.

Pooch, U. W., "Computer Graphics, Interactive Techniques, and Image Processing 1970–1975: A Bibliography," *Computer,* August 46–64 1976.

Schrack, G. F., "Survey: Computer Graphics: A Keyword-Indexed Bibliography for the Years 1976, 1977, and 1978," *Computer Graphics and Image Processing* **14** 24–79 1980.

Schrack, G. F., "Survey: A Keyword-Indexed Bibliography for the Year 1979," *Computer Graphics and Image Processing* **15** 45–78 1981.

Schrack, G. F., "Survey: A Keyword-Indexed Bibliography for the Year 1980," *Computer Graphics and Image Processing* **18** 145–187 1982.

SELECTED COMPUTER GRAPHICS JOURNALS

Display Technology and Applications, three times per year, IPC Business Press Limited, 205 East 42nd St., New York, N.Y. 10017.

CAD/CAM Digest, monthly, P.O. Box 8100, Dallas, Tex. 75205.

Computer-Aided Design, bimonthly, IPC Business Press Limited, 205 East 42nd St., New York, N.Y. 10017.

Computer Graphics (journal of the ACM Special Interest Group on Computer Graphics), monthly, Association for Computing Machinery, 1133 Ave. of the Americas, New York, N.Y. 10036.

Computer Graphics and Art, yearly, Berkeley Enterprises, Inc., 815 Washington St., Newtonville, Mass. 02160.

Computer Graphics and Image Processing, monthly, Academic Press, Inc., 111 Fifth Ave., New York, N.Y. 10003.

Computer Graphics News (newsletter), monthly, AUI Data Graphics, 1701 K Street NW, Third Floor, Washington, D.C. 20006.

Computer Graphics World, monthly, 54 Mint St., San Francisco, Calif. 94103.

Computers and Graphics, quarterly, Pergamon Press, Inc., Maxwell House, Fairview Park, Elmsford, N.Y. 10523.

Harvard Newsletter on Computer Graphics, biweekly, P.O. Box 89, Sudbury, Mass. 01776.

IEEE Computer Graphics and Applications, quarterly, IEEE Computer Society, 10662 Los Vaqueros Cir., Los Alamitos, Calif. 90720.

Proceedings of the SID, quarterly, Society for Information Display, 654 N. Sepulveda Blvd., Los Angeles, Calif. 90049.

SID Journal, quarterly, Society for Information Display, 654 N. Sepulveda Blvd., Los Angeles, Calif. 90049.

SELECTED COMPUTER JOURNALS OR MAGAZINES WITH OCCASIONAL COMPUTER GRAPHICS ARTICLES

Communications of the ACM, monthly, Association for Computing Machinery, 1133 Ave. of the Americas, New York, N.Y. 10036.

Computer, monthly, IEEE Computer Society, 10662 Los Vaqueros Cir., Los Alamitos, Calif. 90720.

Computing Surveys, quarterly, Association for Computing Machinery, 1133 Ave. of the Americas, New York, N.Y. 10036.

Datamation, monthly, Technical Publishing Co., 666 Fifth Ave., New York, N.Y. 10019 (controlled circulation).

Engineering Graphics, monthly, 226 Pasqual Ave., Ventura, Calif. 93003.

Finite Element News, bimonthly, Robinson and Associates, Horton Rd., Woodlands, Winborne, Dorset BH216NB, England.

IBM Systems Journal, quarterly, International Business Machines Corp., Armonk, N.Y. 10504.

IEEE Spectrum, monthly, Institute of Electrical and Electronics Engineers, Inc., 345 E. 47th St., New York, N.Y. 10017.

Infosystems, monthly, Hitchcock Publishing Co., Hitchcock Building, Wheaton, Ill. 60187 (controlled circulation).

Mini-Micro Systems, monthly, 221 Columbus Ave., Boston, Mass. 02116 (controlled circulation).

SELECTED MAGAZINES FOR PERSONAL COMPUTERS

Byte, monthly, McGraw-Hill Publications Co., 70 Main Street, Peterborough, N.H. 03458

Computer Graphics World, monthly, Advanced Technology Group, Pennwell Publishing Co., 1714 Stockton Street, San Francisco, Calif. 94133.

Creative Computing, monthly, 39 E. Hanover Ave., Morris Plains, N.J. 07950.

McWorld, monthly, PC World Communications, Inc., 555 De Haro Street, San Francisco, Calif. 94107.

PC World, monthly, PC World Communications, Inc., 555 De Haro Street, San Francisco, Calif. 94107.

PC Tech Journal, monthly, Ziff-Davis Publishing Co., One Park Ave., New York, N.Y. 10016.

PC Magazine, bimonthly, Ziff-Davis Publishing Co., One Park Ave., New York, N.Y. 10016.

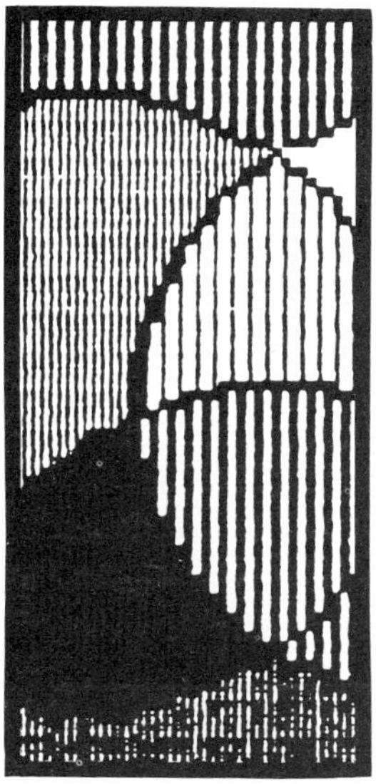

CHAPTER TWO
Graphics Programming

This chapter is concerned mainly with the software system of the IBM PC. The software system is a set of graphics commands used by an application program to generate pictures on a display monitor and to handle graphical interaction. We will examine first how we can access and control the screen memory to create a graphics image. In the process, we will review the BASIC graphics commands available on the IBM PC. We will then discuss how to develop a high-speed graphics program by interfacing with machine language subroutines.

2.1 MEMORY-MAPPED GRAPHICS IN TEXT MODE

As we mentioned in Section 1.2.4, graphics images on the PC are created with pixels controlled through a memory-mapped display format. Each memory location corresponds to a screen location. With the memory-mapped screen, we can read and write display data directly, simply by accessing the display memory that resides in the 16K-byte display buffer of the color/graphics adapter.

To develop our ability to apply the color and graphics capability of the PC to our needs, it is important to know how to access and control the screen display memory. Each memory location is one byte in size. How this byte is displayed on the screen depends on the mode of graphics operation.

2.1.1 MEMORY REQUIREMENT

We will consider the text mode first. For each screen location, there are two bytes in memory. Together, these two bytes specify what is to be displayed (character), and how it is to be shown (colors). Thus every display character position is defined by the following 2-byte character/attribute format.

Display character code byte	Attribute byte
7 6 5 4 3 2 1 0	7 6 5 4 3 2 1 0

There are 2000 characters on the screen in 80-column mode (80 × 25). Because each character takes two bytes, 4000 bytes are needed for the screen memory in text mode (2000 bytes for 40 × 25 mode).

Display character code byte. Each byte has 8 bit positions and can thus store 256 different values, or represent 256 different characters. When bytes are used to hold characters, some code must be used to determine which numeric value represents which character. The most common code is ASCII. Since ASCII has only 128 different codes and its characters are stored inside 8-bit bytes, there is room for another 128 codes. These other codes are sometimes called extended ASCII. The ASCII codes are standardized, but extended ASCII codes vary from computer to computer. (You will recall from Section 1.3.2 that when the color/graphics adapter is operating in a text mode, it forms characters by converting ASCII codes in its character generator into any of 256 display characters.) Table 2.1 shows the relationship between the ASCII codes (in both decimal and hexadecimal) and their associated characters for the PC. (See Appendix A for hexadecimal conversion table.) For example, if we have a bit pattern of 01000001 for the display character code byte, we can convert it to a decimal (or hexadecimal) value of 65 as follows:

7	6	5	4	3	2	1	0	**Bit position**
0	1	0	0	0	0	0	1	**Bit pattern**
2^7	2^6	2^5	2^4	2^3	2^2	2^1	2^0	**Power of two**
128	64	32	16	8	4	2	1	**Decimal value**
	65							

From Table 2.1 we know that the letter "A" has the decimal value of 65. Thus assigning the decimal value 65 to the character code byte is equivalent to storing the letter "A" in memory.

Attribute byte. Besides an 8-bit character code, every character position on the screen also has an 8-bit attribute code. The attribute byte specifies the

TABLE 2.1 ASCII character codes for the PC

DECIMAL VALUE	➡	0	16	32	48	64	80	96	112	128	144	160	176	192	208	224	240
⬇	HEXA-DECIMAL VALUE	0	1	2	3	4	5	6	7	8	9	A	B	C	D	E	F
0	0	BLANK (NULL)	►	BLANK (SPACE)	0	@	P	`	p	Ç	É	á	░	└	╨	∝	≡
1	1	☺	◄	!	1	A	Q	a	q	ü	æ	í	▒	┴	╤	β	±
2	2	☻	↕	"	2	B	R	b	r	é	Æ	ó	▓	┬	╥	Γ	≥
3	3	♥	‼	#	3	C	S	c	s	â	ô	ú	│	├	╙	π	≤
4	4	♦	¶	$	4	D	T	d	t	ä	ö	ñ	┤	─	╘	Σ	⌠
5	5	♣	§	%	5	E	U	e	u	à	ò	Ñ	╡	┼	╒	σ	⌡
6	6	♠	▬	&	6	F	V	f	v	å	û	a̲	╢	╞	╓	μ	÷
7	7	•	↨	'	7	G	W	g	w	ç	ù	o̲	╖	╟	╫	τ	≈
8	8	◘	↑	(	8	H	X	h	x	ê	ÿ	¿	╕	╚	╪	Φ	°
9	9	○	↓	)	9	I	Y	i	y	ë	Ö	⌐	╣	╔	┘	Θ	●
10	A	◙	→	*	:	J	Z	j	z	è	Ü	¬	║	╩	┌	Ω	•
11	B	♂	←	+	;	K	[	k	{	ï	¢	½	╗	╦	█	δ	√
12	C	♀	∟	,	<	L	\	l	¦	î	£	¼	╝	╠	▄	∞	n
13	D	♪	↔	—	=	M	]	m	}	ì	¥	¡	╜	═	▌	φ	²
14	E	♫	▲	.	>	N	∧	n	~	Ä	₧	«	╛	╬	▐	∈	■
15	F	☼	▼	/	?	O	_	o	△	Å	ƒ	»	┐	╧	▀	∩	BLANK FF

colors of the character and its background, the intensity of the colors, and whether the character is displayed continuously or blinking (see Fig. 2.1). To see what this code does, we must first see that each character symbol consists of the character itself (called foreground) and the rectangular area immediately surrounding it (called the background). The lower four bits (bits 0, 1, 2, and 3) of the attribute byte determine the foreground color of the character; bits 4, 5, and 6 determine the background color; and bit 7 determines whether or not the character blinks. Figure 2.1 also shows the attribute-byte formats for displaying characters in color.

The individual bits in this attribute byte actually control individual colors (R, G, B), which are then combined in an additive manner by the video circuitry to make the foreground or background. (Pigments or filters rely on a subtractive color scheme. When colors are combined by that method, they provide less light.)

In alpha modes, each display position is defined by a character code/attribute pair. The character code is always the even-addressed byte, the attribute is the next higher odd-addressed byte.

Attribute byte

7	6	5	4	3	2	1	0
I/B	Red	Grn	Blu	I	Red	Grn	Blu
Background				Foreground			

Attribute byte format

Bit 0–3	Foreground color
Bits 4–6	Background color
Bit 7	Background intensity

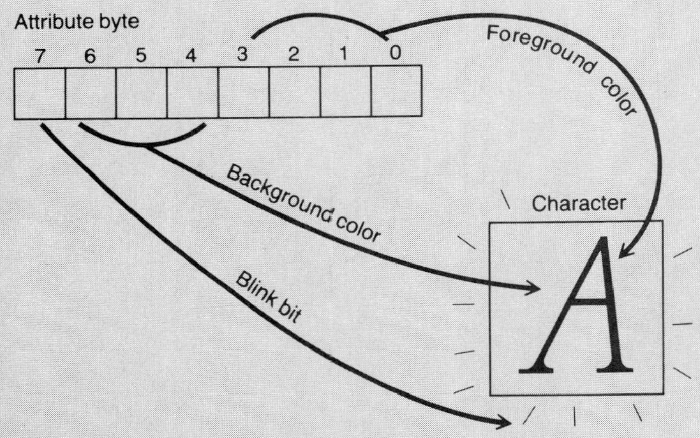

FIGURE 2.1 Attribute byte format used in text mode

Since four bits are allotted to the foreground color, 16 different numbers (0 through 15) can be represented. These color code schemes are exactly the same as those shown in Table 1.8. Thus 16 colors are possible for the character itself. Since only three bits are assigned to the background color, however, only eight colors (0 through 7) can be represented in the background of a character. Because of the way the bits are arranged, the following formula can be used to compute the color code attribute for a character position:

$$\text{Attribute value} = 128(\text{blink}) + 16(\text{background color code}) + \text{foreground color code} \quad \textbf{(2.1)}$$

where blink is 0 for a nonblinking character and 1 for a blinking character. For example, if we want to write a *nonblinking* character in *red* foreground and *blue* background, the corresponding attribute value would be

$$\text{Attribute value} = 128(0) + 16(1) + 4 = 20.$$

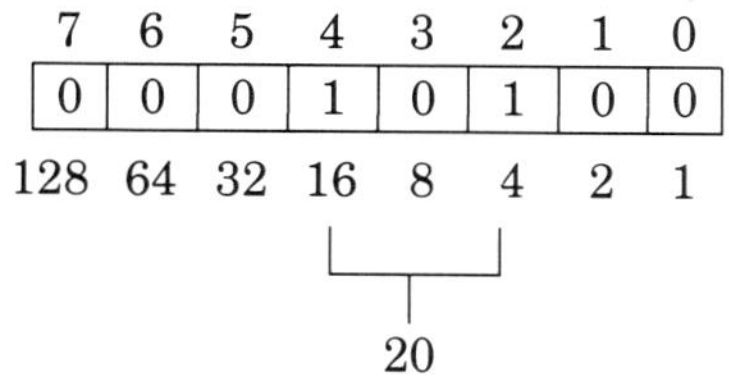

As we discussed in Section 1.3.5, the Color Select Register controls the screen border color in text mode, allowing one of the 16 colors listed in Table 1.8. Since the Color Select Register has its own memory to store the border color information, this color information is not mapped into the display buffer.

When we turn on power to the computer, the color/graphics adapter sets the entire screen to a normal intensity, nonblinking display of white characters on a black background. By specifying new attribute values, however, we can change these settings at any selected positions on the screen. We will show how this is done in the next section.

2.1.2 MEMORY MAPPING

Each character position on the screen in text mode is assigned two bytes in a special area of memory called the display buffer. Recall that the chips that contain this memory are physically on the color/graphics adapter; in this sense, the adapter acts like a 16K byte extension of the system's main memory.

Offset. Because of the nature of computer arithmetic and notation, data elements are often numbered starting from zero for the first element; this is called zero-origin or base. Counting from zero is done particularly when figuring a memory location relative to some starting point. For the color graphics, the storage begins at &HB800 (see Table 1.4). The relative location from this base is referred to as an *offset.* Starting from any base location in memory, the first byte is at offset *zero,* and the next byte is at offset *one.*

The mapping. In text mode, the first two bytes of the display buffer are mapped to the upper left corner of the screen (the first character position). The next two bytes are mapped to the next character position—just to the right of the first character position. This process continues across the first row of

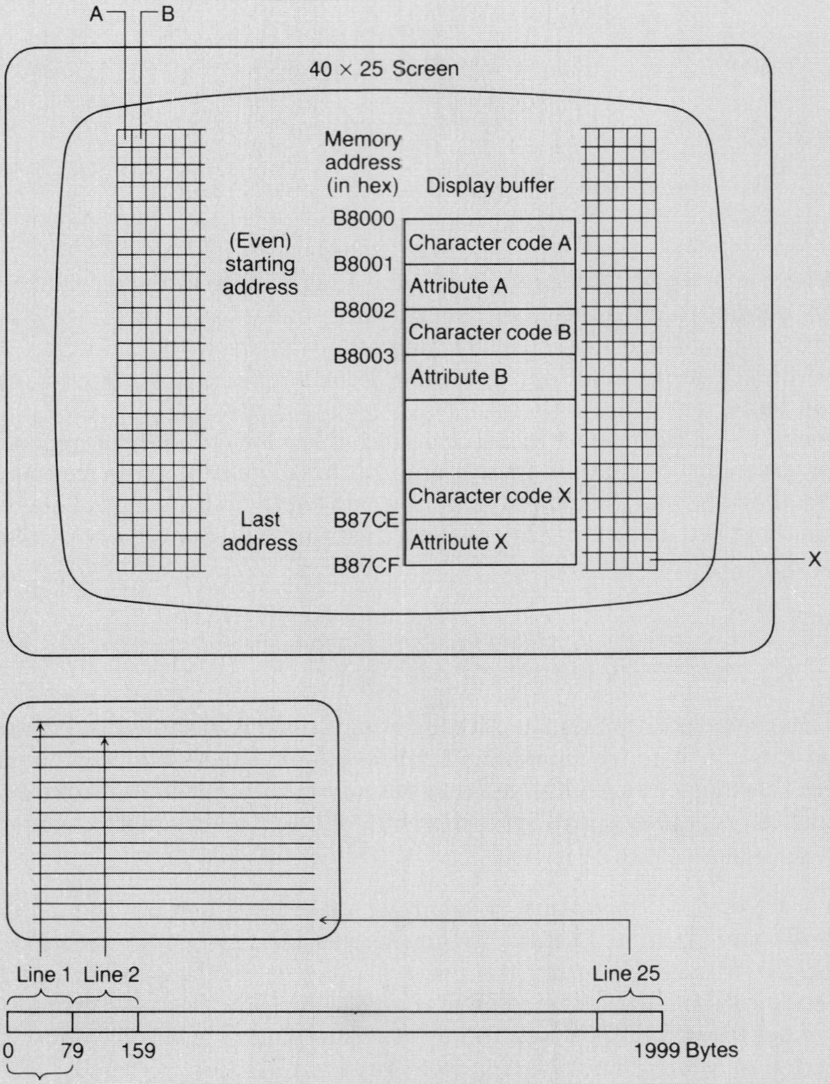

FIGURE 2.2 Display memory map in text mode. (Example of a 40 × 25 screen.)

characters. At the end of each row, the memory map wraps around so that the first column of the next line is mapped to a pair of bytes following the last column of the preceding line. This pattern continues row by row to the bottom of the screen. The complete process of memory mapping is illustrated in Fig. 2.2. Note that the first of each pair of bytes (which contains a character) has an *even* address location, whereas the corresponding attribute byte has an *odd* address. (The starting address of the display buffer is programmable through the 6845 CRT Controller, but it must be an even address.)

For any given character position, we can use the following formula to compute the position of the corresponding bytes in the screen memory:

$$\begin{aligned} &\text{Character Address:} \quad \text{First byte} = 2(\text{WIDTH})(\text{Row} - 1) + 2(\text{Column} - 1) \\ &\text{Attribute Address:} \quad \text{Second byte} = \text{First byte} + 1 \end{aligned} \qquad \textbf{(2.2)}$$

where WIDTH=40 or 80.

Here we must use the IBM PC convention by which rows and columns are numbered beginning with 1 rather than 0. The address formulas above, however, give the memory offsets— that is, the number of bytes from the beginning of a segment of memory. These addresses must be provided to access that memory.

2.1.3 ACCESSING MEMORY FROM BASIC

Using PEEK and POKE statements. The BASIC statements PEEK and POKE are the tools for exploring the screen memory map. The PEEK and POKE statements access a specific memory location relative to the defined segment. On the PC, the DEF SEG statement will set the current segment to point at the beginning of the graphics screen.Then PEEK or POKE will define the actual physical address of its operation as an offset into this segment. In specific, the PEEK (n) statement returns the byte read from memory position n. The POKE n, m statement writes a byte into a memory location n, where n represents the offset from the current segment (as defined by the DEF SEG statement) and m represents the data to be written. The values of n and m can be specified in either decimal or hexadecimal.

For example, suppose we want to write the character "A" in the fourth column and third row of the screen. The character is to be in red foreground and blue background color. We can do this as follows:

Step 1: Locate the address of the block to print "A" using Eq. (2.2):

$$\begin{aligned} \text{Character address} &= 80(3 - 1) + 2(4 - 1) = 166 \\ \text{Attribute address} &= 166 + 1 \qquad\qquad\quad = 167 \end{aligned}$$

Step 2: Determine the character code value and attribute value using Table 2.1 and Eq. (2.1):

ASCII code value for "A" = 65 (Table 2.1)

Attribute value {nonblinking, red foreground, blue background} = 20 [Eq. (2.1)]

Step 3: Set the current segment to point at the beginning of the graphics screen:

```
DEF SEG = &HB800
```

(The display buffer is at absolute address B8000 hex. Since segments are specified on 16-byte boundaries, the last hex digit is dropped on DEF SEG specification.)

Now, whatever we POKE into memory in the address range B800: 0000 to B800: 3FFF (or 0 to 16384) immediately affects what is displayed on the screen. The following BASIC program illustrates a means of accessing and moving the screen memory in the text mode.

```
 10 CLS                       'CLEAR THE SCREEN
 20 SCREEN 0: WIDTH 40        'SET THE SCREEN IN TEXT MODE
 30 DEF SEG = &HB800          'DEFINE CURRENT SEGMENT
 40 POKE 166, 65              'WRITE "A"
 50 POKE 167, 20              'SET THE ATTRIBUTE COLOR
 60 A = PEEK (166)            'READ CHARACTER "A"
 70 B = PEEK (167)            'READ THE ATTRIBUTE
 80 POKE 1832, A              'WRITE ANOTHER "A"
 90 POKE 1833, B              'SET THE ATTRIBUTE
100 END
```

When the program is executed, we will see a nonblinking character "A" printed on the screen in two locations, as shown in Fig. 2.3.

We can also add a border color to the screen (outside the text area) by adding the following statement to the program.

```
OUT &H3D9, 14    'YELLOW BORDER
```

Using the COLOR statement. In BASIC, the COLOR statement allows us to select the foreground and background colors for characters and the screen border color with a single statement. The full syntax in text mode is

```
COLOR [foreground] [,[background] [,border]]
```

where foreground = an integer expression that indicates the foreground color code in the range of 0 to 15 (add 16 to the numbers to have blinking characters),

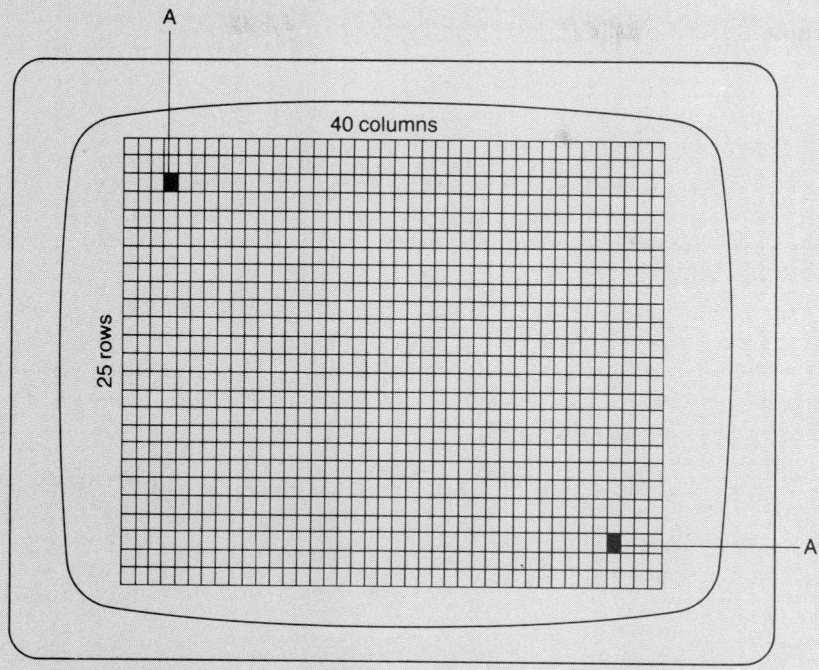

FIGURE 2.3 Memory-mapped character display on the IBM PC

background = an integer expression in the range 0 to 7 for the background color,

border = an integer expression in the range 0 to 15, defining the color for the border screen.

All integer numbers above should correspond to the color codes given in Table 1.8. As with the color/graphics adapter, we can make the character blink by adding 16 to the number of the desired foreground color. For example, the statement COLOR 14 + 16, 2, 4 sets a blinking yellow foreground, a blue background, and a red border screen. This is summarized in Table 2.2.

2.1.4 MULTIPLE TEXT PAGES

As we discussed before, when the memory map uses two bytes per displayed character, it takes up 4000 bytes in the 80 × 25 text mode. In the 40 × 25 text mode, the map is half as big, using only 2000 bytes. The display buffer has 16K bytes and thus is big enough for either four or eight complete text pages.

TABLE 2.2 BASIC color codes in text mode

Code decimal†	Color		
	Foreground	Color/effect background	Border‡
0	Black	Black	Black
1	Blue	Blue	Blue
2	Green	Green	Green
3	Cyan (greenish blue)	Cyan	Cyan
4	Red	Red	Red
5	Magenta (purplish)	Magenta	Magenta
6	Brown	Brown	Brown
7	White	White	White
8	Gray		Gray
9	Light blue		Light blue
10	Light green		Light green
11	Light cyan		Light cyan
12	Light red		Light red
13	Light magenta		Light magenta
14	Yellow		Yellow
15	Bright white		Bright white
16	Black		
17	Blinking blue		
18	Blinking green		
19	Blinking cyan		
20	Blinking red		
21	Blinking magenta		
22	Blinking brown		
23	Blinking white		
24	Blinking gray		
25	Blinking light blue		
26	Blinking light green		
27	Blinking light cyan		
28	Blinking light red		
29	Blinking light magenta		
30	Blinking yellow		
31	Blinking bright white		

†Code decimal numbers 16–31 are obtained with bit 7 on.

‡Controlled by Color Select Register.

AVAILABLE FROM ADDISON-WESLEY

Save time and keep keyboarding errors out of your programs!

A complete set of the programs in INTERACTIVE MICROCOMPUTER GRAPHICS by Chan S. Park is available on disk for $49.95.

Equipment you will need:

Hardware	IBM PC or XT, Color Monitor, Color/Graphics Adapter, Disk Drive, DOS 2.0
Memory	64K minimum

To order, use the handy card below

INTERACTIVE MICROCOMPUTER GRAPHICS

by Chan S. Park (#05541)

☐ I am interested in a licensing agreement available for $175 for the software to accompany the above title. Please send the licensing agreement form to:

Name ______________________________

Title ______________________________

Affiliation ______________________________

Department ______________________________

Address ______________________________

City ____________________ State _____ Zip _______

Telephone (____) ______________________________

INTERACTIVE MICROCOMPUTER GRAPHICS

by Chan S. Park (#05541)

Please send me:

_______ (qty) **INTERACTIVE MICROCOMPUTER GRAPHICS** software disk(s) at $49.95 each (#05537-6)

☐ Check enclosed. (Please include local state sales tax. Addison-Wesley will pay postage and handling.)

In a hurry, call 617-944-8660 for credit card orders only. Visa and MasterCard accepted.

Name ______________________________

Affiliation ______________________________

Address ______________________________

City ____________________ State _____ Zip _______

Telephone (____) ______________________________

NO POSTAGE
NECESSARY
IF MAILED
IN THE
UNITED STATES

BUSINESS REPLY CARD
FIRST CLASS PERMIT NO. 11 READING, MA.

Postage Will Be Paid By Addressee

ADDISON-WESLEY
PUBLISHING COMPANY, INC.
Attn: Tom Robbins
Reading, Massachusetts U.S.A. 01867

NO POSTAGE
NECESSARY
IF MAILED
IN THE
UNITED STATES

BUSINESS REPLY CARD
FIRST CLASS PERMIT NO. 11 READING, MA.

Postage Will Be Paid By Addressee

ADDISON-WESLEY
PUBLISHING COMPANY, INC.
Attn: Tom Robbins
Reading, Massachusetts U.S.A. 01867

The PC uses this extra memory when it is not needed for graphics displays by providing the text mode with multiple screen images in memory. These multiple images are called pages.

The display pages are numbered 0 through 3 for the 80 × 25 text mode or 0 through 7 for the 40 × 25 text mode. Page zero is located at the beginning of the display memory, followed by the other pages. The beginning of each page is located at a round number in binary notation. For example, in the 80 × 25 text mode, each page needs 4000 bytes. Page 0 then begins at relative location 0 in the color/graphics memory (or in hexadecimal, location &HB800). Page 1, however, does not begin immediately following page 0, at relative location 4000. Instead, it begins at the next kilobyte boundary, at a displacement of 4K, or 4096 bytes (1K = 1024). Thus, 96 bytes of memory are left unused in each page. Figure 2.4 shows how the pages are laid out in the display memory.

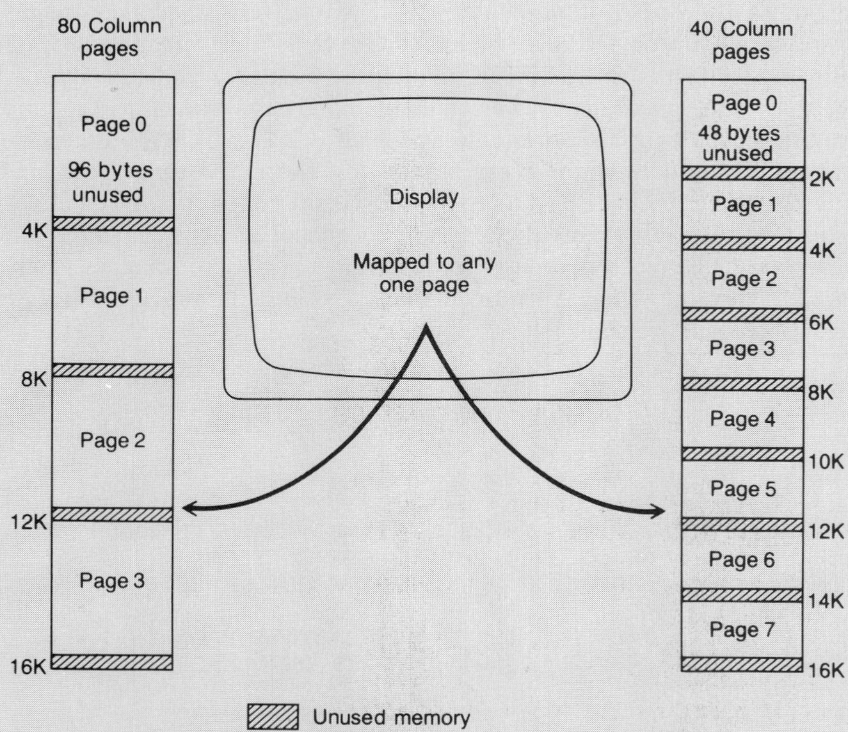

FIGURE 2.4 Multiple text pages in text mode

Control over the display pages is also provided in BASIC by the following statements:

```
SCREEN 0 [,[burst] ],[apage] [,vpage]]]
```

where

0 = a numeric expression resulting in text mode at current width (40 or 80).

burst = a numeric expression which enables color. In the text mode, a zero value disables color (black and white images only); any numeral value not zero allows color images.

apage = an integer expression in the range 0 to 7 for width 40, or 0 to 3 for width 80. It selects the page to be written to by output statements to the screen. It is called the "active page."

vpage = an integer expression in the same range as apage above. It selects which page is to be displayed on the screen. This "visual page" may be different from the active page.

For example, the BASIC statement "SCREEN 0, 1, 0, 0," selects text mode with color and sets both the active and visual pages to 0. If only *apage* and *vpage* are specified, the effect is that of changing display pages for viewing. By manipulating active and visual pages, we can display one page while building another. For example, the BASIC statement "SCREEN , , 1, 2" will make the mode and color burst remain unchanged, while setting the active page to 1 and the display page to 2. This allows us to switch visual pages instantaneously.

The following program illustrates the concept of creating multiple text pages in text mode. We will create two text pages in 40-column mode, each page containing the following short text. Each text begins at the 10th row and 15th column. The program is as follows.

Page 0	Page 1
10 [J. M. White]	10 [A. B. Black]
15	15

```
10 CLS
20 SCREEN 0,0,0: WIDTH 40          'SET BOTH ACTIVE AND VISUAL
30 SCREEN 0,1,0,0: COLOR 1,2,14    PAGES TO ZERO
40 LOCATE 10,15: PRINT             'WRITE ONTO PAGE 0
   "J. M. WHITE"
50 SCREEN 0,1,1,0                  'SET ACTIVE PAGE TO 1
60 LOCATE 10,15: PRINT             'WRITE ONTO PAGE 1
   "A. B. BLACK"
70 SCREEN 0,1,0,0                  'DISPLAY PAGE 0
80 IF INKEY$ = "" THEN 80          'PAUSE: HIT ANY KEY TO CONTINUE
90 SCREEN 0,1,1,1                  'DISPLAY PAGE 1
```

2.2 MEMORY-MAPPED GRAPHICS IN GRAPHICS MODE

2.2.1 MEMORY REQUIREMENT

We will first examine the memory needs of high-resolution graphics. If all we need to specify about a pixel is whether it is on or off, a single bit is enough to control a single pixel. In high-resolution graphics, there are 640 × 200, or 128,000 pixels. To control them all using one bit per pixel, we need 128,000 bits. With eight bits to a byte, we would need 80 bytes per line and 16,000 per screen. That is almost the entire memory capacity of the color/graphics adapter. Thus only 384 bytes are left unused (16K = 16,384 bytes). Since there is not much memory left, there is no way to assign colors to the pixels (other than to assign the colors black or white by turning the pixel off or on).

In medium-resolution mode, however, there are only half as many pixels on the screen. Since both resolutions use 16K bytes of display buffer to represent the screen image, we can dedicate two bits to each pixel. Two bits (C0, C1), taken together, can specify four different values (0, 1, 2, and 3), providing four colors in the medium-resolution graphics mode. Figure 2.5 shows how the display buffer formats pixels into bytes in each graphics mode.

2.2.2 MEMORY MAPPING

In graphics modes, the display buffer is organized into two blocks of 8K bytes each. Strange as it seems, all the even raster lines are stored in the first 8K of the screen memory map and all the odd raster lines in the next 8K. This is done because the 6845 CRT Controller draws all the even lines first and all the odd lines second, a practice known as *interlacing*. If we plan to do graphics from a language with no graphics commands, such as FORTRAN, Pascal, or assembly language, we must account for interlacing when plotting points.

Figure 2.6 summarizes the graphics memory map and pixel formats. For example, with high-resolution graphics as an example, there are 100 even-numbered raster lines and another 100 odd-numbered lines. Eighty bytes are used to control each raster line. The very first bit controls pixel (0,0); the next controls (0,1); the next (0,2); and so on to the last pixel of line 0 (0,639). This pixel is then followed by (2,0), (2, 1), and so on. Finally, the end of the even-line block is reached, and, on the next kilobyte boundary, the odd line block begins.

Experimenting with the POKE command will make this interlacing clearer. For example, the following BASIC program will plot two points, one

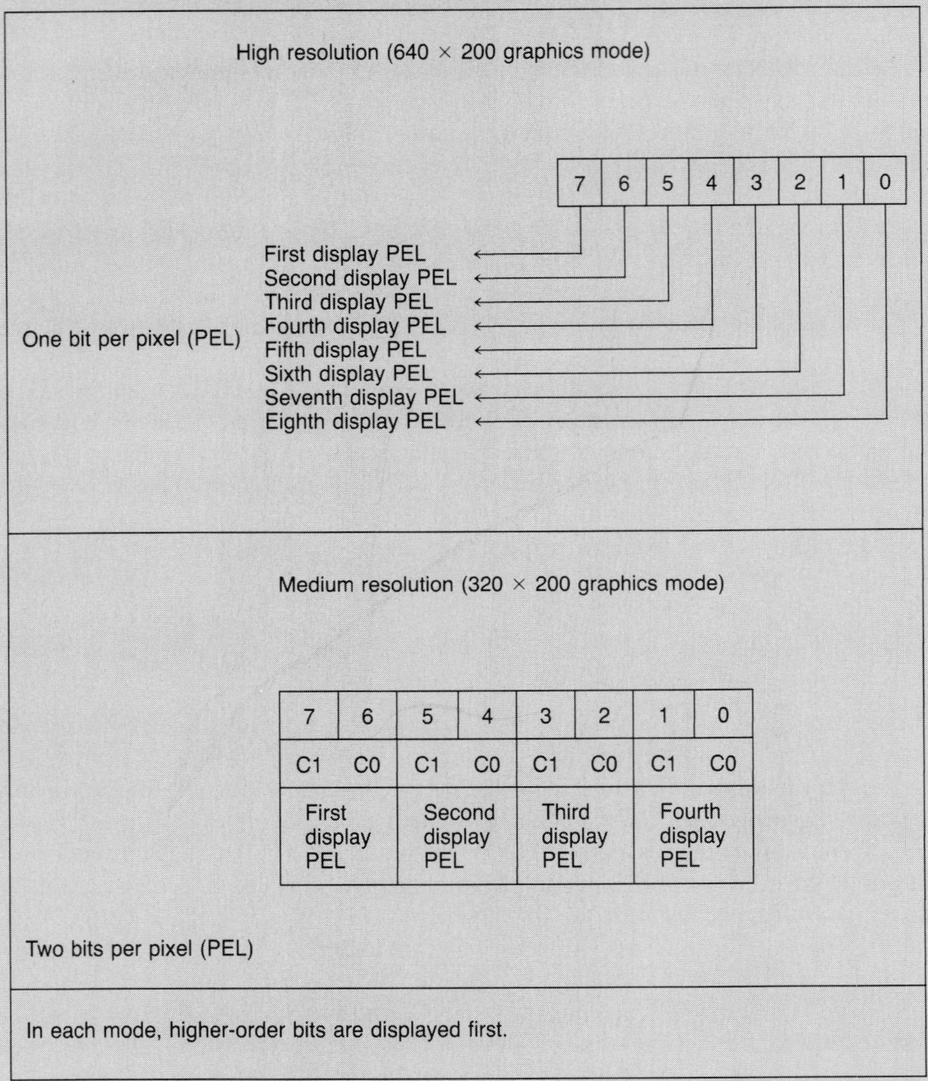

FIGURE 2.5 Bit assignments in graphics modes

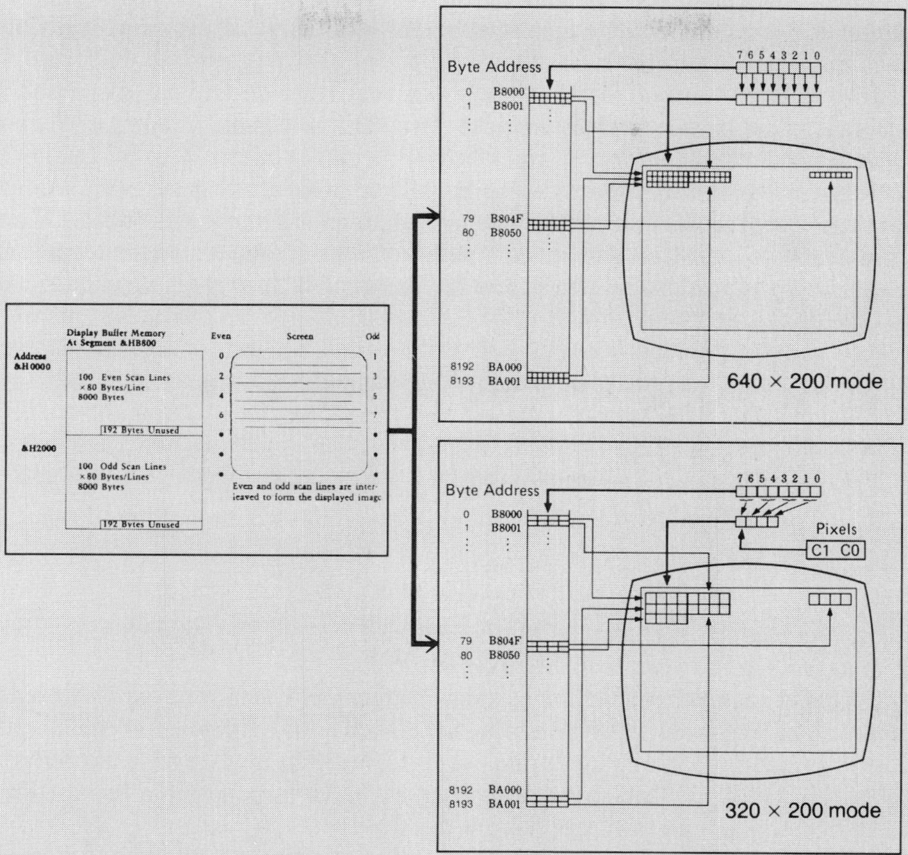

FIGURE 2.6 **Memory mapping in graphics modes. (From M. Waite and C. L. Morgan, *Graphics Primer for the IBM PC,* Osborne/ McGraw-Hill, 1983.)**

directly above the other:

```
10    SCREEN 2
20    DEF SEQ = &HB800
30    POKE 500, 3
40    POKE 500 + &H2000, 3
```

The 8K difference (&H2000) between their locations is the offset between the even and odd sections of the screen memory.

2.2.3 ACCESSING MEMORY FROM BASIC

Using PEEK and POKE Statements. We need first to program the Color Select Register to assign the background color for the pixels we will turn off, and the palette number for the pixels we will turn on. As we discussed in Section 1.3.5, the Color Select Register is a 6-bit write-only register with an I/O address of &H3D9 (or 985 in decimal). It can be written to by using the BIOS routine or BASIC. We will use BASIC to program this register. We can select the background color from any one of 16 colors shown in Table 1.8 and one of the two palettes shown in Table 2.3. For example, to select a blue background and assign palette 1, the bit pattern for this register should look like the following:

```
          5 4 3 2 1 0
         |1|0|0|0|0|1|   33 (decimal)
          ↑ ↑
   Palette  |  I R G B
         Normal intensity
```

To set this value from BASIC, the following statements can be used:

```
10   SCREEN 1, 0
20   OUT &H3D9, 33
```

Once this value is programmed in, the register will set the background to blue and pick palette 1 to control the pixel colors.

Colors in medium resolution can now be formed by combining bits from the Color Select Register with two pixel bits—C1 and C0—from the display buffer. Recall that the display buffer formats four pixels per byte as was shown in Fig. 2.5. With two bits taken together we have four possible bit patterns, giving decimal values ranging from 0 to 3.

When C1 and C0 are both "0," the pixel is not activated and has to take the background color of the screen. If this is the case, the adapter scans through the bit pattern stored in the Color Select Register to determine the background color.

When C1 and C0 give a decimal value other than 0, the pixel is to be turned on. Then the adapter scans through the bit pattern stored in the Color Select Register to determine from which palette the pixel will select the foreground color. For a given palette, these numerical values correspond to the color codes in the palette. The following program will turn on three pixels with different colors on the screen.

```
10 CLS: SCREEN 1, 0
20 OUT &H3D9, 33          'SET BACKGROUND COLOR
30 DEF SEG = &HB800       'AND SELECT PALETTE 1
40 POKE 0, 0
50 POKE 80, 64
60 POKE 160, 128
70 POKE 240, 192
```

TABLE 2.3 Medium-resolution (320 × 200) color sets

CSR bit 4 (Int)	Pixel data C1 (Red)	C0 (Green)	CSR bit 5 (Blue)	IRGB color number	Color name	BASIC Palette number	BASIC Color code
(0)	0	0	(0)		Background	Palette 0	0
0	0	1	0	2	Green		1
0	1	0	0	4	Red		2
0	1	1	0	6	Brown		3
(0)	0	0	(1)		Background	Palette 1	0
0	0	1	1	3	Cyan		1
0	1	0	1	5	Magenta		2
0	1	1	1	7	White		3
(1)	0	0	(0)		Background	Palette 2	
1	0	1	0	10	Light green		
1	1	0	0	12	Light red		
1	1	1	0	14	Yellow		
(1)	0	0	(1)		Background	Palette 3	
1	0	1	1	11	Light cyan		
1	1	0	1	13	Light magenta		
1	1.	1	1	15	Intense white		

Note: Palettes 2 and 3 cannot be accessed from the COLOR graphics statement. We must use the BIOS routine (or OUT statement) to access these additional palettes. CSR stands for Color Select Register.

Source: T. V. Hoffmann, "The IBM Color/Graphics Adapter," Reprinted from *PC Technical Journal* **1** (1), 1983. Copyright © 1983, Ziff-Davis Publishing Company.

In 640 × 200 mode, the display buffer stores the information about the status of each pixel—on or off. As we mentioned earlier, one bit controls one pixel in memory mapping; in high resolution there is no room to assign colors to the pixels. Thus the adapter first scans through the status of each pixel on the screen, then passes the information to the Color Select Register to determine the foreground color for the "on" pixels. To program an intensified red foreground color to the register in high-resolution graphics mode, the bit pattern should look like

5	4	3	2	1	0	
0	0	1	1	0	0	12
		I	R	G	B	

To set this value from BASIC, the following statement can be used:

```
10    SCREEN 2
20    OUT &H3D9, 12
```

Using the COLOR statement. In graphics mode, the COLOR statement in BASIC has a slightly different syntax. The full syntax for the COLOR statement in the medium-resolution graphics mode is

COLOR [background] [,palette]

where

background = a numeric expression specifying the background color. The colors allowed for background are 0 through 15, as shown in Table 1.8.

palette = numeric expression ranging from 0 to 1 that selects the palette of colors shown in Table 2.3.

The color selected for background may be the same as any of the palette colors. The palette gives us a choice between the two sets of colors that work with subsequent graphics commands such as PSET, PRESET, LINE, CIRCLE, PAINT, and DRAW. (These commands will be discussed in later sections.) Once the palette number is specified by the COLOR statement, we should select one of the three colors specified in that palette. No COLOR statement is permitted in high-resolution graphics mode.

2.3 IBM PC GRAPHICS BASIC COMMANDS

Up to this point, we have explored how to access and control the screen memory by using POKE and PEEK statements. Certainly these BASIC statements are useful for exploring the screen memory map, but they are not convenient for creating complex graphics images. Several graphics commands are available on the IBM PC that can be used to create complicated graphics images with relative ease. Even though these commands are a subset of the BASIC Language, they are written in machine level code and are fast enough to use in the normal graphics environment. In this section, we will briefly introduce these graphics commands with examples explaining what they are and how to use them in generating computer graphics. To begin with, we will discuss how to specify coordinates in BASIC graphics.

2.3.1 SPECIFYING COORDINATES AND STATEMENT FORMAT

Graphics coordinates. Any graphics statements require information about where we want to draw on the screen. We give this information in the form of coordinates. Coordinates are in the form (x, y), where x is the horizontal position and y is the vertical position. This form is known as the *absolute form* and refers to the actual coordinates of the point on the screen, without regard to the last point referenced. In our discussion in graphics commands, the expression (x, y) will always denote the coordinates of a point.

There is another way to indicate coordinates, known as *relative form*. Using this form we tell BASIC where the point is relative to the last point referenced. This form looks like:

```
STEP (x offset, y offset)
```

where x offset and y offset represent the horizontal and vertical positions from the last point referenced. (The "last point referenced" is set by each graphics command.) We will give examples of how to use both forms of coordinates when we discuss each graphics command.

Color convention. In the medium resolution mode, *color* is a value between 0 and 3: Color 0 selects the background color, while 1, 2, and 3 each select a color from the palette chosen in the COLOR statement. The default is the foreground color, color number 3. In high-resolution mode, 0 selects black and 1 selects white. If the color is omitted, the foreground color is assumed. All other color-related parameters in the graphics commands will follow this color convention.

2.3.2 PSET AND PRESET STATEMENTS

PSET is the simplest graphics statement. It sets a pixel to a selected color. The command is

```
PSET (x,y) [,color]
PRESET (x,y) [,color]
```

Square brackets around a quantity indicate that the quantity is optional. Any element within the syntax statement that is omitted retains its previous value. In this command, color is optional.

PRESET is similar to PSET. It differs only in that, if no color parameter is given to PRESET, the background color 0 is selected. The PRESET (x, y) statement will then draw a point on the screen in background color, an action perceived as an erasure by the user. Thus PSET (x, y), 0 is identical to PRESET (x, y).

The following example demonstrates how these commands can be used in plotting points on the screen:

```
10 SCREEN 1,0              'SET MEDIUM RESOLUTION IN COLOR
20 COLOR 1,0               'SET BACKGROUND BLUE, PALETTE 0
30 PSET (3,10), 2          'PUT DOT IN RED
40 PSET STEP (7,-5)        'PUT ANOTHER DOT IN RED AT (10,5)
50 PRESET (3,10)           'ERASE DOT AT (3,10)
```

Note: PSET STEP in line 40 specifies relative coordinates.

Almost any graphic functions can be performed with PSET and PRESET. Lines, circles, and other shapes are composed of a series of pixels strung together to create the desired form. Of course, it is faster and easier to draw a square with a single command than to position and draw each of the pixels individually. LINE and CIRCLE statements are such composite commands.

2.3.3 LINE STATEMENT

The LINE statement can connect two points with a line (solid or dotted) or draw a box on the screen. The LINE statement can even draw filled boxes. The full syntax for this LINE statement is as follows:

```
LINE [(x1,y1)]-(x2,y2)[,[color] [,B[F]][,style]]
```

Once again, square brackets indicate various levels of options. Pairs $(x1, y1)$, $(x2, y2)$ are the coordinates of two connecting points. The use of the color option is identical to that of the PSET command. Option "B" draws an unfilled box, whereas "BF" draws a box filled with the selected color. The last option, "style," is a 16-bit integer mask used to draw a dotted line across the screen. It is available only in the BASIC 2.0 or higher version. The "style" option is used for normal lines and boxes, but cannot be used with filled boxes (BF).

The simplest form of the LINE command is as follows:

```
LINE - (x2,y2)
```

If no starting point $(x1, y1)$ is specified, the PC will draw a line from the last point referenced to the point $(x2, y2)$ in the foreground color. Suppose we want to draw a series of lines, each line beginning where the previous line ended. To do this we can use a series of LINE statements, like this:

```
10 SCREEN 1,0                       'SET MEDIUM RESOLUTION IN COLOR
20 COLOR 0,0                        'BLACK BACKGROUND, PALETTE 0
30 LINE (30,100)-(100,120)          'DRAW A TRIANGLE
40 LINE    -(130,100)
50 LINE    -(30,100)
```

(See Fig. 2.7a.) The following example will draw a box filled with the color selected. In this case, the two sets of coordinates $(x1, y1)$ and $(x2, y2)$ represent the opposite diagonal corner points of the box (see Fig. 2.7b).

```
10 SCREEN 1,0
20 COLOR 1,1
30 LINE (0,0)-(100,100),2,BF
```

To format the display line, we assign bits to the "style" option. Because "style" is 16 bits wide, the pattern for a dotted line looks like this:

1 0 1 0 1 0 1 0 1 0 1 0 1 0 1 0

This is equal to AAAA in hexadecimal notation because hex A = 1010. We can create our own patterns by experimenting with arrangements of the 16-bit assignment. A series of lines, each with fatter dashes, would be assigned by

1 1 0 0 1 1 0 0 1 1 0 0 1 1 0 0 (&HCCCC)
1 1 1 0 1 1 1 0 1 1 1 0 1 1 1 0 (&HEEEE)
1 1 1 1 1 0 0 0 1 1 1 1 1 0 0 0 (&HF8F8)
1 1 1 1 1 1 1 1 0 0 0 0 0 0 0 0 (&HFF00)

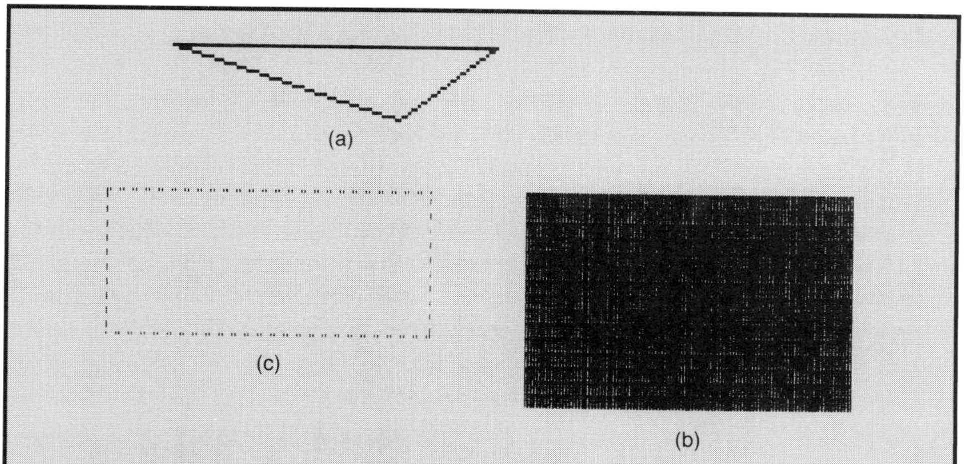

FIGURE 2.7 Line statements used to draw (a) a triangle, (b) a box filled in magenta, (c) a cyan box with dashes.

To draw a cyan box with dashes, we might execute the following:

```
10 SCREEN 1,0
20 COLOR 0,1
30 LINE (100,100)-(200,140), 1, BF, &HCCCC
```

(See Fig. 2.7c.) The last point referenced after a LINE statement can also be used as a base to draw a line. For example,

```
LINE(100,100)-STEP(50,-30)
```

will draw a line from (100,100) to (150,70). Note that in BASIC release 2.0, out-of-range coordinates are not visible on the viewing surface. This is called *line clipping* because the image that is outside of the coordinate range is "clipped" at the boundaries of the viewing surface. This is a very useful feature in computer graphics, as we will see in Chapter 3.

2.3.4 CIRCLE STATEMENT

The CIRCLE statement draws circles, arcs, and ellipses, providing an easy way to construct curved shapes. The full syntax for the CIRCLE command is

CIRCLE(*x*,*y*),*r*[,color[,start,end[,aspect]]]

The coordinates (x,y) are for the center of the circle, and r (radius) is the distance from the center to the outer edge of the circle, as measured in pixels on the screen. *Color* is the color of the circle; it is an optional parameter that defaults to Color 3. *Start* and *end* are the two ends of the arc to be drawn, and are specified in *radians* (see Fig. 2.8). If these two parameters are omitted, the whole circle will be drawn. The last parameter, called the aspect, is the ratio of the radius in the y direction to the radius in the x direction (height/width), which allows the command to be used to draw an ellipse. In a true circle, the aspect ratio is always 1. For a monitor such as the IBM PC Color Graphics unit, whose pixel lengths are not the same in both the x and y directions (i.e., 320×200), we need to adjust the aspect ratio to get a true circle. In medium resolution the default aspect ratio is 5/6; the slight shortening of the y axis produces the visual effect of a circle. All aspect ratios in high-resolution mode should be half of those used in medium-resolution mode to produce the same images with the default aspect ratio of 5/12 (see Fig. 2.9). If aspect >1, then r is the y radius. That is, the radius is measured in pixels in the vertical direction. If aspect <1, r is the x radius.

The CIRCLE statement also can draw wedges (or pie slices). A wedge is nothing more than an arc with lines connecting the end points to the center of the circle. With the CIRCLE statement, if either the start or the end is a negative number, that point is connected to the center of the circle. If both points are negative, a wedge is formed. The following will demonstrate the use

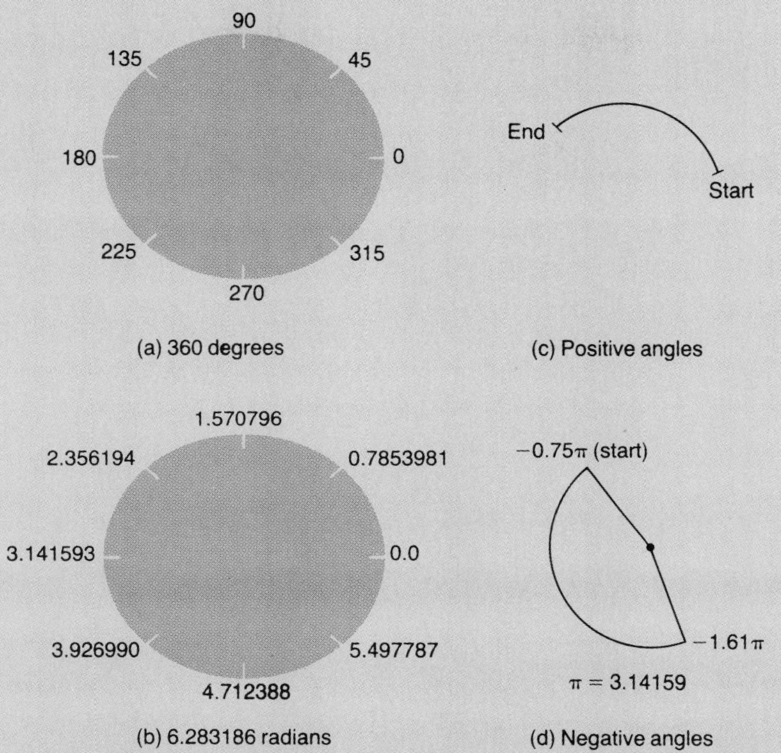

FIGURE 2.8 Specifying circle parameters

of the CIRCLE command:

```
10 CLS
20 SCREEN 1,0
30 COLOR 0,1
40 PI=3.141593
50 CIRCLE (100,100),30                 ' DRAW A CIRCLE IN WHITE
60 CIRCLE (100,100),30,,,,5/18         ' DRAW A HORIZONTAL ELLIPSE
                                         IN WHITE
70 CIRCLE (100,100),30,2,1.2*PI,1.7*PI      ' DRAW AN ARC
80 CIRCLE (100,100),30,2,-1.3*PI,-1.7*PI    ' DRAW A WEDGE
```

Note: Line 60 shows how in BASIC a parameter is skipped over by omitting it between commas: ,,, skips two parameters.

The last point referenced after a circle is drawn is the center of the circle, and points that are off the screen are not drawn (see Fig. 2.10).

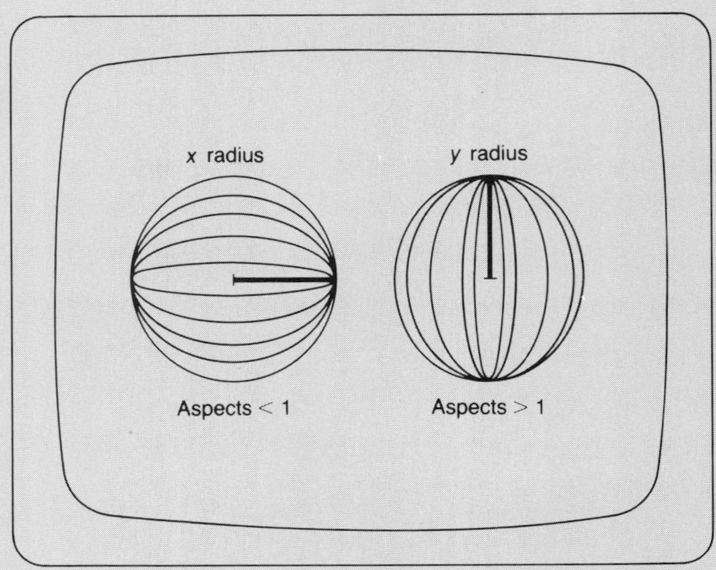

FIGURE 2.9 Effect of aspect ratio value on ellipses

2.3.5 PAINT STATEMENT

The PAINT statement fills in an area on the screen with selected color. The complete syntax format is

```
PAINT (x,y) [,paint][,boundary]
```

The coordinates (x, y) are for the point within the area to be filled in. *Paint* can be either a numeric or a string expression. If it is a numeric expression, it is the color to be painted with. If it is a string expression, then a specified pattern is *tiled,* or embedded, in a painted figure. The figure should be drawn in the *boundary* color. (The figure to be filled in is the figure with edges of boundary color.)

Paint tiling. The method of designing patterns is to represent the string expression by the tile mask. The tile mask is always 8 bits wide and it must be a string expression of the form:

```
CHR (HEXADECIMAL NUMBERS REPRESENTING THE 8-BIT PATTERN)
```

The string expression may contain up to 64 bytes. The structure of the string expression appears in Fig. 2.11. The tile pattern is repeated uniformly over the entire system. Because there is only one bit per pixel in high resolution (see

Section 2.2.1), a point is plotted at every position in the bit mask that has a value of 1. For example, if we design the tile mask with three bytes having the following bit patterns,

	7	6	5	4	3	2	1	0	bit position
Tile byte 0	1	1	0	0	0	1	0	1	CHR$(&HC5), 197
Tile byte 1	0	1	0	1	1	0	1	0	CHR$(&H5A), 90
Tile byte 2	0	1	1	1	1	1	1	0	CHR$(&H7E), 126

we can translate these bit patterns into a string expression,

```
TILE$ = CHR$(&HC5) + CHR$(&H5A) + CHR$(&H7E).
```

The program below will demonstrate how to tile a box with the tile mask designed above.

```
10 CLS : SCREEN 2 : KEY OFF
20 LINE (100,100) - (400,180),,B
30 TILE$ = CHR$(&HC5) + CHR$(&H5A) + CHR$(&H7E)
40 PAINT (300,140), TILE$
50 END
```

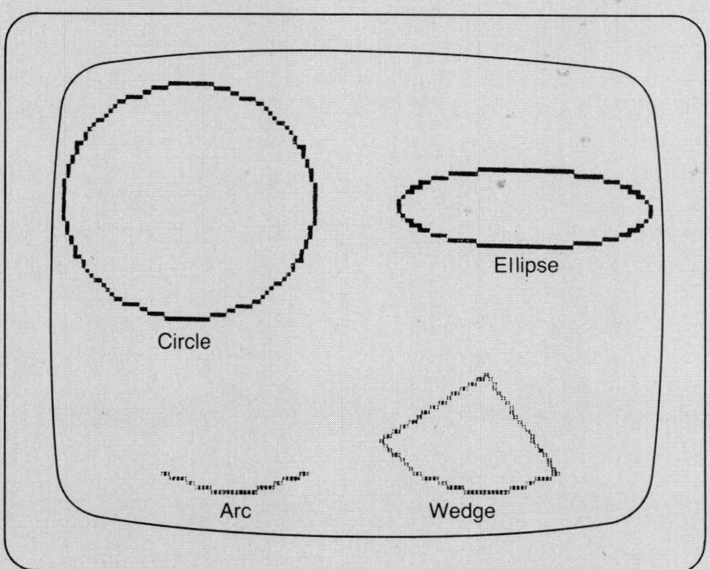

FIGURE 2.10 Effects of CIRCLE statement (circle, ellipse, arc, and wedge)

	7	6	5	4	3	2	1	0	Bit position
BYTE 0	x	x	x	x	x	x	x	x	
BYTE 1	x	x	x	x	x	x	x	x	
BYTE 2	x	x	x	x	x	x	x	x	
BYTE 3	x	x	x	x	x	x	x	x	
.	.	.	.	.	.	.	.	.	
.	.	.	.	.	.	.	.	.	
.	.	.	.	.	.	.	.	.	
BYTE 62	x	x	x	x	x	x	x	x	
BYTE 63	x	x	x	x	x	x	x	x	

x = 0 or 1 binary bit.

FIGURE 2.11 The structure of tile pattern in PAINT (640 × 200 mode)

In this case, PAINT at coordinate (300,140) will begin by plotting byte 1. This pattern appears on the screen as shown in Fig. 2.12.

The method of designing patterns in medium resolution is different from the method used in high resolution. One medium-resolution tile byte describes only four pixels, since medium resolution has only two bits per pixel (see Section 2.2.1). Every two bits of the tile byte now can describe one of four

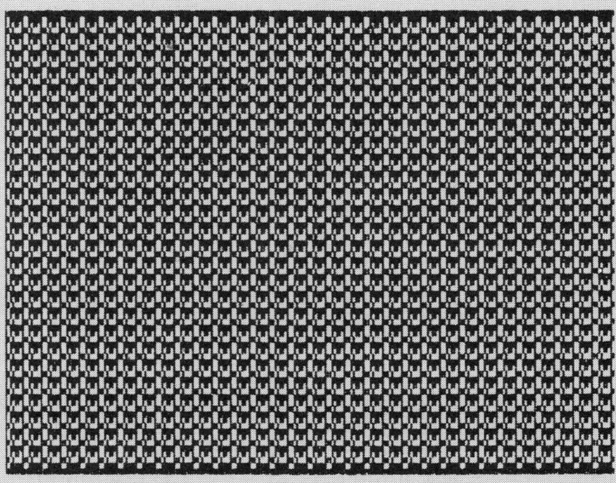

FIGURE 2.12 Effect of tiling in 640 × 200 graphics mode

TABLE 2.4 The tile patterns in 320 × 200 graphics mode

Color palette 0	Color palette 1	Color number in binary	Pattern to draw solid line in binary	Pattern to draw solid line in hexadecimal
Green	Cyan	01	01010101	&H55
Red	Magenta	10	10101010	&HAA
Brown	White	11	11111111	&HFF

Source: *IBM PC Basic Reference Manual*

possible colors associated with each of the four pixels to be plotted. Table 2.4 shows the binary and hexadecimal values associated with the given colors.

The following example demonstrates how to tile a circle area in medium resolution with two lines of red and one line of green (see Fig. 2.13).

```
10 CLS : SCREEN 1,0 : KEY OFF
20 COLOR 0,0
30 TILE$ = CHR$(&HAA) + CHR$(&HAA) + CHR$(&H55)
40 CIRCLE (160,100), 50, 3
50 PAINT (160,100), TILE$, 3
60 END
```

2.3.6 DRAW STATEMENT

The DRAW statement draws an object as specified by a string. The syntax format is

```
DRAW string
```

The DRAW statement employs a *graphics definition language* (GDL) to draw combinations of straight lines and points. The language commands are contained in the string expression *string*. The string defines an object, which is drawn when BASIC executes the DRAW statement. During execution, BASIC examines the value of *string* and interprets single letter commands from the string. These commands are detailed in Table 2.5.

Move and draw commands. The global move command M has two different modes, relative and absolute. These modes correspond to and perform in much the same way as the relative and absolute modes for the PSET, LINE, and CIRCLE statements. Relative mode is indicated by a signed integer and absolute mode, by an unsigned integer.

The command string can consist of a single move command or several such commands joined together in the same string. It is also possible to put semi-

FIGURE 2.13 Painting circle with tile pattern (320 × 200 mode)

colons between move commands and to put spaces anywhere throughout the command string. Since the effects of several draw statements are cumulative, we do not have to pack all our move commands into one command string.

There are eight local move commands: U, D, L, R, E, F, G, and H. Table 2.5 also shows which direction each of these local move commands moves the point. There are three possible forms for the syntax for these local move commands: the letter itself; the letter followed by an unsigned integer constant; and the letter followed by an "=" sign, the variable name. A letter by itself indicates a move by one unit in the indicated direction. A letter followed by either an unsigned constant or by an "= variable name" allows us to move that many units in that direction.

Prefix commands. The B and N prefixes can be used with either the global (M) or local move commands. The B prefix causes the next command to be executed as a move without draw, whereas the N prefix causes the current position to remain as it was before the command was executed.

Action commands. There are six action commands, allowing us to set colors and draw figures. The syntax of these commands is shown in Table 2.5. The C command stands for color, and it sets the color for all subsequent move commands until the next C command. The A command sets the angle for all subsequent move commands until the next A command. Only four angles are allowed: 0, 90, 180, and 270 degrees. The TA command turns figures through 360°, in slices as small as one degree. A positive angle rotates an image

TABLE 2.5 DRAW statement—graphics definition language

Control command	Format	Effect	Parameter
Move and draw	M x,y	To specified point (x,y)	x,y, = absolute coordinates
	M $+x, +y$	To specified point $(X + x, Y + y)$	X, Y = last referenced point $+x, +y$ = relative coordinates
	Un	Up [↑]	n rows'
	Dn	Down [↓]	n rows'
	Rn	Right [→]	n columns'
	Ln	Left [←]	n columns'
	En	Diagonally up and right [↗]	n = diagonal distance
	Fn	Diagonally down and right [↘]	n = diagonal distance
	Gn	Diagonally down and left [↙]	n = diagonal distance
	Hn	Diagonally up and left [↖]	n = diagonal distance
Prefix	B [Move and Draw]	Do not draw on the next move	
	N [Move and Draw]	Return to current point after next move	
Action	A n	Rotate all subsequent moving and drawing counterclockwise	n = rotation angle 0 = 0 2 = 180 1 = 90 3 = 270
	TA n	Turn angle n	n = rotation angle $-360 \leqslant n \leqslant 360$ $n > 0$ counterclockwise $n < 0$ clockwise
	S n	Scale subsequent distances	n = scale factor $1 \leq n \leq 255$
	C n	Select color from given palette	n = 0 or 1 (640 × 200 mode) = 0, 1, 2, or 3 (320 × 200 mode)
	P paint, bound	Paint or fill in area	paint = paint color bound = boundary color
	X variable	Execute subcommands from another string	variable = a string variable that contains more subcommands

counterclockwise and a negative angle, clockwise. TA followed by another TA is not cumulative; each resets the angle for subsequent images. When objects are rotated by the specified angle, they are drawn with the aspect ratio of 4/3. This means that rotated objects are drawn in such a way as to prevent them from looking distorted if we happen to be using an ideal display monitor.

The S command sets scale factor, allowing us to scale objects. The scale factor must be between 0 and 255. The P command allows us to set figure color to *paint* and border color to *boundary*.

Finally, the X command acts like a subroutine call—that is, it causes the named command string to be executed immediately. In the command syntax, the letter is followed by a semicolon. The semicolon must be present so that BASIC knows when the name of the string has ended. We will illustrate how to use the DRAW statement with two short examples below. The following program draws a green triangle with a red border on a blue background. The default starting position is the center of the screen. (See Fig. 2.14).

```
10 CLS
20 SCREEN 1,0 : COLOR 1,0
30 DRAW "C2 TA30 U49 TA150"
40 DRAW "U50 TA270 U50"
50 DRAW "TA60 BU25 P1,2"
```

The following program, which demonstrates how to use the X subcommand, rotates a box around a central point to produce a decorative wheel (see Fig. 2.15).

```
10 CLS
20 SCREEN 1,0 : COLOR 1,1
30 BOX$ = "U40 R48 D40 L48"
40 FOR I = 1 TO 360 STEP 20
50 DRAW "TA = I ; XBOX$ ;"
60 NEXT I
```

2.3.7 WINDOW STATEMENT AND CLIPPING

The WINDOW statement allows us to redefine the coordinates of the screen. In other words, WINDOW allows us to draw objects in a new coordinate space (the *world coordinate system*) that is not bounded by the logical limits of the screen (the *physical coordinate system*). Subsequent graphics are scaled to the new coordinates. The complete syntax of the command is

```
WINDOW[[SCREEN](x1,y1)-(x2,y2)]
```

The $(x1, y1)$ and $(x2, y2)$ are user-defined coordinates called world coordinates. This rectangular region in the world coordinate space is called a *window*. When the statement is in effect, BASIC converts the world coordinate pairs into the appropriate physical coordinate pairs for display within the screen.

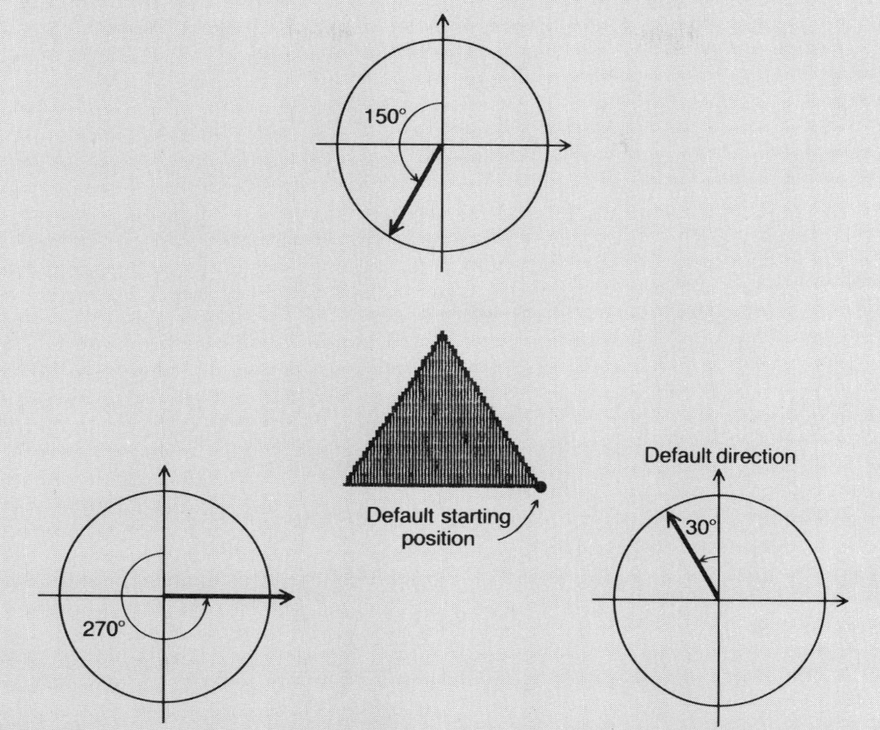

FIGURE 2.14 Triangle drawn by using DRAW statements. The default starting position is the center of the screen.

Without the WINDOW statement, the PC screen is configured so that the upper left-hand corner is labeled (0,0) and the lower right-hand corner is labeled either (319,199) in medium resolution or (639,199) in high resolution.

When WINDOW statement such as WINDOW (−10,−10) − (10,10) is executed, the upper left corner of the screen receives the coordinates (−10,10) and the lower right corner, the coordinates (10,−10). When the following program is executed, we obtain Fig. 2.16.

```
10 CLS
20 SCREEN 1,0 : COLOR 1,0
30 WINDOW (-10,-10)-(10,10)
40 LINE (-5,-5)-(5,5),,B
50 LINE (0,0) - (4,5), 1
```

Note that the figure is the normal orientation for Cartesian coordinates, with

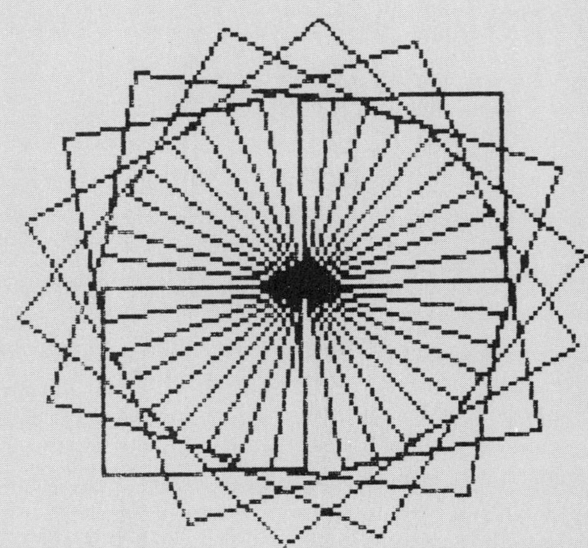

FIGURE 2.15 A decorative wheel created by using the X subcommand

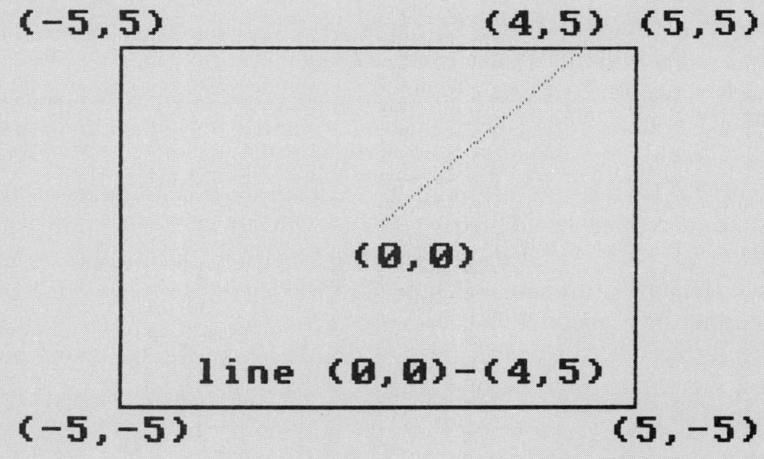

FIGURE 2.16 Effect of the WINDOW statement: The WINDOW statement converts the screen coordinates into Cartesian coordinates.

x increasing to the right and y increasing upwards. Note also that the screen center (0,0) is located in the middle of the screen.

When the SCREEN attribute is included, the coordinates are not inverted. In that case, a statement such as WINDOW (−10,−10) − (10,10) defines the screen to look like Fig. 2.17. This can be verified by executing the following program.

```
10 CLS
20 SCREEN 1,0 : COLOR 1,0
30 WINDOW SCREEN (-10,-10) - (10,10)
40 LINE (-5,-5) - (5,5),,B
50 LINE (0,0) - (4,5), 1
```

The WINDOW statement uses *line clipping,* a process by which points referenced outside the window are made invisible to the viewing area. Thus any object lying partially inside and partially outside the window is cut off so that only the points referenced inside the window appear to the viewer. (This clipping capability becomes very critical when we manipulate graphical images, as we will discuss in Chapter 3.)

WINDOW also allows us to "zoom" and "pan." If a window is used with coordinates larger than an image, the entire image will appear in miniature.

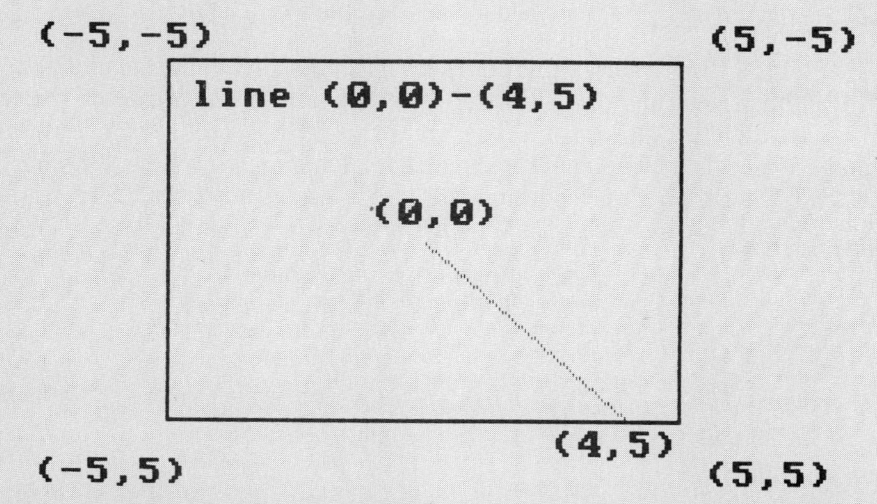

FIGURE 2.17 Effect of the WINDOW SCREEN statement: The WINDOW SCREEN statement converts the Cartesian coordinates into the IBM PC device coordinates.

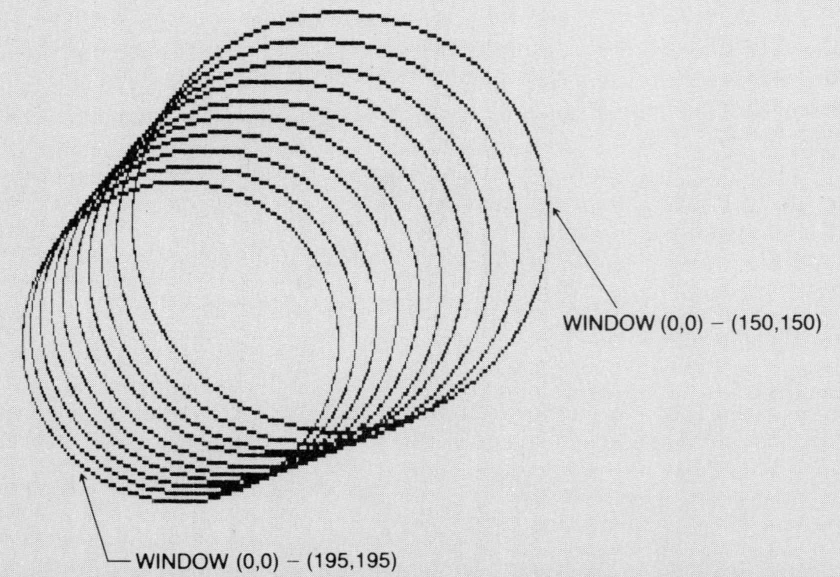

FIGURE 2.18 A series of circles drawn by varying the parameters of the WINDOW statement

Choosing window coordinates smaller than an image forces clipping and allows only a portion of the image to be displayed and magnified. By changing window sizes, we can zoom in until an object occupies the entire screen, or pan out until the image is nothing but a spot on the screen. The following program demonstrates both the clipping and zooming features of the WINDOW statement. The output result is shown in Fig. 2.18.

```
10 CLS: SCREEN 2 : KEY OFF
20 FOR I=1 TO 10
30 X=200-5*I: Y=200-5*I
40 WINDOW (0,0) - (X,Y)
50 GOSUB 80
60 NEXT I
70 END
80 CIRCLE (100,100),30
90 RETURN
```

2.3.8 VIEW STATEMENT AND VIEWPORT PLANNING

The VIEW statement allows us to define subsets of the viewing surface, called viewports, onto which graphical contents are mapped. The complete syntax is

```
VIEW[[SCREEN][(x1,y1)-(x2,y2)[,[color][,[boundary]]]] ]
```

Optional parameters allow the viewport to be filled and bordered with a specified color. The pairs $(x1, y1)$, $(x2, y2)$ are the upper left $(x1, y1)$ and lower right $(x2, y2)$ coordinates of the viewport defined on the screen. These must be defined within the actual limits of the screen. The parameter "color" fills the defined viewport with color and the parameter "boundary" (a color in the range 0 to 3) draws a boundary line around the viewport. If the SCREEN argument is omitted, all points plotted are relative to the viewport. That is, $x1$ and $y1$ are *added* to the x and y coordinate before the point is plotted on the screen. If the SCREEN argument is included, all the points plotted are *absolute* and may be inside or outside the screen limits. We can define multiple viewports, but only one viewport can be active at a time. RUN and SCREEN statements disable the viewports.

VIEW also scales objects by placing them in smaller or larger viewports. The coordinates of the viewport are determined by the last executed WINDOW statement and objects are scaled to fit the viewport. For example, this program

```
10 CLS: SCREEN 1,0: COLOR 1,0
20 WINDOW (50,50)-(350,200)                 'Starting Viewport
30 LINE (50,50)-(350,200),,B
40 GOSUB 100
50 VIEW (20,20)-(150,100),1,3               'Viewport 1
60 GOSUB 100
70 VIEW (200,150)-(300,190),1,2             'Viewport 2
80 GOSUB 100
90 END
100 CIRCLE (240,150),40,2,,,5/18
110 CIRCLE (240,150),40,2,,,1
120 RETURN
```

defines normal Cartesian coordinates with $(0, 0)$ as the lower left point, draws two circles in red, defines a portion of the screen as a green viewport with a brown border, and draws the same two circles but in a second viewport. This result is shown in Fig. 2.19. Note that the circles have been scaled into different viewports.

2.3.9 GET AND PUT STATEMENTS

The GET and PUT statements can be used for high-speed object motion and are very useful in computer animation. GET reads the colors of the points within the specified rectangle into the array and PUT writes the colors onto a specified area of the screen. The syntax of the commands is

```
GET (x1,y1)-(x2,y2),arrayname
PUT (x3,y3),arrayname[,action]
```

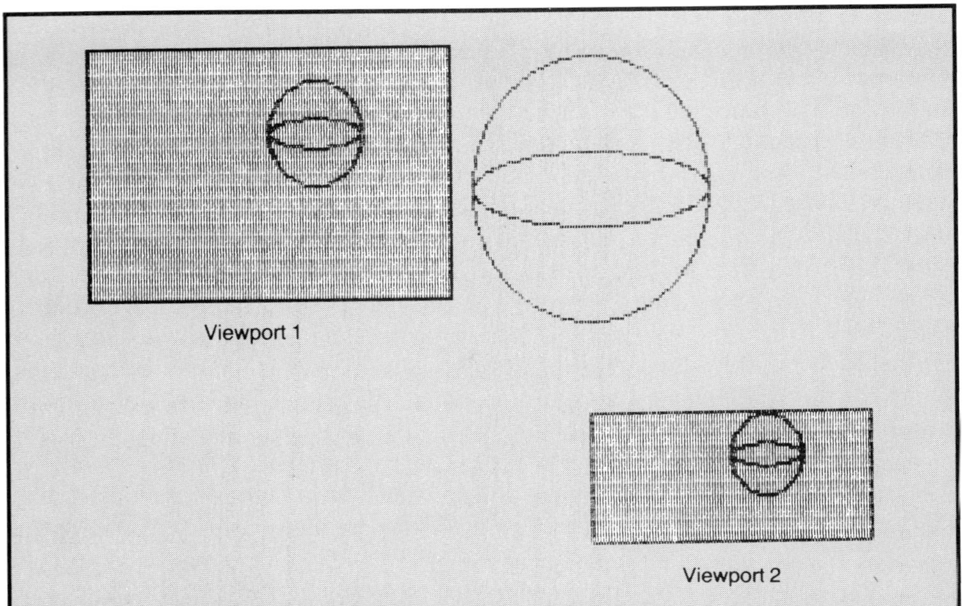

FIGURE 2.19 Effect of VIEW statement (setting multiple viewports)

GET statement. We will first discuss the GET statement. The specified rectangle has opposite corners $(x1, y1)$ and $(x2, y2)$. The array is used as a place to hold the image; it must be numeric, and may be any precision. The array must be dimensioned and defined before the GET statement is used.

The rectangular area of the screen that the GET statement captures can be of any size and at any location. We must, however, specify a numeric array that is large enough to hold the screen data the GET statement will read. We can use the following formula to calculate the array size required.

$$\text{Number of bytes} = 4 + \text{INT}[(x \cdot \text{B} + 7)/8]y \qquad \textbf{(2.3)}$$

where B = bits per pixel (2 in medium resolution, and 1 in high resolution).

x = length of the horizontal side of the rectangle

y = length of the vertical side of the rectangle

For example, if we were to execute

```
GET (10,10)-(19,19), ARRAY
```

in medium-resolution mode, the array would have to be dimensioned to hold 34 bytes.

$$4 + \text{INT}[(10 * 2 + 7)/8]10 = 34 \text{ bytes.}$$

The bytes per element of an array are: 2 for integer, 4 for single precision, and 8 for double-precision. Therefore, we could use an integer array with at least 17 elements so that we may dimension ARRAY(17).

PUT statement. Coordinates $(x3, y3)$ define where the upper left corner of the image will be placed. *Arrayname* is the array in which the image has been saved and action, the only optional parameter, selects one of the five ways in which the image may be put onto the screen. Valid values for *action* are PSET, PRESET, XOR, OR, and AND. XOR is the default setting if no value is selected. The last point referenced is $(x3, y3)$.

PUT with the PSET action displays the exact image stored in the array with the GET statement, erasing what was there before.

The PRESET action is similar to the PSET action, but puts a negative of the image onto the screen. In medium resolution, colors 0 and 3 are negatives of each other, as are colors 1 and 2. In high resolution, colors 0 and 1 are negatives of each other.

The AND, XOR, and OR actions each blend array and screen colors according to different rules, which are summarized in Table 2.6. For example, the AND action would blend a cyan point (color 1) with a white point (color 3) and get a cyan point (color 1). The OR action would blend cyan and white and get white, whereas the XOR action would get magenta from cyan and white.

The effect of one PUT with the XOR action against background color is to place the image on the screen. The effect of another PUT with the XOR with the same image in the same location is to *erase* it. Therefore, the XOR actions can be used to erase an image as well as draw it. The following example will demonstrate some of the features of the GET and PUT statements discussed above (see Fig. 2.20 for the program output).

```
10  CLS:SCREEN 1,0
20  COLOR 1,0
30  WINDOW (-4,-4)-(4,4)
40  VIEW (60,15)-(260,175),,3
50  CIRCLE (0,-1),1.5                        'Create Venn diagram
60  CIRCLE (-.87,.5),1.5
70  CIRCLE (.87,.5),1.5
80  PAINT (0,2),CHR$(&H33),3                 'Fill in the sections
90  PAINT (0,-1),CHR$(&HAA),3
100 PAINT (-.87,.5),CHR$(&H55),3
110 PAINT (0,1),CHR$(&H11),3
120 PAINT (-.87,-.5),CHR$(&HFF),3
130 PAINT (.87,-.5),CHR$(&H22),3
140 PAINT (0,0),CHR$(&HCC),3
150 WINDOW : VIEW                            'Restore window and viewport
160 DIM ARRAY (1204)                         'See Eq.(2.3)
170 GET (120,60)-(200,120),ARRAY             'Curve out an area
180 CLS
190 PUT (10,10),ARRAY, PRESET                'Put the image in negative color
200 END
```

TABLE 2.6 PUT statement color blending suffixes

Array color	PSET screen color 0 1 2 3	PRESET screen color 0 1 2 3	AND screen color 0 1 2 3	OR screen color 0 1 2 3	XOR screen color 0 1 2 3
0	0 0 0 0	3 3 3 3	0 0 0 0	0 1 2 3	0 1 2 3
1	1 1 1 1	2 2 2 2	0 1 0 1	1 1 3 3	1 0 3 2
2	2 2 2 2	1 1 1 1	0 0 2 2	2 3 2 3	2 3 0 1
3	3 3 3 3	0 0 0 0	0 1 2 3	3 3 3 3	3 2 1 0

Note: PSET plots exactly as captured. PRESET plots a negative image (colors 0 and 3 are negatives of each other, so are 1 and 2).

2.3.10 BSAVE AND BLOAD COMMANDS

The BSAVE statement saves portions of the computer's memory on the specified device, while the BLOAD statement loads a memory image file into memory. BLOAD and BSAVE are thus useful for loading and saving machine language programs (which can be called using the CALL statement). In computer graphics, BSAVE and BLOAD can also be used to save or restore an image of the screen by moving it to or from the disk. The syntax for each command is

```
BSAVE filespace, offset, length

BLOAD filespace [ ,offset]
```

where filespace is a filename, offset is the address at which saving or loading a screen image file will start, and length is the length of the screen image to be saved.

As explained in Section 2.1.3, the address of the 16K screen buffer for the color/graphics adapter is &HB800. The DEF SEG statement is then used to establish the segment address to the start of the screen buffer. The offset of 0 and the length of &H4000 specifies that the entire 16K screen buffer is to be saved on the default disk drive.

```
10 CLS: SCREEN 2
20 DEF SEG = &HB800
30 CIRCLE (320,100), 50
40 PAINT (320,100)
50 BSAVE "PICTURE", 0, &H4000
60 END
```

Once a file has been created with BSAVE, the screen can be restored within seconds using the BLOAD statement. The following example loads the image file, PICTURE, from the default disk drive onto memory.

```
BLOAD "PICTURE", 0
```

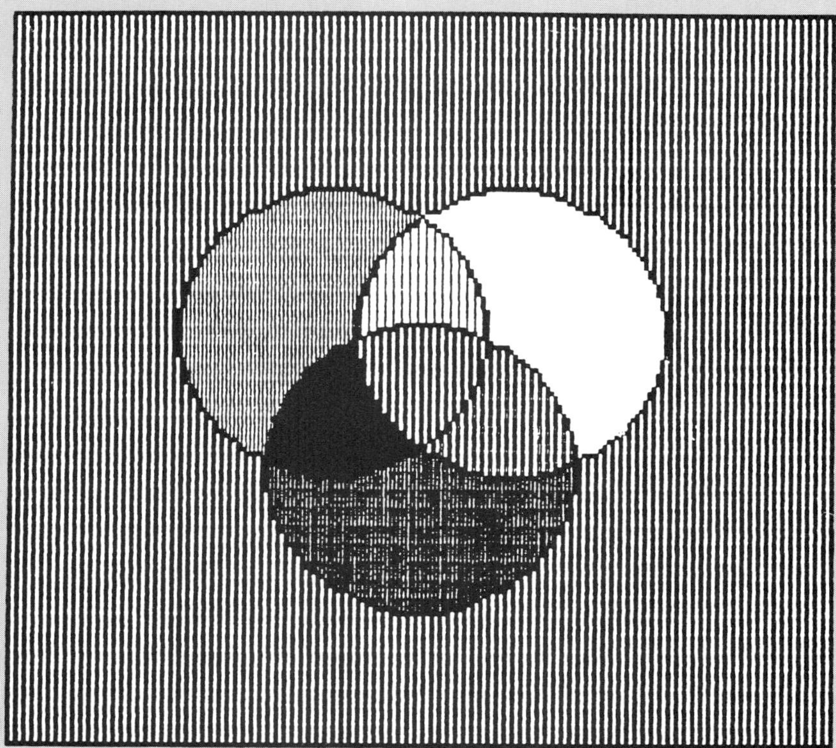

PUT (10,10), ARRAY, PRESET

Negative image

FIGURE 2.20 Effect of GET and PUT statements

2.4 ADVANCED GRAPHICS PROGRAMMING†

As we have seen, BASIC is an Englishlike high-level language in which programs are easy to write, understand, debug, and maintain. It is not always efficient, however, and can be too slow for applications where speed is critical, such as real-time graphics programming. In this case, the user should control the processor as directly as possible to take full advantage of its capabilities. This is possible only if the user has a firm understanding of the configuration of the system he or she is operating and the relevant characteristics of its hardware and software.

Machine languages produce the most efficient programs because they can directly control the memory, but they are difficult to use. We rarely write programs directly in machine language for the PC. Instead, we use assembly language, which is a symbolic version of machine language. Its instructions consist of easy-to-remember combinations of letters, each of which can be exactly translated into a single machine language instruction. Thus execution speed is greatly improved over execution with BASIC programming.

PC BASIC gives us the best of both worlds. We can use BASIC for parts of the program that are not speed sensitive, and then use a CALL statement or USR function in the BASIC program to branch to a machine language program for the segments that require maximum execution speed. In this section, we will demonstrate how to link an assembly language subroutine to a BASIC program. This linking is very important when one is writing structured and efficient programs that combine the simplicity and flexibility of BASIC with the power of the assembly language. The following application, a simple drawing processor, demonstrates this technique.

2.4.1 PROGRAM DESIGN DRAWING PROCESSOR

Suppose we want a graphics program that allows the user to draw simple pictures freely without writing any graphics program. (A complete graphics program that draws elaborate pictures will be developed in Chapter 8.)

Our intention here is to write a graphics program in BASIC that interfaces with a machine language subroutine. We will call the graphics program DRAWING PROCESSOR. The DRAWING PROCESSOR program has two program segments: the main program segment written in BASIC and the subroutine segment written in assembly language. We will call this main program SDRAW and its assembly language subroutine, KBDRAW. The SDRAW program then handles the input/output features of the DRAWING PROCESSOR and passes keyboard inputs to the KBDRAW program, which controls the drawing process.

†This section can be skipped without loss of continuity.

SDRAW plays the role of a supervisor for DRAWING PROCESSOR. As shown below, it is menu-driven, with four options from which to select. When either of the first two options is selected, a call is made to the assembly language subroutine KBDRAW and control over the keyboard is given to the user, either to create a new picture on the screen (option 1) or to modify an existing one (option 2).

```
                         SCREEN DRAWING
                       PRIMARY OPTION MENU


OPTIONS AVAILABLE :

                      -DRAW A NEW PICTURE...1
                      -MODIFY A PICTURE.....2
                      -DISPLAY A PICTURE....3
                      -EXIT ................4



ENTER OPTION NUMBER?
```

The KBDRAW subroutine then provides nine function keys, which set any pixel on the screen, move the pixel dot, plot the points in specified directions, and change both the foreground and background colors. A complete list of these functions is given in Table 2.7. The program logic is provided in Fig. 2.21 and a complete listing of the code is shown at the end of the section. In the sections ahead, we will present the steps involved in developing KBDRAW and linking KBDRAW to SDRAW. In particular, we will describe in detail:

- How to allocate memory for the subroutines (KBDRAW),
- How to get the machine language subroutine (KBDRAW) into memory, and
- How to call the subroutine from BASIC (SDRAW) and pass parameters to it (KBDRAW).

2.4.2 THE STEPS IN DEVELOPING AN ASSEMBLY LANGUAGE SUBROUTINE

In writing an assembly language program for the IBM PC, the user must have a thorough understanding of (1) the operation of the 8088 processor and its instruction set, (2) input and output programming, especially interrupt handling, (3) the IBM Macro Assembler, (4) the DOS, and (5) the software monitor,

TABLE 2.7 Function keys for DRAWING PROCESSOR

Key	Function	Instructions
[F1]	To select background color. Default: black	After pressing key [F1], a digit key between 0 and 9.
[F2]	To select color palette Default: palette 0	After pressing key [F2], press a digit key, either 0 or 1.
[F3]	To select dot color. Default: 1 = green 2 = red 3 = yellow	After pressing key [F3], press a digit key, either 1, 2, or 3.
[F4]	To locate a pixel on the screen. Default: upper left corner pixel (0, 0)	After pressing key [F4], enter (1) the x-coordinates (000–319) by pressing three digits in sequence, then immediately (2) the y-coordinates (000–199) by pressing three digits in sequence.
[F5]	To select the x and y increments (in pixels). Defaults: x increment = 1 y increment = 1	After pressing key [F5], press 1) a digit between 0 and 9 to set the x increment, 2) a digit between 0 and 9 to set the y increment.
[F6]	To draw	Use the cursor keys in the numeric pad (to the right of the keyboard) to move the dot in the direction indicated by the arrow.
[F7]	To move the dot without drawing.	Same as [F6].
[F8]	Not used.	——
[F9]	To move the dot to the home position (upper left corner).	Press key [F9].
[F10]	To terminate the drawing and save the picture under the filename specified before. (Control returns to the BASIC program.)	Press key [F10].

Note: Unless specified, the numeric pad cannot be used.

which provides the code necessary to interface with the system hardware. Three steps are necessary for the development of an assembly program:

1. Editing the source program (user-written program) using the text editor EDLIN,
2. Assembling the source program using the Macro Assembler to create its object code, and
3. Linking the object code to create an executable load module that can be executed any time its name is entered to the system.

Our concern here is how to link a subroutine written in assembly language to a main BASIC program. We will call these programs KBDRAW.ASM and

SDRAW.BAS. To perform this task, the three steps outlined above should be followed, bearing in mind that the load module produced should be loaded *high* in memory so that it won't be overlaid. Otherwise, some bad surprises might occur! The following log session will help to clarify these steps.

Editing the source program. The IBM PC text editor is called EDLIN and is invoked from DOS by entering the EDLIN command (after the DOS prompt) and pressing the [ENTER] key (denoted here by ↵]). This text editor allows the user to edit an ASCII source program of his or her assembly code and save it on diskette if desired. In our case, the source program is edited under the name KBDRAW.ASM.

Assuming that DOS is in control and drive b contains the diskette where KBDRAW.ASM will be saved, enter the EDLIN command after the DOS

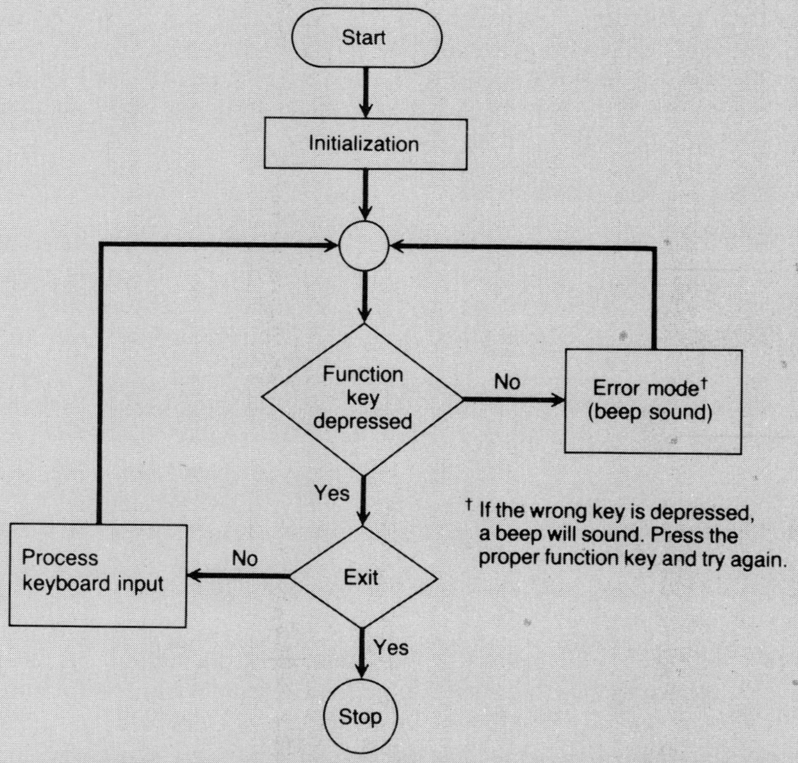

FIGURE 2.21 Programming logic for DRAWING PROCESSOR

prompt, then the file name (here KBDRAW.ASM) and press [↵]. DOS will put us in the Edit mode and prompt us with the message:

```
NEW FILE
*_
```

where "New File" means we are editing a new file, the asterisk "*" is the EDLIN prompt and the underline "_" is the cursor position on the screen. (If you are editing a file that already exists, the message "New File" will be replaced by the message, "End of Input File".)

EDLIN allows several commands to be used: insert (I), list (L), append (A), write (W), and delete (D); replace text (R) and search text (S); end edit and save program (E); and quit editing without saving anything (Q). (For a detailed explanation of these commands, refer to the IBM PC DOS manual.)

The editing of our program KBDRAW.ASM was done using some of these commands. (The complete listing of the program is shown at the end of this section.)

Assembling the source program. In the assembly step, the object code of the source program is generated. In this code, the instructions are translated to their binary representations and the external symbols are flagged to be resolved in the linking step. To assemble the KBDRAW.ASM program, the following command line

```
MASM KBDRAW,,CON:,CON:;
```

can be used. This will create an object file KBDRAW.OBJ with listings of the source program (and its object code) and the cross-reference list. These listings are directed to the user's terminal and may be echoed to the printer if a hard copy is desired. (Just press the CNTL and PRTSC keys before the command is invoked.) Any error in the assembly will be automatically displayed. In this case, the source and its cross-reference listings will be valuable in debugging. For more details about MASM, refer to the *IBM Macro Assembler Manual.*

Linking the object code. Once the object code is generated and free from any assembly error, it can be linked to other subroutines (if any) by invoking the LINK program:

```
LINK KBDRAW ,,CON:/H;
```

This line command will create a load module under the file name KBDRAW.EXE and display (and may also print) the map of the load module. The map will prove useful for linking with a BASIC program. Note here the specification of the H switch. This directs the DOS to load the load module in memory as high as possible so that it won't be overlaid. If this parameter is omitted, there may be undesirable results.

The map of KBDRAW.EXE shows that the program code length is 0174H bytes (H for hexadecimal base system) and the program entry point (the address of the first executable instruction in the program) is at 0000:003B. The length 0174H should be recorded for later use.

```
A>link kbdraw, ,con:/h;

IBM Personal Computer Linker
Version 1.10 (C)Copyright IBM Corp 1982


Start    Stop     Length   Name                    CLASS
00000H   00173H   0174H    CSEG                    CODE
00180H   0097FH   0800H    STACK                   STACK

Program entry point at 0000:003B
```

2.4.3 LINKING AN ASSEMBLY SUBROUTINE TO A BASIC PROGRAM

To link KBDRAW to SDRAW, the system program DEBUG can be used. As shown in Table 2.8, DEBUG is first executed under DOS by entering the line command,

```
DEBUG BASIC.COM
```

After receiving control, DEBUG will load the BASIC program at some entry point CS:IP where CS is a register, and IP is the instruction pointer (here 04B5:0100) and display the ready prompt _. Enter the command R to display the contents of all of the registers and condition flags. Record their values, because they should be restored later. Now load into memory the load module of the application (file KBDRAW.EXE, assumed to be on drive b.) by entering two commands:

```
N B:KBDRAW.EXE
L
```

This will load KBDRAW.EXE high in memory at an entry point CS:IP, which can be found by displaying the registers using the R command. In this case, KBDRAW.EXE has been loaded at CS:IP = 1F68:003B. Record this value because it is the address at which KBDRAW will be called in SDRAW, the BASIC program. While doing this, look at the contents of this entry and make sure that it is the first executable instruction in KBDRAW.

At this point, both BASIC and KBDRAW are loaded in memory ready to be linked. First, control must be returned to BASIC by restoring the registers to their contents when BASIC was first loaded. Use the R command to restore

TABLE 2.8 Logging procedure: DEBUG

```
B>DEBUG BASIC.COM
-R
AX=0000  BX=0000  CX=2C80  DX=0000  SP=FFF0  BP=0000  SI=0000  DI=0000
DS=04B5  ES=04B5  SS=04B5  CS=04B5  IP=0100   NV UP DI PL NZ NA PO NC
04B5:0100 E9032A          JMP     2B06
-N B:KBDRAW.EXE
-L
-R
AX=0000  BX=0000  CX=0980  DX=0000  SP=0800  BP=0000  SI=0000  DI=0000
DS=04B5  ES=04B5  SS=1F80  CS=1F68  IP=003B   NV UP DI PL NZ NA PO NC
1F68:003B 2E              SEG     CS
1F68:003C C606010001      MOV     B,[0001],01                CS:0001=01
-R CX
CX 0980
:2C80
-R SP
SP 0800
:FFF0
-R SS
SS 1F80
:04B5
-R CS
CS 1F68
:04B5
-R IP
IP 003B
:0100
-R
AX=0000  BX=0000  CX=2C80  DX=0000  SP=FFF0  BP=0000  SI=0000  DI=0000
DS=04B5  ES=04B5  SS=04B5  CS=04B5  IP=0100   NV UP DI PL NZ NA PO NC
04B5:0100 E9032A          JMP     2B06
-G
DIRECT STATEMENT IN FILE
OK
DEF SEG=&H1F68
OK
BSAVE "B:KBDRAW.EXE",0,&H174
OK
SYSTEM

PROGRAM TERMINATED NORMALLY
-Q
```

Notes: (1) Prefix - indicates the current cursor position.
(2) Either lowercase or uppercase characters can be used in programming.

them one at a time and then check that they have indeed been restored. Second, enter the command G (for Go) to put the system under BASIC control. BASIC will prompt us with OK. In the direct mode, enter the statements

```
DEF SEG=&H1F68
OK (BASIC prompt)
```

and

```
BSAVE "B:KBDRAW.EXE",0, &H174
OK (BASIC prompt)
```

In the first statement, 1F68 is the segment address at which KBDRAW .EXE was loaded earlier in memory. In the second statement, KBDRAW.EXE is saved on drive b as a core image starting at offset 0 for a length of 174 (hexadecimal) bytes. (This length was found earlier in the load map.)

To return control to DEBUG, enter the BASIC command, SYSTEM. If a normal return has been done, DEBUG will prompt us with the message,

```
Program terminated normally.
```

At this point, the linking process is complete and DEBUG can be terminated by entering the Quit command, q, which will return control to DOS.

After the core image "B:KBDRAW.EXE" has been saved, the assembly language subroutine KBDRAW can be called from the BASIC program SDRAW at any time needed by including the following three statements in the program (see Program 2.1).

```
520 DEF SEG=&H1F68      'Segment KBDRAW
530 KBDRAW=&H3B         'Load point for KBDRAW
540 CALL KBDRAW
```

Before making any of these calls, however, the core image "B:KBDRAW" must be loaded into memory. This is done by the following BASIC statements:

```
230 DEF SEG=&H1F68
240 BLOAD "B:KBDRAW.EXE",0
```

To restore the code segment register (CS) to that of BASIC, be sure to follow these two statements by

```
150 DEF SEG :
```

The proper sequence of these BASIC statements is shown in Program 2.1.

2.4.4 APPLICATION EXAMPLE

The DRAWING PROCESSOR presented in this section is by no means a complete, sophisticated one. It is used only to demonstrate that by combining BASIC and assembly language the user can expect to develop powerful applications that take full advantage of the machine he or she is using.

The picture in Fig. 2.22, drawn using KBDRAW, could have been generated through BASIC. Our intention here was to describe how BASIC interfaces with machine language subroutines.

The reader is encouraged to seek some hands-on experience by editing, assembling, and linking the application program (Program 2.1). Many improvements are possible—only the user's imagination dictates how much can be done.

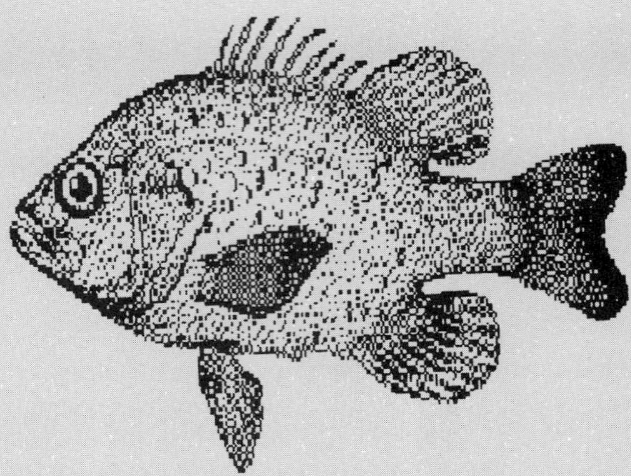

FIGURE 2.22 Fish drawn by the DRAWING PROCESSOR program

```
100 ' Program 2.1: Drawing Processor
110 KEY OFF:SCREEN 0,1:WIDTH 80:COLOR 11,0:CLS
120 DFLT=0
130 DEF SEG=&H1F68
140 BLOAD "b:kbdraw.exe",0
150 DEF SEG:
160 MSG1$="Screen Drawing":MSG2$="Draw a New Picture":MSG3$="Modify a Picture"
170 MSG4$="Display a Picture"
180 GOSUB 350:ON NUM GOTO 190,260,290,660
190 CLS:MSG$=MSG1$:GOSUB 650:PRINT:MSG$=MSG2$:GOSUB 650
200 LBLANK=5:GOSUB 470
210 GOSUB 480
220 SCREEN 1,0:COLOR 0,1:CLS
230 GOSUB 510
240 GOSUB 570
250 GOTO 180
260 CLS:MSG$=MSG3$:GOSUB 590
270 GOSUB 550:GOSUB 520:GOSUB 570
280 GOTO 180
290 CLS:MSG$=MSG4$:GOSUB 590
300 GOSUB 550
310 DEF SEG=0:POKE 1050,PEEK(1052)
320 V$=INKEY$:IF V$="" THEN 320
330 WIDTH 80:SCREEN 0,1:COLOR 11,0:CLS
340 GOTO 180
350 LOCATE 2,1
360 LOCATE 2,1:FOR I=1 TO 80:PRINT"*";:NEXT
370 LOCATE 25,1:FOR J=1 TO 80:PRINT"*";:NEXT
380 A$="Screen Drawing":LOCATE 5,(80-LEN(A$))/2,1:PRINT A$;
390 A$="Primary Option Menu":LOCATE 6,(80-LEN(A$))/2,1:PRINT A$;
400 PRINT:PRINT:PRINT:PRINT:PRINT:LOCATE ,10:PRINT"Options available :":PRINT
410 LOCATE ,29:COLOR 14:PRINT"- draw a new picture...1"
420 LOCATE ,29:PRINT"- Modify a picture.....2"
430 LOCATE ,29:PRINT"- Display a picture....3"
440 LOCATE ,29:PRINT"- exit.................4"
450 COLOR 11:PRINT:PRINT:PRINT:LOCATE ,10:INPUT "Enter option number ";NUM
460 RETURN
470 FOR I=1 TO LBLANK:PRINT:NEXT:RETURN
```

PROGRAM 2.1 Drawing processor

```
480 LOCATE ,10:COLOR 14 :INPUT "Enter Filename(8 char. max.)";FILE$:PRINT
490 LOCATE ,10:INPUT "Enter Extension(3 char. max.)";EXT$:PRINT
500 LOCATE ,10:INPUT "Enter Drive <a or b>";DR$:RETURN
510 SCREEN 1,0:COLOR 0,0:CLS
520 DEF SEG=&H1F68
530 KBDRAW=&H3B
540 CALL KBDRAW:RETURN
550 SCREEN 1,0:COLOR 0,0:CLS:DEF SEG=&HB800
560 BLOAD DR$+":"+FILE$+"."+EXT$,0:DFLT=1:RETURN
570 DEF SEG=&HB800:BSAVE DR$+":"+FILE$+"."+EXT$,0,&H4000
580 DFLT=1:WIDTH 80:SCREEN 0,1:COLOR 11,0:CLS:RETURN
590 CLS:GOSUB 650
600 LBLANK=5:GOSUB 470
610 IF DFLT=0 THEN GOTO 480
620 LOCATE ,10:COLOR 14:INPUT  "current filename <y or n>";ANS$
630 IF ANS$<>"y" THEN GOTO 480
640 RETURN
650 LOCATE 5,(80-LEN(MSG$))/2,1:PRINT MSG$:RETURN
660 COLOR 7:CLS:PRINT"End of Session,BYE"
    End of input file
```

```
*          Subroutine: KBDRAW
comment *
           Set_bgnd:    to select the background color from 8 different colors
           set_pal:     to select one of 2 palettes,palette 0 or 1 to allow
                        different colors.
           dot_col:     to select the pixel color.
           locate:      to set a pixel on the screen.
           inc:         select the increments (in pixels) in the x's and y's
                        directions.
           mov_d_on:    to set a pixel while moving.
           mov_d_off:   to move to a given point without setting the pixel
*
d
stack      segment para     stack 'stack'    ;setting the stack
           db      256      dup('stack   ')
stack      ends
cseg       segment para     public 'code'
           assume  cs:cseg,ss:stack
           c_byte  db       10                ;initialize the constants
           flag    db       1
           b_color db       0
           f_color db       1
           d_color db       1
           x_delta dw       1
           y_delta dw       1
a1         label   word
           dw      offset   set_bgnd          ;setting pointer table
           dw      offset   set_pal
           dw      offset   dot_col
           dw      offset   locate
           dw      offset   inc
           dw      offset   mov_d_on
           dw      offset   mov_d_off
           dw      offset   a2
           dw      offset   start
           dw      offset   exit
           dw      offset   a2
           dw      offset   a2
           dw      offset   north_west
           dw      offset   north
           dw      offset   north_east
           dw      offset   to_err
           dw      offset   west
           dw      offset   to_err
           dw      offset   east
           dw      offset   to_err
           dw      offset   south_west
           dw      offset   south
           dw      offset   south_east
           dw      offset   to_err
           dw      offset   to_err
all        equ     $-a1
           public  kbdraw
kbdraw     proc    far                        ;main procedure
start:
           mov     flag,1
```

PROGRAM 2.1 (continued)

```
        mov     cx,00                           ;setting pointer table
        mov     dx,00
a2:     cmp     flag,1                          ;dot in turned mode off mode ?
        mov     al,0
        je      c1                              ;yes,dot at the background color
        mov     al,f_color                      ;no,set the foreground color
c1:     mov     ah,0ch
        int     10h                             ;set color graphics mode
        mov     ah,1
        int     16h                             ;polling keyboard for character
        pushf
        pop     ax
        test    ax,0060h                        ;character available ?
        jz      dispach                         ;yes
        cmp     flag,1                          ;no
        mov     al,f_color
        je      c2
        mov     al,0
c2:     mov     ah,0ch
        int     10h
        push    cx
        mov     cx,2000
delay:  loop    delay                           ;delay for dot blinking
        pop     cx
        jmp     a2
dispach:        mov     ah,0                    ;a char. is available in buffer
        int     16h                             ;read its scan code
        sub     ah,59                           ;key f1 through f10 depressed ?
        jc      to_err                          ;no, error!
        mov     al,ah                           ;yes,set up its pointer
        xor     ah,ah
        sal     ax,1
        cmp     ax,18                           ;function key f10 is pressed ?
        je      exit                            ;yes,terminate the session.
        mov     si,ax
        jmp     word ptr cs:[si+offset a1]      ;jump to the desired
                                                ;function entry
to_err: call    error
        jmp     a2
exit:
        ret
set_bgnd:       mov     bh,0                    ;to set background color
        call    a3
        mov     b_color,bl
        jmp     a2
set_pal:        mov     bh,1                    ;function to set palette
        call    a3
        jmp     a2
locate:                                         ;function to locate a pixel
        mov     si,2
rep:    mov     cx,3
        xor     bx,bx
rep1:   mov     ah,0
        int     16h
        sub     al,30h
        cbw
        add     ax,bx
        cmp     cx,1
        je      around
        mul     c_byte
around: mov     bx,ax
        loop    rep1
        push    bx
        dec     si
        cmp     si,0
        jne     rep
        pop     dx
        pop     cx
        mov     flag,1
        mov     al,f_color
        mov     ah,0ch
        int     10h
        jmp     a2
inc:    mov     ah,0                            ;function to increment x or y
        int     16h
        sub     al,30h
        xor     ah,ah
        mov     x_delta,ax
        mov     ah,0
        int     16h
        sub     al,30h
```

PROGRAM 2.1 (continued)

```
                xor     ah,ah
                mov     y_delta,ax
                jmp     a2
mov_d_on:               mov     flag,0          ;function to turn on pixel
                jmp     a2
mov_d_off:              mov     flag,1          ;function to turn off pixel
                jmp     a2
north_west:             sub     cx,x_delta      ;move dot to north_west
north:          sub     dx,y_delta              ;move dot in north direction
                jmp     a2
north_east:             sub     dx,y_delta      ;move dot to north_east
east:           add     cx,x_delta              ;move dot in east direction
                jmp     a2
south_west:             add     dx,y_delta      ;move dot to south_west
west:           sub     cx,x_delta              ;move dot in west direction
                jmp     a2
south_east:             add     cx,x_delta      ;move dot to south_east
south:          add     dx,y_delta              ;move dot in south direction
                jmp     a2
dot_col:                mov     ah,0            ;set dot color
                int     16h
                sub     al,30h
                mov     f_color,al
                mov     d_color,al
                jmp     a2
a3              proc    near                    ;procedure to select palette
                mov     ah,0
                int     16h
                sub     al,30h
                mov     bl,al
                mov     ah,0bh
                int     10h
                ret
a3              endp
error           proc    near                    ;error procedure,sound beep
                push    dx
                mov     dl,07h
                mov     ah,2
                int     21h
                pop     dx
                ret
error           endp
kbdraw          endp
cseg            ends
                end     kbdraw
```

PROGRAM 2.1 Drawing processor

2.5 SUMMARY

In this chapter we examined how to access and control the PC screen memory to create a graphics image. As we have seen, PC graphics images are created with pixels and controlled through a memory-mapped display format. Each memory location corresponds to a screen location. With the memory-mapped screen, we can read and write display data directly by accessing the display memory. This feature provides an easier means of manipulating the contents of pictures.

We then reviewed several BASIC graphics commands available on the PC. This will prepare readers at the earliest possible moment to write their own simple programs and thus deepen their understanding of the graphics capabilities of microcomputers.

For most programming applications, the slight degradation of performance caused by the use of BASIC is not noticeable. In areas like computer animation, however, program execution speed can be critical, and a BASIC program may not be fast enough to be practical. To improve program efficiency, we introduced a technique whereby one writes a graphics program in BASIC that interfaces with a machine language subroutine.

EXERCISES

2.1 Write a program to draw a line segment with its two endpoints specified, using the PSET statement. Compare its execution speed with that of the LINE statement.

2.2 Write a program that uses the PSET statement to draw a circle centered at (a, b) with radius r. Note the circle equation given in Fig. 2.23.

2.3 Write a program to draw an ellipse using the PSET statement. Recall that an ellipse is represented by $(x - a)^2/A^2 + (y - b)^2/B^2 = 1$, as shown in Fig. 2.24.

2.4 Write a program to produce a pattern similar to the one given in Fig. 2.25. Assume that the outer circle has radius A and the disc has radius B. The disc is always in contact with the circle. The disc is rotated counterclockwise, but must always touch the outer circle. Note the mathematical relationships among the parameters that control the shape of the disc, given in Fig. 2.26.

2.5 Write a program to draw the cardioid shown in Fig. 2.27. The mathematical formula is given in Fig. 2.28.

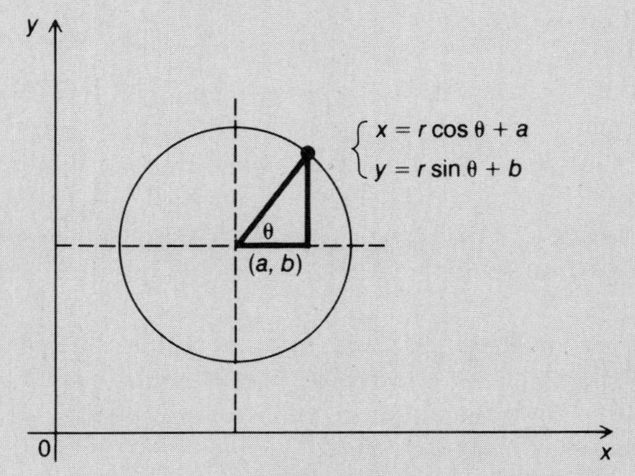

FIGURE 2.23

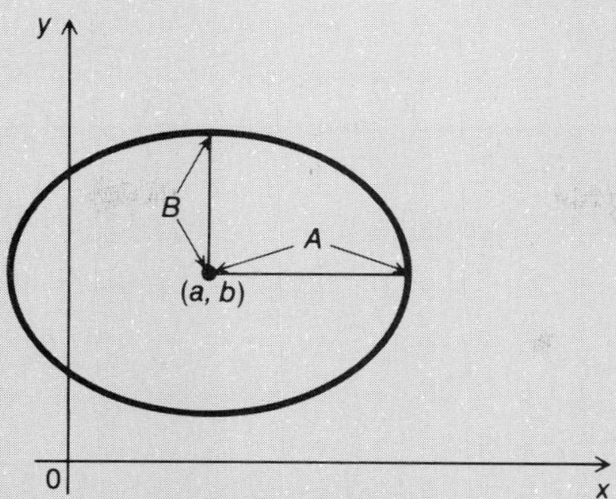

FIGURE 2.24

FIGURE 2.25

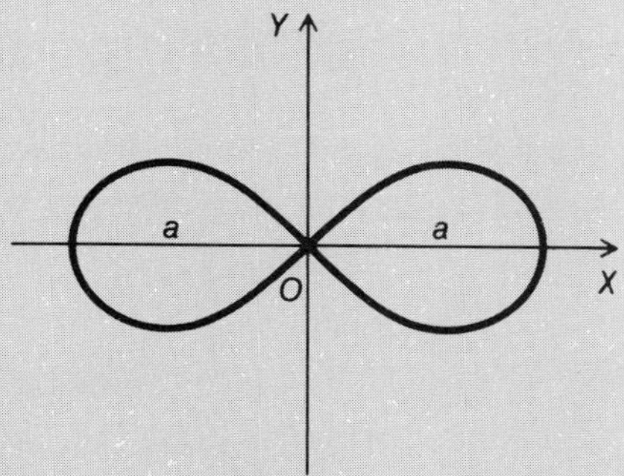

$(x^2 + y^2)^2 = a^2(x^2 - y^2),$

$r^2 = a^2 \cos 2\theta$

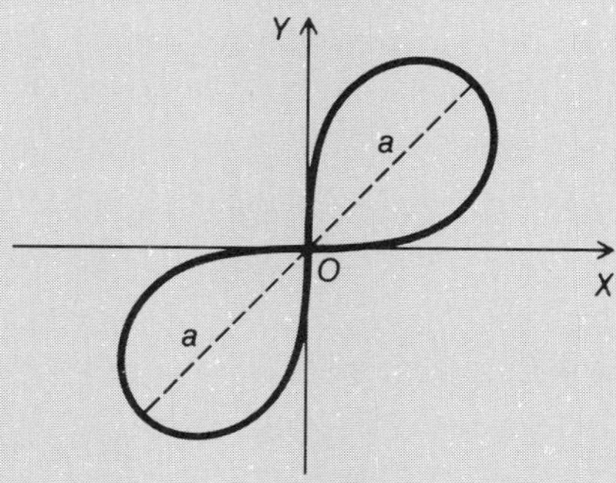

$(x^2 + y^2)^2 = 2a^2 xy,$

$r^2 = a^2 \sin 2\theta$

FIGURE 2.26

FIGURE 2.27

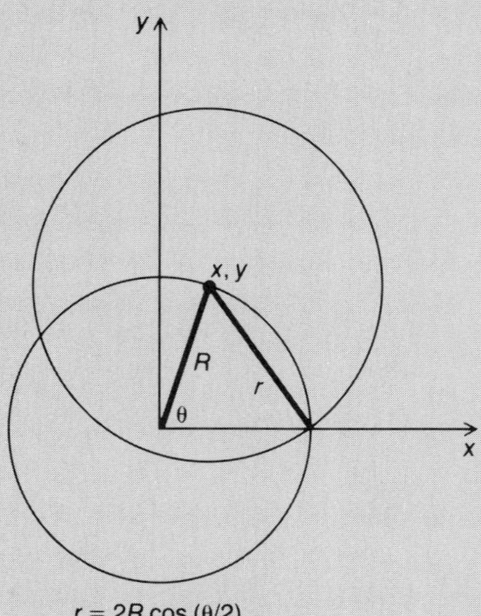

$r = 2R \cos(\theta/2)$

FIGURE 2.28

REFERENCES

1. *IBM PC Macro Assembler Manual,* IBM Corporation, P.O. Box 1328, Boca Raton, Fla. 33432, 1981.
2. *IBM PC BASIC Manual* (Version 2.00) IBM Corporation, P.O. Box 1328, Boca Raton, Fla. 33432, 1983.
3. Morgan C. L., "Bluebook of Assembly Routines for the IBM PC," *The Waite Group Book,* 1984.
4. Brack F. R., "Linking Assembly Subroutines to BASIC Programs," *PC Technical Journal,* **1** (6) 118–40, 1984.

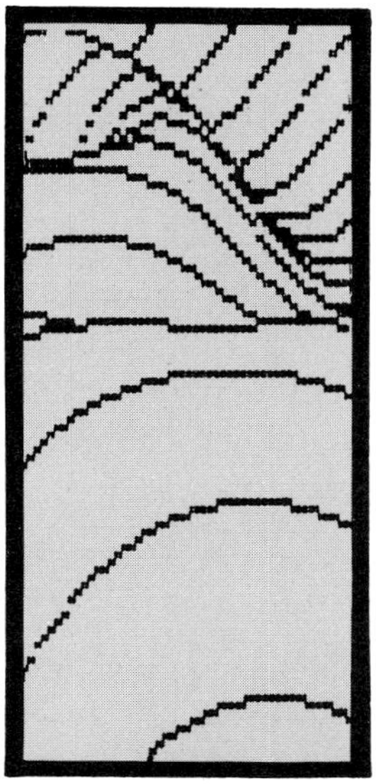

PART TWO
Mathematical Elements for Computer Graphics

The purpose of Part Two is to introduce the basic two-dimensional (2-D) and three-dimensional (3-D) geometrical transformations used in computer graphics. The translation, scaling, and rotation transformations discussed here are essential to many graphics applications and will be referred to extensively in succeeding chapters. Mathematical elements for producing perspective views are discussed, and algorithms for removing hidden edges and surfaces of 3-D objects are also reviewed.

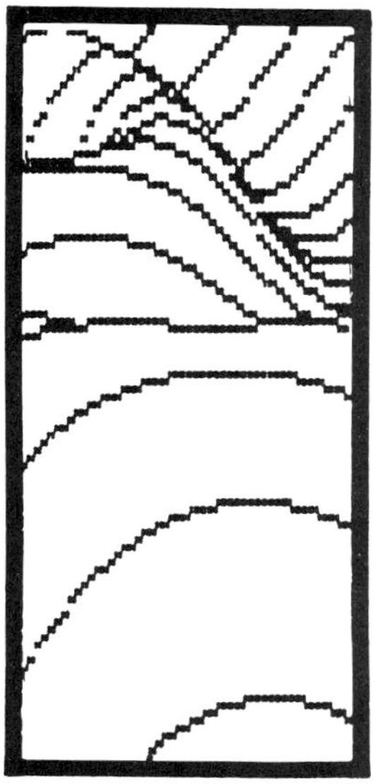

CHAPTER THREE

Mathematical Elements in 2-D Computer Graphics

Now that we have discussed computer graphics in general, we will explore the methods used to project an image (described in terms of Cartesian coordinates) onto a graphics screen and to manipulate that image. We often want to enlarge the scale of a picture so that detail appears more clearly or reduce it so that more of the picture is visible. We may need to rotate a picture through some angle to get a better view of the object. These manipulations or transformations are basic to computer graphics and can be accomplished by using geometric transformation techniques. In this chapter, we examine the fundamentals of the mathematics underlying computer graphics by considering the representation and transformation of points, lines, and objects in the two-dimensional (2-D) plane. We then apply these techniques to representing a 2-D object on a graphics screen.

3.1 TRANSFORMATION OF POINTS

When we represent a point P in a 2-D display screen by its coordinates (x, y), the transformed point $P' = (x', y')$ is expressed as the product of a point P with a general 2×2 transformation matrix T:

$$T = \begin{bmatrix} A & B \\ C & D \end{bmatrix}.$$

More precisely, we have the expression of P' as

$$P' = PT = (x,y)\begin{bmatrix} A & B \\ C & D \end{bmatrix} = [(Ax + Cy), \quad (Bx + Dy)] \tag{3.1}$$

This mathematical description means simply that the effect of the transformation is determined by the proper choice of values for parameters A, B, C, and D in the matrix T. We will examine several situations to see how this choice affects the position of the transformed point, P'.

3.1.1 IDENTITY

With $B = C = 0$ and $A = D = 1$, the T matrix becomes an identity matrix:

$$(x',y') = (x,y)\begin{bmatrix} 1 & 0 \\ 0 & 1 \end{bmatrix} = (x,y). \tag{3.2}$$

As we can see, an *identity transformation* leaves the coordinates of P unchanged.

3.1.2 SCALING

Now consider the case where $D = 1$ but $B = C = 0$ as before:

$$(x',y) = (x,y)\begin{bmatrix} A & 0 \\ 0 & 1 \end{bmatrix} = (Ax,y). \tag{3.3}$$

This transformation "stretches" the original coordinates in the X direction. (See Fig. 3.1a.) On the other hand, the T matrix with $A = 1$ and $B = C = 0$ produces a change in scale, or *scaling*, only in the Y direction:

$$(x',y') = (x,y)\begin{bmatrix} 1 & 0 \\ 0 & D \end{bmatrix} = (x,Dy). \tag{3.4}$$

The effect of this transformation is shown in Fig. 3.1(b).

With only $B = C = 0$, the T matrix and its effect on the transformed coordinates are expressed by

$$(x',y') = (x,y)\begin{bmatrix} A & 0 \\ 0 & D \end{bmatrix} = (Ax,Dy). \tag{3.5}$$

This type of matrix yields a scale change in both the X and Y directions, as shown in Fig. 3.1(c). If $A \neq D$, a distortion occurs. If $A = D$, then uniform scaling is effected.

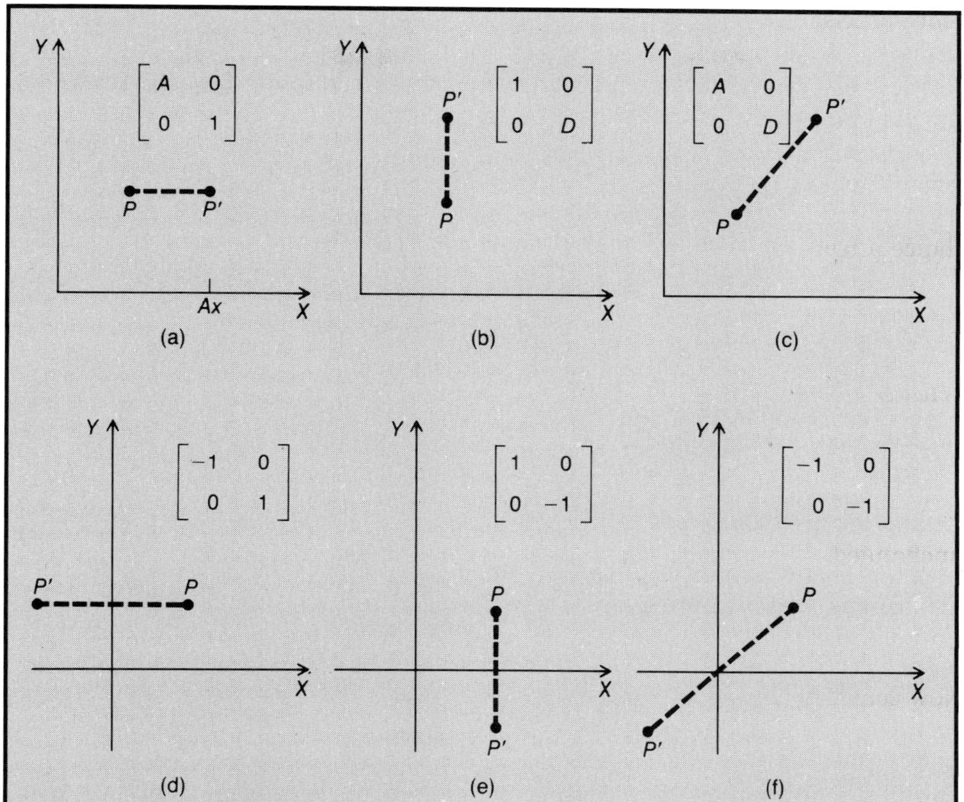

FIGURE 3.1 Transformation of points

3.1.3 REFLECTION

Reflection occurs when either A or D, or both, are negative in the T matrix. As shown in Figs. 3.1(d) and 3.1(e), *reflection* of a point through the X axis or Y axis involves generating a mirror image of the point on the opposite side of respective axis. To see this transformation, we consider $B = C = 0$, $A = -1$ and $D = 1$.

$$(x', y') = (x, y)\begin{bmatrix} -1 & 0 \\ 0 & 1 \end{bmatrix} = (-x, y). \tag{3.6}$$

In this case, reflection about the Y axis occurs. On the other hand, if $B = C = 0$, $A = 1$ and $D = -1$, then reflection about the X axis occurs. If $A =$

$D = -1$ and $B = C = 0$, then reflection about the origin $(0,0)$ occurs. The effects of these transformations are shown in Figs. 3.1(d), 3.1(e), and 3.1(f), respectively. Note that scaling and reflection of the coordinates involve only the diagonal terms of the transformation matrix.

3.1.4 SHEAR

Suppose that we have a T matrix where $A = D = 1$ and $C = 0$ such that

$$(x'y') = (x,y)\begin{bmatrix} 1 & B \\ 0 & 1 \end{bmatrix} = (x, Bx + y). \tag{3.7}$$

This transformation leaves the X coordinate of the point P unchanged, while y' becomes a linear function of x and y. This type of transformation is referred to as a *shear* in the direction of y. An x shear is simply represented by

$$(x',y') = (x,y)\begin{bmatrix} 1 & 0 \\ C & 1 \end{bmatrix} = (x + Cy, y). \tag{3.8}$$

These two shearing effects are shown in Figs. 3.2(a) and 3.2(b). (The effect of shearing will be more evident when we get to lines and objects.) Note that the *off-diagonal* terms produce the shearing effect on the coordinates of the point P.

3.1.5 ROTATION

Points can be rotated through some angle θ about the origin. In matrix form, we represent this rotation as:

$$\begin{aligned}(x',y') &= (x,y)\begin{bmatrix} \cos\theta & \sin\theta \\ -\sin\theta & \cos\theta \end{bmatrix} \\ &= (x\cos\theta - y\sin\theta, \quad x\sin\theta + y\cos\theta).\end{aligned} \tag{3.9}$$

Postive angles are measured *counterclockwise* from X toward Y. When points are rotated through clockwise angles (negative angles), we simply use $-\theta$ in lieu of θ in Eq. (3.9). Note also that $\cos(-\theta) = \cos\theta$ and $\sin(-\theta) = -\sin\theta$. Thus the effect of rotation through a clockwise angle θ is

$$\begin{aligned}(x',y') &= (x,y)\begin{bmatrix} \cos\theta & -\sin\theta \\ \sin\theta & \cos\theta \end{bmatrix} \\ &= (x\cos\theta + y\sin\theta, \quad -x\sin\theta + y\cos\theta).\end{aligned} \tag{3.10}$$

The effect of the individual components of this rotation matrix is not immediately clear. We can easily explore the components, however, by examining Fig. 3.3. Figure 3.3 indicates that the point P rotates through a positive angle θ to produce the new point P'. Note that the distances from the origin $(0,0)$ to

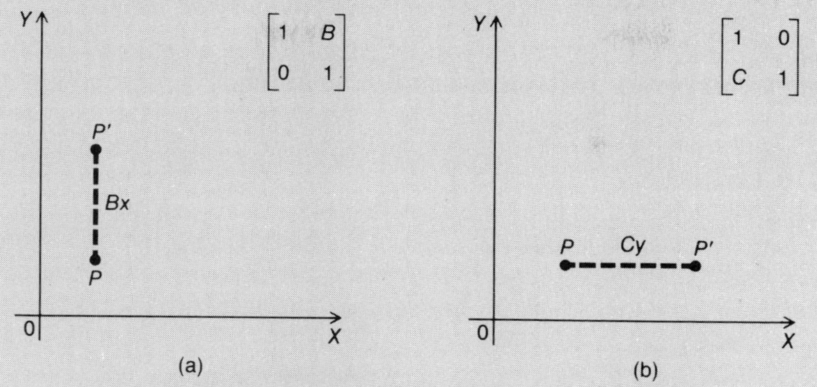

FIGURE 3.2 Shearing effects on points

P and P' are equal. This is because the rotation is about the origin. With these distances labeled r in the figure, we obtain the relations

$$x = r \cos \phi, \qquad y = r \sin \phi$$

and

$$x' = r \cos(\theta + \phi) = r \cos \phi \cos \theta - r \sin \phi \sin \theta = x \cos \theta - y \sin \theta$$
$$y' = r \sin(\theta + \phi) = r \cos \phi \sin \theta + r \sin \phi \cos \theta = x \sin \theta + y \cos \theta$$

Thus we confirm the result in Eq. (3.9).

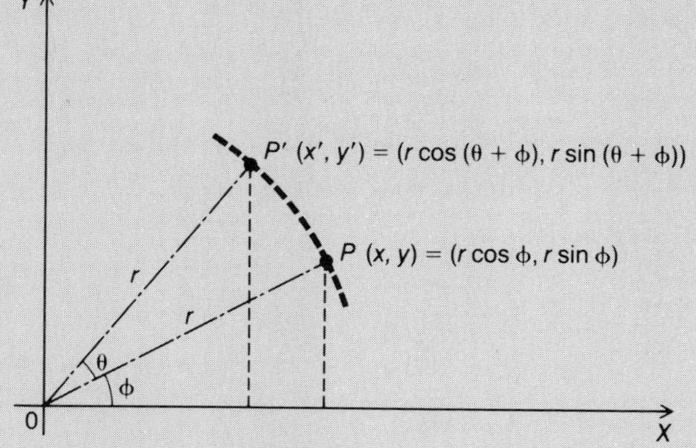

FIGURE 3.3 Rotation of a point in 2-D space

3.2 TRANSFORMATION OF LINES AND OBJECTS

A straight line is made up of two position vectors that specify the coordinates of its endpoints. A line transformation can be accomplished simply by transforming the endpoints and drawing a new line between the transformed endpoints. This principle holds for all the transformations we have observed, from scaling to rotation.

If we view an object as being made up of several lines, we see that an object can be transformed by identifying all the vertices where two lines join and applying Eq. (3.1) to each vertex of the object. If the object of interest consists of n vertices (coordinates of its endpoints), the general transformation is expressed as:

$$\underset{\text{object coordinates}}{\text{Transformed}}\qquad\qquad \underset{\text{coordinates}}{\text{Original object}}\qquad \underset{\text{matrix}}{\text{Transformation}}$$

$$\begin{bmatrix} P_1' \\ P_2' \\ \cdot \\ \cdot \\ \cdot \\ P_n' \end{bmatrix} = \begin{bmatrix} x_1' & y_1' \\ x_2' & y_2' \\ \cdot & \cdot \\ \cdot & \cdot \\ \cdot & \cdot \\ x_n' & y_n' \end{bmatrix} = \begin{bmatrix} x_1 & y_1 \\ x_2 & y_2 \\ \cdot & \cdot \\ \cdot & \cdot \\ \cdot & \cdot \\ x_n & y_n \end{bmatrix} \cdot \begin{bmatrix} A & B \\ C & D \end{bmatrix}. \tag{3.11}$$

3.2.1 SCALING

As an example, consider the triangle shown in Fig. 3.4(a), which is defined by its three vertices, (0, 0), (30, 0), and (15, 30). If the triangle is to be enlarged to twice its original size, we simply choose $A = D = 2$. To see the effect of this overall scaling, we compute

$$\begin{bmatrix} P_1' \\ P_2' \\ P_3' \end{bmatrix} = \begin{bmatrix} 0 & 0 \\ 30 & 0 \\ 15 & 30 \end{bmatrix} \begin{bmatrix} 2 & 0 \\ 0 & 2 \end{bmatrix} = \begin{bmatrix} 0 & 0 \\ 60 & 0 \\ 30 & 60 \end{bmatrix}.$$

Note that the enlargement is relative to the origin of the $X\ Y$ coordinate system. (See Fig. 3.4(b).)

3.2.2 ROTATION

To rotate an object with n vertices through a counterclockwise angle about the origin of the coordinate system, we compute

$$\begin{bmatrix} P_1' \\ \cdot \\ \cdot \\ \cdot \\ P_n' \end{bmatrix} = \begin{bmatrix} x_1 & y_1 \\ \cdot & \cdot \\ \cdot & \cdot \\ \cdot & \cdot \\ x_n & y_n \end{bmatrix} \begin{bmatrix} \cos\theta & \sin\theta \\ -\sin\theta & \cos\theta \end{bmatrix}. \tag{3.12}$$

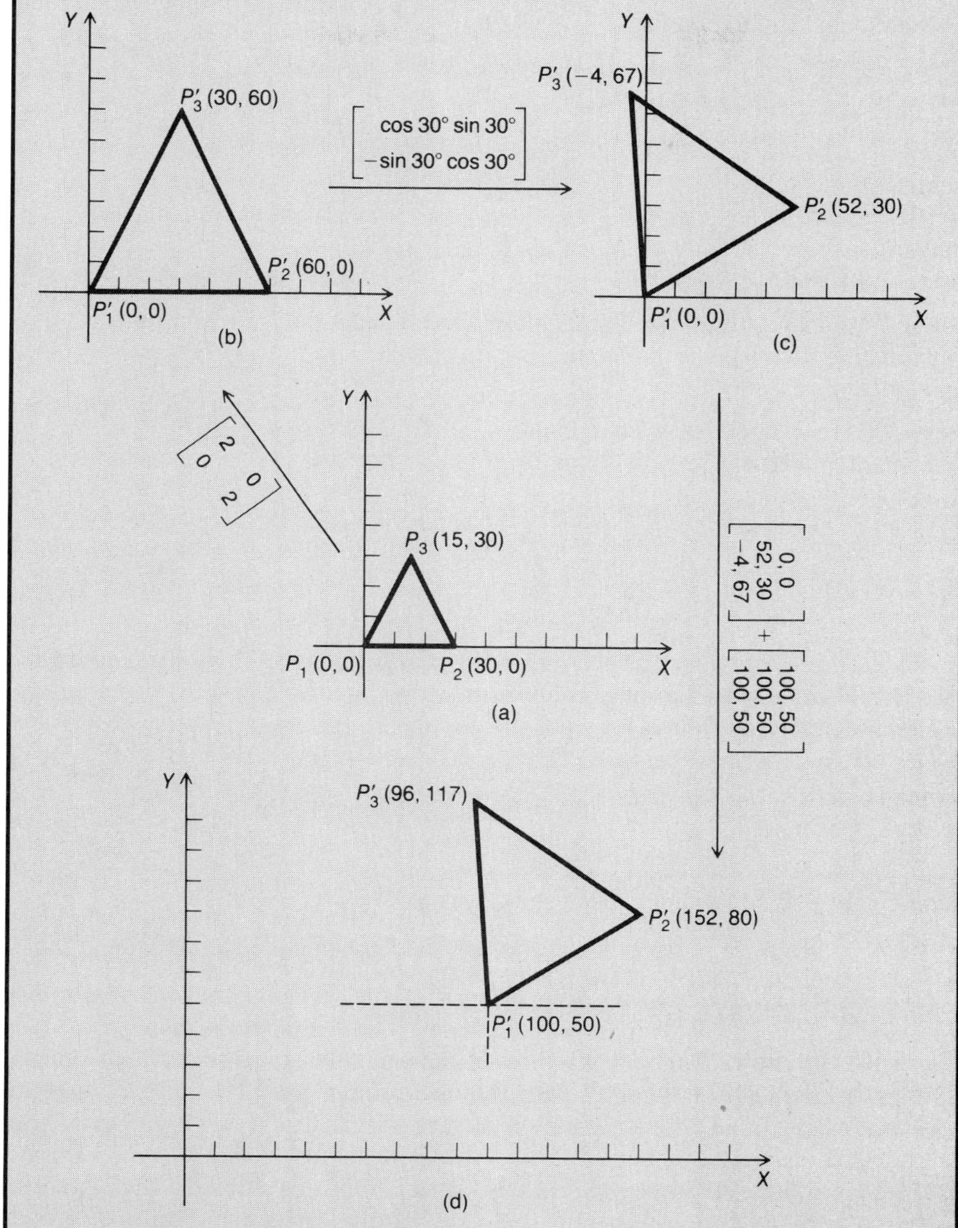

FIGURE 3.4 **Transformation of triangles in 2-D space: (a) initial position, (b) scaling, (c) rotation, and (d) translation**

The triangle shown in Fig. 3.4(b), when rotated 30° (0.5236 radian) counterclockwise about the *origin*, is expressed by

$$\begin{bmatrix} P_2' \\ P_2' \\ P_3' \end{bmatrix} = \begin{bmatrix} 0 & 0 \\ 60 & 0 \\ 30 & 60 \end{bmatrix} \begin{bmatrix} 0.8660 & 0.5 \\ & \\ -0.5 & 0.8660 \end{bmatrix} = \begin{bmatrix} 0 & 0 \\ 52 & 30 \\ -4 & 67 \end{bmatrix}.$$

The rotated triangle is shown in Fig. 3.4(c).

3.2.3 TRANSLATION

An object can be *translated* (shifted on the plane) simply by adding a component of magnitude to each vertex of the object. The matrix format of object translation is

$$\begin{matrix} \text{Translated} \\ \text{coordinates} \end{matrix} = \begin{matrix} \text{Original} \\ \text{coordinates} \end{matrix} + \begin{matrix} \text{Translation} \\ \text{magnitude} \end{matrix}$$

$$\begin{bmatrix} P_1' \\ \cdot \\ \cdot \\ \cdot \\ P_n' \end{bmatrix} = \begin{bmatrix} x_1 & y_1 \\ \cdot & \cdot \\ \cdot & \cdot \\ \cdot & \cdot \\ x_n & y_n \end{bmatrix} + \begin{bmatrix} T_x & T_y \\ \cdot & \cdot \\ \cdot & \cdot \\ \cdot & \cdot \\ T_x & T_y \end{bmatrix}. \tag{3.14}$$

As an example, consider the triangle shown in Fig. 3.4(c). If we want to translate it 100 units to the right and 50 units up ($T_x = 100, T_y = 50$), we calculate the new vertices as follows:

$$\begin{bmatrix} P_1' \\ P_2' \\ P_3' \end{bmatrix} = \begin{bmatrix} 0 & 0 \\ 52 & 30 \\ -4 & 67 \end{bmatrix} + \begin{bmatrix} 100 & 50 \\ 100 & 50 \\ 100 & 50 \end{bmatrix} = \begin{bmatrix} 100 & 50 \\ 152 & 80 \\ 96 & 117 \end{bmatrix}.$$

The effect of this transformation is illustrated in Fig. 3.4(d).

3.2.4 LIMITATIONS OF STANDARD COORDINATE SYSTEM

There are two limitations to applying the general 2 × 2 matrix in transforming an object. First, all of the transformations we have used thus far have been centered at (0, 0), so that as each of the transformations was applied to the origin, it remained unchanged. Thus, rotation about arbitrary points is not provided by these methods. Similarly, reflections are effected through the X axis, the Y axis, or the origin, but not through arbitrary points or lines.

Second, we have treated the constants of translation differently from those of scaling and rotation (the first as addition, the others as multiplications). In computer graphics, many transformations cannot be represented by just one of the matrices described above, but as combinations of several. A sequence of matrix operations must thus be performed. In doing so, different matrix forms can cause difficulty. For mathematical convenience, we want to treat them in a homogeneous way so that all basic transformations can be combined through multiplications. The introduction of a homogeneous coordinate system will permit us to circumvent these limitations.

3.3 HOMOGENEOUS COORDINATE SYSTEMS

In homogeneous coordinate systems, point (x, y) is represented as (x, y, H) for any nonzero scale factor H. Then the normalized homogeneous coordinate representation of the point (x, y) is $(x/H,\ y/H,\ 1)$. Since H can be any nonzero constant, we usually select $H = 1$ so that the division will never be required. As a result, the point with homogeneous coordinate $(x, y, 1)$ has the Cartesian coordinate (x, y). We will adopt this normalized convention for the remainder of this book.

3.3.1 REVISED TRANSFORMATION MATRIX

The most obvious effect of introducing the homogeneous coordinates is that the previous 2×2 transformation matrix must be expanded. Since points are expressed by three element row vectors, the 2×2 matrix is now expanded to a 3×3 matrix:

$$\begin{bmatrix} A & B \\ C & D \end{bmatrix} \longrightarrow \begin{bmatrix} A & B & 0 \\ C & D & 0 \\ 0 & 0 & 1 \end{bmatrix}. \qquad \textbf{(3.15)}$$

To add a translation property to the 3×3 matrix, we simply change the third-row elements from $(0\ 0\ 1)$ to $(L\ M\ 1)$, which effects a linear translation of points through L units horizontally and M units vertically. Thus a generalized matrix will always be of the form

$$T = \begin{bmatrix} A & B & 0 \\ C & D & 0 \\ L & M & 1 \end{bmatrix}. \qquad \textbf{(3.16)}$$

The third column vector in the 3×3 matrix allows us to combine the translation, scaling, and rotation operations in multiplications. The effect of the transformations on a point (x, y) can then be described by

$$(x', y', 1) = (x, y, 1) \cdot T$$

or

$$x' = Ax + Cy + L \qquad \text{and} \qquad y' = Bx + Dy + M\,.$$

In the following sections, we will show how this matrix form simplifies the sequential transformation process.

3.3.2 TRANSLATION

When only translation is considered, the matrix given in Eq. (3.16) is further simplified:

$$\begin{bmatrix} 1 & 0 & 0 \\ 0 & 1 & 0 \\ L & M & 1 \end{bmatrix}. \tag{3.17}$$

To illustrate the translation process, let us consider a triangle whose three vertices are defined as (15, 30), (60, 30), and (30, 60). Translating this triangle through (20, 50) generates new position vectors:

$$P' = \begin{bmatrix} 15 & 30 & 1 \\ 60 & 30 & 1 \\ 30 & 60 & 1 \end{bmatrix} \begin{bmatrix} 1 & 0 & 0 \\ 0 & 1 & 0 \\ 20 & 50 & 1 \end{bmatrix} = \begin{bmatrix} 35 & 80 & 1 \\ 80 & 80 & 1 \\ 50 & 110 & 1 \end{bmatrix}.$$

What would happen if we moved the translated triangle another 30 units in the x direction and 10 units in the y direction? The net translation is

$$P'' = P' \begin{bmatrix} 1 & 0 & 0 \\ 0 & 1 & 0 \\ 30 & 10 & 1 \end{bmatrix} = P \begin{bmatrix} 1 & 0 & 0 \\ 0 & 1 & 0 \\ 20+30 & 50+10 & 1 \end{bmatrix}.$$

As we can see, the net translation is additive even though the sequential translations are multiplicative. In general, we can show that

$$\begin{bmatrix} 1 & 0 & 0 \\ 0 & 1 & 0 \\ L_1 & M_1 & 1 \end{bmatrix} \begin{bmatrix} 1 & 0 & 0 \\ 0 & 1 & 0 \\ L_2 & M_2 & 1 \end{bmatrix} = \begin{bmatrix} 1 & 0 & 0 \\ 0 & 1 & 0 \\ L_1 + L_2 & M_1 + M_2 & 1 \end{bmatrix}. \tag{3.18}$$

3.3.3 SCALING

The scaling matrix of Eq. (3.5) is represented in a 3×3 matrix as

$$\begin{bmatrix} A & 0 & 0 \\ 0 & D & 0 \\ 0 & 0 & 1 \end{bmatrix}. \tag{3.19}$$

Whereas successive translations are additive, successive scalings are multiplicative:

$$\underset{\text{First scaling}}{\begin{bmatrix} A_1 & 0 & 0 \\ 0 & D_1 & 0 \\ 0 & 0 & 1 \end{bmatrix}} \underset{\text{Second scaling}}{\begin{bmatrix} A_2 & 0 & 0 \\ 0 & D_2 & 0 \\ 0 & 0 & 1 \end{bmatrix}} = \underset{\text{Combined scaling}}{\begin{bmatrix} A_1A_2 & 0 & 0 \\ 0 & D_1D_2 & 0 \\ 0 & 0 & 1 \end{bmatrix}}. \tag{3.20}$$

3.3.4 ROTATION

A rotation through an angle θ in the homogeneous coordinate system is produced by

$$\begin{bmatrix} \cos\theta & \sin\theta & 0 \\ -\sin\theta & \cos\theta & 0 \\ 0 & 0 & 1 \end{bmatrix}. \tag{3.21}$$

We can further show that two successive rotations are additive.

$$\underset{\text{First rotation}}{\begin{bmatrix} \cos\theta_1 & \sin\theta_1 & 0 \\ -\sin\theta_1 & \cos\theta_1 & 0 \\ 0 & 0 & 1 \end{bmatrix}} \underset{\text{Second rotation}}{\begin{bmatrix} \cos\theta_2 & \sin\theta_2 & 0 \\ -\sin\theta_2 & \cos\theta_2 & 0 \\ 0 & 0 & 1 \end{bmatrix}}$$

$$= \overset{\text{Combined rotation}}{\begin{bmatrix} \cos(\theta_1+\theta_2) & \sin(\theta_1+\theta_2) & 0 \\ -\sin(\theta_1+\theta_2) & \cos(\theta_1+\theta_2) & 0 \\ 0 & 0 & 1 \end{bmatrix}} \tag{3.22}$$

3.3.5 INVERSES OF TRANSFORMATIONS

Consider the following two translation matrices.

$$T_1 = \begin{bmatrix} 1 & 0 & 0 \\ 0 & 1 & 0 \\ -L & -M & 1 \end{bmatrix}, \qquad T_2 = \begin{bmatrix} 1 & 0 & 0 \\ 0 & 1 & 0 \\ L & M & 1 \end{bmatrix}.$$

The matrices T_1 and T_2 have opposite effects. That is, multiplication by matrix T_1 causes a translation through $(-L, -M)$, while multiplication by T_2 causes a translation through (L, M). Successive multiplications by T_1 and T_2 will produce an identity transformation, which leaves the point unchanged. We can easily verify this:

$$T_1T_2 = \begin{bmatrix} 1 & 0 & 0 \\ 0 & 1 & 0 \\ -L & -M & 1 \end{bmatrix}\begin{bmatrix} 1 & 0 & 0 \\ 0 & 1 & 0 \\ L & M & 1 \end{bmatrix} = \begin{bmatrix} 1 & 0 & 0 \\ 0 & 1 & 0 \\ 0 & 0 & 1 \end{bmatrix}. \quad \textbf{(3.23)}$$

Pairs of matrices whose product is an identity matrix I are referred to as *inverses*. In general, the inverse of a matrix T is denoted as T^{-1}; therefore, $T_2 = T_1^{-1}$. Many of the transformation matrices discussed in the previous sections have inverses, and their computations are rather straightforward. For example, the matrix

$$R(30°) = \begin{bmatrix} \cos 30° & -\sin 30° & 0 \\ \sin 30° & \cos 30° & 0 \\ 0 & 0 & 1 \end{bmatrix} = \begin{bmatrix} 0.866 & -0.5 & 0 \\ 0.5 & 0.866 & 0 \\ 0 & 0 & 1 \end{bmatrix},$$

represents a rotation of 30° counterclockwise. It has an inverse

$$R(30°)^{-1} = R(-30°) = \begin{bmatrix} 0.866 & 0.5 & 0 \\ -0.5 & 0.866 & 0 \\ 0 & 0 & 1 \end{bmatrix},$$

which represents a rotation of 30° clockwise. We can easily verify that their matrix product is $R(30°) \cdot R(-30°) = I$.

3.3.6 TRANSFORMING A COORDINATE SYSTEM

Up to this point, we have discussed transformations of a set of points into another set of points within the same coordinate system. An alternative, but equivalent, way of transforming a set of points is to change the coordinate system. To show how this is done, we will examine two special cases.

We begin by considering Fig. 3.5(a). The point P' is produced by rotating point P through a *counterclockwise* angle of 30°. On the other hand, rotating the coordinate system XY through a *clockwise* angle of 30° results in the new coordinate system $X'Y'$, as seen in Fig. 3.5(b). This new coordinate system can provide another means of referencing point P. More specifically, the position of P' relative to the XY coordinate system is identical to the position of point P relative to the rotated coordinate system $X'Y'$. The matrix required to represent the transformation of a coordinate system is thus the *inverse* of that needed to transform points within a coordinate system. This relationship will be very useful in our development of computer graphics techniques.

As a second example, consider Fig. 3.5(c), where point P (3, 3) (as defined in the XY coordinate system) can have its position specified by (3.5, 2.5) in the $X'Y'$ coordinate system. The transformation required from coordinate system

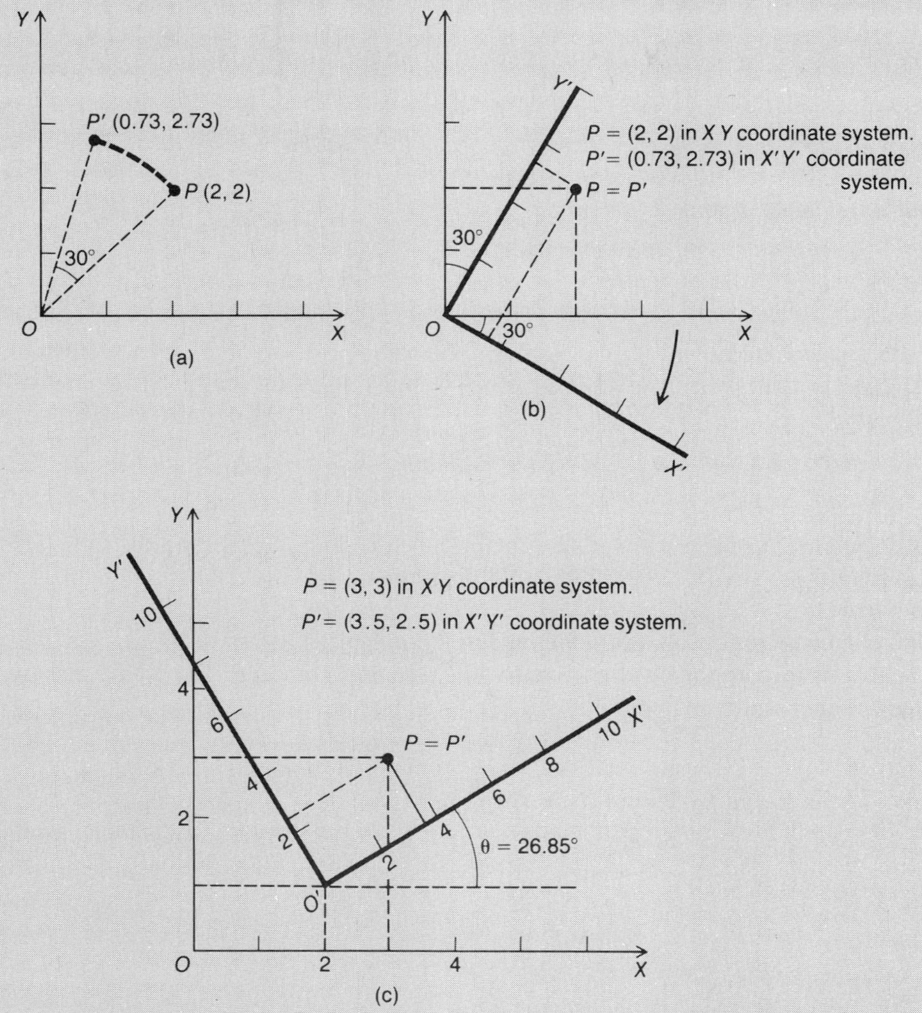

FIGURE 3.5 **Relationship between (a) transforming a point, (b) transforming a coordinate system, and (c) point *P* and two coordinate systems**

XY to $X'Y'$ can be determined by first translating the origin to O′, then scaling both coordinate axes, and finally rotating the $X'Y'$ coordinate system through a *clockwise* angle of θ. In matrix product form, this is equivalent to

$$T = \begin{bmatrix} 1 & 0 & 0 \\ 0 & 1 & 0 \\ -2 & -1 & 1 \end{bmatrix} \begin{bmatrix} 2 & 0 & 0 \\ 0 & 2 & 0 \\ 0 & 0 & 1 \end{bmatrix} \begin{bmatrix} \cos\theta & -\sin\theta & 0 \\ \sin\theta & \cos\theta & 0 \\ 0 & 0 & 1 \end{bmatrix}$$
$$= \begin{bmatrix} 2\cos\theta & -2\sin\theta & 0 \\ 2\sin\theta & 2\cos\theta & 0 \\ -4\cos\theta - 2\sin\theta & 4\sin\theta - 2\cos\theta & 1 \end{bmatrix}. \quad (3.24)$$

Thus we obtain

$$P' = (3, 3, 1) \cdot T = (2\cos\theta + 4\sin\theta, \quad -2\sin\theta + 4\cos\theta, \quad 1).$$

If the angle θ is known, we can easily obtain the position of P'. In our example, P' (3.5, 2.5) is known instead. Therefore we may solve for θ by letting $\sin\theta = u$ and $\cos\theta = (1 - u^2)^{1/2}$. (Note that $\sin^2\theta + \cos^2\theta = 1$.) Given the relationships

$$2\cos\theta + 4\sin\theta = 3.5,$$
$$-2\sin\theta + 4\cos\theta = 2.5,$$

substituting the simultaneous equations in terms of u and rearranging terms yields $18.5\,u^2 + 10\,u - 8.25 = 0$. Solving the equation for u gives 0.45014, or $\theta = 26.85°$.

As can be expected, transformation from coordinate system $X'Y'$ to XY is done by simply applying the inverse of Eq. (3.24). In general, if we define T as product of n matrices

$$T = T_1 \cdot T_2 \cdot \cdots T_{n-1} \cdot T_n$$

then T^{-1} is found by the relationship

$$T^{-1} = T_n^{-1} \cdot T_{n-1}^{-1} \cdot \cdots T_2^{-1} \cdot T_1^{-1}. \quad (3.25)$$

Thus we obtain

$$T^{-1} = \begin{bmatrix} \cos\theta & \sin\theta & 0 \\ -\sin\theta & \cos\theta & 0 \\ 0 & 0 & 1 \end{bmatrix} \begin{bmatrix} 1/2 & 0 & 0 \\ 0 & 1/2 & 0 \\ 0 & 0 & 1 \end{bmatrix} \begin{bmatrix} 1 & 0 & 0 \\ 0 & 1 & 0 \\ 2 & 1 & 1 \end{bmatrix}$$
$$= \begin{bmatrix} 1/2\cos\theta & 1/2\sin\theta & 0 \\ -1/2\sin\theta & 1/2\cos\theta & 0 \\ 2 & 1 & 1 \end{bmatrix}.$$

To find P, we may multiply P' by T^{-1}:

$$P = P' \cdot T^{-1} = (1.75\cos\theta - 1.25\sin\theta + 2, \quad 1.75\sin\theta + 1.25\cos\theta + 1, 1)$$
$$= (3, 3, 1).$$

This method of transforming a coordinate system is particularly useful when multiple objects, each defined in its own coordinate system, are combined to represent their coordinates in a single, global coordinate system. (This geometric transformation is often referred to as an *instance transformation.*)

3.4 SEQUENTIAL 2-D TRANSFORMATIONS

The introduction of homogeneous coordinates in the previous section provides us with a means for combining the primitive translation, rotation, and scaling matrices to produce desired general results. This section shows how such a combination can be used to obtain the rotation of an object about an arbitrary point or the reflection of an object about an arbitrary axis.

3.4.1 2-D ROTATION ABOUT AN ARBITRARY POINT

Previously we considered rotations as occurring about the origin. Now we consider the rotation of an object about an arbitrary point Q (q_1, q_2). Because we only know how to rotate about the origin, we convert our original problem into three different problems. This requires a sequence of three set transformations.

Step 1: Translate the center of rotation to the origin.

$$T_1 = \begin{bmatrix} 1 & 0 & 0 \\ 0 & 1 & 0 \\ -q_1 & -q_2 & 1 \end{bmatrix}$$

Step 2: Perform the desired rotation.

$$R(\theta) = \begin{bmatrix} \cos\theta & \sin\theta & 0 \\ -\sin\theta & \cos\theta & 0 \\ 0 & 0 & 1 \end{bmatrix}$$

Step 3: Translate the result back to the original center of Q.

$$T_2 = \begin{bmatrix} 1 & 0 & 0 \\ 0 & 1 & 0 \\ q_1 & q_2 & 1 \end{bmatrix}$$

The net effect of the three transformations is the product of the matrices above:

$$T = T_1 R(\theta)\, T_2 =$$

$$\begin{bmatrix} \cos\theta & \sin\theta & 0 \\ -\sin\theta & \cos\theta & 0 \\ q_1(1 - \cos\theta) + q_2 \sin\theta & q_2(1 - \cos\theta) - q_1 \sin\theta & 1 \end{bmatrix} \qquad (3.26)$$

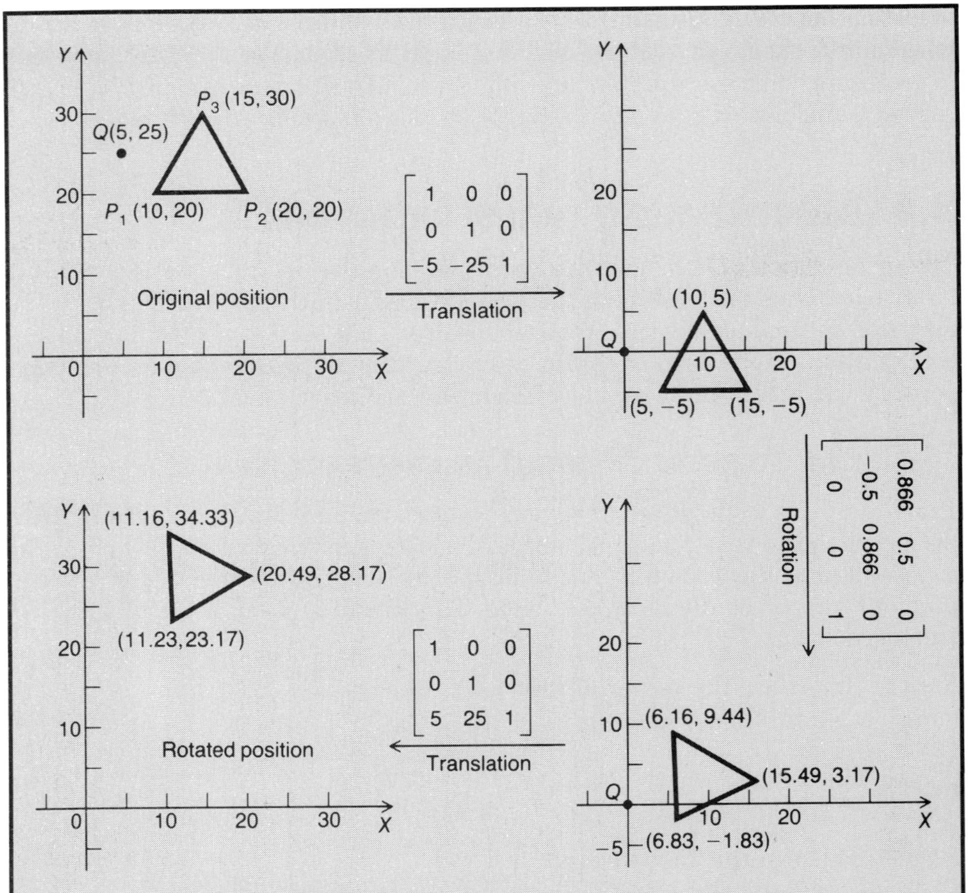

FIGURE 3.6 Two-D rotation about an arbitrary point

As an example, we consider a triangle defined by the vertices (10, 20), (20, 20), and (15, 30) and assume a rotation about point Q (5, 25) through a counterclockwise angle of 30°. The step-by-step transformation procedure is shown in Fig. 3.6, the final vertices being (11.83, 23.17), (20.49, 28.17), and (11.16, 34.33).

3.4.2 REFLECTION ABOUT AN ARBITRARY AXIS

Suppose we want to find a reflection of a triangle about the axis $y = a + bx$. We can again derive the transformed coordinates from combinations of the primitive transformations. The steps in the reflection about the arbitrary axis $y = a + bx$ are as follows.

Step 1: Translate the origin to $(0, a)$. (See Fig. 3.7b.)

$$T_1 = \begin{bmatrix} 1 & 0 & 0 \\ 0 & 1 & 0 \\ 0 & -a & 1 \end{bmatrix}$$

Step 2: Rotate the axis through a *clockwise* angle θ such that the axis line $(y = a + bx)$ lies on the X axis. The angle θ is easily computed, as the slope of the arbitrary axis is b: $\cos\theta = 1/r$, $\sin\theta = b/r$, where $r = (b^2 + 1)^{1/2}$. Substituting these parameters into Eq. (3.21) yields

$$R(-\theta) = \begin{bmatrix} 1/r & -b/r & 0 \\ b/r & 1/r & 0 \\ 0 & 0 & 1 \end{bmatrix}.$$

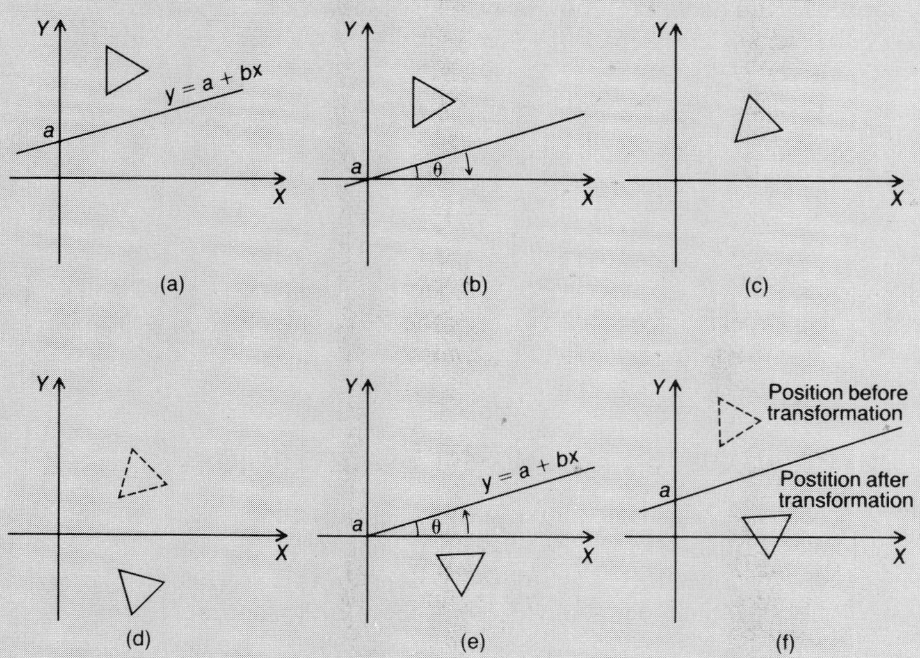

FIGURE 3.7 Reflection around an arbitrary axis: (a) original figure, (b) translation, (c) rotation, (d) reflection, (e) rotation, and (f) translation

The situation after the rotation is shown in Fig. 3.7(c).

Step 3: Reflect the object about the X axis, as shown in Fig. 3.7(d).

$$T_2 = \begin{bmatrix} 1 & 0 & 0 \\ 0 & -1 & 0 \\ 0 & 0 & 1 \end{bmatrix}$$

Step 4: Apply the inverse of step 2. (See Fig. 3.7(e).)

$$R(\theta) = \begin{bmatrix} 1/r & b/r & 0 \\ -b/r & 1/r & 0 \\ 0 & 0 & 1 \end{bmatrix}$$

Step 5: Apply the inverse of step 1. (See Fig. 3.7(f).)

$$T_1^{-1} = \begin{bmatrix} 1 & 0 & 0 \\ 0 & 1 & 0 \\ 0 & a & 1 \end{bmatrix}$$

The purpose of steps 4 and 5 is to return the object to its original coordinate system. The provisional coordinate systems created by steps 1, 2, and 3 are used only as intermediate steps in the process. The complete transformation that represents these five steps is

$$T = T_1 R(-\theta) T_2 R(\theta) T_1^{-1}$$

$$= \begin{bmatrix} 1 & 0 & 0 \\ 0 & 1 & 0 \\ 0 & -a & 1 \end{bmatrix} \begin{bmatrix} \cos 2\theta & \sin 2\theta & 0 \\ \sin 2\theta & -\cos 2\theta & 0 \\ 0 & 0 & 1 \end{bmatrix} \begin{bmatrix} 1 & 0 & 0 \\ 0 & 1 & 0 \\ 0 & a & 1 \end{bmatrix}. \quad \textbf{(3.29)}$$

This sequence is illustrated in Fig. 3.7. In the sections ahead, we will develop a computer program that will perform the 2-D viewing transformations and plot the resulting image on the graphics screen.

3.5 VIEWPORT PLANNING OF 2-D GRAPHICS

Up to this point, we have manipulated 2-D objects through various transformations in an abstract space. We call this abstract space the *world coordinate system* (or Standard Coordinate System). In this section, we will discuss a method for transforming world coordinates into coordinates the graphics screen can use, the *screen display coordinates*. To do so, we need three viewing operation techniques: window clipping, window-to-viewport mapping, and generating device-dependent physical screen coordinates.

3.5.1 WINDOW CLIPPING

Window and viewport. The rectangular boundary of the area of interest in the world coordinate system is called the *window;* the corresponding translation to the screen area is referred to as the *viewport.* In other words, we use the window to define what we want to display, and use the viewport to specify where on the screen to put it. Figure 3.8 illustrates the relationship between the window and the viewport.

As seen in Fig. 3.8, the window selected by the user usually does not include all the graphic data generated in the data base. If the program does not check for visibility before it sends the data to the display device, the coordinates of points may be outside the screen. Therefore, clipping is done before the display instructions are sent to the screen in order to eliminate the portions of the picture that are outside the window.

Clipping points. Clipping a point can be done by simply comparing its coordinates with the window boundaries. If the point lies outside the window boundaries, it is not plotted. (See Fig. 3.8.) If the X coordinate boundaries of the window are at $x_{w \cdot \min}$ and $x_{w \cdot \max}$, and the y coordinate boundaries are at $y_{w \cdot \min}$ and $y_{w \cdot \max}$, the following conditions must be met if a point at (x, y) is to be

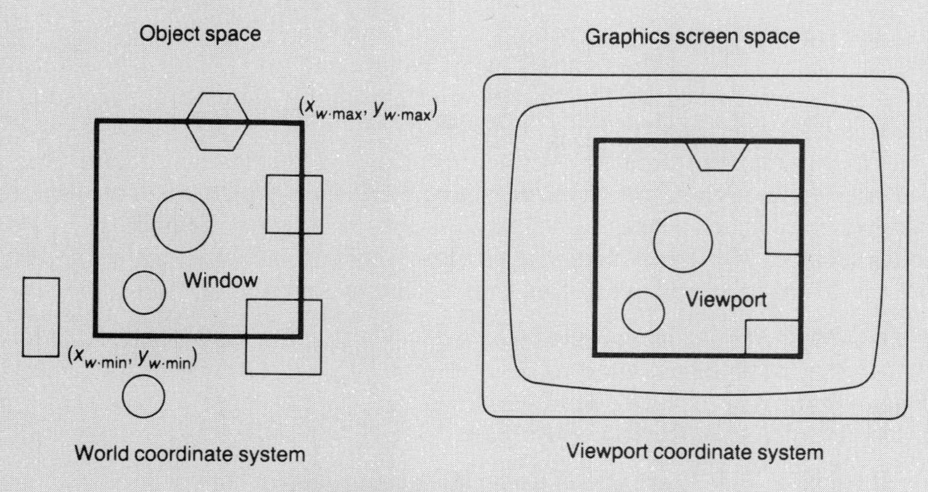

FIGURE 3.8 Window vs viewport

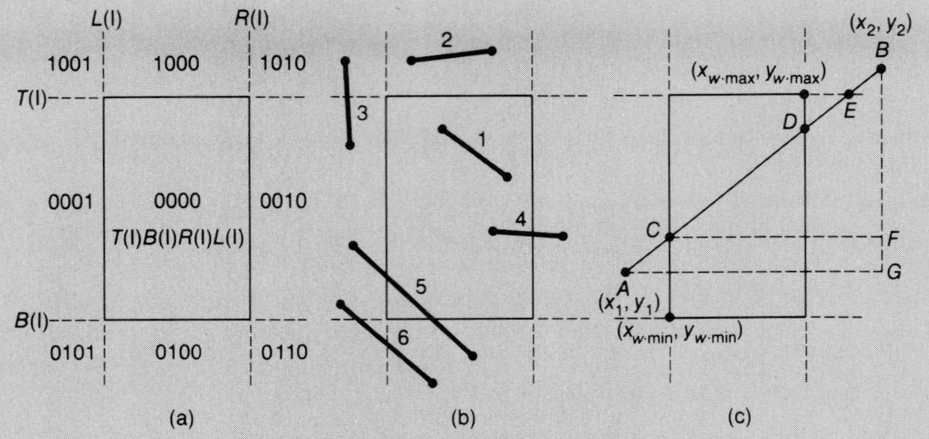

FIGURE 3.9 Clipping line segments

visible:

$$x_{w \cdot \min} \leq x \leq x_{w \cdot \max},$$

$$y_{w \cdot \min} \leq y \leq y_{w \cdot \max}.$$

Clipping lines. Line clipping is much more difficult because it requires checking and classifying a line as visible, partially visible, or invisible. For example, part of line may be in the window even though both end points of the line are outside the window area. The following line-clipping algorithm is based upon the Cohen-Sutherland Clipping Algorithm [3].

To illustrate the sequence of the algorithm, we consider Fig. 3.9(a), where the window is divided into nine regions by the four lines that determine the window boundaries. Each endpoint of the line is assigned a computer bit code that indicates whether it is on the window, above it, below it, to its right or to its left. More precisely, we define four variables for each endpoint:

$T(I)$—Point I is above window.
$B(I)$—Point I is below window.
$R(I)$—Point I is to the right of window.
$L(I)$—Point I is to the left of window.

Each variable code is set to 1 (TRUE) if a given relation between the end point and the window is true. Otherwise the variable code is 0 (FALSE). The visibility status of the line is then determined by a logical comparison of the variable codes for its two endpoints.

- If both endpoints (1 and 2) lie inside the window, the entire line segment is visible. (See line segment 1 in Fig. 3.9(b).) This condition arises when both variable codes satisfy the equation

$$T(1) + B(1) + R(1) + L(1) + T(2) + B(2) + R(2) + L(2) = 0. \qquad \textbf{(3.31)}$$

- If both endpoints lie outside of any same boundary line, the entire line is invisible. (See line segments 2 and 3.) This condition is detected by checking the sum of the products of each corresponding variable code to determine if it is nonzero.

$$[T(1)T(2)] + [B(1)B(2)] + [R(1)R(2)] + [L(1)L(2)] \neq 0. \qquad \textbf{(3.32)}$$

- If both endpoints are outside the window area and do not have any matching position characteristic, the status of the line cannot be determined immediately. The necessary condition for this is

$$[T(1)T(2)] + [B(1)B(2)] + [R(1)R(2)] + [L(1)L(2)] = 0. \qquad \textbf{(3.33)}$$

  In this case, there are two possibilities: the line segment is partially visible, or the line segment is totally invisible. (See line segments 5 and 6 in Fig. 3.9(b).) If one endpoint is on the window and the other is off the window, the line is partially visible. (See line segment 4 in Fig. 3.9(b).)

Whenever we observe the condition described in Eq. (3.33), we must subdivide the line segment by finding the point of intersection of the line with one edge of the window and discarding the part that lies off the window. For example, the line *AB* in Fig. 3.9(c) would be subdivided at *C* and the portion *AC* eliminated. Since each line is intersected by a window edge that is vertical or horizontal, the intersection point's *X* or *Y* coordinate can be obtained quite easily. For example, in identifying the interesection coordinates associated with the point *C* $(x_{w \cdot \min}, y)$, we consider in Fig. 3.9(c) the right triangles *ABG* and *CBF*. These are similar triangles for which

$$\frac{BG}{AG} = \frac{BF}{CF} = \frac{y_2 - y_1}{x_2 - x_1} = \frac{y_2 - y}{x_2 - x_{w \cdot \min}}. \qquad \textbf{(3.34)}$$

Rearranging the terms gives us

$$y = y_2 - \frac{y_2 - y_1}{x_2 - x_1} \cdot (x_2 - x_{w \cdot \min}) \qquad \textbf{(3.35)}$$

Now endpoints *A* and *C* are known. Since both points lie on the outside of the same boundary line, the line segment *AC* is invisible and discarded. We test the remaining line segment *CB* and cannot accept or reject it immediately. We calculate the intersection point *D* and discard *DB*. Finally we test *CD* and accept it. (A line clipping subroutine is not necessary on the IBM PC: The LINE graphic statement provides the line clipping in BASIC release 2.0.)

3.5.2 WINDOW-TO-VIEWPORT MAPPING

After clipping an image to the window boundary, the next step is to map that image to the viewport. Changing the point of view is also possible through a sequence of window-to-viewport transformations.

To understand the procedure, consider Fig. 3.10. Here, the point (x_w, y_w) maps to the point (x_v, y_v) in such a way as to retain its relative position within the enclosing rectangle. With the variables defined as in Fig. 3.10, transforming the window coordinates to the viewpoint coordinates is equivalent to translating (x_w, y_w) through $(x_{w \cdot \min}, y_{w \cdot \min})$, performing an appropriate scaling, and then translating from the world coordinate system to the new coordinate system (viewport). Thus a sequence of three primitive transformations is necessary:

$$[x_v, y_v, 1] = [x_w, y_w, 1]\begin{bmatrix} 1 & 0 & 0 \\ 0 & 1 & 0 \\ -x_{w \cdot \min} & -y_{w \cdot \min} & 1 \end{bmatrix}\begin{bmatrix} S_1 & 0 & 0 \\ 0 & S_2 & 0 \\ 0 & 0 & 1 \end{bmatrix} \cdot \begin{bmatrix} 1 & 0 & 0 \\ 0 & 1 & 0 \\ x_{v \cdot \min} & y_{v \cdot \min} & 1 \end{bmatrix} \tag{3.36}$$

$$= [S_1(x_w - x_{w \cdot \min}) + x_{v \cdot \min}, S_2(y_w - y_{w \cdot \min}) + y_{v \cdot \min}, 1]$$

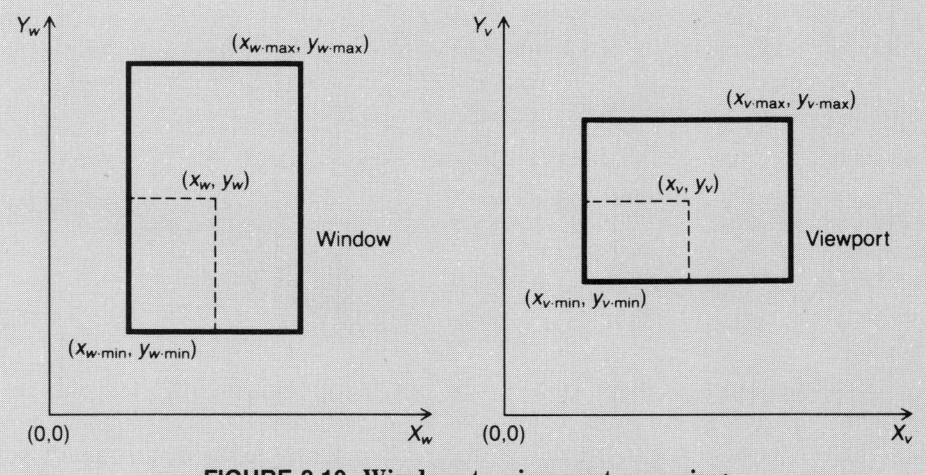

FIGURE 3.10 Window to viewport mapping

To preserve proportions (i.e., the relative position within the enclosing rectangle), the scale factors S_1 and S_2 may be set to

$$S_1 = \frac{x_{v \cdot \max} - x_{v \cdot \min}}{x_{w \cdot \max} - x_{w \cdot \min}} \tag{3.37}$$

and

$$S_2 = \frac{y_{v \cdot \max} - y_{v \cdot \min}}{y_{w \cdot \max} - y_{w \cdot \min}} \tag{3.38}$$

[Note that if $S_1 \neq S_2$, then we will get a distorted shape.]
Once the viewport parameters are provided, we can easily compute the viewport coordinates

$$x_v = S_1(x_w - x_{w \cdot \min}) + x_{v \cdot \min} \tag{3.39}$$

$$y_v = S_2(y_w - y_{w \cdot \min}) + y_{v \cdot \min} \tag{3.40}$$

It is quite obvious that both window and viewport coordinates will be exactly the same when we choose $S_1 = S_2 = 1$.

3.5.3. GENERATING PHYSICAL DEVICE COORDINATES

The graphic display screen provided by most microcomputers has a coordinate axis system (pixel) whose location and orientation differs somewhat from the standard mathematical graphics orientation. This difference is shown in Fig. 3.11. To interpret the screen coordinates in terms of the usual Cartesian coordinate system (viewport coordinate system) we need to reorient and relocate points through transformation.[†] Since the display screen of microcomputers like the IBM PC has the y axis upside down, the point (x_v, y_v) on the viewport coordinate can be considered a reflection of the point (x_v, y_v) through the X axis. Because the origin $(0, 0)$ is located at the upper left-hand corner of the screen, we must translate the origin to an onscreen location through (L, M). Thus the corresponding device coordinates are computed as

$$[x_s, y_s, 1] = [x_v, y_v, 1]\begin{bmatrix} 1 & 0 & 0 \\ 0 & -1 & 0 \\ 0 & 0 & 1 \end{bmatrix}\begin{bmatrix} 1 & 0 & 0 \\ 0 & 1 & 0 \\ \mathrm{L} & \mathrm{M} & 1 \end{bmatrix} \tag{3.41}$$
$$(x_s, y_s, 1) = (x_v + L, M - y_v, 1)$$

[†]For computers such as Chromatics, this transformation is not required because the video screens are already addressed in the Cartesian coordinate system. In this case,
$$(x_s, y_s, 1) = (x_v, y_v, 1).$$

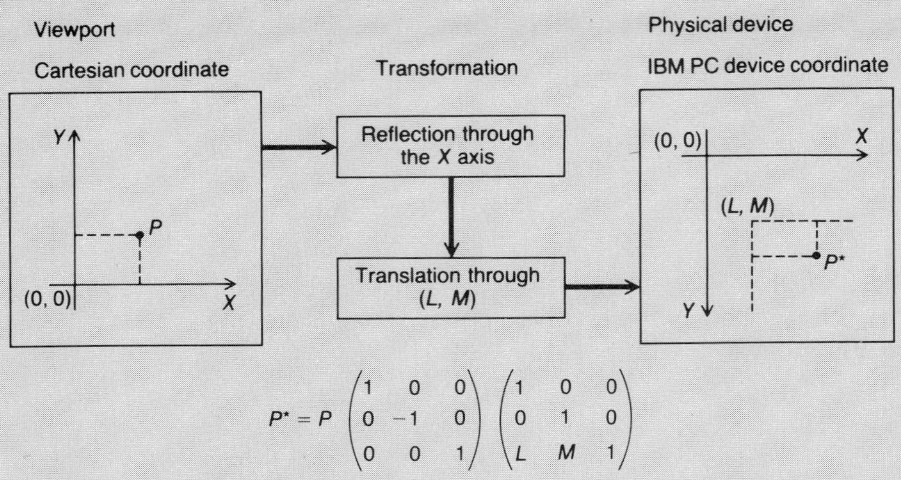

FIGURE 3.11 Transformation process from the viewport coordinate system to the IBM PC device coordinate system

or

$$\begin{aligned} x_s &= S_1(x_w - x_{w \cdot \min}) + x_{v \cdot \min} + L \\ y_s &= S_2(y_{w \cdot \min} - y_w) - y_{v \cdot \min} + M \end{aligned} \tag{3.42}$$

We will use the latter form [Eq. (3.42)] for most of the sample programs in this book. The scaling parameters, S_1 and S_2, in Eq. (3.42) are designed for computer screens with an aspect ratio of 1:1, which implies that the horizontal and vertical scales are the same. However, differences between these scales are fairly common among microcomputers. For example, the IBM PC medium-resolution graphic mode is based on a grid of 320 × 200, which suggests that a horizontal unit is equivalent to 200/320 of a vertical unit. In computer graphics, it is frequently important that the horizontal and vertical scales be equidistant so that a square will appear to have all sides of equal lengths, and so that all points of a circle will appear to be the same distance from the center. This requirement can be met by adjusting the x_s coordinate in Eq. (3.42).

$$x_s = SCF[S_1(x_w - x_{w \cdot \min}) + x_{v \cdot \min} + L] \tag{3.43}$$

where SCF = screen scaling adjustment factor.

Since each graphics monitor comes with different screen combinations, the scaling factor must be determined according to the physical size of the screens character display zone. Figure 3.12 indicates the maximum raster display areas obtainable on a range of monitor sizes. For example, the character display zone of the Amdek Color II Monitor has a horizontal length of 240 mm and a vertical length of 180 mm. Thus one way to determine the appropriate scaling factor (*SCF*) for the monitor is as follows.

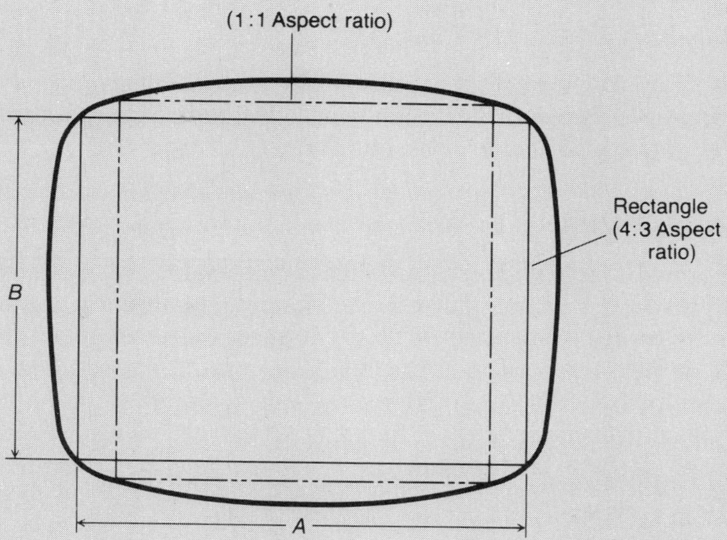

Diagonal screen size	A (mm)	B (mm)	Square (mm)	Typical monitor
9″	148	111	118	Portable IBM PC
12″	216	162	172	
13″	240	180	191	IBM PC
16″	283	213	226	
19″	348	261	276	TV
20″	356	267	283	
21″	368	276	293	
23″	408	306	324	TV

FIGURE 3.12 Raster dimensions as functions of screen size

Step 1: Given the graphic resolution (320 × 200), compute the ratios H and V:

$$H = \frac{\text{Horizontal length}}{\text{Maximum number of horizontal points}} = \frac{240 \text{ mm}}{320}$$

$$V = \frac{\text{Vertical length}}{\text{Maximum number of vertical points}} = \frac{180 \text{ mm}}{200}.$$

Step 2: Compute the SCF

$$SCF = \frac{V}{H} = 1.2,$$

and multiply the horizontal coordinate by the SCF in planning the viewport. In high resolution mode, where the horizontal points are doubled (640), the scale factor would be 2.4.

3.5.4 ZOOMING

Having obtained a screen graphics image from a database, we may want to examine a portion of a graph in detail. For example, we might want to magnify the portion to the full screen size. To do so, we specify a rectangle on the display screen that defines the portion of the current picture that should be shown as the next picture (see Fig. 3.13). Note that this rectangle is *not* the window itself, but its transformed viewport image on the screen. Since we only redraw the graphic contents in the square, a new window may be defined within the old window.

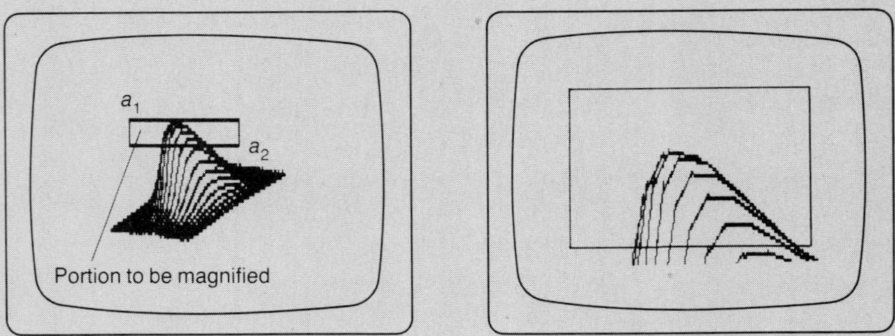

FIGURE 3.13 Viewing transformation in zooming

One intuitive but time-consuming approach is to find the new window parameters in the world coordinate system, $(x'_{w \cdot \min}, y'_{w \cdot \min})$ and $(x'_{w \cdot \max}, y'_{w \cdot \max})$. These correspond to the off-diagonal screen coordinates (x_{a_1}, y_{a_1}) and (x_{a_2}, y_{a_2}) of the rectangle on the screen. Then we reset the viewport parameters $(x'_{v \cdot \min}, y'_{v \cdot \min})$ according to the size of screen desired. The window-clipping routine is thus applied to the new window boundaries. Substituting new window and viewport parameters into Eq. (3.42), we obtain new screen coordinates.

The transformation process to obtain the newly defined points $(x'_{w \cdot \min}, y'_{w \cdot \min})$ and $(x'_{w \cdot \max}, y'_{w \cdot \max})$ for the given screen coordinates is simply to apply the inverses of Eqs. (3.41) and (3.36) in that sequence. Then we can represent the net effect of the inverse transformation as

$$T = \begin{bmatrix} 1 & 0 & 0 \\ 0 & -1 & 0 \\ L & M & 1 \end{bmatrix} \begin{bmatrix} 1 & 0 & 0 \\ 0 & 1 & 0 \\ -x_{v \cdot \min} & -y_{v \cdot \min} & 1 \end{bmatrix} \begin{bmatrix} 1/S_1 & 0 & 0 \\ 0 & 1/S_2 & 0 \\ 0 & 0 & 1 \end{bmatrix} \cdot \begin{bmatrix} 1 & 0 & 0 \\ 0 & 1 & 0 \\ x_{w \cdot \min} & y_{w \cdot \min} & 1 \end{bmatrix}$$

Given screen coordinates (x_{a_1}, y_{a_1}), to find $(x'_{w \cdot \min}, y'_{w \cdot \min})$ we compute

$$(x'_{w \cdot \min}, y'_{w \cdot \min}, 1) = (x_{a_1}, y_{a_1}, 1) \cdot T \tag{3.44}$$

A more efficient approach is to save the entire screen image when the first picture is generated. Then, one specifies the square on the display screen defining the part of the picture to be enlarged, reads only the graphic contents of the square, and redraws them on the screen. Saving and moving portions of the computer's memory using the specified device usually require a machine language program. (The effect of zooming can be obtained by using either WINDOW or VIEW statements for the IBM PC. See Sections 2.3.7 and 2.3.8.)

3.6 SCREEN DISPLAY FOR 2-D GRAPHICS ON IBM PC

We now know how to manipulate 2-D pictures, but we have not yet discussed how to develop a computer program that will actually do this. The purpose of this section is to develop a series of computer programs based on the concepts explained in the previous sections.

3.6.1 PROGRAM STRUCTURE

Inputting world coordinates. Figure 3.14 illustrates the 2-D viewing and plotting process. As a first step toward a computer program we need to provide

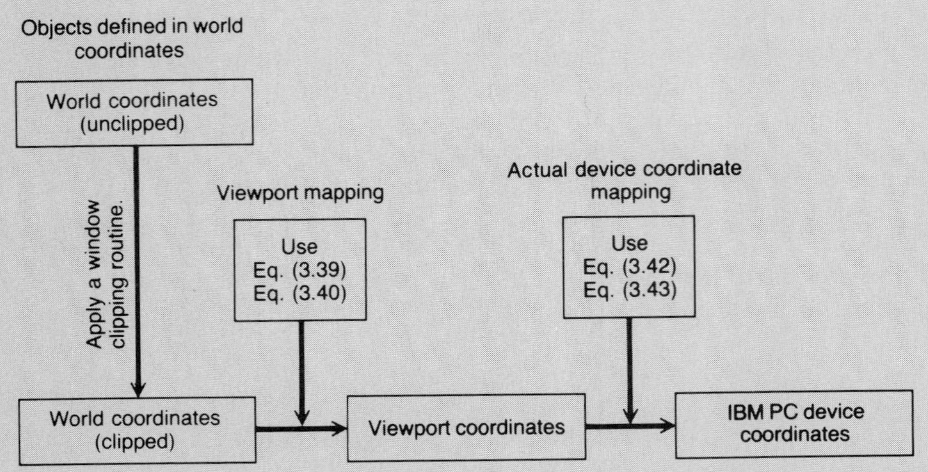

FIGURE 3.14 Two-D viewing process extended to include the IBM PC device coordinate system

a mechanism for furnishing data to it. There are three possible mechanisms for providing the data to create a 2-D picture. First, data may be entered manually through the keyboard as required or provided through DATA statements in the program. Second, a set of data files may be created according to the input format of the model so that the user needs only to link the data file to the 2-D graphics program. (We will discuss the details of creating data files in Chapter 6.) Third, the program itself may contain line statements that generate coordinate points through mathematical relationships such as $y = f(x)$ or $(x = f(t),\ y = g(t))$. This latter method is used frequently when plotting a picture based on well-defined mathematical functions.

2-D Transformation matrix generator. Once the method of inputting coordinate data has been established, the next step is to interface with the user about the types of transformations required. As was seen in Section 3.4, several combinations of primitive transformations may need to be performed for the object to be displayed in proper location and shape. Combining several primitive transformation matrices can be quite tedious if this has to be done by hand. Program 3.1 handles this task by simply designating the type of transformation and then having the computer do the matrix multiplications. Recall from Eq. (3.16) that the nine matrix elements control the shape of the 2-D object. Since the third column vector elements in the 3×3 matrix are fixed, only six parameters remain to be specified (A, B, C, D, L, and M). Program 3.1 essentially computes these six matrix elements. With these six elements specified, we can easily compute the transformed coordinates.

```
100 ' Program 3.1: Subroutine to Determine the Transformation Matrix
110     CLS: KEY OFF : SCREEN 2
120 '----- Type of Transformation ---------
130 LOCATE 2,20: PRINT"TRANSFORMATION MENU":PRINT
140 PRINT TAB(20)"1. Translation"
150 PRINT TAB(20)"2. Scaling"
160 PRINT TAB(20)"3. Reflection"
170 PRINT TAB(20)"4. Rotation"
180 PRINT TAB(20)"5. Combined Transformations"
190 PRINT: PRINT TAB(25)"< Input Choice >";:INPUT Q1
200 ON Q1 GOSUB 250,280,320,450,520
210 DEF FNX(X,Y)=A*X + C*Y + L          ' FNX(X,Y) : Transformed X coordinate
220 DEF FNY(X,Y)=B*X + D*Y + M          ' FNY(X,Y) : Transformed Y Coordinate
230 RETURN
240 END
250 '-------- TRANSLATION ------------
260 PRINT: PRINT TAB(20)"< Translation thru (L,M) > ";:INPUT L,M
270 A=1:B=0:C=0:D=1  : RETURN
280 '-------- SCALING       ------------
290 PRINT:PRINT TAB(20)"< Scaling Factors for X,Y >";:INPUT A,D
300 PRINT TAB(20)"< Shear Factors for  B,C >";:INPUT B,C
310 L=0:M=0               : RETURN
320 '-------- REFLECTION  ------------
330 PRINT:PRINT TAB(20)"REFLECTION MENU"
340 PRINT TAB(20)"1. Reflection thru X-axis"
350 PRINT TAB(20)"2. Reflection thru Y-axis"
360 PRINT TAB(20)"3. Reflection thru Origin"
370 PRINT:PRINT TAB(20)"< Input Choice >";:INPUT Q2
380 IF Q2=1 THEN 410
390 IF Q2=2 THEN 420
400 A=-1:D=-1: GOTO 430
410 A=1: D=-1: GOTO 430
420 A=-1: D=1
430 B=0: C=0: L=0: M=0
440 RETURN
450 '-------- ROTATION    --------------
460 PRINT: PRINT TAB(20)"  Rotation Angle(Degree) : + for counterclockwise,"
470        PRINT TAB(20)"                           - for clockwise.";
480 INPUT DEGREE
490 Q3=DEGREE*3.14159/180
500 A=COS(Q3):B=SIN(Q3):C=-B:D=A:L=0:M=0
510 RETURN
520 '------ COMBINED TRANSFORMATIONS ----------
530 PRINT:PRINT TAB(20)"Number of Transformations Required";
540 INPUT NT
550 FOR I=1 TO NT
560      PRINT:PRINT TAB(20) I": Type of Transformation - < 1,2,3,or 4>";
570      INPUT Q4
580      ON Q4 GOSUB 250,280,320,450
590      IF I=1 THEN 680 ELSE 600
600      A2=A:B2=B:C2=C:D2=D:L2=L:M2=M
610      A=A1*A2 + B1*C2
620      B=A1*B2 + B1*D2
630      C=C1*A2 + D1*C2
640      D=C1*B2 + D1*D2
650      L=L1*A2 + M1*C2 + L2
660      M=L1*B2 + M1*D2 + M2
670      IF I= NT  THEN 700
680      A1=A:B1=B: C1=C:D1=D:L1=L:M1=M
690 NEXT I
700 RETURN
```

PROGRAM 3.1 **Subroutine to determine the transformation matrix**

Clipping. As discussed in Section 3.5.1, we need to specify the window parameters to define what we want to display. Depending upon the graphic contents, either points or lines, we apply the appropriate window-clipping routine. This routine applies an accept–reject test to each transformed world coordinate.

Viewport planning and plot. All accepted points or lines are now subject to plotting on the screen. We need to plan the viewport by specifying $(x_{v \cdot \min}, y_{v \cdot \min})$ and $(x_{v \cdot \max}, y_{v \cdot \max})$, which define the image area on the screen. These parameters will be inputs to the program, along with the screen scaling factor. When all the viewing parameters are defined, we can easily compute the screen coordinates from Eq. (3.43). We are then ready to plot these coordinates on the screen.

3.6.2 ILLUSTRATIVE EXAMPLE

Rotating a triangle. As a first example of the use of transformation matrices with the display, we will look at a program that rotates a triangle through an arbitrary point. Consider a triangle at the origin of the world coordinate system, defined by the following points and lines:

Lines	Points (x, y)
$\overline{P_1P_2}$	$P_1(10, 20)$
$\overline{P_2P_3}$	$P_2(20, 20)$
$\overline{P_3P_1}$	$P_3(15, 30)$

We want to rotate the triangle through the arbitrary point Q (5, 25). (This example was previously shown in Fig. 3.6.) As discussed in Section 3.4.1, we need three transformation steps to rotate the triangle.

Program 3.2 will plot each intermediate transformed triangle and the resulting rotated triangle. These are shown in Fig. 3.15.

Nested octagons. As a second example of the use of transformation matrices, we will plot a sequence of nested octagons through different viewports to generate the image in Fig. 3.16 in several steps.

Step 1: We first center the octagon at the origin (0, 0) and fix the position of one of the eight vertices. From simple geometry, we know that consecutive vertices of the octagon are separated by a central angle of 45°. Thus, the second vertex can be derived by rotating the first vertex through 45°. In our example, the first vertex is positioned at (30, 0). From Eq. (3.21), we obtain the second vertex (21.21, 21.21), assuming the rotation is 45° counterclockwise. The third vertex is then calculated by rotating the vertex through another 45°. In like manner, we obtain the rest of the vertices. (See Fig. 3.16(a).)

```
10 ' Program 3.2 : Object Rotation through an Arbitrary Point
15 CLS: KEY OFF: SCREEN 2
20 '----- Input Screen Parameters --------
25 INPUT " Enter center coordinates (CX,CY) for plot ="; CX,CY
30 INPUT " Enter Screen Scaling Factor (SCF) ="; SCF
35 GOSUB 100 : CLS
40 ' ---- Input World Coordinates --------
45 FLAG = 0
50 FOR I=1 TO 4
55 READ X,Y
60  XS = SCF*FNX(X,Y) + CX
65  YS = CY - FNY(X,Y)
70 IF FLAG > 0 THEN 80
75 LINE (XS,YS)-(XS,YS): FLAG = 1 : GOTO 85     'line clipping is provided
80 LINE -(XS,YS)                                'through the LINE statements.
85 NEXT I
90 END
95 DATA 10,20,20,20,15,30,10,20
96 ' ---- attach Program 3.1 -----
```

PROGRAM 3.2 Object rotation through an arbitrary point

```
Enter center coordinates (CX,CY) for plot =? 320,100
Enter Screen Scaling Factor (SCF) =? 2.4

TRANSFORMATION MENU

1. Translation
2. Scaling
3. Reflection
4. Rotation
5. Combined Transformations

    < Input Choice >? 5

Number of Transformations Required? 3

 1 : Type of Transformation - < 1,2,3,or 4>? 1

< Translation thru (L,M) > ? -5,-25

 2 : Type of Transformation - < 1,2,3,or 4>? 4

  Rotation Angle(Degree) : + for counterclockwise,
                           - for clockwise.? 30

 3 : Type of Transformation - < 1,2,3,or 4>? 1

< Translation thru (L,M) > ? 5,25
```

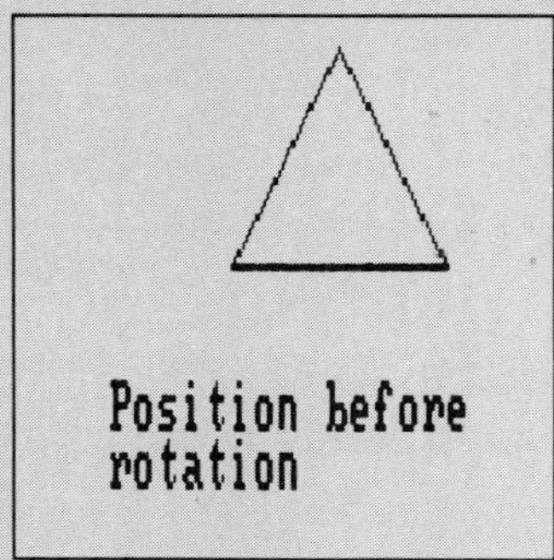

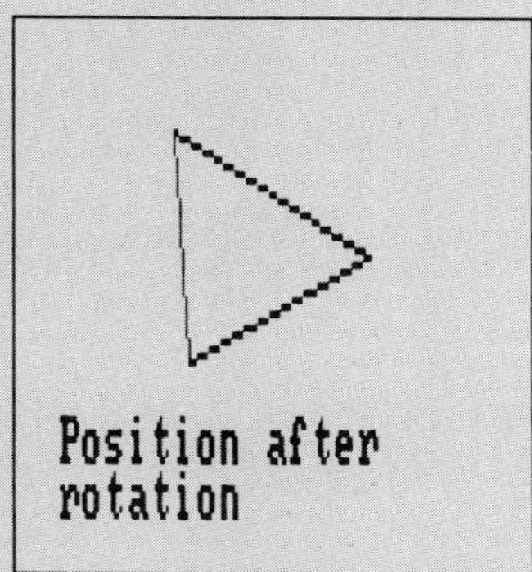

FIGURE 3.15 Rotating a triangle through an arbitrary point

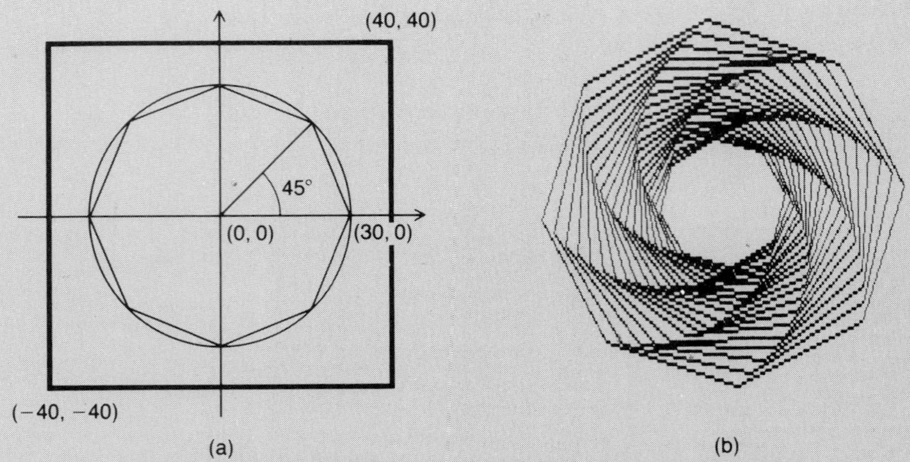

FIGURE 3.16 Plot of nested octagons through the 2-D viewing transformations: (a) octagon defined in world coordinates, and (b) nested octagons drawn by the IBM PC

Step 2: Because the graph is simple, we can skip the window-clipping routine by setting the window parameters at $(-40, -40)$ and $(40, 40)$, placing the eight vertices inside of the window. To translate the window contents (octagon) to a viewport, we set the viewport parameters at $(40, 40)$ and $(200, 200)$. (See Section 3.5.3.) Then we can use Eq. (3.42) to compute the screen coordinates. First we calculate S_1 and S_2 using Eqs. (3.37) and (3.38):

$$S_1 = \frac{200 - 40}{40 - (-40)} = 2;$$

$$S_2 = \frac{200 - 40}{40 - (-40)} = 2.$$

For the first vertex of the octagon, $(30, 0)$, the viewport coordinates are

$$x_v = 2[30 - (-40)] + 40 = 180,$$

$$y_v = 2[0 - (-40)] + 40 = 120.$$

The PC device coordinates are then

$$x_s = x_v + L = 180 + 0 = 180,$$

$$y_s = -y_v + M = -120 + 199 = 79.$$

We can further scale the coordinate x_s by using Eq. (3.43):

$$x_s = SCF \cdot x_s = 2.4x_s = 432 .$$

Step 3: After computing and mapping viewport coordinates to the screen, we will now connect each vertex to an adjacent one by the LINE statements. Thus we obtain one complete octagon on the screen.

Step 4: We now add program lines to generate a sequence of octagons nested within the first one (drawn in step 3). Each is slightly smaller than the previous one and slightly rotated counterclockwise. The decrease in size can be obtained by multiplying by Eq. (3.19). To rotate each octagon slightly, we use Eq. (3.21). Thus the transition from one octagon to the next (scaled and rotated) is effected by

$$(x', y', 1) = (x, y, 1)\begin{bmatrix} A & 0 & 0 \\ 0 & D & 0 \\ 0 & 0 & 1 \end{bmatrix}\begin{bmatrix} \cos\theta & \sin\theta & 0 \\ -\sin\theta & \cos\theta & 0 \\ 0 & 0 & 1 \end{bmatrix},$$

where $A = D$. The equivalent programming statements are

$$x' = x \cdot A \cdot \cos(\theta) - y \cdot A \cdot \sin(\theta),$$

$$y' = x \cdot A \cdot \sin(\theta) + y \cdot A \cdot \cos(\theta).$$

```
100 ' Program 3.3: nested Octagons
110 CLS: KEY OFF: SCREEN 2
120 PI = 3.14159
130 XWMIN=-40: YWMIN=-40                              'Set window
140 XVMIN=40 : YVMIN = 40                             'Set viewport
150 S1 =2     : S2=2    : SCF = 2.4                   'Set scale factors
160 L=0 : M=199                                       'Translation parameters
170 XW=30: YW=0
180 C=COS(PI/4): S=SIN(PI/4)
190 CN=COS(PI/36): SN=SIN(PI/36) : SF = .95
200 FOR J= 1 TO 20                                    'Draw 20 nested octagons
210       IF J=1 THEN 240
220       XW = SF*XW*CN - SF*YW*SN
230       YW = SF*XW*SN + SF*YW*CN
240       FOR I=0 TO 8                                'Draw single octagon
250           XS=S1*(XW-XWMIN) + XVMIN + L
260           XS=SCF*XS
270           YS=S2*(YWMIN-YW) - YVMIN + M
280           IF I=0 THEN PSET (XS,YS)
290           LINE -(XS,YS)
300           XN=XW*C -YW*S: YW=XW*S +YW*C : XW=XN
310       NEXT I
320 NEXT J
```

PROGRAM 3.3 Nested octagons

```
100 ' Program 3.4: An alternate method to draw nested octagons
110 CLS: KEY OFF: SCREEN 2
120 PI = 3.14159: SCF=2.4
130 WINDOW (-75,-75) - (75,75)
140 VIEW (150,0 )-(340,190)
150 XW=30: YW=0
160 C=COS(PI/4): S=SIN(PI/4)
170 CN=COS(PI/36): SN=SIN(PI/36) : SF = .95
180 FOR J= 1 TO 20
190       IF J=1 THEN 220
200       XW = SF*XW*CN - SF*YW*SN
210       YW = SF*XW*SN + SF*YW*CN
220       FOR I=0 TO 8
230            XS=XW
240            XS=SCF*XS
250            YS=YW
260            IF I=0 THEN PSET (XS,YS)
270            LINE -(XS,YS)
280            XN=XW*C -YW*S: YW=XW*S +YW*C : XW=XN
290       NEXT I
300 NEXT J
310 END
```

PROGRAM 3.4 An alternate method to draw nested octagons

In our example, we assume $A = 0.95$ and $\theta = 5°$. We then use Program 3.3 to draw the nested octagons.

As we presented in Section 2.3.8 and Section 2.3.9, WINDOW and VIEW statements can be used to map the world coordinates into the PC's screen coordinates. Program 3.4 draws the same nested octagons by using the WINDOW and VIEW statements. (See Fig. 3.16.)

3.7 SUMMARY

The purpose of this chapter was to introduce the basic 2-D geometrical transformations used in computer graphics. The translation, scaling, and rotation transformations discussed in this chapter are essential to many graphics applications and will be referred to extensively in later chapters. The homogeneous coordinate system was introduced here as one means of facilitating the transformation process.

We also discussed the concept of the window-to-viewport transformation. We used the window to define what we want to display and used the viewport to specify where to put it on the screen. In order to speed up the transformation, we used a clipping algorithm to clip the graphic content to any rectangular boundary. The efficient implementation of window-to-viewport transformation clips first, using the window as clipping region, and then performs the transformation of Eq. (3.42) on the lines that are at least partially visible. When a small portion of a very large picture is being displayed, the advantage of performing clipping before transformation is considerable.

EXERCISES

3.1 Consider a triangle defined by its three vertices, $(20, 40)$, $(50, 50)$, and $(30, 60)$.

a) Find the reflection of the triangle about the arbitrary axis $y = b - (b/a)x$, where a and b are positive constants.

b) Rotate the triangle in (a) through a counterclockwise angle of θ about point Q (c, d).

c) Let $a = 10$, $b = 15$, $c = 5$, $d = 50$, and $\theta = 45°$. By using the transformation matrices derived above, find the final coordinates of the vertices.

3.2 Suppose we define our window as $(-20, -20) - (60, 60)$ in the world coordinate system. We consider a line segment whose two endpoints are given by $(-30, 0)$ and $(80, 40)$.

a) Clip the line segment to the window boundary. Find all the intersection points.

b) Assume that the viewport is defined by $(10, 30) - (200, 130)$. Find the viewport coordinates for the intersection points.

3.3 Write a program that performs the line clipping procedure given in Section 3.5.1. Can you extend the program to perform polygon clipping? (Note that polygons are made of line segments.)

3.4 Write a program that performs the zooming and panning operation.

3.5 Write a program that draws the picture shown in Fig. 3.17, then extend the program to draw the picture shown in Fig. 3.18.

a) There are 20 nested squares within the base square, each slightly smaller than the previous one, and slightly rotated. The size of the squares may be controlled by the matrix of Eq. (3.19). To rotate each square slightly, use the rotation transformation matrix of Eq. (3.21). Identify the appropriate scaling factor and rotation angle.

b) To obtain the pattern in Fig. 3.18, use the reflection transformation matrix. For the IBM PC users: Can you get the pattern using the GET and PUT statements?

3.6 Write a program that draws the side view of a wheel shown in Fig. 3.19. Expand the program to show the wheel rolling clockwise across the screen from left to right. Consider the following specific cases:

a) How would you control the speed of the wheel movement?

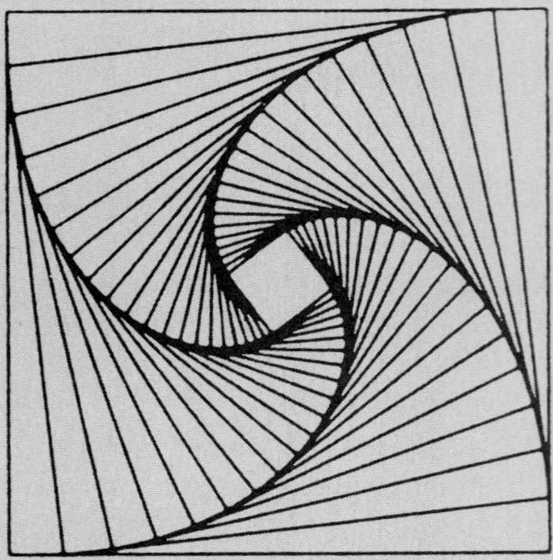

FIGURE 3.17

FIGURE 3.18

FIGURE 3.19

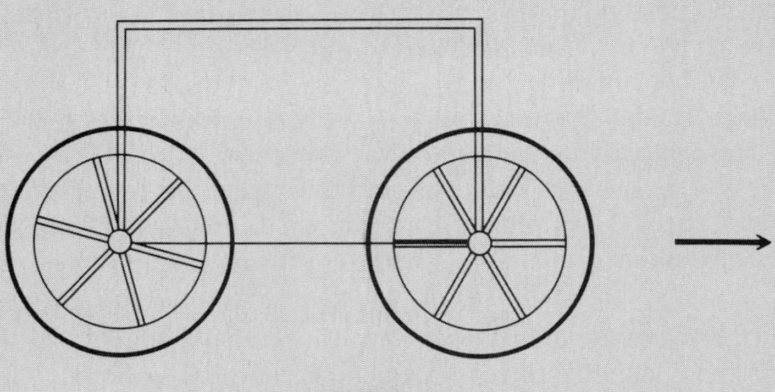

FIGURE 3.20

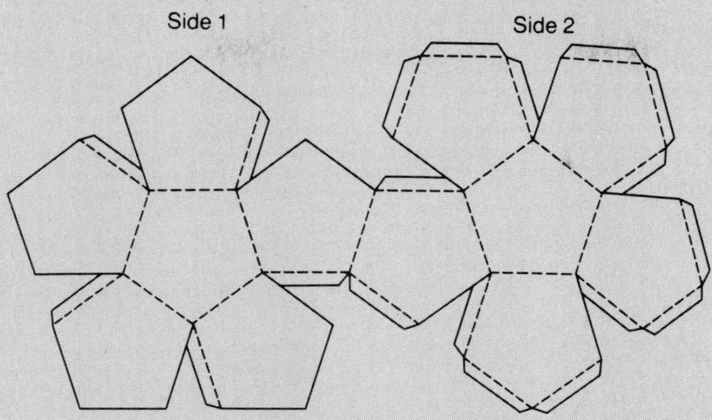

FIGURE 3.21

b) For the IBM PC users: Can we simulate the wheel movement by using the GET and PUT statements?

c) Add another wheel to the problem, and simulate the motion of both wheels (see Fig. 3.20).

3.7 Write a program to draw the dodecahedron shown in Fig. 3.21. Note that we need only define the coordinates of the first pentagon vertices on each side.

REFERENCES

1. Angell, I. O., *A Practical Introduction to Computer Graphics,* Macmillan, London, 1982.

2. Chasen, S. H., *Geometric Principles and Procedures for Computer Graphics Applications,* Prentice-Hall, Englewood Cliffs, N.J., 1978.

3. Foley, J. D., and A. Van Dam, *Fundamentals of Interactive Computer Graphics,* Addison-Wesley, Reading, Mass., 1982.

4. Lemke, H. U., "Two-Dimensional Graphics and Image Processing," *Computer Graphics, State of the Art Report, Series 8,* **2** (5) 166–89, 1980.

5. Liming, R. A., *Mathematics for Computer Graphics,* Aero Publishers, Fallbrook, Calif., 1979.

6. Myers, R. E., *Microcomputer Graphics for the Apple® Computer,* Addison-Wesley, Reading, Mass., 1982.

7. Newman, W. M., and R. F. Sproull, *Principles of Interactive Computer Graphics,* McGraw-Hill, New York, 1979.

8. Rogers, D. F., and J. A. Adams, *Mathematical Elements for Computer Graphics,* McGraw-Hill, New York, 1976.

9. Scott, J. E., *Introduction to Interactive Computer Graphics,* Wiley, New York, 1982.

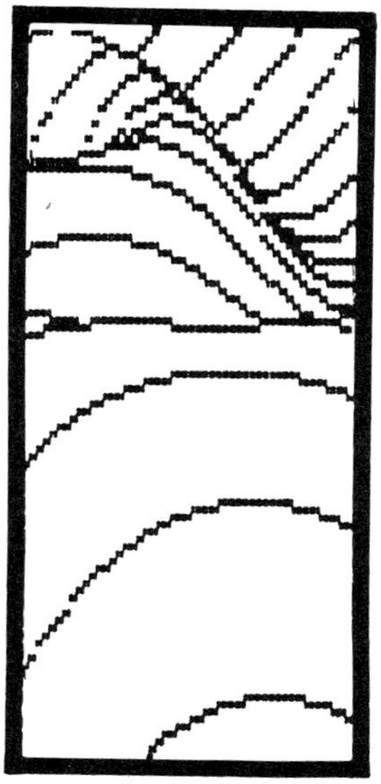

CHAPTER FOUR
Mathematical Elements in 3-D Graphics

This chapter focuses on the viewing techniques used to present three-dimensional (3-D) graphics as a wire frame drawing or a shaded picture. The 3-D viewing process introduces additional complexity to the display techniques. Unfortunately, the computer display screen is a 2-D space, so we must devise a mechanism for displaying 3-D objects in a 2-D space. This is done by introducing perspective projections that transform 3-D objects onto a 2-D projection plane. Thus this chapter is devoted primarily to projections and 3-D transformations, explaining what they are and how their mathematical elements relate.

4.1 COORDINATE SYSTEMS

To represent a point in a 3-D world, we need a 3-D coordinate system. We choose one that requires three mutually perpendicular (orthogonal) axes. The 3-D coordinate system can be viewed as the 2-D coordinate system (XY plane) augmented by a Z axis through the origin, resulting in two additional planes (the XZ plane and the YZ plane). Two orientations are possible when we elect to augment the Z axis. If the Z axis points toward the viewer's eye, the associated coordinate system is referred to as the *right-handed system*. Similarly, a coordinate system with the Z axis pointing away from the viewer is referred to as the *left-handed system*. These two orientations are shown in Fig. 4.1. As a matter of convention, we use the right-handed coordinate system as our world coordinate system.

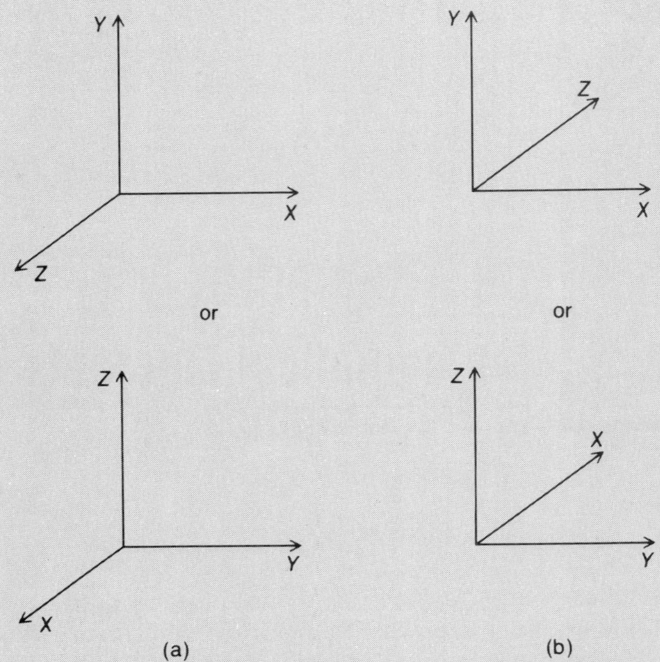

FIGURE 4.1 Coordinate systems: (a) right-handed system and (b) left-handed system

4.1.1. POINT REPRESENTATION IN 3-D WORLD

There are two common ways to represent points in a 3-D world: the rectangular coordinate system and the spherical coordinate system.

Rectangular coordinate system. Points are identified by ordered triples (x, y, z) of numbers with X, Y and Z coordinates providing the directed distance from the point to the YZ, XZ, and XY planes. (See Fig. 4.2.)

Spherical coordinate system. In this system, each point is represented by an ordered triple of numbers (D, θ, ϕ). The distance from the point P to the origin is D. The angle between line $\overline{OP}$ and the positive direction of the Z axis is ϕ. The angle between the positive direction of the X axis and the line $\overline{OP'}$ (projection of $\overline{OP}$ onto the XY plane) is θ. This angle is measured in a counter-clockwise direction from the X axis.

4.1.2 RELATIONSHIP BETWEEN THE RECTANGULAR AND SPHERICAL COORDINATE SYSTEMS

Because both rectangular and spherical coordinate systems are used interchangeably in computer graphics, it is often necessary to convert between the two systems. From elementary trigonometry, we can establish the following relationships between the two system coordinates.

$$\begin{aligned} x &= D \cdot \sin \phi \cos \theta, \\ y &= D \cdot \sin \phi \sin \theta, \\ z &= D \cdot \cos \phi \end{aligned} \tag{4.1}$$

and

$$\begin{aligned} D &= \sqrt{x^2 + y^2 + z^2}, \\ \theta &= \tan^{-1}(y/x), \\ \phi &= \cos^{-1}(z/D). \end{aligned}$$

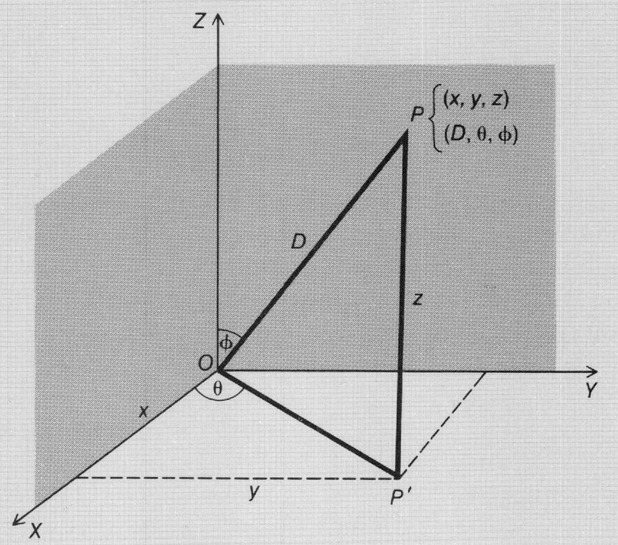

FIGURE 4.2 Relationship between the rectangular and spherical coordinate systems

For example, the point $(4, 2, 3)$ in the rectangular coordinate system is equivalent to point (5.4, 27°, 56°) in the spherical coordinate system.

We will adopt the convention of identifying the *viewpoint* (location of the viewer's eye) by its spherical coordinates. This convention will permit easy manipulation of the viewpoint location, as we will see later in this chapter.

4.2 TRANSFORMATION MATRIX

As in Chapter 3, we will adopt the homogeneous coordinate system for 3-D transformations. As a matter of convention, we will use the rectangular coordinate system to represent the position vector (x, y, z). The generalized 4×4 transformation matrix for a point in a 3-D homogeneous coordinate system is

$$\begin{bmatrix} A & B & C & 0 \\ D & E & F & 0 \\ G & H & I & 0 \\ \hline L & M & N & 1 \end{bmatrix}. \tag{4.2}$$

and can be partitioned into three submatrices:

$$\left[\begin{array}{c|c} \begin{matrix} \text{I} \\ (3 \times 3) \end{matrix} & \begin{matrix} \text{III} \\ 4 \\ \times \\ 1 \end{matrix} \\ \hline \begin{matrix} \text{II} \\ (1 \times 3) \end{matrix} & \end{array}\right] \tag{4.3}$$

Submatrix I allows us to perform scaling, shearing, reflection, and rotation of 3-D objects. Submatrix II produces linear translation, and Submatrix III permits us to combine the translation and transformation in multiplication form. We will discuss various properties of these submatrices in this section and show their effects on the pyramid shown in Fig. 4.3.

4.2.1 3-D TRANSLATION

The transformation that translates a point (x, y, z) to a new point (x', y', z') through (L, M, N) is expressed by

$$[x', y', z', 1] = [x, y, z, 1] \begin{bmatrix} 1 & 0 & 0 & 0 \\ 0 & 1 & 0 & 0 \\ 0 & 0 & 1 & 0 \\ \hline L & M & N & 1 \end{bmatrix} \tag{4.4}$$

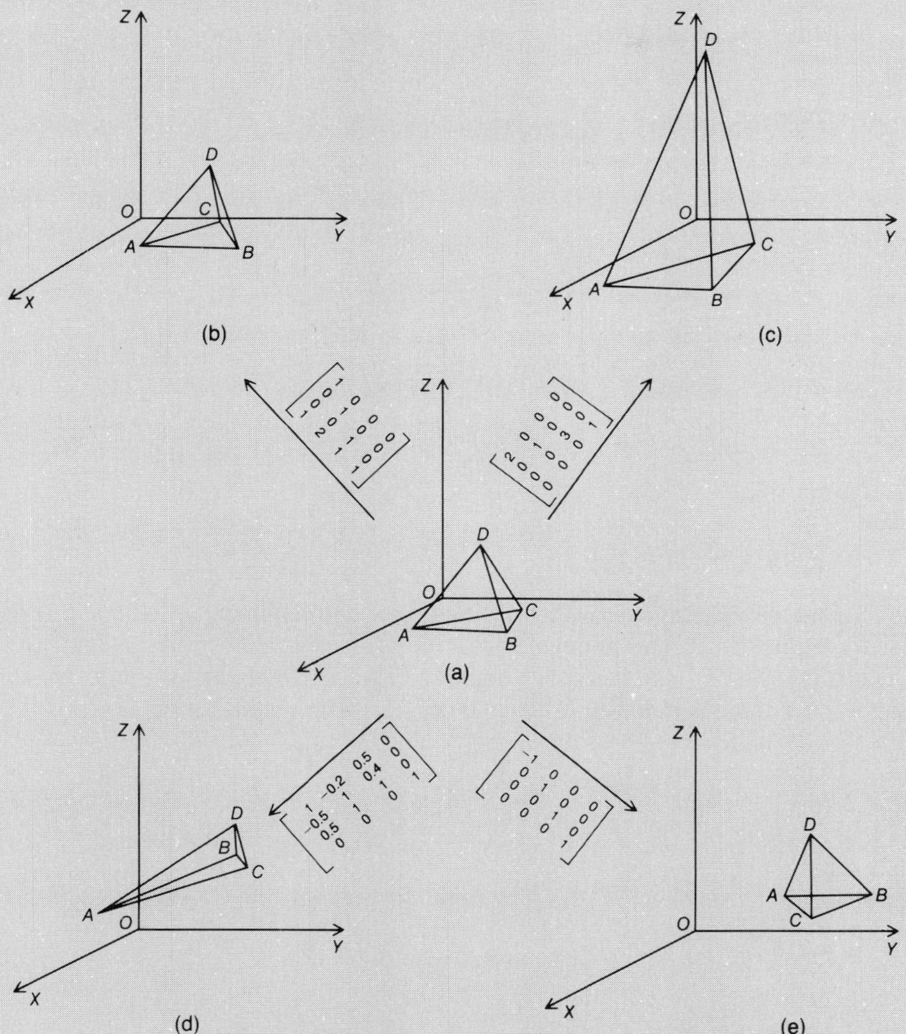

FIGURE 4.3 **Three-dimensional transformations: (a) original position, (b) translation, (c) scaling, (d) shearing, and (e) reflection**

where L, M, and N are the distances to be moved from x, y, and z, respectively. Figure 4.3(b) shows the effect of the 3-D translation of a pyramid through 1, 2, and 1 units in the X, Y, and Z directions, respectively.

4.2.2 3-D SCALING

The diagonal terms of the general 4×4 transformation matrix provide scaling transformations:

$$[x', y', z', 1] = [x, y, z, 1] \left[\begin{array}{ccc|c} A & 0 & 0 & 0 \\ 0 & E & 0 & 0 \\ 0 & 0 & I & 0 \\ \hline 0 & 0 & 0 & 1 \end{array}\right]. \tag{4.5}$$

Equation (4.5) indicates that we can scale each of the coordinates individually to control movement along any of the coordinate axes. Overall scaling is simply obtained by setting $A = E = I$. If the object is to be enlarged by a factor of two, we simply choose $A = E = I = 2$. The effects of local scalings are shown in Fig. 4.3(c).

4.2.3 3-D SHEARING

In Chapter 3, 2-D shearing was obtained from the off-diagonal terms in the left 2×2 submatrix of the generalized 2-D transformation matrix. Shearing in 3-D is a simple extension of 2-D shearing. The off-diagonal terms in the upper left 3×3 submatrix of Eq. (4.2) produce the effect of shearing:

$$[x', y', z', 1] = [x, y, z, 1] \left[\begin{array}{ccc|c} 1 & B & C & 0 \\ D & 1 & F & 0 \\ G & H & 1 & 0 \\ \hline 0 & 0 & 0 & 1 \end{array}\right]. \tag{4.6}$$

A 3-D shear on the pyramid is shown in Fig. 4.3(d).

4.2.4 3-D REFLECTION

An object is reflected through a plane by manipulating the diagonal elements in the 3-D transformation matrix. As discussed in Chapter 3, an object is reflected through a plane by generating a mirror image of all points of the object on the opposite side of the plane. For an example, in a reflection through the XY plane, only the Z coordinate values of the object's position vectors will be affected, and these will be reversed in sign. The transformation matrix for this reflection is

$$\begin{bmatrix} 1 & 0 & 0 & 0 \\ 0 & 1 & 0 & 0 \\ 0 & 0 & -1 & 0 \\ 0 & 0 & 0 & 1 \end{bmatrix}. \tag{4.7}$$

Similarly, for a reflection through the YZ plane the matrix is

$$\begin{bmatrix} -1 & 0 & 0 & 0 \\ 0 & 1 & 0 & 0 \\ 0 & 0 & 1 & 0 \\ 0 & 0 & 0 & 1 \end{bmatrix}, \tag{4.8}$$

and for a reflection through the XZ plane, it is

$$\begin{bmatrix} 1 & 0 & 0 & 0 \\ 0 & -1 & 0 & 0 \\ 0 & 0 & 1 & 0 \\ 0 & 0 & 0 & 1 \end{bmatrix}. \tag{4.9}$$

The reflection of the pyramid through the YZ plane is shown in Fig. 4.3(e).

4.2.5 3-D ROTATION

Before considering the general case of 3-D rotation about an arbitrary axis, we will examine rotations about the X, Y, Z coordinate axes. Let us consider first a rotation about the X axis. In this case, the X dimensions do not change so the transformation matrix will have zeros in the third row and third column, except for unity on the main diagonal. The other terms are determined by considering the rotation of the 2-D object shown in Eq. (3.9), which is a simple rotation about the Z axis in 3-D. This leads to the following transformation matrix for a rotation of angle θ about the Z axis:

$$\begin{bmatrix} \cos\theta & \sin\theta & 0 & 0 \\ -\sin\theta & \cos\theta & 0 & 0 \\ 0 & 0 & 1 & 0 \\ 0 & 0 & 0 & 1 \end{bmatrix}. \tag{4.10}$$

As a matter of convention, we measure the rotation angle θ counterclockwise about the origin when looking at the origin from a point on the positive X axis.

The transformation matrices that effect rotations of angle θ about the X axis and Y axis are

$$R(\theta)_x = \begin{bmatrix} 1 & 0 & 0 & 0 \\ 0 & \cos\theta & \sin\theta & 0 \\ 0 & -\sin\theta & \cos\theta & 0 \\ 0 & 0 & 0 & 1 \end{bmatrix} \tag{4.11}$$

and

$$R(\theta)_y = \begin{bmatrix} \cos\theta & 0 & -\sin\theta & 0 \\ 0 & 1 & 0 & 0 \\ \sin\theta & 0 & \cos\theta & 0 \\ 0 & 0 & 0 & 1 \end{bmatrix}. \tag{4.12}$$

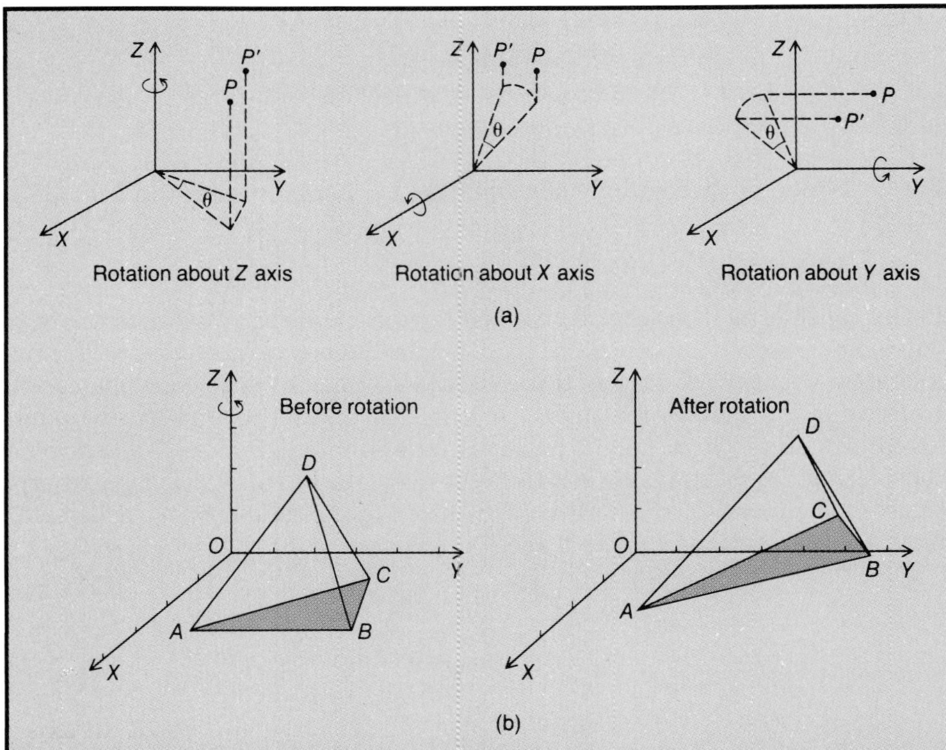

FIGURE 4.4 Three-dimensional rotations: (a) rotation of a point and (b) rotation of an object

Three-dimensional rotations about each axis of an orthogonal axis system are represented in Fig. 4.4.

As an example of 3-D rotation, let us consider the pyramid given in Fig. 4.3(a). Now the pyramid is to be rotated 30° (counterclockwise) about the Z axis. Using Eq. (4.10), we find the new coordinates

$$\begin{bmatrix} A' \\ B' \\ C' \\ D' \end{bmatrix} = \begin{bmatrix} 3 & 1 & 0 & 1 \\ 3 & 5 & 0 & 1 \\ 1 & 4 & 0 & 1 \\ 2 & 3 & 3 & 1 \end{bmatrix} \begin{bmatrix} 0.866 & 0.5 & 0 & 0 \\ -0.5 & 0.866 & 0 & 0 \\ 0 & 0 & 1 & 0 \\ 0 & 0 & 0 & 1 \end{bmatrix}$$

$$= \begin{bmatrix} 2.1 & 2.37 & 0 & 1 \\ 0.1 & 5.83 & 0 & 1 \\ 1.13 & 3.96 & 0 & 1 \\ 0.232 & 3.60 & 3 & 1 \end{bmatrix}.$$

The effect of the transformation is shown in Fig. 4.4(b).

Suppose the same pyramid is rotated through −30° (clockwise) about the Z axis. With $\theta = -30$ and Eq. (4.10), we have

$$R(-30°) = \begin{bmatrix} 0.866 & -0.5 & 0 & 0 \\ 0.5 & 0.866 & 0 & 0 \\ 0 & 0 & 1 & 0 \\ 0 & 0 & 0 & 1 \end{bmatrix}.$$

How about multiplying both transformation matrices, $R(30°)_z$ and $R(-30°)_z$? This is an inverse matrix of I:

$$R(30°) \cdot R(-30°) = \begin{bmatrix} 0.866 & 0.5 & 0 & 0 \\ -0.5 & 0.866 & 0 & 0 \\ 0 & 0 & 1 & 0 \\ 0 & 0 & 0 & 1 \end{bmatrix} \begin{bmatrix} 0.866 & -0.5 & 0 & 0 \\ 0.5 & 0.866 & 0 & 0 \\ 0 & 0 & 1 & 0 \\ 0 & 0 & 0 & 1 \end{bmatrix}$$

$$= \begin{bmatrix} 1 & 0 & 0 & 0 \\ 0 & 1 & 0 & 0 \\ 0 & 0 & 1 & 0 \\ 0 & 0 & 0 & 1 \end{bmatrix} = R(30°) \cdot R(30°)^{-1} = I.$$

This implies that the rotation matrix for a *clockwise angle* about an axis is equivalent to the inverse $[R(\theta)^{-1}]$ of the rotation matrix for a *counterclockwise* angle about the same axis $[R(\theta)]$. The example above is not an isolated case, but represents a general principle which we will find valuable in computer graphics. This principle implies that

$$R(\theta)_z^{-1} = R(-\theta)_z = \begin{bmatrix} \cos\theta & -\sin\theta & 0 & 0 \\ \sin\theta & \cos\theta & 0 & 0 \\ 0 & 0 & 1 & 0 \\ 0 & 0 & 0 & 1 \end{bmatrix}, \tag{4.13}$$

$$R(\theta)_x^{-1} = R(-\theta)_x = \begin{bmatrix} 1 & 0 & 0 & 0 \\ 0 & \cos\theta & -\sin\theta & 0 \\ 0 & \sin\theta & \cos\theta & 0 \\ 0 & 0 & 0 & 1 \end{bmatrix}, \tag{4.14}$$

and

$$R(\theta)_y^{-1} = R(-\theta)_y = \begin{bmatrix} \cos\theta & 0 & \sin\theta & 0 \\ 0 & 1 & 0 & 0 \\ -\sin\theta & 0 & \cos\theta & 0 \\ 0 & 0 & 0 & 1 \end{bmatrix}. \tag{4.15}$$

It is also important to note that, in general, the order of multiplication will affect the final result. This is because 3-D rotations are *noncommutative*. To see this, consider a rotation θ_1 about the Z axis followed by another rotation θ_2 about the X axis:

$$R(\theta_1)_z \cdot R(\theta_2)_x = \begin{bmatrix} \cos\theta_1 & \sin\theta_1\cos\theta_2 & \sin\theta_1\sin\theta_2 & 0 \\ -\sin\theta_1 & \cos\theta_1\cos\theta_2 & \cos\theta_1\sin\theta_2 & 0 \\ 0 & -\sin\theta_2 & \cos\theta_2 & 0 \\ 0 & 0 & 0 & 1 \end{bmatrix}. \tag{4.16}$$

With the reverse operation (i.e., a rotation θ_2 about the X axis followed by a rotation θ_1 about the Z axis), we have

$$R(\theta_2)_x \cdot R(\theta_1)_z = \begin{bmatrix} \cos\theta_1 & \sin\theta_1 & 0 & 0 \\ -\cos\theta_2\sin\theta_1 & \cos\theta_2\cos\theta_1 & \sin\theta_2 & 0 \\ \sin\theta_2\sin\theta_1 & -\sin\theta_2\cos\theta_1 & \cos\theta_2 & 0 \\ 0 & 0 & 0 & 1 \end{bmatrix}. \tag{4.17}$$

Comparison of the results confirms that they are not the same. Thus the fact that rotations are noncommutative must be kept in mind when 3-D matrix multiplications are involved.

4.2.6 CHANGE OF COORDINATE SYSTEM

Up to this point, we have discussed only the transformation of a point or a set of points into another set of points, with both sets still in the *same coordinate system*. In this case, the coordinate system remains unchanged, and the object is transformed with respect to the origin of the coordinate system. In computer graphics, it is often desirable to establish a new coordinate system without altering the position of a point or object. This involves *transforming a coordinate system*. In such cases, we can reference points in terms of both the original coordinate system and the transformed coordinate system. To see this, consider Fig. 4.5, where point P has coordinates $(2, 3, 4)$ in the XYZ coordinate system but $(1, 2, 2)$ in the $X'Y'Z'$ coordinate system.

The transformation from coordinate system XYZ to $X'Y'Z'$ is obtained by translating the origin O' to O. Since the origin O' for the $X'Y'Z'$ system is located at $(1, 1, 2)$, the desired translation is

$$P' = P \cdot T = (2, 3, 4, 1)\begin{bmatrix} 1 & 0 & 0 & 0 \\ 0 & 1 & 0 & 0 \\ 0 & 0 & 1 & 0 \\ -1 & -1 & -2 & 1 \end{bmatrix} = (1, 2, 2, 1)\,.$$

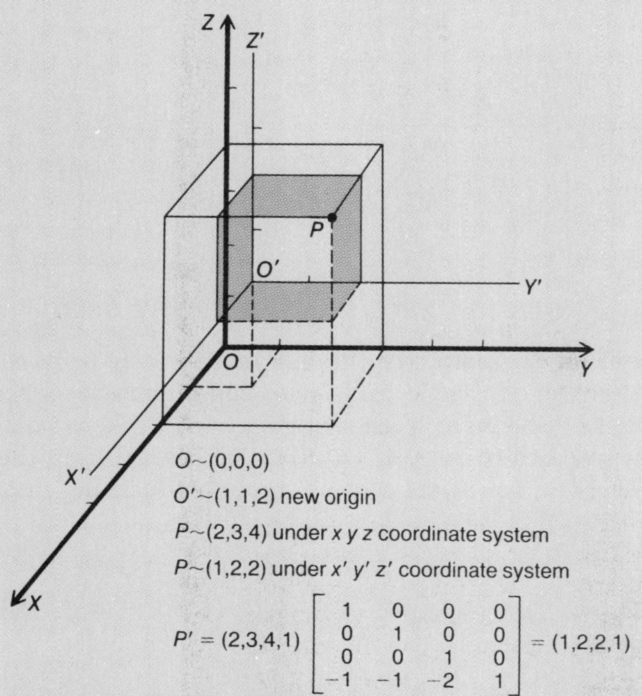

FIGURE 4.5 Point *P* and two different coordinate systems

Now consider the effect of rotating the coordinate system through a *clockwise* angle of 30° about the Z axis. The resulting coordinate system $X'Y'Z'$ is shown in Fig. 4.6(b). Note that the physical position of point P remains unchanged. Suppose we rotate the point only through a *counterclockwise* angle of 30° about the Z axis, retaining the orientation and directions of the original coordinate axes. This is shown in Fig. 4.6(a).

Now it is clear that the position of the rotated point P' relative to the XYZ coordinate system is the same as the position of point P relative to the rotated coordinate system $X'Y'Z'$. Thus the matrix required to represent the transformation of a coordinate axis is the *inverse* of that needed to transform points within an unaltered coordinate system. To see this, we assume that point P in Fig. 4.6(a) is positioned at $(1,3,2)$. From Eq. (4.10), the transformation matrix to find rotated point P' is

$$P' = P \cdot R(30°)_z = (1,3,2,1)\begin{bmatrix} \cos 30° & \sin 30° & 0 & 0 \\ -\sin 30° & \cos 30° & 0 & 0 \\ 0 & 0 & 1 & 0 \\ 0 & 0 & 0 & 1 \end{bmatrix}$$

$$= (-0.63, 3.1, 2, 1).$$

These results are based on rotation through a *counterclockwise* angle about the Z axis. The position of point P relative to the rotated coordinate system $X'Y'Z'$ through a *clockwise* angle about the Z' axis will be $(-0.63, 3.1, 2, 1)$. This example is not a special case, but represents a general principle that we will use in obtaining a 2-D representation of a 3-D object.

4.2.7 3-D ROTATION ABOUT AN ARBITRARY AXIS

A rotation about an arbitrary axis through an arbitrary point can be derived from combinations of the basic transformation techniques discussed in the previous sections. We begin by considering Fig. 4.7(a) where we want to rotate point P about the arbitrary axis OJ that passes through the origin. Let us further define $Q(q_1, q_2, q_3)$ as a point through which the rotation axis OJ passes.

Direction cosines. To determine the direction of the axis of rotation, we need three direction cosines: $\cos\alpha$, $\cos\beta$, and $\cos\gamma$. (The angles α, β, and γ are identified in Fig. 4.7(b).) The direction cosines of the rotation axis have a simple interpretation. Referring to Fig. 4.7(b), we note that triangle OAQ is a right triangle with right angle at A; then $\cos\alpha = q_1/r$. Since we know that

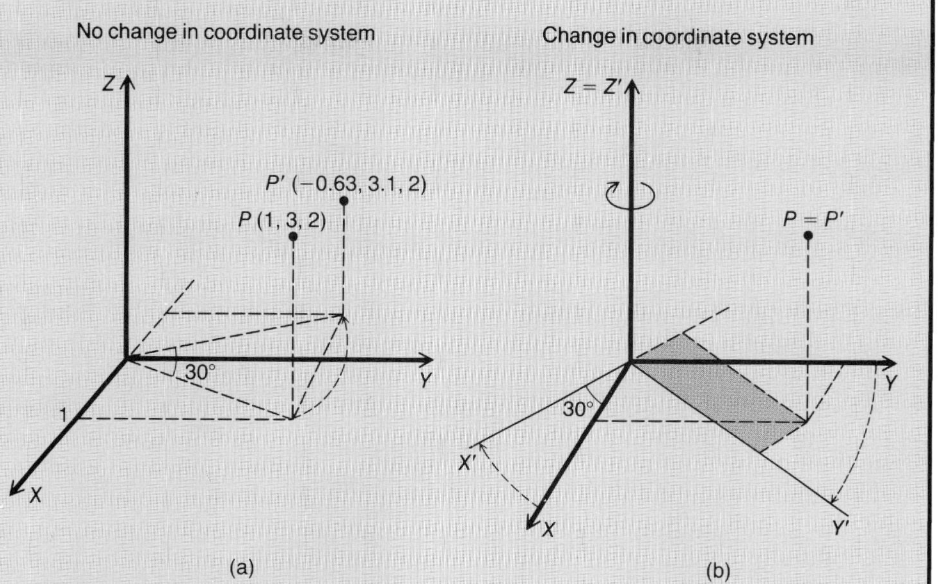

FIGURE 4.6 **Transformation as a change of coordinate systems: (a) a rotation about axis through a counterclockwise angle of 30° and (b) a rotation of the coordinate system about the axis through a clockwise angle of 30°**

$r = (q_1^2 + q_2^2 + q_3^2)^{1/2}$, we can redefine the direction cosines as follows:

$$\begin{aligned}\cos\alpha &= \frac{q_1}{r} = \frac{q_1}{(q_1^2 + q_2^2 + q_3^2)^{1/2}},\\ \cos\beta &= \frac{q_2}{r} = \frac{q_2}{(q_1^2 + q_2^2 + q_3^2)^{1/2}},\\ \cos\gamma &= \frac{q_3}{r} = \frac{q_3}{(q_1^2 + q_2^2 + q_3^2)^{1/2}}.\end{aligned} \tag{4.18}$$

From these it follows that

$$\cos^2\alpha + \cos^2\beta + \cos^2\gamma = \frac{q_1^2 + q_2^2 + q_3^2}{r^2} = 1. \tag{4.19}$$

Another important property of the direction cosines is that if we choose numbers a, b, and c that are proportional to the direction cosines (called direction numbers), we can also establish the relationship between them. Let us consider Fig. 4.7(c). A vector **k** can be represented with an initial point at the origin of a rectangular coordinate system and components of (a, b, c) in the

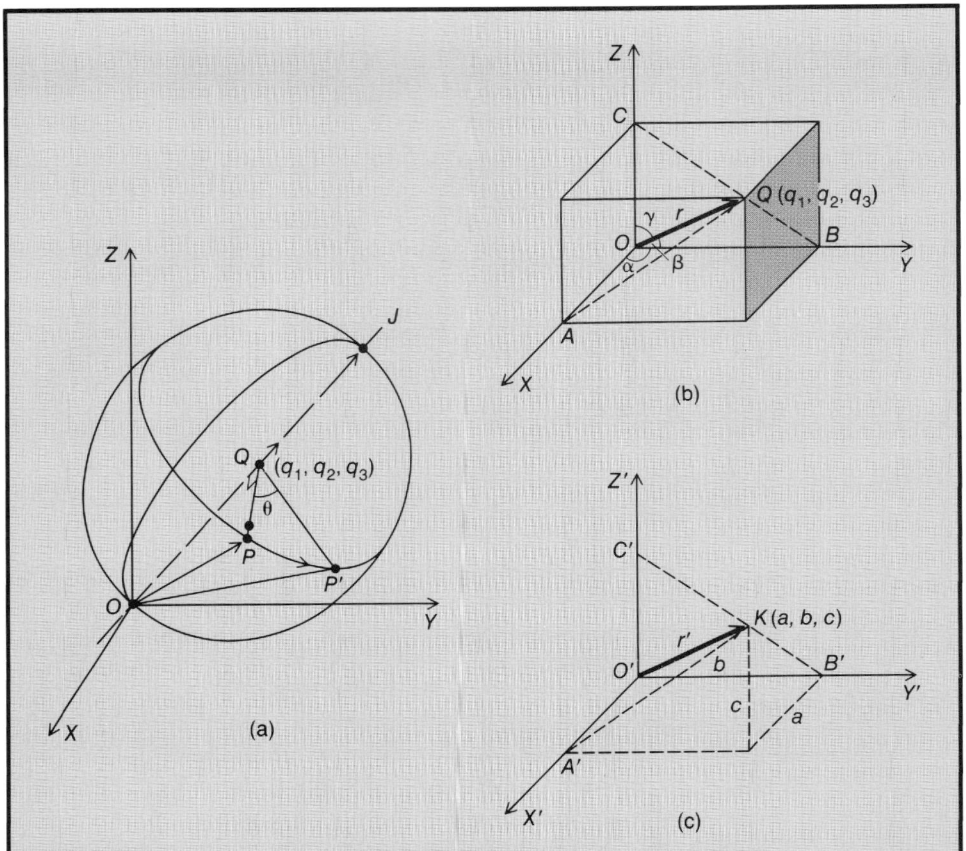

FIGURE 4.7 Three-dimensional rotation about an arbitrary axis *OJ* and direction cosines: (a) rotation of point *P* about the *OJ* axis by the angle *θ*, (b) and (c) direction cosines

direction of the positive X', Y', and Z' axes. Further, we choose the values for A, B, and C in such a way that $a = \cos\alpha$, $b = \cos\beta$, and $c = \cos\gamma$, where α, β, and γ are defined as before. Then length $\overline{O'K}$ is

$$r' = (a^2 + b^2 + c^2)^{1/2} = (\cos^2\alpha + \cos^2\beta + \cos^2\gamma)^{1/2} = 1\,. \tag{4.20}$$

Triangle $O'A'K$ is a right triangle with right angle at A'; then $\cos\alpha' = \cos\alpha/r' = \cos\alpha/1 = \cos\alpha$. Similarly, we can prove that $\cos\beta' = \cos\beta$ and $\cos\gamma' = \cos\gamma$, indicating that $\overline{OQ}$ and $\overline{O'K}$ have the same direction cosines.

Transformation matrix. Once the direction cosines of the axis OJ are identified, we may take the following steps to rotate point P through an angle θ about this OJ axis.

Step 1: Translate the object into a new coordinate system where Q becomes the new origin. In our notation, the intermediate axis systems are each referred to as $X'Y'Z'$; the final $X'Y'Z'$ axis system is the standard coordinate system XYZ. The effect of this translation is given by the following matrix T_1:

$$T_1 = \begin{bmatrix} 1 & 0 & 0 & 0 \\ 0 & 1 & 0 & 0 \\ 0 & 0 & 1 & 0 \\ -q_1 & -q_2 & -q_3 & 1 \end{bmatrix}.$$

Step 2: Align the QJ axis with the Z' axis. This is done in two steps—a rotation about the X' axis, and a rotation about the Y' axis. Since both Figs. 4.7(b) and 4.7(c) are identical in terms of the direction of OJ, we will use Fig. 4.7(c) to determine the necessary rotation angles along the

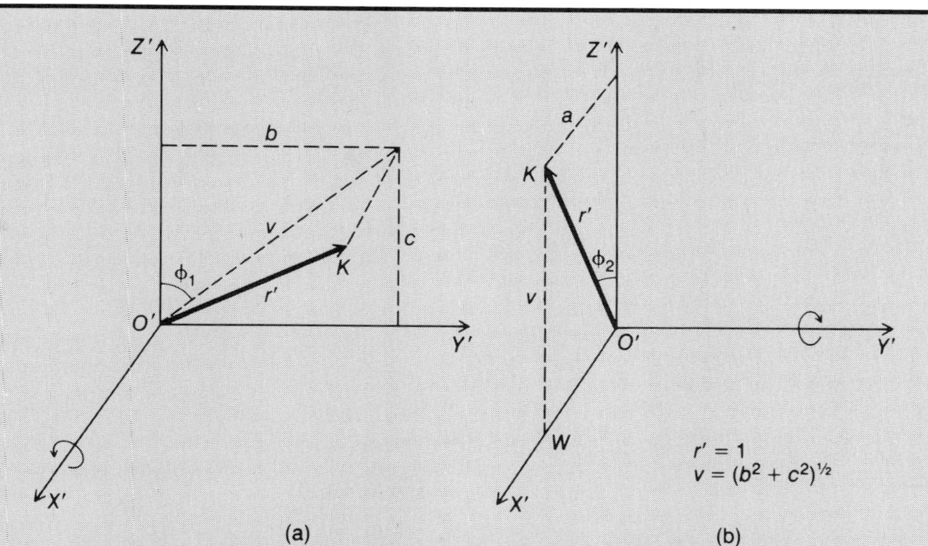

FIGURE 4.8 Two rotations are required to align the point $K(a, b, c)$ with the Z' axis: (a) rotation about the X' axis and (b) rotation about the Y' axis

axes. If we project $\overline{O'K}$ onto the $Y'Z'$ plane, we obtain Fig. 4.8(a). If we rotate $\overline{O'K}$ through the counterclockwise angle ϕ_1 about the X' axis, $\overline{O'K}$ will lie in the $X'Z'$ plane. From this we compute

$$\cos\phi_1 = \frac{c}{v},$$

$$\sin\phi_1 = \frac{b}{v},$$

where $v = (b^2 + c^2)^{1/2}$. By inserting these parameters into Eq. (4.11), we obtain the transformation matrix of this rotation:

$$R_1 = \begin{bmatrix} 1 & 0 & 0 & 0 \\ 0 & c/v & b/v & 0 \\ 0 & -b/v & c/v & 0 \\ 0 & 0 & 0 & 1 \end{bmatrix}.$$

The situation after the first rotation is shown in Fig. 4.8(b). The rotation angle ϕ_2 can be determined in a similar manner. Note, however, that $\overline{O'K} = r' = 1$. This implies that the length $\overline{KW}$ becomes v: $\overline{O'K} = [(\overline{KW})^2 + a^2]^{1/2} = r'$, $r' = (a^2 + b^2 + c^2)^{1/2} \rightarrow (\overline{KW})^2 = b^2 + c^2 = v^2$. Thus we measure ϕ_2 clockwise so that

$$\cos(-\phi_2) = \cos(\phi_2) = v,$$

$$\sin(-\phi_2) = -\sin(\phi_2) = -a.$$

These parameters, when inserted into Eq. (4.12), yield

$$R_2 = \begin{bmatrix} v & 0 & a & 0 \\ 0 & 1 & 0 & 0 \\ -a & 0 & v & 0 \\ 0 & 0 & 0 & 1 \end{bmatrix}.$$

Thus the rotation of $\overline{O'K}$ through the clockwise angle ϕ_2 about the Y' axis will align $\overline{O'K}$ with the Z' axis.

Step 3: Perform the desired rotation θ about the Z' axis of the new coordinate system. The resulting transformation matrix is

$$R_z(\theta) = \begin{bmatrix} \cos\theta & \sin\theta & 0 & 0 \\ -\sin\theta & \cos\theta & 0 & 0 \\ 0 & 0 & 1 & 0 \\ 0 & 0 & 0 & 1 \end{bmatrix}.$$

Recall that the θ above is measured in a counterclockwise angle. If a clockwise rotation is desirable, we simply replace θ in $R_z(\theta)$ with $-\theta$.

Step 4: Return the object to its original coordinate system. To do this, we apply the inverse of Step 2 and the inverse of Step 1. The inverse order must be preserved in exact sequence, R_2^{-1} followed by R_1^{-1} and T_1^{-1}.

The complete transformation representing the four steps is

$$T = T_1 \cdot R_1 \cdot R_2 \cdot R_z(\theta) \cdot R_2^{-1} \cdot R_1^{-1} \cdot T_1^{-1}$$
$$= R_1 \cdot R_2 \cdot R_z(\theta) \cdot R_2^{-1} \cdot R_1^{-1}$$

The complete concatenation can also be represented by one transformation matrix:

$$T = \begin{bmatrix} A & B & C & 0 \\ D & E & F & 0 \\ G & H & I & 0 \\ 0 & 0 & 0 & 1 \end{bmatrix} \tag{4.21}$$

where

$$A = a^2 + (1 - a^2)\cos\theta,$$
$$B = ab(1 - \cos\theta) + c\sin\theta,$$
$$C = ac(1 - \cos\theta) - b\sin\theta,$$
$$D = ab(1 - \cos\theta) - c\sin\theta,$$
$$E = b^2 + (1 - b^2)\cos\theta,$$
$$F = bc(1 - \cos\theta) + a\sin\theta,$$
$$G = ac(1 - \cos\theta) + b\sin\theta,$$
$$H = bc(1 - \cos\theta) - a\sin\theta,$$
$$I = c^2 + (1 - c^2)\cos\theta,$$
$$a = \cos\alpha = q_1/r,$$
$$b = \cos\beta = q_2/r,$$
$$c = \cos\gamma = q_3/r,$$
$$r = (q_1^2 + q_2^2 + q_3^2)^{1/2}.$$

Finally, we compute a rotated position of point P as

$$P' = [x, y, z, 1] \cdot T \tag{4.22}$$

Numerical example. To demonstrate the computational procedure involved, we take an example where the parameters for P, Q, and θ are given as follows:

$$P(x, y, z) = (1, 2, 3),$$
$$Q(q_1, q_2, q_3) = (4, 8, 5),$$
$$\theta = 30^\circ \text{ (counterclockwise)}.$$

Then from Eq. (4.18), the direction cosines are

$$\cos \alpha = \frac{4}{\sqrt{105}} = 0.39036 = a \,,$$

$$\cos \beta = \frac{8}{\sqrt{105}} = 0.78072 = b \,,$$

$$\cos \gamma = \frac{5}{\sqrt{105}} = 0.48795 = c \,,$$

$$r = (4^2 + 8^2 + 5^2)^{1/2} = \sqrt{105} \,,$$

and $\cos(30°) = 0.866$, $\sin(30°) = 0.5$. Inserting these parameters into Eq. (4.21) gives us

$$T = \begin{bmatrix} 0.886 & 0.285 & -0.365 & 0 \\ -0.203 & 0.948 & 0.246 & 0 \\ 0.416 & -0.144 & 0.898 & 0 \\ 0 & 0 & 0 & 1 \end{bmatrix} .$$

Thus we obtain

$$P' = (1, 2, 3, 1) \cdot T = (1.73, 1.75, 2.83, 1)$$

Relation to the rotation about the standard axis. We can easily confirm that rotations about the standard coordinate axes [such as those given by Eqs. (4.10) through (4.12)] are special cases of the general rotation matrix. To demonstrate this, let us consider the case where rotation about the Z axis is to be performed. For this special case, no coordinate translation is required because the rotation is to be made about the standard axis. Therefore $Q = (0, 0, 0)$ and $OJ = OZ$. The direction cosines are computed as

$$\cos \alpha = \cos 90° = 0 = a \,,$$

$$\cos \beta = \cos 90° = 0 = b \,,$$

$$\cos \gamma = \cos 0° = 1 = c \,.$$

When we insert these numeric values into Eq. (4.21), the rotation matrix T becomes

$$\begin{bmatrix} \cos \theta & \sin \theta & 0 & 0 \\ -\sin \theta & \cos \theta & 0 & 0 \\ 0 & 0 & 1 & 0 \\ 0 & 0 & 0 & 1 \end{bmatrix} .$$

We can quickly confirm that the matrix is identical with that given by Eq. (4.10).

4.3 VIEWING IN THREE DIMENSIONS

Up to this point, we have manipulated 3-D objects through various transformations. In this section, we will discuss how to actually display the 3-D objects on a computer graphics screen. Since a graphics screen is a 2-D space, we need some means of obtaining a 2-D representation of a 3-D object. Perspective projection is used to create a 2-D screen image that simulates the way we would see a real 3-D object. We will discuss two types of perspective projection — the central projection and the arbitrary projection. Once we obtain the perspective projection of a 3-D object onto a 2-D plane, a transformation from the world coordinate system to the *eye coordinate system* becomes necessary. The purpose of this *viewing transformation* is to calculate the position on the display screen of each point on the image of the 3-D object.

4.3.1 CENTRAL PROJECTION

Figure 4.9 illustrates the central projection frequently used in computer graphics. In a central projection, the viewpoint (the center of projection) is always located on one of the world coordinate axes, whereas the eye coordinate axes are established at the center of projection. We assume that the center of projection is located on the Z axis. This means that the line of sight is aligned with the Z axis of the world coordinate system so that the display screen is parallel to the XY plane. Then a perspective display is obtained by simply projecting each point of an object onto the display screen as shown in Fig. 4.9.

We adopt the convention that the eye coordinate system is a left-handed coordinate system. We represent the eye coordinate system in terms of (x_e, y_e, z_e): the Z_e axis points toward the origin of the world coordinate system, the X_e axis to the right, and the Y_e axis up. We can then align the X_e and Y_e axes with the X_s and Y_s axes of the display screen. (See Fig. 4.9.) As we discussed in the previous section, the world coordinate system for points is normally represented with right-handed systems.

We also adopt the convention of identifying the viewpoint in terms of its spherical coordinates. This convention permits easy control over the location of the viewpoint (viewer's eye). Using the notations given in Section 4.1.2, we recall:

D = distance from the viewpoint to the origin of the world coordinate system where the object is to be positioned.

(θ,ϕ) = direction from which the viewer will see the object.

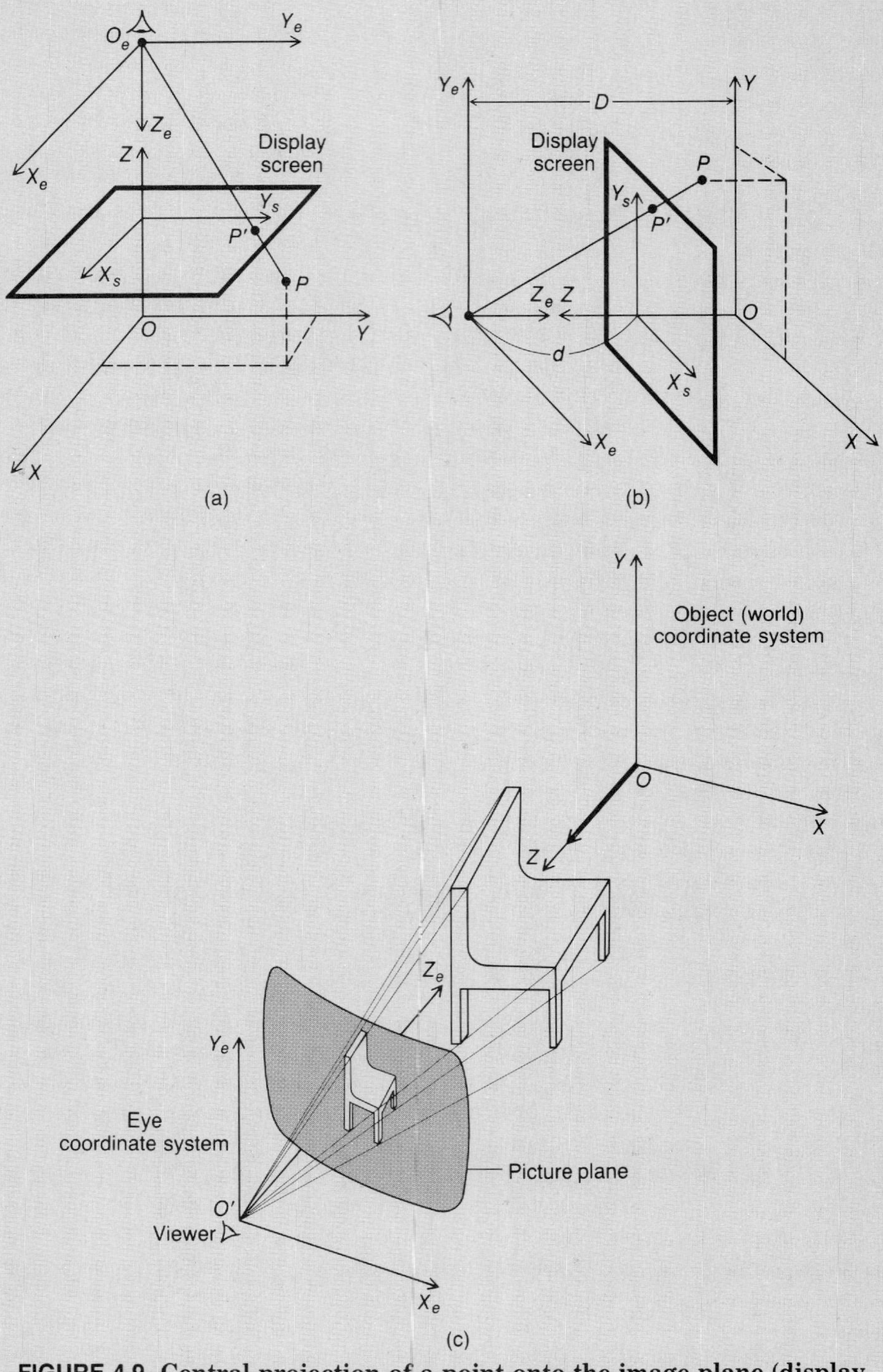

FIGURE 4.9 **Central projection of a point onto the image plane (display screen): (a) and (b) are equivalent representations of the central projection and (c) is the central projection of an object.**

In a central projection, the viewpoint is located on the Z_e axis, which is aligned with one of the world coordinate axes. For our example in Fig. 4.9, the viewpoint is aligned with the Z axis. In this case the X_eY_e plane is parallel to the XY plane, giving zero values to (θ, ϕ). Thus the central projection viewpoint may be expressed by the position $(D, 0, 0)$ in the spherical coordinate system.

Viewing transformation. To calculate the position on the display screen of the image of a point, we must first transform the point from the world coordinate system into the eye coordinate system, which has its origin at the viewpoint and its Z_e axis pointed in the direction of the origin of the world coordinate system.

Let $P(x, y, z)$ be the point in the world coordinate system. When we observe the point P at the viewpoint O_e, the X and Y dimensions do not change. Since the viewpoint is at a distance D from the XY plane, the corresponding Z_e coordinate is simply $D - z$. Thus the conversion of P to the eye coordinate system can be achieved by

$$(x_e, y_e, z_e) = (x, y, D - z) \tag{4.23}$$

This relation was obtained by intuitive observation, but the same result can be obtained through formal viewing transformations. To convert point P in the world coordinate system into a point in the eye coordinate system, we will use four steps.

Step 1: Translate the origin to the viewpoint:

$$T_1 = \begin{bmatrix} 1 & 0 & 0 & 0 \\ 0 & 1 & 0 & 0 \\ 0 & 0 & 1 & 0 \\ 0 & 0 & -D & 1 \end{bmatrix}$$

Step 2: Reverse the direction of Z_e:

$$T_2 = \begin{bmatrix} 1 & 0 & 0 & 0 \\ 0 & 1 & 0 & 0 \\ 0 & 0 & -1 & 0 \\ 0 & 0 & 0 & 1 \end{bmatrix}$$

Step 3: Determine the combined transformation matrix:

$$T = T_1 \cdot T_2 = \begin{bmatrix} 1 & 0 & 0 & 0 \\ 0 & 1 & 0 & 0 \\ 0 & 0 & -1 & 0 \\ 0 & 0 & D & 1 \end{bmatrix}$$

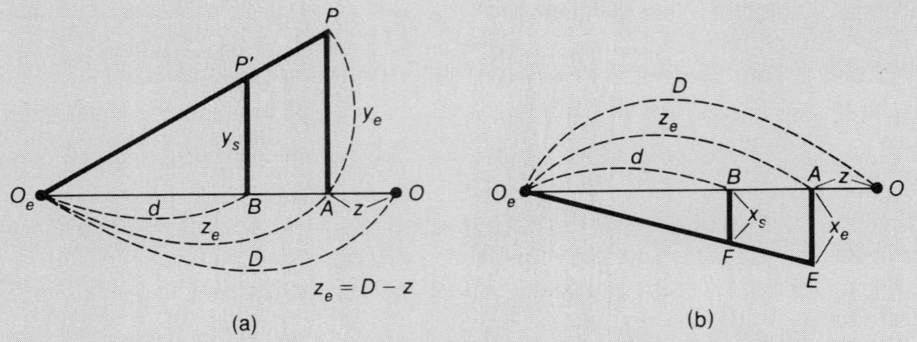

FIGURE 4.10 Relations among the projection parameters

Step 4: Identify the eye coordinates:

$$(x_e, y_e, z_e, 1) = (x, y, z, 1)\begin{bmatrix} 1 & 0 & 0 & 0 \\ 0 & 1 & 0 & 0 \\ 0 & 0 & -1 & 0 \\ 0 & 0 & D & 1 \end{bmatrix} \tag{4.24}$$

$$= (x, y, D - z, 1)$$

This result is identical to Eq. (4.23).

Conversion to screen coordinates. The screen coordinates (x_s, y_s) of the projected image of the point P measured in eye coordinates (x_e, y_e, z_e) are easily computed by considering the Y_eZ_e plane drawn in Fig. 4.10(a). The construction of the Y_eZ_e plane is based on Fig. 4.9(b). We also introduce a parameter d representing the distance between the display screen and the viewpoint. Note that the triangles AO_eP and BO_eP' are similar. This gives us the relationship

$$\frac{y_s}{d} = \frac{y_e}{z_e} \rightarrow y_s = d\,\frac{y_e}{z_e} = d\,\frac{y}{D - z}. \tag{4.25}$$

To find x_s, we consider Fig. 4.10(b), which is constructed from the X_eZ_e plane given in Fig. 4.9(b). Triangles AO_eE and BO_eF are also similar, so we again establish

$$\frac{x_s}{d} = \frac{x_e}{z_e} \rightarrow x_s = d\,\frac{x_e}{z_e} = d\,\frac{x}{D - z}. \tag{4.26}$$

It is worth noting from both Eqs. (4.25) and (4.26) that

- Since y_s and x_s are both linear functions of d, moving the display screen closer to the viewer will result in a smaller projected image.
- Increasing D will move the viewer away from the object being observed, which will cause the object to appear smaller when d is fixed.
- Central projection does not require a complicated viewing transformation procedure because the viewpoint is aligned with the world coordinate system.
- A further simplification can be obtained by moving the display screen into the XY plane of the world coordinate system ($D = d$), and moving the viewpoint toward infinity. With $D \to \infty$ and $D = d$, we have the trivial solution

$$x_s = x \qquad \text{and} \qquad y_s = y\,. \tag{4.27}$$

This projection is called *orthographic*. The orthographic projection is a special form of the *parallel projection*, in which parallel lines in the 3-D object are transformed into parallel lines in its image.

4.3.2 PROJECTION THROUGH AN ARBITRARY VIEWPOINT

Now we want to place the viewpoint at some arbitrary point in 3-D space. We still position the display screen at a distance d from the viewpoint. The display screen is also assumed to be perpendicular to the line connecting the viewer's eye with the origin. The eye coordinate system orients the axes so that the viewer's line of sight (Z_e axis) is directed toward the origin of the world coordinate system. Again the X_e axis points to the right and the Y_e axis points upward. Figure 4.11 shows the difference between central projection and projection through an arbitrary viewpoint.

In identifying the screen coordinates (x_s, y_s) associated with the point $P(x, y, z)$, we perform tasks similar to those performed in the central projection:

Task 1: Through viewing transformations, identify the eye coordinates (x_e, y_e, z_e) associated with a point having world coordinates (x, y, z).
Task 2: Identify the screen coordinates (x_s, y_s) associated with eye coordinates (x_e, y_e, z_e).

Viewing transformations. The conversion of the world coordinates to eye coordinates requires a series of viewing transformations. Further individual viewing transformation is accomplished by transforming the coordinate system. This is because the physical location of the point P is fixed, but our viewpoint is referenced through the eye coordinate system. As discussed

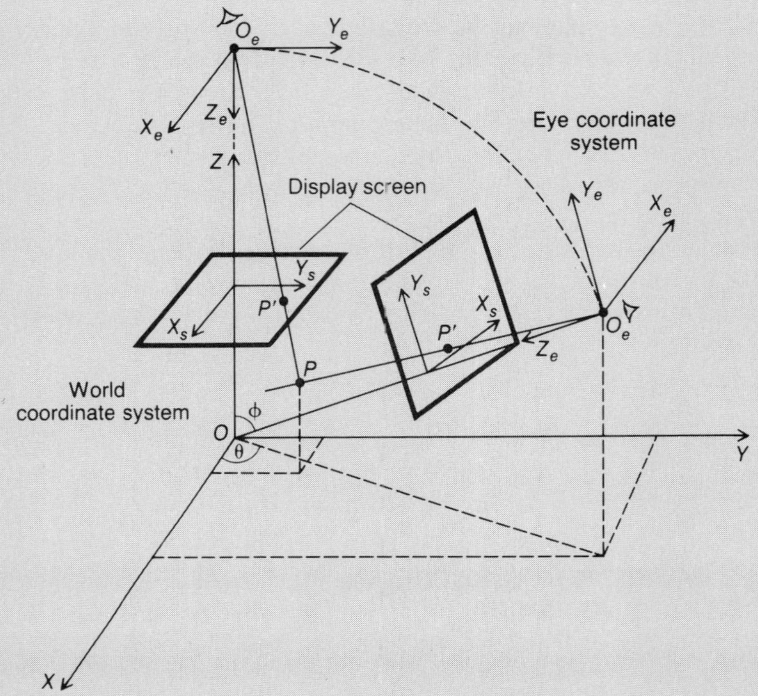

FIGURE 4.11 The perspective projection of point *P* onto the display screen

in Section 4.2.6, transforming a coordinate system is the inverse of the corresponding transformation that moves a point. We will need four viewing transformations, whose effect can be viewed as obtaining a sequence of new coordinate systems with the eye coordinate system as the final result. For notational convenience, we refer to the intermediate axis systems as X', Y', Z', with the final X', Y', Z' axis system being the eye coordinate system X_e, Y_e, Z_e. The reader must understand the difference between the transformation of points and the transformation of coordinate axes. The former alters the physical position of the point, while the latter does not. Let us first identify the viewpoint O_e (see Fig. 4.11) by the spherical coordinates (D, θ, ϕ). From Eq. (4.1), we know that these are $(x = D \cdot \sin\phi \cos\theta,\ y = D \cdot \sin\phi \sin\theta,\ z = D \cdot \cos\phi)$ where (D, θ, ϕ) is defined as before. Then we perform the transformations as follows.

Step 1: Translate origin to O_e so as to establish a new coordinate system at the viewpoint. (See Fig. 4.12(a).) The required transformation matrix is

$$T_1 = \begin{bmatrix} 1 & 0 & 0 & 0 \\ 0 & 1 & 0 & 0 \\ 0 & 0 & 1 & 0 \\ -D \cdot \sin\phi\cos\theta & -D \cdot \sin\phi\cos\theta & -D \cdot \cos\phi & 1 \end{bmatrix}.$$

Step 2: Rotate the axis system about the Z' axis through the *clockwise* angle $90 - \theta$. The rotation results in the Y' axis intersecting the Z axis. (See Fig. 4.12(b).) The transformation matrix will have the same result as rotating a point about the Z axis through the *counterclockwise* angle $90 - \theta$. Knowing that $\sin(90 - \theta) = \cos\theta$ and $\cos(90 - \theta) = \sin\theta$ and using matrix (4.10), we find

$$T_2 = \begin{bmatrix} \sin\theta & \cos\theta & 0 & 0 \\ -\cos\theta & \sin\theta & 0 & 0 \\ 0 & 0 & 1 & 0 \\ 0 & 0 & 0 & 1 \end{bmatrix}.$$

Step 3: Rotate the axis system again about the X' axis through the *counterclockwise* angle $180 - \phi$ so that the Z' axis is directed toward the origin of the world coordinate system. (See Fig. 4.12(c).) This transformation is equivalent to rotating a point about the X axis through the *clockwise* angle $180 - \phi$. Since $\sin(180 - \phi) = \sin\phi$ and $\cos(180 - \phi) = -\cos\phi$, the effect of this transformation is simply

$$T_3 = \begin{bmatrix} 1 & 0 & 0 & 0 \\ 0 & -\cos\phi & -\sin\phi & 0 \\ 0 & \sin\phi & -\cos\phi & 0 \\ 0 & 0 & 0 & 1 \end{bmatrix}.$$

Step 4: Convert to a left-handed coordinate system, reversing the direction of the X' axis so that the axis system conforms to the conventions of the eye coordinate system. (See Fig. 4.12(d).) The effect is

$$T_4 = \begin{bmatrix} -1 & 0 & 0 & 0 \\ 0 & 1 & 0 & 0 \\ 0 & 0 & 1 & 0 \\ 0 & 0 & 0 & 1 \end{bmatrix}.$$

This completes the four basic transformations needed to establish the viewing

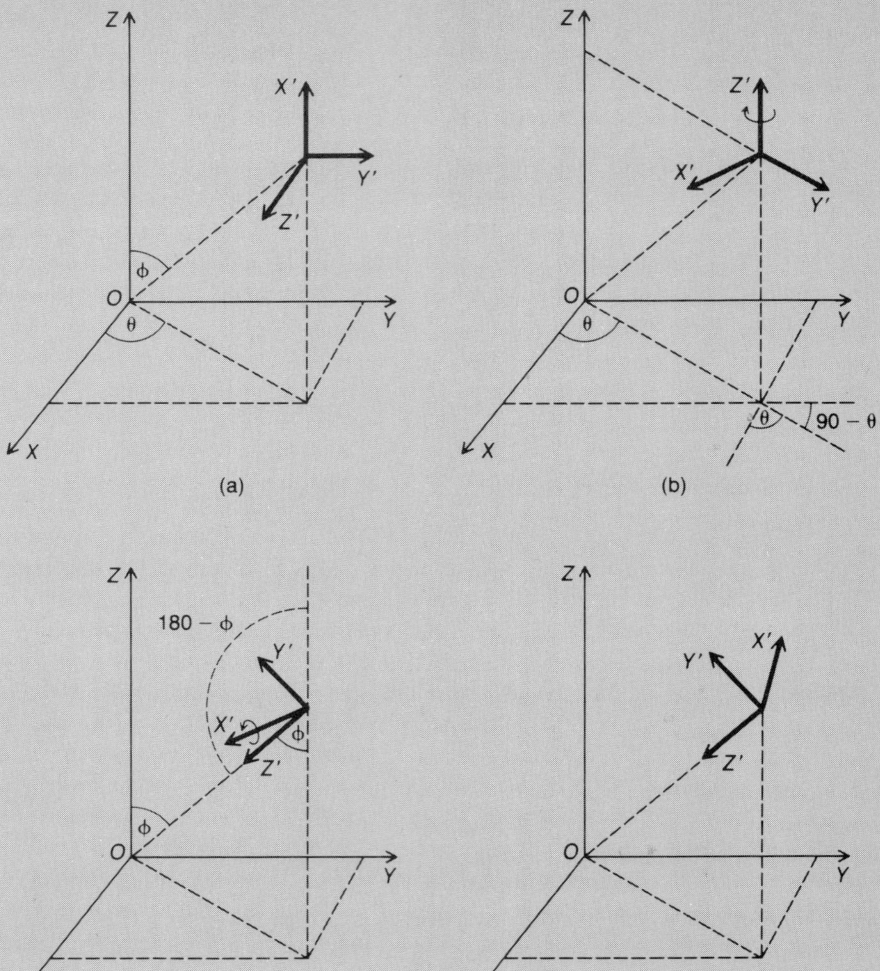

FIGURE 4.12 Four steps in establishing the viewing transformation from the world coordinates to the eye coordinates

transformation T. That is,

$$T = T_1 \cdot T_2 \cdot T_3 \cdot T_4$$

$$= \begin{bmatrix} -\sin\theta & -\cos\theta\cos\phi & -\cos\theta\sin\phi & 0 \\ \cos\theta & -\sin\theta\cos\phi & -\sin\theta\sin\phi & 0 \\ 0 & \sin\phi & -\cos\phi & 0 \\ 0 & 0 & D & 1 \end{bmatrix}. \quad \textbf{(4.28)}$$

Thus if the world coordinates (x, y, z) of a point are known, the eye coordinates (x_e, y_e, z_e) are readily obtained as

$$(x_e, y_e, z_e, 1) = (x, y, z, 1) \cdot T$$

or

$$\begin{aligned} x_e &= -x\sin\theta + y\cos\theta, \\ y_e &= -x\cos\theta\cos\phi - y\sin\theta\cos\phi + z\sin\phi, \\ z_e &= -x\cos\theta\sin\phi - y\sin\theta\sin\phi - z\cos\phi + D. \end{aligned} \quad \textbf{(4.29)}$$

Once the eye coordinates are known, it is a simple matter to calculate the screen coordinates (x_s and y_s) from Eqs. (4.25) and (4.26).

$$x_s = d\left(\frac{x_e}{z_e}\right), \qquad y_s = d\left(\frac{y_e}{z_e}\right). \quad \textbf{(4.30)}$$

Finally, we can show that the transformation matrix for central projection [Eq. (4.24)] is a special case of Eq. (4.29) where $\theta = 270°$ and $\phi = 0°$. That is, substituting these values into Eq. (4.28) yields

$$\begin{bmatrix} 1 & 0 & 0 & 0 \\ 0 & 1 & 0 & 0 \\ 0 & 0 & -1 & 0 \\ 0 & 0 & D & 1 \end{bmatrix},$$

the transformation matrix for the central projection.

Relationships among parameters. It is important to understand how each of the viewing parameters (d, θ, ϕ, and D) affect the image generated on the display screen.

- Varying the values of θ and ϕ permits us to view an object from different angles. (See Fig. 4.11.)
- Changing the value of D (the distance from the viewer to the origin) permits us to move the viewer closer to the object or further away. (See Fig. 4.10.)

- When a viewpoint (D, θ, ϕ) is fixed, changes in d affect the size of the image on the display screen. If the screen is closer to the viewer (d is decreased), the size of the projected screen image will be decreased. [See Eqs. (4.25) and (4.26) and Fig. 4.10.]
- Since both D and d control the size of the screen image, we may be able to establish some relationships between them. When an object is close to the viewer, it appears larger than when it is farther away because it occupies a larger proportion of the field of view. For example, a perspective view of a cube will cause the edges close to the viewer to appear larger than edges farther away. To reduce this effect of perspective viewing, we may increase the value of D so as to decrease the perceived size of the image. To simply magnify the reduced image without reintroducing the effect of perspective, we may increase d.

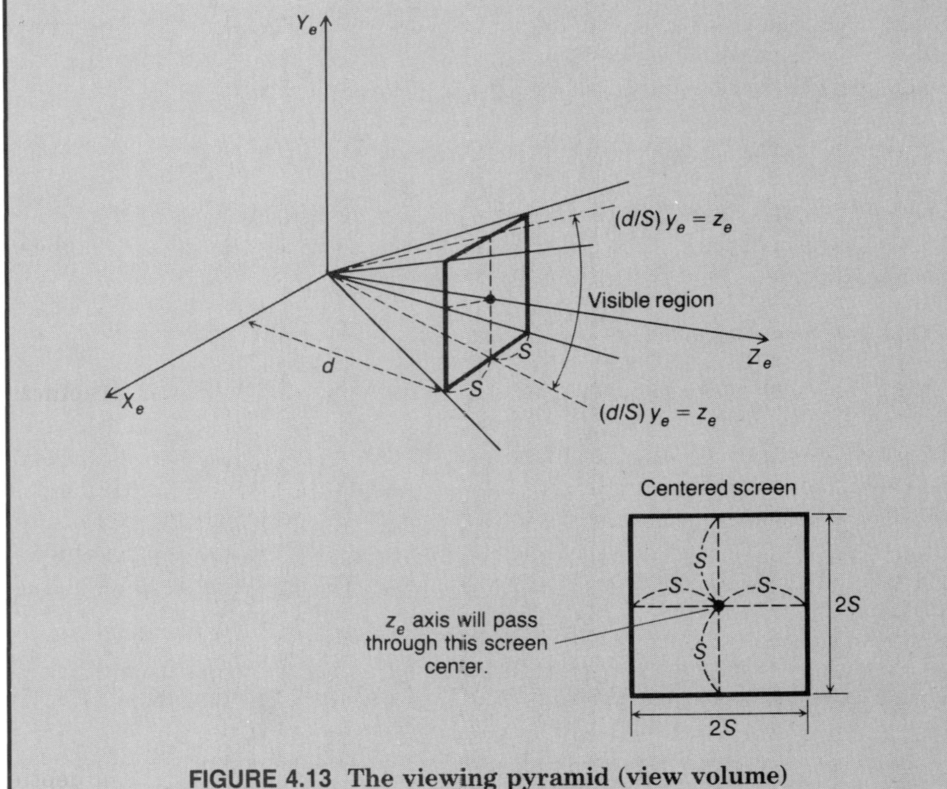

FIGURE 4.13 The viewing pyramid (view volume)

4.3.3 HOMOGENEOUS SCREEN COORDINATE SYSTEM

Rather than varying the parameter values of D and d to control the size of the screen image, we can convert the x_s and y_s values into dimensionless fractions by dividing them by the centered screen size S (when the origin is located at the center of the screen). This results in a new screen coordinate system where

$$x_s = \left(\frac{d}{S}\right)\frac{x_e}{z_e}, \tag{4.31}$$

$$y_s = \left(\frac{d}{S}\right)\frac{y_e}{z_e}. \tag{4.32}$$

The viewing pyramid shown in Fig. 4.13 specifies a region of the eye coordinate system in which objects must lie if they are to be visible. For a fixed viewpoint, only the ratio (d/S) will control the projected image on the screen. The effect of this ratio is analogous to that of the focal length of a camera lens, which determines how much of a scene will be included in the picture. If the ratio is small, it is analogous to using a small focal length to take a picture. The resulting image is similar to that of a wide-angle lens. On the other hand, a large value of (d/S) specifies a long focal length, yielding a limited "telephoto" view.

It is also important to note that the division of the screen coordinates by S yields new limits

$$-1 \leqslant x_s \leqslant 1, \tag{4.33}$$

$$-1 \leqslant y_s \leqslant 1. \tag{4.34}$$

4.4. PERSPECTIVE DEPTH

In this section, we will discuss an important aspect of computer graphics: creating images of 3-D objects that are realistic. The depth (distance) information of a point (or an object) provides the basis for producing this visual realism. In this section, we will introduce the mathematical elements involved in measuring depth. We will use this depth information in removing hidden lines (or surfaces) and in developing 3-D clipping algorithms. (The use of depth value in 3-D clipping will be discussed in Section 4.5; the development of the hidden line removal algorithms will be presented in Chapter 5.)

4.4.1 DEPTH MEASURE FOR A PARALLEL PROJECTION

The depth of each point in the image we produce on the screen must be available to determine which surfaces hide lines and other surfaces. The basic depth comparison is equivalent to the following question: Given $P_1 = (x_1, y_1, z_1)$ and

$P_2 = (x_2, y_2, z_2)$, does either point obscure the other? This question can be reduced to: Are P_1 and P_2 on the same projector (i.e., ray emanating from the viewpoint)? If the answer is yes, a comparison of z_1 and z_2 tells us which point is closer to the viewer. Otherwise, neither point can obscure the other.

Before introducing the depth calculations, we may recall the viewing transformations given in Section 4.3.2. We used two steps in identifying the screen coordinates. First we transformed the world coordinates into the eye coordinates, then the eye coordinates into the screen coordinates:

$$(x, y, z) \rightarrow (x_e, y_e, z_e) \rightarrow (x_s, y_s).$$

An orthographic (parallel) projection can be viewed as a central projection (see Section 4.3.1) with the viewpoint located at the infinite horizon of the Z axis. In this type of projection, where $x = x_e = x_s$, $y = y_e = y_s$, and $z_e = D - z$, depth comparison is simplified. The z coordinate alone can determine the relative depth of any point. Since z and z_e are inversely related, the smaller the z_e, the closer the point lies to the observer.

For a perspective projection, however, depth comparison is more complicated, because projecting points onto the display screen involves rays emanating from the viewpoint at various angles (i.e., projectors). Since the viewing transformation "distorts" the image of objects so that portions of an object are smaller in order to appear farther away, the depth comparison by z_e-coordinates has to be modified.

4.4.2 DEPTH MEASURE FOR A PERSPECTIVE PROJECTION

First, we will augment the 2-D screen coordinate system (X_s, Y_s) to a 3-D system (X_s, Y_s, Z_s). In this augmented system, the Z_s-coordinate will be calculated so as to retain depth information without changing the interpretation of the x_s and y_s values. If we were to display a point (x_s, y_s, z_s) on a conventional computer screen, we could use the values of x_s and y_s directly and ignore the z_s coordinate.

Second, recall that a straight line in the eye coordinate system transforms into a straight line in the screen coordinate system. This is done simply by transforming its endpoints and then redrawing the line between the transformed endpoints. For the 3-D screen coordinate system, the same transformation property is equally applicable—that is, planes in the eye coordinate system transform into planes in the screen coordinate system. Thus we may transform z_e values along with x_e and y_e values so that a plane equation in eye coordinates transforms into a plane equation in screen coordinates

$$Ax_e + By_e + Cz_e + D = 0 \tag{4.35}$$

$$\rightarrow A'x_s + B'y_s + C'z_s + D' = 0. \tag{4.36}$$

We can determine the unknown coefficients in the plane equation if three vertices on the plane are known.

For a perspective projection, we obtain the values for x_s and y_s,

$$x_s = \left(\frac{d}{S}\right)\frac{x_e}{z_e} \quad \text{and} \quad y_s = \left(\frac{d}{S}\right)\frac{y_e}{z_e},$$

where d is the distance between the viewpoint and the display screen. Substituting values for x_s and y_s into Eq. (4.36) and solving for z_s gives

$$z_s = \alpha - \frac{\beta}{z_e}, \tag{4.37}$$

where $\alpha = -D'/C'$ and $\beta = (d/C'S)(A'x_e + B'y_e)$.

Since the plane equation in screen coordinates is not known in advance, we may adopt the procedure given by Newman and Sproull [9] in choosing α and β:

- We limit our viewing scope by specifying z_e values in the range $K_1 \leqslant z_e \leqslant K_2$. The truncated viewing pyramid in the eye coordinate system is shown in Fig. 4.14.

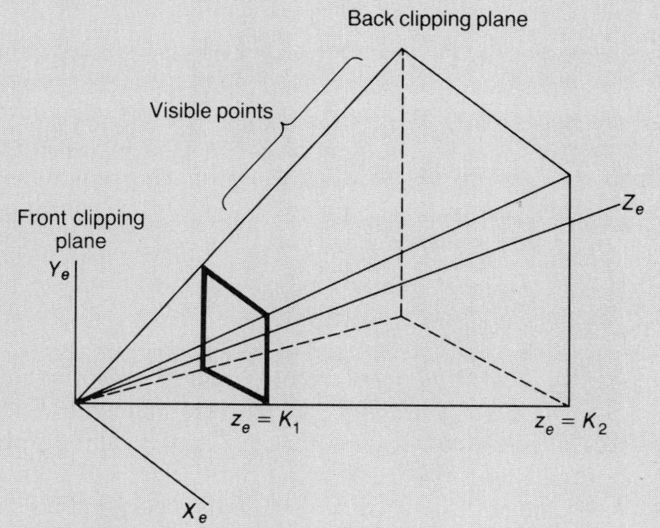

FIGURE 4.14 Truncated view volume in the eye coordinate system. (Visible points must have $K_1 \leqslant z_e \leqslant K_2$.)

- We map $z_e = K_1$ into the smallest z_s value and $z_e = K_2$ into the largest. Values outside this range will have no representation in the screen coordinate system. As a convention, we adopt $0 \leq z_s \leq 1$.
- Since $z_s = 0 \rightarrow z_e = K_1$ and $z_s = 1 \rightarrow z_e = K_2$, we obtain two linear equations:

$$0 = \alpha - \frac{\beta}{K_1},$$

$$1 = \alpha - \frac{\beta}{K_2},$$

and solve for α and β. This gives us

$$\alpha = \frac{K_2}{K_2 - K_1} \quad \text{and} \quad \beta = \frac{K_1 K_2}{K_2 - K_1}.$$

- We find z_s by substituting α and β into Eq. (4.37)

$$z_s = \frac{K_2(z_e - K_1)}{(K_2 - K_1)z_e}, \qquad 0 \leq z_s \leq 1 \tag{4.38}$$

- When two points are compared for depth, the point with the smaller z_s will lie closer to the viewer.

4.5 VIEWPORT PLANNING FOR 3-D GRAPHICS

Three-dimensional viewport planning involves clipping the contents of the data against the boundaries of the desired view. This clipping process is to ensure that only the visible portions of the picture are transformed into plotting instructions for the display device. The clipping boundaries for 3-D graphics are the faces of the viewing pyramid. (See Fig. 4.14.)

4.5.1 THREE-DIMENSIONAL CLIPPING

If we want to specify a limited view volume, we simply introduce a *front clipping plane* and a *back clipping plane*, such as that shown in Fig. 4.14. Both clipping planes are parallel to the view plane (display plane), and both are specified by a distance along the view plane normal from the view reference point. In other words, these planes are assumed to be perpendicular to the line of sight (Z_e axis).

Point clipping. Three conditions must be met for an individual point to be visible within the truncated pyramid. From Eqs. (4.31) through (4.34), we obtain

$$-1 \leq x_s \leq 1 \rightarrow -z_e \leq \left(\frac{d}{S}\right)x_e \leq z_e \rightarrow -w \leq x_e \leq w, \tag{4.39}$$

$$-1 \leq y_s \leq 1 \rightarrow -z_e \leq \left(\frac{d}{S}\right)y_e \rightarrow \leq z_e - w \leq y_e \leq w, \tag{4.40}$$

where

$$w = \left(\frac{S}{d}\right)z_e \quad \text{and} \quad w > 0.$$

From Eq. (4.38) we introduce an additional clipping limit,

$$0 \leq z_s \leq 1 \rightarrow K_1 \leq z_e \leq K_2. \tag{4.41}$$

If a point fails the test, it is not displayed. If it satisfies the three conditions, Eqs. (4.31) and (4.32) are applied to the eye coordinates to determine the position of the point on the display screen. In fact, the net results of Eqs. (4.31), (4.32), and (4.38) are to map the truncated viewing pyramid into a standard viewport in the screen coordinate system.

Line clipping. As we saw in 2-D clipping, lines cannot be processed as easily as points. Lines must be clipped against the limits of the viewing pyramid defined in Eqs. (4.39) through (4.41). Figure 4.15 depicts the view volume with limits imposed by Eqs. (4.39) through (4.41).

We can derive a 3-D clipping algorithm by extending the 2-D scheme described in Section 3.5.1. The algorithm determines whether an endpoint of the line lies outside the boundaries of the view volume by computing a six-bit code for each endpoint. For endpoint I, we define:

$T(I)$—point is above view volume, $y_e > w$
$B(I)$—point is below view volume, $y_e < -w$
$R(I)$—point is right of view volume, $x_e > w$
$L(I)$—point is left of view volume, $x_e < -w$
$BH(I)$—point is behind view volume, $z_e > K_2$
$F(I)$—point is in front of view volume, $z_e < K_1$.

If the statement is true, the corresponding bit code is 1. Otherwise, the bit code is set to 0. We consider the following three cases:

Case 1: If we observe

$$\begin{aligned} &T(1) + B(1) + R(1) + L(1) + BH(1) + F(1) \\ &+ T(2) + B(2) + R(2) + L(2) + BH(2) + F(2) = 0, \end{aligned} \tag{4.42}$$

then both endpoints lie inside the view volume and we accept the entire line.

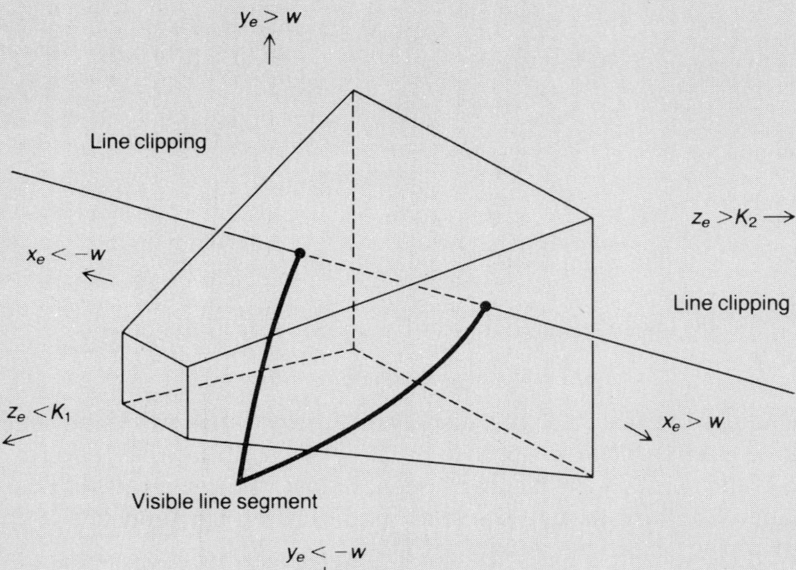

FIGURE 4.15 Three-dimensional clipping. Lines that pass through the view volume must be clipped before the perspective division is performed.

Case 2: If we observe

$$\begin{aligned} &T(1) \cdot T(2) + R(1) \cdot R(2) + L(1) \cdot L(2) \\ &+ B(1) \cdot B(2) + BH(1) \cdot BH(2) + F(1) \cdot F(2) \neq 0, \end{aligned} \tag{4.43}$$

then both endpoints lie on the invisible side of one of the planes and the entire line is rejected.

Case 3: Otherwise the status of the line cannot be determined immediately. In this case, we must compute the point(s) of intersection of the line with the planes of the view volume.

Using a parametric representation of a line defined by its two endpoints in the eye coordinate system, we can easily determine the point of intersection between the line and one of the planes of the view volume. If we denote $P_1(x_{e_1} y_{e_1} z_{e_1})$ and $P_2(x_{e_2} y_{e_2} z_{e_2})$ as the eye coordinates of the two endpoints, the parametric equations are

$$x_e = (x_{e_2} - x_{e_1}) \cdot t + x_{e_1},$$

$$y_e = (y_{e2} - y_{e1}) \cdot t + y_{e1}, \tag{4.44}$$

$$z_e = (z_{e2} - z_{e1}) \cdot t + z_{e1},$$

and $0 \leqslant t \leqslant 1$. As t is allowed to vary from 0 to 1, these three equations give the coordinates of all points on the line.

To calculate the intersection of a line with the top plane of the view volume, we replace the variable y_e with the boundary value w and solve for t. This gives

$$\begin{aligned}(y_{e2} - y_{e1})t + y_{e1} &= w \\ &= (S/d)z_e && \text{[See Eq. (4.40).]} \\ &= (S/d)[(z_{e2} - z_{e1})t + z_{e1}] && \text{[See Eq. (4.44).]}\end{aligned}$$

$$t = \frac{(S/d)z_{e1} - y_{e1}}{(y_{e2} - y_{e1}) - (S/d)(z_{e2} - z_{e1})} \tag{4.45}$$

If t is outside the interval from 0 to 1, the intersection is outside the view volume. Otherwise, substituting this value of t into Eq. (4.44) yields the point of intersection.

Other intersections are calculated in a similar fashion. There is, of course, a risk that we will invest our effort in computing the eye coordinates of points that may be discarded in the clipping test; however, the clipping algorithm is much easier to implement in the eye coordinate system than in the world coordinate system.

Once the point of intersection is found, we use this point to replace the endpoint that was on the invisible side of the plane. Then we compute the screen coordinates of the endpoints of the clipped line segment.

As an example, we consider a line segment defined by its two endpoints in the eye coordinate system $P_1(x_{e_1}, y_{e_1}, z_{e_1}) = (1, 6, 2)$ and $P_2(x_{e_2}, y_{e_2}, z_{e_2}) = (4, -2, 5)$. For simplicity we assume $S = d(S/d \rightarrow 1)$ and $4 \leqslant z_e \leqslant 10$. For point P_1 we compute $w = (S/d)z_{e_1} = 2$. For point P_2 we have $w = (S/d)z_{e_2} = 5$. Computing a six-bit code for each endpoint gives

$$\begin{aligned} T(1) &= 1 & T(2) &= 0 \\ B(1) &= 0 & B(2) &= 0 \\ R(1) &= 0 & R(2) &= 0 \\ L(1) &= 0 & L(2) &= 0 \\ BH(1) &= 0 & BH(2) &= 0 \\ F(1) &= 1 & F(2) &= 0 \end{aligned}$$

We quickly confirm that P_1 is outside the view volume but P_2 is inside. This indicates that we have only one point of intersection to compute. [Note that neither condition (4.42) nor condition (4.43) is met.]

We will first check the possibility of intersection with the top plane of the view volume. From Eq. (4.45) we compute $t = 4/11$. Since $0 < t < 1$, the top plane contains the point of intersection. From Eq. (4.44) we compute the coordinates of the possible point of intersection:

$$x_e = (4 - 1)(4/11) + 1 = 23/11,$$

$$y_e = (-2 - 6)(4/11) + 6 = 34/11,$$

$$z_e = (5 - 2)(4/11) + 2 = 34/11.$$

It is premature to conclude that this is the point of intersection. Why? Remember that our front clipping plane is at $z_e = 4 > 34/11$. Thus we cannot see this point of intersection. We have to test further to find the true intersection point. If we compute t values for the remaining planes, we obtain the following.

Plane	t	**Visibility**
Top	4/11	No $\left(z_e = \dfrac{34}{11} < 4\right)$
Bottom	−3/5	No
Right	undefined	No
Left	−1/6	No
Back	3	No
Front	2/3	Yes ($z_e = 4$)

The point of intersection with the front clipping plane is computed as

$$x_e = (4 - 1)(2/3) + 1 = 3,$$

$$y_e = (-2 - 6)(2/3) + 6 = 2/3,$$

$$z_e = (5 - 2)(2/3) + 2 = 4.$$

The point (3, 2/3, 4) represents the true point of intersection.

Before we leave this section, we must consider the special case when $w = 0$. In Eqs. (4.39) through (4.41), the limits are stated so as to guarantee that w is always positive. In fact, we can allow w to take any value. If $w = 0$, a point lies in the plane of the viewpoint ($z_e = 0$). In particular, if $w < 0$ the viewer is placed within the object, so that any images drawn with such a viewpoint must be processed by a line clipping subroutine. Interested readers should consult reference [4].

4.5.2 VIEWPORT MAPPING

After clipping a picture against the view volume, the final step is to map it to the viewport. Since the perspective transformation gives the 2-D screen coordinates, we can adopt the procedure used in Section 3.5 for the viewport mapping. The actual screen coordinates on the physical device are also found by applying Eqs. (3.36) through (3.42).

Alternatively, we may convert to device coordinates by specifying the location of the viewport in which the image is centered. For the *PC*, we may use

$$\begin{aligned} x_s &= SCF[(d/S)(x_e/z_e)V_x + L] \\ y_s &= -(d/S)(y_e/z_e)V_y + M \end{aligned} \qquad (4.46)$$

where the four viewport parameters are given in *center-size* notation: the viewport is centered at (L, M) and is $2V_x$ units wide and $2V_y$ units high. The derivation of Eq. (4.46) assumes that the image on the screen plane is *square*—i.e., that V_x is the same as V_y. [Compare Eq. (4.46) with Eq. (3.42) and Eq. (3.43).]

4.6 SCREEN DISPLAY OF 3-D GRAPHICS

We conclude this chapter by presenting two computer programs that demonstrate the concepts discussed in the previous sections. The first program draws a perspective view of a cube; the second draws surfaces specified by a mathematical function of the form $z = f(x, y)$.

4.6.1 PERSPECTIVE VIEW OF A CUBE

Consider a cube centered at the origin of the world coordinate system and defined by the following vertices:

Vertex number	World coordinates (x, y, z)
1	(1, 1, −1)
2	(1, 1, 1)
3	(1, −1, 1)
4	(1, −1, −1)
5	(−1, 1, −1)
6	(−1, −1, −1)
7	(−1, −1, 1)
8	(−1, 1, 1)

We will observe this cube from a point (12.5, 53.13°, 46.85°) with the viewing axis Z_e pointed directly at the origin of the world coordinate system. We intend to fill a 13½ inch (252 mm) computer screen (diagonal measurement). The display screen has a 20 cm × 20 cm viewing area and is designed to be viewed from 40 cm away. We assume that the computer screen has 320 × 200 addressable pixel positions (medium resolution mode on an IBM PC). Thus $D = 12.5$, $\theta = 53.13°$, $\phi = 46.85°$, $d = 40$, and $S = 10$. (See Fig. 4.13 to learn how S value is determined.)

For a sample calculation, we take vertex 1. Using Eq. (4.28), we compute the corresponding eye coordinates as:

$$\sin(\theta) = 0.8,\ \cos(\theta) = 0.6,\ \sin(\phi) = 0.73, \text{ and } \cos(\phi) = 0.684\,,$$

$$x_e = -(1)(0.8) + (1)(0.6) = -0.2\,,$$

$$y_e = -(1)(0.6)(0.684) - (1)(0.8)(0.684) + (-1)(0.73) = -1.688\,,$$

$$z_e = -(1)(0.6)(0.73) - (1)(0.8)(0.73) - (-1)(0.684) + 12.5 = 12.162\,.$$

Using Eqs. (4.31) and (4.32), we compute the screen coordinates

$$x_s = \left(\frac{40}{10}\right)\left(\frac{-0.2}{12.162}\right) = -0.066\,,$$

$$y_s = \left(\frac{40}{10}\right)\left(\frac{-1.688}{12.162}\right) = -0.555\,.$$

The depth value z_s also can be computed using the fact that the z_e values for all vertices of the cube range between 10.794 and 14.205. Therefore we may set K_1 to 10 and K_2 to 15 to ensure that all the vertices are inside the truncated viewing pyramid. Using Eq. (4.38), we can calculate z_s for vertex 1:

$$z_s = \frac{15(12.162 - 10)}{(15 - 10)12.162} = 0.533.$$

The screen coordinates for the remaining vertices can be computed in a similar fashion, as summarized in Table 4.1. A review of the z_s column in Table 4.1 indicates that vertex 2 lies closest to the viewer ($z_s = 0.22$) and vertex 6 lies farthest from the viewer ($z_s = 0.888$).

The final step is to find the physical coordinates on the specific device, the IBM PC. Since we intend to draw the cube on the screen with medium resolution mode (320 × 200), we may define the screen coordinates for vertex 1, using Eq. (4.46).

$$x_s = 1.2[(-0.066)(100) + 160] = 184.08$$

$$y_s = -(-0.555)(100) + 100 = 155.5.$$

Note that the viewport is given in center-size notation.

Program 4.1 will plot the perspective view of the cube. Changing the viewing parameters in the program will provide a variety of perspective views of the cube, as shown in Fig. 4.16.

Although we must apply the clipping routine to each edge of the cube, it is apparent from Table 4.1 that all of the vertices lie within the viewing pyramid. Thus the clipping algorithm will eventually accept each line.

TABLE 4.1 Viewing transformation

Vertex number	World coordinate			Eye coordinate			Screen coordinate			†Device coordinate (IBM PC)	
	x	y	z	x_e	y_e	z_e	x_s	y_s	z_s	x_s	y_s
1	1	1	−1	−0.2	−1.688	12.162	−0.066,	−0.555	0.533	184.1	155.5
2	1	1	1	−0.2	−0.228	10.794	−0.075,	−0.085	0.220	183.1	108.5
3	1	−1	1	−1.401	0.866	11.962	−0.469,	0.289	0.492	135.8	71.1
4	1	−1	−1	−1.401	−0.573	13.329	−0.421	−0.178	0.749	141.6	117.8
5	−1	1	−1	−1.4	−0.867	13.037	0.429	−0.266	0.699	243.5	126.6
6	−1	−1	−1	0.199	0.227	14.205	0.056	0.064	0.888	198.8	93.6
7	−1	−1	1	0.199	1.687	12.837	0.062	0.525	0.663	199.5	47.5
8	−1	1	1	1.4	0.592	11.670	0.479	0.203	0.429	249.6	79.7

†$SCF = 1.2$, $V_x = V_y = 100$, $L = 160$, $M = 100$. [See Eq. (4.46).]

```
100 ' Program 4.1 : Draw a Cube
110 '  NV = Number of Vertices : NS = Number of Surfaces
130 '  NPS(J) = Number of vertices to form surface J
140 '
150 CLS : KEY OFF : SCREEN 1,0 : COLOR 1,2
160          GOSUB 210
170          GOSUB 280
180          GOSUB 530
190          GOSUB 660
200 END
210 '------ DEFINE VIEWING PARAMETERS ------
220        D=12.5: VD=40   : THETA=53.13: PHI=46.85: TX= 160: TY=100 : S=10
230        PI=3.141593     :SCF=1.2        : VX=100    : VY=100
240        THETA=THETA*PI/180 : PHI=PHI*PI/180
250        SN1=SIN(THETA) : SN2=SIN(PHI) :CN1=COS(THETA) :CN2=COS(PHI)
260        NV=8 : K1=10: K2=15: W=K2/(K2-K1)
270 RETURN
280 '------ VERTEX ARRAY  ---------
290        DIM V(8,3), EC(8,3), SC(8,3)
300        FOR J=1 TO NV
310             READ X,Y,Z
320             V(J,1)=X: V(J,2)=Y: V(J,3)=Z
330             GOSUB 410
340             EC(J,1)=XE: EC(J,2)=YE: EC(J,3)=ZE
350             GOSUB 460
360             SC(J,1)= XS   : SC(J,2)= YS   : SC(J,3)=ZS
370       NEXT J
380 RETURN
390        DATA 1,1,-1, 1,1,1, 1,-1,1, 1,-1,-1
400        DATA -1,1,-1, -1,-1,-1, -1,-1,1, -1,1,1
410 '------ EYE COORDINATES  ---------
420        XE= -X*SN1 + Y*CN1
430        YE= -X*CN1*CN2 - Y*SN1*CN2 + Z*SN2
440        ZE= -X*SN2*CN1 - Y*SN2*SN1 - Z*CN2 + D
450 RETURN
460 '----   SCREEN COORDINATES -------
470        XS=(VD/S)*(XE/ZE)                                  ' See Eq.(4.31)
480        YS=(VD/S)*(YE/ZE)                                  ' See Eq.(4.32)
490        ZS=W*(1- K1/ZE)                                    ' See Eq.(4.38)
500             XS=XS*VX + TX     : XS=SCF*XS                 ' PC device coordinates
510             YS=-YS*VY + TY                                ' See Eq.(4.46)
520 RETURN
530 '------   SURFACE ARRAY    ----------
540 DIM SF(6,5),NPS(6)
550 NS=6
560 FOR I=1 TO NS: READ NPS(I): NEXT I
570      FOR J=1 TO NS
580           FOR K=1 TO NPS(J)
590                READ SF(J,K)
600           NEXT K
610      NEXT J
620 RETURN
630 DATA 5,5,5,5,5,5
640 DATA 1,2,3,4,1, 1,5,8,2,1, 5,6,7,8,5, 4,3,7,6,4, 2,8,7,3,2, 1,4,6,5,1
660 '------   PLOT    ---------------
670 FOR J=1 TO NS
680           FOR K=1 TO NPS(J)
690                NN=SF(J,K)
700                A=SC(NN,1) : B= SC(NN,2)
710                IF K=1 THEN PSET (A,B): GOTO 730
720                LINE - (A,B)
730           NEXT K
740 NEXT J
750 RETURN
```

PROGRAM 4.1 Draw a cube

4.6.2 SURFACES OF THE FORM $z = f(x, y)$

Graphs of points (x, y, z) that satisfy functions $z = f(x, y)$ may be plotted using the processes discussed in previous sections. Unlike Program 4.1, in which we provide the coordinates of points as DATA, the points will be generated by a program segment. Program 4.2 illustrates this process by generating an image that represents the surfaces as a sequence of wire-frame curves. The program will plot the function $z = 7 \cdot e^{-.1(x^2+y^2)}$. A smoother surface would result from calculating more points on each curve, but would also result in an increase in execution time.

Figure 4.17 shows a variety of views of the function with choices of different viewing parameters. As different viewing positions are selected, the images become muddled by overlapping curves. The program generates a transparent surface. This gives us the illusion that we can see through the near parts of the surface to the farther parts that lie behind. If we could somehow avoid drawing the hidden surfaces, we might obtain more realistic images. The next chapter will provide general approaches to this problem.

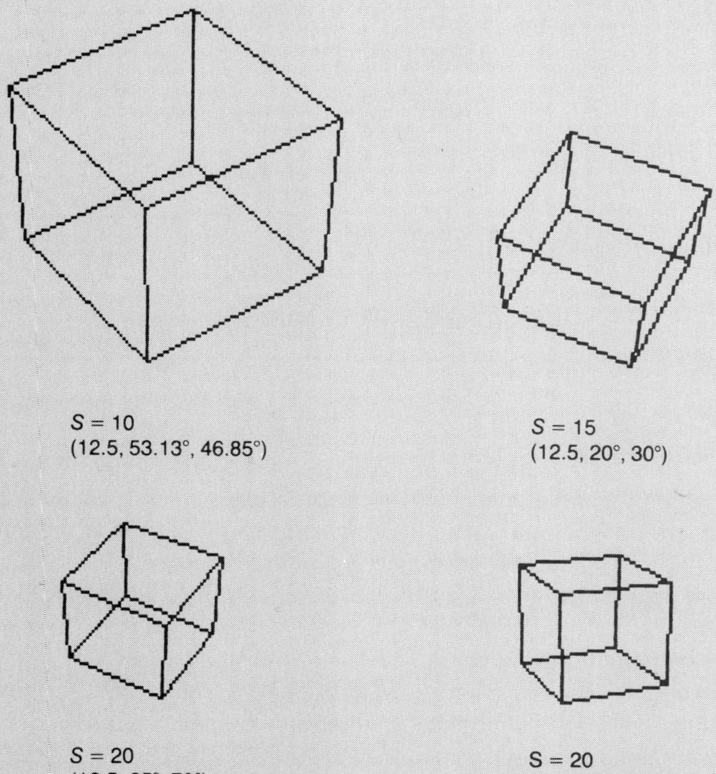

S = 10
(12.5, 53.13°, 46.85°)

S = 15
(12.5, 20°, 30°)

S = 20
(12.5, 65°, 70°)

S = 20
(12.5, 65°, 70°)

FIGURE 4.16 Perspective projections of the cube at various viewing angles

```
10 ' Program 4.2: Plot of 3-D Functions
20 ' (D,theta,phi) = Viewpoint
30 ' VD = Distance of the Projection Plane from the XY Plane.
40 '  S = Centered screen size. (see Eq.(4.31).
50 CLS: KEY OFF
60 SCREEN 1,0 : COLOR 1,2
70 '
80     GOSUB 110
90     GOSUB 170
100 END
110 '------- Define Viewing Parameters ---------
120         TX= 160: TY = 100: PI = 3.141593 : SCF= 1.2
130         D= 30: VD=420: THETA=  0: PHI= 70 : S=2
140         THETA=THETA*PI/180 : PHI=PHI*PI/180
150         SN1=SIN(THETA) : SN2=SIN(PHI) : CN1=COS(THETA): CN2=COS(PHI)
160 RETURN
170 '------- Define the 3-D function to plot ------
180 DEF FNZ(X,Y) = 7*EXP(-.1*(X*X + Y*Y))
190 FOR X=8 TO -8 STEP -1
200        FLAG =0
210        FOR Y=-8 TO 8 STEP .5
220               Z=FNZ(X,Y)
230               GOSUB 290
240               GOSUB 340
250               GOSUB 420
260        NEXT Y
270 NEXT X
280 RETURN
290 '-------- Compute Eye Coordinates --------------
300        XE= -X*SN1 + Y*CN1
310        YE= -X*CN1*CN2 - Y*SN1*CN2 + Z*SN2
320        ZE= -X*SN2*CN1 - Y*SN2*SN1 - Z*CN2 + D
330 RETURN
340 ' -------- Compute Screen Coordinates -----------
350 ' We assume s1 = s2 = 1 so that both window and viewport coordinates
360 ' will be exactly same. [see Eqs. (3.39) and (3.40).]
370        XS= (VD/S)*(XE/ZE)                          ' Viewport coordinates
380        YS= (VD/S)*(YE/ZE)
390        XS= XS + TX     : XS= SCF*XS                ' PC device coordinates
400        YS= -YS + TY
410 RETURN
420 '---------- Plotting Routine ---------------------
430 IF XS<0 OR XS>319 OR YS<0 OR YS>199 THEN FLAG=0 : GOTO 460
440 IF FLAG=0 THEN PSET (XS,YS): FLAG=1 : GOTO 460
450 LINE - (XS,YS)
460 RETURN
```

PROGRAM 4.2 Plot of 3-D functions

4.7 SUMMARY

The techniques we developed in this chapter for expressing 3-D object transformations are extensions of the 2-D techniques presented in Chapter 3. Two important aspects of the 2-D transformation are retained: (1) a transformation is expressed as a single 4×4 matrix, and (2) complex transformations can be combined to yield a single matrix that has the same effect as the sequence of individual transformations.

We introduced the perspective projections to create the 2-D screen image that simulates a real 3-D object. A viewing transformation (from the world coordinate system to the eye coordinate system) is the first step in the perspective transformation. After the viewing transformation is completed, points and lines outside the field of vision must be excluded. The viewing pyramid has an opening angle of approximately 60°. This defines a window on the picture plane. The boundary of this window usually coincides with the edges of the

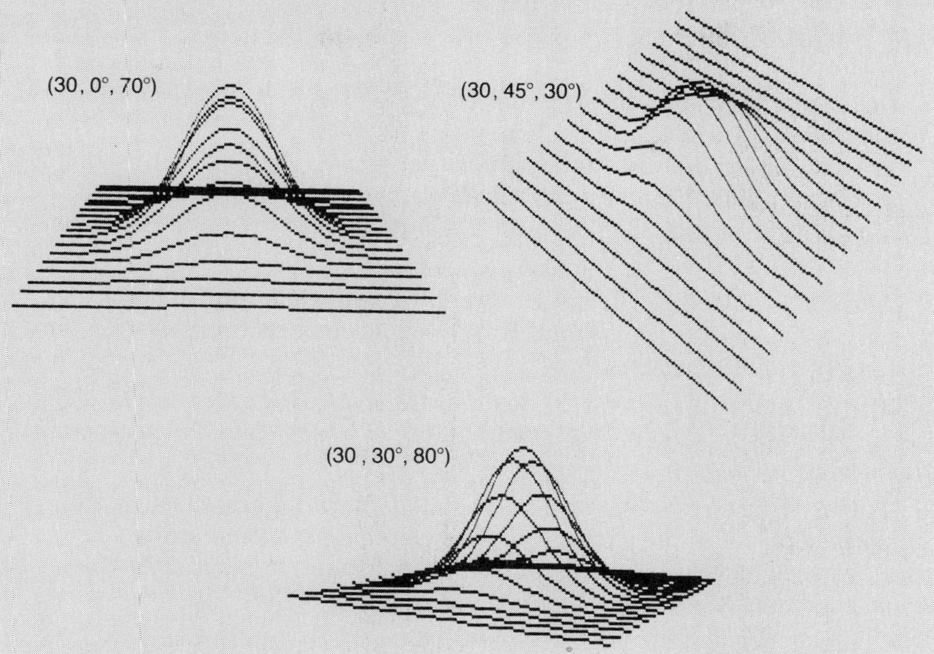

FIGURE 4.17 Three-dimensional surfaces at various viewing angles

display device, such as the CRT screen. All portions of the image outside this window are mathematically clipped and removed from the scene.

We finally introduced the homogeneous screen coordinate system to calculate the screen positions of the projected 3-D images. This sequence of operations forms the basis for the perspective transformation and can be combined into a single matrix multiplication that includes viewing transformation, clipping, and perspective division. Many graphic display devices have now implemented this matrix multiplication in the hardware.

EXERCISES

4.1 We observed in Chapter 3 that two successive 2-D rotations are additive: $R(\theta_1) \cdot R(\theta_2) = R(\theta_1 + \theta_2)$. Can you say the same for two successive 3-D rotations?

4.2 Program 3-D clipping algorithms for
a) parallel projection,
b) perspective projection.

4.3 You are given a line in 3-D going from $P_1(-5, 4, 2)$ to $P_2(5, -6, 18)$ $S = d$, $K_1 = 0$, $K_2 = 10$, and $(D, \theta, \phi) = (10, 30°, 60°)$.
a) Clip the line in 3-D using parametric Eq. (4.44), then project it onto the projection plane. Find the clipped endpoints on the plane.
b) Can we first project the line onto a 2-D plane and then clip it against a 2-D window?

4.4 Develop a routine similar to Program 3.1 that generates a 4×4 transformation matrix from an arbitrary sequence of scaling, rotation, and translation transformations.

4.5 Can you calculate a point (x_e, y_e, z_e) in the eye coordinate system if the screen coordinates (x_s, y_s, z_s) are given? In other words, does the perspective transformation have an inverse?

4.6 Can we transform a 3-D object so that the parallel projection of the transformed object is the same as the perspective projection of the untransformed object? If so, develop the transformation matrix for this viewing operation.

4.7 A cube is defined by eight vertices: $A(0, 0, 0)$, $B(1, 0, 0)$, $C(1, 1, 0)$, $E(0, 0, 1)$, $F(1, 0, 1)$, $G(1, 1, 1)$ and $H(0, 1, 1)$.
a) Find the cube's parallel projection after it is rotated by 60° about the diagonal axis joining the points $(0, 0, 0)$ and $(1, 1, 1)$.
b) Repeat the question in (a) for the cube's perspective projection, assuming that $S = d$ and $(D, \theta, \phi) = (10, 60°, 30°)$.

4.8 Write a program to plot each of the objects in Figs. 4.18–4.23. Their coordinates are defined in the rectangular coordinate system.
a) Elliptic cone with axis as z axis (Fig. 4.18):

$$\frac{x^2}{a^2} + \frac{y^2}{b^2} = \frac{z^2}{c^2}.$$

b) Hyperboloid of one sheet (Fig. 4.19):

$$\frac{x^2}{a^2} + \frac{y^2}{b^2} - \frac{z^2}{c^2} = 1.$$

c) Elliptic paraboloid (Fig. 4.20):

$$\frac{x^2}{a^2} + \frac{y^2}{b^2} = \frac{z}{c}.$$

d) Hyperbolic paraboloid (Fig. 4.21; note orientation of axes):

$$\frac{x^2}{a^2} - \frac{y^2}{b^2} = \frac{z}{c}.$$

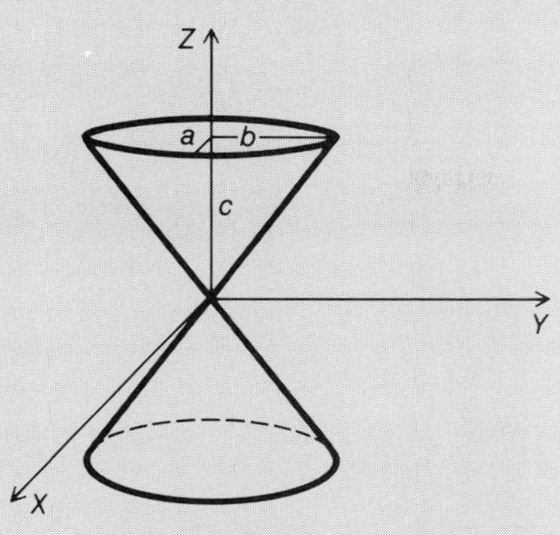

FIGURE 4.18

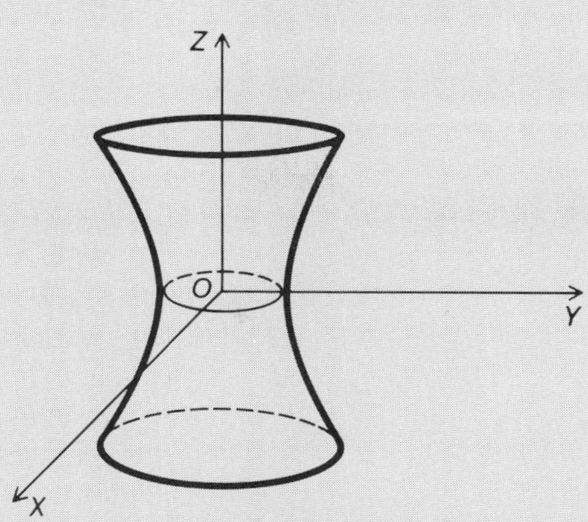

FIGURE 4.19

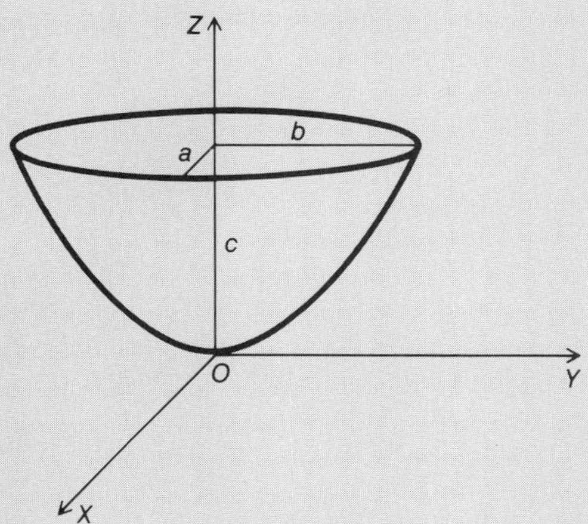

FIGURE 4.20

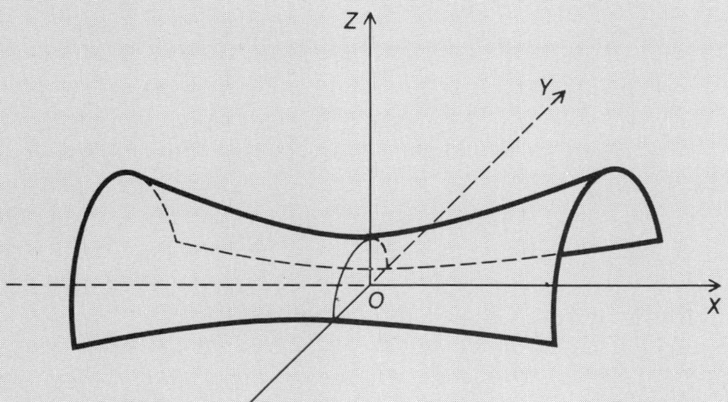

FIGURE 4.21

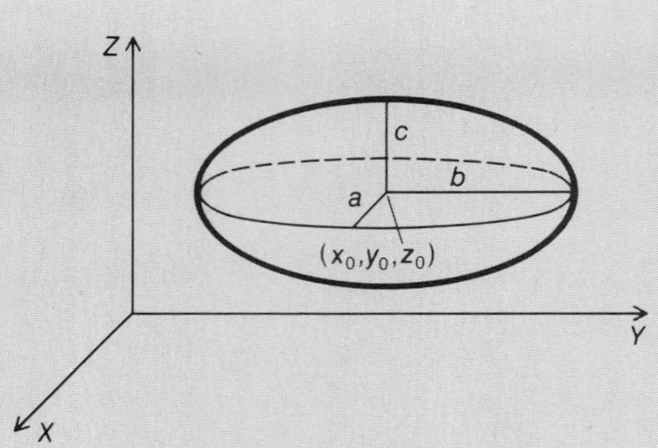

FIGURE 4.22

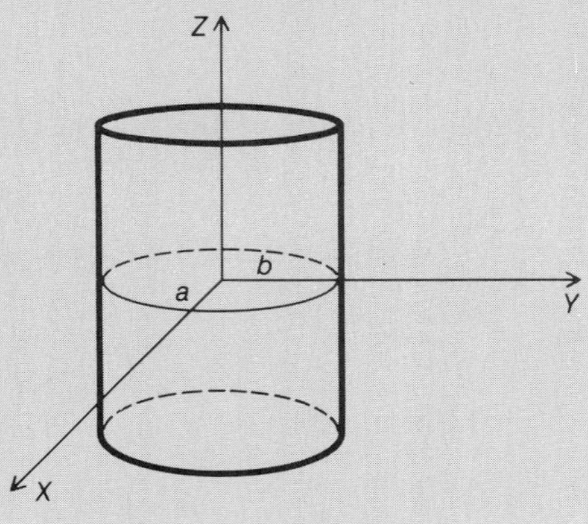

FIGURE 4.23

e) Equation of ellipsoid with center (x_0, y_0, z_0) and semi-axes a, b, and c (Fig. 4.22):

$$\frac{(x - x_0)^2}{a^2} + \frac{(y - y_0)^2}{b^2} + \frac{(z - z_0)^2}{c^2} = 1 .$$

f) Elliptic cylinder with axis as z axis (Fig. 4.23):

$$\frac{x^2}{a^2} + \frac{y^2}{b^2} = 1$$

where a and b are semi-axes of the elliptic cross section. If $b = a$, it becomes a circular cylinder of radius a.

4.9 The sphere shown in Fig. 4.24 has the following equation in rectangular coordinates:

$$(x - x_0)^2 + (y - y_0)^2 + (z - z_0)^2 = R^2$$

where the sphere has center (x_0, y_0, z_0) and radius R. With this equation in mind, write a program that draws a sphere such as that shown in Fig. 4.25.

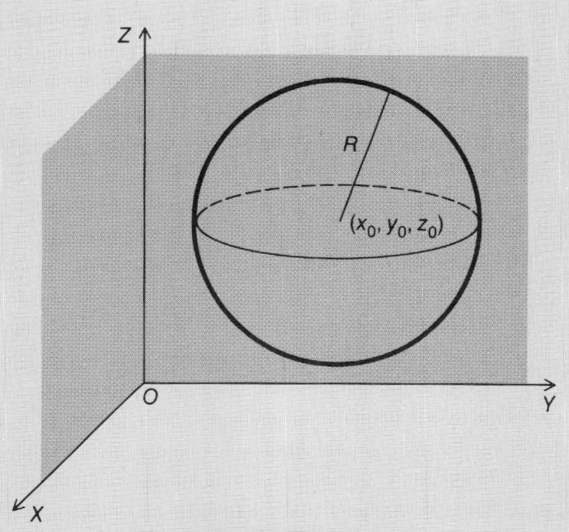

FIGURE 4.24

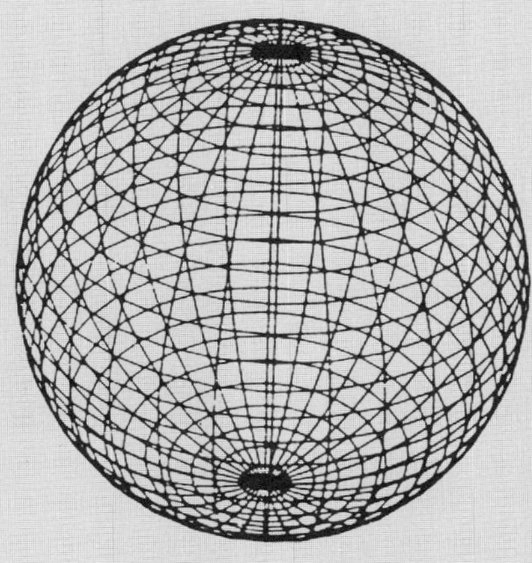

FIGURE 4.25

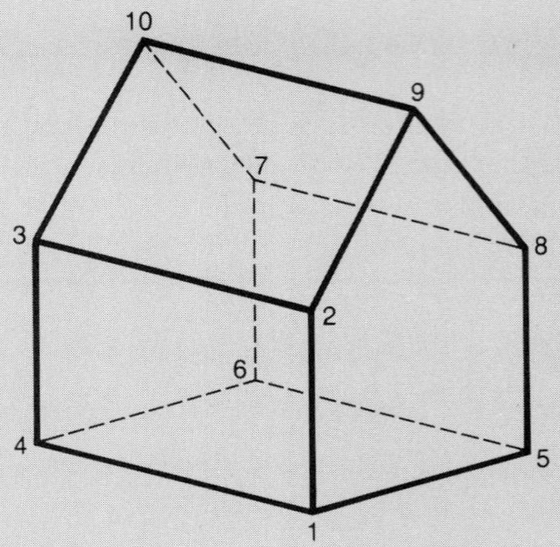

Vertex	Coordinates		
1	5	7	−5
2	5	7	5
3	5	−7	5
4	5	−7	−5
5	−5	7	−5
6	−5	−7	−5
7	−5	−7	5
8	−5	7	5
9	0	7	8
10	0	−7	8

FIGURE 4.26

4.10 Write a program to plot the following functions:

a) $z = 3\cos[0.05(x^2 - y^2)]$

b) $z = 3\cos[0.05(x^2 + y^2)]$

4.11 Write a program to draw the house shown in Fig. 4.26. The data are adapted from Roy E. Myers, *Microcomputer Graphics for the Apple® Computer,* © 1982, Addison-Wesley Pub. Co. Inc., Reading, Mass. Reprinted with permission.

a) Plot the perspective view of the house at $(40, 0°, 0°)$ $(40, 45°, 60°)$, and $(40, 130°, 45°)$, respectively.

b) What would happen if we specify a view angle ϕ greater than 90° [for example, $(40, 30°, 150°)$]?

c) Now scale the Z axis by 2 and repeat the question (a).

REFERENCES

1. Anton, H., *Elementary Linear Algebra* (3rd ed.), Wiley, New York, 1981.

2. Ahuja, D. V., "Geometry for Construction and Display," *The IBM Systems Journal,* **7** (3), 1968.

3. Blinn, J. F., "A Homogeneous Formulation for Lines in 3-Space," *Computer Graphics,* **11** (2), 192–198, 1977.

4. Blinn, J. F., and M. E. Newell, "Clipping Using Homogeneous Coordinates," *Computer Graphics,* **12** (3), 245–251, August 1978.

5. Curlbom, I., and J. Paciorek, "Geometric Projection and Viewing Transformation," *Computer Surveys,* **1** (4), 465–502, 1978.

6. Foley, J. D., and A. Van Dam, *Fundamentals of Interactive Computer Graphics,* Addison-Wesley, Reading, Mass., 1982.

7. Grotch, S. L., "Three-Dimensional and Stereoscopic Graphics for Scientific Data Display and Analysis," *IEEE Computer Graphics and Applications,* **3** (8) 31–43, November 1983.

8. Myers, R. E., *Microcomputer Graphics for the Apple® Computer,* Addison-Wesley, Reading, Mass., 1982.

9. Newman, W. M., and R. F. Sproull, *Principles of Interactive Computer Graphics,* McGraw-Hill, New York, 1979.

10. Rogers, D. F., and J. A. Adams, *Mathematical Elements for Computer Graphics,* McGraw-Hill, New York, 1976.

11. Rosenfield, R. F., "Homogeneous Coordinates and Projective Planes in Computer Graphics," *IEEE Computer Graphics and Applications,* **1** (1) 50–55, January 1981.

12. Verdina, J., *Projective Geometry and Point Transformations,* Allyn and Bacon, Boston, 1971.

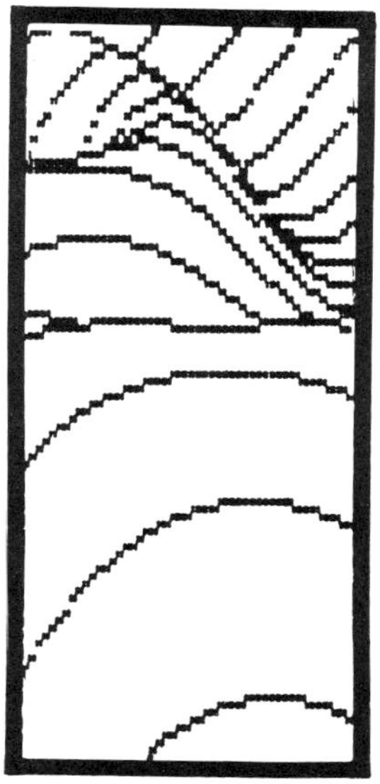

CHAPTER FIVE

Hidden Line and Surface Removals

Creating realistic images of 3-D objects often requires removal of hidden lines or surfaces. To do this, we must develop methods for identifying those surfaces and line segments that are visible or partly visible and those that are invisible. Then we display the visible portions of the object and eliminate the portions that are hidden from our view. Comprehensive development of such hidden line (or surface) removal algorithms requires large amounts of computer time and memory. These are limiting factors on most microcomputers. A general-purpose hidden line algorithm would be very inefficient. In general, it is much more effective for the programmer to adapt the techniques to each specific application. For this reason, we will limit our discussion to some basic, but useful, algorithms implemented on a microcomputer.

Before introducing the theory of operation, we will give two important practical assumptions. The first assumption is that if an object has *contour* faces, we will use line segments to approximate them by polygons. This is because the primary graphical primitive is the line segment. The second assumption is that all polygon faces are *flat*. This means that the vertices of the bounding polygon all lie on the same plane. This property will facilitate the comparison of the geometrical relationships among the polygons.

5.1 THE VISIBILITY OF SINGLE CONVEX OBJECT

If we deal with only one object, and that object is convex, we can solve the visibility problem by examining the directions of the *normals* to the faces of the object. Here the *face normal* is defined as a vector perpendicular to the plane of the face. A convex object is defined as one in which the line segments joining any pair of points in the object are wholly contained in the object (e.g., cube, sphere, pyramid, and so forth). Similarly, a convex polygon is one in which the line segments joining any pair of points in the polygon are wholly contained in the polygon (e.g., rectangle, triangle, circle, hexagon, and so forth).

5.1.1 APPROACH TO THE VISIBILITY PROBLEM

Consider a solid object such as a cube. (See Fig. 5.1a.) The cube has eight vertices, twelve edges, and six faces. Each face is a flat surface with a polygonal boundary. As we look at the cube from the viewpoint P, only two or three of the faces are visible to us. The others face away from us. To avoid drawing the hidden lines and surfaces of the cube, we need a visibility test to distinguish the visible lines from the hidden lines.

In developing the visibility test, we introduce two orientation vectors associated with each surface, the surface-normal vector and the line-of-sight vector. They will be denoted by boldface lowercase letters. We define a surface-normal vector $\mathbf{n}$ as an outward-pointing vector, normal (i.e., perpendicular) to the surface. A line-of-sight vector $\boldsymbol{\ell}$ represents the line passing through the viewpoint and the start point of the surface-normal vector. (See Fig. 5.2.) We will

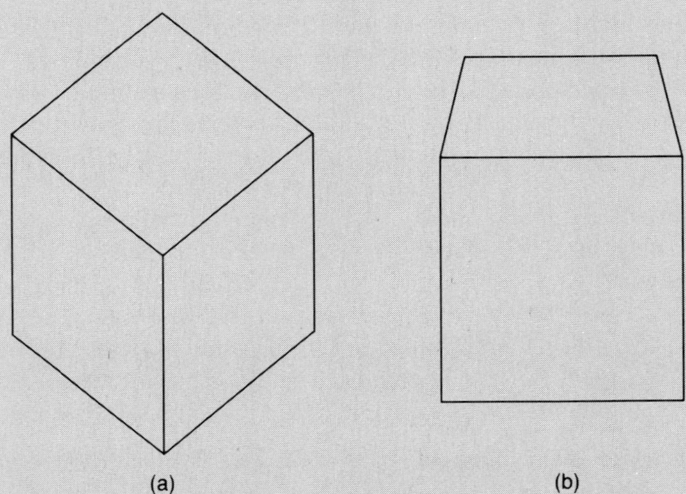

FIGURE 5.1 Number of visible surfaces of a cube: (a) has three sides visible and (b) has only two sides visible.

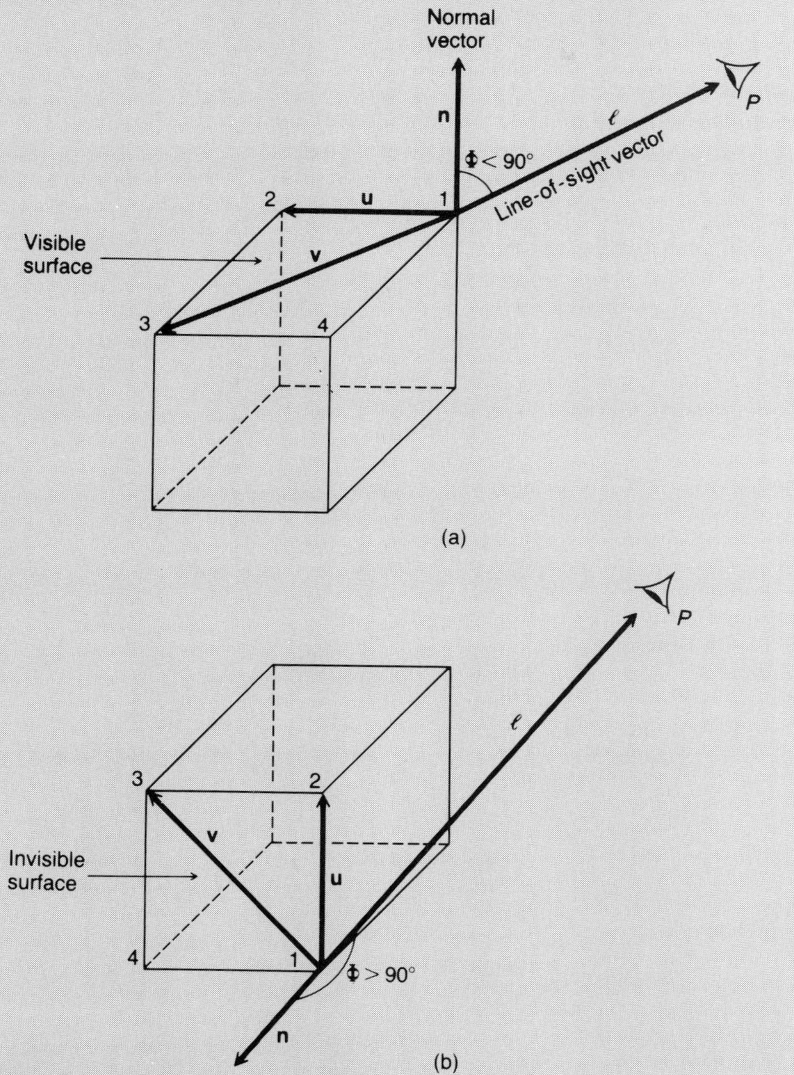

FIGURE 5.2 Normal and line of sight vectors that define the visibility

calculate the angle Φ between **n** and ℓ. If this angle is between 0° and 90°, the surface is visible and should be displayed. If it is greater than 90°, the surface is facing away from the viewer; it is invisible and should not be displayed. In the pages ahead, we will show how to compute the normal vectors and the angles between the orientation vectors.

Surface-normal vector. To compute the normal vector associated with a surface, we need to number the vertices of each surface of the cube in a *counterclockwise* direction. For a given surface, the starting vertex is arbitrary, but it is important that the remaining vertices of the surface be numbered in a counterclockwise direction, as viewed from outside the cube, facing the surface. (See Fig. 5.2.) After numbering the vertices, the next step is to identify vector **u**, directed from vertex number 1 to vertex number 2, and vector **v**, directed from vertex number 1 to vertex number 3. The cross product, $\mathbf{u} \times \mathbf{v}$, will be normal to the surface and directed outward. (If the points are assigned in a *clockwise* direction, the vector $\mathbf{n} = \mathbf{u} \times \mathbf{v}$ will point *inward*). In linear algebra, the cross product of two vectors is defined

$$\begin{aligned} \mathbf{n} &= \mathbf{u} \times \mathbf{v} \\ &= (bf - ce, cd - af, ae - bd) \end{aligned} \tag{5.1}$$

where

$$\mathbf{u} = (a, b, c), \quad \text{and} \quad \mathbf{v} = (d, e, f).$$

Suppose we identify the vertices of the front surface of a cube shown in Fig. 5.3 as follows:

Vertex number	Coordinates (**x**, *y*, *z*)
1	(1, 1, −1)
2	(1, 1, 1)
3	(1, −1, 1)
4	(1, −1, −1)

Since

$$\mathbf{u} = (1, 1, 1) - (1, 1, -1) = (0, 0, 2),$$

$$\mathbf{v} = (1, -1, 1) - (1, 1, -1) = (0, -2, 2),$$

the normal vector is

$$\mathbf{n} = \mathbf{u} \times \mathbf{v} = (4, 0, 0).$$

Line-of-sight vector. We compute a line-of-sight vector by extending a line from the viewpoint $P\ (D, \theta, \phi)$ to any point on the object's surface. For convenience, we normally choose the starting point of the surface-normal vector (vertex 1 in Fig. 5.3). Using Eq. (4.1), we identify the viewpoint in terms of its

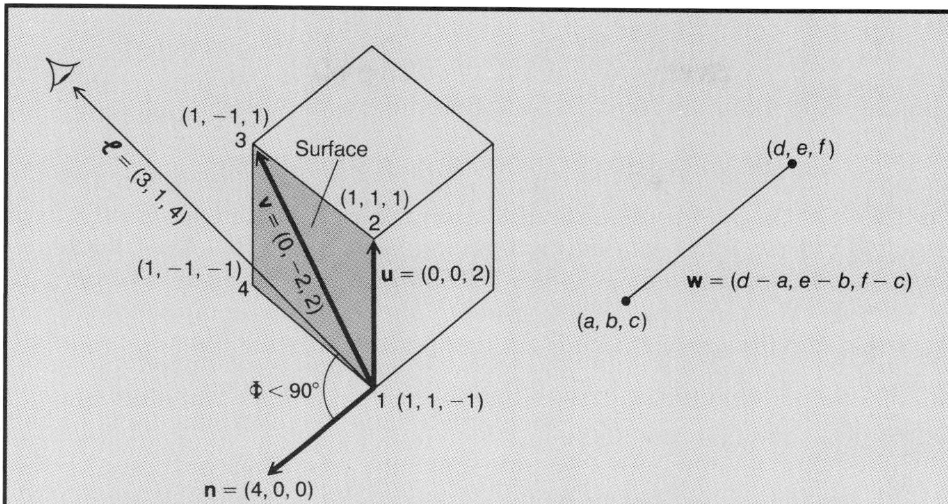

FIGURE 5.3 Visibility test applied to the first surface of the cube

spherical coordinates. Then ℓ is:

$$\ell = (D \sin \phi \cos \theta, D \sin \phi \sin \theta, D \cdot \cos \phi) - (x_1, y_1, z_1) \tag{5.2}$$

where (x_1, y_1, z_1) are the coordinates for vertex 1.

Assuming a viewpoint at $(5.4, 27°, 56°) = (4, 2, 3)$, we compute $\ell = (4, 2, 3) - (1, 1, -1) = (3, 1, 4)$.

Visibility test. We define the dot product of vectors **n** and ℓ as

$$\mathbf{n} \cdot \ell = (n_1, n_2, n_3) \cdot (\ell_1, \ell_2, \ell_3) = n_1\ell_1 + n_2\ell_2 + n_3\ell_3 \tag{5.3}$$

From linear algebra, we know that the dot product in Eq. (5.3) also has the property

$$\begin{aligned} \mathbf{n} \cdot \ell &= |\mathbf{n}| \cdot |\ell| \cdot \cos \Phi \\ \Phi &= \arccos\left(\frac{\mathbf{n} \cdot \ell}{|\mathbf{n}|\,|\ell|}\right), \end{aligned} \tag{5.4}$$

where

$$|\mathbf{n}| = \text{length of } \mathbf{n},$$

$$|\ell| = \text{length of } \ell,$$

$$\Phi = \text{angle between } \mathbf{n} \text{ and } \ell.$$

For a visible surface, Φ will be between 0° and 90° and $\mathbf{n} \cdot \ell > 0$. For a hidden surface, Φ will be between 90° and 180° and $\mathbf{n} \cdot \ell < 0$. Thus in our previous example the dot product yields

$$\mathbf{n} \cdot \ell = (4,0,0) \cdot (3,1,4) = 12 > 0.$$

Since $\mathbf{n} \cdot \ell > 0$, the surface will be visible from a viewpoint at $(4,2,3)$.

5.1.2 DEVELOPMENT OF COMPUTER PROGRAM

To illustrate the use of surface orientation in eliminating hidden lines, we will discuss Program 5.1, which draws the cube shown in Fig. 5.3. The cube has six surfaces: top, bottom, and four sides. The 12 edges are defined by 8 vertices. We will present the program in six segments. (The complete listing of the program begins at the bottom of this page.)

Segment 1: vertex array. We first identify the eight vertices of the cube in terms of their rectangular coordinates, numbering them as shown in Fig. 5.4(a):

Vertex number	Coordinates x, y, z
1	(1, 1, −1)
2	(1, 1, 1)
3	(1, −1, 1)
4	(1, −1, −1)
5	(−1, 1, −1)
6	(−1, −1, −1)
7	(−1, −1, 1)
8	(−1, 1, 1)

```
10 ' Program 5.1 : Single Object with Hidden Lines Removed
20 CLS : KEY OFF : SCREEN 2
30      GOSUB 110
40      GOSUB 180
50      GOSUB 410
60      GOSUB 540
70      GOSUB 660
80      GOSUB 770
90      GOSUB 940
100 END
110 REM : DEFINE VIEWING PARAMETERS
120     D=5.4: VD=200 : THETA=27 : PHI=56 : TX= 320: TY=100
130     PI=3.141593   : SCF=2.4
140     THETA=THETA*PI/180 : PHI=PHI*PI/180  : S= 2
150     SN1=SIN(THETA) : SN2=SIN(PHI) :CN1=COS(THETA) :CN2=COS(PHI)
160     NV=8 : K1=7: K2=10: W=K2/(K2-K1)
170 RETURN
180 REM : VERTEX ARRAY
190     DIM V(8,3), EC(8,3), SC(8,3)
200     FOR J=1 TO NV
210         READ X,Y,Z
220         V(J,1)=X: V(J,2)=Y: V(J,3)=Z
230         GOSUB 310
240         EC(J,1)=XE: EC(J,2)=YE: EC(J,3)=ZE
250         GOSUB 360
```

PROGRAM 5.1 Single Object with Hidden Lines Removed

```
260             SC(J,1)= XS   : SC(J,2)= YS   : SC(J,3)=ZS
270       NEXT J
280 RETURN
290         DATA 1,1,-1, 1,1,1, 1,-1,1, 1,-1,-1
300         DATA -1,1,-1, -1,-1,-1, -1,-1,1, -1,1,1
310 REM : EYE COORDINATES
320         XE= -X*SN1 + Y*CN1
330         YE= -X*CN1*CN2 - Y*SN1*CN2 + Z*SN2
340         ZE= -X*SN2*CN1 - Y*SN2*SN1 - Z*CN2 + D
350 RETURN
360 REM : SCREEN COORDINATES
370         XS=(VD/S)*(XE/ZE)
380         YS=(VD/S)*(YE/ZE)
390         ZS=W*(1- K1/ZE)
400 RETURN
410 REM : SURFACE ARRAY
420 DIM SF(6,5),NPS(6)
430 NS=6
440 FOR I=1 TO NS: READ NPS(I): NEXT I
450       FOR J=1 TO NS
460             FOR K=1 TO NPS(J)
470                   READ SF(J,K)
480             NEXT K
490       NEXT J
500 RETURN
510 DATA 5,5,5,5,5,5
520 DATA 1,2,3,4,1, 1,5,8,2,1, 5,6,7,8,5, 4,3,7,6,4
530 DATA 2,8,7,3,2, 1,4,6,5,1
540 REM : NORMAL ARRAY
550 DIM N(6,3),U(3),W(3)
560       FOR J=1 TO NS
570             FOR K=1 TO 3
580                   U(K)= V(SF(J,2),K) - V(SF(J,1),K)
590                   W(K)= V(SF(J,3),K) - V(SF(J,1),K)
600             NEXT K
610             N(J,1)= U(2)*W(3) - W(2)*U(3)
620             N(J,2)= U(3)*W(1) - W(3)*U(1)
630             N(J,3)= U(1)*W(2) - W(1)*U(2)
640       NEXT J
650 RETURN
660 REM : VISIBILITY TEST
670 DIM VSF(6)
680 XP= D*SN2*CN1 : YP= D*SN2*SN1 : ZP= D*CN2
690       FOR J=1 TO NS
700             LX=XP - V(SF(J,1),1)
710             LY=YP - V(SF(J,1),2)
720             LZ=ZP - V(SF(J,1),3)
730             T= N(J,1)*LX + N(J,2)*LY + N(J,3)*LZ
740             IF T <= 0 THEN VSF(J)=0 ELSE VSF(J)=1
750       NEXT J
760 RETURN
770 REM: VISIBLE EDGE ARRAY
780       M=1
790       FOR J=1 TO NS
800             IF VSF(J)=0 THEN  920
810             E1= SF(J,1)
820             FOR K=2 TO NPS(J)
830                   E2=SF(J,K)
840                   FOR L=1 TO M
850                         IF E(L,1)=E2 AND E(L,2)=E1 THEN E(L,3)=2: E(L,4)=J:
                            GOTO 890
860                   NEXT L
870                   E(M,1)=E1: E(M,2)=E2: E(M,3)=1: E(M,4)=J
880                   M=M+1
890                   E1=E2
900             NEXT K
910             NVE=M-1
920       NEXT J
930 RETURN
940 REM : PLOT
950       FOR J=1 TO NVE
960         IF E(J,3)=0 THEN 1010
970         F1=E(J,1): F2=E(J,2)
980         A=SC(F1,1):B=SC(F1,2): C=SC(F2,1):D=SC(F2,2)
990         A=SCF*A+TX : B=TY-B : C=SCF*C+TX : D=TY-D
1000        LINE (A,B) - (C,D)
1010      NEXT J
1020 RETURN
```

PROGRAM 5.1 (continued)

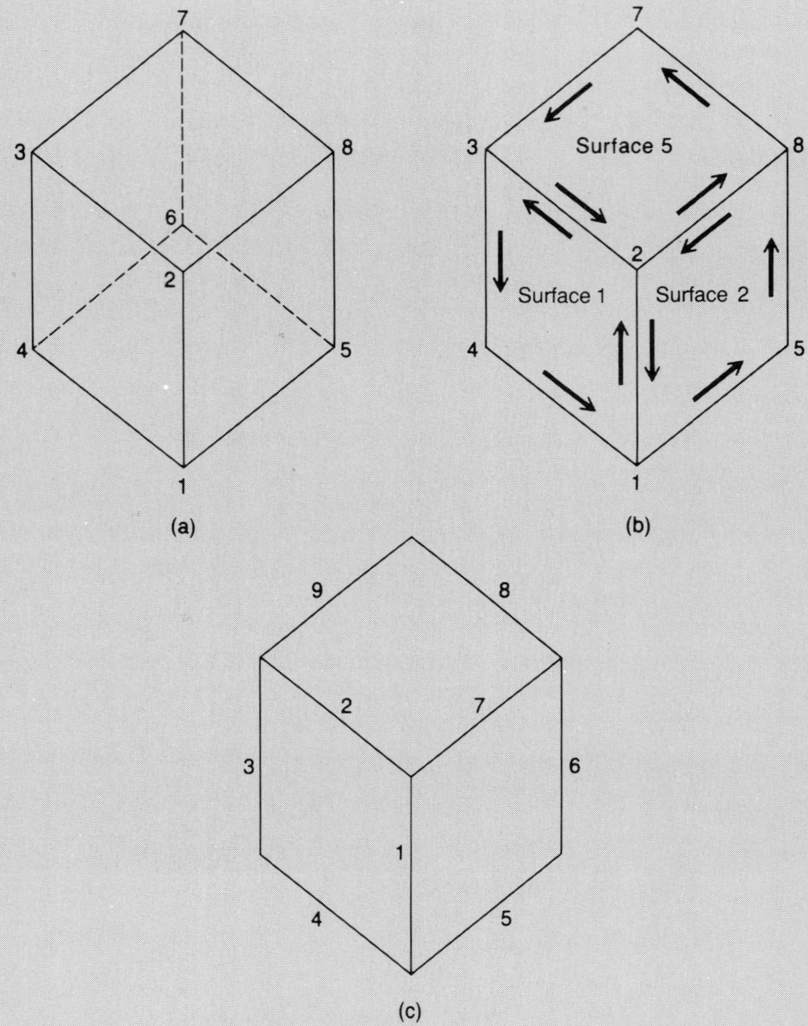

FIGURE 5.4 Definition of (a) vertices, (b) surfaces, and (c) edges for the cube

We introduce a two-dimensional array $V(I,J)$, where I is the vertex number $(1 \sim 8)$ and J is the coordinate identified $(1 \sim 3)$. For example, $V(1,1)$ is the X-coordinate of vertex 1, $V(1,2)$ the Y-coordinate of vertex 1, and $V(1,3)$ the Z-coordinate of vertex 1.

Program segment 1 defines the various viewing parameters and loads the vertex coordinates into a two-dimensional vertex array. As the coordinates of the vertices are read, the screen coordinates of each point are calculated. For each I, $SC(I,1)$ and $SC(I,2)$ are the screen coordinates x_s and y_s for vertex I.

Segment 2: surface array. As shown in Fig. 5.4(b), there are six surfaces in the cube. We identify these surfaces by vertex number. Since we draw each surface by connecting the appropriate vertices, we introduce array $SF(I,J)$ to identify surface I and the vertices (J) that define the surface. For example, for surface 1, we connect vertex 1 to 2 to 3 to 4 to 1 and save these numbers as $SF(1,1) = 1$, $SF(1,2) = 2$, $SF(1,3) = 3$, $SF(1,4) = 4$ and $SF(1,5) = 1$ respectively. For surface 2, we connect vertex 1 to 5 to 8 to 2 to 1. The other surfaces are defined in a similar manner. The complete array is shown in Table 5.1. In filling the $SF(I,J)$ array for each surface, the vertices must be identified *counterclockwise* as they appear from *outside* the cube. Saving vertices in this manner will ensure that the normal vectors are directed outward. Program segment 2 basically assigns vertices into the $SF(I,J)$ array for each surface.

Segment 3: normal vector array. Having saved the coordinates of all the vertices and identified the surfaces defined by them, we can easily compute the normal vector associated with each surface. As shown in Eq. (5.1), the calculation is based on the fact that the cross product of two vectors is normal to the plane containing the two vectors.

Each surface has four vertices in the cube. We find **u** by extending a line from the first to the second of these vertices, and **v**, by extending a line from the first to the third vertex. We use Eq. (5.1) to compute the cross product **u** × **v**. We then save the coordinates of the normal vectors **n** in the normal

TABLE 5.1 Surface array

I (Surface)	*J* (Points to be connected)				
	1	2	3	4	5
1	1	2	3	4	1
2	1	5	8	2	1
3	5	6	7	8	5
4	4	3	7	6	4
5	2	8	7	3	2
6	1	4	6	5	1

TABLE 5.2 Normal array $N(I, J)$

I (Surface)	*J*		
	1 (x)	2 (y)	3 (z)
1	4	0	0
2	0	4	0
3	−4	0	0
4	0	−4	0
5	0	0	4
6	0	0	−4

array $N(I,J)$. $N(I,1)$, $N(I,2)$, and $N(I,3)$ are the X, Y, and Z components of the normal vector to surface I. The complete array is shown in Table 5.2.

Segment 4: line-of-sight vector. For each surface, we choose a line-of-sight vector ℓ from the starting vertex on the surface normal to the viewpoint (x_e, y_e, z_e). We introduce variables LX, LY, and LZ to compute the ℓ vector coordinates, and define $\ell = (LX, LY, LZ)$. The complete arrays are shown in Table 5.3.

Segment 5: the visibility test. We are now ready to apply the visibility test to each surface of the cube. We compute the dot product of $\mathbf{n} \cdot \ell$ for each surface. This should look like Table 5.4.

Segment 6: edge array. As seen in segment 5, only three surfaces are visible, and each visible surface is defined by four edges. As seen in Fig. 5.4(c), however, edges such as 3, 4, 5, 6, 8, and 9 are each a boundary of one visible surface. Therefore, we need only nine edges to define the three visible surfaces, even though each individual cube surface needs four edges.

We will introduce the edge array $E(I,J)$. For each edge I, we will save four numbers: First, we save the identification numbers of the two endpoints (vertices) of edge I in $E(I,1)$ and $E(I,2)$. Second, we identify the number of visible surfaces for which edge I is a boundary. This number is put in the array $E(I,3)$. If the edge is a boundary of two visible surfaces, then the value of $E(I,3)$ is 2. Third, we identify the surface number to which the edge belongs, and store the information in $E(I,4)$. If the edge belongs to more than one surface, the first surface encountered will be saved. With the edges labeled as in Fig. 5.4(c), the complete edge array looks like Table 5.5. No view of the cube will show more than 9 edges, even though the cube is defined by 12 edges.

TABLE 5.3 Calculation of line-of-sight vector array

	J			Eye coordinate	–	First vertex
Surface, *I*	1(x)	2(y)	3(z)	(x_e, y_e, z_e)	–	(x_1, y_1, z_1)
1	3	1	4	(4, 2, 3)	–	(1, 1, −1)
2	3	1	4	(4, 2, 3)	–	(1, 1, −1)
3	5	1	4	(4, 2, 3)	–	(−1, 1, −1)
4	3	3	4	(4, 2, 3)	–	(1, −1, −1)
5	3	2	2	(4, 2, 3)	–	(1, 1, 1)
6	3	1	4	(4, 2, 3)	–	(1, 1, −1)

TABLE 5.4 Visibility test results

Surface, *I*	***N*(*I*, *J*)**	***L***	***N*(*I*, *J*) · *L***	**Visibility**
1	(4, 0, 0)	(3, 1, 4)	12	Visible
2	(0, 4, 0)	(3, 1, 4)	4	Visible
3	(−4, 0, 0)	(5, 1, 4)	−20	Invisible
4	(0, −4, 0)	(3, 3, 4)	−12	Invisible
5	(0, 0, 4)	(3, 2, 2)	8	Visible
6	(0, 0, −4)	(3, 1, 4)	−16	Invisible

TABLE 5.5 Edge array *E* (*I*, *J*)

Surface, *I*	***J***			
	1	2	3	4
1	1	2	2	1
2	2	3	2	1
3	3	4	1	1
4	4	1	1	1
5	1	5	1	2
6	5	8	1	2
7	8	2	2	5
8	8	7	1	5
9	7	3	1	5

Note: $J = 1$ and 2 are endpoints;
$J = 3$ is the edge type;
$J = 4$ is the surface.

Further, we observe that the *outer* edges of the cube (edges 3, 4, 5, 6, 8, and 9) all have $E(I,3) = 1$. On the other hand, the *inner* edges of the cube (1, 2, 7) all have $E(I,3) = 2$. The distinction between inner and outer edges is not necessary when we are drawing a single object. This distinction becomes important, however, when we draw more than one object (see Section 5.2).

Program segment 6 basically fills the edge array. The endpoints of each edge are read from the surface array and saved in the edge array, and a flag is set to 1. If an edge is encountered for a second time, the flag is reset to 2.

Segment 7: plotting the object. We are now ready to plot the visible edges. Program segment 7 identifies the visible edges, reads the endpoints associated with the visible edges, and finally plots the edges. Now we can obtain a variety of views of the cube by varying the viewpoint parameters, as demonstrated in Fig. 5.5.

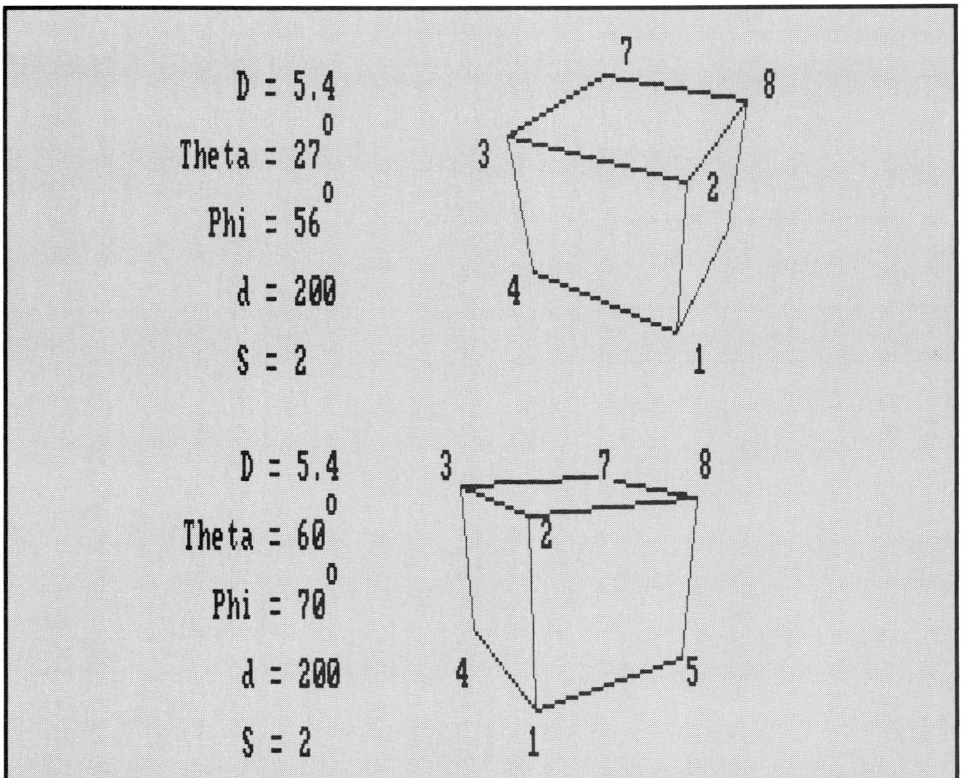

FIGURE 5.5 Two different views of the cube with hidden lines removed

5.2 THE VISIBILITY OF SEVERAL OBJECTS

The surface orientation described in the previous section permits one to draw the visible portions of a single convex object. In this section, we will present algorithms for drawing several objects with hidden lines removed. When more than one object is drawn, it is necessary to identify those portions that are hidden by a closer object, in addition to determining the visible portions of individual objects.

Algorithms for removing hidden parts from images of several objects operate either in *object space* or *image space*. An object space algorithm uses the geometrical relationships among the objects in the scene to determine the hidden parts. An image space algorithm, on the other hand, operates on the final 2-D image to determine what is visible within each raster pixel. This method is designed to operate on a raster-scan graphical device. We will discuss image space algorithms in Section 5.5.

The two approaches used separately generally lead to algorithms with different performance characteristics and hardware requirements. Object space methods are used primarily in hidden line algorithms, whereas image space methods are used in hidden surface algorithms.

The algorithm to be developed in this section, however, operates partly in the object space and partly in the image space. The algorithm uses the object space to determine the hidden parts of individual objects, but uses the image space to identify the geometrical relationships among the visible objects. This combined approach gives more satisfactory results on a microcomputer.

5.2.1 GEOMETRIC COMPUTATIONS

The surface orientation introduced in Section 5.1 is the basis for the hidden line removal technique developed in this section. The geometric method for hidden line removal consists of three major steps.

Step 1: We apply the *visibility test* to each solid object to identify the hidden surfaces of the object.

Step 2: We apply a series of relationship tests to determine the geometric relationships among the potentially visible faces of all the objects in the scene. There are three possibilities for each pair of polygons: two polygons that intersect, one polygon that completely surrounds another, and two polygons that do not overlap at all. The first relationship test is a prescreening test, referred to as the *minimax* test. The purpose of this test is to detect pairs of polygons that cannot possibly overlap.

Step 3: If the minimax test indicates a possible (but not proven) overlap, we test the two polygons further to determine if their polygon edges intersect or if one is completely surrounded by the other. The *intersection test* is done first. This checks each line segment that is an edge

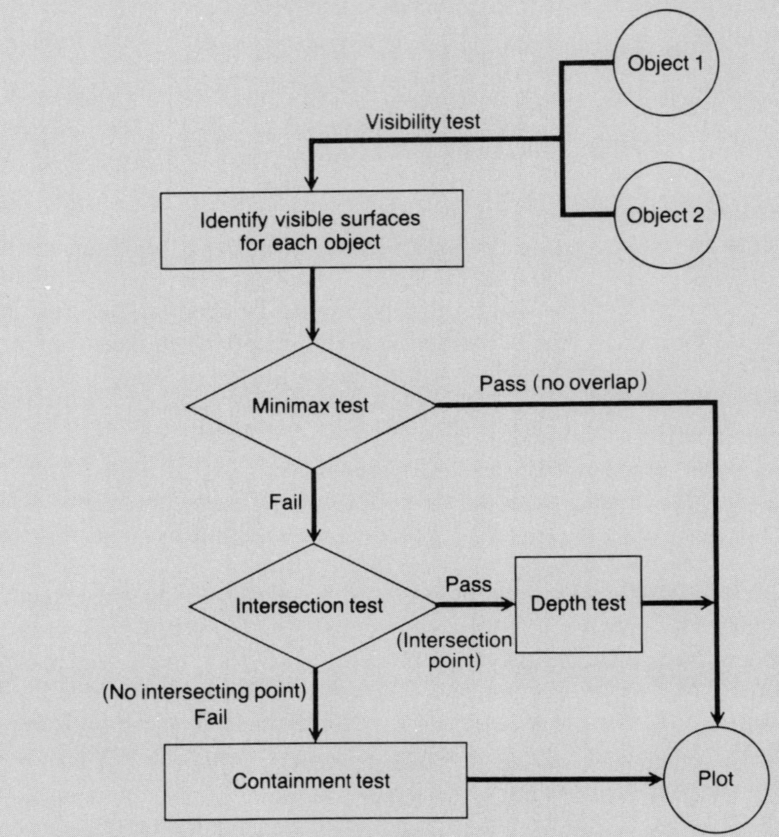

FIGURE 5.6 Logical sequence of tests used in hidden line elimination

of one polygon to see if it intersects the line segments that are edges of the other polygon. Having identified the pair of overlapping polygons, we then apply a *depth test* (or priority test) to determine which polygon is visible and which is hidden from a particular point of view. If there is no intersection between two polygons, we have two possibilities: either one polygon completely surrounds the other, or they do not overlap at all. To test if one polygon surrounds the other, we use the *containment test.* If the test indicates that one polygon is surrounded by the other, the surrounded polygon will not be visible.

It is important to note that the visibility test is performed in the object space, whereas both the relationship and depth tests are performed in the image space. Figure 5.6 summarizes the logical sequence of tests involved in developing the hidden line elimination algorithm. In the pages ahead, we will discuss the procedures involved in each test in more detail. Since we already discussed the visibility test in Section 5.1, we will begin with the minimax test.

5.2.2 MINIMAX TEST

Consider two closed polygons A and B in the image plane, which will be projections of two surfaces of 3-D objects. (See Fig. 5.7). For each polygon, we find the maximum and minimum values of the X-coordinate and the maximum and minimum values of the Y-coordinate, respectively. These maximum and minimum coordinate values are then compared. If at least one of the following statements is true, then polygons A and B cannot possibly overlap:

$$\begin{aligned} \max x_A &< \min x_B, \\ \max x_B &< \min x_A, \\ \max y_A &< \min y_B, \\ \max y_B &< \min y_A, \end{aligned} \tag{5.5}$$

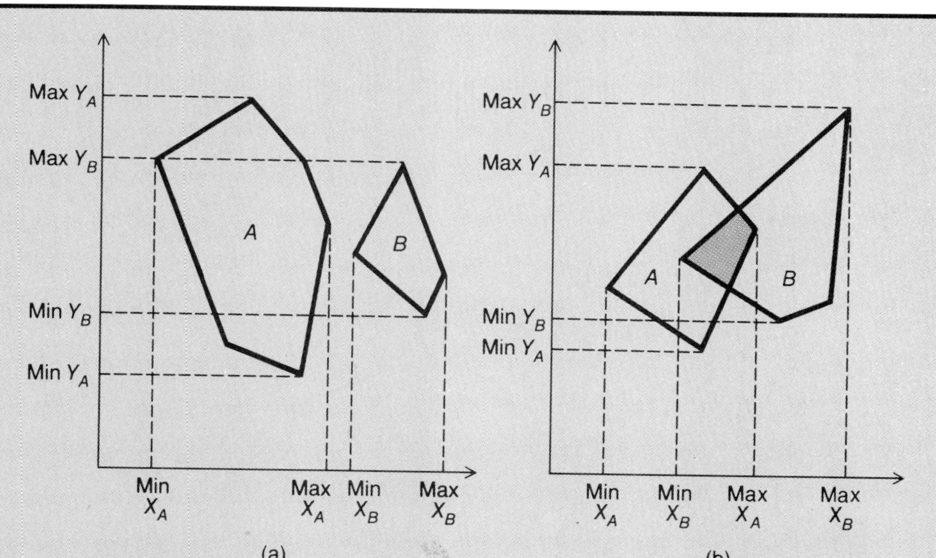

FIGURE 5.7 Minimax test: (a) cannot overlap and (b) overlap possible but not proven

where

$$x_j = X \text{ coordinate for polygon } j \ (j = A, B),$$

$$y_j = Y \text{ coordinate for polygon } j \ (j = A, B).$$

If we applied the minimax test to the pairs of polygons shown in Fig. 5.8, the test would indicate (but not prove) that each pair of polygons overlaps. It is obvious, however, that the pairs of polygons shown in Figs. 5.8(d) and 5.8(e) do not actually overlap. Because this test is inconclusive, we have to test the polygons further to determine if their edges intersect or if one is completely surrounded by the other. The test for an intersection is less complex, so it is done first.

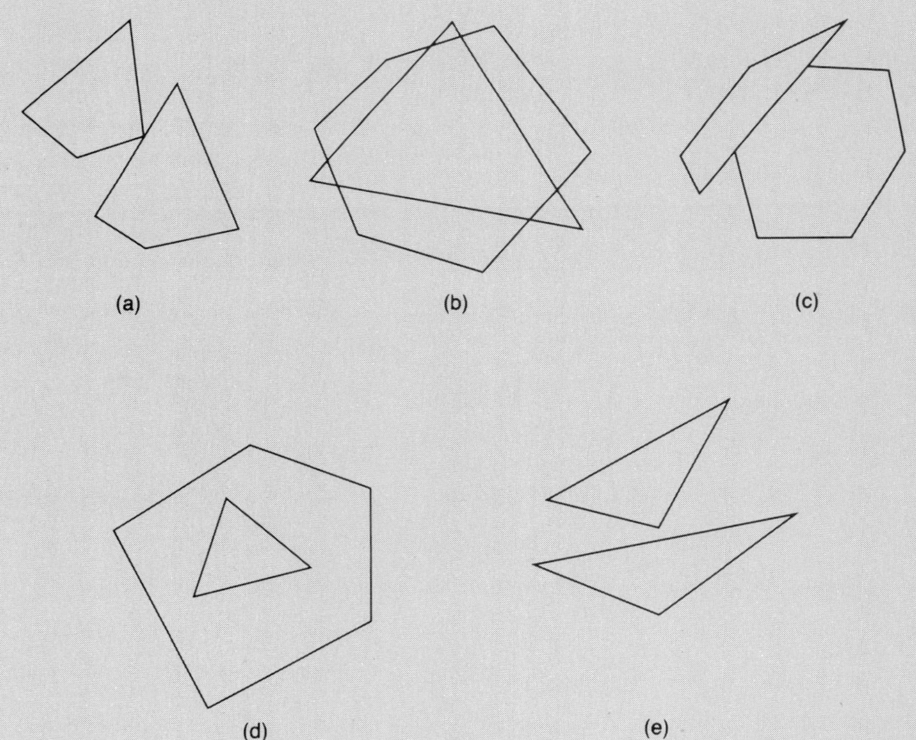

FIGURE 5.8 Possibilities of determining the distinguished point in the intersection of two polygons: (a) unique point, (b) multiple points, (c) infinitely many points, (d) nested set (no point), and (e) no overlap

5.2.3 INTERSECTION TEST

From linear algebra, we can easily obtain formulas for the point of intersection between two lines and for the intersection of two line segments. We present here the two formulas, which will be useful for our intersection test.

Intersection of two lines. Given two line equations L and L',

$$\begin{aligned} L&: A_1x + B_1y + C_1 = 0 \qquad (A_1, B_1 \text{ both not zero}) \\ L'&: A_2x + B_2y + C_2 = 0 \qquad (A_2, B_2 \text{ both not zero}), \end{aligned} \tag{5.6}$$

there are three possibilities:

1. The lines L and L' may be parallel, in which case there is no intersection. This condition arises when the determinant
$$\begin{vmatrix} A_1 & B_1 \\ A_2 & B_2 \end{vmatrix} = A_1B_2 - B_1A_2 = 0\,.$$
2. The lines L and L' may coincide, in which case there are infinitely many points of intersection. This situation arises if $A_1/A_2 = B_1/B_2 = C_1/C_2$.
3. Otherwise, we have a point of intersection (x_i, y_i) with the coordinates
$$x_i = \frac{B_1C_2 - B_2C_1}{A_1B_2 - A_2B_1}, \qquad y_i = \frac{C_1A_2 - C_2A_1}{A_1B_2 - A_2B_1}. \tag{5.7}$$

Intersection of two line segments. Suppose that we define two line segments G and G' on line L and L', respectively. Line segment G is given by its two endpoints (x_1, y_1) and (x_2, y_2); line segment G' is given by (x_1', y_1') and (x_2', y_2'). Let L and L' intersect in the point $I = (x_i, y_i)$ as before. Then the two segments G and G' do not intersect at point I if one of the following conditions is satisfied.

$$\begin{aligned} &x_i < A_1, \quad x_i > B_1, \quad x_i < C_1, \quad x_i > D_1, \\ &y_i < A_2, \quad y_i > B_2, \quad y_i < C_2, \quad y_i > D_2. \end{aligned} \tag{5.8}$$

where

$$\begin{aligned} &A_1 = \min(x_1, x_2); \quad B_1 = \max(x_1, x_2); \quad C_1 = \min(x_1', x_2'); \quad D_1 = \max(x_1', x_2') \\ &A_2 = \min(y_1, y_2); \quad B_2 = \max(y_1, y_2); \quad C_2 = \min(y_1', y_2'); \quad D_2 = \max(y_1', y_2') \end{aligned}$$

Otherwise, the two line segments G and G' intersect. A graphical illustration is shown in Fig. 5.9. We will apply these rules to our edge intersection test.

Edge intersection test. Our task is not only to find out whether two edges overlap but also to find a point of intersection between the edges of the two

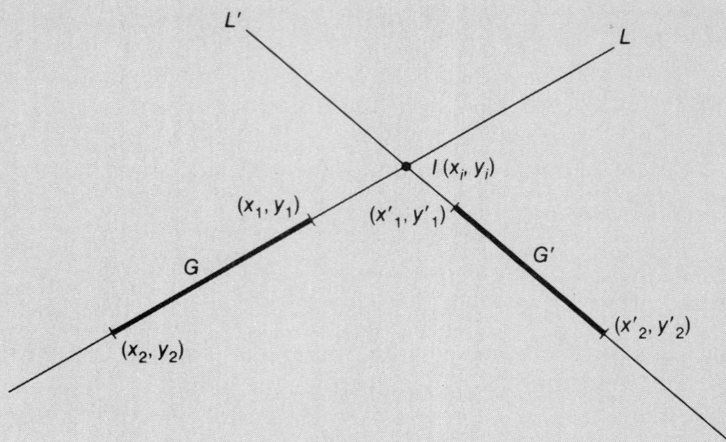

FIGURE 5.9 Edge intersection test

polygons. Since an edge is defined by its two endpoints, or vertices, we develop the equation of the edge by first specifying its endpoints.

Let points (x_1, y_1) and (x_2, y_2) be the endpoints of an edge of polygon A. The equation of the edge line is

$$y = y_1 + m(x - x_1), \tag{5.9a}$$

where

$$m = (y_2 - y_1)/(x_2 - x_1).$$

Or expressed differently,

$$mx - y + (y_1 - mx_1) = 0.$$

Similarly, let points (x_1', y_1') and (x_2', y_2') be the endpoints of an edge of polygon B. Then the equation of the edge line is

$$m'x - y + (y_1' - m'x_1') = 0, \tag{5.9b}$$

where

$$m' = (y_2' - y_1')/(x_2' - x_1').$$

To find the point of edge intersection, we proceed as follows:

Step 1: Compute the determinant,

$$\begin{vmatrix} m & -1 \\ m' & -1 \end{vmatrix} = m' - m.$$

If $m' - m = 0$, the two edge lines are parallel; go to step 5. Otherwise, go on to step 2.

Step 2: If $m/m' = 1 = (y_1 - mx_1)/(y_1' - m'x_1')$, the two edge lines coincide; go to step 5. Otherwise, go on to step 3.

Step 3: Compute a point of intersection (x_i, y_i) using Eq. (5.7).

$$x_i = \frac{(y_1 - y_1') - (mx_1 - m'x_1')}{m' - m},$$
$$y_i = \frac{(y_1 - mx_1)m' - (y_1' - m'x_1')m}{m' - m}. \tag{5.9c}$$

Step 4: Apply the conditions set by Eq. (5.8) to determine if the two edges do intersect at point $I(x_i, y_i)$.

Step 5: Choose another edge from polygon B and repeat the process. If no edges are left to compare, stop.

5.2.4 CONTAINMENT TEST

When there is no intersection between the two polygons, either one polygon completely surrounds the other or they do not overlap at all. To distinguish between these cases, we test the vertices of one polygon for containment in the other polygon. Elementary geometry provides two well-known procedures for performing such a test.

Test by calculating a sum of angles. We calculate the sum of angles from a vertex point (test point) of polygon A along imaginary lines drawn to every vertex of polygon B. (See Fig. 5.10.) Let $P_j = (x_j, y_j)$ denote the jth vertex of polygon B, where $j = 1, \ldots n$ and $P_n = P_1$. We number the polygon vertices in the counterclockwise direction as before. Let P_t be a point that will be tested for inclusion in polygon B.

Let $\overline{\mathbf{P}_t\mathbf{P}_j}$ denote a line segment connecting P_t with P_j. Let α_j denote the angle between $\overline{\mathbf{P}_t\mathbf{P}_j}$ and $\overline{\mathbf{P}_t\mathbf{P}_{j+1}}$, measured from $\overline{\mathbf{P}_t\mathbf{P}_j}$ to $\overline{\mathbf{P}_t\mathbf{P}_{j+1}}$. We must preserve the arithmetic sign in measuring α_j. For instance, if we measure the angle clockwise, we assign a negative sign to the angle. If we measure counterclockwise, we assign a positive sign. We compute α_j for *all* j and calculate $\Sigma\, \alpha_j$. Now we can complete the containment test:

- If $\Sigma\, \alpha_j = 0$, the point P_t is outside polygon B.
- If $\Sigma\, \alpha_j = 360°$, the point P_t is inside polygon B.

To illustrate the procedure, consider Fig. 5.10(a). We will calculate α_1. Since vertices P_1 (30, 80), P_2 (40, 50) and P_t (60, 40) are involved, we first com-

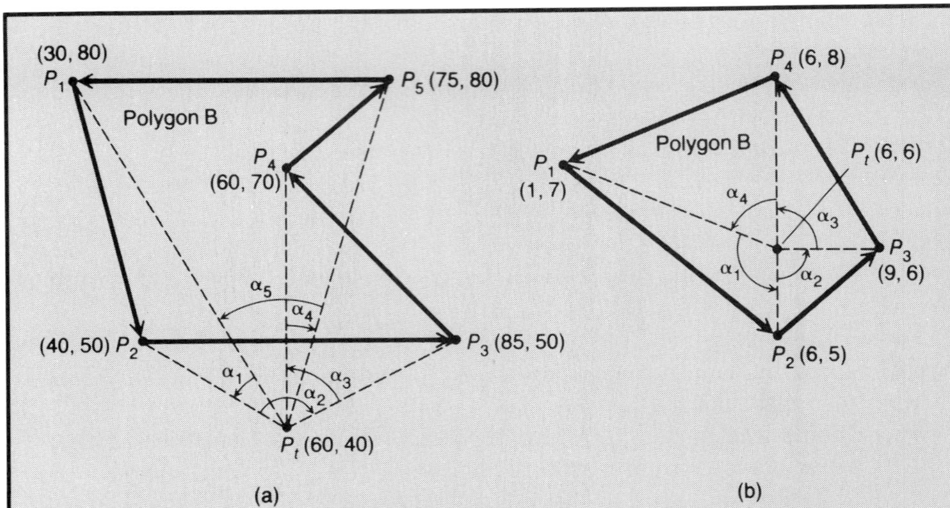

FIGURE 5.10 Containment test by calculating a sum of angles

pute two vectors, $\overline{\mathbf{P}_t\mathbf{P}_1}$ and $\overline{\mathbf{P}_t\mathbf{P}_2}$, and their lengths $|\overline{\mathbf{P}_t\mathbf{P}_1}|$ and $|\overline{\mathbf{P}_t\mathbf{P}_2}|$:

$$\overline{\mathbf{P}_t\mathbf{P}_1} = (30,80) - (60,40) = (-30,40)\,.$$

$$\overline{\mathbf{P}_t\mathbf{P}_2} = (40,50) - (60,40) = (-20,10)\,,$$

$$|\overline{\mathbf{P}_t\mathbf{P}_1}| = \sqrt{(-30)^2 + 40^2} = 50\,,$$

$$|\overline{\mathbf{P}_t\mathbf{P}_2}| = \sqrt{(-20)^2 + 10^2} = 22.36\,.$$

Then we compute the dot product of the vectors:

$$\overline{\mathbf{P}_t\mathbf{P}_1} \cdot \overline{\mathbf{P}_t\mathbf{P}_2} = (-30,40) \cdot (-20,10) = 1000\,.$$

Using Eq. (5.4), we compute α_1 by

$$\alpha_1 = \cos^{-1} \frac{1000}{(50) \cdot (22.36)} = 26.56^\circ\,.$$

We compute α_2 in a similar manner. Angle α_2 is measured in the clockwise direction, so it is in fact a negative angle. This computation gives us $\alpha_2 = -124.3^\circ$. We repeat the process for the rest of α_j and then find $\Sigma\,\alpha_j = 0$. This result implies that the test point P_t is *outside* polygon B.

The containment test is repeated for each vertex point of polygon A. Polygon A surrounds polygon B when every vertex of A is inside B. The result is inconclusive when every vertex of A is outside B, because polygon A

may surround polygon B. In this case, the entire procedure must be done again with the roles of A and B reversed to determine the relationship between the two polygons.

Test by the half-plane method. This alternative procedure is to determine which half-plane of polygon B contains the test point (in polygon A). From analytic geometry, we know that the line connecting two points P, and Q divides the XY plane into two half-planes. The half-plane on the left when looking along vector $\overline{\mathbf{PQ}}$ is defined as the *left half-plane;* that on the right is referred to as the *right half-plane.*

We may view each polygon edge (connecting two vertices P_j and P_{j+1}) as a line vector dividing the XY plane. We define the test point as P_t as before, and work to determine which half-plane contains P_t. This is accomplished by first defining two vectors, **u** and **v**, as shown in Fig. 5.11. Vector **u** extends from P_j to P_t, the point to be tested. Vector **v**, on the other hand, extends from P_j to P_{j+1}. Then we can say:

- If P_t is in the right half-plane of line $\overline{\mathbf{P}_j\mathbf{P}_{j+1}}$ (and thus outside polygon B), then $\mathbf{u} \times \mathbf{v}$ is a negative multiple of $(0, 0, 1)$.
- If P_t is in the left half-plane of line $\overline{\mathbf{P}_j\mathbf{P}_{j+1}}$(and thus inside polygon B), then $\mathbf{u} \times \mathbf{v}$ is a positive multiple of $(0, 0, 1)$.

These statements are mathematically precise, but we express them differently for our convenience in computer programming.

Let $P_j = (a, b)$, $P_{j+1} = (c, d)$, and $P_t = (e, f)$. Then $\mathbf{u} = (e - a, f - b)$ and $\mathbf{v} = (c - a, d - b)$. The cross product $\mathbf{u} \times \mathbf{v}$ is defined only for 3-D vectors, however. Therefore, we expand vectors **u** and **v** into 3-D space, adding a zero Z-coordinate to each vector. In other words, a 2-D vector on the XY plane is equivalent to a 3-D vector having a zero Z-coordinate. This gives

$$\mathbf{u} = (e - a, f - b, 0) \quad \text{and} \quad \mathbf{v} = (c - a, d - b, 0) .$$

From Eq. (5.1), the cross product is

$$\mathbf{u} \times \mathbf{v} = (0, 0, (e - a)(d - b) - (f - b)(c - a)) . \tag{5.10}$$

The condition for which the cross product is a positive multiple of $(0, 0, 1)$ is $(e - a)(d - b) > (f - b)(c - a)$. Thus

- if $(e - a)(d - b) > (f - b)(c - a)$, then P_t is contained in the left half-plane of line $\overline{\mathbf{P}_j\mathbf{P}_{j+1}}$.
- if $(e - a)(d - b) < (f - b)(c - a)$, then P_t is contained in the right half-plane of line $\overline{\mathbf{P}_j\mathbf{P}_{j+1}}$.

To complete the containment test, we repeat this procedure for each edge of polygon B. Since the polygon boundaries have a counterclockwise orientation,

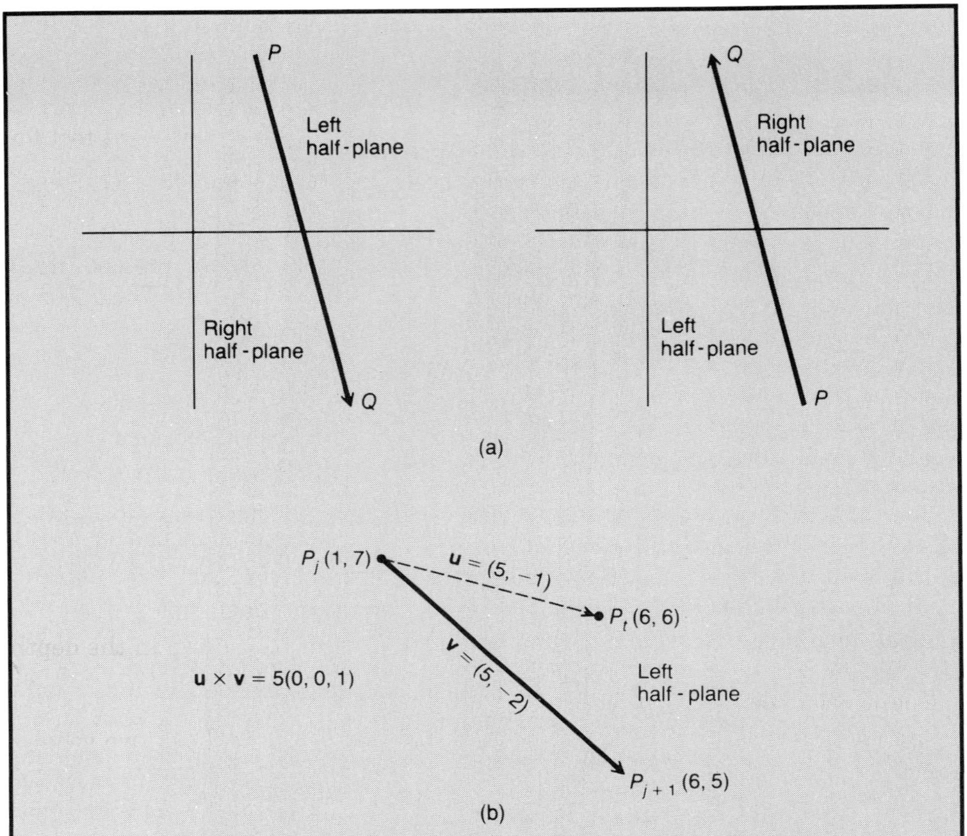

FIGURE 5.11 Containment test by a half-plane method

we conclude:

- P_t is inside polygon B if it lies in the left half-plane of each edge of the polygon.
- P_t is outside polygon B if it lies in the right half-plane of *at least* one boundary edge.

To illustrate the computational procedure, consider Fig. 5.10(b). For edge $\overline{\mathbf{P}_1\mathbf{P}_2}$ and test point P_t, we compute the cross product for the two vectors, **u** and **v**:

$$\mathbf{u} = (6 - 1, 6 - 7) = (5, -1),$$

$$\mathbf{v} = (6 - 1, 5 - 7) = (5, -2),$$

and
$$\mathbf{u} \times \mathbf{v} = (5, -2, 0) \times (5, -1, 0) = (0, 0, 5)$$
$$= 5(0, 0, 1),$$

which is a positive multiple of (0, 0, 1). We can easily verify from Fig. 5.11(b) that P_t is indeed in the left half-plane. We can repeat the containment test for edges $\overline{\mathbf{P}_2\mathbf{P}_3}$, $\overline{\mathbf{P}_3\mathbf{P}_4}$, and $\overline{\mathbf{P}_4\mathbf{P}_1}$ and quickly confirm that P_t lies in the left half-plane for each edge tested. Thus P_t is inside polygon B.

The half-plane method is computationally more attractive; therefore, we adopt this method in our hidden line algorithm. It must be understood, however, that the half-plane method works only for *convex* polygons. [The polygon shown in Fig. 5.10(a) is not convex. The half-plane method will not work for this polygon.]

5.2.5 DEPTH TEST

In Section 4.4, we introduced a method for measuring the depth of each point in the perspective image. The depth value z_s was calculated by transforming a plane in the eye coordinate system into a corresponding plane in the screen coordinate system.

Plane equation. As seen in Eqs. (4.35) and (4.36), the first step in the depth test is to determine the unknown coefficients of the plane equation that defines the polygon surface. To do this, let $P_j(x_j, y_j, z_j), j = 1, 2, 3$, be such vertices on the polygon surface. If these vertices are not collinear, we can identify two vectors $\mathbf{u}$ and $\mathbf{v}$ associated with the plane. (To be consistent with the surface-normal vector, we will identify the three vertices in the counterclockwise direction.)

$$\mathbf{u} = \overline{\mathbf{P}_1\mathbf{P}_2} = (x_2, y_2, z_2) - (x_1, y_1, z_1) = (x_2 - x_1,\ y_2 - y_1,\ z_2 - z_1)$$
$$\mathbf{v} = \overline{\mathbf{P}_1\mathbf{P}_3} = (x_3,\ y_3,\ z_3) - (x_1,\ y_1,\ z_1) = (x_3 - x_1,\ y_3 - y_1,\ z_3 - z_1)$$

Then we know from plane analytic geometry that the cross product $\mathbf{u} \times \mathbf{v}$ provides the coefficients of the plane passing through (x_1, y_1, z_1). Recall that a plane equation takes the form

$$Ax + By + Cz + D = 0. \qquad \textbf{(5.11)}$$

The coefficients (A, B, C) are determined as

$$(A, B, C) = \mathbf{u} \times \mathbf{v}. \qquad \textbf{(5.12)}$$

Using Eq. (5.1), we find the expressions for the coefficients as follows:

$$A = y_1(z_2 - z_3) + y_2(z_3 - z_1) + y_3(z_1 - z_2),$$
$$B = z_1(x_2 - x_3) + z_2(x_3 - x_1) + z_3(x_1 - x_2),$$
$$C = x_1(y_2 - y_3) + x_2(y_3 - y_1) + x_3(y_1 - y_2),$$

and

$$D = -Ax_1 - By_1 - Cz_1 . \tag{5.13}$$

Priority. Two calculations are sufficient to show which overlapping polygon lies closer to the viewer. The first calculation determines an intersection point of the polygons. (Polygons may intersect more than once, but we need only one intersection to apply the depth test.) The second calculation is to find the z_s value of each polygon at the intersection point. These calculations are as follows:

- Let (x_i, y_i) be the screen coordinates of the intersection point.
- Determine the plane equations that define the polygons in the screen coordinate system:

$$a_1x_s + b_1y_s + c_1z_s + d_1 = 0 \qquad \text{for polygon 1},$$

$$a_2x_s + b_2y_s + c_2z_s + d_2 = 0 \qquad \text{for polygon 2}.$$

- Substituting $x_s = x_i$ and $y_s = y_i$, we solve for z_s.
- Compare the z_s values. The polygon with a smaller z_s value lies closer to the viewer. Thus the entire polygon should be visible. (A numerical example explaining these calculations will be given in Section 5.3.10.)

In the next section, we will demonstrate the operational and computational procedures of this hidden line algorithm by developing a sample computer program.

5.3 PROGRAM DEVELOPMENT OF DRAWING TWO CONVEX OBJECTS

We will use the two objects, a cube and a pyramid, shown in Fig. 5.12 to illustrate the calculations that are necessary for the development of the hidden line algorithm discussed in Section 5.2. The program is long, so we will present it in several segments, explaining the purpose of each segment.

5.3.1 THE MAIN PROGRAM

Program 5.2 has twelve subroutines and five additional nested subroutines. Basically, the main program controls and directs the steps to follow upon completing each specific test or computation. Figure 5.13 shows the sequential steps for the hidden line algorithm. The complete listing of the program is shown on pages 207–210.

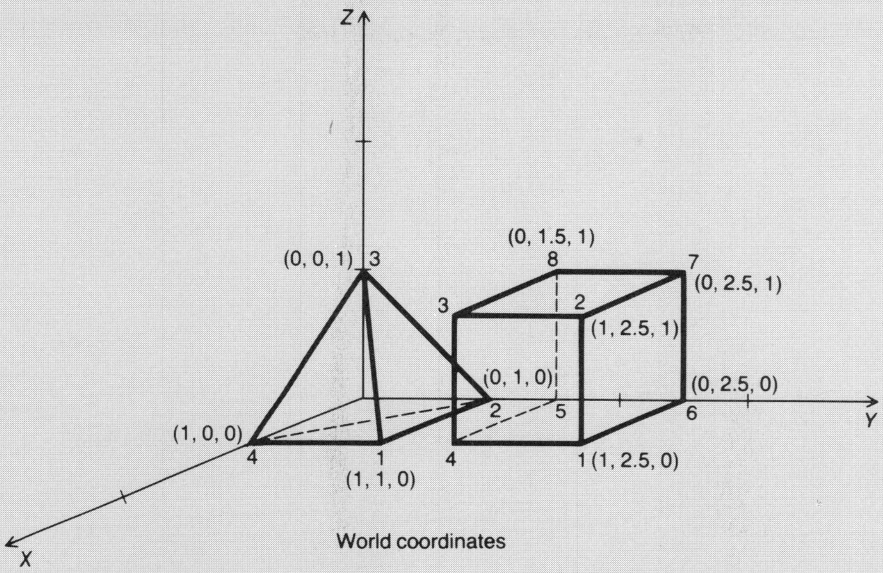

FIGURE 5.12 Two convex objects, pyramid and cube, defined in the world coordinate system

```
10 ' Program 5.2 : Hidden Line Elimination - Two Objects
20 CLEAR
30 CLS : KEY OFF : SCREEN 2
40       GOSUB 170
50       GOSUB 230
60       GOSUB 500
70       GOSUB 670
80       GOSUB 810
90       GOSUB 940
100      GOSUB 1140
110      IF OVERLAP=0 THEN 120 ELSE 130
120      FOR LL=1 TO 2 :GOSUB 1300:NEXT LL: END
130      GOSUB 1390
140      GOSUB 2090
150      GOSUB 2240
160   END
170 REM : DEFINE VIEWING PARAMETERS
180      D=10 : VD=500 : THETA=57 : PHI=68 : TX= 320: TY=100
190      PI=3.141593    :SCF=2.4
200      THETA=THETA*PI/180 : PHI=PHI*PI/180  : S = 1.5
210      SN1=SIN(THETA) : SN2=SIN(PHI) :CN1=COS(THETA) :CN2=COS(PHI)
220 RETURN
230 REM : VERTEX ARRAY
240 NV(1)=4 : NV(2)=8 : K1=7 : K2=10 : W=K2/(K2-K1)
250 DIM V(2,8,3), EC(2,8,3), SC(2,8,3)
260 FOR I=1 TO 2
270     FOR J=1 TO NV(I)
280          READ X,Y,Z
290          V(I,J,1)=X: V(I,J,2)=Y: V(I,J,3)=Z
300          GOSUB 400
```

PROGRAM 5.2 Hidden Line Elimination — Two Objects

```
310              EC(I,J,1)=XE: EC(I,J,2)=YE: EC(I,J,3)=ZE
320              GOSUB 450
330              SC(I,J,1)=  XS   : SC(I,J,2)= YS   : SC(I,J,3)=ZS
340        NEXT J
350   NEXT I
360   RETURN
370   DATA 1,1,0,0,1,0,0,0,1,1,0,0
380   DATA 1,2.5,0, 1,2.5,1, 1,1.5,1, 1,1.5,0
390   DATA 0,1.5,0, 0,2.5,0, 0,2.5,1, 0,1.5,1
400   REM : EYE COORDINATES
410         XE= -X*SN1 + Y*CN1
420         YE= -X*CN1*CN2 - Y*SN1*CN2 + Z*SN2
430         ZE= -X*SN2*CN1 - Y*SN2*SN1 - Z*CN2 + D
440   RETURN
450   REM : SCREEN COORDINATES
460         XS=(VD/S)*(XE/ZE)                          ' See Eq.(4.31)
470         YS=(VD/S)*(YE/ZE)                          ' See Eq.(4.32)
480         ZS=W*(1- K1/ZE)                            ' See Eq.(4.38)
490   RETURN
500   REM : SURFACE ARRAY
510   DIM SF(2,6,5),NPS(2,6)
520   NS(1)=4 :NS(2)=6
530   FOR I=1 TO 2: FOR J=1 TO NS(I): READ NPS(I,J): NEXT J: NEXT I
540   FOR I=1 TO 2
550        FOR J=1 TO NS(I)
560             FOR K=1 TO NPS(I,J)
570                  READ SF(I,J,K)
580             NEXT K
590        NEXT J
600   NEXT I
610   RETURN
620   DATA 4,4,4,4
630   DATA 5,5,5,5,5,5
640   DATA 1,2,3,1, 2,4,3,2, 4,1,3,4, 1,4,2,1
650   DATA 1,2,3,4,1, 6,7,2,1,6, 5,8,7,6,5, 4,3,8,5,4
660   DATA 4,5,6,1,4, 7,8,3,2,7
670   REM : NORMAL ARRAY
680   DIM N(2,6,3)
690   FOR I=1 TO 2
700        FOR J=1 TO NS(I)
710             FOR K=1 TO 3
720                  U(K)= V(I,SF(I,J,2),K) - V(I,SF(I,J,1),K)
730                  W(K)= V(I,SF(I,J,3),K) - V(I,SF(I,J,1),K)
740             NEXT K
750             N(I,J,1)= U(2)*W(3) - W(2)*U(3)
760             N(I,J,2)= U(3)*W(1) - W(3)*U(1)
770             N(I,J,3)= U(1)*W(2) - W(1)*U(2)
780        NEXT J
790   NEXT I
800   RETURN
810   REM : VISIBILITY TEST
820   DIM VSF(2,6)
830   XP= D*SN2*CN1 : YP= D*SN2*SN1 : ZP= D*CN2
840   FOR I=1 TO 2
850        FOR J=1 TO NS(I)
860             LX=XP - V(I,SF(I,J,1),1)
870             LY=YP - V(I,SF(I,J,1),2)
880             LZ=ZP - V(I,SF(I,J,1),3)
890             T= N(I,J,1)*LX + N(I,J,2)*LY + N(I,J,3)*LZ
900             IF T <= 0 THEN VSF(I,J)=0 ELSE VSF(I,J)=1
910        NEXT J
920   NEXT I
930   RETURN
940   REM: VISIBLE EDGE ARRAY
950   DIM E(2,12,4), NVE(2)
960   FOR I=1 TO 2
970        M=1
980        FOR J=1 TO NS(I)
990             IF VSF(I,J)=0 THEN  1110
1000             E1= SF(I,J,1)
1010             FOR K=2 TO NPS(I,J)
1020                  E2=SF(I,J,K)
1030                  FOR L=1 TO M
1040                       IF E(I,L,1)=E2 AND E(I,L,2)=E1 THEN E(I,L,3)=2:GOTO 1080
1050                  NEXT L
1060                  E(I,M,1)=E1: E(I,M,2)=E2: E(I,M,3)=1: E(I,M,4)=J
1070                  M=M+1
1080                  E1=E2
1090             NEXT K
1100             NVE(I)=M-1
1110        NEXT J
1120  NEXT I
1130  RETURN
1140  REM: MINIMAX TEST
1150  FOR I=1 TO 2
1160       XMX(I)=-999999999#: XMN(I)=999999999#
```

PROGRAM 5.2 (continued)

```
1170      YMX(I)=XMX(I)  :  YMN(I)=XMN(I)
1180      FOR J=1 TO NVE(I)
1190          IF E(I,J,3) <>1 THEN 1260
1200          K=E(I,J,1)
1210          A=SC(I,K,1)  :  B=SC(I,K,2)
1220          IF A > XMX(I) THEN XMX(I)=A
1230          IF A < XMN(I) THEN XMN(I)=A
1240          IF B > YMX(I) THEN YMX(I)=B
1250          IF B < YMN(I) THEN YMN(I)=B
1260      NEXT J
1270 NEXT I
1280          IF (XMX(1)<XMN(2)) OR (XMX(2)<XMN(1)) OR (YMX(1)<YMN(2))
                 OR (YMX(2)<YMN(1))      THEN OVERLAP=0 ELSE OVERLAP=1
1290 RETURN
1300 REM : PLOT
1310      FOR KJ=1 TO NVE(LL)
1320      IF E(LL,KJ,3)=0 THEN 1370
1330      F1=E(LL,KJ,1): F2=E(LL,KJ,2)
1340      A=SC(LL,F1,1):B=SC(LL,F1,2): C=SC(LL,F2,1):D=SC(LL,F2,2)
1350      A=SCF*A + TX:B=TY -B: C=SCF*C + TX : D= TY - D
1360      LINE (A,B) - (C,D)
1370      NEXT KJ
1380 RETURN
1390 REM : DETERMINE OBJECT PRIORITY
1400   I=1 : L=2
1410    FOR J=1 TO NVE(I)
1420              A=E(I,J,1): B=E(I,J,2)
1430              FOR K=1 TO NVE(L)
1440                      IF E(L,K,3) <> 1 THEN 1520
1450                      C=E(L,K,1): D=E(L,K,2)
1460                      GOSUB 1690
1470                      IF NCUT=0 THEN 1520
1480                      GOSUB 1880
1490                      IF DT1 > DT2 THEN 1500 ELSE 1510
1500                      KKK=0:II=1:LL=2: GOSUB 1300: RETURN
1510                      KKK=0:II=2:LL=1: GOSUB 1300: RETURN
1520              NEXT K
1530    NEXT J
1540    GOSUB 1590
1550          IF (ZMN(1) < ZMX(2)) AND (YMX(2)>YMX(1)) THEN LL=2:
                 GOSUB 1300: END
1560          IF (ZMX(2) < ZMN(1)) AND (YMX(1)>YMX(2)) THEN LL=1:
                 GOSUB 1300: END
1570          IF (YMX(2)>YMX(1)) THEN KKK=1:II=1:LL=2: GOSUB 1300: RETURN
1580          IF (YMX(1)>YMX(2)) THEN KKK=1:II=2:LL=1: GOSUB 1300: RETURN
1590 REM: CONTAINMENT TEST
1600  DIM ZMX(2),ZMN(2)
1610    FOR I=1 TO 2
1620              ZMX(I)=0: ZMN(I)=1
1630              FOR J=1 TO NV(I)
1640                      IF SC(I,J,3) > ZMX(I) THEN ZMX(I)=SC(I,J,3)
1650                      IF SC(I,J,3) < ZMN(I) THEN ZMN(I)=SC(I,J,3)
1660              NEXT J
1670    NEXT I
1680    RETURN
1690 REM : INTERSECTION TEST
1700      AX=SC(I,A,1): AY=SC(I,A,2): BX=SC(I,B,1):BY=SC(I,B,2)
1710      CX=SC(L,C,1): CY=SC(L,C,2): DX=SC(L,D,1):DY=SC(L,D,2)
1720      R1=AX-BX: R2=AY-BY: R3=CX-DX: R4=CY-DY
1730      S1=SGN(R1): S2=SGN(R2): S3=SGN(R3): S4=SGN(R4)
1740      A1=AX: B1=BX: A2=AY: B2=BY: C1=CX: D1=DX: C2=CY: D2=DY
1750        IF S1 > 0 THEN A1=BX: B1=AX
1760        IF S2 > 0 THEN A2=BY: B2=AY
1770        IF S3 > 0 THEN C1=DX: D1=CX
1780        IF S4 > 0 THEN C2=DY: D2=CY
1790 REM - MINMAX TEST FOR EDGE OVERLAPPING
1800     IF (B1<C1) OR (D1<A1) OR (B2<C2) OR (D2<A2) THEN NCUT=0: RETURN
1810      M1=R2/R1 : M2=R4/R3 : M3=M2-M1
1820      IF (M3=0) OR (ABS(M3)<=.0001) THEN NCUT=0: RETURN
1830 REM - COMPUTE INTERSECTION POINT
1840      Z0=AY-CY:Z1=M1*AX-M2*CX : Z2=(AY-M1*AX)*M2: Z3=(CY-M2*CX)*M1
1850      XI=(Z0-Z1)/M3  : YI=(Z2-Z3)/M3
1860      IF (XI<A1) OR (XI>B1) OR (XI<C1) OR (XI>D1) OR
          (YI<A2) OR (YI>B2) OR (YI<C2) OR (YI>D2) THEN NCUT=0 ELSE NCUT=1
1870    RETURN
1880 REM - DEPTH TEST
1890 II=I: IJ=J
1900      A1=AX: A2=AY: A3=SC(I,A,3): Q=E(I,J,4)
1910      B1=BX: B2=BY: B3=SC(I,B,3)
1920      GOSUB 1980 : DT1 =DEPTH
1930 II=L: IJ=K
1940      A1=CX: A2=CY: A3=SC(L,C,3): Q=E(L,K,4)
1950      B1=DX: B2=DY: B3=SC(L,D,3)
1960      GOSUB 1980 : DT2 =DEPTH
1970 RETURN
1980 REM - COMPUTE ZS (PLANE NORMAL)
```

PROGRAM 5.2 (continued)

```
1990 FOR JJ=1 TO NPS(II,Q)
2000      IF SF(II,Q,JJ) <> E(II,IJ,2) THEN 2020
2010      KK=SF(II,Q,JJ+1): GOTO 2030
2020 NEXT JJ
2030      C1=SC(II,KK,1): C2=SC(II,KK,2): C3=SC(II,KK,3)
2040      AA=B1-A1: BB=B2-A2: CC=B3-A3: DD=C1-A1: EE=C2-A2: FF=C3-A3
2050      XX=BB*FF-CC*EE: YY=CC*DD-AA*FF: ZZ=AA*EE-BB*DD
2060      T1=XX*A1 + YY*A2 + ZZ*A3
2070      T2=XX*XI + YY*YI
2080      DEPTH=(T1-T2)/ZZ :RETURN
2090 REM - VISIBLE ENDPOINT
2100    DIM ENDPOINT(NVE(II))
2110    FOR J=1 TO NVE(II)
2120              A=E(II,J,1)
2130              FOR K=1 TO NVE(LL)
2140                        IF E(LL,K,3) <> 1 THEN 2200
2150                        C=E(LL,K,1): D=E(LL,K,2)
2160                        AX=SC(II,A,1):AY=SC(II,A,2):
                            CX=SC(LL,C,1):CY=SC(LL,C,2):
                            DX=SC(LL,D,1):DY=SC(LL,D,2)
2170                        V1=DX-CX : V2=DY-CY
2180                        U1=AX-CX : U2=AY-CY :TEST=U2*V1-U1*V2
2190                        IF TEST <=0 THEN ENDPOINT(J)=1:GOTO 2220
2200              NEXT K
2210              ENDPOINT(J)=-1
2220    NEXT J
2230    RETURN
2240 REM : PLOT OF LINE SEGMENT
2250   DIM IX(2),IY(2)
2260    I=II: L=LL
2270    FOR J=1 TO NVE(II)
2280              VI=ENDPOINT(J): NCUT=0 :TCUT=0
2290              A=E(II,J,1): B=E(II,J,2)
2300              FOR K=1 TO NVE(LL)
2310                        IF KKK=1 THEN 2330
2320                        IF E(LL,K,3) <> 1 THEN 2390 ELSE 2340
2330                        IF E(LL,K,3) <> 2 THEN 2390 ELSE 2340
2340                        C=E(LL,K,1): D=E(LL,K,2)
2350                        GOSUB 1690
2360                        IF NCUT=0  THEN 2390 ELSE 2370
2370                        TCUT=TCUT+NCUT
2380                        IX(TCUT)=SCF*XI+TX: IY(TCUT)=TY-YI
2390              NEXT K
2400                        AX=SCF*AX + TX : AY=TY - AY :
                            BX=SCF*BX + TX : BY=TY - BY
2410                        GOSUB 2440
2420    NEXT J
2430    RETURN
2440 REM: PLOT OF VISIBLE EDGE SEGMENT
2450    IF TCUT=0 AND VI=1 THEN LINE (AX,AY)-(BX,BY): RETURN
2460    IF TCUT=0 AND VI=-1 THEN RETURN
2470    IF TCUT=1 AND VI=1 THEN LINE (AX,AY)-(IX(1),IY(1)): RETURN
2480    IF TCUT=1 AND VI=-1 THEN LINE(IX(1),IY(1))-(BX,BY): RETURN
2490    IF  (AX<BX) AND (IX(1) < IX(2)) THEN 2510
2500    IF  (AX>BX) AND (IX(2) < IX(1)) THEN 2510 ELSE  2520
2510    LINE (AX,AY)-(IX(1),IY(1)):LINE (IX(2),IY(2))-(BX,BY): RETURN
2520    LINE (AX,AY)-(IX(2),IY(2)):LINE (IX(1),IY(1))-(BX,BY): RETURN
```

PROGRAM 5.2 Hidden Line Elimination—Two Objects

5.3.2 THE VIEWING PARAMETERS

We will observe the pyramid and cube from the viewpoint $(D, \theta, \phi) = (10, 57°, 68°)$. In rectangular coordinates, the viewpoint is located at $(5.05, 7.78, 37.75)$. We will also position the display screen at $d = 500$. Recall that the viewing parameters D, θ, ϕ, and d control the location and direction of view and the size of the image. Because we are plotting simple objects, we will set our window and viewpoint coordinates equal [see Eqs. (3.39) and (3.40)]. We will use the high-resolution mode (SCREEN 2) and a screen scaling factor (*SCF*) of 2.4.

5.3.3 VERTEX, EYE, AND SCREEN COORDINATE ARRAYS

We first define $NV(I)$ as the number of vertices in object I. The pyramid has four vertices and the cube has eight. We number the vertices as shown in Fig. 5.12. Then we define the parameters $K1$ and $K2$. We may choose the

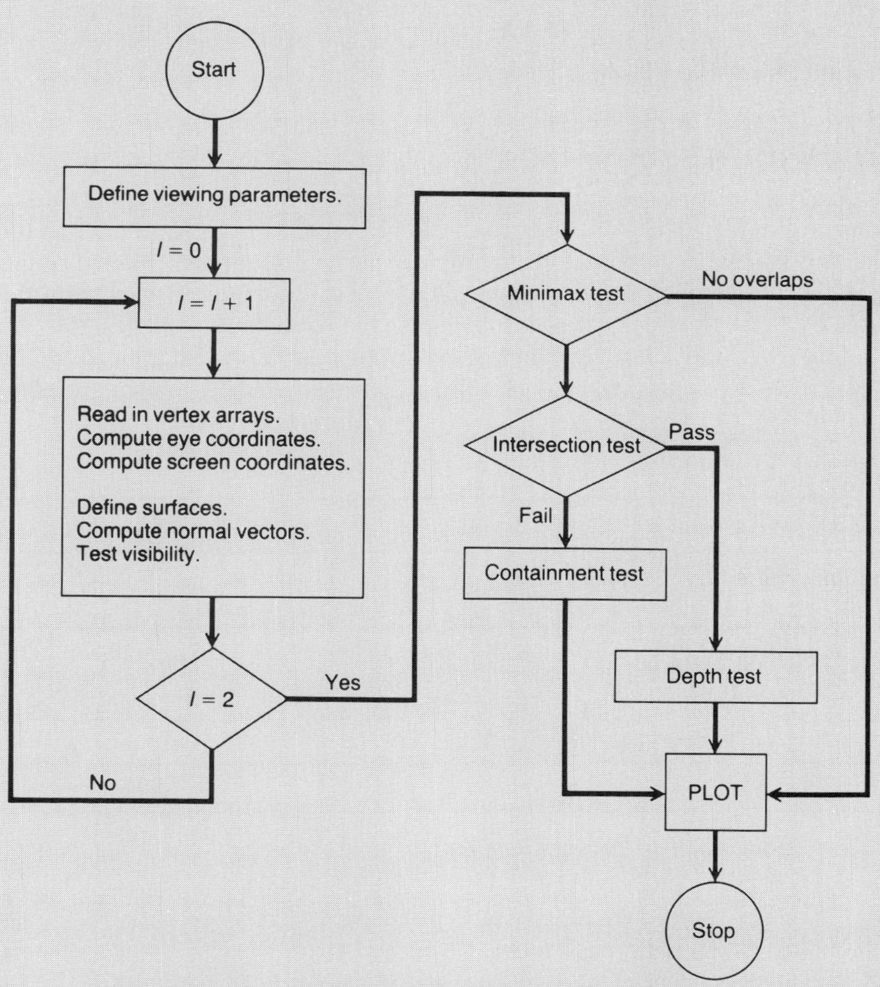

FIGURE 5.13 **Programming logic chart**

values for $K1$ and $K2$ at will. To insure the inclusion of the entire scene, we first compute the z_e coordinate for each vertex and find the smallest and largest z_e values. In our example, the z_e values range between 7.17 and 9.62. Thus setting $K1 = 7$, and $K2 = 10$ will ensure the inclusion of the entire scene. (See Section 4.4.2.)

To compute the eye coordinates, we again use Eq. (4.28); to compute the screen coordinates, we use Eqs. (4.31), (4.32), and (4.38). Thus for given vertex coordinates we compute the coordinates shown in Table 5.6. Recall that the screen coordinates computed here are not the physical device coordinates for the specific device, the IBM PC. We derive these by one more viewing transformation using Eq. (3.42).

5.3.4 THE SURFACE ARRAY

We will have ten surfaces in the scene, four for the pyramid and six for the cube. The surface array $SF(I,J,K)$ serves the same function in Program 5.1 as it did in Section 5.1, with I identifying the object ($I = 1,2$) and K identifying the vertices to be connected for each surface J. Each surface in the pyramid is defined by three vertices, whereas each surface in the cube is defined by four. As before, we will identify the array entries $SF(I,J,1)$ through $SF\{I,J, NPS(I,J)\}$ vertices of surface J of object I, where $NPS(I,J)$ is the number of

TABLE 5.6 Coordinate transformations

Pyramid vertex number	x,	y,	z	x_e,	y_e,	z_e	x_s,	y_s,	z_s
(1)	1,	1,	0	−0.3 ,	−0.52,	8.71	−16.87,	−29.73,	0.656
(2)	0,	1,	0	0.54,	−0.32,	9.22	29.52,	−17.04,	0.803
(3)	0,	0,	1	0 ,	0.92,	9.62	0 ,	48.16,	0.909
(4)	1,	0,	0	−0.84,	−0.21,	9.49	−44.17,	−10.75,	0.875
Cube vertex number									
(1)	1,	2.5,	0	0.52,	−0.99,	7.55	34.62,	−65.52,	0.243
(2)	1,	2.5,	1	0.52,	−0.07,	7.19	36.43,	− 4.34,	0.081
(3)	1,	1.5,	1	−0.03,	0.25,	7.95	− 1.37,	15.83,	0.394
(4)	1,	1.5,	0	−0.03,	−0.68,	8.32	− 1.31,	−40.54,	0.531
(5)	0,	1.5,	0	0.81,	−0.48,	8.83	46.24,	−26.68,	0 691
(6)	0,	2.5,	0	1.36,	−0.79,	8.05	84.50,	−48.75,	0.436
(7)	0,	2.5,	1	1.36,	0.14,	7.68	88.62,	9.22,	0.295
(8)	0,	1.5,	1	0.81,	0.45,	8.45	48.28,	26.94,	0.574

TABLE 5.7 Surface arrays for two objects

Object	*J*	*K*					Object	*J*	*K*				
Pyramid	1	1	2	3	1		Cube	1	1	2	3	4	1
	2	2	4	3	2			2	6	7	2	1	6
	3	4	1	3	4			3	5	8	7	6	5
	4	1	4	2	1			4	4	3	8	5	4
								5	4	5	6	1	4
								6	7	8	3	2	7

TABLE 5.8 Normal array for two objects

Object	*J*	*K*			Object	*J*	*K*		
Pyramid	1	0	1	1	Cube	1	1	0	0
	2	−1	−1	−1		2	0	1	0
	3	1	0	1		3	−1	0	0
	4	0	0	−1		4	0	−1	0
						5	0	0	−1
						6	0	0	1

vertices that define surface J of object I. It is very important to list the vertices in *counterclockwise* order around the surface as seen from outside the object. When complete, the surface arrays should look like Table 5.7.

5.3.5 THE NORMAL ARRAY

We compute the normal array $N(I,J,K)$ as before, with $N(I,J,1)$, $N(I,J,2)$, and $N(I,J,3)$ identifying the three components of the outward pointing normal vector to surface J of object I. The complete arrays are shown in Table 5.8.

5.3.6 VISIBILITY TEST

We are now ready to apply the visibility test to each surface of the objects. For each surface, we choose a line-of-sight vector ℓ extending from the starting point of the surface normal to the viewpoint. Then we compute the dot product $\mathbf{n} \cdot \ell$ and determine the sign of the dot product. We will store the visibility status of each surface J of object I in the $VSF(I,J)$ array (if visible, $VSF(I,J) = 1$; otherwise, $VSF(I,J) = 0$). As shown in Table 5.9, surfaces 1

TABLE 5.9 Pyramid visibility status

Pyramid surface	n			ℓ			n · ℓ	Visibility	VSF(I)
1	0	1	1	4.05	6.78	3.75	10.53	Visible	1
2	−1	−1	−1	5.05	6.78	3.75	−15.57	Invisible	0
3	1	0	1	4.05	7.78	3.75	7.80	Visible	1
4	0	0	−1	4.05	6.78	3.75	− 3.75	Invisible	0

TABLE 5.10 Cube visibility status

Cube surface	n			ℓ			n · ℓ	Visibility	VSF(I)
1	1	0	0	4.05,	5.28	3.75	4.05	Visibile	1
2	0	1	0	5.05,	5.28	3.75	5.28	Visible	1
3	−1	0	0	5.05	6.28	3.75	−5.05	Invisible	0
4	0	−1	0	4.05	6.28	3.75	−6.28	Invisible	0
5	0	0	−1	4.05	6.28	3.75	−3.75	Invisible	0
6	0	0	1	5.05	5.28	2.75	2.75	Visible	1

and 3 are visible in the pyramid. As shown by the results in Table 5.10, surfaces 1, 2, and 6 are visible surfaces in the cube.

5.3.7 VISIBLE EDGE ARRAY

We will introduce $E(I, J, K)$ to represent the edge array. The first array component I will identify the object. For each I, the second array component, J, will identify the number of edges in the object. For each J, component K will save four pieces of information: the endpoints of the edge ($K = 1, 2$), the number of visible surfaces for which the edge is a boundary ($K = 3$), and the surface to which the edge belongs ($K = 4$).

The visible edges are identified by the program in essentially the same manner as in Program 5.1. Upon completion, the edge arrays should look like Table 5.11.

5.3.8 MINIMAX TEST

For each object, we find the maximum and minimum values of the X coordinate and the maximum and minimum values of the Y coordinate. From checking

TABLE 5.11 Visible edge array for two objects

Object	Edge number (J)	Endpoints $K=1$	Endpoints $K=2$	Edge type $K=3$	Surface number $K=4$
Pyramid	1	1	2	1	1
	2	2	3	1	1
	3	3	1	2	1
	4	4	1	1	3
	5	3	4	1	3
Cube	1	1	2	2	1
	2	2	3	2	1
	3	3	4	1	1
	4	4	1	1	1
	5	6	7	1	2
	6	7	2	2	2
	7	1	6	1	2
	8	7	8	1	6
	9	8	3	1	6

the screen coordinate array, we find:

Object 1 = pyramid		**Object 2 = cube**	
max x = 29.52 xmx(1)	max y = 48.16 ymx(1)	max x = 88.62 xmx(2)	max y = 26.94 ymx(2)
min x = −44.17 xmn(1)	min y = −29.73 ymn(1)	min x = −1.37 xmn(2)	min y = −65.52 ymn(2)

The minimax rule given in Eq. (5.5) indicates that the two objects may overlap.

5.3.9 PLOT ROUTINE

If the minimax test indicates no possible overlap between the two objects, we simply plot both objects. The plot subroutine will plot the visible edges of an object by reading the identification numbers of the corresponding endpoints. We will invoke this plot subroutine several times throughout the program. (Note that the viewing transformation from the screen coordinate system to the IBM PC Device Coordinate System is given in line 1350.)

5.3.10 OBJECT PRIORITY

Edges of the farther object may be partly hidden by the closer object; thus we need to classify the objects by their relative positions. Furthermore, the pyramid and cube do not penetrate each other in our example. Our sole interest is to determine which of the objects lies close to the viewer. The object closer to the viewer is defined as the *first priority object.*

Testing sequence. We first check to see if an edge of the pyramid intersects any of the edges of the cube (line 1460). When there is an intersection, we apply the depth test to determine which object is closer to the viewer and thus visible (lines 1480–1510).

The visible edges of the object having first priority may now be drawn (lines 1500–1510). Since the edges are associated with the object having first priority, they could not be hidden by the object having second priority.

When there is no intersection between two objects, we perform the containment test (line 1540). The containment test indicates whether one object completely surrounds the other (lines 1550–1560) or whether they do not overlap at all (lines 1570–1580). We still need to determine the object priority for the contained object. We do this by putting the objects into priority order based on the smallest z_s value for any vertex on each object.

Once again, we draw first the visible edges of the object having first priority. If the object having second priority is contained by the first priority object, it is completely hidden and is not drawn. If the situation is reversed, the outer edges of the second priority object are drawn first, and the inner edges are then checked to see if they interfere visually with the outer edges of the first priority object. Only the visible portions of the inner edges are drawn. (This case will be shown in Section 5.3.13.)

We next present the segment of the computer program that does the priority test. Then we present the nested subroutines with specific numerical examples, which illustrate how edge intersections and depth values are calculated.

Intersection test. Each visible edge of one image (here, the pyramid) is compared against each edge of the other image (cube) to detect intersections (line 1420 and 1450). Once we determine which pair of edges to compare, we identify the respective screen coordinates (lines 1700–1710). Minimax tests on edges can help speed this screening process by determining quickly that two edges cannot possibly intersect (lines 1720–1790). In our example, we will observe two intersections:

	Pyramid	**Cube**	**(x_i, y_i)**
First intersection	Edge 1	Edge 3	−1.320, −25.471
Second intersection	Edge 2	Edge 9	13.168, 19.087

We need only one intersection point to determine the object priority. Once we identify a point of edge intersection, we set NCUT to 1 and return to line 1460. (We will use the first intersection point in the depth test.)

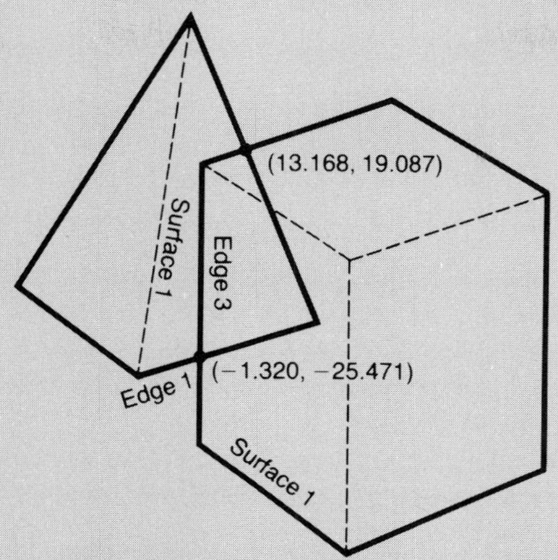

FIGURE 5.14 Intersection test

Depth test. For a pyramid, edge 1 belongs to surface 1 of the object. (See Fig. 5.14.) Since vertices 1, 2, and 3 define the surface, we can use the screen coordinates of these three vertices to determine the plane equation (lines 1900–1910):

Vertex number	x_s	y_s	z_s
1	−16.87	−29.73	0.656
2	29.52	−17.04	0.803
3	0	48.16	0.909

Now using Eq. (5.13), we compute the coefficients of the plane equation that represents the perspective image plane of surface 1 (line 2050):

$$-8.211x_s - 9.242y_s + 3399.316z_s - 2645.498 = 0 .$$

Evaluating z_s at (x_i, x_i) yields the depth value (line 2080).

$$x_s = x_i = -1.320 ,$$

$$y_s = y_i = -25.471 ,$$

$$z_s = 0.7058 = DT1 .$$

For instance, edge 3 belongs to surface 1 of the cube. Four vertices define this surface: 1, 2, 3, and 4. We may use vertices 3, 4, and 1 (or 2, 3, and 4) to find the plane equation (lines 1930–1950):

Vertex number	x_s	y_s	z_s
3	−1.37	15.73	0.399
4	−1.31	−40.54	0.531
1	34.62	−65.52	0.243

The plane equation will be obtained in a manner similar to the previous example. This yields

$$19.56x_s + 4.758y_s + 2023.997z_s - 857.85 = 0 .$$

Evaluating z_s at (x_i, y_i) gives

$$z_s = 0.4965 = DT2 .$$

Clearly, the cube lies closer to the viewer because its depth value, $z_s = 0.4965$, is less than the depth of the pyramid, $z_s = 0.7058$. Therefore, the cube has first priority (line 1490). Once we determine the object priority, we return from the subroutine to the main program (line 130).

5.3.11 VISIBILITY STATUS OF EDGE ENDPOINTS

Three types of edges are associated with the visible surfaces of the object that has second priority. Some edges are completely hidden by a closer object, some are only partly hidden, and others are completely visible. Program line 2120 identifies the first endpoint of each edge of the second priority object. Program lines 2130–2200 refer each endpoint for classification as visible or hidden. We will use Fig. 5.15 to illustrate how endpoint classification is done. In this figure only the outer cube boundaries are plotted and the endpoints of one edge of the pyramid are shown. Note that endpoint (B) (which should be hidden by the cube) is inside the outer boundary of the cube, while point (A) is outside. Since we specified the surface array and stored the information counterclockwise in the edge array, the outside cube boundaries will also have run counterclockwise. Thus the "inside" point (B) lies in the left half-plane of each component of the boundaries (see Section 5.2.4). On the other hand, point (A) is identified as an "outside" point because it is in the right half-plane of at least one boundary component.

Since a point is visible if it is in the right half-plane of *at least* one boundary component, the loop 2130–2200 compares the endpoint (A) (line 2120) with each visible edge of the cube.

For each outside edge CD of the cube (line 2150), two vectors are calculated. (See Fig. 5.15.) Vector $\mathbf{v}$ extends from C to D, and vector $\mathbf{u}$ extends from C to A, the point to be tested. In our example,

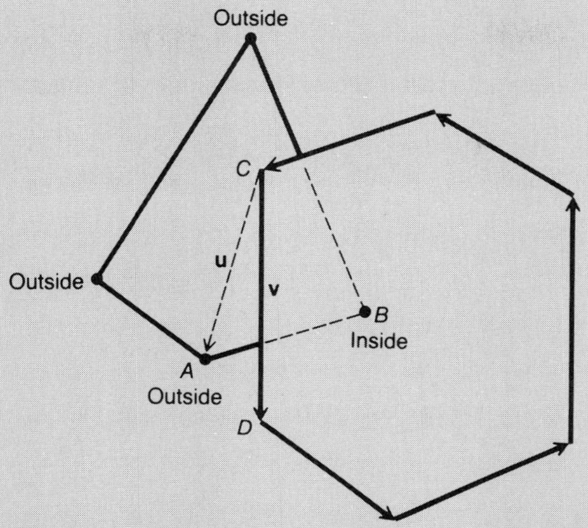

FIGURE 5.15 Endpoint classification for visibility. Outside edges are drawn for the cube.

$$\mathbf{v} = D - C = (-1.31, -40.54) - (-1.37, 15.83) = (0.06, -56.37),$$

$$\mathbf{u} = A - C = (-16.87, -29.73) - (-1.37, 15.83) = (-15.5, -45.56).$$

From Eq. (5.10), the cross product yields

$$\mathbf{u} \times \mathbf{v} = (0, 0, -876.59) = -876.59(0, 0, 1).$$

Since the $\mathbf{u} \times \mathbf{v}$ is a negative multiple of $(0, 0, 1)$, point A is in the right half-plane of CD (and thus outside the cube). In this case, program line 2190 assigns the value 1 to $ENDPOINT(J)$ and testing continues with another point for classification.

If the endpoint J tested is in the left half-plane of each of the outside edges of the cube, we assign the value -1 to $ENDPOINT(J)$. If all visible edge points are classified, then we return from the subroutine.

5.3.12 PLOT OF VISIBLE EDGES OF SECOND PRIORITY OBJECT

Once we have identified the visibility status of each edge point in the second priority object, we are ready to plot the visible edges. The edges of the second priority object can be placed in several categories.

- If the starting endpoint of edge J is visible and no edges of the first priority object intersect edge J, we plot the entire edge segment.
- If $ENDPOINT(J) = -1$ and no edge of the first priority object intersects edge J, edge J is completely invisible and we return from the subroutine.
- If there is only one intersection point, edge J is partially hidden by the first priority object.

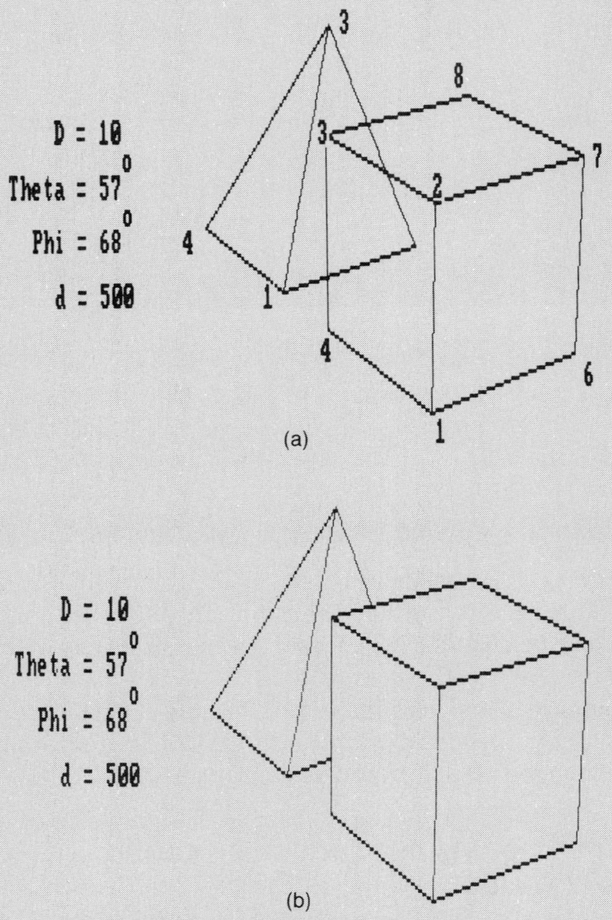

FIGURE 5.16 Plot of the two objects; (a) no overlapping portions removed, and (b) overlapping portions removed

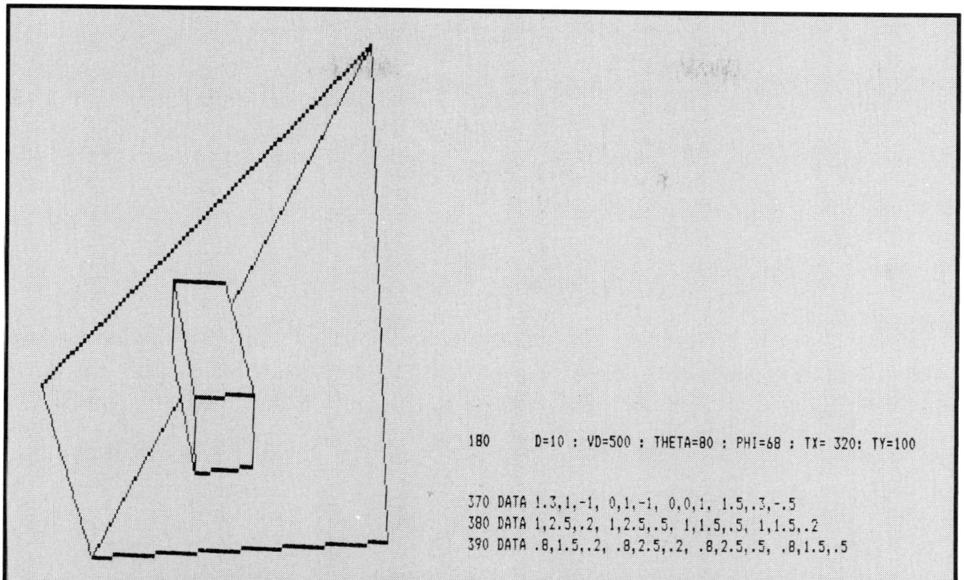

FIGURE 5.17 Containment—cube surrounded by pyramid

- If there are two intersection points, edge *J* will have two separate visible segments. Program lines 2470–2500 identify the visible segments and plot them.

Convex polygons (polygons with interior angles less than 180 degrees) can have no more than two intersection points with a straight line. Therefore, this set of testing rules is sufficient for our example.

Concave polygons, however, can have more than two intersection points with a straight line. Therefore, we modify the plotting segment as follows to incorporate this feature:

- Find all intersection points.
- Sort the intersection points in increasing order of *X* coordinate.
- If *ENDPOINT*(*J*) = 1, plot the edge segment from the starting point to the first intersection point, from the second intersection point to the third intersection point, and so on.
- If *ENDPOINT*(*J*) = −1, plot the edge segment from the first intersection point to the second, the third to the fourth, and so on.
- If there are an even number of intersection points, the end point of the edge is visible. If this is the case, plot the segment between the last intersection point and the edge end point.

5.3.13 GRAPHICS OUTPUT

Upon running the entire program (lines 10–2500), the computer plots the picture shown in Fig. 5.16. By changing viewing parameters such as θ and ϕ, we can create a different view of the objects. For example, changing the view angles (line 180) and vertex coordinates (line 370–390) gives us the picture shown in Fig. 5.17.

5.4 THE MASKING TECHNIQUE

In Section 4.6.2., a program listing was given as an example of how one generates images of the form $z = f(x, y)$. The program was brief, and drew the surface quickly. Unfortunately, it did not eliminate hidden lines. We will now correct this situation by including hidden line capabilities.

5.4.1 THEORY OF OPERATION

We will use the masking technique discussed by Watkins [13]. This technique is based on two premises: (1) lines in the foreground (positive Z direction) are plotted before lines in the background; and (2) a line or a portion of a line is masked (hidden) if it lies within the region bounded by previously plotted lines. Masking is then achieved by maintaining a visible maximum function and a visible minimum function. The portions of each line falling within these bounds are considered hidden. This concept is illustrated in Fig. 5.18. In the next section, we will show how this masking technique can be translated into a hidden line elimination routine.

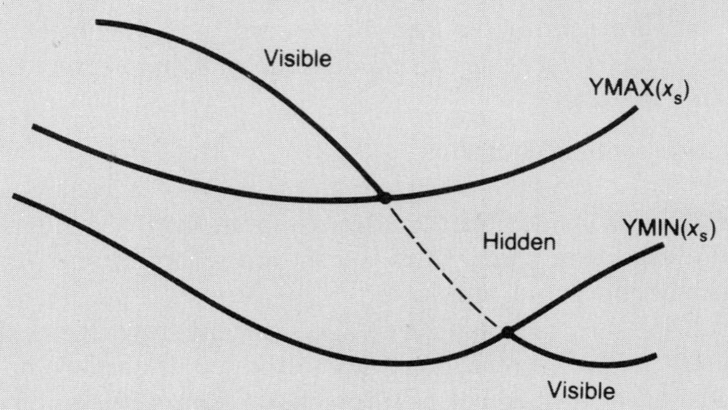

FIGURE 5.18 The concept of the masking technique

```
10 ' Program 5.3: Plot of 3-D Functions with Hidden Lines Removed
20 ' (D,theta,phi) = Viewpoint
30 ' VD = Distance of the Projection Plane from the XY Plane, "d".
40 '  S = Centered screen size. (see Eq.(4.31).
50 ' YMAX(I)= Maximum vertical screen coordinate encountered.
60 ' YMIN(I)= Minimum vertical screen coordinate encountered.
70 ' Flag = The current point is the first of a wire-frame curve (Flag=0).
80 ' Flag1 = The current point is offscreen (Flag1=0).
90 ' Flag2 = The current point is the last referenced point (Flag2=0).
100 '
110 CLS: KEY OFF
120 SCREEN 2
130 DIM YMAX(640), YMIN(640)
140     GOSUB 180
150     GOSUB 240
160     GOSUB 270
170 END
180 '------- Define Viewing Parameters ---------
190       TX= 120: TY = 100: PI = 3.141593 : SCF= 2.4
200       D= 30: VD=420: THETA=30 : PHI= 80 : S=2
210       THETA=THETA*PI/180 : PHI=PHI*PI/180
220       SN1=SIN(THETA) : SN2=SIN(PHI) : CN1=COS(THETA): CN2=COS(PHI)
230 RETURN
240 ' ------- Initialize Ymax and Ymin arrays ------
250 FOR I=1 TO 640 : YMAX(I)=0 : YMIN(I)=199: NEXT I
260 RETURN
270 '------- Define the 3-D function to plot ------
280 DEF FNZ(X,Y) = 7*EXP(-.1*(X*X + Y*Y))
290 FOR X=8 TO -8 STEP -1
300      FLAG =0
310      FOR Y=-8 TO 8 STEP .5
320          Z=FNZ(X,Y)
330          GOSUB 390
340          GOSUB 440
350          GOSUB 520
360      NEXT Y
370 NEXT X
380 RETURN
390 '-------- Compute Eye Coordinates -------------
400      XE= -X*SN1 + Y*CN1
410      YE= -X*CN1*CN2 - Y*SN1*CN2 + Z*SN2
420      ZE= -X*SN2*CN1 - Y*SN2*SN1 - Z*CN2 + D
430 RETURN
440 ' -------- Compute Screen Coordinates -----------
450 ' We assume s1 = s2 = 1 so that both window and viewport coordinates
460 ' will be exactly same. [see Eqs. (3.39) and (3.40).]
470      XS= (VD/S)*(XE/ZE)                         ' Viewport coordinates
480      YS= (VD/S)*(YE/ZE)
490      XS= XS + TX     : XS= SCF*XS               ' PC device coordinates
500      YS= -YS + TY
510 RETURN
520 '---------- Plotting Routine --------------------
530 IF FLAG=0 THEN 540 ELSE 570
540      FLAG= 1 : FLAG2=0
550      OLDX=XS : OLDY=YS
560 RETURN
570      DELTAX=OLDX - XS:IF DELTAX=0 THEN DELTAX=1
580      DELTAY= OLDY - YS
590      SLOPE= DELTAY/DELTAX
600      TEMPY=OLDY
610      NEWX= INT(OLDX) + 1
620      FOR TEMPX =NEWX TO XS
630          FLAG1=1
640          TEMPY=TEMPY + SLOPE
650          IF TEMPX <0 OR TEMPX > 639 THEN FLAG1=0 : FLAG2=0 : GOTO 700
660          IF TEMPY <0 OR TEMPY > 199 THEN FLAG1=0 : FLAG2=0
670          IF TEMPY <= YMIN(TEMPX) THEN 730
680          IF TEMPY >= YMAX(TEMPX) THEN 780
690          FLAG2=0
700      NEXT TEMPX
710      OLDX=XS: OLDY=YS
720 RETURN
730      YMIN(TEMPX)=TEMPY
740      IF FLAG1=0 THEN 770
750      IF FLAG2=0 THEN PSET (TEMPX,TEMPY): FLAG2=1
760      LINE -(TEMPX,TEMPY)
770      IF TEMPY < YMAX(TEMPX) THEN 700
780      YMAX(TEMPX)=TEMPY
790      IF FLAG1=0 THEN 700
800      IF FLAG2=0 THEN PSET (TEMPX,TEMPY): FLAG2=1
810      LINE - (TEMPX,TEMPY)
820      GOTO 700
```

PROGRAM 5.3 Plot of 3-D Functions with Hidden Lines Removed

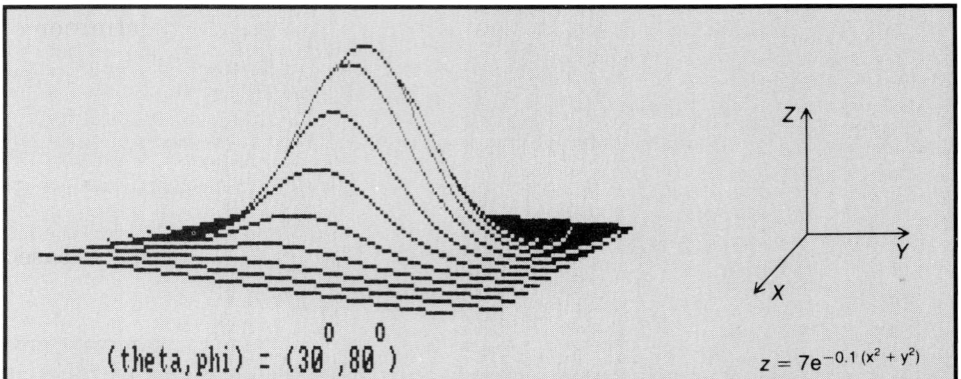

FIGURE 5.19 Plot of the 3-D function with hidden lines removed

5.4.2 PROGRAMMING CONSIDERATIONS

Program 5.3 is an extension of Program 4.2 to include the hidden line routine. As in the beginning of Program 4.2, initialization establishes the viewing and screen parameters and the function to be plotted. Two additional arrays are defined: *YMAX*(*I*) and *YMIN*(*I*). These arrays are used to identify, for each horizontal screen coordinate: (1) the maximum vertical screen coordinate encountered [stored in *YMAX*(*I*)]; and (2) the minimum vertical screen coordinate encountered [stored in *YMIN*(*I*)].

Initially, the value of each *YMAX*(*I*) is zero and the value of each *YMIN*(*I*) is 200 (highest on screen). As coordinates $(x_s y_s)$ are plotted, the values of $YMAX(x_s)$ are reset. As each (x_s, y_s) is considered for plotting, y_s is compared with $YMAX(x_s)$ and $YMIN(x_s)$. If y_s lies between $YMAX(x_s)$ and $YMIN(x_s)$, the coordinate (x_s, y_s) is classified as hidden; otherwise, it is plotted. By executing Program 5.3, we obtain Fig. 5.19. Now compare Fig. 5.19 with Fig. 4.17. The figure looks more pleasing with the hidden lines removed.

5.5 THE IMAGE SPACE ALGORITHMS

Several image space algorithms have been developed [12], but we will discuss only two of them in this section. These are the depth-buffer and scan-line algorithms. Both algorithms are designed for raster displays. They solve the hidden-surface problem, one scan line at a time, processing scan lines from the top to the bottom of the display. The algorithms successively examine a series of windows on the screen. Each window is one scan line high and as wide as the screen. We will use the term *scan conversion* to represent the process of computing the pattern of dots that most closely matches a stored definition of the image.

5.5.1 THE DEPTH-BUFFER ALGORITHM

The depth-buffer algorithm is the simplest of all hidden surface algorithms. It is a brute force approach. Its objective is to independently calculate the intensity (color) of each pixel for the hidden surface displays. The intensity is based on the color of the polygon closest to the viewer.

The algorithm. The algorithm maintains basically two arrays, *INTENSITY* $[x, y]$ and *DEPTH*$[x, y]$ for each pixel (x, y) on the screen. The *INTENSITY* array is a buffer where the color of a pixel is stored. The *DEPTH* array contains the value of z_s for the point nearest to the viewer at each pixel location. The *INTENSITY* array is initialized to the background color and the *DEPTH* array is initialized to 1, the largest representable z_s value [see Eq. (4.41)].

For each polygon, we perform step 1 through step 4 for each point (x, y) inside the polygon:

Step 1: Determine the plane equation that defines the polygon using Eqs. (5.11) through (5.13). Recall that the vertices of the polygon are defined in terms of screen coordinates (x_s, y_s, z_s). This gives the plane equation

$$Ax_s + By_s + Cz_s + D = 0\,.$$

Then solve the plane equation for the variable z_s.

$$z_s = \frac{[-D - Ax_s - By_s]}{C} \tag{5.14}$$

Step 2: Calculate the polygon depth z_s at pixel (x, y). Normally the pixel coordinates (device coordinates) differ from the screen coordinates. If so, we must transform the screen coordinates into the device coordinates. For example, we may transform the screen coordinates into IBM PC device coordinates using Eq. (3.43). For 320 × 200 mode, the coordinates equations are

$$x = 1.2x_s + 160$$

$$y = 100 - y_s\,.$$

Thus computing the depth value at pixel (x, y) is equivalent to evaluating Eq. (5.14) at

$$x_s = \frac{(x - 160)}{1.2} \quad \text{and} \quad y_s = 100 - y\,.$$

Step 3: If $z_s < DEPTH[x, y]$, set $DEPTH[x, y]$ to z_s and $INTENSITY[x, y]$ to the color corresponding to the polygon's shading. Otherwise, no action is taken.

After all the polygons have been considered, the values contained in the *INTENSITY* array represents the solution and can be copied to the display buffer.

It is worth noting that the calculation of z_s for each point on a scan line can be simplified by taking advantage of the fact that a polygon is a flat surface. If we compute z_s at (x, y), we can easily obtain the depth value z_s' at $(x + 1, y)$

$$z_s' = z_s - \frac{A}{C}(\Delta x_s) \tag{5.15}$$

In other words, only one subtraction is required to calculate the depth at $(x + 1, y)$, given the depth z_s at (x, y). For the IBM PC, we may also compute Δx_s at $(x + 1, y)$ as

$$\Delta x_s = \frac{(x + 1 - 160)}{1.2} - \frac{(x - 160)}{1.2} = \frac{1}{1.2}$$

Illustrating example. Figure 5.20 shows the projection of two polygons onto the *XY* plane. Hidden edges are shown as dashed lines. These two polygons are the projected images of surface 1 of the pyramid and surface 1 of the cube in Fig. 5.14. We already computed their plane equations in screen coordinate system in Section 5.3.10. They are

$$\textit{Polygon 1:}\quad -8.211x_s - 9.242y_s + 3399.316z_s - 2645.498 = 0 \tag{5.16a}$$

$$\textit{Polygon 2:}\quad 19.56x_s + 4.758y_s + 2023.997z_s - 857.85 = 0 \tag{5.16b}$$

Assuming a black background, and painting polygon 1 in green and polygon 2 in red, we may assign the color codes as black = 0, green = 1, and red = 2. We then initialize the arrays for all pixels on the screen:

$$INTENSITY[x, y] = 0$$

$$DEPTH[x, y] = 1$$

Now we are ready to scan-convert polygon 1. Solving its plane equation for z_s gives the expression

$$z_s = \frac{2645.498 + 8.211x_s + 9.242y_s}{3399.316} \tag{5.16c}$$

As shown in Fig. 5.21(a), for polygon 1 the y_s coordinate ranges from -29.73 to 48.16, and the x_s coordinate ranges from -16.87 to 29.52. In terms of the PC device coordinate (in 320×200 mode) they are equivalent to $52 \le y \le 130$

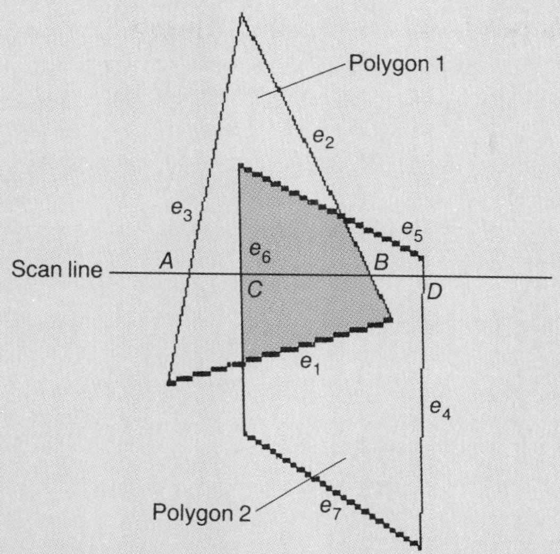

FIGURE 5.20 Two overlapping polygons

and $140 \leq x \leq 195$. Thus, the scan conversion process begins at $y = 52$. The scan line $y = 52$ just touches vertex 3 (160,52) of the polygon, yielding $z_s = 0.656$. Since $z_s < DEPTH[160, 52] = 1$, we update the arrays to have $DEPTH[160, 52] = 0.656$ and $INTENSITY[160, 52] = 1$ (green). This is the only point to evaluate on that line. We increment y by 1 ($y = 53$) and continue the scan conversion process.

By the time the algorithm has progressed down to scan line $y = 110$ (or $y_s = -10$), the scan line intersects the polygon twice, once at A and once at B. To find the intersections of the polygon edges we may use Eq. (5.9). The x_s coordinate of the point of intersection A with $y_s = -10$ is -12.60. Evaluating Eq. (5.16c) at $(-12.60, -10)$ gives $z_s = 0.720$. The screen coordinates for the intersection point B and its depth value can be found similarly: $(x_s, y_s, z_s) = (26.33, -10, 0.814)$.

We then transform these screen coordinates into the PC device coordinates:

$$\text{Point } A = (-12.60, -10) \rightarrow (144, 110)$$

$$\text{Point } B = (26.33, -10) \rightarrow (191, 110)$$

We quickly observe that there are 47 pixels to evaluate on that scan line ($47 = 191 - 144$): Using Eq. (5.15) we can easily compute the depth values for

Polygon 1

Vertex number	x_s, y_s, z_s	Pixel coordinates x, y
(1)	−16.87, −29.73, 0.656	140, 130
(2)	29.52, −17.04, 0.803	195, 117
(3)	0 , 48.16, 0.909	160, 52
Intersection		
A	−12.60, −10.00, 0.720	144, 110
B	26.33, −10.00, 0.814	191, 110

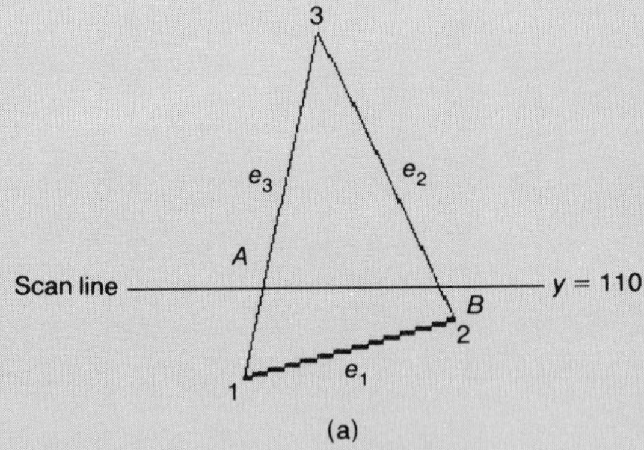

FIGURE 5.21(a) Intersections of polygon 1 with $y=110$ ($y_s = -10$)

Polygon 2

Vertex number	x_s, y_s, z_s	Pixel coordinates x, y
(1)	34.62, −65.52, 0.243	202, 166
(2)	36.43, − 4.34, 0.081	204, 104
(3)	−1.37, 15.83, 0.394	158, 84
(4)	−1.31, −40.54, 0.531	158, 140
Intersection		
C	−1.34, −10.00, 0.460	158, 110
D	36.26, −10.00, 0.097	204, 110

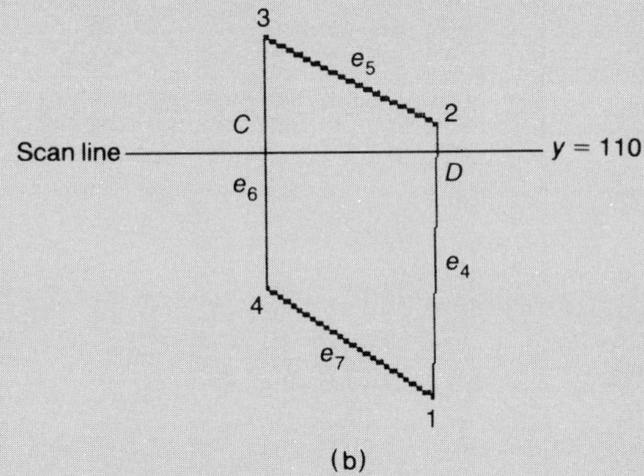

FIGURE 5.21(b) Intersections of polygon 2 with $y = 110$ ($y_s = -10$)

these pixels. For example, the z_s value at point A (144, 110) is 0.720. We then find the z_s value at (145, 110), yielding

$$z_s = 0.720 - (-8.211/3399.316)(1/1.2) = 0.720 + 0.002 = 0.722.$$

Since $z_s < DEPTH[145,110] = 1$, we set $DEPTH[145,110]$ to 0.722 and $INTENSITY[145,110]$ to 1. This process repeats for the remaining pixels on that scan line. Finally, after processing the last scan line $y = 130$, we terminate the scan conversion process for polygon 1.

For polygon 2, the y_s coordinate ranges from -65.53 to 15.83 and the x_s coordinate from -1.37 to 36.43. In terms of the PC coordinates they are equivalent to $84 \leq y \leq 166$ and $158 \leq x \leq 204$. Thus the first scan line begins at $y = 84$. Scan processing proceeds much as before. For scan line $y = 110$, we will examine how the values of the arrays are updated and recorded. The scan line $y = 110$ intersects the edges of polygon 2 twice, at points C and D. The scan conversion process will then begin at point C. The screen coordinates of this intersection and its depth value are

$$(x_s, y_s, z_s) = (1.34, -10, 0.460) \rightarrow (x, y) = (158, 110).$$

Just after we processed polygon 1, the status of the arrays at point C (158, 110) was

$$INTENSITY[158, 110] = 1$$

$$DEPTH[158, 110] = 0.748$$

For polygon 2, we must use Eq. (5.16b). The z_s value at point C is 0.460. Since $z_s < DEPTH[158, 110] = 0.748$, we set $DEPTH[158, 110]$ to 0.460 and $INTENSITY[158, 110]$ to 2 (red). This implies that polygon 2 lies closer to the viewer. Figure 5.22 illustrates how the values of the arrays are updated as we process the remaining pixels on that scan line.

As we move from one scan line to the next, we can compute the new X intersection, just as with scan converting lines:

$$x_{i+1} = x_i + \frac{1}{m} \tag{5.17}$$

where m is the slope of the edge. The slope m is just $\Delta y/\Delta x$, and we have $\Delta y = 1$, so the inverted slope $1/m$ is just Δx.

The depth-buffer algorithm is not always practical because of the enormous size of the depth and intensity arrays. Generating an image with a raster of 320×200 pixels requires 64,000 storage locations for each array. Even though a display buffer may provide memory for the intensity array (e.g., 16K for the IBM PC), the depth array remains large. The scan line coherence algorithm, which we discuss in the next section, capitalizes on various forms of coherence in order to reduce the computing power and memory required to generate an image.

Pixel	[x,y]	[144,110]....	[158,110]....	[181,110]....	[204,110]
Initial value	Depth intensity	1 0	1 0	1 0	1 0
After processing polygon 1	Depth intensity	0.721 1	0.748 1	0.814 1	1 0
After processing polygon 2	Depth intensity	0.721 1	0.460 2	0.190 2	0.097 2
		Polygon 1 ←		→ Polygon 2 ←	

FIGURE 5.22 **Array values after each scan conversion process**

Penetrating polygons. Thus far, no provision has been made for penetrating polygons. Now we can extend the algorithm to handle penetrating polygons, such as those shown in Fig. 5.23. To do this, we simply break up polygon 1 into two parts by introducing false edge e_8. We must then modify the algorithm to find the point of penetration on a scan line as we process it.

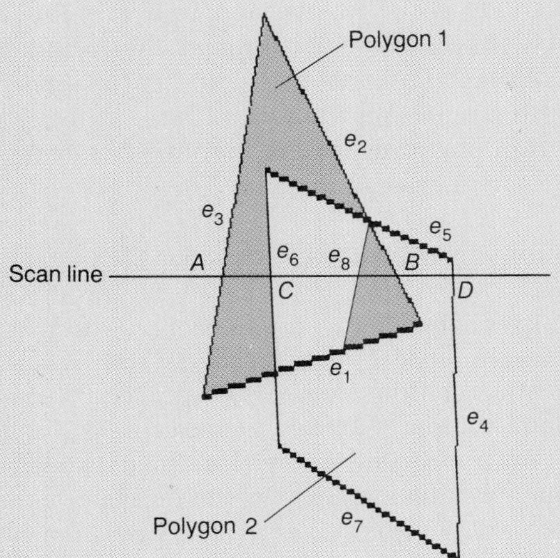

FIGURE 5.23 **Polygon 1 pierces polygon 2 at edge line e_8**

Program 5.4 shows how to translate the algorithm into a computer program. The program is written to process both nonpenetrating and penetrating polygons. With the data given in lines 610–630, we obtain the screen output shown in Fig. 5.24.

```
100 '   Program 5.4: Depth-Buffer Algorithm
110 '   Routine to process either penetrating or nonpenetrating polygons
120 '         BACKGROUND COLOR         = BLUE
130 '         POLYGON 1                = GREEN
140 '         POLYGON 2                = RED
150 '     --------  MAIN ROUTINE  --------
160       CLS: KEY OFF:  SCREEN 0, 1:  WIDTH 80:   COLOR 2, 0
170       PRINT TAB(20) " Specify the types of polygons"
180       PRINT: PRINT TAB(20) "1.  Solid Polygons"
190       PRINT: PRINT TAB(20) "2.  Penetrating Polygons"
200       PRINT: PRINT TAB(20) "Enter Choice ==> "
210       POKE 106, 0
220       CMD$ = INKEY$:  IF CMD$ <> "" THEN 220
230       CMD$ = INKEY$:  IF CMD$ = "" THEN 230
240       IF MID$(CMD$, 1, 1) = "1" THEN SS = 1: GOTO 270
250       IF MID$(CMD$, 1, 1) = "2" THEN SS = 2: GOTO 270
260       GOTO 210
270       CLS:  SCREEN 1, 0:  OUT &H3D9, 1
280       GOSUB 350
290       GOSUB 410
300       GOSUB 750
310       GOSUB 910
320       GOSUB 1060
330       GOSUB 1250
340  END
350 '     --------  DEFINE VIEWING PARAMETERS  --------
360     D = 10:  VD = 500:  THETA = 57:  PHI = 68:  TX = 160:  TY = 100
370     PI = 3.141593:  SCF = 1.2
380     THETA = THETA * PI / 180:  PHI = PHI * PI / 180:  S = 1
390     SN1 = SIN(THETA):  SN2 = SIN(PHI):  CN1 = COS(THETA):  CN2 = COS(PHI)
400 RETURN
410 '     --------  VERTEX ARRAY  --------
420 NV(1) = 3:  NV(2) = 4:  NV(3) = 4:  K1 = 7:  K2 = 10:  W = K2 / (K2 - K1)
430 DIM V(3, 4, 3), EC(3, 4, 3), SC(3, 4, 3), SO(3, 4, 2)
440 FOR I = 1 TO 3
450     FOR J = 1 TO NV(I)
460         READ X, Y, Z
470         V(I, J, 1) = X:  V(I, J, 2) = Y:  V(I, J, 3) = Z
480         GOSUB 640
490         EC(I, J, 1) = XE:  EC(I, J, 2) = YE:  EC(I, J, 3) = ZE
500         GOSUB 690
510         SC(I, J, 1) = XS:  SC(I, J, 2) = YS:  SC(I, J, 3) = ZS
520         SO(I, J, 1) = XS1:  SO(I, J, 2) = YS1
530     NEXT J
540 NEXT I
550 IF SS = 1 THEN LOCATE 2, 15: PRINT "SOLID POLYGONS":  RETURN
560 LOCATE 2, 12: PRINT "PENETRATING POLYGONS"
570 FOR J = 1 TO NV(2)
580     SC(2, J, 1) = SC(3, J, 1): SC(2, J, 2) = SC(3, J, 2):
        SC(2, J, 3) = SC(3, J, 3): SO(2, J, 1) = SO(3, J, 1):
        SO(2, J, 2) = SO(3, J, 2)
590 NEXT J
600 RETURN
610 DATA  1,1,0,  0,1,0,  0,0,1
620 DATA  1,2.5,0,  1,2.5,1,  1,1.5,1,  1,1.5,0
630 DATA  1,1.5,0.5,  0,1.5,0.5,  0,0,0.5,  1,0,0.5
640 '     --------  EYE COORDINATES  --------
650     XE = -X * SN1 + Y * CN1
660     YE = -X * CN1 * CN2 - Y * SN1 * CN2 + Z * SN2
670     ZE = -X * SN2 * CN1 - Y * SN2 * SN1 - Z * CN2 + D
680 RETURN
690 '     --------  SCREEN COORDINATES  --------
700     XS1 = (VD / S) * (XE / ZE)
710     YS1 = (VD / S) * (YE / ZE)
720     ZS = W * (1 - K1 / ZE)
730     XS = XS1 * SCF + TX:   YS = TY - YS1
740 RETURN
750 '     --------  SURFACE ARRAY  --------
```

PROGRAM 5.4 Depth-buffer Algorithm

```
760      DIM SF(2, 1, 5), NPS(2, 1)
770      NS(1) = 1: NS(2) = 1
780      FOR I = 1 TO 2:  FOR J = 1 TO NS(I):  READ NPS(I, J):  NEXT J:  NEXT I
790      FOR I = 1 TO 2
800          FOR J = 1 TO NS(I)
810              FOR K = 1 TO NPS(I, J)
820                  READ SF(I, J, K)
830              NEXT K
840          NEXT J
850      NEXT I
860 RETURN
870 DATA  4
880 DATA  5
890 DATA  1, 2, 3, 1
900 DATA  1, 2, 3, 4, 1
910 '     --------  VISIBLE EDGE ARRAY  --------
920 DIM E(2, 4, 2), VNE(2)
930 FOR I = 1 TO 2
940      M = 1
950      FOR J = 1 TO NS(I)
960          E1 = SF(I, J, 1)
970          FOR K = 2 TO NPS(I, J)
980             E2 = SF(I, J, K)
990             E(I, M, 1) = E1:  E(I, M, 2) = E2
1000             E1 = E2: M = M + 1
1010         NEXT K
1020         NVE(I) = M - 1
1030     NEXT J
1040 NEXT I
1050 RETURN
1060 '     --------  Ymin AND Ymax FOR BOTH POLYGONS  --------
1070     DIM YMIN(2), YMAX(2), XMIN(2), XMAX(2)
1080     FOR I = 1 TO 2
1090         XMIN(I) = SC(I, 1, 1): XMAX(I) = SC(I, 1, 1)
1100         YMIN(I) = SC(I, 1, 2): YMAX(I) = SC(I, 1, 2)
1110         FOR J = 2 TO NV(I)
1120             IF XMIN(I) > SC(I, J, 1) THEN XMIN(I) = SC(I, J, 1)
1130             IF XMAX(I) < SC(I, J, 1) THEN XMAX(I) = SC(I, J, 1)
1140             IF YMIN(I) > SC(I, J, 2) THEN YMIN(I) = SC(I, J, 2)
1150             IF YMAX(I) < SC(I, J, 2) THEN YMAX(I) = SC(I, J, 2)
1160         NEXT J
1170         XMIN(I) = INT(XMIN(I)): XMAX(I) = INT(XMAX(I))
1180         YMIN(I) = INT(YMIN(I)): YMAX(I) = INT(YMAX(I))
1190     NEXT I
1200     IF XMIN(1) > XMIN(2) THEN XL = XMIN(2) ELSE XL = XMIN(1)
1210     IF XMAX(1) > XMAX(2) THEN XU = XMAX(1) ELSE XU = XMAX(2)
1220     IF YMIN(1) > YMIN(2) THEN YL = YMIN(2) ELSE YL = YMIN(1)
1230     IF YMAX(1) > YMAX(2) THEN YU = YMAX(1) ELSE YU = YMAX(2)
1240 RETURN
1250 '     --------  BOUNDARY COORDINATES OF BOTH POLYGONS  --------
1260 DIM ISP(2, 2), DX(2, 2), DEPTH(320), INTENSITY(320)
1270     L3 = 0: LX = XL \ 4: LX1 = LX * 4 + 1
1280     UX = XU \ 4 + 1: DE = 80 - (UX - LX):  UX1 = UX * 4
1290     FOR Y = YL TO YU
1300         C = 0
1310         FOR I = XL TO XU:  DEPTH(I) = 1:  INTENSITY(I) = C: NEXT I
1320         FOR I = 1 TO 2
1330             IF (Y < YMIN(I)) OR (Y > YMAX(I)) THEN 1450
1340             KK = 0
1350             FOR J = 1 TO NVE(I)
1360                 A = E(I, J, 1):  B = E(I, J, 2)
1370                 GOSUB 1490
1380                 IF NCUT <> 1 THEN 1410
1390                 KK = KK + 1: IF I = 1 THEN C = 1 ELSE C = 2
1400                 ISP(I, KK) = INT(XI): DX(I, KK) = (XI - TX) / SCF
1410             NEXT J
1420             IF ISP(I, 1) > ISP(I, 2) THEN SWAP ISP(I, 1), ISP(I, 2):
                                              SWAP DX(I, 1), DX(I, 2)
1430             IF (KK = 0) AND (Y = LB) THEN 1450
1440             GOSUB 1680
1450         NEXT I
1460         GOSUB 1910
1470     NEXT Y
1480 RETURN
1490 '     --------  INTERSECTION TEST  --------
1500     AX = SC(I, A, 1): AY = SC(I, A, 2): BX = SC(I, B, 1): BY = SC(I, B, 2)
1510     CX = 0: CY = Y: DX = 319: DY = Y
```

PROGRAM 5.4 (continued)

```
1520    R1 = AX - BX:   R2 = AY - BY:   R3 = CX - DX:   R4 = CY - DY
1530    S1 = SGN(R1):   S2 = SGN(R2):   S3 = SGN(R3):   S4 = SGN(R4)
1540    A1 = AX: B1 = BX: A2 = AY: B2 = BY: C1 = CX: D1 = DX: C2 = CY: D2 = DY
1550    IF S1 > 0 THEN A1 = BX:  B1 = AX
1560    IF S2 > 0 THEN A2 = BY:  B2 = AY
1570    IF S3 > 0 THEN C1 = DX:  D1 = CX
1580    IF S4 > 0 THEN C2 = DY:  D2 = CY
1590 '      --------  MINMAX TEST FOR EDGE OVERLAPPING  --------
1600    IF (B1 < C1) OR (D1 < A1) OR (B2 < C2) OR (D2 < A2) THEN NCUT = 0:
                                                                  RETURN
1610    M1 = R2 / R1:  M2 = R4 / R3:  M3 = M2 - M1
1620    IF (M3 = 0) OR (ABS(M3) <= .0001) THEN NCUT = 0: RETURN
1630 '      --------  COMPUTE INTERSECTION POINT  --------
1640    Z0 = AY - CY:                Z1 = M1 * AX - M2 * CX:
        Z2 = (AY - M1 * AX) * M2:    Z3 = (CY - M2 * CX) * M1
1650    XI = (Z0 - Z1) / M3:         YI = (Z2 - Z3) / M3
1660    IF (XI < A1) OR (XI > B1) OR (XI < C1) OR (XI > D1) OR (YI < A2) OR
           (YI > B2) THEN NCUT = 0 ELSE NCUT = 1
1670 RETURN
1680 '      --------  UPDATE DEPTH & INTENSITY  --------
1690    XI = DX(I, 1):  YI = TY - Y
1700    GOSUB 1810
1710    X0 = ISP(I, 1):    X1 = ISP(I, 2)
1720    IF ZDEPTH >= DEPTH(X0) THEN 1740
1730        INTENSITY(X0) = C:  DEPTH(X0) = ZDEPTH
1740    X0 = X0 + 1:  RATIO = XX / ZZ
1750    FOR K = X0 TO X1
1760        ZDEPTH = ZDEPTH - RATIO
1770        IF ZDEPTH > DEPTH(K) THEN 1790
1780            DEPTH(K) = ZDEPTH:  INTENSITY(K) = C
1790    NEXT K
1800 RETURN
1810 '      --------  COMPUTE DEPTH  --------
1820    A1 = SO(I, 1, 1):  A2 = SO(I, 1, 2):  A3 = SC(I, 1, 3)
1830    B1 = SO(I, 2, 1):  B2 = SO(I, 2, 2):  B3 = SC(I, 2, 3)
1840    C1 = SO(I, 3, 1):  C2 = SO(I, 3, 2):  C3 = SC(I, 3, 3)
1850    AA = B1 - A1:  BB = B2 - A2:  CC = B3 - A3:
        DD = C1 - A1:  EE = C2 - A2:  FF = C3 - A3
1860    XX = BB * FF - CC * EE: YY = CC * DD - AA * FF: ZZ = AA * EE - BB * DD
1870    T1 = XX * A1 + YY * A2 + ZZ * A3
1880    T2 = XX * XI + YY * YI
1890    ZDEPTH = (T1 - T2) / ZZ
1900 RETURN
1910 '      --------  PLOT  --------
1920    DEF SEG = &HB800
1930    R = Y MOD 2
1940    IF L3 <> 0 THEN 1960
1950    IF R = 1 THEN IO = &H2000 + 80 * (Y-1)/2 + LX :  IE = 80 * (Y+1)/2 + LX
                ELSE IO = &H2000 + 80 * Y / 2 + LX:     IE = 80 * Y / 2 + LX
1960    FOR L1 = LX1 TO UX1 STEP 4
1970        CC = 0:  EX = 64
1980        FOR L2 = 1 TO 4
1990            CC = CC + INTENSITY(L1 + L2 - 1) * EX
2000            EX = EX / 4
2010        NEXT L2
2020        IF R = 1 THEN POKE IO, CC: IO = IO + 1:
                     ELSE POKE IE, CC: IE = IE + 1
2030    L3 = L3 + 1
2040    NEXT L1
2050    IF R = 1 THEN IO = IO + DE ELSE IE = IE + DE
2060 RETURN
```

PROGRAM 5.4 Depth-buffer Algorithm

5.5.2 SCAN-LINE COHERENCE ALGORITHM

This approach is an extension of the depth-buffer algorithm. The difference is that we deal not just with one polygon, but with all the polygons that concurrently define an object. In other words, the algorithm scan-converts all of the polygons in the scene, one scan line at a time. The algorithm proceeds as follows. For *each scan line* we perform step 1 through step 3.

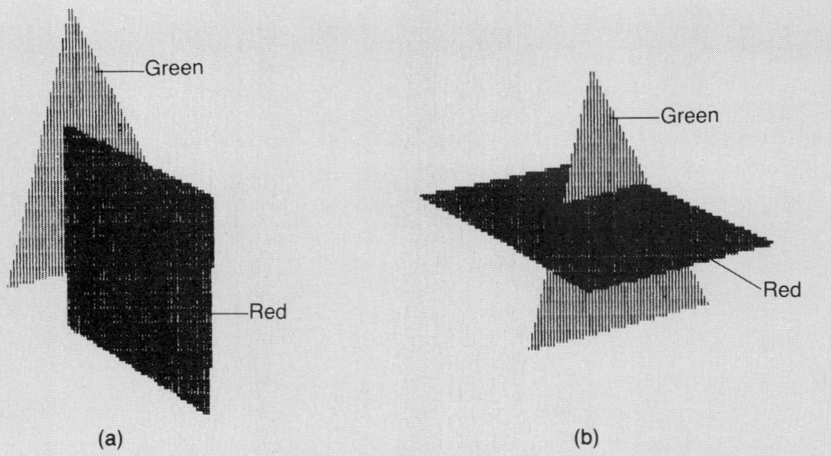

FIGURE 5.24(a) Scan conversion results of nonpenetrating polygons on the IBM PC (320 × 200) and (b) scan conversion results of penetrating polygons on the IBM PC (320 × 200 mode)

Step 1: For all pixels on a scan line, set *DEPTH* $[x]$ to 1 and *INTENSITY* $[x]$ to background color. Note that arrays *DEPTH* and *INTENSITY* have dimension 1.

Step 2: For each polygon in the scene, find all the pixels x on the current scan line y that lie within the polygon. For each of these,

1. Calculate the depth value z_s of the polygon at (x, y).
2. If $z_s <$ *DEPTH* $[x]$, set *DEPTH* $[x]$ to z_s and *INTENSITY* $[x]$ to the color corresponding to the polygon's shading.

Step 3: After all the polygons on that scan line have been considered, the values contained in *INTENSITY* $[x]$ represent the solution and can be displayed.

The algorithm above should work, but it is inefficient because it makes no assumptions about the size or relative positions of surfaces. Such interdependencies are referred to as *coherence.* We will discuss briefly how the algorithm can be improved by introducing the concept of *edge coherence.*

The visibility of an edge changes only when it crosses another edge, as shown in Fig. 5.20. We can take advantage of this property by creating a list of edge segments without intersections. Then we need to check only one point of each segment. For each scan line, we work only with the sets of edges it intersects. We define these edges as the *active edges.* To implement this edge coherence algorithm, we create three tables: an edge table (ET), an active edge table (AET) and a polygon table (PT).

Edge table. We create an edge table containing all of the edges, sorted by their smaller y_s coordinate. The ET is typically built by using a bucket sort with as many buckets as there are scan lines. Within each bucket, edges are kept in order of increasing x_s coordinate of the lower endpoint. Each entry in the ET contains:

1. The x_s coordinate of the endpoint with the smaller y_s coordinate ($x_{s \cdot \min}$).
2. The y_s coordinate of the edge's other endpoint ($y_{s \cdot \max}$).
3. The x_s increment used in stepping from one scan line to the next ($1/m$).
4. The polygon identification, indicating the polygon to which the edge belongs.

For edge e_3 in Fig. 5.20, the entries for the ET look like

Edge e_3	48.16	−16.87	1/4.62	1
	$y_{s \cdot \max}$	$x_{s \cdot \min}$	$1/m$	polygon number

Active edge table. The AET can be constructed in the following manner. As we move to the next scan line, new x_s intersections are calculated using Eq. (5.17). Any new edges intersected by this next scan line are added to the AET, and edges in the AET not intersected by this next scan line are deleted.

Polygon table. The PT may contain the following information for each polygon:

1. The coefficients of the plane equation.
2. Shading or color information for the polygon.
3. A flag that indicates the pointer's location relative to the polygon. [This in/out boolean flag is initialized to false (outside the polygon). It is used during scan line processing.]

Illustrating example. We will apply the algorithm to the example in Fig. 5.20. The sorted ET for this figure contains entries for $e_7, e_4, e_6, e_3, e_1, e_2$, and e_5. The PT has entries for polygon 1 and polygon 2.

The AET is kept in order of increasing x_s. By the time the algorithm has progressed to the scan line $y = 110(y_s = -10)$, the AET contains e_3, e_6, e_2, and e_4, in that order.

The edges are processed from left to right. To process e_3, we first set the flag of polygon 1 to *true*. Thus, the scan is "in" the polygon and the polygon must be considered. Because we are in only one polygon, the polygon must be visible; we therefore paint the span from A to the next edge in the AET, edge e_6. At this point, the flag for polygon 2 also becomes *true* —we are in two polygons. We must now decide whether polygon 1 or polygon 2 is closer to the viewer. We determine this by evaluating the plane equations of both polygons for z_s, at $y = 110$ (or $y_s = -10$) with x_s equal to the intersection of $y_s = -10$ with edge e_6. The intersection value is $(-1.34, -10)$ and is in the AET entry for e_6. Evaluating the plane equations [Eqs. (5.16a) and (5.16b)] at $(-1.34, -10)$ yields

$$z_s = 0.74 \text{ for polygon } 1;$$

$$z_s = 0.46 \text{ for polygon } 2.$$

Since $0.46 < 0.74$, polygon 2 is closer to the viewer. Therefore, the shading for polygon 2 is used for the span to edge e_2. At this point, polygon 1's flag becomes *false* and the scan is again "in" only one polygon, polygon 2, whose shading rule continues all the way to edge e_4. At this point, the scan conversion process terminates and moves to the next scan line.

5.6 SUMMARY

The most difficult and computationally expensive portion of a graphics procedure is the solution of the visible line or visible surface problem. In general, solutions are categorized as object space or image space algorithms. In object space solutions, the calculations are performed in three dimensions and at the maximum precision of the computer. On the other hand, image space algorithms retain the depth information (z_s), but sort the image by pixel position of the picture (x, y). The sorting is done only to the resolution of the display. There are two disadvantages to these image space algorithms. First, information is lost because algorithms sample the visual space and calculate intensities only at discrete sample points. Second, they ignore much of the environmental information, which could be used for shadowing and texturing. Most object space algorithms avoid these problems by maintaining full three-dimensional environmental data and carrying out the computations to the maximum precision of the machine.

EXERCISES

5.1 Consider the house in Fig. 5.25, defined by the accompanying world coordinates.

- **a)** Write a program to draw the house with hidden surfaces removed.
- **b)** Suppose we observe the house at $(15, 60°, 30°)$. Determine which surfaces are visible and which are not.

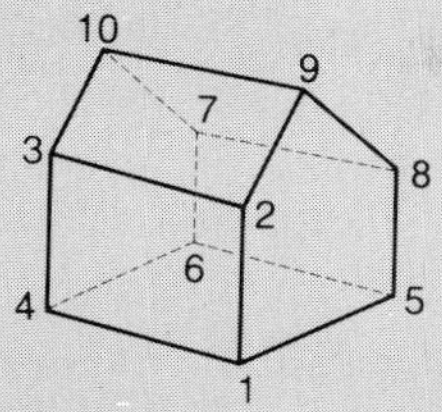

FIGURE 5.25 House

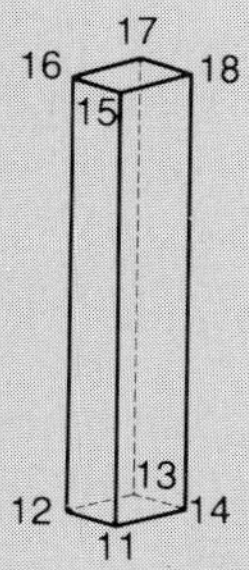

FIGURE 5.26 Chimney

Vertex number	Coordinates x	y	z
1	1	1.2	−1
2	1	1.2	1
3	1	−1.2	1
4	1	−1.2	−1
5	−1	1.2	−1
6	−1	−1.2	−1
7	−1	−1.2	1
8	−1	1.2	1
9	0	1.2	2
10	0	−1.2	2
11	−0.4	−1.2	−1
12	−0.4	−1.8	−1
13	−1	−1.8	−1
14	−1	−1.2	−1
15	−0.4	−1.2	2
16	−0.4	−1.8	2
17	−1	−1.8	2
18	−1	−1.2	2

c) Suppose we add a chimney to the house (Fig. 5.26). How would you modify your program to handle this chimney properly?

(The data for Figs. 5.25 and 5.26 are from Roy E. Myers, *Microcomputer Graphics for the Apple® Computer,* © 1982, Addison-Wesley Pub. Co. Inc., Reading, Mass. Reprinted with permission.)

5.2 Consider the stacked cubes in Fig. 5.27. The vertices of the base cube are identified as: $A(0,0,0)$, $B(2,0,0)$, $C(2,2,0)$, $D(0,2,0)$, $E(0,0,2)$, $F(2,0,2)$, $G(2,2,2)$, and $H(0,2,2)$. The second cube (which is stacked on the base cube) is one-eighth of the base cube in volume; the third cube is one-eighth of the second cube.

a) How can we obtain the coordinates of the second cube from only the vertices of the base cube?

b) Write a program to draw these stacked cubes with hidden lines removed.

c) Suppose that the base cube has a rectangular hole running from the front surface to the back surface. The second and third cubes have holes of the same relative size. How do you draw this hole?

5.3 The following program will draw a hat as shown in Fig. 5.28. The program takes about 20 minutes to complete the picture. The program uses

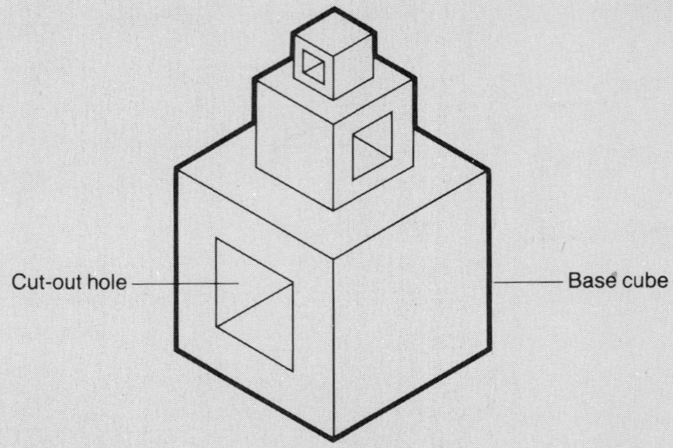

FIGURE 5.27

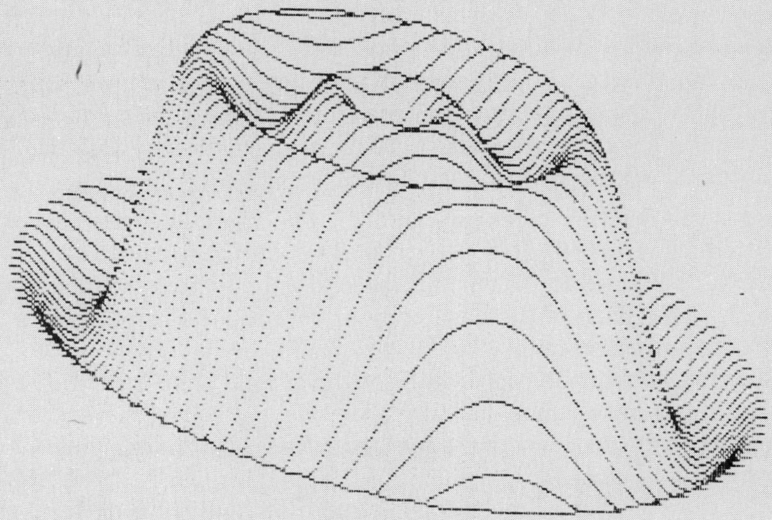

FIGURE 5.28

a blackout technique to eliminate the hidden lines: the hidden portions of the function are drawn, but they are erased again when a closer portion of the function is drawn.

```
100 'PROGRAM TO DRAW A HAT
110 CLS: KEY OFF : SCREEN 1
120 TX=160: TY=100
125 PI=3.1415927#
130 XP=144:XR=1.5*PI
140 YP=56: YR=1:ZP=64
150 XF=XR/XP: YF=YP/YR:ZF=XR/ZP
160 FOR ZI=-TY TO TY-1    STEP 3
170     IF ZI<-ZP OR ZI>ZP GOTO 250
180     ZT=ZI*XP/ZP:ZZ=ZI
190     XL=INT(.5+SQR(XP*XP-ZT*ZT))
200     FOR XI=-XL TO XL
210     XT=SQR(XI*XI + ZT*ZT)*XF:XX=XI
220     YY=(SIN(XT)+.4*SIN(3*XT))*YF
230     GOSUB 270
240     NEXT XI
250 NEXT ZI
260 END
270 XS=XX+ZZ+TX
280 YS=YY-ZZ+TY
290 YS=200-YS
300 PSET(XS,YS),2
310 IF YS=200 GOTO 330
320 LINE (XS,YS+1)-(XS,200),0
330 RETURN
```

a) Discuss how to improve the execution speed of the program.
b) In Section 2.4 we discussed the technique of writing a subroutine in assembly language. Rewrite the program using an assembly language subroutine (if you are familiar with the PC assembly language) and compare the new execution time with the old.

5.4 The surfaces in Fig. 5.29 are defined by the function

$$y = 3 \sin\sqrt{x^2 + z^2}.$$

Knowing this shape of the function, write a program that draws an orthographic projection of a cowboy hat, as shown in Fig. 5.30. If you have a plotter, provide x, y, and z scales with the picture.

5.5 Suppose we want to draw the polygons shown in Fig. 5.31 using the depth-buffer algorithm. What modifications to our drawing procedures will be needed to process such polygons?

5.6 Write a program in a language other than BASIC to perform the depth-buffer algorithm in Section 5.5.1.

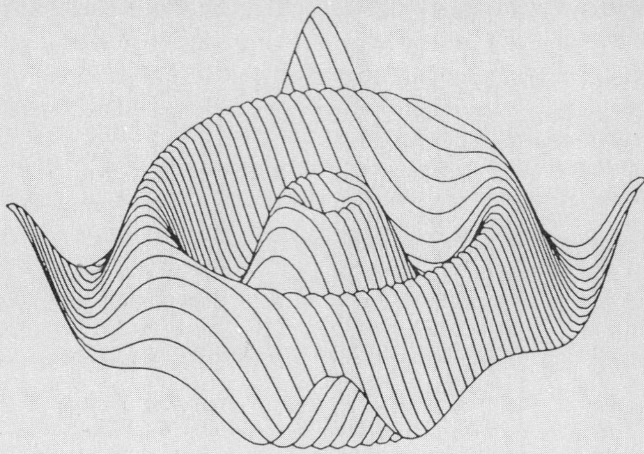

FIGURE 5.29

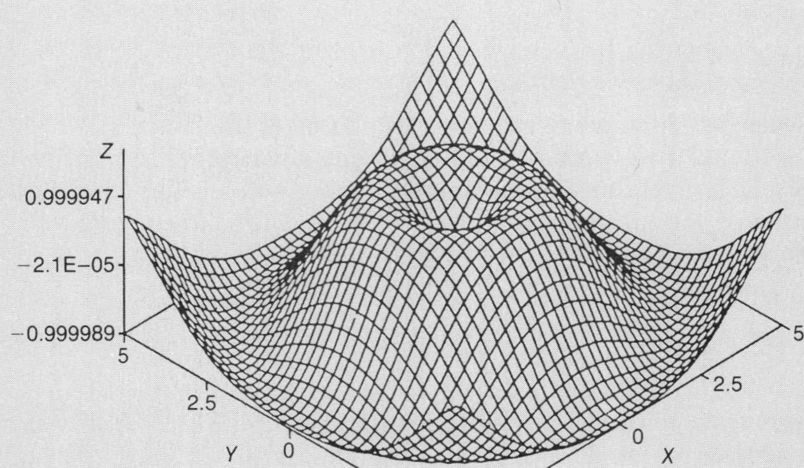

FIGURE 5.30 The cowboy hat

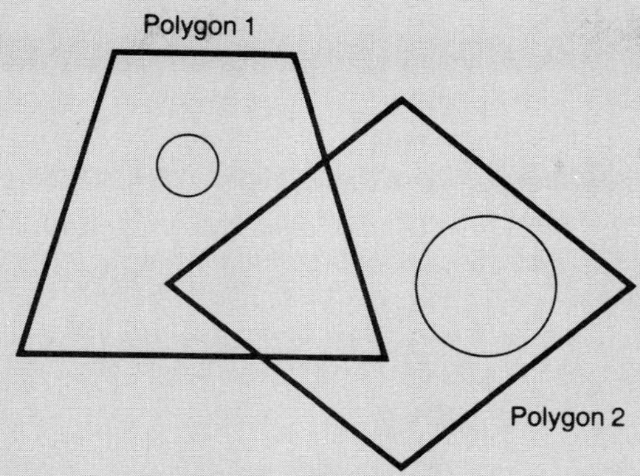

FIGURE 5.31

5.7 Write a program to perform the scan line coherence algorithm discussed in Section 5.5.2.

REFERENCES

1. Barnhill, R. E., and R. F. Riesenfield, *Computer Aided Geometric Design,* Academic Press, New York, 1974.

2. Barsky, B. A., "A Description and Evaluation of Various 3-D Models," *IEEE Computer Graphics and Applications* **4** (1) 38–52, January 1984.

3. Brown, B. E., "Computer Graphics for Large Scale Two- and Three-Dimensional Analysis of Complex Geometries," *Computer Graphics* **13** (2) 33–40, 1979.

4. Brodlie, K. W., *Mathematical Methods in Computer Graphics and Design,* Academic Press, London (edited), 1980.

5. Foley, J. D., and A. Van Dam, *Fundamentals of Interactive Computer Graphics,* Addison-Wesley, Reading, Mass., 1982.

6. Giloi, W. K., *Interactive Computer Graphics,* Prentice-Hall, Englewood Cliffs, N.J., 1978.

7. Greenberg D., A. Marcus, A. H. Schmidt, and V. Gorter, *The Computer Image: Applications of Computer Graphics,* Addison-Wesley, Reading, Mass., 1982.

8. Newman, W. M., and R. F. Sproull, *Principles of Interactive Computer Graphics,* McGraw-Hill, New York, 1979.

9. Parslow, R. D., et al. (eds.), *Computer Graphics: Techniques and Applications,* Plenum Press, New York, 1975.

10. Pavlidis, T., *Algorithms for Graphics and Image Processing,* Computer Science Press, Rockville, Md., 1982.

11. Sowerbutts, W. T. C., "A Surface-Plotting Program Suitable for Microcomputers," *Computer Aided Design* **15** (6) 323–327, November 1983.

12. Sutherland, I. E., R. F. Sproull, and R. A. Schumacker, "A Characterization of Ten Hidden-Surface Algorithms," *Computing Surveys* **6** (1) 1–55, March 1974.

13. Watkins, S. L., "Masked Three-Dimensional Plot Program with Rotations," *Communications of the ACM* **17** (9) 520–523, 1974.

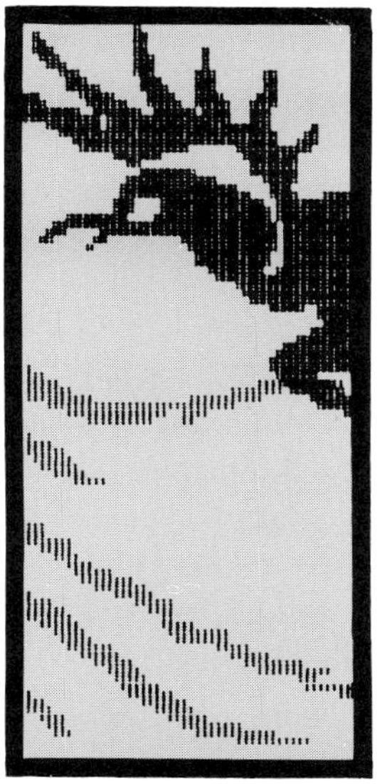

PART THREE
User Interface Design

Part Three serves mainly to show how the basic concepts presented in Part Two can be utilized in designing a simple graphics package. Part Three contains four chapters, which develop a series of general-purpose graphics programs on a microcomputer. Chapter 6 discusses the method of interfacing graphics input data with any graphics routine. Chapter 7 develops a subroutine that performs 2-D plotting; Chapter 8 develops a graphics program that draws a picture through keyboard interfacing only. Chapter 9 presents a 3-D plotter that can translate, rotate, or scale an object through simple menu-driven commands. These programs are intended as examples to explain the principles of user interface design. Readers are encouraged to extend the programs for their own use.

CHAPTER SIX
Interactive Data Editor

As we mentioned briefly in Chapter 3, a first step toward any graphics program is to provide a mechanism for furnishing data to the program. For this purpose, we commonly create a set of data files according to the input format of the model so that the operator needs only to link the data file to the graphics program.

The purpose of this chapter is to develop a general-purpose data editor program for creating an input data file and editing it when necessary. Good editing features are critical to the graphics program. These features make it possible to avoid restarting or backing up a long data entry sequence when the operator errs in an entry or wishes to modify the data once it has been completely loaded into memory.

6.1 DESIGN PRINCIPLES

We will first describe some of the design principles of DATA EDITOR. These design concepts, based on human engineering principles, are applicable to all of the graphics programs developed in later chapters.

6.1.1 FEEDBACK

Feedback is an important part of an interactive system. Typically, feedback occurs as each command is accepted by the system. For example, a command picked from a menu is highlighted so that the user knows that the action has been accepted. The most useful form of feedback also tells the user that the requested operation has been completed. This is usually done with a new or modified display that explicitly shows the results. Audio feedback such as a beep sound has the same effect. If a requested task will take some time to complete, the program should provide another type of feedback to indicate that the computer is at least working on the problem. The DATA EDITOR program uses several such feedback mechanisms. The complete code follows.

```
10   '------------------------- DATA EDITOR ----------------------------
20   GOSUB 230
30   IF NEWFILE%=1 THEN 80
40   CLS : SCREEN 0,1
50   PRINT "READING ";FILE$;"..."
60   GOSUB 1020
70   NOD%(1)=ROWX%: FOR I%=2 TO COLUMNX% : NOD%(I%)=ROW% : NEXT
80   ROWP%=1 : COLP%=1 :  SAVED%=0 : OLDXPOS%=0 : OLDYPOS%=0
90   GOSUB 440 : GOSUB 730
100  RPOS%=3 : CPOS%=0: GOSUB 2230 : GOSUB 2310
110  IF NEWFILE%=1 THEN 150
120  LOCATE 23,30: PRINT "LISTING...": BEEP
130  GOSUB 840: GOSUB 920
140  LOCATE 23,30: PRINT BLANK2$
150  LOCATE 23,3 : PRINT M$;: BEEP
160  LOCATE 23,55: PRINT M1$
170  LOCATE 23,69: PRINT OLDREP$
180  GOSUB 1580
190  COMMON FD$,PD$,DX%
200  CHAIN CALLFILE$,SL%
210  RETURN
220  '------------------------ INITIALIZING CONSTANTS -------------------
230  OPTION BASE 1 : KEY OFF
240  DIM X.(300,10), COMMAND$(15), NOD%(10)
250  BLANK2$="                                    "
260  OLDREP$="D": M1$="DEFAULT CMD :": BLANK1$="           "
270  M$="COMMAND :" : BLANK$="                   "
280  COMMAND$(1)="r": COMMAND$(2)="c": COMMAND$(3)="d"
290  COMMAND$(4)="u": COMMAND$(5)="s": COMMAND$(6)="k"
300  COMMAND$(7)="i": COMMAND$(8)="f": COMMAND$(9)="b": COMMAND$(10)="o"
310  COMMAND$(11)="e"
320  KEY(11) ON : KEY(14) ON
330  RETURN
340  '------------------------ EXITING EDITOR ---------------------------
350  IF SAVED%=1 OR MODIFIED%=0 THEN 420
360  LOCATE 23,30:PRINT BLANK2$:LOCATE 23,30:BEEP:INPUT "SAVE FILE";REP$
370  IF REP$="N" OR REP$="n" THEN 420
380  LOCATE 23,30: PRINT BLANK2$ : LOCATE 23,30
390  PRINT "SAVING FILE ..." : BEEP
400  GOSUB 1110
410  LOCATE 23,30: PRINT BLANK2$
420  RETURN
430  '------------------------ PRINT INDICES ----------------------------
440  CLS: LOCATE 1,68: PRINT "COMMAND"
450  IF LEFT%=1 THEN LOCATE 3,55: COLOR 0,7: PRINT "NOT ALLOWED": COLOR 7,0
460  LOCATE 3,68 : PRINT "B BACKWARD"
470  IF COL%=1 THEN LOCATE 4,55: COLOR 0,7: PRINT "NOT ALLOWED": COLOR 7,0
480  LOCATE 4,68 : PRINT "C COLUMN"
490  LOCATE 5,68 : PRINT "D DOWN"
500  LOCATE 6,68 : PRINT "E EXIT"
510  IF RIGHT%=1 THEN LOCATE 7,55: COLOR 0,7: PRINT "NOT ALLOWED": COLOR 7,0
520  LOCATE 7,68 : PRINT "F FORWARD"
530  LOCATE 8,68 : PRINT "I INSERT"
540  LOCATE 9,68 : PRINT "K KILL"
550  IF CORDER%=1 THEN LOCATE 10,55: COLOR 0,7: PRINT "NOT ALLOWED": COLOR 7,0
560  LOCATE 10,68: PRINT "O ORDER"
570  LOCATE 11,68: PRINT "R ROW"
580  LOCATE 12,68: PRINT "S SAVE"
590  LOCATE 13,68: PRINT "U UP"
600  LOCATE 22,55: PRINT ORDER$
```

PROGRAM 6.1 DATA EDITOR (AEDIT)

```
610  LOCATE 2,1
620  FOR I%=1 TO 77 : PRINT CHR$(196);: NEXT
630  LOCATE 21,1
640  FOR I%=1 TO 77 : PRINT CHR$(196);: NEXT
650  FOR I%=1 TO 23
660       LOCATE I%,1: PRINT CHR$(179)
670       LOCATE I%,78: PRINT CHR$(179)
680       LOCATE I%,28: PRINT CHR$(179)
690       LOCATE I%,53: PRINT CHR$(179)
700       NEXT
710  RETURN
720  '------------------------ PRINT DATA ON SCREEN ------------------------
730  FOR I%=1 TO 18
740       LOCATE I%+2,2,1,7,7
750       PRINT USING "###";I%+18*(ROWP%-1); : PRINT " :"
760       NEXT
770  C%=2*(COLP%-1)
780  IF C%=0 THEN C1$="( Y ) " ELSE C1$="( X"+CHR$(C%+48)+" )"
790  C%=C%+1 : C2$="( X"+CHR$(C%+48)+" )"
800  LOCATE 1,21: PRINT C1$
810  LOCATE 1,46: PRINT C2$
820  RETURN
830  '----------------------- PRINT LEFT COLUMN --------------------------
840  T1%=18*(ROWP%-1)
850  FOR I%=1 TO 18
860       K%=I%+T1% : LOCATE I%+2,7
870       IF K% > NOD%(C%) THEN PRINT "                    " : GOTO 890
880       IF COLP%=1 THEN PRINT USING "################.###";X.(K%,1)
              ELSE IF C% <= COLUMNX% THEN
                  PRINT USING "################.###";X.(K%,C%)
890       NEXT I%
900  RETURN
910  '-------------------------- PRINT RIGHT COLUMN -----------------------
920  T1%=18*(ROWP%-1)
930  FOR I%=1 TO 18
940       K%=I%+T1%
950       LOCATE I%+2,32
960       IF K% > NOD%(C%+1) THEN PRINT "                    " : GOTO 980
970       IF C%+1 <= COLUMNX% THEN
              PRINT USING "################.###";X.(K%,C%+1)
980       NEXT I%
990  BEEP
1000 RETURN
1010 '------------------------ READING FILE ------------------------------
1020 OPEN FILE$ FOR INPUT AS #2
1030 INPUT #2,ROWX%,ROW%,COLUMNX%
1040 KEEP%=0
1050 FOR J%=1 TO COLUMNX%
1060      IF J%<>1 THEN FOR I%=1 TO ROW% : INPUT #2,X.(I%,J%) : NEXT I% ELSE
              FOR I%=1 TO ROWX% : INPUT #2,X.(I%,1) : NEXT I%
1070      NEXT J%
1080 CLOSE #2
1090 RETURN
1100 '------------------------ SAVE X & Y VALUES ------------------------
1110 ROWX%=NOD%(1) : ROW%=NOD%(2)
1120 OPEN FILE$ FOR OUTPUT AS #1
1130 PRINT #1,ROWX%;ROW%;COLUMNX%
1140 FOR J%=1 TO COLUMNX%
1150      IF J%<>1 THEN FOR I%=1 TO ROW% : PRINT #1,X.(I%,J%);: NEXT I%
              ELSE FOR I%=1 TO ROWX% : PRINT #1,X.(I%,1);: NEXT I%
1160      NEXT J%
1170 CLOSE #1 : SAVED%=1
1180 RETURN
1190 '------------------------ SCROLL DOWN ------------------------------
1200 MID$(REP$,1)=" " : PG%=VAL(REP$)
1210 IF PG%=0 THEN PG%=1
1220 ROWP%=ROWP%+PG%
1230 QUIT%=1
1240 GOSUB 730
1250 RPOS%=3 : CPOS%=0: GOSUB 2230 : GOSUB 2310
1260 GOSUB 840 : GOSUB 920: RETURN
1270 '------------------------ SCROLL UP --------------------------------
1280 MID$(REP$,1)=" " : PG%=VAL(REP$)
1290 IF PG%=0 THEN PG%=1
1300 ROWP%=ROWP%-PG%
1310 IF ROWP% < 1 THEN ROWP%=1
1320 QUIT%=1
1330 GOSUB 730
1340 RPOS%=3 : CPOS%=0: GOSUB 2230 : GOSUB 2310
1350 GOSUB 840 : GOSUB 920: RETURN
```

PROGRAM 6.1 (continued)

```
1360 '------------------------  SCROLL RIGHT  ----------------------------
1370 IF RIGHT%=1 THEN GOSUB 2920 : GOTO 1450
1380 MID$(REP$,1)=" " : PG%=VAL(REP$)
1390 IF PG%=0 THEN PG%=1
1400 COLP%=COLP%+PG%
1410 QUIT%=1
1420 GOSUB 730
1430 RPOS%=3 : CPOS%=0: GOSUB 2230 : GOSUB 2310
1440 GOSUB 840 : GOSUB 920
1450 RETURN
1460 '------------------------  SCROLL LEFT  -----------------------------
1470 IF LEFT%=1 THEN GOSUB 2920 : GOTO 1560
1480 MID$(REP$,1)=" " : PG%=VAL(REP$)
1490 IF PG%=0 THEN PG%=1
1500 COLP%=COLP%-PG%
1510 IF COLP% < 1 THEN ROWP%=1
1520 QUIT%=1
1530 GOSUB 730
1540 RPOS%=3 : CPOS%=0: GOSUB 2230 : GOSUB 2310
1550 GOSUB 840 : GOSUB 920
1560 RETURN
1570 '-----------------------  CHANGE DATA  -------------------------------
1580 LOCATE 23,69: PRINT BLANK1$: LOCATE 23,69: PRINT OLDREP$
1590 LOCATE 23,12 : PRINT BLANK$
1600 LOCATE 23,12: INPUT REP$ : IF REP$="" THEN REP$=OLDREP$
1610 REP2$=LEFT$(REP$,1)
1620 T1%=ASC(REP2$)
1630 IF T1% >= 43 AND T1% <= 57 THEN 1690
1640 T1%=T1% OR 32 : REP2$=CHR$(T1%)
1650 GOSUB 2350
1660 IF VALID%=0 THEN 1580 ELSE VALID%=0: OLDREP$=REP$
1670 ON FLAG% GOSUB 2070,2280,1200,1280,380,2480,2670,1370,1470,2430,350
1680 IF REP2$<>"e" THEN 1580 ELSE 2050
1690 WHILE REP2$<>"e"
1700      NEWDATA=VAL(REP$)
1710      IF QUIT%=1 OR OLDXPOS%=0 THEN QUIT%=0: GOTO 1720 ELSE
               LOCATE OLDXPOS%,OLDYPOS%,0:
               PRINT USING "################.###";OLDDATA
1720      LOCATE 23,12: PRINT BLANK$
1730      R%=RPOS%-2+18*(ROWP%-1)
1740      IF CPOS%<>0 THEN X.(R%,C%+1)=NEWDATA: YPOS%=32: FLAG%=1 ELSE
               IF C%=1 THEN X.(R%,1)=NEWDATA: YPOS%=7: FLAG%=2 ELSE
                    X.(R%,C%)=NEWDATA: YPOS%=7: FLAG%=3
1750      ON FLAG% GOTO 1760,1820,1790
1760      IF R% > NOD%(C%+1) THEN NOD%(C%+1)=R%
1770      IF C%+1 > COLUMNX% THEN COLUMNX%=C%+1
1780      GOTO 1840
1790      IF R% > NOD%(C%) THEN NOD%(C%)=R%
1800      IF C% > COLUMNX% THEN COLUMNX%=C%
1810      GOTO 1840
1820      IF R% > NOD%(1) THEN NOD%(1)=R%
1830      IF C% > COLUMNX% THEN COLUMNX%=C%
1840      XPOS%=R%-18*(ROWP%-1)+2
1850      LOCATE XPOS%,YPOS% : COLOR 4,0,0
1860      PRINT USING "################.###";NEWDATA : MODIFIED%=1
1870      SAVED%=0 : COLOR 7,0,0
1880      IF ORDER%=1 THEN FWD%=1 : GOSUB 2080 : GOTO 1910
1890      IF CPOS%=1 THEN FWD%=1 : GOSUB 2080
1900      GOSUB 2280
1910      OLDYPOS%=YPOS%:OLDXPOS%=XPOS%: OLDDATA=NEWDATA
1920      LOCATE 23,69: PRINT BLANK1$: LOCATE 23,69: PRINT OLDREP$
1930      LOCATE 23,12: PRINT BLANK$
1940      LOCATE 23,12: INPUT REP$ :IF REP$="" THEN REP$=OLDREP$
1950      REP2$=LEFT$(REP$,1)
1960      IF REP2$="" THEN REP2$=OLDREP$ : GOTO 2000
1970      T1%=ASC(REP2$)
1980      IF T1% >= 43 AND T1% <= 57 THEN 1690
1990      T1%=T1% OR 32 : REP2$=CHR$(T1%)
2000      GOSUB 2350
2010      IF VALID%=0 THEN 1580 ELSE VALID%=0: OLDREP$=REP$
2020      ON FLAG% GOSUB 2070,2280,1200,1280,380,2480,2670,1370,1470,2430,350
2030      IF REP2$<>"e" THEN 1920 ELSE 2040
2040      WEND
2050 RETURN
2060 '--------------------------  ROW INDEXING  --------------------------
2070 MID$(REP$,1)=" " : FWD%=VAL(REP$) : IF FWD%=0 THEN FWD%=1
2080 OLDRPOS%=RPOS% : RPOS%=RPOS%+FWD% : PG%=0
2090 IF RPOS%=20 THEN SOUND 400,3
2100 IF RPOS%>2 THEN 2160
```

PROGRAM 6.1 (continued)

```
2110 IF RPOS%<3 THEN RPOS%=RPOS%+18: PG%=PG%+1: GOTO 2110
2120 IF ROWP%=1 THEN RPOS%=3 : GOTO 2210
2130 ROWP%=ROWP%-PG% : IF ROWP%<1 THEN ROWP%=1: RPOS%=3
2140 QUIT%=1 : GOSUB 730: GOSUB 840: GOSUB 920: GOSUB 2310
2150 GOTO 2230
2160 IF RPOS%<21 THEN 2210
2170 IF RPOS%>20 THEN RPOS%=RPOS%-18: PG%=PG%+1: GOTO 2170
2180 ROWP%=ROWP%+PG%
2190 QUIT%=1 : GOSUB 730: GOSUB 840: GOSUB 920: GOSUB 2310
2200 GOTO 2230
2210 LOCATE OLDRPOS%,2,0 : PRINT USING "###";OLDRPOS%-2+18*(ROWP%-1);
2220 PRINT " :"
2230 COLOR 0,7 : LOCATE RPOS%,2,0 : PRINT USING "###";RPOS%-2+18*(ROWP%-1);
2240 PRINT " :"
2250 COLOR 7,0
2260 RETURN
2270 '------------------------ COLUMN INDEXING --------------------------
2280 IF COL%=1 THEN GOSUB 2920 : GOTO 2330
2290 CPOS%=CPOS%+1 : IF CPOS%>1 THEN CPOS%=0
2300 IF CPOS%=0 THEN LOCATE 1,46,0 : PRINT C2$
        ELSE LOCATE 1,21,0 : PRINT C1$
2310 COLOR 0,7 : IF CPOS%=0 THEN LOCATE 1,21,0 : PRINT C1$ ELSE
        LOCATE 1,46,0 : PRINT C2$
2320 COLOR 7,0
2330 RETURN
2340 '------------------------ CHECK COMMANDS ---------------------------
2350 I%=0
2360 WHILE I%<11 AND VALID%=0
2370     I%=I%+1
2380     IF REP2$=COMMAND$(I%) THEN FLAG%=I%: VALID%=1
2390     WEND
2400     IF VALID%=0 THEN GOSUB 2920
2410 RETURN
2420 '--------------------------- CHANGE ORDER --------------------------
2430 IF CORDER%=1 THEN GOSUB 2920 : GOTO 2460
2440 IF ORDER%=1 THEN ORDER%=0: ORDER$="COLUMN ORDER"
        ELSE ORDER%=1 : ORDER$="ROW    ORDER"
2450 LOCATE 22,55: PRINT ORDER$: BEEP
2460 RETURN
2470 '------------------------ DELETE DATA ------------------------------
2480 MID$(REP$,1)=" ": COUNT%=VAL(REP$): IF COUNT%=0 THEN COUNT%=1
2490 IF ORDER%=0 THEN N%=2 ELSE N%=1
2500 LOCATE 23,30: PRINT "DELETING";COUNT%*N%;" DATA...": BEEP
2510 LOCATE 23,12: PRINT BLANK$
2520 R%=RPOS%-2+18*(ROWP%-1)
2530 FOR J%=1 TO N%
2540     IF CPOS%<>0 THEN T1%=C%+1: FLAG%=2 ELSE
            IF C%=1 THEN T1%=1:FLAG%=1 ELSE T1%=C%: FLAG%=1
2550     FOR I%=R%+COUNT% TO NOD%(T1%)
2560         X.(I%-COUNT%,T1%)=X.(I%,T1%)
2570         NEXT I%
2580     NOD%(T1%)=NOD%(T1%)-COUNT%
2590     T1%=CPOS%
2600     ON FLAG% GOSUB 840, 920
2610     IF ORDER%=0 THEN GOSUB 2280
2620     NEXT J%
2630 MODIFIED%=1
2640 LOCATE 23,30: PRINT BLANK2$: BEEP
2650 RETURN
2660 '---------------------- INSERT DATA -------------------------------
2670 MID$(REP$,1)=" ": COUNT%=VAL(REP$): IF COUNT%=0 THEN COUNT%=1
2680 IF ORDER%=0 THEN N%=2 ELSE N%=1
2690 LOCATE 23,30: PRINT "INSERT";COUNT%*N%;" DATA...": BEEP
2700 LOCATE 23,12: PRINT BLANK$
2710 R%=RPOS%-2+18*(ROWP%-1)
2720 FOR J%=1 TO N%
2730     IF CPOS%<>0 THEN T1%=C%+1: FLAG%=2: YPOS%=32 ELSE
            IF C%=1 THEN T1%=1: FLAG%=1: YPOS%=7 ELSE T1%=C%: FLAG%=1: YPOS%=7
2740     FOR I%=NOD%(T1%)+COUNT% TO R%+COUNT% STEP -1
2750         X.(I%,T1%)=X.(I%-COUNT%,T1%)
2760         NEXT I%
2770     FOR I%=R% TO R%+COUNT%-1 : X.(I%,T1%)=0! : NEXT I%
2780     NOD%(T1%)=NOD%(T1%)+COUNT%
2790     T1%=CPOS%
2800     ON FLAG% GOSUB 840, 920
2810     FOR I%=R% TO R%+COUNT%-1
2820         IF I%+2>20 THEN 2840 ELSE LOCATE I%+2,YPOS%
2830         COLOR 0,7: PRINT "                    "
2840         NEXT I%
```

PROGRAM 6.1 (continued)

```
2850      COLOR 7,0
2860      IF ORDER%=0 THEN GOSUB 2280
2870      NEXT J%
2880 MODIFIED%=1
2890 LOCATE 23,30: PRINT BLANK2$: BEEP
2900 RETURN
2910 '------------------------ ERROR MESSAGE ----------------------------
2920 LOCATE 23,30: PRINT "INVALID COMMAND..."
2930 FOR F=300 TO 500 STEP 100
2940     SOUND F,2
2950     SOUND 32767,2
2960     NEXT
2970 LOCATE 23,30: PRINT BLANK2$
2980 RETURN
```

PROGRAM 6.1 DATA EDITOR (AEDIT)

6.1.2 CONSISTENCY

The position on the screen of items such as menu, commands, and feedback is important; we normally designate a fixed portion of the screen for each of them. This consistency allows the user to build "muscle memory" that helps in picking the desired menu item quickly. Other examples of consistency are in the use of color coding and abbreviations. Colors should always convey information in the same way (e.g., a red character means change in input data). Keyboard labels or global commands in a character-string oriented language should be abbreviated with a constant-length string (e.g., CIRCLE → CIRL → C, ANGLE → ANGL → A).

6.1.3 MINIMAL MEMORIZATION

An important principle is to make necessary memorization as simple as possible and to avoid it whenever possible. Some examples are displaying system status messages that indicate the current mode of operation and using short forms of commands for keyboard-oriented graphics systems (e.g., ERASE → E). The order of positional parameters should be left fluid whenever possible.

6.2 COMPUTER PROGRAMMING LOGIC

The general programming logic for DATA EDITOR is shown in Fig. 6.1. This DATA EDITOR program is written in BASIC and requires the IBM PC DOS 2.00 to run the program. The DATA EDITOR program uses some BASIC statements available only on the IBM PC. Users with other microcomputers, however, will find the program relatively simple to convert. If the operator uses a color/graphics monitor, some of the inputs and commands will be displayed in color, to accentuate the specific information shown on the screen. The defini-

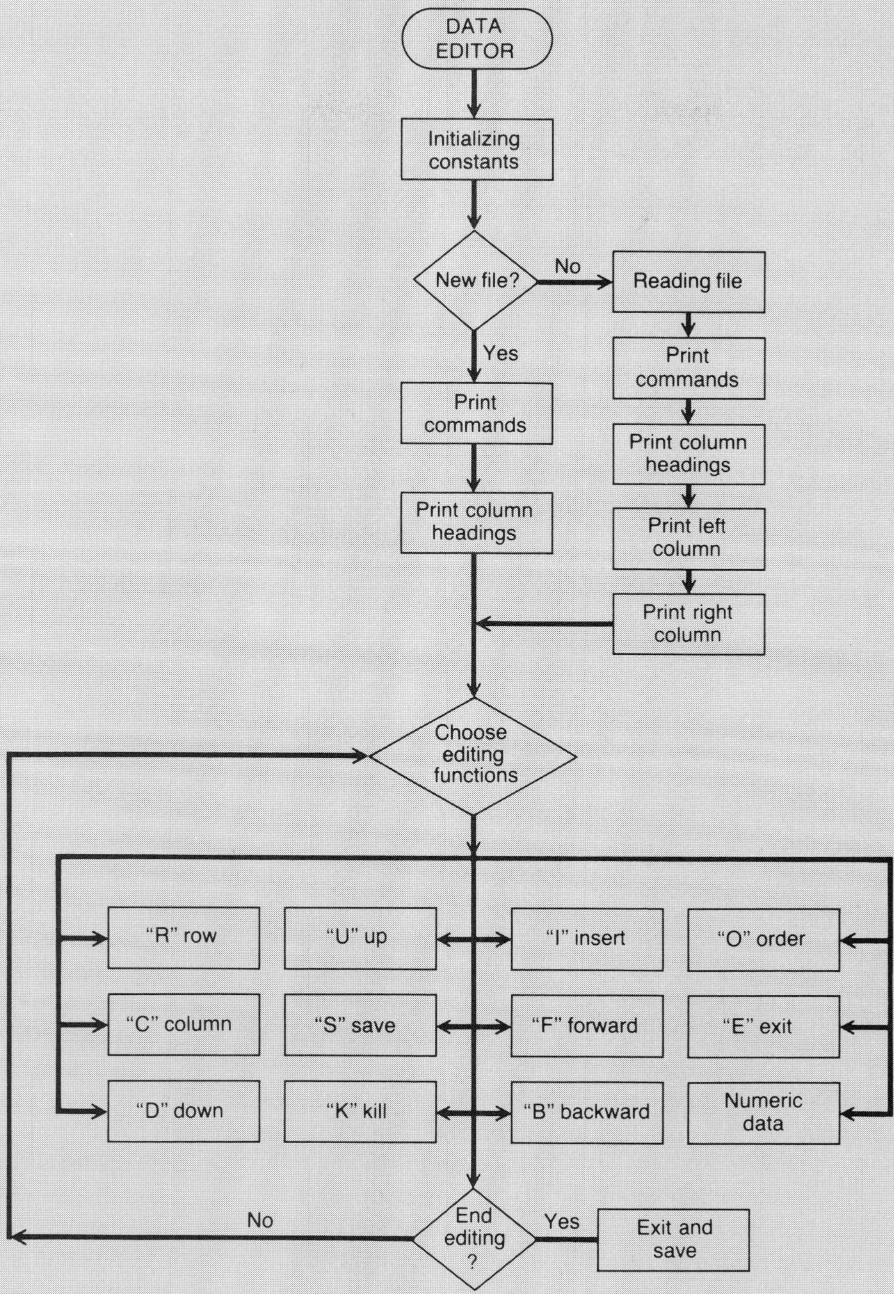

FIGURE 6.1 Programming logic for DATA EDITOR

tions of the variable names used in the DATA EDITOR program are located on pages 261 and 262.

6.3 DESCRIPTION OF DATA EDITOR

When we call DATA EDITOR, we are asked to assign a file name to the data file to be created. The IBM DOS requires that we refer to a file by its name in retrieving the information. The following rules govern the names we assign to files:

- A complete file name consists of two parts separated by a period (i.e., name . extension).
- The name should be less than eight characters long; the extension (when used) can be no more than three characters long.
- For our example, we will use the file name "PLOT.DAT" and

Input file name = ? PLOT.DAT

6.3.1 DISPLAY FORMAT

To begin our keyboard input, we simply press the [ENTER] key. This refers to the key marked "↵" on the IBM PC keyboard and sometimes called [RETURN]. In a moment, DATA EDITOR will display the form shown in Fig. 6.2.

The numbers 1 through 18 in Fig. 6.2 are row indices that show us which row entry we are in. The (Y) and ($X1$), ($X2$)...etc. on the first line are the column headings. As a matter of convention, the Y column is always considered to contain a dependent variable. In a specific plotting example, column X may represent the month and column Y may represent demand. Two pointers on the screen represent a row and column position respectively. The place where the two pointers cross is the entry position of a data element. The movements of the two pointers are controlled by the "C" and "R" commands, which will be explained in the next section.

The bottom line is divided into three parts. From left to right, these are the command area, the message area, and the default status area. In the command area, we will see a prompt "COMMAND:?" and a screen cursor blinking. This is the place where we enter commands or data. The message area is the area where system messages are displayed. The "COLUMN ORDER" displayed in the default status area means that we are going to fill in columns (Y) and ($X1$) before we change to the next row. The "DEFAULT CMD:D" means that the current default command is "D" (scroll down one page). To use the default command, we simply press the [ENTER] key.

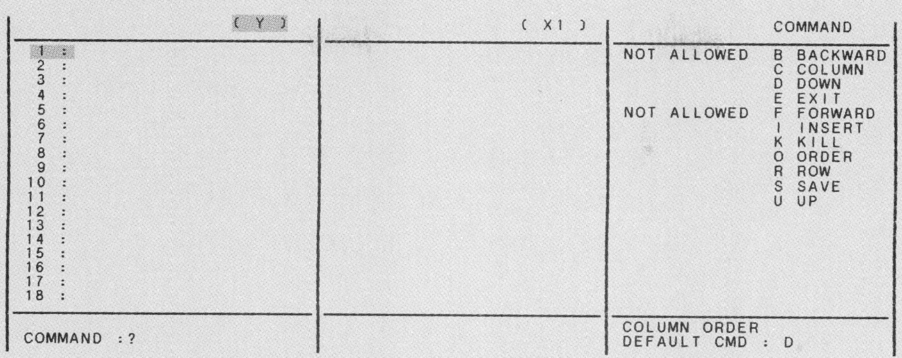

FIGURE 6.2 Screen format for EDITOR

6.3.2 EDITING COMMANDS

Command keys. We will explain the various editing commands with the IBM PC keyboard diagram shown in Fig. 6.3. The IBM keyboard is an expanded version of the more familiar typewriter keyboard. All of the customary keys are in their normal places, but a number of additional characters are also included.

To the left of the standard keyboard are the function keys. To the right of the standard keyboard is the cursor pad with keys to move the cursor, either back and forth on a line or up and down on the screen. We will freeze the function keys and cursor pad keys in DATA EDITOR, however, and only use the standard keyboard to enter editing commands. Eleven editing commands are used in DATA EDITOR. The meaning of each keyboard input is summarized in Table 6.1.

Column and row order. Since the row and column pointers automatically change position as soon as new data are entered, it is important to know the order in which they change (i.e., column order or row order). COLUMN ORDER mode is like a text editor's line edit mode; ROW ORDER mode is like the corresponding word edit mode. If we are entering data in COLUMN ORDER mode, we will enter two column data items in the same row (line) before we get to the next row (line). On the other hand, if we are entering data in ROW ORDER mode, we will enter data in every row in the current column. In other words, COLUMN ORDER means that we enter data in a horizontal direction and ROW ORDER means in a vertical direction. The mode operates in the same way when we are using the "INSERT" and "KILL" commands.

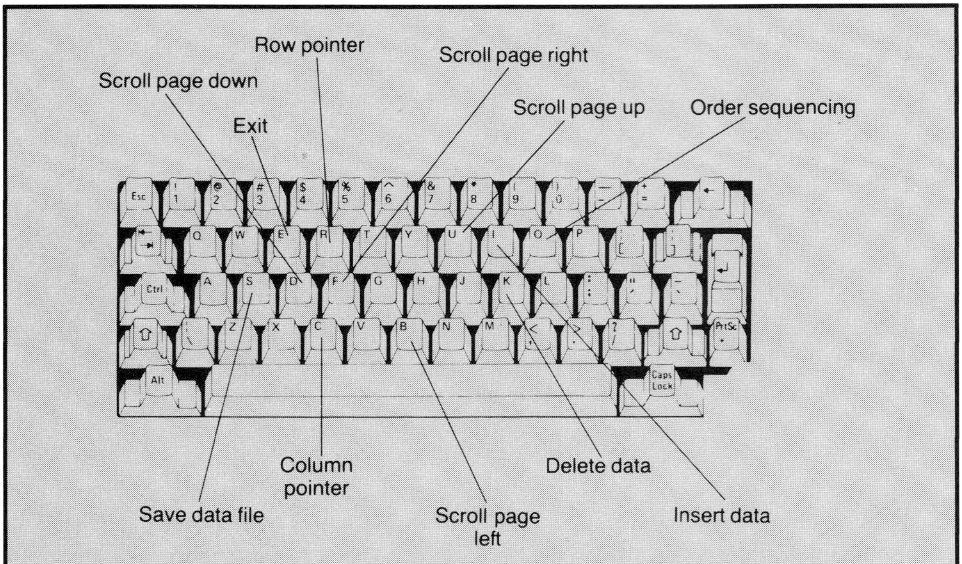

FIGURE 6.3 Editing command keys on the IBM PC keyboard

6.4 EDITING EXAMPLES

Now we will look at some simple examples illustrating the functions of DATA EDITOR. Suppose we have the following three sets of input data:

Y	*X*
123.0	1
0.8	2
−378.0	3

6.4.1 INPUT IN COLUMN ORDER

Suppose we are in COLUMN ORDER mode (check the default status area to make sure). If we want to input the above six data points, we can do it as follows:

```
COMMAND  :  ?  123<RETURN>
COMMAND  :  ?  1<RETURN>
COMMAND  :  ?  .8<RETURN>
COMMAND  :  ?  2<RETURN>
COMMAND  :  ?  -378<RETURN>
COMMAND  :  ?  3<RETURN>
```

TABLE 6.1 Description of editing commands

Key		Description
C	*	Column pointer: Enter "C" to move the column pointer from one column to another.
R	*	Row pointer: Enter "R" to move the row pointer to the next row position. If the row pointer is currently in the last row, entering "R" will put the row pointer in the first row. Enter "R5" to move the pointer down 5 rows. Enter "R-3" to move the row pointer up 3 rows. Any positive or negative integer can follow "R" to represent the number of rows up or down, counting the current row.
D	*	Scroll page down: Enter "D" to get to the next page. Enter "D*n*" to scroll down *n* pages, where *n* is a positive integer.
U	*	Scroll page up: Enter "U" to get to the previous page. Enter "U*n*" to scroll up *n* pages, where *n* is a positive integer.
B	*	Scroll page left: Enter "B" to get to the next page to the left of the current text page. Enter "B*n*" to scroll left *n* text pages, where *n* is a positive number.
F	*	Scroll page right: Enter "F" to get to the right of the current text page. Enter "F*n*" to scroll right *n* text pages, where *n* is a positive number.
I	*	Insert data: Enter "I" to insert a data element in front of the current entry pointed to by the column and row pointers. Enter "I*n*" to insert *n* data elements in front of the current entry, where *n* is a positive number.
K	*	Kill (delete) data: Enter "K" to delete the entry currently pointed to by the column and row pointers. Enter "K*n*" to kill *n* data elements starting from the current entry, where *n* is a positive number.
O	*	Order sequencing: Enter "O" to flip the operation order (mode) from row order to column order. Enter "O" again to flip it back.
S	*	Save data file: Enter "S" to save the file created or modified. We must specify the file name, but do *not* specify a disk drive name here, because there is already a default drive name specified at the beginning of the program.
E	*	Exit editor: Enter "E" to exit the data editor and go back to the main options menu.

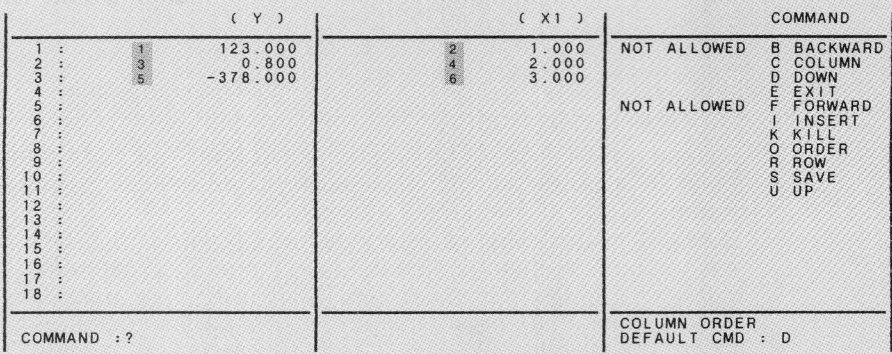

FIGURE 6.4 Input in column order: Data are entered in column by column.

We don't have to worry about the row or column pointers because they are automatically positioned in column order. All we have to do is to type in the data, and we will see the data we just entered appear in their proper positions. When we have finished, the screen should look like Fig. 6.4. The number in front of each entry is the order in which that particular number appeared on the screen.

6.4.2 INPUT IN ROW ORDER

If instead we want to input data in row order, the first thing we should do is make sure we are in ROW ORDER mode. If not, we should use the "O" command to change the order. Then we enter data as follows:

```
COMMAND  :  ?  123<RETURN>
COMMAND  :  ?  .8<RETURN>
COMMAND  :  ?  -378<RETURN>
COMMAND  :  ?  C<RETURN>
COMMAND  :  ?  R-3<RETURN>
COMMAND  :  ?  1<RETURN>
COMMAND  :  ?  2<RETURN>
COMMAND  :  ?  3<RETURN>
```

Notice that as soon as we finish entering data for *Y*, we have to move the column pointer over to the *X* column so we can enter data for *X*. After we change the column pointer, we still have to change the row pointer to point to the first row because the row pointer is now pointing at the fourth row. To return the row pointer to the first row, we can either use "R-3" or enter "R-1" and press the [ENTER] key repeatedly until the row pointer reaches the first row. When we have finished, the screen looks like that shown in Fig. 6.5.

6.4.3 DELETE DATA

Let us assume that the row pointer is currently pointing at row 4 and that the column pointer is pointing at column (Y). If we want to delete the first set of (X, Y) values and we are again in COLUMN ORDER mode, we can do it in the following sequence:

```
COMMAND  :  ? R-3<ENTER>
COMMAND  :  ? K
```

The result resembles that shown in Fig. 6.6(a). Note that if we had used "K2" instead of "K", we would have killed two sets of data. A message "deleting 4 data..." would also displayed in the message area. With our input above, however, "K" has become the default command from this point on. If we want to kill more data, we simply press [ENTER].

If we repeat what we did above but change the order to ROW ORDER, we will only delete one element of data instead of one set of data. The result will look like that shown in Fig. 6.6(b).

6.4.4 INSERT DATA

To insert data elements, we first move the pointers to the place where the data are to be inserted. For example, we want to insert data elements (7, 1.5)

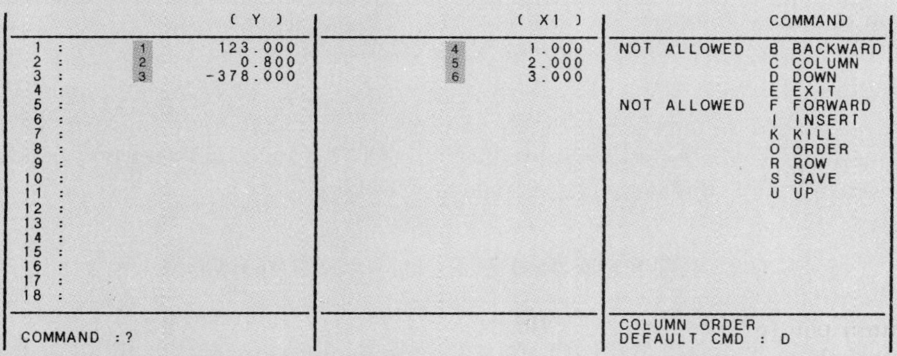

FIGURE 6.5 Input in row order: Data are entered in row sequence.

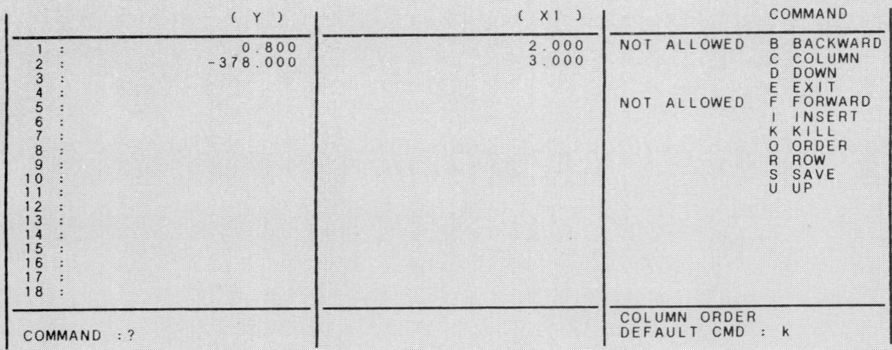

FIGURE 6.6(a) Delete in row order

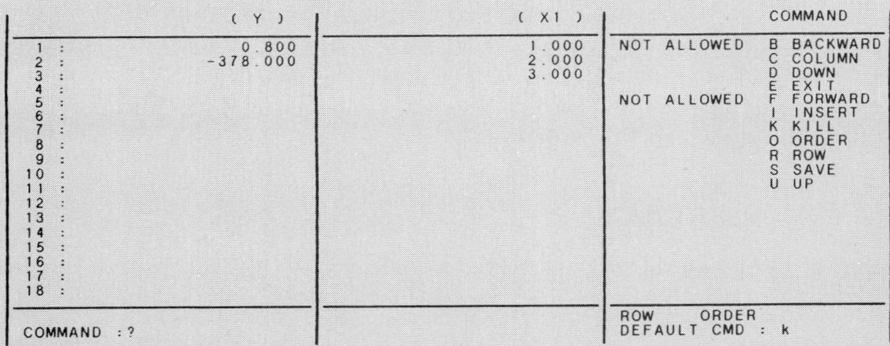

FIGURE 6.6(b) Delete in column order

between rows 1 and 2. We assume that we are in COLUMN ORDER mode. We then move the row pointer at row 2 and press "I" key to acknowledge the insert command. The computer then provides a blank row space between rows 1 and 2. We are ready to insert data elements. (See Fig. 6.7.)

6.4.5 CHANGE DATA AND SCROLL PAGES VERTICALLY

Suppose we have a data file containing 48 sets of (X, Y) values. We want to change the Y value in the 40th row from 437 to 450. We are on the first data page (see Fig. 6.8a). The 40th row is on the third page of the data. To get to the third page, we enter "D2" at the command area. The third page of the data file looks like that shown in Fig. 6.8(b). We now use the pointers to locate 437 and change it to 450:

```
COMMAND : ? R4
COMMAND : ? 450
```

After all the changes are made, we can save the file and then exit the editor.

6.4.6 CHANGE DATA AND SCROLL PAGES HORIZONTALLY

If there are more than two column entries in the data files, we can scroll the pages horizontally using the "F" and "B" commands. "F" scrolls pages from right to left; "B" scrolls pages from left to right. We will demonstrate how to use the "F" and "B" commands in Chapter 11.

6.4.7 EDIT (EXAMINE) OLD FILE

Once we have created an input data file through DATA EDITOR, we can also access and modify it. When this option is chosen, we see a prompt for the input file name:

```
INPUT FILE NAME = ?  PLOT.DAT
```

We answer the name of the file we want to edit, and in so doing access DATA EDITOR. Figure 6.8(a) is then displayed on the screen. From this point on, we

```
                    ( Y )   |               ( X1 )  |                      COMMAND
  1 :             123.000   |                1.000  | NOT ALLOWED      B BACKWARD
  2 :                       |                       |                  C COLUMN
  3 :               0.800   |                2.000  |                  D DOWN
  4 :            -378.000   |                3.000  |                  E EXIT
  5 :                       |                       | NOT ALLOWED      F FORWARD
  6 :                       |                       |                  I INSERT
  7 :                       |                       |                  K KILL
  8 :                       |                       |                  O ORDER
  9 :                       |                       |                  R ROW
 10 :                       |                       |                  S SAVE
 11 :                       |                       |                  U UP
 12 :                       |                       |
 13 :                       |                       |
 14 :                       |                       |
 15 :                       |                       |
 16 :                       |                       |
 17 :                       |                       |
 18 :                       |                       |
                            |                       | COLUMN ORDER
 COMMAND  : ?               |                       | DEFAULT CMD  :  I
```

FIGURE 6.7 Insert data elements

```
        ( Y )              ( X1 )                   COMMAND
 1 :   143.000             1.000   NOT ALLOWED   B BACKWARD
 2 :   138.000             2.000                 C COLUMN
 3 :   195.000             3.000                 D DOWN
 4 :   225.000             4.000                 E EXIT
 5 :   175.000             5.000   NOT ALLOWED   F FORWARD
 6 :   389.000             6.000                 I INSERT
 7 :   454.000             7.000                 K KILL
 8 :   618.000             8.000                 O ORDER
 9 :   564.000             9.000                 R ROW
10 :   564.000            10.000                 S SAVE
11 :   327.000            11.000                 U UP
12 :   235.000            12.000
13 :   189.000            13.000
14 :   326.000            14.000
15 :   289.000            15.000
16 :   293.000            16.000
17 :   279.000            17.000
18 :   552.000            18.000
                                   COLUMN ORDER
COMMAND :?                         DEFAULT CMD : D
```

(a)

```
        ( Y )              ( X1 )                   COMMAND
37 :   332.000            37.000   NOT ALLOWED   B BACKWARD
38 :   244.000            38.000                 C COLUMN
39 :   320.000            39.000                 D DOWN
40 :   437.000            40.000                 E EXIT
41 :   544.000            41.000   NOT ALLOWED   F FORWARD
42 :   830.000            42.000                 I INSERT
43 :  1011.000            43.000                 K KILL
44 :  1081.000            44.000                 O ORDER
45 :  1400.000            45.000                 R ROW
46 :  1123.000            46.000                 S SAVE
47 :   713.000            47.000                 U UP
48 :   487.000            48.000
49 :
50 :
51 :
52 :
53 :
54 :
                                   COLUMN ORDER
COMMAND :?                         DEFAULT CMD : D2
```

(b)

FIGURE 6.8 Scrolling data pages (a) data page 1 and (b) data page 3

can modify any data element by using a sequence of editing commands as given in Table 6.1.

DATA EDITOR is a general-purpose program designed for entering data in a graphics program. We need only to write the graphics program and then link DATA EDITOR to the graphics program. We will develop a 2-D plotter in the next chapter to demonstrate this application.

6.5 SUMMARY

The success with which we design and construct application programs depends on the flexibility of the user interface, the part of the program that determines how the user and the computer communicate. In this chapter we briefly discussed three components of an interactive system: feedback, consistency, and minimal memorization. We then incorporated these elements into the DATA EDITOR program, organizing the displayed image to convey the information as effectively as possible.

```
--------------------- VARIABLE LIST ---------------------
ARRAYS      :

X.                   : DATA BUFFER.
COMMAND$             : LIST OF VALID COMMANDS.
NOD%                 : NUMBER OF DATA IN EACH COLUMN.

INTEGERS    :

C%                   : COLUMN NUMBER.
COL%                 : FLAG INDICATING COLUMN POINTER STATUS.
CPOS%                : COLUMN POSITION IN DATA EDITOR.
DX%                  : NUMBER OF OPTIONS BYPASSED.
FLAG%                : FLAG INDICATING OPTION CHOSEN.
I%                   : SENTINEL NUMBER.
J%, K%               : SENTINEL NUMBERS.
LEFT%                : FLAG INDICATING THE "SCROLL LEFT" STATUS.
MODIFIED%            : FLAG INDICATING CHANGE OF DATA.
NEWFILE%             : FLAG INDICATING A NEW FILE BEING CREATED.
ORDER%               : FLAG INDICATING THE INPUT ORDER.
PG%                  : PAGES SCROLLED.
QUIT%                : FLAG INDICATING "QUIT CHECKING OLD DATA."
R%                   : ROW NUMBER OF DATA EDITOR.
ROWP%                : NTH PAGE OF FILE DISPLAYED.
RPOS%                : ROW POSITION OF CURSOR.
SAVED%               : FLAG INDICATING THE FILE BEING SAVED.
T1%                  : TEMPORARY STORAGE.

REALS       :

NEWDATA              : NEW DATA TO BE ENTERED.
OLDDATA              : PREVIOUS DATA ENTERED.

CHARACTERS  :

ANS$                 : KEYBOARD INPUT FROM USER.
BLANK$               : BLANK SPACES.
BLANK1$              : BLANK SPACES.
```

PROGRAM 6.1 DATA EDITOR—AEDIT[†]

[†]*Note:* The DATA EDITOR program cannot be run by itself. This is a utility program linked to other graphics programs.

```
BLANK2$        : BLANK SPACES.
C1$            : FIRST COLUMN HEADING.
C2$            : SECOND COLUMN HEADING.
FD$            : DISK DRIVE USED FOR THE DATA FILES.
FILE$          : FILE NAME.
M$             : "COMMAND"
M1             : "DEFAULT CMD :"
ORDER$         : MESSAGE NOTIFYING THE INPUT ORDER.
PD$            : DISK DRIVE USED FOR THE PACKAGE.
REP$           : RESPONSE FROM USER.
PG%            : PAGES SCROLLED.
```

PROGRAM 6.1 DATA EDITOR—AEDIT

REFERENCES

1. Chang, S. K., and T. L. Kunii, "Pictorial Data Base Design," *Computer* **14** (11) 13–21, November 1981.

2. Dube, R. P., and M. R. Smith, "Managing Geometric Information with a Data Base Management System," *IEEE Computer Graphics and Applications* **3** (7) 57–62, October 1983.

3. Encarnacao, J., ed., "Computer Aided Design: Modeling, Systems Engineering, CAD-Systems," *Lecture Notes in Computer Science No. 89,* Springer Verlag, New York, 1980.

4. Haber, R. N., and L. Wilkinson, "Perceptual Components of Computer Display," *IEEE Computer Graphics and Applications* **2** (3) 23–34, May 1982.

5. Haber, R. N., "How We Remember What We See," *Scientific American,* May 1970.

6. Marcus, A., "Designing the Face of an Interface," *IEEE Computer Graphics and Applications* **2** (1) 23–29, January 1982.

7. McCleary, G. F., "An Effective Graphics Vocabulary," *IEEE Computer Graphics and Applications* **3** (2) 46–53, March/April 1983.

8. Swezey, R. W., and E. G. Davis, "A Case Study of Human Factors Guidelines in Computer Graphics," *IEEE Computer Graphics and Applications* **3** (8) 21–30, November 1983.

CHAPTER SEVEN
Interactive 2-D Plotter

The purpose of this chapter is to show how a simple graphics routine can be used to make computer output more meaningful and useful. Microcomputers can now present a great variety of information in the form of graphs, pictures, maps, and models. We will primarily, however, focus on plotting techniques for two-dimensional graphs. To enter or edit the data, we will use the DATA EDITOR routine developed in Chapter 6.

7.1 PLOTTING FEATURES ENVISIONED

Several features constitute a good plotting routine. First, it should be a subroutine that, when called, plots data generated in the main program with minimum user interaction. Second, it should provide several plotting options, such as lines, bars, steps, and curves. Third, it should allow the user to plot multiple data files on the same chart to obtain comparative graphs. Fourth, it should provide scaling options (automatic or manual) so that the user can manipulate the size of the graph. Fifth, the hard copy output should have enough resolution to allow interpretation of the data. Last, but not least, the user should be able to access and edit the data files with relative ease. We will present a plotting routine called PLOTTER developed with these features in mind.

7.2 DESIGN PRINCIPLES

We will first introduce a few more design principles pertaining to PLOTTER, in addition to the principles discussed in Section 6.1.

7.2.1 HIERARCHY OF COMMANDS

If there are too many commands to display in a menu, we can group them into different phases or modes. Each phase contains a group of logically related commands. If a menu is used for command entry, then the "main" menu may be selected to choose a phase. Naturally, the name of the current phase or subphase should be displayed so that the user always knows the context in which commands will be performed. Another group of logically related commands will be displayed for the next phase of command selection. The PLOTTER graphics commands will be based upon such a hierarchical command structure.

7.2.2 ACCOMMODATION OF ERRORS

We all make mistakes when working with computers; we often press wrong keys. We must provide easy and convenient ways to correct these mistakes. In other words, the user should be able to abort the current command or keyboard input before it has been completed. The system should then be restored to the stage before the aborted command was entered. Another useful method of accommodating errors is to design the graphics system so that the program ignores all inputs except the specified characters. Providing cancellation of commands requires extra programming effort, particularly for commands that make major changes to data structures. The extra efficiency is worth this effort, however. The PLOTTER program has several of these convenient error-correction mechanisms.

7.3 COMPUTER PROGRAMMING LOGIC

The general programming logic for PLOTTER is shown in Fig. 7.1. PLOTTER is designed to run on an IBM PC with the minimum configuration of 64K RAM, disk drive, and color/graphics adapter monitor. An IBM PC graphics printer is also required if the user desires a hard copy. The software required is DOS 2.0 and BASICA.

Program 7.1, which lists the complete code for PLOTTER, appears at the end of this chapter along with definitions of the variable names used in

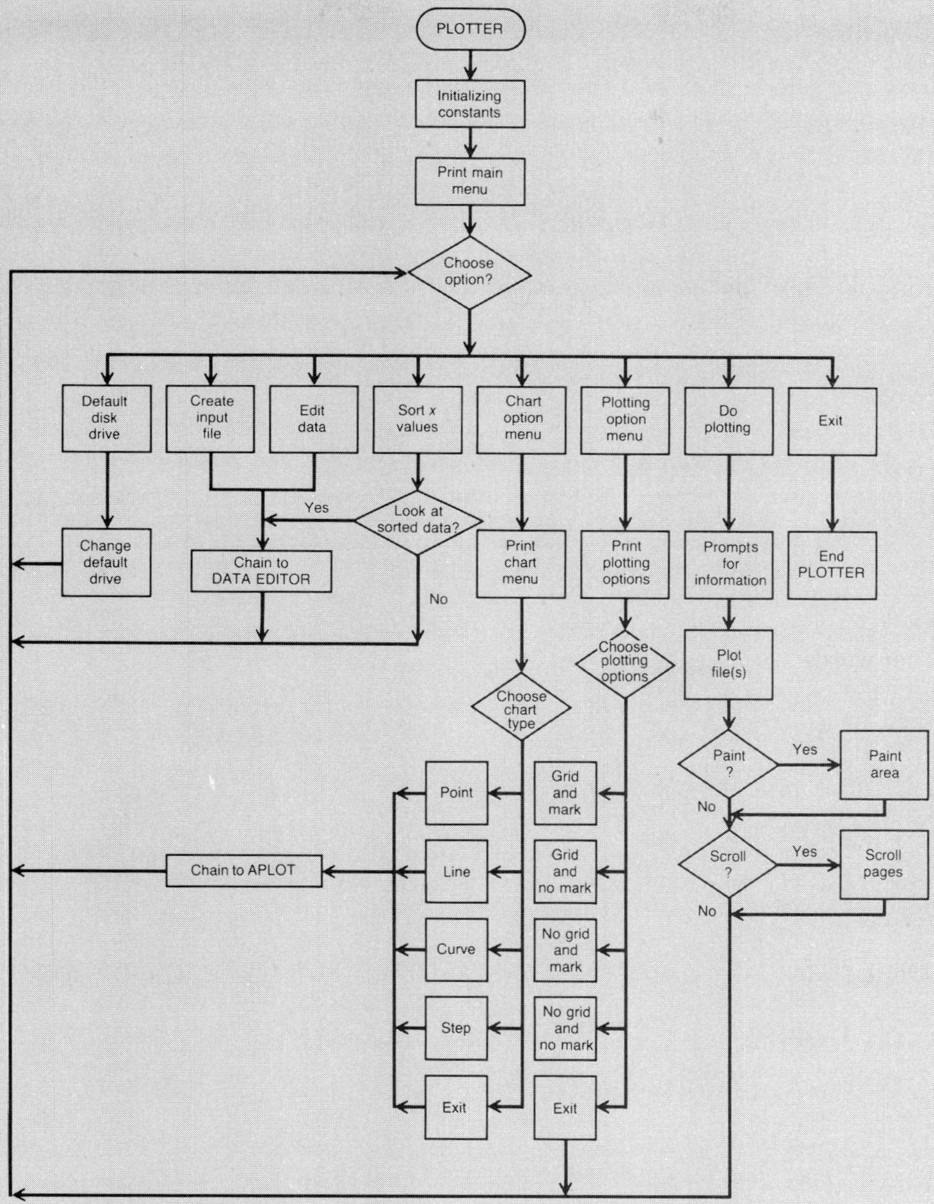

FIGURE 7.1 Programming logic of 2-D PLOTTER

the program. Program 7.2 is a general-purpose plotter that is chained to PLOTTER (like a subroutine) to provide various plotting features. We call this program APLOT. Programs such as WINTERS and REGRESSION (developed in later chapters) require APLOT linked to plot the results.

7.4 CASE EXAMPLE

We will explain how to run the PLOTTER with the following example. The demand for a diet soft drink packaged in a 48-oz nonreturnable bottle is seasonal. A large portion of the demand occurs during the summer and early fall. Historical data for four years (1980–1983) are available as shown in Table 7.1. (This embellished example is based on material from [5]). We are interested in plotting the demand pattern over the four-year period.

TABLE 7.1 Monthly demand for a 48-oz soft drink, in hundreds of cases

Year	Month(X)	Demand(Y)	Year	Month(X)	Demand(Y)
1980	1	143	1982	25	359
	2	138		26	264
	3	195		27	315
	4	225		28	361
	5	175		29	414
	6	389		30	647
	7	454		31	836
	8	618		32	901
	9	564		33	1104
	10	564		34	874
	11	327		35	683
	12	235		36	352
1982	13	189	1983	37	332
	14	326		38	244
	15	289		39	320
	16	293		40	437
	17	279		41	544
	18	552		42	830
	19	674		43	1011
	20	827		44	1081
	21	1000		45	1400
	22	502		46	1123
	23	512		47	713
	24	300		48	487

7.5 DESCRIPTION OF 2-D PLOTTER

When we load and execute the program, we see the following prompt on the screen:

```
WHICH DISK DRIVE DOES CONTAIN PLOTTER, AEDIT, AND APLOT?
DRIVE A IS ON YOUR LEFT,
DRIVE B IS ON YOUR RIGHT,
DRIVE C IS YOUR HARD (FIXED) DISK DRIVE.
ENTER [ A, B, OR C ]?
```

We then specify the drive where the diskette containing PLOTTER, APLOT, and AEDIT is located. These programs should be located in a single diskette.

7.5.1 MENU SELECTION THROUGH CURSOR PAD

When the program is started, the menu appears on the screen.

```
******  INTERACTIVE PLOTTING MENU  ******          STATUS
                                               -------------------
*       _ CHANGE DEFAULT DISK DRIVE      *
*       _ CREATE INPUT FILE              *     DEFAULT DRIVE   = B:
*       _ EDIT(EXAMINE) DATA             *     USER OPTIONS    :
*       _ SORT X VALUES                  *     CURVE
*       _ CHART OPTION MENU              *     NO GRID
*       _ PLOTTING OPTION MENU           *     MARK
*       _ DO PLOTTING                    *
*       _ EXIT                           *

*****************************************
```

The menu contains eight items to pick from. We use the "↑" and "↓" keys to position the cursor and pick the menu item. We will use the [ENTER] key to select options after we have positioned the cursor in front of the desired menu item. The cursor will only move within the cursor path. Thus if the cursor is positioned at the exit option and the "↓" key is pressed, the cursor will return to the starting cursor position, "CHANGE DEFAULT DISK DRIVE". Furthermore, the computer responds only to the cursor movement keys (↑, ↓) and the [ENTER] key in the menu selection stage. This feature is extremely useful in preventing the user from entering erroneous inputs accidentally. Another useful feature of this menu selection scheme is that the menu items are arranged in the order of normal procedures, and once the user has selected a menu item, the cursor will automatically advance to the next item in the menu. This minimizes the cursor movement required of the user and at the same time guides the user through the normal procedure flow.

7.5.2 DEFAULT SYSTEM STATUS MESSAGES

System status messages are shown at the middle of the right-hand side of the screen. These have the following meanings:

- *Default Drive:* This message tells which disk drive we are using to store or retrieve data. The default drive in this menu is B:; thus whatever files created will be stored on the diskette in drive B:.
- *Chart Type:* The default chart type is curve. For the data provided, cubic spline interpolation will be performed.
- *Plotting Option:* The default plotting option is "No Grid." This means that no grid lines will be imposed on the plot.
- *Mark:* The default mark option is "Mark." This means that all data points will be marked.

7.5.3 CHANGING DEFAULT DISK DRIVE

We can use this option to change the default disk drive from A: to B: or from B: to A:. (If there is a hard disk, we can also change it to C: or D:.) This option makes the program flexible under different disk drive systems, and is particularly useful for users who are forced to retrieve information from a single disk drive. Subroutine 1240 will effect this menu option. Note that since a default disk drive is always assumed, we should not put the device name (A: or B:) in the file specification any longer.

7.5.4 CREATING INPUT FILE

We use this option when we want to create an input file that contains the data to be plotted later. After choosing this option, we see the prompt "INPUT FILE NAME = ?" and must assign a file name to the data file to be created. We will use the file name PLOT1.DAT for our example:

```
INPUT FILE NAME =? PLOT1.DAT
```

Immediately after we type in the input file name, PLOTTER will chain the DATA EDITOR program discussed in Chapter 6. After entering 48 data elements in Table 7.1, the computer screen should look like that shown in Fig. 7.2.

7.5.5 EDITING (EXAMINING) OLD FILE

Once we create an input data file by using either DATA EDITOR or some other database program, we can access and modify the data file. When this option is chosen, we see a prompt for the file name:

```
INPUT FILE NAME = ?
```

We answer the name of the file we want to edit (examine), and the system puts us back in DATA EDITOR. All the commands remain the same as those described in Chapter 6.

```
         ( Y )              ( X1 )                 COMMAND
 1 :    143.000              1.000   NOT ALLOWED  B BACKWARD
 2 :    138.000              2.000                C COLUMN
 3 :    195.000              3.000                D DOWN
 4 :    225.000              4.000                E EXIT
 5 :    175.000              5.000   NOT ALLOWED  F FORWARD
 6 :    389.000              6.000                I INSERT
 7 :    454.000              7.000                K KILL
 8 :    618.000              8.000                O ORDER
 9 :    564.000              9.000                R ROW
10 :    564.000             10.000                S SAVE
11 :    327.000             11.000                U UP
12 :    235.000             12.000
13 :    189.000             13.000
14 :    326.000             14.000
15 :    289.000             15.000
16 :    293.000             16.000
17 :    279.000             17.000
18 :    552.000             18.000
                                     COLUMN ORDER
COMMAND :?                           DEFAULT CMD : D
```

```
         ( Y )              ( X1 )                 COMMAND
19 :    674.000             19.000   NOT ALLOWED  B BACKWARD
20 :    827.000             20.000                C COLUMN
21 :   1000.000             21.000                D DOWN
22 :    502.000             22.000                E EXIT
23 :    512.000             23.000   NOT ALLOWED  F FORWARD
24 :    300.000             24.000                I INSERT
25 :    359.000             25.000                K KILL
26 :    264.000             26.000                O ORDER
27 :    315.000             27.000                R ROW
28 :    361.000             28.000                S SAVE
29 :    414.000             29.000                U UP
30 :    647.000             30.000
31 :    836.000             31.000
32 :    901.000             32.000
33 :   1104.000             33.000
34 :    874.000             34.000
35 :    683.000             35.000
36 :    352.000             36.000
                                     COLUMN ORDER
COMMAND :?                           DEFAULT CMD : D
```

```
         ( Y )              ( X1 )                 COMMAND
37 :    332.000             37.000   NOT ALLOWED  B BACKWARD
38 :    244.000             38.000                C COLUMN
39 :    320.000             39.000                D DOWN
40 :    437.000             40.000                E EXIT
41 :    544.000             41.000   NOT ALLOWED  F FORWARD
42 :    830.000             42.000                I INSERT
43 :   1011.000             43.000                K KILL
44 :   1081.000             44.000                O ORDER
45 :   1400.000             45.000                R ROW
46 :   1123.000             46.000                S SAVE
47 :    713.000             47.000                U UP
48 :    487.000             48.000
49 :
50 :
51 :
52 :
53 :
54 :
                                     COLUMN ORDER
COMMAND :?                           DEFAULT CMD : D
```

FIGURE 7.2 Data file—PLOT1.DAT

7.5.6 SORTING X VALUES

If the X values of the input data are not in ascending order, we should use this option to sort the X values before we make any attempt to plot the data (unless we only want to plot the data points without connecting them with lines or curves). When this option is chosen, we will see:

```
ENTER FILE NAME TO BE SORTED :? PLOT1.DAT
READING FILE B:PLOT1.DAT... (SYSTEM MESSAGE)
SORTING... (SYSTEM MESSAGE)
SORTED FILE B:PLOT1.DAT BEING SAVED     (SYSTEM MESSAGE)
WANT TO LOOK AT SORTED DATA?
```

First we must enter the name of the file to be sorted. Then we enter "N" if we don't want to look at the sorted data; otherwise we hit the [ENTER] key. Note that the sorted file is saved under the same file name as the original (unsorted) file in our example.

7.5.7 CHART TYPE OPTION

There are three different ways to connect two successive points in the plot, as shown in the chart option menu:

```
******   CHART OPTION MENU   ******

*         _ LINE                  *
*         _ POINT                 *
*         _ CURVE                 *
*         _ STEP                  *
*         _ EXIT                  *

***********************************
```

Choosing the point option leaves data points unconnected. The default chart option is curve. When we use the curve option in connecting two successive points, we get a cubic spline interpolation. (In Section 7.7, we will briefly summarize the mathematical algorithm that performs the cubic spline interpolation.)

7.5.8 PLOTTING OPTIONS

Four types of plotting options are available in PLOTTER. The default mode plots the data with marks but with no grid lines embedded on the chart. To choose another plotting option, we enter the plotting option menu, move the screen cursor to the desired option, and hit the [ENTER] key to activate it.

```
******   PLOTTING OPTION MENU   ******
*     _     GRID &     MARK           *
*     _     GRID & NO  MARK           *
*     _  NO GRID &     MARK           *
*     _  NO GRID & NO  MARK           *
*     _  EXIT                         *
***************************************
```

7.5.9 PLOTTING EXECUTION

Plot of single data file. After you have created a data file, made sure that the X values are in ascending order, and determined the chart type and plotting option, you are now ready to execute the plotting command. You need several pieces of information in designing the layout of a plot such as that shown in Fig. 7.3.

The heading, X title, and Y title must be provided by the user. These will help explain what the graph represents. The heading and X title are limited

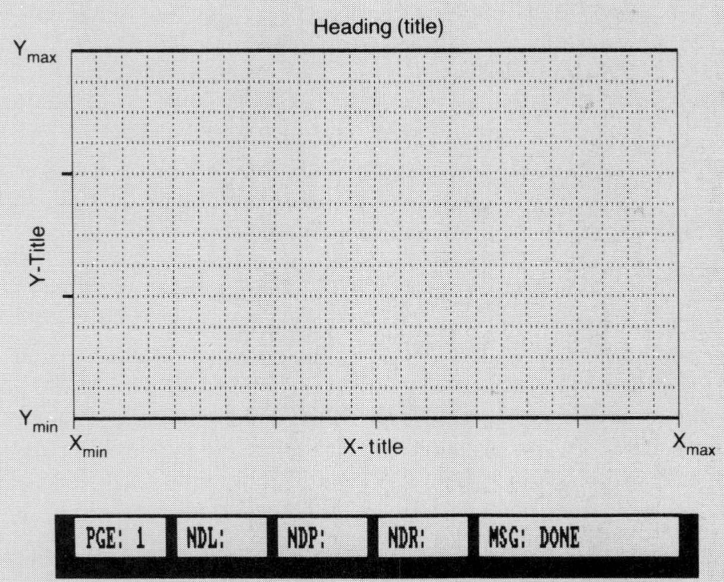

FIGURE 7.3 Information required in designing a screen layout

to 60 characters or less; the Y title is limited to 15 characters or less. Characters that exceed these limits will be truncated.

The maximum and minimum variable values (xmin, xmax, ymin, and ymax) can be provided either by the user or by default. If default lower bounds and upper bounds are used, all data points will be chosen to fill one single graph. If we think it would be too crowded with all the data points in one graph, we can divide the data into several graph pages. The number of pages we will have depends on the range (the difference between xmax and xmin) we set for one graph.

Plot of multiple graph pages. If we have more than one page of graph, we can use the "←" and "→" keys to scroll the graph pages back and forth. The number in the PGE box tells us which *graph page* we're on. The number in the NDP box tells us the *number of data points plotted* on the current page. The number in the NDL box tells us the *number of data points to the left* of the current page. The number in the NDR box tells us the *number of data points to the right* of the current page. The MSG box gives us the *system message*. Of course, when NDR = 0 we can no longer scroll to the right; when NDL = 0 we can no longer scroll to the left. Otherwise, a message "NO MORE DATA" will be displayed. For our PLOT1.DAT example, we may proceed as follows:

```
NUMBER OF DATA FILE(S) TO BE PLOTTED ON THE SAME PLOT =? 1
ENTER FILE NAME(S) :
FILE # 1 =? PLOT1.DAT
HEADING FOR THE PLOT =? MONTHLY DEMAND FOR SOFT DRINK
                        (UNIT: 1000)
X TITLE FOR THE PLOT =? MONTH
Y TITLE FOR THE PLOT =? CASES
MINIMUM X VALUE = [DEFAULT: 1 ]? 0
MAXIMUM X VALUE = [DEFAULT: 48 ]? 48
MINIMUM Y VALUE = [DEFAULT: 138 ]? 100
MAXIMUM Y VALUE = [DEFAULT: 1400 ]? 1500
```

Scaling the graph. The PLOTTER will provide automatic scaling for either X or Y. Whenever this automatic scaling is preferred, we simply use default minimum and maximum values for the X or Y axis by pressing the [ENTER] key for each corresponding prompt. If we don't want to provide the heading, X title, or Y title, we can also press the [ENTER] key to neglect the prompt.

Painting the graph. Once we have obtained a plot, we may want to color in or paint the area under the curve. To do this, we simply press "P." Normally, the painted curve gives a more distinctive look than its unpainted counterpart. When more than one data file are plotted, this paint command does not function.

Plot of multiple data files on the same chart. We can plot up to ten data files on the same graph page. We do not recommend, however, plotting more than three data files on the same graph because of the resulting confusion.
The way to do multiple plots is as follows:

```
NUMBER OF DATA FILE(S) TO BE PLOTTED ON THE SAME PLOT =? 2
ENTER FILE NAME(S):
FILE # 1 =? PLOT1.DAT
FILE # 2 =? PLOT2.DAT

HEADING FOR THE PLOT =?
X TITLE FOR THE PLOT =?
Y TITLE FOR THE PLOT =?
MINIMUM X VALUE = [DEFAULT:          ]?
MAXIMUM X VALUE = [DEFAULT:          ]?
MINIMUM Y VALUE = [DEFAULT:          ]?
MAXIMUM Y VALUE = [DEFAULT:          ]?
```

Note that if the Y value of a data point is outside the range specified by the user, that particular point will not be plotted on the graph. We can examine this by looking at the NDP box.

Changing the foreground color. Once we obtained a plot, we can change the foreground color by pressing the function key [F1]. The default foreground color is *green* with black background. Fifteen different foreground colors are possible. To change the foreground color we press the [F1] key successively until we encounter the desired foreground color. Note that we cannot change the background color in high resolution.

Dumping the screen graphics to printer. We can print the contents of a graphics display screen on an IBM PC Graphics Printer. To do this, we proceed as follows:

1. When the system is on, enter the following DOS commands, assuming the DOS diskette in Disk Drive A.

```
A > GRAPHICS    [ENTER]
A > BASICA      [ENTER]
```

2. Run the PLOTTER program and obtain a desired plot. To print the plot, press and hold either Shift key, and then press the PrtSc key; then release both of them.

Dumping the screen graphics to Hewlett-Packard plotter. We can also dump the screen plot to 7470A HP-Plotter. Once we obtained a plot, we simply press the "D" key. Then the program starts translating the screen graphics into the HP-GL (Hewlett-Packard Graphics Language) and drives the HP Plotter for plotting. This option is available only through the program diskette provided in this book.

Return to main menu. We press the [ENTER] key to go back to the main menu.

7.6 PLOTTING EXAMPLES

We will demonstrate several features of PLOTTER by using the data file shown earlier in this chapter (the soft drink demand data in Table 7.1). Since we have four types of charts, four types of plots, and a paint option, we have 28 different ways to plot the same data file. This is a very powerful feature of PLOTTER. We will show just a few examples in this section.

Figure 7.4 shows several variations in plotting the PLOT1.DAT. file. In this example, we packed all 48 months of data into a single graph. Note Fig. 7.4(f). This figure is drawn by the HP 7470A Plotter using PLOTTER.

Figure 7.5 shows scrolling the graph pages. Figure 7.5(a) plots the first 12 months' sales trend. To plot the second 12 months' sales trend, we simply press the "→" key to obtain Fig. 7.5(b), which is page 2 of the PLOT1.DAT file. Figure 7.5(b) also indicates that the current graph contains 12 data points (NDP), that there are 24 more data points to be plotted (NDR), and that we examined 12 data points before reaching the current plot (NDL). These are very useful features in computer graphics because a busy human being tends to forget things in a short period of time.

Figure 7.6 shows an example of plotting two data files on the same graph. In addition, Fig. 7.6 shows another feature of PLOTTER: a solid zero line added whenever the plot contains both positive and negative Y values. When the plot contains both positive and negative X values, a vertical solid zero line will also be plotted.

7.7 CUBIC SPLINE INTERPOLATION

In curve fitting such as that required to connect the data points on our displayed graph, a piecewise polynomial approximation that uses nth polynomials is called an nth spline interpolation. The spline function most commonly used is the cubic spline function.

A spline function can be considered an analytical french curve. A french curve is a manual graphics tool often used as an aid in plotting curves. If the draftsperson is skilled in its use, the resulting curve will go smoothly through the data points. The following mathematical function should yield similar results.

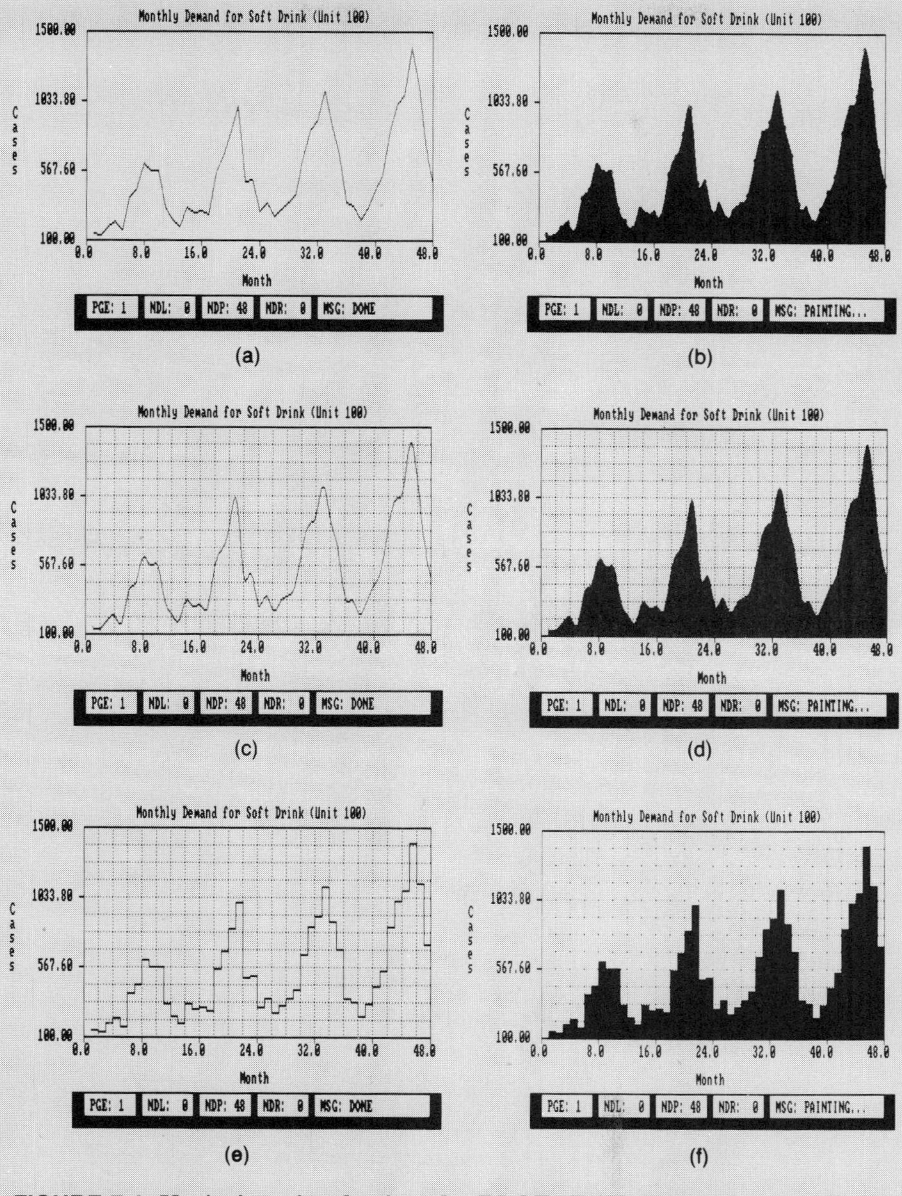

FIGURE 7.4 Variations in plotting the PLOT1.DAT: (a)-(e) obtained from IBM PC graphics printer; (f) obtained from HP 7470 A plotter

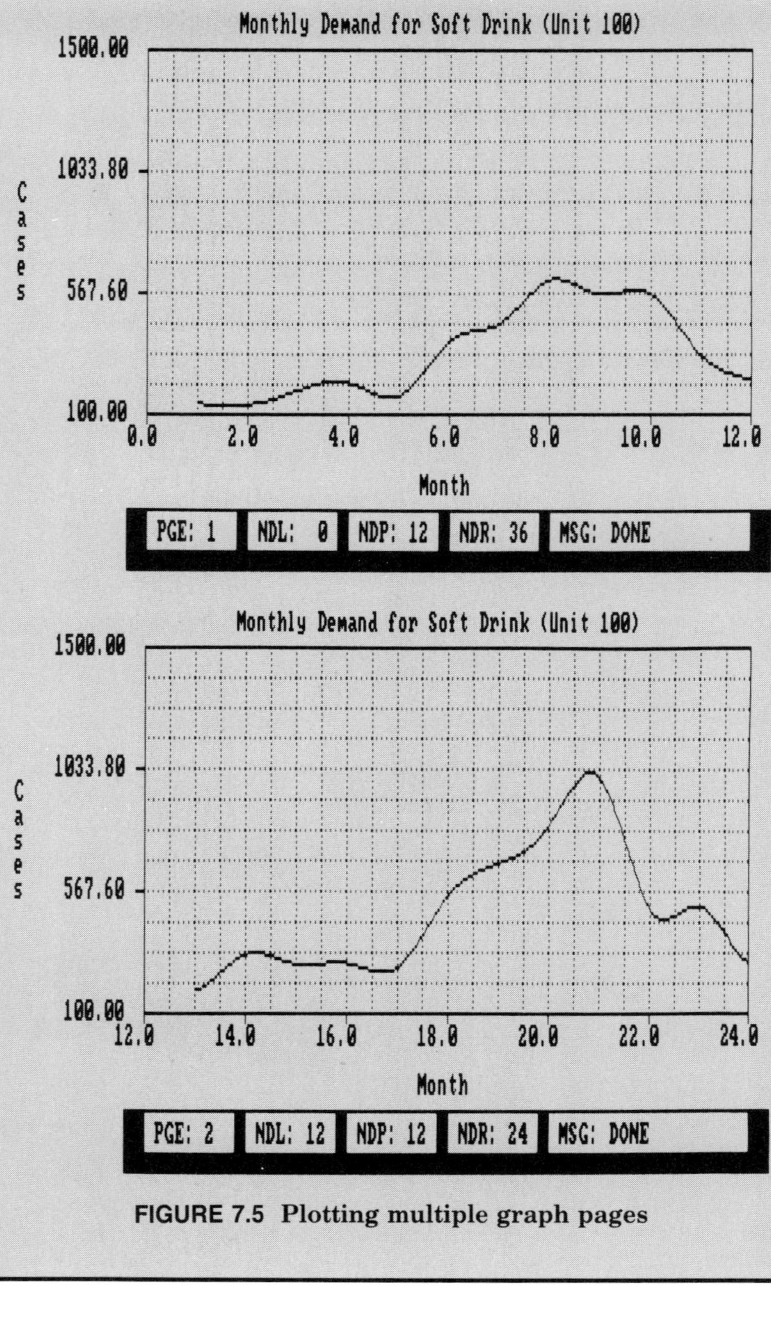

FIGURE 7.5 Plotting multiple graph pages

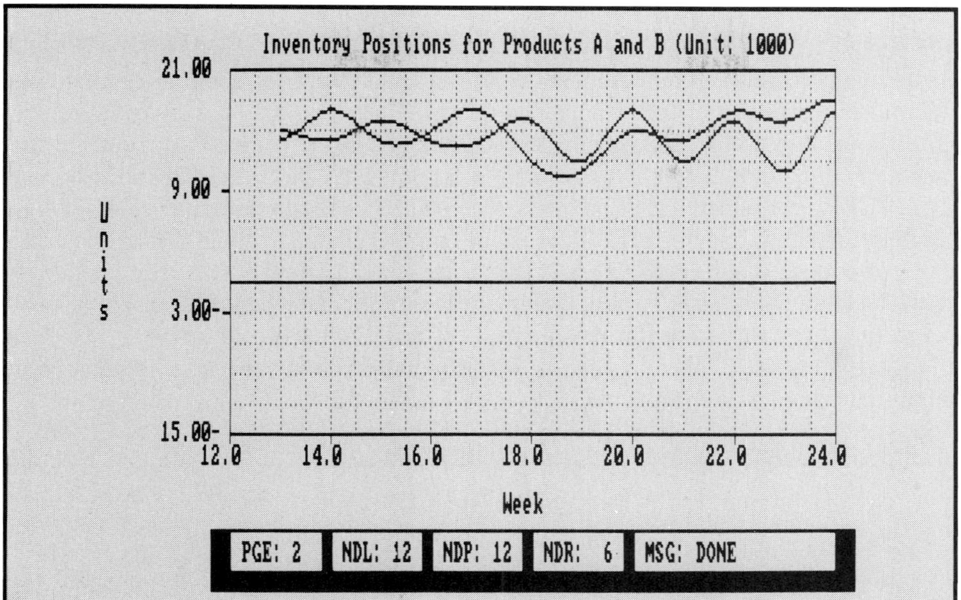

FIGURE 7.6 Plotting multiple files

Given a function $f(x)$ defined on interval $[a, b]$ and a set of measurements at $x_0, x_1, \ldots, x_n$ $(a = x_0 < x_1 < \ldots < x_n = b)$ and $f(x_0), f(x_1), \ldots, f(x_n)$, a cubic spline interpolant, S, for $f(x)$ is a function that satisfies the following conditions (where S_j' and S_j'' represent the first and second derivative of S evaluated at x_j, respectively):

1. S is a cubic polynomial, denoted S_j, on the subinterval $[x_j, x_{j+1}]$ for each $j = 0, 1, \ldots, n - 1$; $S_j(x) = a_j + b_j(x - x_j) + c_j(x - x_j)^2 + d_j(x - x_j)^3$ and $S(x) = S_j(x)$ for $x_j \leq x \leq x_{j+1}$.
2. $S(x_j) = f(x_j)$ for each $j = 0, 1, \ldots, n$.
3. $S_{j+1}(x_{j+1}) = S_j(x_{j+1})$ for each $j = 0, 1, \ldots, n - 2$.
4. $S_{j+1}'(x_{j+1}) = S_j'(x_{j+1})$ for each $j = 0, 1, \ldots, n - 2$.
5. $S_{j+1}''(x_{j+1}) = S_j''(x_{j+1})$ for each $j = 0, 1, \ldots, n - 2$
6. $S''(x_0) = S''(x_n) = 0$ for boundary conditions.

Our objective is to determine the unknown coefficients in $S_j(x)$. We will use the algorithm outlined in [2]. The program lines 1860-2120 in APLOT (Program 7.2) determine these unknown coefficients (a_j, b_j, c_j, and d_j).

7.8 SUMMARY

In this chapter we demonstrated how a simple graphics routine can be used to make computer output more meaningful and useful. We introduced two additional elements in user interface design: hierarchy of commands and accommodation of errors. One point which emerges from the worked program, PLOTTER, is the impact of hardware characteristics on user-interface design. For best results, user interfaces must be compatible with these characteristics. It is of course feasible to design user interfaces that will function on a wide variety of devices. This may be essential for applications that must be portable from one hardware configuration to another. Such user interfaces are relatively difficult to design, however, and the results are rarely as good as when a specific device is chosen.

```
----------------------- VARIABLE LIST -----------------------

ARRAYS     :

A             : INTEGER STORAGE USED IN CUBIC INTERPOLATION.
B             : FIRST ORDER COEFFICIENT OF CUBIC POLYNOMIAL.
C             : SECOND ORDER COEFFICIENT OF CUBIC POLYNOMIAL.
D             : THIRD ORDER COEFFICIENT OF CUBIC POLYNOMIAL.
FILESTK$      : INPUT FILES STACK.
H             : DIFFERENCE OF SUCCESSIVE X VALUES.
L             : INTERMEDIATE STORAGE USED IN CUBIC INTERPOLATION.
PGSTK%        : PAGE STACK.
U             : INTERMEDIATE STORAGE USED IN CUBIC INTERPOLATION.
X             : X VALUES.
XSTK%         : STACK USED TO STORE FIRST AND LAST POINTS FOR
                PAINTING.
Y             : Y VALUES.
Z             : INTERMEDIATE STORAGE USED IN CUBIC INTERPOLATION.

INTEGERS   :

BOTTOM%       : THE LAST DATA ENTRY TO BE PRINTED.
COUNT%        : NUMBER OF POINTS PLOTTED.
CPOS%         : COLUMN POSITION IN DATA EDITOR.
DELTAY%       : DEVIATION IN Y DIRECTION FROM ORIGIN.
DX%           : NUMBER OF OPTIONS BYPASSED.
FIRST%        : LINE NUMBER OF FIRST OPTION.
FIRSTX%       : X COORDINATE OF FIRST POINT.
FIRSTY%       : Y COORDINATE OF FIRST POINT.
FLAG%         : FLAG INDICATING OPTION CHOSEN.
FWD%          : NUMBER OF ROWS FOWARDED.
HDPOS%        : CENTER POSITION OF HEADING.
I%            : SENTINEL NUMBER.
```

PROGRAM 7.1 2-D PLOTTER

```
INTERVALX%   : LENGTH OF X INTERVAL.
INTERVALY%   : LENGTH OF Y INTERVAL.
J%, K%, L%   : SENTINEL NUMBERS.
LAST%        : LINE NUMBER OF LAST OPTION.
LASTX%       : X COORDINATE OF LAST POINT DRAWN IN A PAGE.
LASTY%       : Y COORDINATE OF LAST POINT DRAWN IN A PAGE.
MODIFIED%    : FLAG INDICATING CHANGE OF DATA.
MFWD%        : MAXIMUM LINES WHICH CAN BE FORWARDED IN ONE PAGE.
NEWFILE%     : FLAG INDICATING A NEW FILE BEING CREATED.
NOD%         : NUMBER OF DATA.
NOF%         : NUMBER OF FILES.
OLDX%        : X COORDINATE OF PREVIOUS POINT.
OLDY%        : Y COORDINATE OF PREVIOUS POINT.
OLDXPOS%     : PREVIOUS X PRINT POSITION.
OLDYPOS%     : PREVIOUS Y PRINT POSITION.
ORIGINX%     : X COORDINATE OF ORIGIN.
ORIGINY%     : Y COORDINATE OF ORIGIN.
P%           : STARTING POSITION OF HEADING.
PG%          : PAGES SCROLLED.
PTR%         : POINTER OF DATA PLOTTED.
R%           : ROW NUMBER OF DATA EDITOR.
ROWP%        : NTH PAGE OF FILE DISPLAYED.
RPOS%        : ROW POSITION OF CURSOR.
SAVED%       : FLAG INDICATING THE FILE BEING SAVED.
STKPTR%      : STACK POINTER.
SX%          : X PRINT POSITION OF MESSAGE.
SY%          : Y PRINT POSITION OF MESSAGE.
T1%, T2%     : TEMPORARY STORAGE.
TEMP4%       : TEMPORARY STORAGE.
X%           : X COORDINATE.
XPOS%        : X PRINT POSITION.
Y%           : Y COORDINATE.
YPOS%        : Y PRINT POSITION.

REALS       :

NEWDATA      : NEW DATA TO BE ENTERED.
OLDDATA      : PREVIOUS DATA ENTERED.
RANGE        : X RANGE IN A PAGE.
XINC         : INCREMENT OF X INDEX.
XINDEX       : X INDEX.
XMAX         : MAXIMUM X VALUE IN FIRST GRAPH PAGE.
XMIN         : MINIMUM X VALUE IN FIRST GRAPH PAGE.
T1, T2, T3   : TEMPORARY STORAGE.
TEMP         : TEMPORARY STORAGE.
TEMP2        : TEMPORARY STORAGE.
TEMP3        : TEMPORARY STORAGE.
YMAX         : MAXIMUM Y VALUE IN A PAGE.
YMIN         : MINIMUM Y VALUE IN A PAGE.
YINDEX       : INDICES ON Y AXIS.
```

PROGRAM 7.1 (continued)

CHARACTERS:

ANS$	:	KEYBOARD INPUT FROM USER.
BLANK$	:	BLANK SPACES.
FD$	:	DISK DRIVE USED FOR FILES.
FILE$	:	FILE NAME.
GRD$	:	GRID OPTION.
M$	:	''COMMAND.''
MRK$	:	MARK OPTION.
OPT$	:	OPTION CHOSEN.
REP$	:	RESPONSE FROM USER.
REP2$	:	RESPONSE FROM USER.

PROGRAM 7.1 2-D PLOTTER

```
10    '  Program 7.1 PLOTTER
20    CLS: SCREEN 2 : KEY OFF : WIDTH 80: LOCATE 10,1
30    PRINT "Which disk drive does contain PLOTTER ,AEDIT and APLOT ?"
40    PRINT "Drive A is on your left,"
50    PRINT "Drive B is on your right,"
60    PRINT "Drive C is your hard (fixed) disk drive." : BEEP
70    INPUT "ENTER [ A, B, or C ]";PD$ : PD$=PD$+":" : FD$="B:"
80    GRD$="NO GRID" : MRK$="MARK    "
90    OPT$="CURVE    "
100   GOSUB 220
110   GOSUB 390
120   X%=5+DX%: Y%=16: LOCATE X%,Y%,1,0,7
130   FIRST%=5 : LAST%=12
140   ANS$=INKEY$ : IF ANS$="" THEN 140
150   IF ANS$=CHR$(0)+CHR$(80) THEN IF X%<LAST% THEN X%=X%+1 ELSE X%=FIRST%
160   IF ANS$=CHR$(0)+CHR$(72) THEN IF X%>FIRST% THEN X%=X%-1 ELSE X%=LAST%
170   LOCATE X%,Y%: IF ANS$<>CHR$(13) THEN 140
180   FLAG1%=CSRLIN : FLAG1%=FLAG1%-4
190   ON FLAG1% GOSUB 1250,610,610,1290,730,990,1740,1980
200   IF FLAG1%<>1 THEN GOTO 110 ELSE GOTO 120
210   '---------------------- INITIALIZING CONSTANTS ---------------------
220   DIM X(300),Y(300),B(300),C(300),D(300)
230   DIM FILESTK$(10)
240   OUT 985,6
250   SX%=5 : SY%=55
260   M$="COMMAND :"
270   BLANK$="                                        "
280   B$="            "
290   SCREEN 0,1 : CLS
300   HDPOS%=48
310   KEY(1) ON: ON KEY(1) GOSUB 340
320   RETURN
330   '--------------------- CHANGE FOREGROUND COLOR ---------------------
340   FG%=FG%+1
350   IF FG% > 15 THEN FG%=1
360   OUT 985,FG%
370   RETURN
380   '---------------------- PRINT MAIN OPTIONS MENU --------------------
390   CLS: SCREEN 0,1: LOCATE 3,1
400   PRINT TAB(10) "******  INTERACTIVE PLOTTING MENU  ******"
410   PRINT
420   PRINT TAB(10) "*      _ CHANGE DEFAULT DISK DRIVE        *"
430   PRINT TAB(10) "*      _ CREATE INPUT FILE                *"
440   PRINT TAB(10) "*      _ EDIT(EXAMINE) DATA               *"
450   PRINT TAB(10) "*      _ SORT X VALUES                    *"
460   PRINT TAB(10) "*      _ CHART OPTION MENU                *"
470   PRINT TAB(10) "*      _ PLOTTING OPTION MENU             *"
480   PRINT TAB(10) "*      _ DO PLOTTING                      *"
490   PRINT TAB(10) "*      _ EXIT                             *": BEEP
```

PROGRAM 7.1 PLOTTER

```
500  PRINT
510  PRINT TAB(10) "****************************************"
520  LOCATE 3,65,1 : PRINT "STATUS"
530  LOCATE 4,55 : PRINT "------------------------"
540  LOCATE SX%,SY% : PRINT "DEFAULT DRIVE       = "+FD$
550  LOCATE SX%+2,SY% : PRINT "USER OPTIONS        :"
560  LOCATE SX%+3,SY% : PRINT OPT$
570  LOCATE SX%+4,SY% : PRINT GRD$
580  LOCATE SX%+5,SY% : PRINT MRK$
590  RETURN
600  '------------------------- DATA EDITOR ------------------------------
610  CLS : BEEP
620  INPUT "INPUT FILE NAME =";FILE$ : FILE$=FD$+FILE$
630  IF FLAG1%=2 THEN NEWFILE%=1 ELSE NEWFILE%=0
640  DX%=FLAG1%
650  SL%=100: ORDER%=0 : ORDER$="COLUMN ORDER"
660  LEFT%=1 : RIGHT%=1
670  CHAINFILE$=PD$+"AEDIT.BAS"
680  CALLFILE$=PD$+"PLOTTER.BAS"
690  COMMON NEWFILE%,FILE$,CALLFILE$,DX%,SL%,FD$,PD$,RIGHT%,
            LEFT%,ORDER%,ORDER$
700  CHAIN CHAINFILE$
710  RETURN
720  '------------------------- CHART OPTION MENU -------------------------
730  CLS : LOCATE 6,1
740  PRINT TAB(20) "******  CHART OPTION MENU  ******"
750  PRINT
760  PRINT TAB(20) "*       _ LINE                   *"
770  PRINT TAB(20) "*       _ POINT                  *"
780  PRINT TAB(20) "*       _ CURVE                  *"
790  PRINT TAB(20) "*       _ STEP                   *"
800  PRINT TAB(20) "*       _ EXIT                   *"
810  PRINT
820  PRINT TAB(20) "**********************************": BEEP
830  X%=8: Y%=27: LOCATE X%,Y%,1,0,7
840  FIRST%=8 : LAST%=12
850  ANS$=INKEY$ : IF ANS$="" THEN 850
860  IF ANS$=CHR$(0)+CHR$(80) THEN IF X%<LAST% THEN X%=X%+1 ELSE X%=FIRST%
870  IF ANS$=CHR$(0)+CHR$(72) THEN IF X%>FIRST% THEN X%=X%-1 ELSE X%=LAST%
880  LOCATE X%,Y%: IF ANS$<>CHR$(13) THEN 850
890  FLAG%=CSRLIN : FLAG%=FLAG%-7
900  ON FLAG% GOSUB 930,940,950,960,970
910  DX%=5
920  RETURN
930  OPT$="LINE     " : RETURN
940  OPT$="POINT    " : RETURN
950  OPT$="CURVE    " : RETURN
960  OPT$="STEP     " : RETURN
970  RETURN
980  '------------------------- PLOTTING OPTION MENU ----------------------
990  CLS : SCREEN 0,1: LOCATE 6,1
1000 PRINT TAB(20) "******  PLOTTING OPTION MENU  ******"
1010 PRINT
1020 PRINT TAB(20) "*      _    GRID &    MARK         *"
1030 PRINT TAB(20) "*      _    GRID & NO MARK         *"
1040 PRINT TAB(20) "*      _ NO GRID &    MARK         *"
1050 PRINT TAB(20) "*      _ NO GRID & NO MARK         *"
1060 PRINT TAB(20) "*      _ EXIT                      *"
1070 PRINT
1080 PRINT TAB(20) "************************************": BEEP
1090 X%=8 : Y%=26 : LOCATE X%,Y%,1,0,7
1100 FIRST%=8 : LAST%=12
1110 ANS$=INKEY$ : IF ANS$="" THEN 1110
1120 IF ANS$=CHR$(0)+CHR$(80) THEN IF X%<LAST% THEN X%=X%+1 ELSE X%=FIRST%
1130 IF ANS$=CHR$(0)+CHR$(72) THEN IF X%>FIRST% THEN X%=X%-1 ELSE X%=LAST%
1140 LOCATE X%,Y%: IF ANS$<>CHR$(13) THEN 1110
1150 FLAG%=CSRLIN : FLAG%=FLAG%-7
1160 ON FLAG% GOSUB 1190,1200,1210,1220,1230
1170 DX%=6
1180 RETURN
1190 GRD$="GRID    ": MRK$="MARK    " : RETURN
1200 GRD$="GRID    ": MRK$="NO MARK" : RETURN
1210 GRD$="NO GRID": MRK$="MARK    " : RETURN
1220 GRD$="NO GRID": MRK$="NO MARK" : RETURN
1230 RETURN
1240 '------------------------ CHANGE DEFAULT DRIVE ---------------------
1250 IF FD$="A:" THEN FD$="B:" ELSE IF FD$="B:" THEN FD$="C:" ELSE FD$="A:"
1260 LOCATE 5,76: PRINT FD$ : BEEP
```

PROGRAM 7.1 (continued)

```
1270 RETURN
1280 '------------------------- SORTING ------------------------------------
1290 CLS: INPUT "ENTER FILE NAME TO BE SORTED :";FILE$ : FILE$= FD$+FILE$
1300 PRINT "READING FILE "+FILE$+"..." : BEEP
1310 GOSUB 1520
1320 PRINT "SORTING..."
1330 L%=2 : K%=NOD%-1 : R%=NOD%
1340 WHILE (L%<=R%)
1350      FOR J%=R% TO L% STEP -1
1360           IF (X(J%-1)>X(J%)) THEN SWAP X(J%),X(J%-1):
                    SWAP Y(J%),Y(J%-1):K%=J%
1370           NEXT
1380      L%=K%+1
1390      FOR J%=L% TO R%
1400           IF (X(J%-1)>X(J%)) THEN SWAP X(J%),X(J%-1):
                    SWAP Y(J%),Y(J%-1):K%=J%
1410           NEXT
1420      R%=K%-1
1430      WEND
1440 CLS :BEEP
1450 PRINT "SORTED FILE ";FILE$;" BEING SAVED..." :GOSUB 1630
1460 DX%=4
1470 BEEP: INPUT "WANT TO LOOK AT SORTED DATA";ANS$:ANS$=ANS$+"y"
1480 ANS$=LEFT$(ANS$,1) : T1%=ASC(ANS$) OR 32 : ANS$=CHR$(T1%)
1490 IF ANS$<>"n" THEN GOSUB 650
1500 RETURN
1510 '------------------------- READING FILE ------------------------------
1520 OPEN FILE$ FOR INPUT AS #2
1530 INPUT #2,NOD%,T1%,T2%
1540 FOR J%=1 TO NOD%
1550      INPUT #2,Y(J%)
1560      NEXT
1570 FOR J%=1 TO NOD%
1580      INPUT #2,X(J%)
1590      NEXT
1600 CLOSE #2
1610 RETURN
1620 '------------------------- SAVE X AND Y ------------------------------
1630 OPEN FILE$ FOR OUTPUT AS #1
1640 PRINT #1,NOD%,NOD%,2
1650 FOR J%=1 TO NOD%
1660      PRINT #1,Y(J%);
1670      NEXT
1680 FOR J%=1 TO NOD%
1690      PRINT #1,X(J%);
1700      NEXT
1710 CLOSE #1
1720 RETURN
1730 '------------------------- INITIALIZING PLOTTER ----------------------
1740 CLS: INPUT "NUMBER OF DATA FILE(S) TO BE PLOTTED ON THE SAME PLOT =";NOF%
1750 PRINT "ENTER FILE NAME(S) :" : BEEP
1760 FOR I%=1 TO NOF%
1770      PRINT "FILE #";:PRINT USING "##";I%; :INPUT " =";FILE$
1780      FILE$=FD$+FILE$
1790      FILESTK$(I%)=FILE$
1800      CURVE$(I%)=OPT$
1810      NEXT
1820 PFILE$=PD$+"PLOTTER.BAS": FILE2$=PD$+"APLOT.BAS"
1830 SL%=100
1840 CHAIN FILE2$,30,ALL
1850 DX%=7
1860 RETURN
1870 '--------------------- SYSTEM STATUS BOXES ----------------------------
1880 LINE(142,164)-(215,178),,B
1890 LINE(223,164)-(295,178),,B
1900 LINE(303,164)-(375,178),,B
1910 LINE(383,164)-(455,178),,B
1920 LINE(463,164)-(622,178),,B
1930 LINE(127,164)-(638,184),,B
1940 PAINT(128,165),1,1
1950 LOCATE 22,20 : PRINT "PGE:  ": LOCATE 22,30: PRINT "NDL:    ":LOCATE 22,40:
     PRINT "NDP:   ":LOCATE 22,50:PRINT "NDR:   ":LOCATE 22,60:
     PRINT "MSG:              "
1960 LOCATE 22,24: PRINT USING"##";STKPTR%
1970 RETURN
1980 END
```

PROGRAM 7.1 PLOTTER

```
10    ' Program 7.2 -------------- APLOT ---------------------------------
20    DIM X(300), Y(300), B(300), C(300), D(300)
30    KEY OFF : SCREEN 2
40    HDPOS%=44 : B$="                    "
50    KEY(1) ON : ON KEY(1) GOSUB 110 : OUT 985,2
60    GOSUB 260
70    OPT$=CURVE$(1)
80    ERASE X,Y,FILESTK$,CURVE$,B,C,D
90    CHAIN PFILE$,SL%,ALL
100   '----------------------- CHANGE FOREGROUND COLOR --------------------
110   FG%=FG%+1
120   IF FG%>15 THEN FG%=1
130   OUT 985,FG%
140   RETURN
150   '------------------------ READING FILE -----------------------------
160   OPEN FILE$ FOR INPUT AS #2
170   INPUT #2,NOD%,T1%,T2%
180   FOR J%=1 TO NOD%
190        INPUT #2,Y(J%)
200        NEXT
210   FOR J%=1 TO NOD%
220        INPUT #2,X(J%)
230        NEXT
240   CLOSE #2
250   RETURN
260   '------------------------ INITIALIZING PLOTTER ---------------------
270   FOR L%=1 TO NOF%
280        FILE$=FILESTK$(L%)
290        GOSUB 160
300        IF L%=1 THEN XMIN=X(1): XMAX=XMIN: YMIN=Y(1): YMAX=YMIN
310        FOR I%=1 TO NOD%
320             IF X(I%)<XMIN THEN XMIN=X(I%) ELSE IF X(I%)>XMAX THEN XMAX=X(I%)
330             IF Y(I%)<YMIN THEN YMIN=Y(I%) ELSE IF Y(I%)>YMAX THEN YMAX=Y(I%)
340             NEXT I%
350        NEXT L%
360   INPUT "HEADING FOR THE PLOT =";HEAD$
370   T1%=LEN(HEAD$) : IF T1%>60 THEN HEAD$=LEFT$(HEAD$,60)
380   INPUT "X TITLE FOR THE PLOT =";XTITLE$
390   T1%=LEN(XTITLE$) : IF T1%>60 THEN XTITLE$=LEFT$(XTITLE$,60)
400   INPUT "Y TITLE FOR THE PLOT =";YTITLE$
410   T1%=LEN(YTITLE$) : IF T1%>15 THEN YTITLE$=LEFT$(YTITLE$,15)
420   PRINT "MINIMUM X VALUE = [DEFAULT:";XMIN;"]";: INPUT T1$
430   IF T1$<>"" THEN TEMP=VAL(T1$) ELSE TEMP=XMIN
440   IF TEMP<=XMIN THEN OK%=1 ELSE OK%=0
450   IF T1$<>"" THEN TEMP3=XMIN: XMIN=TEMP
460   PRINT "MAXIMUM X VALUE = [DEFAULT:";XMAX;"]";: INPUT T1$
470   IF T1$<>"" THEN XMAX=VAL(T1$)
480   PRINT "MINIMUM Y VALUE = [DEFAULT:";YMIN;"]";: INPUT T1$
490   IF T1$<>"" THEN YMIN=VAL(T1$)
500   PRINT "MAXIMUM Y VALUE = [DEFAULT:";YMAX;"]";: INPUT T1$
510   IF T1$<>"" THEN YMAX=VAL(T1$)
520   RANGE=XMAX-XMIN
530   IF OK%=1 THEN PTR%=1: STKPTR%=1: PGSTK%(1)=1 ELSE GOSUB 580
540   CLS : SCREEN 2
550   GOSUB 840
560   RETURN
570   '------------------------ SET PAGES --------------------------------
580   TEMP2=(TEMP-TEMP3)/RANGE+1 : PG%=INT(TEMP2)
590   STKPTR%=PG%+1
600   FOR I%=1 TO STKPTR%
610        T2=TEMP-RANGE*(I%-1)
620        J%=1
630        WHILE X(J%)<T2
640             J%=J%+1
650             WEND
660        PGSTK%(PG%-I%+2)=J%
670   NEXT I%
680   PTR%=PGSTK%(STKPTR%)
690   RETURN
700   '------------------------ PLOT WITHOUT GRID ------------------------
710   LINE(ORIGINX%,ORIGINY%)-(ORIGINX%+6*INTERVALX%,TEMP4%),1,B
720   X%=ORIGINX%
```

PROGRAM 7.2 APLOT†

†*Note:* APLOT cannot be run by itself. This is a utility subroutine similar to AEDIT.

```
730  FOR I%=1 TO 25
740       IF ((I%-1) MOD 4 =0) THEN LINE(X%,132)-(X%,135)
750       X%=X%+INTERVALX%/4
760       NEXT
770  T1%=ORIGINX%-8 : T2%=ORIGINY%
780  FOR I%=1 TO 2
790       T2%=T2%+INTERVALY%
800       LINE(T1%,T2%)-(ORIGINX%,T2%)
810       NEXT
820  RETURN
830  '------------------------  PLOTTING ROUTINES  ------------------------
840  ORIGINY%=12 : ORIGINX%=142 : INTERVALX%=80 : INTERVALY%=40
850  TEMP4%=ORIGINY%+3*INTERVALY%
860  GOSUB 2300
870  VIEW(0,0)-(639,163) : CLS : VIEW
880  LOCATE 22,65: PRINT "PLOTTING..." : BEEP
890  GOSUB 710
900 IF LEFT$(GRD$,1)="G" THEN GOSUB 2410
910 X%=ORIGINX% : Y%=ORIGINY%
920 FOR L%=1 TO NOF%
930      IF NOF%=1 THEN 960
940      FILE$=FILESTK$(L%)
950      GOSUB 160
960      XINDEX=XMIN
970      GOSUB 1410
980      IF L% = 1 THEN GOSUB 1120
990      IF L% <> NOF% THEN PTR%=PGSTK%(STKPTR%)
1000     NEXT L%
1010 LOCATE 22,65: PRINT B$: LOCATE 22,65: PRINT "DONE" : BEEP
1020 ANS$=INKEY$ : IF ANS$="" THEN 1020
1030 IF ANS$<>CHR$(0)+CHR$(77) THEN 1060
1040 IF NOD%-PTR%+1 <=0 THEN LOCATE 22,65: PRINT "NO MORE DATA" : BEEP:
       FOR I%=1 TO 500 : NEXT: LOCATE 22,65: PRINT B$: GOTO 1020
1050 STKPTR%=STKPTR%+1: LOCATE 22,24: PRINT USING "##";STKPTR%:
     XMIN=XMAX: XMAX=XMAX+RANGE: PGSTK%(STKPTR%)=PTR%:GOTO 870
1060 IF ANS$<>CHR$(0)+CHR$(75) THEN 1090
1070 IF STKPTR%<=1 THEN LOCATE 22,65: PRINT "NO MORE DATA" : BEEP:
       FOR I%=1 TO 500: NEXT : LOCATE 22,65: PRINT B$: GOTO 1020
1080 XMAX=XMIN : XMIN=XMAX-RANGE: STKPTR%=STKPTR%-1: LOCATE 22,24:
       PRINT USING"##";STKPTR%: PTR%=PGSTK%(STKPTR%):GOTO 870
1090 IF ANS$="P" OR ANS$="p" THEN GOSUB 1740 : GOTO 1020
1100 RETURN
1110 '------------------------  FIND ZERO LINE  ---------------------------
1120 IF (YMAX*YMIN <0) THEN TEMP=(-1*YMIN/(YMAX-YMIN))*120 ELSE 1190
1130 DELTAY%=CINT(TEMP)
1140 LINE(ORIGINX%,TEMP4%-DELTAY%)-(ORIGINX%+6*INTERVALX%,TEMP4%-DELTAY%)
1150 IF (XMAX*XMIN <0) THEN TEMP=(-1*XMIN/(XMAX-XMIN))*480 ELSE 1190
1160 DELTAX%=CINT(TEMP)
1170 LINE(ORIGINX%+DELTAX%,ORIGINY%)-(ORIGINX%+DELTAX%,TEMP4%)
1180 '------------------------  PRINT INDECIES  ---------------------------
1190 YINDEX=YMAX
1200 TEMP=(YMAX-YMIN)/3
1210 P%=LEN(HEAD$) : P%=HDPOS%-(P%*.5)
1220 LOCATE 1,1: PRINT TAB(P%) HEAD$
1230 FOR I%=1 TO 4
1240      PRINT USING "##############.##-";YINDEX
1250      IF (I%<>4) THEN FOR J%=1 TO 4 : PRINT : NEXT J%
1260      IF (I%<3) THEN YINDEX=YINDEX-TEMP ELSE YINDEX=YMIN
1270      NEXT I%
1280 XINDEX=XMIN : XINCR=(XMAX-XMIN)/24
1290 PRINT USING "#####################.#";XINDEX;
1300 FOR I%=1 TO 6
1310      XINDEX=XINDEX+XINCR*4
1320      PRINT USING "########.#";XINDEX; : NEXT I%
1330 P%=LEN(XTITLE$) : P%=HDPOS%-(P%*.5)
1340 LOCATE 20,1: PRINT TAB(P%) XTITLE$
1350 T1%=LEN(YTITLE$) : P%=9-(T1%*.5)
1360 FOR I%=1 TO T1%
1370      T1$=MID$(YTITLE$,I%,1): LOCATE P%+I%,6: PRINT T1$
1380      NEXT
1390 RETURN
1400 '------------------------  LOCATE POINTS ON PLOT  --------------------
1410 TEMP2=1/(YMAX-YMIN): TEMP3=1/(XMAX-XMIN)
1420 IF MRK$="" THEN MRK$="MARK   "
1430 REP2$=LEFT$(MRK$,1)
1440 T%=L% : REP$=LEFT$(CURVE$(L%),1)
1450 IF T% > 3 THEN T%=T%-3 : GOTO 1450
```

PROGRAM 7.2 (continued)

```
1460 IF REP$="C" THEN GOSUB 1870
1470 COUNT%=0 : NDP%=0
1480 WHILE (PTR%<=NOD%) AND (X(PTR%) <= XMAX)
1490      IF X(PTR%) < XMIN THEN 1650
1500      IF Y(PTR%) < YMIN OR Y(PTR%) >YMAX THEN 1650
1510      NDP%=NDP%+1
1520      TEMP1=ABS((X(PTR%)-XMIN)*TEMP3)*480
1530      TEMP=ABS((Y(PTR%)-YMIN)*TEMP2)*120
1540      DELTAY%=CINT(TEMP) : DELTAX%=CINT(TEMP1)
1550      OLDY%=Y% : OLDX%=X%
1560      Y%=TEMP4%-DELTAY% : X%=ORIGINX%+DELTAX%
1570      IF COUNT%=0 THEN OLDY%=Y% : OLDX%=X%: PSET(X%,Y%):
              FIRSTX%=X%: FIRSTY%=Y%: COUNT%=1
1580      IF REP$="P" THEN 1600 ELSE IF REP$="S" THEN LINE-(X%,OLDY%)
1590      LINE-(X%,Y%),1
1600      IF REP2$<>"M" AND REP$<>"P" THEN 1630
1610      IF T%=1 THEN CIRCLE(X%,Y%),2,1,0,6.28,5/12 ELSE IF T%=2 THEN
              LINE(X%,Y%)-(X%+6,Y%): LINE-(X%+3,Y%-3): LINE-(X%,Y%) ELSE
              LINE(X%,Y%)-(X%+6,Y%-3),1,B : PSET(X%,Y%)
1620      GOTO 1640
1630      PSET(X%,Y%)
1640      IF REP$="C" THEN GOSUB 2140
1650      PTR%=PTR%+1
1660      WEND
1670 LOCATE 22,34
1680 PRINT USING"###";PGSTK%(STKPTR%)-1
1690 LOCATE 22,44: PRINT USING "###";NDP%: LOCATE 22,54
1700 PRINT USING"###";NOD%-PTR%+1
1710 LASTX%=X% : LASTY%=Y%
1720 RETURN
1730 '------------------------- PAINTING ------------------------------
1740 IF REP$="P" OR NOF%>1 THEN 1850
1750 LOCATE 22,65: PRINT "PAINTING..." : BEEP
1760 COUNT%=0
1770 LINE(LASTX%,LASTY%)-(LASTX%,ORIGINY%+3*INTERVALY%)
1780 LINE(FIRSTX%,FIRSTY%)-(FIRSTX%,ORIGINY%+3*INTERVALY%)
1790 FOR K%=FIRSTX% TO LASTX%
1800      COLOR1%=POINT(K%,129)
1810      IF COLOR1%=1 THEN COUNT%=COUNT%+1 : XSTK%(COUNT%)=K%
1820      IF COUNT%=2 THEN T1%=(XSTK%(2)+XSTK%(1))*.5 : PAINT(T1%,131),1,1:
              COUNT%=0
1830      NEXT
1840 LOCATE 22,65: PRINT B$: LOCATE 22,65: PRINT "DONE": BEEP
1850 RETURN
1860 '----------------------- CUBIC INTERPOLATION ----------------------
1870 DIM H(200),A(200),L(200),U(200),Z(200)
1880 FOR I%=1 TO NOD%-1
1890      H(I%)=X(I%+1)-X(I%)
1900      NEXT
1910 FOR I%=2 TO NOD%-1
1920      T1=Y(I%+1)*H(I%-1)
1930      T2=Y(I%)*(X(I%+1)-X(I%-1))
1940      T3=Y(I%-1)*H(I%)
1950      A(I%)=3*(T1-T2+T3)/(H(I%-1)*H(I%))
1960      NEXT I%
1970 L(1)=1 : U(1)=0 : Z(1)=0
1980 FOR I%=2 TO NOD%
1990      L(I%)=2*(X(I%+1)-X(I%-1))-H(I%-1)*U(I%-1)
2000      U(I%)=H(I%)/L(I%)
2010      Z(I%)=(A(I%)-H(I%-1)*Z(I%-1))/L(I%)
2020      NEXT I%
2030 L(NOD%)=1 : Z(NOD%)=0 : C(NOD%)=0
2040 FOR J%=NOD%-1 TO 1 STEP -1
2050      C(J%)=Z(J%)-U(J%)*C(J%+1)
2060      T1=(Y(J%+1)-Y(J%))/H(J%)
2070      T2=H(J%)*(C(J%+1)+2*C(J%))/3
2080      B(J%)=T1-T2
2090      D(J%)=(C(J%+1)-C(J%))/(3*H(J%))
2100      NEXT J%
2110 ERASE H,A,L,U,Z
2120 RETURN
2130 '----------------------- PLOT CUBIC --------------------------
2140 IF PTR%+1 > NOD% OR X(PTR%+1) > XMAX THEN 2280
2150 T1=(XMAX-XMIN)/480 : T2=X(PTR%)
2160 TEMP1=ABS((X(PTR%+1)-XMIN)*TEMP3)*480
2170 DELTAX%=CINT(TEMP1)
2180 XNEXT%=ORIGINX%+DELTAX%
```

PROGRAM 7.2 (continued)

```
2190 X%=X%+2
2200 IF X% >= XNEXT% THEN 2280
2210 T2=T2+2*T1
2220 T4=T2-X(PTR%)
2230 T3=Y(PTR%)+B(PTR%)*T4+C(PTR%)*T4*T4+D(PTR%)*T4*T4*T4
2240 TEMP=ABS((T3-YMIN)*TEMP2)*120
2250 DELTAY%=CINT(TEMP) : Y%=TEMP4%-DELTAY%
2260 IF Y%>132 THEN Y%=132 ELSE IF Y%<12 THEN Y%=12
2270 LINE-(X%,Y%) : GOTO 2190
2280 RETURN
2290 --------------------  SYSTEM STATUS BOXES  ---------------------------
2300 LINE(142,164)-(215,178),,B
2310 LINE(223,164)-(295,178),,B
2320 LINE(303,164)-(375,178),,B
2330 LINE(383,164)-(455,178),,B
2340 LINE(463,164)-(622,178),,B
2350 LINE(127,164)-(638,184),,B
2360 PAINT(128,165),1,1
2370 LOCATE 22,20 : PRINT "PGE:   ": LOCATE 22,30: PRINT "NDL:    ":LOCATE 22,40:
     PRINT "NDP:    ":LOCATE 22,50:PRINT "NDR:    ":LOCATE 22,60:
     PRINT "MSG:                "
2380 LOCATE 22,24: PRINT USING"##";STKPTR%
2390 RETURN
2400 '------------------------  PLOT WITH GRIDS  --------------------------
2410 FOR I%=1 TO 11
2420      T1%=ORIGINY%+I%*10
2430      LINE(143,T1%)-(623,T1%),,,&H4444
2440      NEXT I%
2450 FOR I%=1 TO 23
2460      T1%=ORIGINX%+I%*20
2470      LINE(T1%,12)-(T1%,132),,,&HAAAA
2480      NEXT I%
2490 RETURN
2500 END
```

PROGRAM 7.2 APLOT

REFERENCES

1. Berg, C. R., "Computer Graphics Display: Windows for Process Control," *IEEE Computer Graphics and Applications* **3** (3) 43–55, May–June 1983.

2. Burden, R. L., J. D. Faires, and A. C. Reynolds, *Numerical Analysis,* 2nd ed., Prindle, Weber, and Schmidt, Boston, 1981 (Chapter 3).

3. Caporal, P. M., and G. J. Hahn, "Tools for Automated Statistical Graphics," *IEEE Computer Graphics and Applications* **1** (4) 72–82, October 1981.

4. Gust, R. L., "Designing Effective Business Graphics," *IEEE Computer Graphics and Applications* **1** (4) 33–36, July 1983.

5. Montgomery, D. C., and L. A. Johnson, *Forecasting and Time Series,* McGraw-Hill, New York, 1976 (Chapter 5).

6. Takeuchi, H., and A. H. Schmidt, "New Promise of Computer Graphics," *Harvard Business Review* **58** 121–131, January-February 1980.

7. Vinberg, A., and J. E. George, "Computer Graphics and Business Executive — The New Management Team," *IEEE Computer Graphics and Applications* **1** (1) 57–71, January 1981.

CHAPTER EIGHT
Interactive Computer-Aided Design

The replacement of paper as a drafting medium is perhaps one of the most widely claimed advantages of a graphics system. A graphics system that presents the proper tools for image creation and manipulation can make a user much more productive. For instance in an engineering drawing environment, repetitive construction components do not have to be redrawn but can be instantaneously called forth from storage.

In this chapter, we will develop a general-purpose interactive drawing tool called DRAWER and demonstrate its versatility as a *computer-aided design* tool. DRAWER is basically a graphics program developed on the IBM PC that turns the screen into an automated sketch pad—that is, it allows the user to draw elaborate pictures freely without writing any graphics program. DRAWER still assumes a 2-D drawing environment, but we will add several new features such as the use of function keys and cursor pad in designing graphics commands.

8.1 USING THE COMPUTER AS A DESIGNER'S AID

Computer graphics are an essential tool for designers in many disciplines, such as engineering drawing, artwork, fashion, textiles, carpeting, and similar areas. For example, complex fabric patterns involving several figures can be automatically generated by the computer graphics system. These patterns can be displayed in any combination to determine the overall effect, and many alternative designs can be tried in less time than is required to draw a single pattern manually. This type of computer assistance promotes the designer's imagination and creativity. With a sophisticated graphics system, the computer design can be sent directly to production via control programs that manufacture fabrics.

A technique such as the example above in which designer and computer blend into a problem-solving team is often referred to as *computer-aided design*. The remaining sections of this chapter examine how we develop a graphics system useful as a designer's tool, utilizing the best characteristics of human beings and machines [1].

8.2 DESIGN PRINCIPLES

As in the previous two chapters, we will develop a series of graphics commands using the keyboard as the sole input device. However, we will take a somewhat different approach to displaying information on the screen. First, we will introduce the use of function keys in graphics commands. Second, we will design the screen in such a way that menu-driven commands, prompts, and status messages will be displayed along with the graphical information.

8.2.1 SCREEN LAYOUT

One of the first decisions that must be made regarding graphics display concerns how the screen area is to be used. In many applications, the screen is simply not large enough to accommodate menus, prompts, and other messages. The need to optimize the use of screen space will normally call for a screen division into at least four windows: one for a menu, a second containing the status messages, a third for prompts, and a fourth as the drawing area. Here the windows are rectangular screen regions whose positions and dimensions are set by the user. The boundaries of the windows can be tailored to each graphics program. Figure 8.1 shows the layout of the screen to be used in the development of DRAWER.

8.2.2 INFORMATION DISPLAY

Once we determine the overall layout of the screen, we must decide how to show menus, window boundaries, and status messages. Also, object representations must accurately display all relevant attributes of the objects.

Graphics commands. In designing graphics commands, we must pay special attention to conventions familiar to the user. At the same time, we must be as

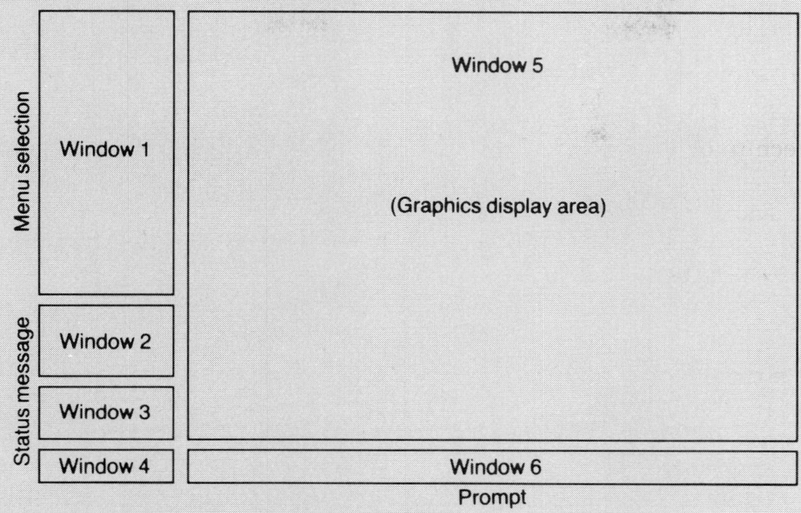

FIGURE 8.1 **Screen layout for DRAWER**

economical as possible in the use of screen space. This often leads to a situation where we cannot exactly match standard graphics conventions. If this happens, it is necessary to experiment with different representations in order to find one that satisfies the user. In Fig. 8.2, Window 1 contains 24 single-character commands. We quickly observe that some of the letter symbols deviate from the standard conventions. For instance, we normally use "S" (SAVE) command to save a file. In our example, however, "S" sets the speed of the leading dot; therefore, we must use "F" (FILE) instead. We will always experience problems like this when we use single-character commands. We could use multicharacter strings to design the graphics commands, but these are not as convenient to use as a single-character command program. We can also use single numbers to represent each command; however, numbers do not help the user memorize the commands.

Status messages. We will reserve three windows on the screen to display the status messages. Window 2 will record and print the X and Y coordinates of the leading dot (cursor position in graphics mode). It simply pinpoints the current position of the leading dot in the absolute coordinates on the screen. As we move the dot from one position to another, this window provides easily accessed information something like a digital meter at a gas station:

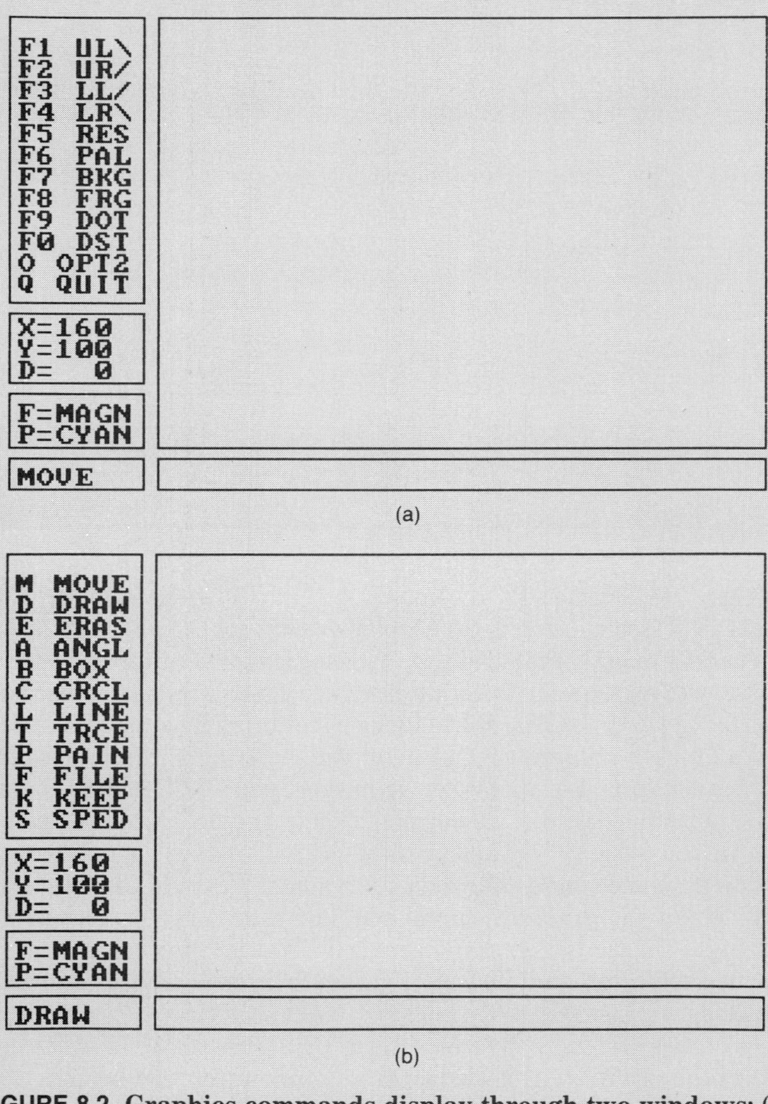

FIGURE 8.2 Graphics commands display through two windows: (a) option 1 menu and (b) option 2 menu

as we pump gasoline into the car tank, we know exactly how much gasoline has flowed into it at any moment just by glancing at the meter. This coordinate information becomes very useful in placing an object at a precise location on the screen.

Window 3 on the screen displays color information about the leading dot and foreground. Displaying the current color mode helps the user select what colors to use for both leading dot and picture drawn. Window 4 displays the drawing mode we're currently in. There are three drawing modes in DRAWER—"DRAW", "MOVE", and "ERASE".

Feedback. Since DRAWER's command language is relatively simple, and the computer's response is very rapid, we will use a beep sound as command feedback. This will provide unobtrusive confirmation that the user's commands are being received. The user learns to rely on this sound as confirmation and will notice its absence at once.

DRAWER will use prompts to assist the user in selecting the next command in a multimode command language, where the choice of permissible parameters may not be obvious. We need another window to display a printed message for these prompts. Window 6 in Fig. 8.1 serves this purpose.

8.2.3 PROGRAMMING LOGIC

The general programming logic for DRAWER is shown in Fig. 8.3. DRAWER is written in IBM PC advanced BASIC (BASICA) and requires a minimum configuration of 64K RAM, color/graphics adapter, and monitor. Also required is DOS 2.0. The complete computer program appears at the end of this chapter, along with detailed documentation.

8.3 MENU-DRIVEN COMMANDS

In Fig. 8.2, the first window lists keyboard commands that are aided by a set of function keys. Function keys provide several advantages in developing a graphics system such as DRAWER: (1) faster operation is possible because no time is lost in selecting the function key, and (2) the function key is conceptually simple and easily understood, particularly if it is labeled with the name of the function it performs.

8.3.1 MENU SELECTION

All available commands in DRAWER are grouped under two main menu options. Menu Option 1 lists ten function keys that control the powerful graph-

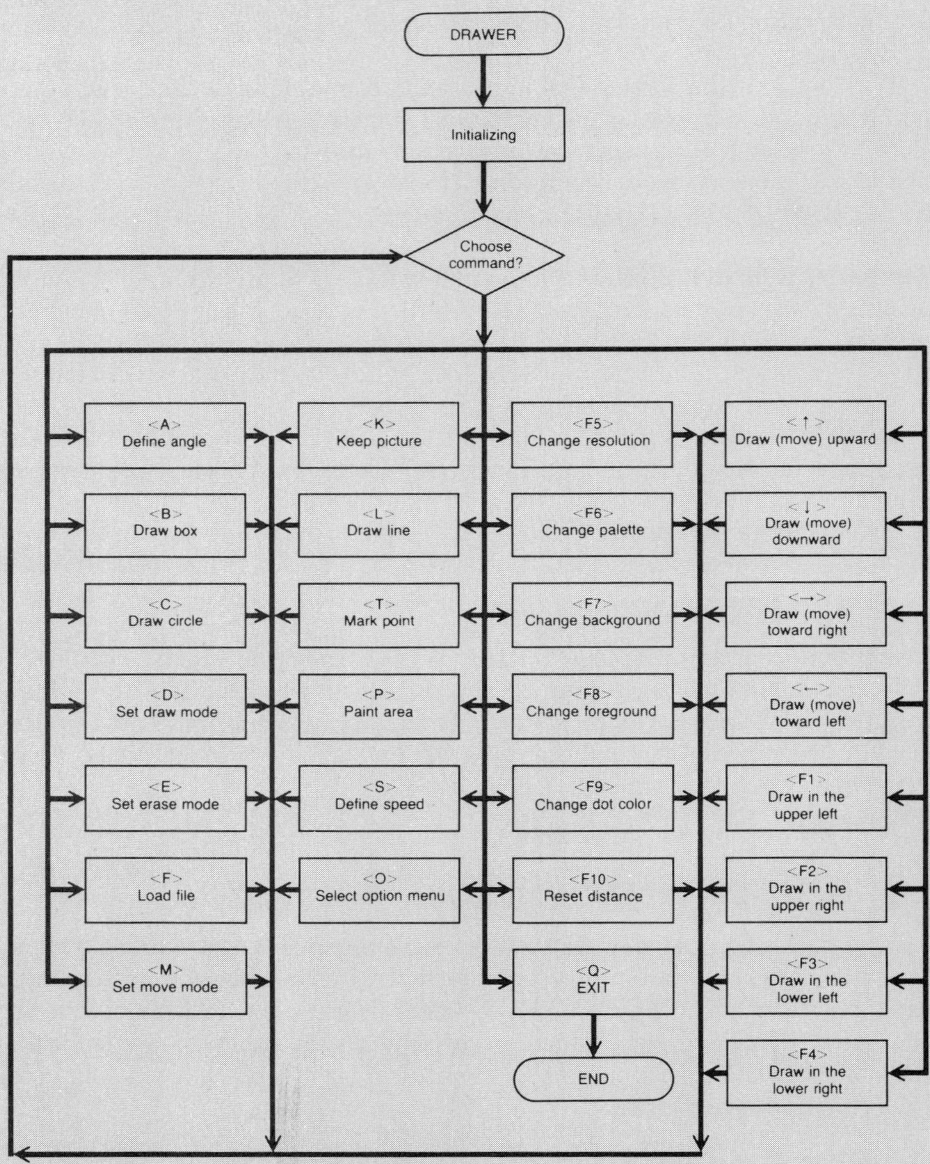

FIGURE 8.3 Programming logic for DRAWER

ics mode manipulation features of DRAWER. (See Fig. 8.2a.) Each function key often controls more than one function. Menu Option 2 contains three additional graphics modes and ten graphics functions. (See Fig. 8.2b.) The "O" key is to switch between Option 1 and Option 2 for the menu selection. The default menu option is Option 1 when the program is executed. (This menu design principle was introduced in Section 7.2.1.)

8.3.2 CURSOR CONTROL

Eight keys are assigned to move the cursor around the screen, four from the cursor pad and another four from the function keys. These are summarized in Table 8.1, along with the IBM PC Keyboard diagram.

TABLE 8.1 Cursor movement

Key		Movement direction	
Up arrow	[↑]	Up	
Down arrow	[↓]	Down	
Right arrow	[→]	Right	
Left arrow	[←]	Left	
	[F1]	Diagonally up and left	[↖]
	[F2]	Diagonally up and right	[↗]
	[F3]	Diagonally down and left	[↙]
	[F4]	Diagonally down and right	[↘]

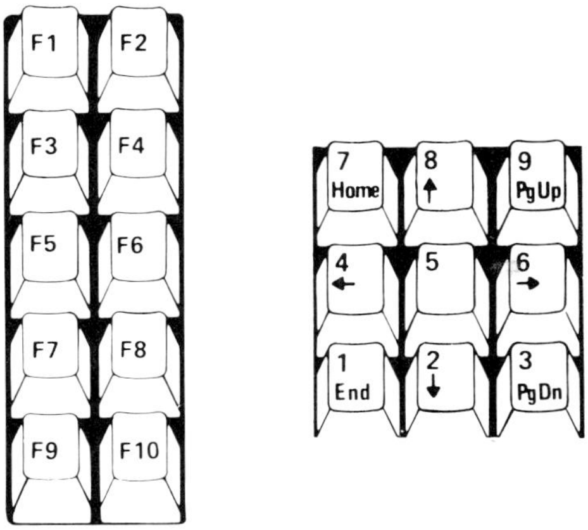

8.4 MODE SELECTION

Two modes are available, graphics mode and color mode. The graphics mode contains four submodes to choose from; the color mode contains another four submodes that define color combinations.

8.4.1 GRAPHICS MODE SELECTION

Four graphics submodes are available for manipulating a picture: DRAW, ERASE, MOVE, and SCREEN. The default mode is the "DRAW" mode. When we press the "D," "M," or "E" key from the keyboard, the mode in effect will be displayed in Window 4 of the screen. (See Fig. 8.2.)

DRAW mode. The DRAW mode draws a point at the cursor (leading dot) position on the screen.

ERASE mode. The ERASE mode erases a point at the specified position on the screen. As we press this key, the ERASE mode will be displayed in Window 4 as ERASE. *It is important to understand that ERASE mode works only when the background color is black* (0). Therefore, it is a good idea to keep the screen in black BACKGROUND mode during ordinary drawing. Once we finish drawing, we can change the background color to one other than black.

MOVE mode. The MOVE mode moves, but does *not* plot or erase any points. We press the "M" key to effect this mode. We can only move around the screen by using the four movement keys on the cursor pad (↑, ↓, ←, →).

SCREEN mode. The SCREEN mode sets the screen attributes used by the subsequent statements. The default mode is the medium resolution graphics mode. Pressing the [F5] key while in the medium-resolution graphics mode changes the screen to the high-resolution graphics mode, and vice versa. Switching from medium-resolution mode to high-resolution mode (or vice versa) clears the graphics screen. In other words, all the graphical contents in the display window (Window 5) will be lost. Thus the [F5] key can be used to clear the screen.

8.4.2 COLOR MODE SELECTION

Four submodes are available for setting the color attributes in medium resolution graphics.

PALETTE mode. The PALETTE mode sets the palette colors. Two palettes are available in the IBM PC graphics mode, 0 and 1. The default mode is

TABLE 8.2 Mode selection

Mode type	Key	Description	Status line display
Graphics	D	Draw	DRAW
	M	Move	MOVE
	E	Erase	ERASE
	[F5]	Screen resolution	
Color	[F6]	Palette	
	[F7]	Background	
	[F8]	Foreground	Color selected
	[F9]	Leading dot	Color selected

Palette 0. Pressing the [F6] key while in Palette 0 mode switches to Palette 1 mode, and vice versa. The colors selected when we choose each palette are

Color	Palette 0	Palette 1
1	Green	Cyan
2	Red	Magenta
3	Brown	White

BACKGROUND mode. The BACKGROUND mode sets the background colors. Any of the palette colors may be selected for background. The default background color is black. We can change the background color by successively pressing the [F7] key until we encounter the desired background color.

FOREGROUND mode. The FOREGROUND mode sets the foreground color (i.e., the color of the picture itself). We can select the desired foreground color by successively pressing the [F8] key. The FOREGROUND mode selects the color from the current palette defined by the COLOR statement in DRAWER.

LEADING DOT mode. The LEADING DOT mode sets the color of the leading dot. It is a good idea to give the leading dot a color different from the foreground color. This dot pinpoints quickly where the current graphic cursor is located on the screen. We use the [F9] key to effect this mode and select the color by successively pressing the [F9] key. Table 8.2 summarizes these modes.

8.5 GRAPHICS COMMANDS

There are eight graphic function commands from which to choose. These are displayed in Window 1 on the screen.

8.5.1 TRACE COMMAND

This command is used to mark a point on the screen. Pressing the "T" key causes a beep sound to acknowledge the receipt of the command. The computer then records the current cursor coordinates.

8.5.2 RESET COMMAND

DRAWER automatically computes the length of the line segment drawn and displays it in Status Window 2 along with the current X and Y coordinates. The length is reset to zero when D is greater than 999. We use the [F10] key to reset the meter to zero whenever we need to measure the distance between two points.

8.5.3 SPEED COMMAND

We can change the speed of the cursor by pressing the "S" key. The program will then prompt us to enter a positive number. The default is 1. Entering a value greater than 1 makes the cursor move faster than normal. (A value of 10 is the largest value it is practical to enter.)

8.5.4 LINE COMMAND

This command is used to draw a line on the screen, after two endpoints have been specified by the trace command. If only one point is marked and the line command is entered, the computer draws a line from the last point referenced (marked) to the current marked point, in the color defined by the current color mode. To draw lines BC and CD shown in Fig. 8.4(a), where the initial cursor is located at point A, we can take the following steps:

Step 1: Set the program in MOVE mode by pressing the "M" key.
Step 2: Move the cursor from point A to point B by using cursor pad keys (↑, ↓, ←, →).
Step 3: Mark the position of point B by pressing the "T" key. (We will hear a short beep sound.)
Step 4: Move the cursor to point C, and mark the position by pressing the "T" key. (We will hear another beep sound.)
Step 5: Press the "L" key to draw a line between point B and point C.
Step 6: Move the cursor to point D, and press the "L" key to connect points C and D. (Recall that the computer will always use the last two marked points.)

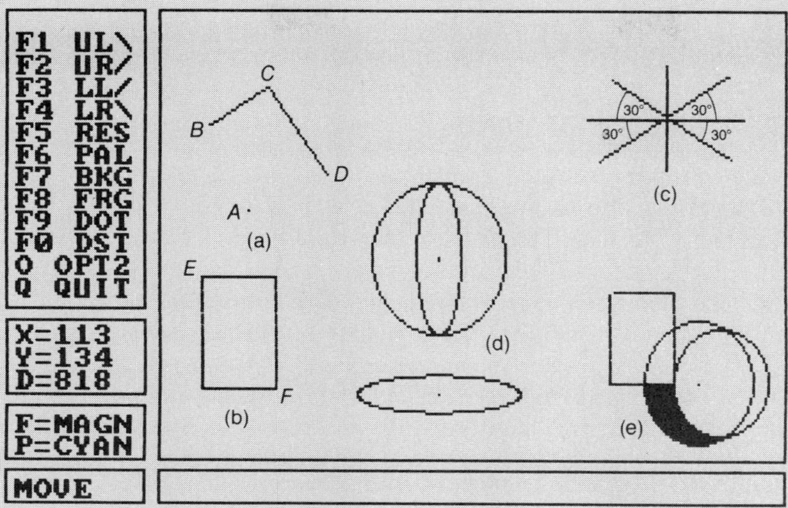

FIGURE 8.4 Examples of DRAWER's commands

8.5.5 BOX COMMAND

This command draws a rectangle when the position of two of its diagonal corners are marked by the user. To draw the rectangle shown in Fig. 8.4(b), the following steps may be taken:

Step 1: Make sure that MOVE mode is in effect.
Step 2: Move the cursor to point E, and mark the position.
Step 3: Move the cursor to point F, and mark the position.
Step 4: Press the "B" key to draw the rectangle.

8.5.6 ANGLE COMMAND

This command is used in conjunction with function keys [F1], [F2], [F3], and [F4] when we draw or erase a line with a slope measured in degrees from the *horizontal* axis. To execute this command, we first press the "A" key, which prompts an angle input in Window 6, accompanied by a beep sound. Then we simply type an angle input and press the [ENTER] key. From this point on, the drawing is in ANGLE mode. We use the movement function keys to draw a sloped line. The default angle is 45 degrees, but an angle may be specified in the range between 0 and 90 degrees. We must be in DRAW mode to draw a sloped line. If we happen to be in ERASE mode, any points on the sloped line will be erased. Figure 8.4(c) shows 30-degree lines sloping in four different directions.

8.5.7 CIRCLE COMMAND

We use this command to draw a circle or an ellipse by specifying the starting and ending angles, the radius, and the aspect ratio (the ratio between the x radius and the y radius). The default starting angle is 0 degree (three-o'clock position); whereas the default ending angle is 360 degrees (the same place). The angles are measured *counterclockwise.* The default for aspect ratio is 1 in medium resolution and 5/12 in high resolution. These values produce a *visual circle* with a standard screen aspect ratio of 4/3. If the aspect ratio is less than one, then the radius assumed in the circle command is the x radius. That is, the radius is measured in the horizontal direction. If the aspect ratio is greater than one, then the radius is the y radius. We draw a circle or an ellipse with the following procedure:

Step 1: Measure the radius on the screen by using the trace command. To measure a radius with a specified length, use the [F10] key to set the distance meter to zero, and mark the starting point. Then move the cursor until the meter reads the specified length in coordinate, and mark the ending point. The computer records this length as a radius for future circle or ellipse plottings.

Step 2: Move the cursor to the center of the circle or ellipse.

Step 3: Press the "C" key to prompt the circle command. Then enter the *starting* and *ending* angles, and the aspect ratio. To draw a circle, simply press [ENTER] to these three prompts.

Figure 8.4(d) shows a circle and two ellipses with a radius of 22 and an aspect ratio of 3. Note that no clipping is provided by the DRAWER program. Thus the radius should be set within the limit of Window 5.

8.5.8 PAINT COMMAND

We use this command to fill in a screen area with the selected color. Two prompt messages are displayed: the color to be painted and the color of the boundary. The colors should be given in numbers, from 0 to 3. In medium resolution, this color is the color from the current palette. Zero (0) is the background color. Note that we can paint a closed area only if it is surrounded by one boundary color. If the boundary is not completely closed, we will mess up the whole picture. When we want to paint a closed area, we should first move the dot into the closed area and make sure that the color of the dot is not the same as that of the boundary. Otherwise nothing will be painted. Be sure to select a

TABLE 8.3 Summary of graphics function commands

Key	Command	Function
T	Trace	Marks a point and picks its coordinates on the screen.
L	Line	Draws a line connecting two marked endpoints.
B	Box	Draws a box with two diagonal marked corner points.
A	Angle	Sets an angle in a line drawing.
C	Circle	Draws an ellipse with given *radius, starting/ending angle,* and *aspect ratio.*
P	Paint	Sets the *color* to be painted and the *boundary* color.
S	Speed	Sets the cursor speed.
[F10]	Reset	Resets the distance meter to zero.

proper color for the boundary. It is a good practice to save the picture before painting the picture. Figure 8.4(e) shows an example with a portion of the picture painted. Table 8.3 summarizes the graphics function commands used in DRAWER.

8.6 UTILITY COMMANDS

Two utility commands are provided in DRAWER, the Keep and File commands.

8.6.1 KEEP COMMAND

This utility command is used to save *only* the picture on the screen, excluding any status messages and other command menus displayed on the screen. Therefore, the technique used in saving the picture is different from just saving the total screen image, which was described in Chapter 2. Approximately 15 K of diskette storage is needed for any one picture. (See the program segment that performs this task, Subroutine 1910 in Program 8.1.) We may use eight characters or less for the file name with or without extension; however, the disk drive name should never be added because we already specified the drive name in the beginning of the program. To effect this command, we press the "K" key on the keyboard.

8.6.2 FILE COMMAND

This utility command is used to load an image file from a diskette into the drawing area on the screen. Note that only the graphics files created by

DRAWER can be viewed by this command. This command will *not* erase any contents already on the screen. Thus an image file can be called and superimposed on the current screen image. This is a very powerful feature in creating a picture based on repetitive elements. To load the image file created by DRAWER, we simply press the "F" key and specify the name of the file to be called forth. We will give an example of how to use these utility commands in the later section.

8.7 STATUS MESSAGES

Whenever we are creating a picture, the status window will be visible on the left-hand side of the screen. This is our reference for a number of elements related to the picture drawn on the screen. Typical information displayed on the window is as follows:

X = __ : The absolute X coordinate of the dot.
Y = __ : The absolute Y coordinate of the dot.
D = __ : The length of the line segment drawn. (D is reset to zero when D is greater than 999.)
F = __ : The current foreground color, which will be the color of the lines drawn.
P = __ : The color of the leading dot.

The status messages about X, Y, and D keep track of the relative position of points in a drawing. We can use this information to determine the various distances between points. Note that in high-resolution mode, no F and P information is displayed.

8.8 MULTILAYERED DRAWINGS

We will conclude this chapter by demonstrating an example of how to save and superimpose a portion of a picture to produce a desired end picture. Consider the birds in Fig. 8.5(a), which can be obtained by using various drawing commands provided in DRAWER. First, we draw bird A as shown in Fig. 8.5(b) and save it under the file name of BIRD1 as follows:

> Press the "K" key from the keyboard. The program responds by asking us to assign the file name for the picture to be saved. Do this by entering "BIRD1". It takes about the same time to save the picture, no matter how complex it may be. It is because the entire display screen (Window 5) is being saved.

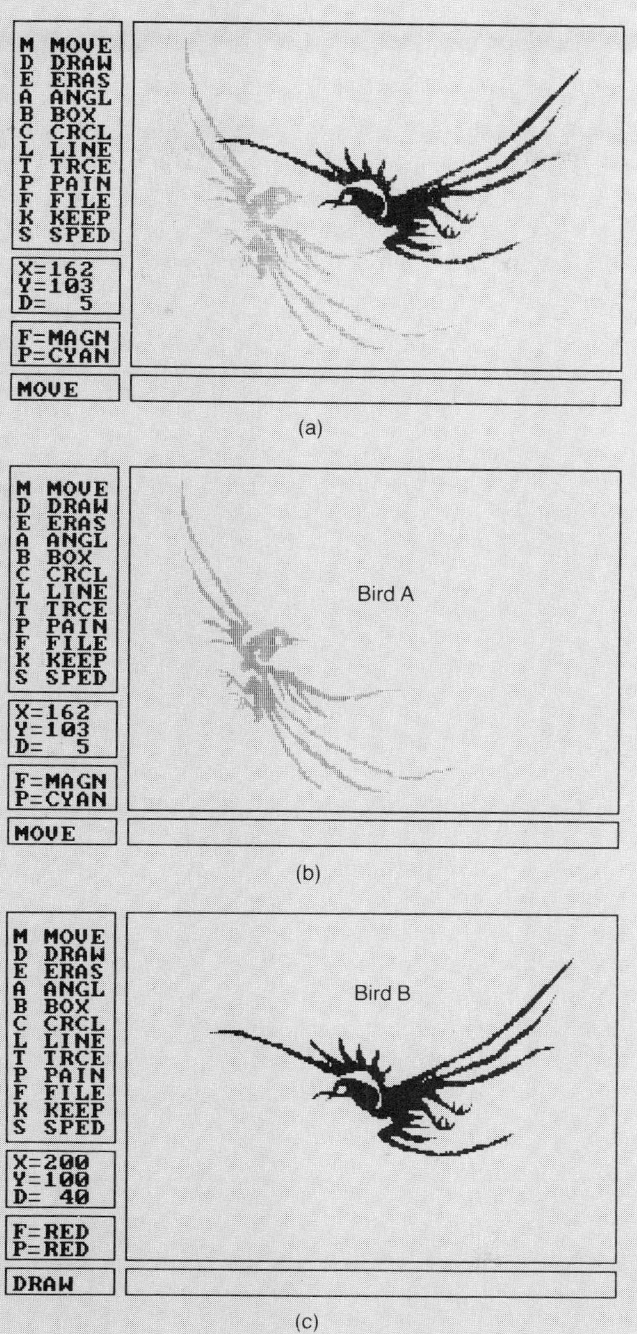

FIGURE 8.5 Combining image files

Now we clear the screen by pressing the [F5] key twice, then draw bird *B* as shown in Fig. 8.5(c). Upon completion, we follow the same procedure as for bird *A*; this time using the file name BIRD2.

Now we are ready to combine the two birds in the same picture frame by superimposing the two files. Since the second bird is already on the screen, we simply load file BIRD1 into memory. More precisely,

> Press the "F" key from the keyboard, and then enter the file name by typing in BIRD1. It will take some time to load the file. When the file is loaded, the computer will superimpose the graphic image file BIRD1 over the current screen, resulting in Fig. 8.5(a). This is saved as BIRD3.

Color plates 1–4 show how these birds appear in color on the screen. These pictures were obtained by varying the foreground and background colors. Color plate 4 shows the bird picture with a set of Chinese characters. Color plates 5–8 show examples of typical oriental artwork drawn by DRAWER.

8.9 SUMMARY

The principal argument in favor of the use of graphical displays is their effectiveness in displaying information. This poses a problem for the user interface designer: how should information be presented on the display in a manner that promotes the most effective interaction between user and computer? This is the central issue in information display as a component of user-interface design. This chapter attempted to answer some of these questions by optimizing the use of screen space. In the worked program DRAWER, the screen was devoted entirely to displaying the form being designed and the command menu. Several new picture manipulation features were introduced in this chapter, such as the use of function keys and cursor pad in designing graphics commands. In designing DRAWER, we have not yet incorporated the transformation concepts discussed in Part Two. The next chapter will expand our drawing environment to a 3-D world by incorporating the depth transformation techniques.

```
---------------------- VARIABLES LIST --------------------
ARRAYS       :
  COLSTR$    : FOREGROUND COLORS AVAILABLE.
  COMMAND$   : VALID COMMANDS TABLE.
  PIC%       : STORAGE FOR SCREEN IMAGE.
```

PROGRAM 8.1 DRAWER

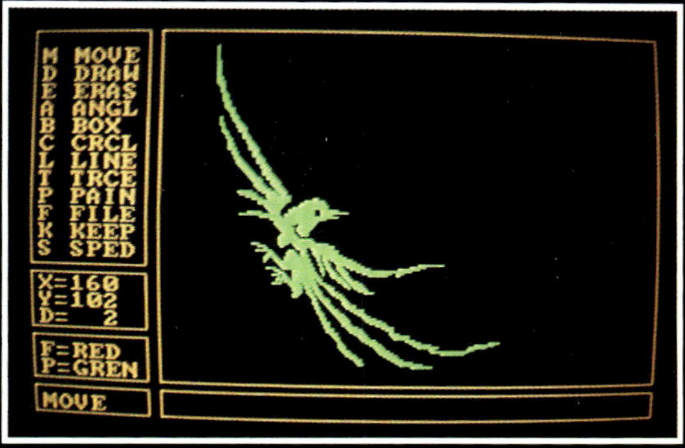
M MOVE
D DRAW
E ERAS
A ANGL
B BOX
C CRCL
L LINE
T TRCE
P PAIN
F FILE
K KEEP
S SPED
X=160
Y=102
D= 2
F=RED
P=GREN
MOVE

F1 UL\
F2 UR/
F3 LL/
F4 LR\
F5 RES
F6 PAL
F7 BKG
F8 FRG
F9 DOT
F0 DST
O OPT2
Q QUIT
X=160
Y=103
D= 3
F=RED
P=GREN
MOVE
千山我独行
不必相送

M MOVE
D DRAW
E ERAS
A ANGL
B BOX
C CRCL
L LINE
T TRCE
P PAIN
F FILE
K KEEP
S SPED
X=160
Y=102
D= 2
F=RED
P=GREN
MOVE

F1 UL\
F2 UR/
F3 LL/
F4 LR\
F5 RES
F6 PAL
F7 BKG
F8 FRG
F9 DOT
F0 DST
O OPT2
Q QUIT
X=160
Y=103
D= 3
F=MAGN
P=CYAN
MOVE

F1 UL\
F2 UR/
F3 LL/
F4 LR\
F5 RES
F6 PAL
F7 BKG
F8 FRG
F9 DOT
F0 DST
O OPT2
Q QUIT
X=160
Y=103
D= 3
F=RED
P=GREN
MOVE

M MOVE
D DRAW
E ERAS
A ANGL
B BOX
C CRCL
L LINE
T TRCE
P PAIN
F FILE
K KEEP
S SPED
X=160
Y=104
D= 4
F=MAGN
P=CYAN
MOVE

F1 UL\
F2 UR/
F3 LL/
F4 LR\
F5 RES
F6 PAL
F7 BKG
F8 FRG
F9 DOT
F0 DST
O OPT2
Q QUIT
X=160
Y=100
D= 0
F=MAGN
P=CYAN
DRAW

F1 UL\
F2 UR/
F3 LL/
F4 LR\
F5 RES
F6 PAL
F7 BKG
F8 FRG
F9 DOT
F0 DST
O OPT2
Q QUIT
X=160
Y=100
D= 0
F=MAGN
P=CYAN
DRAW

```
INTEGERS      :

  ACUMX%      : ACCUMULATIVE DEVIATION IN X DIRECTION.
  ACUMY%      : ACCUMULATIVE DEVIATION IN Y DIRECTION.
  BG%         : BACKGROUND COLOR.
  COLOR1%     : COLOR OF THE LEADING DOT.
  COLOR2%     : CURRENT FOREGROUND COLOR.
  COLOR3%     : COLOR OF THE SURROUNDING FRAME.
  COLOR4%     : COLOR TO BE PAINTED WITH.
  COLOR5%     : COLOR OF THE BOUNDARY.
  DIST%       : DISTANCE MOVED OR DRAWN.
  FLAG%       : FLAG FOR MENU OPTION SELECTION.
  I%, J%      : SENTINEL NUMBERS.
  PCOLOR%     : PREVIOUS FOREGROUND COLOR.
  PL%         : PALETTE.
  RES%        : RESOLUTION.
  SPEED%      : MAGNITUDE OF INCREMENT OF LINE SEGMENT.
  TEMP1%      : TEMPORARY STORAGE.
  TEMP2%      : TEMPORARY STORAGE.
  TEMP3%      : TEMPORARY STORAGE.
  TEMP4%      : TEMPORARY STORAGE.
  VALID%      : FLAG FOR TESTING COMMANDS.
  X%          : CURRENT X COORDINATE.
  XLAST%      : PREVIOUS X COORDINATE.
  X1%         : X COORDINATE OF FIRST POINT MARKED.
  X2%         : X COORDINATE OF SECOND POINT MARKED.
  Y%          : CURRENT Y COORDINATE.
  YLAST%      : PREVIOUS Y COORDINATE.
  Y1%         : Y COORDINATE OF FIRST POINT MARKED.
  Y2%         : Y COORDINATE OF SECOND POINT MARKED.

REALS         :

  A           : ANGLE BETWEEN HORIZONTAL LINE AND LINE DRAWN.
  AYINC       : ACCUMULATIVE DEVIATION IN Y DIRECTION.
  HASP        : ELLIPSE ASPECT IN HIGH RESOLUTION.
  LAST        : ENDING ANGLE FOR DRAWING ELLIPSE.
  LST         : TEMPORARY STORAGE FOR ENDING ANGLE.
  START       : STARTING ANGLE FOR DRAWING ELLIPSE.
  YINC        : DEVIATION IN Y DIRECTION.

CHARACTERS    :

  ANS$        : KEYBOARD INPUT.
  B$          : BLANKS.
  PD$         : DISK DRIVE USED.
```

PROGRAM 8.1 (continued)

```
10   ' Program 8.1: DRAWER  --  MAIN PROGRAM  ----------------------------
20   GOSUB 100
30   GOSUB 1300
40   VALID%=0
50   ANS$=INKEY$ : IF ANS$="" THEN 50 ELSE GOSUB 340
60   IF VALID%=0 THEN 50
70   ON FLAG% GOSUB 2150,790,750,620,720,1160,2040,810,1210,1920,2250,670,
               1700,2540
80   GOTO 40
90   '-----------------------  INITIALIZING  ----------------------------
100  CLS : SCREEN 0 : WIDTH 80 : KEY OFF
110  PRINT "WHICH DISK DRIVE CONTAINS THE GRAPHICS IMAGE FILE (IF ANY)"
120  INPUT "(DRIVE A IS ON YOUR LEFT) <ENTER A OR B, (C FOR HARD DISK)>";PD$
130  PD$=PD$+":"
140  DIM PIC%(7150), COLSTR$(1,3), COMMAND$(20)
150  COMMAND$(1)="m" : COMMAND$(2)="l" : COMMAND$(3)="t"
160  COMMAND$(4)="s" : COMMAND$(5)="b" : COMMAND$(6)="a"
170  COMMAND$(7)="f" : COMMAND$(8)="c" : COMMAND$(9)="p"
180  COMMAND$(10)="k" : COMMAND$(11)="d" : COMMAND$(12)="e"
190  COMMAND$(13)="o": COMMAND$(14)="q"
200  COLSTR$(0,1)="GREN" : COLSTR$(0,2)="RED " : COLSTR$(0,3)="BRWN"
210  COLSTR$(1,1)="CYAN" : COLSTR$(1,2)="MAGN" : COLSTR$(1,3)="WITE"
220  KEY(1) ON : KEY(2) ON : KEY(3) ON : KEY(4) ON : KEY(5) ON
230  KEY(6) ON : KEY(7) ON : KEY(8) ON : KEY(9) ON : KEY(10) ON
240  KEY(11) ON : KEY(12) ON : KEY(13) ON : KEY(14) ON
250  ON KEY(1) GOSUB 980 : ON KEY(2) GOSUB 1070 : ON KEY(3) GOSUB 1010
260  ON KEY(4) GOSUB 1040 : ON KEY(5) GOSUB 1280 : ON KEY(6) GOSUB 1730
270  ON KEY(7) GOSUB 1780 : ON KEY(8) GOSUB 1810 : ON KEY(9) GOSUB 1870
280  ON KEY(10) GOSUB 960
290  ON KEY(11) GOSUB 400 : ON KEY(12) GOSUB 540
300  ON KEY(13) GOSUB 510 : ON KEY(14) GOSUB 430
310  RES%=1 : BG%=0 : PL%=1 : PI=3.141593 : B$="
320  RETURN
330  '-----------------------  CHECK COMMAND  ---------------------------
340  TEMP1%=ASC(ANS$) OR 32 : ANS$=CHR$(TEMP1%)
350  I%=0 : WHILE I%<14 AND VALID%=0 : I%=I%+1
360  IF ANS$=COMMAND$(I%) THEN FLAG%=I% : VALID%=1
370  WEND
380  RETURN
390  '-------------------  DRAW OR ERASE UPWARDS  -----------------------
400  Y%=Y%-SPEED% : AYINC=Y%+.5
410  GOTO 440
420  '-------------------  DRAW OR ERASE DOWNWARDS  ---------------------
430  Y%=Y%+SPEED% : AYINC=Y%+.5
440  LINE-(X%,Y%),COLOR2% : PSET(X%,Y%),COLOR1%
450  LOCATE 16,4 :PRINT USING "###";Y%
460  DIST%=DIST%+ABS(Y%-YLAST%) : IF DIST%>999 THEN DIST%=0
470  LOCATE 17,4 : PRINT USING "###";DIST%
480  YLAST%=Y%
490  RETURN
500  '-------------------  DRAW OR ERASE TOWARDS RIGHT  -----------------
510  X%=X%+SPEED%
520  GOTO 550
530  '-------------------  DRAW OR ERASE TOWARDS LEFT  ------------------
540  X%=X%-SPEED%
550  LINE-(X%,Y%),COLOR2% : PSET(X%,Y%),COLOR1%
560  LOCATE 15,4 :PRINT USING "###";X%
570  DIST%=DIST%+ABS(X%-XLAST%) : IF DIST%>999 THEN DIST%=0
580  LOCATE 17,4 : PRINT USING "###";DIST%
590  XLAST%=X% : YLAST%=Y%
600  RETURN
610  '-------------------  SET DRAWING SPEED  ---------------------------
620  LOCATE 22,10: BEEP : INPUT "S";SPEED% : LOCATE 22,10: PRINT B$
630  IF A=0 THEN A=.25*PI
640  IF RES%=1 THEN YINC=SPEED%*TAN(A) ELSE YINC=.5*SPEED%*TAN(A)
650  RETURN
660  '-------------------  SET VISIBILITY  ------------------------------
670  IF MOVE%=1 THEN GOSUB 2250
680  COLOR2%=BG%
690  LOCATE 22,2 : PRINT "ERASE" : BEEP
700  RETURN
710  '-------------------  DRAW A RECTANGLE  ----------------------------
720  LINE(X1%,Y1%)-(X2%,Y2%),COLOR2%,B : PSET(X%,Y%),COLOR1%
730  RETURN
740  '-------------------  MARK POINT  ----------------------------------
750  X1%=X2% : Y1%=Y2% : X2%=X% : Y2%=Y%
760  PSET(X%,Y%),COLOR3% : COLOR4%=COLOR3%
```

PROGRAM 8.1 (continued)

```
770  RETURN
780  '-------------------- DRAW A LINE ----------------------------------
790  LINE (X1%,Y1%)-(X2%,Y2%),COLOR2% : PSET(X%,Y%),COLOR1%: RETURN
800  '-------------------- DRAW A CIRCLE --------------------------------
810  TEMP1%=(X2%-X1%) : TEMP2%=Y2%-Y1%
820  TEMP3%=TEMP1%*TEMP1%+TEMP2%*TEMP2% : TEMP4=SQR(TEMP3%)
830  RADIUS%=INT(TEMP4)
840  LOCATE 22,10: BEEP: INPUT "STARTING ANGLE =";START
850  IF START=0 THEN FIRST=0 ELSE FIRST=START/360*2*PI
860  LOCATE 22,10: PRINT B$
870  LOCATE 22,10: BEEP: INPUT "ENDING ANGLE =";LST
880  LOCATE 22,10: PRINT B$
890  IF LST=0 THEN LAST=2*PI ELSE LAST=LST/360*2*PI
900  LOCATE 22,10: BEEP: INPUT "ASPECT =";ASP
910  LOCATE 22,10: PRINT B$
920  IF ASP=0 THEN IF RES%=1 THEN ASP=LASP ELSE ASP=HASP
930  CIRCLE(X%,Y%),RADIUS%,COLOR2%,FIRST,LAST,ASP
940  RETURN
950  '------------------ RESET DISTANCE COUNTER -------------------------
960  DIST%=0 :LOCATE 17,4 : PRINT USING "###";DIST% : RETURN
970  '------------- DRAW LINES IN UPPER LEFT DIRECTION ------------------
980  AYINC=AYINC-YINC: X%=X%-SPEED% : Y%=INT(AYINC)
990 GOTO 1080
1000 '------------- DRAW LINES IN LOWER LEFT DIRECTION ------------------
1010 AYINC=AYINC+YINC: X%=X%-SPEED% : Y%=INT(AYINC)
1020 GOTO 1080
1030 '------------- DRAW LINES IN LOWER RIGHT DIRECTION -----------------
1040 AYINC=AYINC+YINC: X%=X%+SPEED% : Y%=INT(AYINC)
1050 GOTO 1080
1060 '------------- DRAW LINES IN UPPER RIGHT DIRECTION -----------------
1070 AYINC=AYINC-YINC: X%=X%+SPEED% : Y%=INT(AYINC)
1080 LINE-(X%,Y%),COLOR2% : PSET(X%,Y%),COLOR1%
1090 LOCATE 15,4 :PRINT USING "###";X% : LOCATE 16,4 :PRINT USING "###";Y%
1100 ACUMX%=X%-XLAST% : ACUMY%=Y%-YLAST%: TEMP1%=ACUMX%*ACUMX%+ACUMY%*ACUMY%
1110 DIST%=DIST%+SQR(TEMP1%): IF DIST%>999 THEN DIST%=0
1120 LOCATE 17,4 : PRINT USING "###";DIST%
1130 XLAST%=X% : YLAST%=Y%
1140 RETURN
1150 '------------- DRAW LINES WITH GIVEN ANGLES -----------------------
1160 LOCATE 22,10: BEEP : INPUT "ANGLE =";A : A=A/360*2*PI
1170 IF RES%=1 THEN YINC=SPEED%*TAN(A) ELSE YINC=.5*SPEED%*TAN(A)
1180 AYINC=Y%+.5
1190 LOCATE 22,10: PRINT B$ : RETURN
1200 '----------------- PAINT A CLOSED AREA ----------------------------
1210 LOCATE 24,10: IF RES%=1 THEN FOR I%=1 TO 3: PRINT I%;:
         PRINT COLSTR$(PL%,I%);: NEXT ELSE PRINT "0 : BLACK  1 : WHITE";
1220 LOCATE 22,10: BEEP: IF RES%=1 THEN INPUT "PAINT COLOR =<1,2 OR 3>";COLOR4%
       ELSE INPUT "PAINT COLOR =<0 OR 1>";COLOR4%
1230 LOCATE 22,10: PRINT B$
1240 LOCATE 22,10: BEEP : IF RES%=1 THEN INPUT "BOUNDARY COLOR =<1,2 OR 3>";
       COLOR5% ELSE INPUT "BOUNDARY COLOR =<0 OR 1>";COLOR4%
1250 LOCATE 22,10: PRINT B$: LOCATE 24,10: PRINT B$;
1260 PAINT(X%,Y%),COLOR4%,COLOR5% : RETURN
1270 '----------------- CHANGE RESOLUTIONS -----------------------------
1280 IF RES%=1 THEN RES%=2 ELSE RES%=1
1290 '----------------- INITIALIZING PARAMETERS ------------------------
1300 SCREEN RES%,0 :CLS : IF RES%=1 THEN COLOR BG%,PL%
1310 IF RES%=1 THEN COLOR1%=1 : COLOR2%=2 : COLOR3%=3 : PCOLOR%=COLOR2%
     ELSE COLOR1%=1 : COLOR2%=1 : COLOR3%=1 : PCOLOR%=COLOR2%
1320 IF RES%=1 THEN YINC=1! ELSE YINC=.5
1330 X%=160: Y%=100: X1%=X% : X2%=X% : Y1%=Y% : Y2%=Y%
1340 AYINC=Y%+.5 : SPEED%=1
1350 XLAST%=X% : YLAST%=Y% : DIST%=0: MENU1%=1
1360 LASP=1! : HASP=5/12
1370 GOSUB 1540
1380 IF RES%=1 THEN LINE(66,0)-(319,160),COLOR3%,B: LINE(66,164)-(319,176),
       COLOR3%,B ELSE LINE(66,164)-(639,176),COLOR3%,B:
       LINE(66,0)-(639,160),COLOR3%,B
1390 LINE(4,0)-(60,106),COLOR3%,B
1400 LINE(4,110)-(60,136),COLOR3%,B
1410 LINE(4,140)-(60,160),COLOR3%,B
1420 LINE(4,164)-(60,176),COLOR3%,B
1430 PSET(X%,Y%),COLOR1%
1440 LOCATE 15,2 : PRINT "X=" USING "###";X% : LOCATE 16,2
1450 PRINT "Y=" USING "###";Y%
1460 LOCATE 17,2 : PRINT "D=" USING "###";DIST%
```

PROGRAM 8.1 (continued)

```
1470 LOCATE 22,2
1480 IF MOVE%=0 THEN PRINT "DRAW " ELSE PRINT "MOVE "
1490 IF RES%=2 THEN 1690
1500 LOCATE 19,2: PRINT "F=";COLSTR$(PL%,COLOR2%)
1510 LOCATE 20,2 : PRINT "P=";COLSTR$(PL%,COLOR1%)
1520 RETURN
1530 '------------------ MENU 1 ----------------------------------------
1540 LOCATE 2,2 : PRINT "F1 UL"+CHR$(92): LOCATE 3,2 : PRINT "F2 UR"+CHR$(47)
1550 LOCATE 4,2 : PRINT "F3 LL"+CHR$(47): LOCATE 5,2: PRINT "F4 LR"+CHR$(92)
1560 LOCATE 6,2 : PRINT "F5 RES" : LOCATE 7,2 : PRINT "F6 PAL"
1570 LOCATE 8,2 : PRINT "F7 BKG" : LOCATE 9,2 : PRINT "F8 FRG"
1580 LOCATE 10,2 : PRINT "F9 DOT" : LOCATE 11,2 : PRINT "F0 DST"
1590 LOCATE 12,2 : PRINT "O OPT2" : LOCATE 13,2 : PRINT "Q QUIT"
1600 MENU1%=1 : BEEP: RETURN
1610 '------------------ MENU 2 ----------------------------------------
1620 LOCATE 2,2 : PRINT "M MOVE" : LOCATE 3,2 : PRINT "D DRAW"
1630 LOCATE 4,2 : PRINT "E ERAS" : LOCATE 5,2 : PRINT "A ANGL"
1640 LOCATE 6,2 : PRINT "B BOX " : LOCATE 7,2 : PRINT "C CRCL"
1650 LOCATE 8,2 : PRINT "L LINE" : LOCATE 9,2 : PRINT "T TRCE"
1660 LOCATE 10,2 : PRINT "P PAIN" : LOCATE 11,2 : PRINT "F FILE"
1670 LOCATE 12,2 : PRINT "K KEEP" : LOCATE 13,2 : PRINT "S SPED"
1680 MENU1%=0 : BEEP : RETURN
1690 '------------------- CHANGE MENU ------------------------------------
1700 IF MENU1%=1 THEN GOSUB 1620 : MENU1%=0 ELSE GOSUB 1540: MENU1%=1
1710 RETURN
1720 '------------------- CHANGE PALETTE ------------------------------
1730 IF PL%=0 THEN PL%=1 ELSE PL%=0
1740 IF RES%=1 THEN LOCATE 19,4 : PRINT COLSTR$(PL%,COLOR2%)
1750 IF RES%=1 THEN LOCATE 20,4 : PRINT COLSTR$(PL%,COLOR1%)
1760 COLOR BG%,PL% : RETURN
1770 '------------------- CHANGE BACKGROUND COLOR ----------------------
1780 IF BG%<15 THEN BG%=BG%+1 ELSE BG%=0
1790 COLOR BG%,PL% : RETURN
1800 '------------------- CHANGE FOREGROUND COLOR ----------------------
1810 IF COLOR2%=BG% THEN 1850
1820 IF COLOR2%<3 THEN COLOR2%=COLOR2%+1 ELSE COLOR2%=1
1830 PCOLOR%=COLOR2%
1840 IF RES%=1 THEN LOCATE 19,4 : PRINT COLSTR$(PL%,COLOR2%)
1850 RETURN
1860 '--------- CHANGE COLOR OF LEADING DOT ---------------------------
1870 IF COLOR1%<3 THEN COLOR1%=COLOR1%+1 ELSE COLOR1%=1
1880 PSET(X%,Y%),COLOR1%
1890 IF RES%=1 THEN LOCATE 20,4 : PRINT COLSTR$(PL%,COLOR1%)
1900 RETURN
1910 '---------------------- SAVE PICTURES -----------------------------
1920 LOCATE 22,10: BEEP: INPUT "FILE=";FILE$
1930 FILE$=PD$+FILE$ : LOCATE 22,10: PRINT B$
1940 LOCATE 22,10: PRINT "SAVING PICTURE...": BEEP
1950 PSET(X%,Y%),COLOR2%
1960 OPEN FILE$ FOR OUTPUT AS #1
1970 IF RES%=1 THEN GET(67,1)-(318,159),PIC% ELSE GET(67,1)-(638,160),PIC%
1980 FOR I%=0 TO 7150
1990 PRINT #1,PIC%(I%);: NEXT
2000 CLOSE #1
2010 LOCATE 22,10: PRINT B$: BEEP
2020 RETURN
2030 '---------------------- CALL PICTURES -----------------------------
2040 LOCATE 22,10: BEEP: INPUT "FILE=";FILE$
2050 FILE$=PD$+FILE$ : LOCATE 22,10: PRINT B$
2060 LOCATE 22,10: PRINT "LOADING PICTURE...": BEEP
2070 OPEN FILE$ FOR INPUT AS #2
2080 FOR I%=0 TO 7150 : INPUT #2,PIC%(I%) : NEXT
2090 CLOSE #2
2100 PUT (67,1),PIC%,OR
2110 PSET(X%,Y%),COLOR1%
2120 LOCATE 22,10: PRINT B$: BEEP
2130 RETURN
2140 '----------------------- MOVE MODE --------------------------------
2150 MOVE%=1
2160 IF COLOR2%<>PCOLOR% THEN COLOR2%=PCOLOR%
2170 ON KEY(11) GOSUB 2330
2180 ON KEY(14) GOSUB 2360
2190 ON KEY(12) GOSUB 2440
2200 ON KEY(13) GOSUB 2470
2210 LOCATE 22,2 : PRINT "MOVE " : BEEP
2220 COLOR4%=BG%
2230 PSET(X%,Y%) : RETURN
```

PROGRAM 8.1 (continued)

```
2340 GOTO 2370
2350 '------------------------ MOVE  DOWN  -----------------------------
2360 Y%=Y%+SPEED% : AYINC=Y%+.5
2370 PSET(X%,YLAST%),COLOR4%
2380 COLOR4%=POINT(X%,Y%) : PSET(X%,Y%),COLOR1%
2390 LOCATE 16,4 :PRINT USING "###";Y%
2240 '---------------------- DRAW MODE  ---------------------------------
2250 MOVE%=0
2260 IF COLOR2%<>PCOLOR% THEN COLOR2%=PCOLOR%
2270 ON KEY(11) GOSUB 400 : ON KEY(12) GOSUB 540
2280 ON KEY(13) GOSUB 510 : ON KEY(14) GOSUB 430
2290 COLOR2%=PCOLOR%
2300 BEEP: LOCATE 22,2: PRINT "DRAW "
2310 RETURN
2320 '------------------------ MOVE  UP  --------------------------------
2330 Y%=Y%-SPEED% : AYINC=Y%+.5
2400 DIST%=DIST%+ABS(Y%-YLAST%) : IF DIST%>999 THEN DIST%=0
2410 LOCATE 17,4 : PRINT USING "###";DIST%
2420 YLAST%=Y% : RETURN
2430 '------------------------ MOVE  LEFT  ------------------------------
2440 X%=X%-SPEED%
2450 GOTO 2480
2460 '------------------------ MOVE  RIGHT  -----------------------------
2470 X%=X%+SPEED%
2480 PSET(XLAST%,Y%),COLOR4%
2490 COLOR4%=POINT(X%,Y%) : PSET(X%,Y%),COLOR1%
2500 LOCATE 15,4 :PRINT USING "###";X%
2510 DIST%=DIST%+ABS(X%-XLAST%) : IF DIST%>999 THEN DIST%=0
2520 LOCATE 17,4 : PRINT USING "###";DIST%
2530 XLAST%=X% : YLAST%=Y% : RETURN
2540 END
```

PROGRAM 8.1 DRAWER

REFERENCES

1. Besant, C. B., *Computer-Aided Design and Manufacture,* Halsted Press, New York, 1980.

2. Edmonds, E. A., A. Schappo, and S. A. R. Scrivener, "Image Handling in Two-Dimensional Design," *IEEE Computer Graphics and Applications* **2** (5) 75–88, July 1982.

3. Grigg, P. J., "A CAD Interface for Textile Design," *Computer Aided Design* **15** (1) January 1983.

4. Lodding, K. N., "Iconic Interfacing," *IEEE Computer Graphics and Applications* **3** (2) 11–20, March-April 1983.

5. Lucido, A. P., "Software Systems for Computer Graphics," *Computer* **9** (8) 23–32, August 1976.

CHAPTER NINE

Interactive 3-D Plotter

The previous two chapters were concerned with creating graphics in a 2-D environment. The 2-D system we examined had many simplifying characteristics in its database and mathematical elements that produced fairly good performance and short response times.

The purpose of this chapter is to expand our programming effort to a 3-D environment. As we learned from Chapter 4, the necessary mathematical transformations are quite complex. Consequently, the system and database needed for such manipulations are quite laborious to design. Once implemented, however, interactive computer graphics becomes a powerful tool that increases a user's productivity greatly. For instance, with the proper database design a new view of an object requires only that the user state the request in a precise form, such as a rotation about an axis. Rotation or translation of one object relative to another is also easily performed. We will show how such manipulations can be performed through a 3-D graphics program, 3-D PLOTTER.

9.1 PROJECTION METHOD ADOPTED

As we discussed in Chapter 4, the 3-D viewing process produces additional complexity in obtaining the graphics image on the screen. This is because the display screen is a 2-D space—we cannot actually display 3-D objects, only their projections. Projectional transformations are generally quite expensive

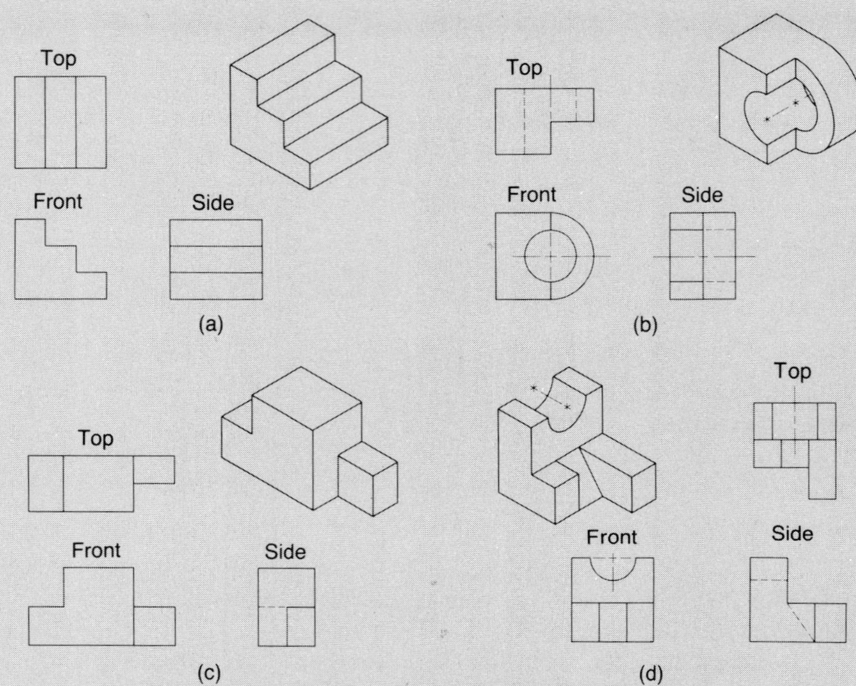

FIGURE 9.1 Parallel projections of 3-D objects: top, front, and side views. (Artwork courtesy of James A. Leach, Auburn University.)

computationally; they are also slow in execution if all the programming is done in BASIC.

Since generating a perspective view of a given object may require the projectional transformation of a large number of points, we will use a special case of *central projection,* that is *parallel projection.* The use of parallel projection will not simplify the programming effort, but it will keep the resulting execution time within reasonable limits. The most common types of parallel projections are the *front* (elevation), *top* (plan), and *side* (elevation) projections. These projections are often referred to as *orthographic projections* — that is, projections in which the projection plane is perpendicular to a principal axis (the direction of projection). Figure 9.1 shows the construction of each of these three projections. Orthographic projections are often used in *engineering drawings* to depict machine parts, assemblies, and buildings because distances and angles can be measured from them. One of the weaknesses of using only orthographic projections is that the 3-D nature of the projected object can be difficult to perceive sometimes because each projection depicts only one face of the object. We can circumvent this difficulty to some extent, however, by providing a rotated view of the object. We take this approach in the 3-D PLOTTER program.

9.2 PROGRAM DESIGN

9.2.1 SCREEN LAYOUT

When a great deal of information must be displayed to the user, it should be presented in a structured form so that the user can perceive and understand it with no confusion. As we demonstrated in Chapter 8, we structure the information by dividing the viewing surface into different areas where different spe-

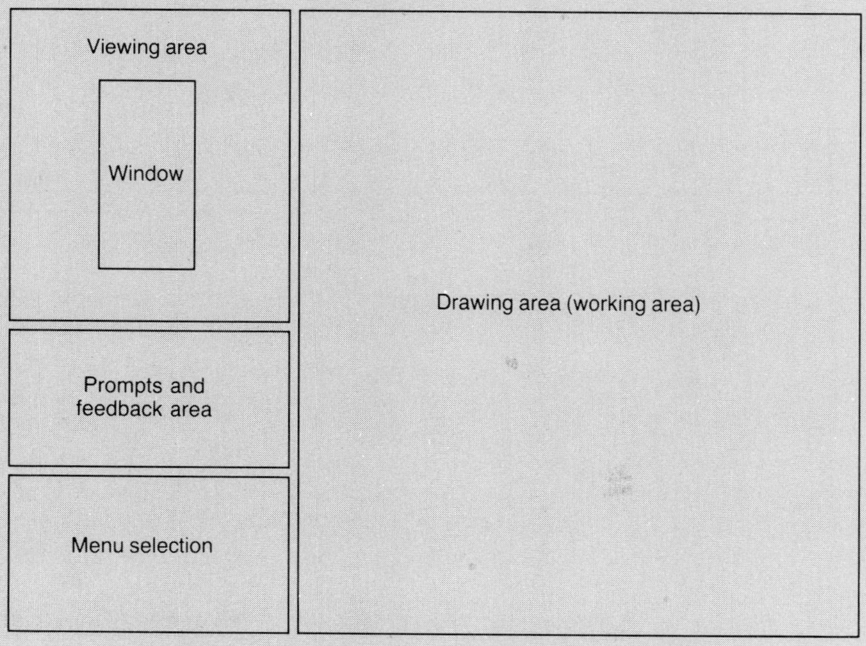

FIGURE 9.2 Screen layout of 3-D PLOTTER

cific types of information can be presented. Prompts, system status, commands, and the graphical representation itself each have their own areas. This provides an uncluttered and organized display presentation and allows the user to locate relevant information. Figure 9.2 shows the overall screen layout used with 3-D PLOTTER.

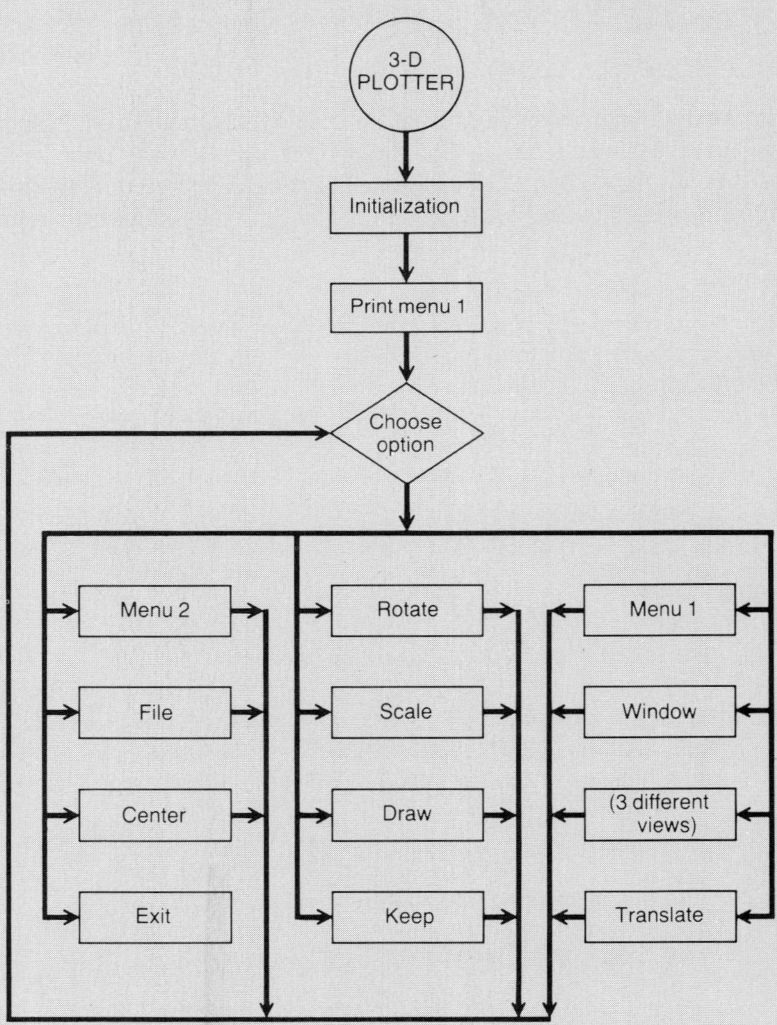

FIGURE 9.3 Programming logic for 3-D PLOTTER

9.2.2 ZOOM CAPABILITY

We will provide a zoom capability in 3-D object manipulations. This feature permits the user to decrease visual clutter by enlarging a small area of the display to expose details not otherwise distinguishable. The ability to zoom (or "window") in or out from a given part of the drawing area also partially overcomes the physical limitations of the screen size. When an enlarged part of the original drawing is being displayed, however, the original drawing must be retained in some way so that the enlarged portion can be placed in its overall context. The area for retaining the original drawing is referred to as the *viewing area* and the area for displaying the transformed drawings is referred to as the *work area.* The small square inside the viewing area indicates which part of the overall drawing is being shown. (This can be done even more effectively with two monitor displays: one for the overview, the other for the enlarged portion. This is the approach commonly used in a sophisticated CAD environment.)

9.2.3 RESOLUTION QUALITY

Greater screen resolution provides more aesthetically pleasing images, more accurate placement of points within the drawing, and finer drawings on a small surface. For this reason, we will use the high-resolution graphics mode on the IBM PC for 3-D PLOTTER. We do lose colors in high-resolution mode, however, so there will be no color-related commands in 3-D PLOTTER.

9.2.4 PROGRAMMING LOGIC

The general programming logic for 3-D PLOTTER is shown in Fig. 9.3. 3-D PLOTTER is written in IBM PC Advanced BASIC (BASICA) and requires a minimum configuration of 64 K RAM, color/graphics adapter, monitor, and DOS 2.00. The complete computer program appears at the end of this chapter, along with detailed documentation. In Fig. 9.3, note that the program requires an input data file for an object to de plotted by 3-D PLOTTER. In the next section, we will discuss how to create an input data file for 3-D PLOTTER.

9.3 CREATING A DATA FILE FOR 3-D PLOTTER

We may use either DATA EDITOR (Chapter 6) or the EDLIN editor of the IBM PC DOS 2.00 to create the data file, which is linked to 3-D PLOTTER later. Since the data entries are rather simple, however, we could easily write a short program that creates the data file for 3-D PLOTTER. Three short programs will be provided for this purpose.

9.3.1 DATA FILE FOR A SOLID OBJECT

The file structure consists of four data elements for each vertex of the object, the world coordinates (x, y, z) and a flag. The flag simply identifies whether the vertex being defined is the starting point for drawing the object. We assign 0 if the vertex is the starting point; otherwise, we assign 1. If the flag of the current vertex is 0, no attempt will be made to draw a line from the previous vertex (if any) to the current vertex. Otherwise, a line will be drawn between the two vertices. Here 0 and 1 work like MOVE and DRAW commands in DRAWER.

To understand the input format, consider the two objects shown in Fig. 9.4. The triangle has three vertices, but we need to enter four vertices to draw all the sides (the fourth vertex is the same as the first vertex). Similarly, we need to enter five vertices to draw the rectangle. The four data elements for each vertex might look like this:

Triangle: $(20, 30, 10, 0)$, $(10, 20, 10, 1)$, $(30, 20, 10, 1)$, $(20, 30, 10, 1)$
Rectangle: $(35, 25, 5, 0)$, $(45, 25, 5, 1)$, $(45, 15, 5, 1)$, $(35, 15, 5, 1)$, $(35, 25, 5, 1)$

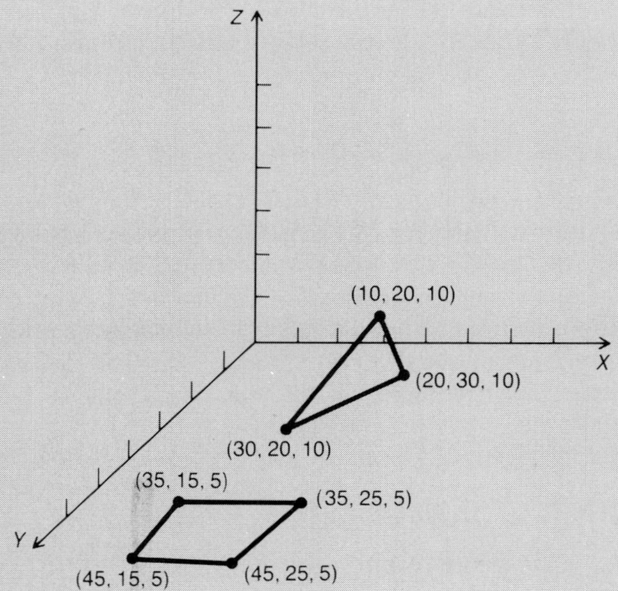

FIGURE 9.4 Two 3-D polygons and their vertices as defined in world coordinates

```
10 ' Program DGEN1 : Data Generation Routine for 3-D Objects
20 CLS
30 PRINT "PLEASE ENTER INPUT FILE NAME"
40 PRINT "EXAMPLE - B:ABC.DAT"
50 INPUT "====>";FILE$
60 PRINT "NOW, ENTER X, Y, Z, AND FLAG"
70 PRINT "FLAG FOR MOVE IS 0 AND FLAG FOR LINE IS 1"
80 PRINT "TO END INPUT, TYPE 0,0,0,-1 <ENTER>"
90 PRINT "EXAMPLE - 10,20,-10,0 <ENTER>"
100 OPEN FILE$ FOR OUTPUT AS #2
110 WHILE FLAG<>-1
120      INPUT X,Y,Z,FLAG
130      IF FLAG=-1 THEN 150
140      PRINT #2,X,Y,Z,FLAG
150      WEND
160 CLOSE
170 END
```

PROGRAM DGEN1 Data Generation Routine for 3-D Objects

Program DGEN1 creates a data file for a solid object. When we execute DGEN1, the program will ask for a data file name to assign. We then enter the X, Y, and Z coordinates and the flag for each vertex. To end the entries to DGEN1, we simply type "$0, 0, 0, -1$". Table 9.1 shows a typical user interface for creating a data file through DGEN1.

9.3.2 DATA FILE FOR A 3-D FUNCTION

Wire-frame form. Unlike the procedure for solid 3-D objects, we will not provide the coordinates of surface points through the keyboard, but will generate them by a program. Program DGEN2 illustrates this.

The program generates an image that represents the surface as a sequence of wire-frame curves. Obviously, the image obtained by the program depends on the function selected (line 160). To execute DGEN2, we need six pieces of information. The parameters Xmin, Xmax, Ymin, and Ymax are necessary to specify the range of the x and y values in the function $z = f(x, y)$. We also need to provide the step sizes for each variable, the x increment and y increment. A smoother surface will result from decreasing the step size, thereby calculating more points on each curve. (This also results in an increase in execution time.) The 3-D PLOTTER program will plot up to 1500 points.

Crosshatched surface. In plotting a 3-D function, we may use a crosshatched square in lieu of the wire-frame curve. Figure 9.5 compares a wire-frame curve with a crosshatched square in drawing the same 3-D function. Crosshatched squares often produce a more pleasing image than the wire-frame curve, one that shows the significant characteristics of the surface. To generate the input data for a 3-D function based on the crosshatch form, we can use the following program, DGEN3.

```
5 ' Program. DGEN2: Routine to generate input data for a 3-D function
                     ( Wire-frame Curve)
10  DEF FNZ(X,Y)=7*EXP(-.1*(X*X+Y*Y))              'User provided function
20  FLAG=0
30  CLS: PRINT "ENTER OUTPUT FILE NAME :"
40  PRINT "<EXAMPLE : B:ABC.DAT>"
50  INPUT "======>";FILE$
60  PRINT
70  INPUT "XMIN =";XMIN
80  INPUT "XMAX =";XMAX
90  INPUT "X INCREMENT =";XINC
100 INPUT "YMIN =";YMIN
110 INPUT "YMAX =";YMAX
120 INPUT "Y INCREMENT =";YINC
130 OPEN FILE$ FOR OUTPUT AS #2
140 FOR Y=YMIN TO YMAX STEP YINC
150     FOR X=XMIN TO XMAX STEP XINC
160         Z=FNZ(X,Y)
170         PRINT #2,X;Z;Y;FLAG;
180         IF FLAG=0 THEN FLAG=1
190         NEXT X
200     FLAG=0
210     NEXT Y
220 CLOSE
```

PROGRAM DGEN2 Routine to Generate Input Data for a 3-D Function (Wire-frame Curve)

```
5 'Program DGEN3: Routine to generate input data for a 3-d Function
                  ( Cross-hatched form)
10  DEF FNZ(X,Y)=7*EXP(-.1*(X*X+Y*Y))
20  FLAG=0
30  CLS: PRINT "ENTER OUTPUT FILE NAME :"
40  PRINT "<EXAMPLE : B:ABC.DAT>"
50  INPUT "======>";FILE$
60  PRINT
70  INPUT "XMIN =";XMIN
80  INPUT "XMAX =";XMAX
90  INPUT "X INCREMENT =";XINC
100 INPUT "YMIN =";YMIN
110 INPUT "YMAX =";YMAX
120 INPUT "Y INCREMENT =";YINC
130 OPEN FILE$ FOR OUTPUT AS #2
140 FOR Y=YMIN TO YMAX STEP YINC
150     FOR X=XMIN TO XMAX STEP XINC
160         Z=FNZ(X,Y)
170         PRINT #2,X;Z;Y;FLAG;
180         IF FLAG=0 THEN FLAG=1
190         NEXT X
200     FLAG=0
210     NEXT Y
220 FLAG=0
230 FOR X=XMIN TO XMAX STEP XINC
240     FOR Y=YMIN TO YMAX STEP YINC
250         Z=FNZ(X,Y)
260         PRINT #2,X;Z;Y;FLAG;
270         IF FLAG=0 THEN FLAG=1
280         NEXT Y
290     FLAG=0
300     NEXT X
310 CLOSE
320 END
```

PROGRAM DGEN3 Routine to Generate Input Data for a 3-D Function (Crosshatched form)

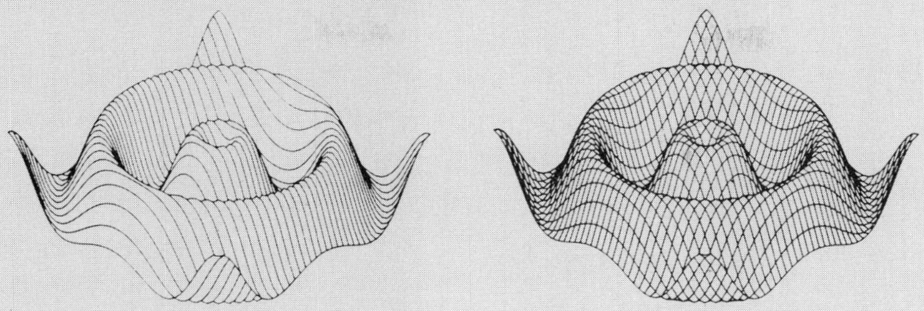

(a) (b)

FIGURE 9.5 Types of 3-D function plots: (a) wire frame and (b) crosshatched (meshed)

9.4 DESCRIPTION OF COMMANDS

9.4.1 MAIN MENU SELECTION

Ten graphics commands are available to the user. Six of them are grouped under the two primary menus. Menu 1 contains three graphics commands—file, center, and exit. Menu 2 contains the other three commands—window, 3-view, and transl. The four remaining commands are rotate, scale, draw, and keep. The latter four commands are displayed at all times on the screen. Thus a total of eight commands are shown on the screen at any moment, including the menu option.

The program displays a small circle in the option menu, which we call the *menu cursor.* We use the cursor movement keys (↑, ↓, ←, →) to move the menu cursor. To choose an option (or command) we simply move the cursor to the desired option (or command) and press the [ENTER] key. The actual screen layout under each menu option should look like this:

When Menu 1 is in effect

_ MENU 2	_ ROTATE
_ FILE	_ SCALE
_ CENTER	_ DRAW
_ EXIT	_ KEEP

When Menu 2 is in effect

_ MENU 1	_ ROTATE
_ WINDOW	_ SCALE
_ 3-VIEW	_ DRAW
_ TRANSL	_ KEEP

9.4.2 MENU-DRIVEN GRAPHICS COMMANDS

We will explain the commands through an example. Suppose we have the 3-D object shown in Fig. 9.6, defined by 34 vertices. We use DGEN1 to create an

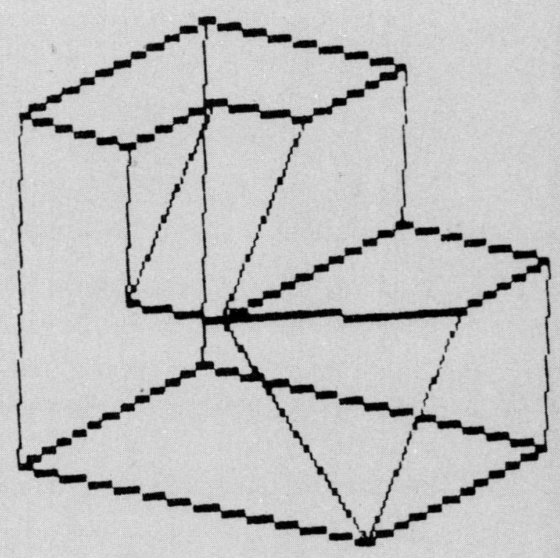

FIGURE 9.6 A 3-D object in world coordinate system

input data file, 3D1.DAT, for the 3-D object. We retrieve the data file from disk drive B on the IBM PC. The data file should look like Table 9.1.

Having created the input file, we are ready to execute 3-D PLOTTER. When the program is loaded, the screen will immediately display the layout shown in Fig. 9.7.

Center command. The first message we read from the screen is "AUTO CENTERING ON". This means that the object coordinates will be automatically scaled and centered in the viewing and the work areas. If we want to scale, center, or translate the object manually, we pick and enter the center command in Menu 1 to turn the automatic (auto) centering off. The default command leaves the auto centering on. If we want to return to the auto-centering-on mode while we are in the auto-centering-off mode, we again pick and enter the center command in Menu 1.

File command. This command loads a data file from the disk into memory. When this command is selected, we are first asked to enter the name of the file containing the data for plotting. In our example, we respond by typing in "B:3D1.DAT". Then 3-D PLOTTER loads 3D1.DAT from disk drive B into memory and displays a front view of the 3-D object in the viewing area. (See Fig. 9.8a). The picture shown in this viewing area serves as the reference picture upon which future transformations are based.

TABLE 9.1 Data file (3D1.DAT)

X	*Y*	*Z*	Flag
0	64	0	0
25	64	0	1
25	35	0	1
47	35	0	1
82	0	0	1
0	0	0	1
0	64	0	1
0	64	−70	1
47	64	−70	1
47	64	−32	1
25	64	−32	1
25	64	0	1
0	64	0	1
25	64	−32	0
25	35	0	1
47	64	−32	0
47	35	0	1
0	0	0	0
0	0	−70	1
82	0	−70	1
82	0	0	1
0	64	−70	0
0	0	−70	1
47	64	−70	0
47	35	−70	1
82	35	−70	1
82	0	−70	1
47	35	−70	0
47	35	0	1
82	35	−70	0
82	35	−35	1
82	0	0	1
47	35	0	1
82	35	−35	1

```
PLEASE ENTER INPUT FILE NAME
EXAMPLE-B:ABC.DAT
===>? B:3D1.DAT
NOW, ENTER X, Y, Z, AND FLAG
FLAG FOR MOVE IS 0 AND FLAG
  FOR LINE IS 1
TO END INPUT, TYPE 0,0,0,-1
  <ENTER>
EXAMPLE-10,20,-10,0 <ENTER>
?
```

Draw command. After specifying a sequence of translation, rotation, and scaling, we choose this option to draw the transformed picture in the work area.

Translation command. When this command is selected, the program prompts the user to enter TX, TY, and TZ, which represent the movement's

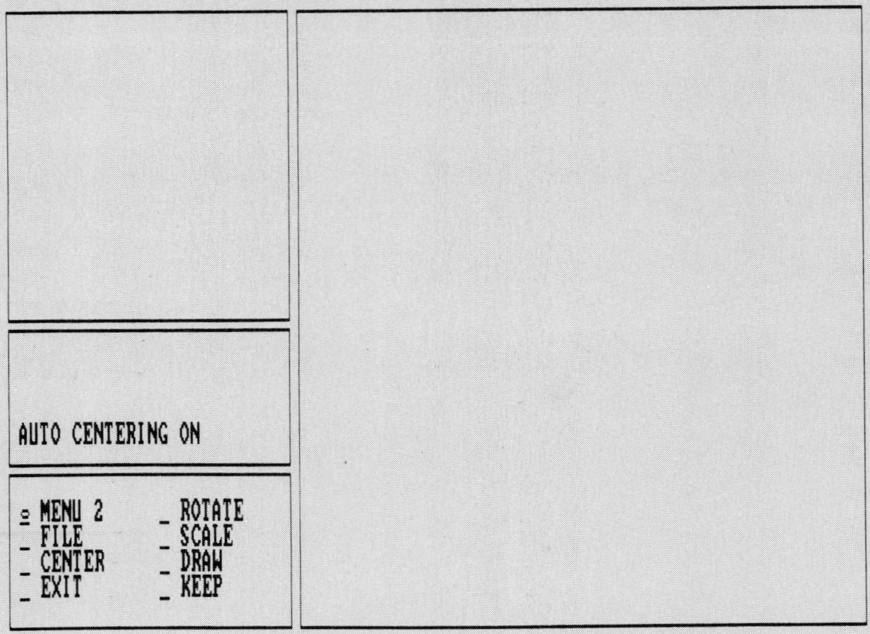

FIGURE 9.7 Screen layout display

components in the X, Y, and Z directions, respectively. To effect this command, we first turn off the auto centering mode. We then enter the translation command, specify TX, TY, and TZ, and enter the draw command to display the translated picture in the work area. For our example, with TX = 50, TY = 50, and TZ = 0, we obtain Fig. 9.8(b). (See Section 4.2.1 for a mathematical explanation of translation.)

Rotate command. When this command is selected, the program prompts the user for rotations about the X, Y, and Z axes. Note that all positive angles rotate *counterclockwise* (see Section 4.2.5). In our example, we respond to the prompts as follows:

```
ROTATION ABOUT X =  0
ROTATION ABOUT Y =  0
ROTATION ABOUT Z = 30
```

Then we enter the draw command to plot the rotated view of the 3-D object shown in the viewing area. Figure 9.8(c) illustrates this transformation.

Scale command. We enter this command if we want to enlarge or shrink a picture in the viewing area. The program then prompts the user to enter SX, SY, and SZ, which represent the scaling in the X, Y, and Z directions, respectively. In our example, we respond to the prompts as follows: SX = 0.5, SY = 1, SZ = 1. Then we enter the draw command to display the scaled picture in the work area. Figure 9.8(d) illustrates this process.

By specifying negative scaling factors, we can create a reflected picture. For example, by entering SX = −1, SY = 1, and SZ = 1, a reflection through the YZ plane occurs.

Keep command. When this command is entered, the picture in the viewing area is replaced by the picture in the work area. Later manipulations will then be based on this new picture. In other words, the picture in the work area becomes the reference picture for future manipulations.

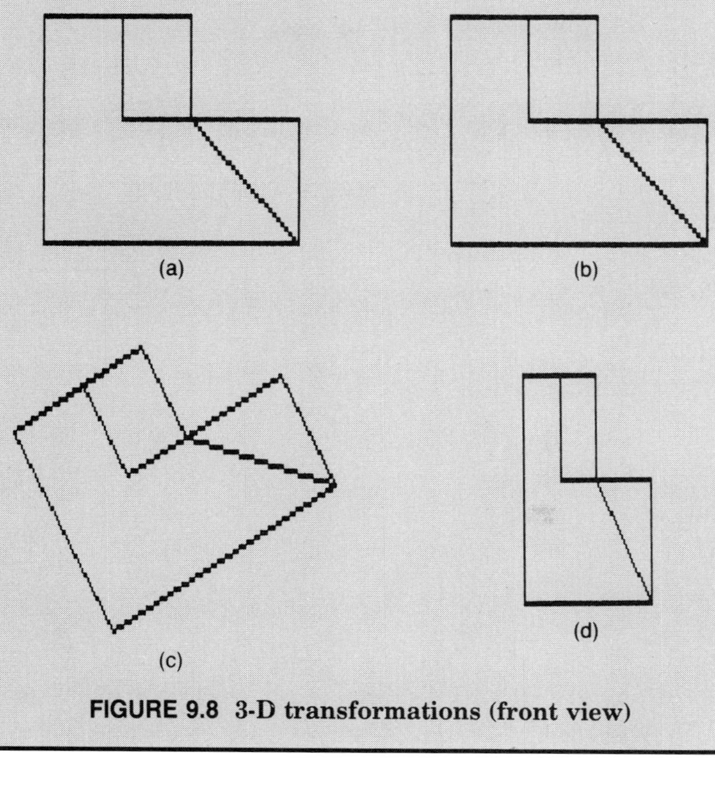

FIGURE 9.8 3-D transformations (front view)

Window (zoom) command. If we want to look at only a portion of the picture in the work area, we can give the window command and display only the portion we are interested in. When this command is in effect, a dot appears in the viewing area. We use the cursor pad keys to control the movement of this dot. To specify a window, we mark two diagonal corner points by moving the dot to each corner and hitting the [ENTER] key before moving on. After two corner points are marked, a rectangular window is drawn, and the windowed portion of the object is drawn in the work area. To draw another picture or choose another command, we hit a key (*any key*). This restores the viewing area picture to the work area. An example of "windowing" or "zooming" is illustrated in Fig. 9.9.

3-view command. When this command is entered, the program divides the work area into four windows, displaying the top (plan), front (elevation), side (elevation), and a rotated view of the 3-D object shown in the viewing area. This

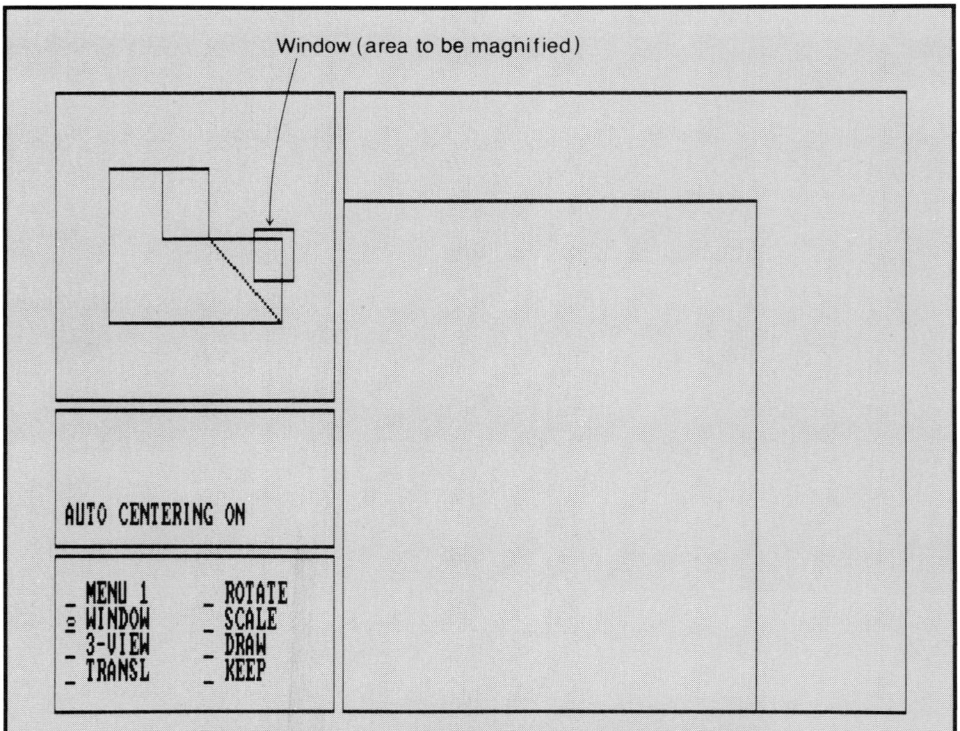

FIGURE 9.9 Zooming feature of 3-D PLOTTER

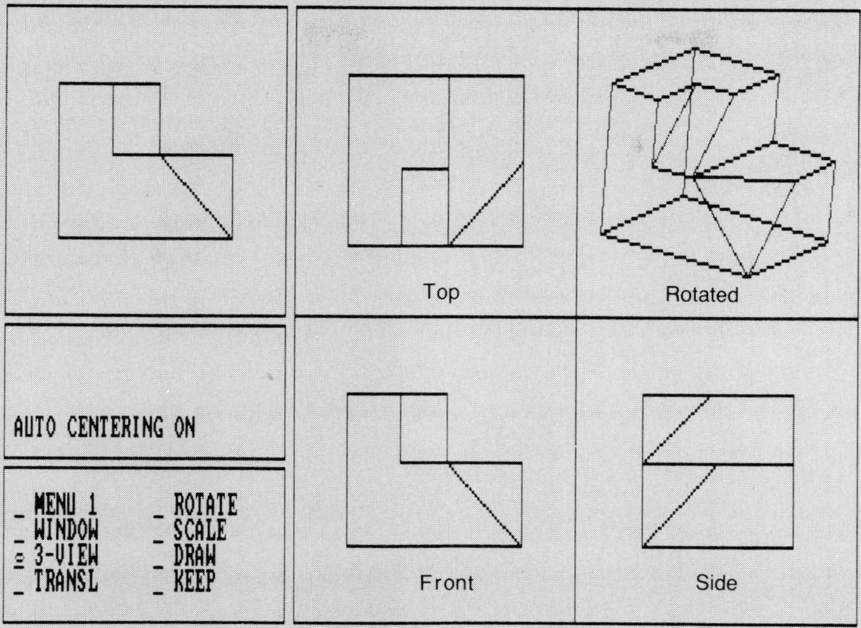

FIGURE 9.10 Three different views

is one of the most powerful features of 3-D PLOTTER and enables the user to view the same object from different angles. Figure 9.10 depicts these views for the object shown in the viewing area. Note that the rotated view in the upper right corner of the work area is obtained by rotating the object in the viewing area 20 degrees about the X axis, -30 degrees about the Y axis, and -15 degrees about the Z axis. These rotation angles are predetermined in the program.

9.5 DRAWING A 3-D FUNCTION

We will conclude this chapter by demonstrating the use of 3-D PLOTTER in plotting a 3-D function, $z = f(x,y)$. We will give the example in several steps.

Step 1: We must first create an input file. We will generate the data elements for this figure through a program (either DGEN2 or DGEN3). For this demonstration, we will use DGEN2, thus drawing a wire-frame surface.

The function is $z = 7e^{-0.1(x^2+y^2)}$. Upon loading DGEN2, we must provide the file name and the six parameters discussed in Section 9.3. We name the data file 3D2.DAT and save it using disk drive B.

```
ENTER OUTPUT FILE NAME :
<EXAMPLE : B:ABC.DAT>
======>? B:3D2.DAT

XMIN =? -8
XMAX =? 8
X INCREMENT =? 1
YMIN =? -8
XMAX =? 8
Y INCREMENT =? 1
```

After receiving six parameters such as those above, DGEN2 generates and writes the data elements to the disk drive specified.

Step 2: We now execute 3-D PLOTTER. When the menus are displayed, we enter the file command to load the data file created, B:3D2.DAT. A front

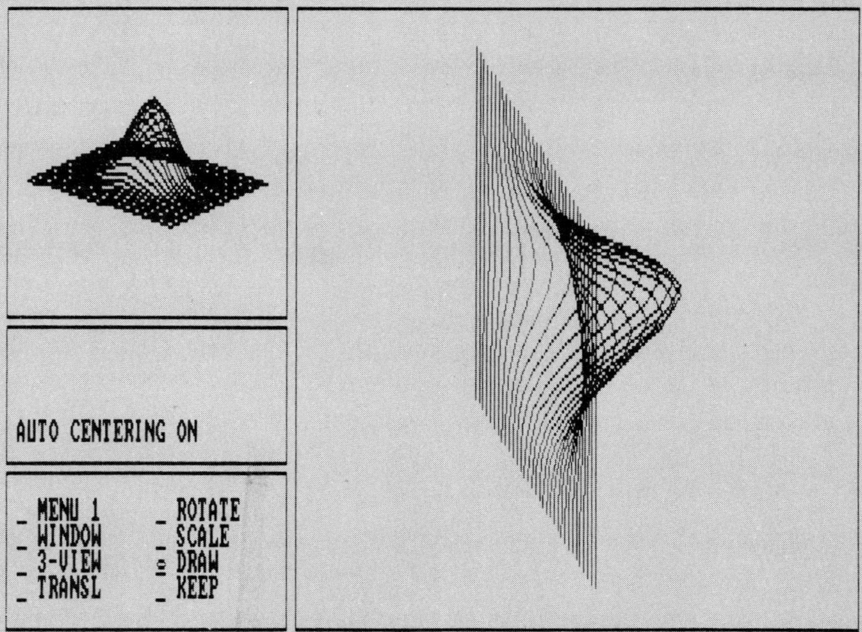

FIGURE 9.11 Rotated view of the 3-D function

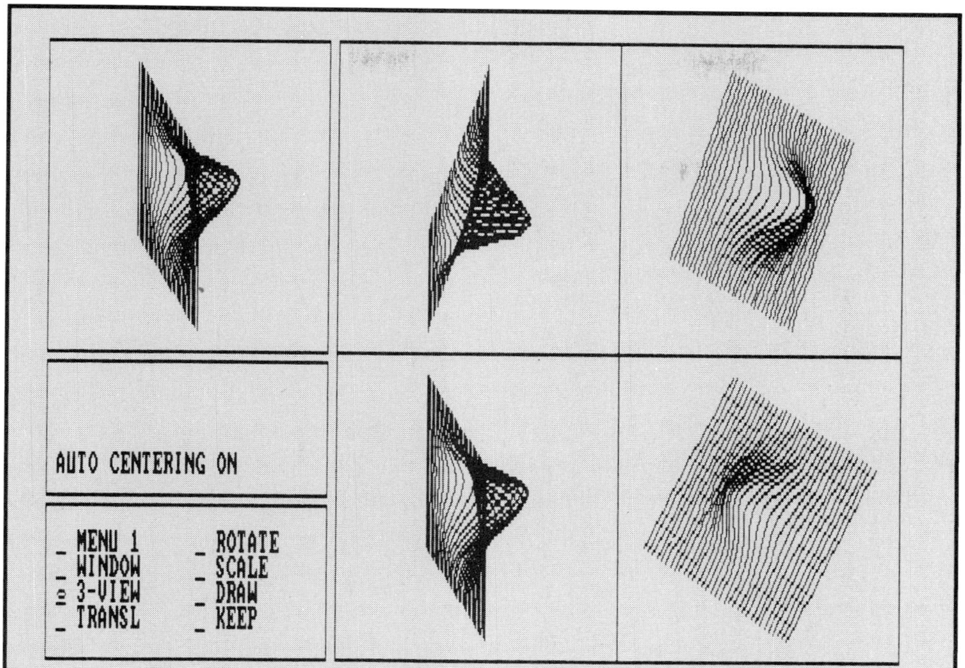

FIGURE 9.12 Three additional views

view of the function is displayed in the viewing area. To get a better view of the function, we can rotate the original picture 20 degrees about the X axis, -30 degrees about the Y axis, and -15 degrees about the Z axis. When the transformation is complete, we use the draw command to display the rotated view of the object in the work area. This is shown in Fig. 9.11.

Step 3: Now we use the keep command to replace the original picture in the viewing area by the rotated picture in the work area. Then we enter the 3-V command to display the other four views of the rotated picture. This is shown in Fig. 9.12. (Figure 9.13 shows a crosshatched form of the function.)

As different viewing positions are selected, the viewer may become badly confused by overlapping curves in the image. This is because no provision is made to eliminate the hidden lines in 3-D PLOTTER. To obtain more pleasing images, we must develop methods for identifying those surfaces and line segments that are visible (or partly visible) and those that are invisible (see

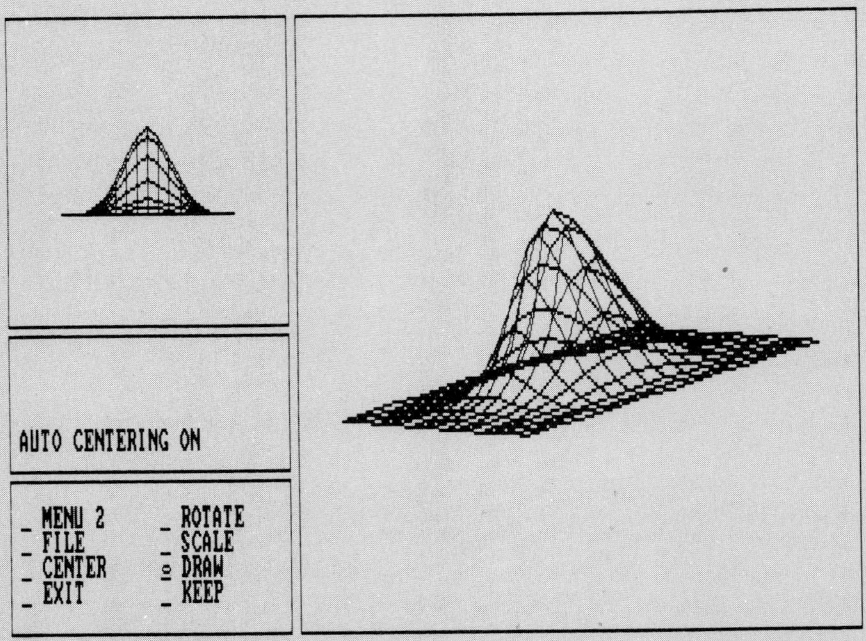

FIGURE 9.13 A crosshatched form ($Z = 7e^{-0.1(x^2+y^2)}$)

Chapter 5). We could easily incorporate one of the algorithms discussed in Chapter 5 into 3-D PLOTTER.

If a hidden-line algorithm written in BASIC were included in 3-D PLOTTER, however, the program would become very inefficient (slow in execution). Machine-level (assembly language) subroutines that perform the hidden line calculations would be preferred. The use of such subroutines greatly increases the execution speed of programs.

9.6 SUMMARY

In this chapter we expanded our programming effort and user-interface design principles to a 3-D environment. The mathematical functions that perform the various stages of viewing transformations are rather complex. Consequently, the system and user interface needed for 3-D object displays required a quite laborious design effort. The most difficult aspect was the design of the overall screen layout. The 12 × 12 inch screen does not provide enough room for both the drawing area and the image buffer. We solved this problem by providing a zooming feature so that the user can control the object size. Care in the design of user interfaces is always rewarded. The result of such care is the satisfying knowledge that computer graphics is being used to enhance our capability and creativity.

```
------------------------ VARIABLES LIST ------------------------

ARRAYS           :

    CENTER1      : CENTER OF THE ORIGINAL PICTURE.
    CENTER2      : CENTER OF THE NEW PICTURE.
    COORD        : COORDINATES OF THE ORIGINAL OBJECT.
    COORD2       : COORDINATES OF THE TRANSFORMED OBJECT.
    CTM          : CURRENT TRANSFORMATION MATRIX.
    FLAG%        : FLAGS INDICATING MOVE OR DRAW.
    R            : ROTATION MATRIX FOR X, Y AND Z.
    RX           : ROTATION MATRIX FOR X AXIS.
    RY           : ROTATION MATRIX FOR Y AXIS.
    RZ           : ROTATION MATRIX FOR Z AXIS.
    S            : SCALING MATRIX FOR X, Y AND Z.
    T            : TRANSLATION MATRIX FOR X, Y AND Z.
    TEMP         : TEMPORARY STORAGE.
    X%           : X COORDINATE.
    Y%           : Y COORDINATE.

INTEGERS         :

    C%           : COLUMN POSITION FOR PRINTING.
    CENTER%      : FLAG INDICATING WHETHER AUTO CENTERING IS ON.
    COLOR1%      : COLOR OF PREVIOUS POINT.
    FLAG%        : FLAG FOR CHOOSING MENU OPTIONS.
    I%, J%, K%   : SENTINEL NUMBERS.
    LX%          : X COORDINATE ON THE LEFT PART OF MENU.
    MARK%        : NUMBER OF POINTS MARKED.
    MAXY%        : MAXIMUM Y COORDINATE.
    MENU1%       : FLAG INDICATING WHETHER MENU 1 IS BEING USED.
    MINY%        : MINIMUM Y COORDINATE.
    NOP%         : NUMBER OF POINTS TO BE DRAWN.
    OLDX%        : PREVIOUS X COORDINATE.
    OLDY%        : PREVIOUS Y COORDINATE.
    OX%          : X COORDINATE OF OPTION CURSOR.
    OY%          : Y COORDINATE OF OPTION CURSOR.
    R%           : ROW POSITION FOR PRINTING.
    SPEED%       : INCREMENT OF DOT MOVEMENT.
    X%           : X COORDINATE.
    Y%           : Y COORDINATE.
```

PROGRAM 9.1 3-D PLOTTER

```
REALS            :

    MAX          : MAXIMUM VALUE.
    MIN          : MINIMUM VALUE.
    RANGE        : RANGE OF THE PICTURE.
    SX           : SCALING IN X DIRECTION.
    SY           : SCALING IN Y DIRECTION.
    SZ           : SCALING IN Z DIRECTION.
    T1, T2, T3   : TEMPORARY STORAGE.
    TEMP         : TEMPORARY STORAGE.
    THETAX       : ROTATION ABOUT X AXIS.
    THETAY       : ROTATION ABOUT Y AXIS.
    THETAZ       : ROTATION ABOUT Z AXIS.
    TX           : TRANSLATION IN X DIRECTION.
    TY           : TRANSLATION IN Y DIRECTION.
    TZ           : TRANSLATION IN Z DIRECTION.

CHARACTERS       :

    ANS$         : ANSWER FROM USER.
    BLANK$       : BLANKS.
    CENTER$      : STATUS OF AUTO CENTERING OPTION.
    D$           : ''DOWN.''
    L$           : ''LEFT.''
    OPT1$        : NAME OF OPTION 1.
    OPT2$        : NAME OF OPTION 2.
    OPT3$        : NAME OF OPTION 3.
    OPT4$        : NAME OF OPTION 4.
    OPT5$        : NAME OF OPTION 5.
    OPT6$        : NAME OF OPTION 6.
    OPT7$        : NAME OF OPTION 7.
    OPT8$        : NAME OF OPTION 8.
    R$           : ''RIGHT.''
    U$           : ''UP.''
```

PROGRAM 9.1 3-D PLOTTER

```
5    ' Program 9.1 : 3-D PLOTTER
10   '--------------------------- MAIN PROGRAM ----------------------------
20   OPTION BASE 1 : KEY OFF
30   DIM CENTER1(3), CENTER2(3), X%(2), Y%(2)
40   DIM COORD(1500,3), COORD2(1500,3),FLAG%(1500), R(4,4)
50   DIM CTM(4,4),RX(4,4),RY(4,4),RZ(4,4),TEMP(4,4), T(4,4), S(4,4)
60   GOSUB 220
70   ANS$=INKEY$ : IF ANS$="" THEN 70
80   IF ANS$=CHR$(13) THEN 160
90   IF ANS$<>U$ AND ANS$<>D$ AND ANS$<>L$ AND ANS$<>R$ THEN 70
100  OLDX%=OX% : OLDY%=OY%
110  IF ANS$=D$ THEN OY%=OY%+8 ELSE IF ANS$=U$ THEN OY%=OY%-8 ELSE
         IF ANS$=L$ THEN OX%=LX% ELSE IF ANS$=R$ THEN OX%=RX%
```

PROGRAM 9.1 3-D PLOTTER

```
120  IF OY% > MAXY% THEN OY%=156 : OX%=RX% ELSE IF OY% < MINY% THEN
        OY%=180 : OX%=LX%
130  CIRCLE(OLDX%,OLDY%),3,0,0,2*PI,5/12
140  CIRCLE(OX%,OY%),3,,0,2*PI,5/12
150  GOTO 70
160  FLAG%=(OY%-148)/8
170  IF OX%=RX% THEN FLAG%=FLAG%+4
180  IF MENU1%=1 THEN ON FLAG% GOSUB 2320,1520,1480,3060,550,1070,1230,2450
         ELSE ON FLAG% GOSUB 2380,2700,2540,910,550,1070,1230,2450
190  WINDOW SCREEN(0,0)-(639,199) : VIEW
200  GOTO 70
210  '------------------------ INITIALIZING -----------------------------
220  SCREEN 2 : CLS
230  LINE(0,0)-(210,96),,B
240  LINE(0,99)-(210,141),,B
250  LINE(0,144)-(210,192),,B
260  LINE(217,0)-(639,192),,B
270  GOSUB 2380
280  PI=3.141593 : BLANK$="                              "
290  WINDOW SCREEN(0,0)-(639,199) : VIEW
300  RX(1,1)=1! : RX(4,4)=1!
310  RY(2,2)=1! : RY(4,4)=1!
320  CTM(1,1)=1! : CTM(2,2)=1! : CTM(3,3)=1! : CTM(4,4)=1!
330  RZ(3,3)=1! : RZ(4,4)=1!
340  T(1,1)=1! : T(2,2)=1! : T(3,3)=1! : T(4,4)=1!
350  S(4,4)=1! : CENTER$="AUTO CENTERING ON " : CENTER%=1 : SPEED%=10
360  LOCATE 17,2 : PRINT CENTER$
370  OX%=12 : OY%=156 : LX%=12 : RX%=116 : MAXY%=180 : MINY%=156
380  CIRCLE(OX%,OY%),3,,0,2*PI,5/12
390  U$=CHR$(0)+CHR$(72) : D$=CHR$(0)+CHR$(80)
400  L$=CHR$(0)+CHR$(75) : R$=CHR$(0)+CHR$(77)
410  RETURN
420  '------------------------- PRINT FORMAT ----------------------------
430  R%=20 : C%=2
440  LOCATE R%,C%   : PRINT "_ "+OPT1$
450  LOCATE R%+1,C% : PRINT "_ "+OPT2$
460  LOCATE R%+2,C% : PRINT "_ "+OPT3$
470  LOCATE R%+3,C% : PRINT "_ "+OPT4$
480  C%=15
490  LOCATE R%,C%   : PRINT "_ "+OPT5$
500  LOCATE R%+1,C% : PRINT "_ "+OPT6$
510  LOCATE R%+2,C% : PRINT "_ "+OPT7$
520  LOCATE R%+3,C% : PRINT "_ "+OPT8$
530  RETURN
540  '------------------------ ROTATION --------------------------------
550  LOCATE 14,2 : BEEP : INPUT "ROTATION ABOUT X";THETAX
560  LOCATE 15,2 : BEEP : INPUT "ROTATION ABOUT Y";THETAY
570  LOCATE 16,2 : BEEP : INPUT "ROTATION ABOUT Z";THETAZ
580  LOCATE 14,2 : PRINT BLANK$ : LOCATE 15,2 : PRINT BLANK$
590  LOCATE 16,2 : PRINT BLANK$
600  LOCATE 14,2 : PRINT "ROTATING..." : BEEP
610  IF THETAX=0 THEN 700
620  T1=COS(THETAX*PI/180) : T2=SIN(THETAX*PI/180)
630  RX(2,2)=T1 : RX(2,3)=T2 : RX(3,2)=-1*T2 : RX(3,3)=T1
640  FOR I%=1 TO 4
650      FOR J%=1 TO 4
660          R(I%,J%)=RX(I%,J%)
670          NEXT J%
680      NEXT I%
690  GOSUB 1690
700  IF THETAY=0 THEN 790
710  T1=COS(THETAY*PI/180) : T2=SIN(THETAY*PI/180)
720  RY(1,1)=T1 : RY(1,3)=-1*T2 : RY(3,1)=T2 : RY(3,3)=T1
730  FOR I%=1 TO 4
740      FOR J%=1 TO 4
750          R(I%,J%)=RY(I%,J%)
760          NEXT J%
770      NEXT I%
780  GOSUB 1690
790  IF THETAZ=0 THEN 880
800  T1=COS(THETAZ*PI/180) : T2=SIN(THETAZ*PI/180)
810  RZ(1,1)=T1 : RZ(1,2)=T2 : RZ(2,1)=-1*T2 : RZ(2,2)=T1
820  FOR I%=1 TO 4
830      FOR J%=1 TO 4
840          R(I%,J%)=RZ(I%,J%)
850          NEXT J%
860      NEXT I%
870  GOSUB 1690
880  LOCATE 14,2 : PRINT BLANK$ : BEEP
890  RETURN
```

PROGRAM 9.1 (continued)

```
900  '------------------------ TRANSLATION ------------------------------
910  LOCATE 14,2 : INPUT "TX=";TX
920  LOCATE 15,2 : INPUT "TY=";TY
930  LOCATE 16,2 : INPUT "TZ=";TZ
940  LOCATE 14,2 : PRINT BLANK$ : LOCATE 15,2 : PRINT BLANK$
950  LOCATE 16,2 : PRINT BLANK$
960  LOCATE 14,2 : PRINT "TRANSLATING..." : BEEP
970  T(4,1)=TX : T(4,2)=TY : T(4,3)=TZ
980  FOR I%=1 TO 4
990       FOR J%=1 TO 4
1000           R(I%,J%)=T(I%,J%)
1010           NEXT J%
1020      NEXT I%
1030 GOSUB 1690
1040 LOCATE 14,2 : PRINT BLANK$ : BEEP
1050 RETURN
1060 '------------------------ SCALING ----------------------------------
1070 LOCATE 14,2 : INPUT "SX=";SX
1080 LOCATE 15,2 : INPUT "SY=";SY
1090 LOCATE 16,2 : INPUT "SZ=";SZ
1100 LOCATE 14,2 : PRINT BLANK$ : LOCATE 15,2 : PRINT BLANK$
1110 LOCATE 16,2 : PRINT BLANK$
1120 LOCATE 14,2 : PRINT "SCALING..." : BEEP
1130 S(1,1)=SX : S(2,2)=SY : S(3,3)=SZ
1140 FOR I%=1 TO 4
1150      FOR J%=1 TO 4
1160           R(I%,J%)=S(I%,J%)
1170           NEXT J%
1180      NEXT I%
1190 GOSUB 1690
1200 LOCATE 14,2 : PRINT BLANK$ : BEEP
1210 RETURN
1220 '------------------------ DRAW NEW PICTURE -------------------------
1230 WINDOW (0,0)-(639,607)
1240 VIEW(218,1)-(638,191) : CLS
1250 T3=0
1260 LOCATE 14,2 : PRINT "DRAWING...": BEEP
1270 FOR K%=1 TO NOP%
1280      FOR I%=1 TO 3
1290           FOR J%=1 TO 3
1300                T3=T3+COORD(K%,J%)*CTM(J%,I%)
1310                NEXT J%
1320           COORD2(K%,I%)=T3+CTM(4,I%) : T3=0
1330           NEXT I%
1340      NEXT K%
1350 IF CENTER%=1 THEN GOSUB 2160
1360 FOR I%=1 TO NOP%
1370      IF FLAG%(I%)=1 THEN LINE-(COORD2(I%,1),COORD2(I%,2))
               ELSE PSET(COORD2(I%,1),COORD2(I%,2))
1380      NEXT
1390 LOCATE 14,2 : PRINT BLANK$
1400 FOR I%=1 TO 4
1410      FOR J%=1 TO 4
1420           CTM(I%,J%)=0!
1430           NEXT J%
1440      NEXT I%
1450 CTM(1,1)=1! : CTM(2,2)=1! : CTM(3,3)=1! : CTM(4,4)=1!
1460 RETURN
1470 '----------------------- AUTO CENTERING SWITCH ----------------------
1480 IF CENTER%=1 THEN CENTER%=0 : CENTER$="AUTO CENTERING OFF"
      ELSE CENTER%=1 : CENTER$="AUTO CENTERING ON "
1490 LOCATE 17,2 : PRINT CENTER$
1500 RETURN
1510 '----------------------- PLOT DATA FILES ---------------------------
1520 LOCATE 14,2 : BEEP : INPUT "FILE NAME=";FILE$
1530 LOCATE 14,2 : PRINT BLANK$
1540 OPEN FILE$ FOR INPUT AS #1
1550 NOP%=0
1560 WHILE NOT EOF(1)
1570      NOP%=NOP%+1
1580      INPUT #1,COORD(NOP%,1),COORD(NOP%,2),COORD(NOP%,3),FLAG%(NOP%)
1590      WEND
1600 CLOSE #1
1610 IF CENTER%=1 THEN GOSUB 1850
1620 WINDOW (0,0)-(639,607)
1630 VIEW(1,1)-(209,95) : CLS
1640 FOR I%=1 TO NOP%
1650      IF FLAG%(I%)=1 THEN LINE-(COORD(I%,1),COORD(I%,2))
               ELSE PSET(COORD(I%,1),COORD(I%,2))
```

PROGRAM 9.1 (continued)

```
1660      NEXT
1670 RETURN
1680 '-------------------------  UPDATE CTM MATRIX  -------------------------
1690 T3=0
1700 FOR K%=1 TO 4
1710      FOR I%=1 TO 4
1720           FOR J%=1 TO 4
1730                T3=T3+CTM(K%,J%)*R(J%,I%)
1740                NEXT J%
1750           TEMP(K%,I%)=T3 : T3=0
1760           NEXT I%
1770      NEXT K%
1780 FOR I%=1 TO 4
1790      FOR J%=1 TO 4
1800           CTM(I%,J%)=TEMP(I%,J%)
1810           NEXT J%
1820           NEXT I%
1830 RETURN
1840 '------------------------  FIND ORIGINAL CENTER  ------------------------
1850 LOCATE 14,2 : PRINT "CENTERING..." : BEEP
1860 RANGE=-1
1870 GOSUB 2050
1880 SX=400/RANGE : SY=SX : SZ=SX
1890 FOR I%=1 TO NOP%
1900      COORD(I%,1)=SX*COORD(I%,1)
1910      COORD(I%,2)=SY*COORD(I%,2)
1920      COORD(I%,3)=SZ*COORD(I%,3)
1930      NEXT
1940 CENTER1(1)=CENTER1(1)*SX : CENTER1(2)=CENTER1(2)*SY
1950 CENTER1(3)=CENTER1(3)*SZ
1960 TX=320-CENTER1(1) : TY=304-CENTER1(2) : TZ=0-CENTER1(3)
1970 FOR I%=1 TO NOP%
1980      COORD(I%,1)=COORD(I%,1)+TX
1990      COORD(I%,2)=COORD(I%,2)+TY
2000      COORD(I%,3)=COORD(I%,3)+TZ
2010      NEXT
2020 LOCATE 14,2 : PRINT BLANK$ : BEEP
2030 RETURN
2040 '----------------------  FIND MIN AND MAX  ---------------------------
2050 FOR J%=1 TO 3
2060      MIN=COORD(1,J%) : MAX=MIN
2070      FOR I%=2 TO NOP%
2080           TEMP=COORD(I%,J%)
2090           IF TEMP < MIN THEN MIN=TEMP
                    ELSE IF TEMP > MAX THEN MAX=TEMP
2100           NEXT I%
2110      IF MAX-MIN > RANGE THEN RANGE=MAX-MIN
2120      CENTER1(J%)=(MAX+MIN)*.5
2130      NEXT J%
2140 RETURN
2150 '-----------------------  FIND NEW CENTER  ----------------------------
2160 FOR J%=1 TO 2
2170      MIN=COORD2(1,J%) : MAX=MIN
2180      FOR I%=2 TO NOP%
2190           TEMP=COORD2(I%,J%)
2200           IF TEMP < MIN THEN MIN=TEMP
                    ELSE IF TEMP > MAX THEN MAX=TEMP
2210           NEXT I%
2220      CENTER2(J%)=(MAX+MIN)*.5
2230      NEXT J%
2240 '--------------------  CENTERING PICTURE  --------------------------
2250 TX=320-CENTER2(1) : TY=304-CENTER2(2)
2260 FOR I%=1 TO NOP%
2270      COORD2(I%,1)=COORD2(I%,1)+TX
2280      COORD2(I%,2)=COORD2(I%,2)+TY
2290      NEXT
2300 RETURN
2310 '------------------------  MENU 2  ----------------------------------
2320 MENU1%=0 : OPT1$="MENU 1" : OPT2$="WINDOW"
2330 OPT3$="3-VIEW" : OPT4$="TRANSL"
2340 GOSUB 430
2350 CIRCLE(OX%,OY%),3,,0,2*PI,5/12
2360 RETURN
2370 '------------------------  MENU 1  ----------------------------------
2380 MENU1%=1 : OPT1$="MENU 2" : OPT2$="FILE  "
2390 OPT3$="CENTER" : OPT4$="EXIT  " : OPT5$="ROTATE"
2400 OPT6$="SCALE " : OPT7$="DRAW  " : OPT8$="KEEP  "
2410 GOSUB 430
2420 CIRCLE(OX%,OY%),3,,0,2*PI,5/12
2430 RETURN
```

PROGRAM 9.1 (continued)

```
2440 '------------------------ KEEP IMAGE -----------------------------
2450 FOR I%=1 TO NOP%
2460     FOR J%=1 TO 3
2470         COORD(I%,J%)=COORD2(I%,J%)
2480         NEXT J%
2490     NEXT I%
2500 CENTER1(1)=320 : CENTER1(2)=304
2510 GOSUB 1620
2520 RETURN
2530 '------------------------ 3 VIEWS ---------------------------------
2540 WINDOW (0,0)-(639,607) : VIEW(218,1)-(427,95),,1 : CLS
2550 THETAX=90 : THETAY=0 : THETAZ=0
2560 GOSUB 610
2570 GOSUB 1250
2580 VIEW(218,97)-(427,191),,1 : CLS
2590 GOSUB 1640
2600 VIEW(429,97)-(638,191),,1 : CLS
2610 THETAX=0 : THETAY=-90 : THETAZ=0
2620 GOSUB 610
2630 GOSUB 1250
2640 THETAX=20 : THETAY=-30 : THETAZ=-15
2650 VIEW(429,1)-(638,95),,1 : CLS
2660 GOSUB 610
2670 GOSUB 1250
2680 RETURN
2690 '------------------------ WINDOWING -------------------------------
2700 KEY (11) ON : KEY (12) ON : KEY (13) ON : KEY (14) ON
2710 ON KEY(11) GOSUB 2910
2720 ON KEY(14) GOSUB 2950
2730 ON KEY(12) GOSUB 2990
2740 ON KEY(13) GOSUB 3030
2750 WINDOW (0,0)-(639,607) : VIEW(0,0)-(210,96)
2760 X%=214 : Y%=466 : COLOR1%=POINT(X%,Y%) : MARK%=0
2770 PSET(X%,Y%)
2780 ANS$=INKEY$ : IF ANS$="" THEN 2780
2790 IF ANS$<>CHR$(13) THEN 2780
2800 MARK%=MARK%+1 : X%(MARK%)=POINT(2) : Y%(MARK%)=POINT(3)
2810 PSET(X%(MARK%),Y%(MARK%)) : COLOR1%=1
2820 IF MARK% <>2 THEN 2890
2830 LINE(X%(1),Y%(1))-(X%(2),Y%(2)),,B
2840 CENTER1%=(X%(1)+X%(2))*.5 : CENTER1%(2)=(Y%(1)+Y%(2))*.5
2850 WINDOW (X%(1),Y%(1))-(X%(2),Y%(2)) : GOSUB 1240
2860 ANS$=INKEY$ : IF ANS$="" THEN 2860
2870 GOSUB 1620
2880 KEY(11) OFF : KEY(12) OFF : KEY(13) OFF : KEY(14) OFF : RETURN
2890 GOTO 2780
2900 '------------------------ POINT UP --------------------------------
2910 OLDY%=Y% : Y%=Y%+SPEED% : IF Y%>607 THEN Y%=0
2920 PSET(X%,OLDY%),COLOR1%
2930 COLOR1%=POINT(X%,Y%) : PSET(X%,Y%) : RETURN
2940 '------------------------ POINT DOWN ------------------------------
2950 OLDY%=Y% : Y%=Y%-SPEED%: IF Y%<0 THEN Y%=607
2960 PSET(X%,OLDY%),COLOR1%
2970 COLOR1%=POINT(X%,Y%) : PSET(X%,Y%) : RETURN
2980 '------------------------ POINT LEFT ------------------------------
2990 OLDX%=X% : X%=X%-SPEED% : IF X%<0 THEN X%=639
3000 PSET(OLDX%,Y%),COLOR1%
3010 COLOR1%=POINT(X%,Y%) : PSET(X%,Y%) : RETURN
3020 '------------------------ POINT RIGHT -----------------------------
3030 OLDX%=X% : X%=X%+SPEED% :IF X%>639 THEN X%=0
3040 PSET(OLDX%,Y%),COLOR1%
3050 COLOR1%=POINT(X%,Y%) : PSET(X%,Y%) : RETURN
3060 END
```

PROGRAM 9.1 3-D PLOTTER

REFERENCES

1. Barsky, B. A., "A Description and Evaluation of Various 3-D Models," *IEEE Computer Graphics and Applications* **4** (1) 38–52, 1984.

2. Sowerbutts, W. T. C., "A Surface-Plotting Program Suitable for Microcomputers," *Computer Aided Design* **15** (6) 323–327, November 1983.

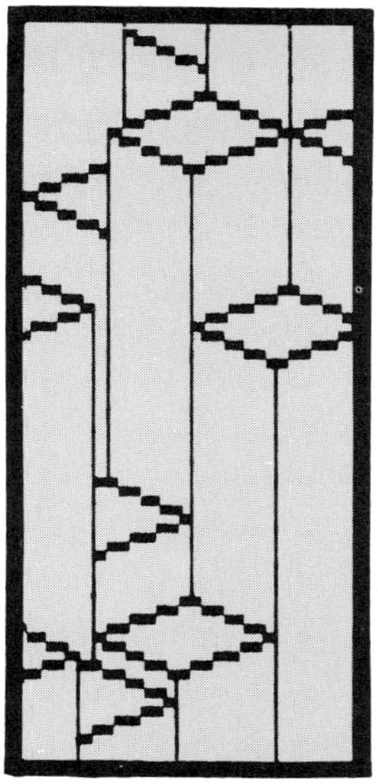

PART FOUR

Graphics Applications in Management Decision Making

In Part Three, we considered efficient design methods for graphics programs. We now look at specific sample applications in greater detail. In Chapter 10, we will demonstrate an automated forecasting system based on the Winters' method. In Chapter 11, we will discuss various plots of regression statistics, which can help the user interpret regression models. Finally, in Chapter 12, we will demonstrate how interactive computer graphics facilitate the understanding of a computer-simulated risk analysis model.

The reader may not be interested in the details or mathematics of each application. However, studying one in detail shows how a new application can be created, using the graphics routines and plots developed in earlier chapters. Graphics makes the applications more understandable and meaningful.

CHAPTER TEN
Interactive Forecasting System

The Winters' method is widely used by production and inventory managers to forecast a seasonal time series. The same technique is frequently applied to other problem areas, including financial planning, investment analysis, facilities planning, and marketing. In the Winters' method, historical data is examined to determine the underlying process generating the variable of interest (assuming that the process is stable) and then using this knowledge to extrapolate the process into the future. The statistical logic is clearly stated, and the operations are mathematical.

In this chapter, we will demonstrate how to develop an automated forecasting system based on the Winters' method and using computer graphics.

10.1 MODEL DEVELOPMENT

The forecasting technique we will present is an exponential smoothing procedure developed by Winters [5] that is best used to forecast a time series with a linear trend and multiplicative seasonal variation. The method assumes that the time series to be forecasted can be adequately represented using the expression

$$y_t = (a + bt)c_t + e_t, \qquad \textbf{(10.1)}$$

where

a = a permanent component (base line),

b = a linear trend component,
c_t = a multiplicative seasonal factor at period t,
e_t = the random error component,
y_t = the forecasted value at period t.

If the model is to be used as a forecasting tool, we must provide estimates of the unknown parameters a, b, and c_t.

10.1.1 UPDATING THE ESTIMATES

We first define the length of the season as L periods. For example, if a season lasts a year, $L = 12$ for a monthly time series and $L = 4$ for a quarterly series. We also define the seasonal factors in such a way that they sum to the length of the season:

$$\sum_{t=1}^{L} c_t = L\,, \tag{10.2}$$

Let us suppose that at the *end* of period $T-1$ we have estimates of the model parameters a, b, and c_t. We denote these estimates as $a(T-1)$, $b(T-1)$, and $c_T(T-L)$. In period T, we obtain a new observation, y_T. We wish to obtain the estimates $a(T)$, $b(T)$, and $c_T(T)$ by updating $a(T-1)$ and $b(T-1)$, the estimates obtained in the previous period, and $c_T(T-L)$, the last estimate of the current seasonal factor (obtained L periods ago).

Permanent component. To update the estimate of the permanent component, we use the following equation:

$$a(T) = \alpha\left[\frac{y_T}{c_T(T-L)}\right] + (1-\alpha)[a(T-1) + b(T-1)] \tag{10.3}$$

where α is a smoothing constant between 0 and 1. Dividing y_T by $c_T(T-L)$ [the estimate of the seasonal factor for period T computed one season (L periods) ago] "deseasonalizes" the data and prevents the seasonal factor from influencing the estimate of the permanent component. The term $[a(T-1) + b(T-1)]$, on the other hand, is simply the average level of the time series at time T, as estimated from the estimates computed in the previous period. Here $a(T)$ can be viewed as the estimate of the intercept of the trend line, when we establish a new origin at the end of the current period.

Trend component. To update the estimate of the trend component, we use the following equation:

$$b(T) = \beta[a(T) - a(T-1)] + (1-\beta)b(T-1) \tag{10.4}$$

where $0 < \beta < 1$ is a second smoothing constant. Here the term $[a(T) - a(T-1)]$ represents the difference between the two successive estimates of the permanent components. This difference and the estimate of the trend made last period yield the new estimate of the trend component in the current period.

Seasonal factor. We obtain the updated estimate of the seasonal factor by using the following equation:

$$c_T(T) = \gamma\left[\frac{y_T}{a(T)}\right] + (1 - \gamma)c_T(T - L), \tag{10.5}$$

where $0 < \gamma < 1$ is a third smoothing constant. Here again we divide y_T by $a(T)$ to isolate the seasonal variation from the observation. Then we obtain the updated estimate by smoothing the estimate of the seasonal factor for the current period T computed L periods ago and the current seasonal variation. Note that we must use the estimate made L periods ago because this was the last possible time we could observe this portion of the seasonal pattern. Note also that the initial values of the seasonal factors add up to L at the outset. As we revise the estimates of the seasonal factors, however, these may not add to the length of the season (as we will observe in our computer output in later sections). We could correct this by normalizing the seasonal factors at the end of every season. This process is not required, but it is often suggested as a possible modification of Winters' method.

Future forecast. Once we obtain these three parameters, we can forecast the observation in any future period $T + \tau$, $\hat{y}_{T+\tau}$, by

$$\hat{y}_{T+\tau} = [a(T) + b(T)\tau]c_{T+\tau}(T + \tau - L). \tag{10.6}$$

Recall that the quantity in parentheses for $a(.)$, $b(.)$ and $c(.)$ indicates the time of computation of the estimate. Thus in order to forecast period $T + \tau$ we need the seasonal factor for period $T + \tau$ that was computed in period $T + \tau - L$. However, if a forecast is to be made for a period more than L periods in the future (so that the index $T + \tau - L$ refers to a seasonal factor that has not yet been computed), the program will reuse the last seasonal factor available.

10.1.2 INITIALIZATION PROCEDURE

To implement the Winters' model, we must provide initial values of the parameters $a(0)$, $b(0)$, and $c_t(0)$ for $t = 1, 2, \ldots, L$, where L is again the number of periods in a season (see Eqs. (10.3) through (10.5).) If historical information is available, several heuristic algorithms are possible. We will use the algorithm described by Montgomery and Johnson [3], which is a slight modification of the original Winters' initialization procedures. In order to estimate $a(0)$ we need to estimate $b(0)$, so we will discuss $b(0)$ first.

Initial trend component $b(0)$. Suppose the last m seasons' data are available and let $\bar{y}_j, j = 1, 2, \ldots, m$, denote the average of the observations during the jth season. Then we compute $b(0)$ by using

$$b(0)=\frac{(\bar{y}_m-\bar{y}_1)}{(m-1)L}\,. \tag{10.7}$$

This equation implies that we need at least two seasons' data for any meaningful estimation of the parameter. Note that the program will use only the first two seasons' data to estimate the initial parameters.

Initial permanent component $a(0)$. To estimate the permanent component at the start of the first period, we use

$$a(0) = \bar{y}_1 - (L/2)b(0)\,. \tag{10.8}$$

Here $\bar{y}_1$ measures the average level of the time series in the first season. The factor $L/2$ represents the middle of the season. Thus the initial estimate $a(0)$ is the average level of the time series at the middle of the first season, less the amount this level has changed from the beginning of the season to the middle of the season.

Initial seasonal factor $c_t(0)$. We compute seasonal factors for each time period $t = 1, 2, \ldots, mL$ using the expression

$$c_t = \frac{y_t}{\bar{y}_i - [(L + 1)/2 - j]b(0)}, \tag{10.9}$$

where $\bar{y}_i$ is the average for a season corresponding to the t index, and j is the position of period t within the season. For example, if $1 \le t \le L$, then $i = 1$; if $L + 1 \le t \le 2L$, then $i = 2$; and if the time series consists of monthly data, $j = 1$ for January, $j = 2$ for February, and so on. We average these m estimates of the seasonal factor to produce a single estimate of the seasonal factor for each period within the season. That is, we obtain

$$\bar{c}_t = \left(\frac{1}{m}\right)\sum_{k=0}^{m-1} c_{t+k}\,, \qquad t = 1, 2, \ldots, L\,. \tag{10.10}$$

Finally, we normalize the seasonal factors so that they add to L. This is accomplished by using

$$c_t(0) = \frac{\bar{c}_t L}{\sum_{t=1}^{L} \bar{c}_t}, \tag{10.11}$$

where $t = 1, 2, \ldots, L$. Note, however, that these estimates are based on a time origin immediately prior to period 1. For forecasting purposes, we normally require that initial estimates of the parameters be made with a time origin at the end of the m seasons of historical data (at the end of period mL). Our program repeatedly smooths the initial estimates using the updating equations until the values at the end of period mL are obtained. The origin of time is then redefined to be the end of the m seasons of historical data.

10.1.3 CHOICE OF SMOOTHING CONSTANTS

Winters' method requires the user to specify values for the smoothing constants in the model for the forecasting system. The smoothing constants act as weighting factors, thereby controlling the number of past realizations of the time series that affect the forecast. For instance, small smoothing values give more weight to past observations; this makes the forecasting system respond slowly to changes in the parameters of the time series. Larger values of the smoothing constant include less historical data; consequently, the forecasting system responds more rapidly.

Several approaches serve as a rational basis for selecting the smoothing constant [3]. In our program we carry out a sequence of trials on a set of actual historical data with different values for combinations of α, β, γ. The forecasts generated by each combination are then compared to the actual observations in the historical time series. The combination minimizing the sum of squared forecast errors is the set of smoothing constants used in the actual forecasting. For example, if three years of monthly observations are available, the program will use the first two years to optimize the smoothing constants and then simulate a forecast for each month of the remaining year to see how the "optimum" smoothing constants respond to new data.

As a general rule, smoothing constants range between 0.01 and 0.3. If the results of a set of trials indicate an optimum value greater than 0.3, the validity of the model should be questioned. The program, therefore, tries all possible combinations of smoothing constants, as follows:

$$\alpha : \text{range } 0 - 0.25, \text{ step size } 0.05$$

$$\beta : \text{range } 0 - 0.20, \text{ step size } 0.05$$

$$\gamma : \text{range } 0 - 0.20, \text{ step size } 0.05$$

Of course, we could change these limits to include larger values, but a large number of relatively uninformative calculations would be made.

10.2 MEASURE OF PERFORMANCE CRITERIA

10.2.1 MEASURES OF FORECAST ERROR

We must accept the fact that no forecasting system can ever produce perfect forecasts of future observations. There will always be some difference between the forecast for the period and the actual realization for that period. This difference is referred to as the forecast error (or residual) for period t and is denoted by

$$\begin{aligned} e_t &= \text{actual value} - \text{forecast value} \\ &= y_t - \hat{y}_t \end{aligned} \tag{10.12}$$

When forecasting is made over several periods, a series of error values is obtained, one for each time period. A summary of these errors provides a basis for measuring the accuracy of the forecast.

Two methods are frequently used as a measure of forecast accuracy. One method is to compute the mean absolute deviation (MAD). This is done simply by computing

$$\text{MAD} = \sum_{t=1}^{n} \frac{|e_t|}{n}. \tag{10.13}$$

Another method is to compute the squared error for each period and average these squared errors for n forecasted periods:

$$\text{MSE} = \sum_{t=1}^{n} \frac{e_t^2}{n}. \tag{10.14}$$

The basic difference between these two measures is that the mean squared error (MSE) penalizes a forecasting technique much more for larger errors than for small errors.

Measures such as MAD and MSE can be used in two ways. First, they can be used to select a forecasting method that produces the most accurate predictions of future values. A common strategy is to simulate historical data and compare the performance of the various methods in forecasting that historical data.

Second, the MAD or MAS can be used to monitor the accuracy of an installed forecasting method. A monitoring device may be needed because a specific forecasting method based on past observations may not remain valid in the future. The underlying data pattern might change in the course of forecasting. Thus it is common to employ a tracking signal test for each period. The *tracking signal* is a statistic computed by dividing an estimate of expected forecast error by a measure of the variability of forecast error, such as an estimate MAD. If the tracking signal deviates from zero by more than a prescribed amount, we must determine whether the forecasting model should be modified to better represent the time series process (see further discussion in [3]). We will not include the tracking test in our computer program, but we suggest it as a possible, useful modification to the Winters' model.

10.2.2 PREDICTION INTERVALS

Having obtained an estimate of future forecast at period t, we wish to make probability statements about the accuracy of the estimated value. To do so, we compute an interval that has a stated probability of containing the actual future value. This range is called a *prediction interval*. This statistical term is often used in lieu of "*confidence interval*," which has the same statistical interpretation but is based only on the data used to fit the forecasting model. (See statistical reasoning in [2].) In our programming, we will use the formula developed by Bowerman and O'Connell [1], which estimates a $(100 - \alpha)$-percent confidence interval made at time T for $\hat{y}_t + \tau$. This is expressed by

$$\hat{y}_{T+\tau} - z_{\alpha/2}\, d_\tau \Delta_w(T) \le y_{T+\tau} \le \hat{y}_{T+\tau} + z_{\alpha/2}\, d_\tau \Delta_w(T), \tag{10.15}$$

where $z_{\alpha/2}$ = the percentage point of the standard normal distribution such that $P\{z \ge z_{\alpha/2}\} = \alpha/2$,

$$d_\tau = 1.25\left[\frac{1 + \dfrac{\theta}{(1+v)^3}[(1 + 4v + 5v^2) + 2\theta(1 + 3v)\tau + 2\theta\tau^2]}{1 + \dfrac{\theta}{(1+v)^3}[(1 + 4v + 5v^2) + 2\theta(1 + 3v) + 2\theta^2]}\right]^{1/2}$$

where

$$\theta = \max\{\alpha, \beta, \gamma\},\ v = (1 - \theta),$$

and

$$\Delta_w(T) = \frac{\displaystyle\sum_{t=1}^{T}\left|\frac{y_t}{c_t(t - L)} - (a(t - 1) + b(t - 1))\right|}{T}.$$

10.2.3 RESIDUAL ANALYSIS

For a given process and forecasting method, the forecast error e_t is considered a random variable having expected value $E(e)$ and variance σ^2. If the forecast

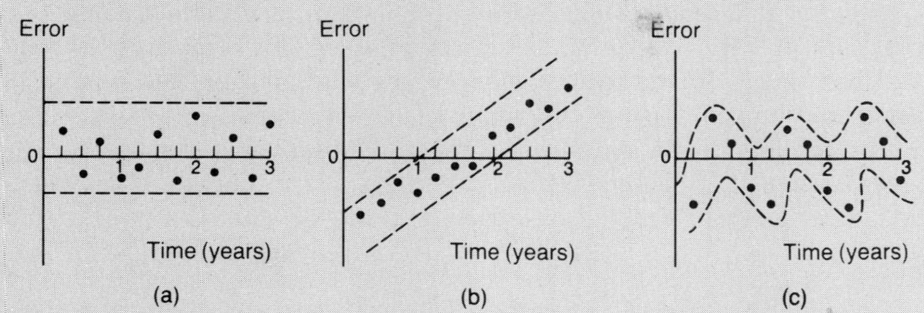

FIGURE 10.1 Residual patterns: (a) random forecast errors, (b) trend not accounted for, and (c) seasonal not accounted for

is unbiased, $E(e) = 0$. Analysis of the residuals, defined by Eq. (10.12), is frequently helpful in checking the assumption that the errors are indeed normally distributed with $E(e) = 0$ and σ^2. One way to check this assumption is to plot the residuals in time sequence. These graphs will usually resemble one of the patterns shown in Fig. 10.1. Pattern (a) in Fig. 10.1 represents the normal situation, while patterns (b) and (c) result from an inadequate model. If the residuals appear as in (b), the forecasting model does not account for an upward trend in time series, which indicates adjustment in β. If a plot of the residuals against time resembles (c), the forecasting model does not appropriately account for a seasonal pattern in the time series.

10.3 DESCRIPTION OF THE WINTERS' PROGRAM

10.3.1 PROGRAMMING LOGIC

The general programming logic for the WINTERS' program is shown in Fig. 10.2. Program 10.1, which lists the complete code for WINTERS, appears at the end of this chapter along with definitions of the variable names used in this program. Note that the WINTERS' program uses both the AEDIT and APLOT programs, which were developed in Chapters 6 and 7, respectively.

Thus these two program files must be available before the user can run the WINTERS' program. No additional programming is required by the user to link these two programs to WINTERS.

10.3.2 FORECASTING EXAMPLE

We will explain how to run the WINTERS' program with the following forecasting example. This is an embellished example of data given in [1]; we present it here for comparison purposes.

Suppose we have three years of historical data (1982–1984) for the demand for a popular soft drink packaged in a 48-oz nonreturnable bottle, as summarized in Table 10.1. A quick examination of the data reveals that much of the demand occurs during the summer and early fall months. Furthermore, the seasonal magnitude appears to grow with the average level of sales, so the Winters' method may be appropriate. We would like to forecast the demand in the next season (1985) based on this time series. We will use the first two years of data to estimate the model parameters, then simulate the forecast for the third year.

10.3.3 MENU SELECTION

When we load and execute the program, we see the following prompt on the screen:

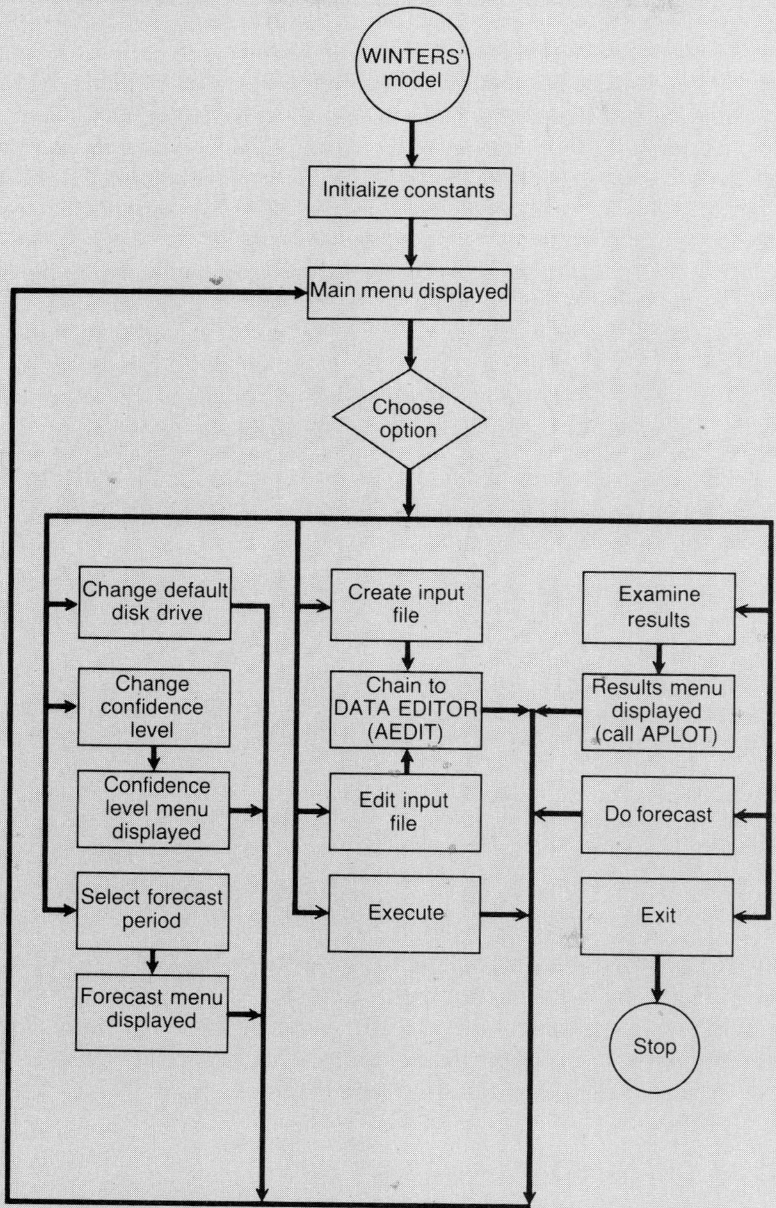

FIGURE 10.2 **Programming logic of WINTERS' model**

TABLE 10.1 Soft drink sales in thousands (bottles)

Year	Month											
	Jan.	Feb.	Mar.	Apr.	May	June	July	Aug.	Sept.	Oct.	Nov.	Dec.
1982	189	229	249	289	260	431	660	777	915	613	485	277
1983	244	296	319	370	313	556	831	960	1152	759	607	371
1984	298	378	373	443	374	660	1004	1153	1388	904	715	441
1985	?											

```
WHICH DISK DRIVE DOES CONTAIN WINTERS?
DRIVE A IS ON YOUR LEFT,
DRIVE B IS ON YOUR RIGHT,
DRIVE C IS YOUR HARD DISK DRIVE.
ENTER [A, B, OR C]?
```

We then specify the drive where the diskette containing WINTERS is located. Be sure to have both AEDIT and APLOT on this drive. After specifying the drive, we see the following menu on the screen:

```
******    WINTERS' MODEL MENU    ******               STATUS
                                            -------------------------

*    _ CHANGE DEFAULT DISK DRIVE         *  DEFAULT DRIVE     = B:
*    _ CHANGE CONFIDENCE LEVEL           *  CONFIDENCE LEVEL  = 95 %
*    _ SELECT FORECAST PERIOD            *  FORECAST PERIOD   = MONTH
*    _ CREATE INPUT FILE                 *
*    _ EDIT(EXAMINE) INPUT DATA          *
*    _ EXECUTE                           *
*    _ EXAMINE RESULTS                   *
*    _ DO FORECASTS                      *
*    _ EXIT                              *

****************************************
```

There are nine menu items from which to pick. We use the [↑] and [↓] keys to position the cursor and pick the menu item by pressing the [ENTER] key. System default status messages are also displayed on the right-hand side of the screen: default drive, confidence level, and forecast period. We will explain each menu option in detail in the following sections.

10.3.4 CHANGING DEFAULT DISK DRIVE

We can use this option (as in the PLOTTER program) to change the default disk drive from A: to B: or from B: to A:. (If there is a hard disk, we can also change it to C: or D:.) This option makes the program flexible under different disk drive systems, and is particularly useful for users who are forced to retrieve information from a single disk drive. Any data file created will be saved on this drive.

10.3.5 CHANGING CONFIDENCE LEVEL

When this option is chosen, a confidence level menu is displayed on the screen:

```
***   CONFIDENCE LEVEL MENU   ***
*           _ 99 %              *
*           _ 98 %              *
*           _ 95 %              *
*           _ 90 %              *
*           _ 80 %              *
*           _ 50 %              *
*           _ EXIT              *
*********************************
```

We move the cursor to the desired confidence level using [↑] and [↓] and press the [ENTER] key to select it. We then return automatically to the main menu. The status message on the right side confirms that the confidence level has been changed.

10.3.6 SELECTING FORECAST PERIOD

We specify the time period for the historical data through the forecast period menu:

```
******   FORECAST PERIOD MENU    ******
*           _ QUARTERLY               *
*           _ MONTHLY                 *
*           _ WEEKLY                  *
*           _ OTHERS                  *
*           _ EXIT                    *
***************************************
```

If the data are given by month, we should make sure the forecast period is set to "MONTH". If the data are given in a period other than quarterly, monthly, or weekly, we should choose the "OTHERS" option. The program will then ask, "HOW MANY PERIODS IN ONE CYCLE?". We may answer 365 if the data are accumulated daily.

10.3.7 CREATING INPUT DATA FILE

When this option is chosen, the program chains the DATA EDITOR program discussed in Chapter 6. In doing so, the WINTERS program transfers control to the DATA EDITOR program and passes variables to it from the current program. We can then create an input data file according to the procedure given in Chapter 6. The input data file for our example, when completed by DATA EDITOR, looks like Fig. 10.3. We will give it the file name "WINTER.DAT". Note that the program saves "WINTER.DAT" on default disk drive.

10.3.8 EDITING INPUT DATA FILE

Once we create an input file by using DATA EDITOR, we can access and modify this data file. When the edit option is chosen, we see a prompt for the file name:

```
INPUT FILE NAME = ?
```

We answer the name of the file we want to edit (examine), and again automatically access DATA EDITOR. All the commands remain the same as those described in Chapter 6.

Editing features such as these are very useful in any forecasting system. For example, we collect five years' data and estimate model parameters based on these data elements. As time advances, we collect more data (say, another year's data) and wish to estimate model parameters based on the most recent five years' data. We then have to delete the first year's data from our input data file. DATA EDITOR will do this for us when the correct sequence of editing commands is specified according to the format shown in Chapter 6.

10.3.9 EXECUTION

When this option is selected, the program will attempt to find the initial smoothing constants and seasonal factors for the Winters' model by reading the input data file specified. Two execution options are available. The first option calls for the user to enter the initial smoothing constants. The program will then compute the seasonal factors and simulate a sequence of one-period-ahead forecasts for the historical data (36 months for our example). The second option requires the program to find the optimal combination of smoothing constants. To find the optimal combination of α, β, γ, the program evaluates the sum of the squared forecast errors for all the combinations of α, β, and γ and selects the combination that minimizes the sum of the squared forecast errors. (See Section 10.3.) At least two seasons' worth of data must be provided for the Winters' model to work. When we desire the second option, we respond to the prompts and receive responses as follows:

```
INPUT FILE NAME =? WINTER.DAT
WANT TO PROVIDE YOUR OWN SMOOTHING FACTORS? N
```

```
                  ( Y )          ( X1 )                  COMMAND
 1 :            189.000                  NOT ALLOWED   B BACKWARD
 2 :            229.000                  NOT ALLOWED   C COLUMN
 3 :            249.000                                D DOWN
 4 :            289.000                                E EXIT
 5 :            260.000                  NOT ALLOWED   F FORWARD
 6 :            431.000                                I INSERT
 7 :            660.000                                K KILL
 8 :            777.000                  NOT ALLOWED   O ORDER
 9 :            915.000                                R ROW
10 :            613.000                                S SAVE
11 :            485.000                                U UP
12 :            277.000
13 :            244.000
14 :            296.000
15 :            319.000
16 :            370.000
17 :            313.000
18 :            556.000

COMMAND  :?                              ROW      ORDER
                                         DEFAULT CMD  :  D
```

```
                  ( Y )          ( X1 )                  COMMAND
19 :            831.000                  NOT ALLOWED   B BACKWARD
20 :            960.000                  NOT ALLOWED   C COLUMN
21 :           1152.000                                D DOWN
22 :            759.000                                E EXIT
23 :            607.000                  NOT ALLOWED   F FORWARD
24 :            371.000                                I INSERT
25 :            298.000                                K KILL
26 :            378.000                  NOT ALLOWED   O ORDER
27 :            373.000                                R ROW
28 :            443.000                                S SAVE
29 :            374.000                                U UP
30 :            660.000
31 :           1004.000
32 :           1153.000
33 :           1388.000
34 :            904.000
35 :            715.000
36 :            441.000

COMMAND  :?                              ROW      ORDER
                                         DEFAULT CMD  :  D
```

FIGURE 10.3 Data file WINTER.DAT

```
FINDING INITIAL FACTORS...
SEARCHING FOR GOOD SMOOTHING CONSTANTS...
```

The program finds the best smoothing constants, computes all relevant statistics, and then returns to the main menu selection. We hear a short beep sound when these tasks are completed.

10.3.10 EXAMINATION OF RESULTS

We select this option when we want to examine the results. Five suboption menus are available:

```
***********  WINTERS' RESULTS MENU  ***********

*   _ TABULATE SMOOTHING FACTORS                *
*   _ TABULATE OBSERVED & FORECAST VALUES       *
*   _ TABULATE FORECAST & CONFIDENCE INTERVAL   *
*   _ PLOT OBSERVED & FORECAST VALUES           *
*   _ PLOT RESIDUAL VS TIME                     *
*   _ EXIT                                      *

************************************************
```

We examine the execution results by successively selecting these suboption menus. After executing each submenu (except "Exit"), the program always returns to the results menu.

Table 10.2, obtained by selecting the first suboption, tabulates the summary information about smoothing values and seasonal factors. The result indicates that the combination of α, β, and γ that minimizes the sum of the squared forecast errors is $\alpha = 0.1$, $\beta = 0.05$, and $\gamma = 0.05$. The smoothed average, trend factor, and seasonal factors represent the statistics at the end of period 36 in our example. We will use these estimates to forecast future values of the time series.

Table 10.3 summarizes the one-period-ahead forecasting results. The program also computes the MAD and MSE statistics. During the first 24 months (from which the model parameters were initially estimated), the forecasts are much closer to the actual observations than during the last 12 months. This can be seen by comparing the MSE during the two periods. For months 1 to 24 MAD is 48.87, while for months 25 to 36 MAD is 60.17. When the two periods are ccmbined (months 1 to 36) MAD is 54.15. Of course, we can expect better

TABLE 10.2 Summary of smoothing statistics

```
-----------------------------------------------------------------------
SMOOTHING CONSTANTS :
    * SMOOTHING CONSTANT FOR AVERAGE      : ALPHA = 0.10
    * SMOOTHING CONSTANT FOR TREND        : BETA  = 0.05
    * SMOOTHING CONSTANT FOR SEASONALITY  : GAMMA = 0.05

SMOOTHED AVERAGE       : (A0) =           736.473
TREND FACTOR           : (B0) =             9.729
SEASONALITY FACTORS :
     F[ 1]=  0.475
     F[ 2]=  0.575
     F[ 3]=  0.589
     F[ 4]=  0.678
     F[ 5]=  0.573
     F[ 6]=  0.979
     F[ 7]=  1.457
     F[ 8]=  1.660
     F[ 9]=  1.951
     F[10]=  1.264
     F[11]=  0.988
     F[12]=  0.585
-----------------------------------------------------------------------
```

TABLE 10.3 Forecasted vs. observed values

PERIOD	OBSERVED	FORECAST	RESIDUAL
1	189.000	189.586	-0.586
2	229.000	235.168	-6.168
3	249.000	245.879	3.121
4	289.000	289.914	-0.914
5	260.000	250.461	9.539
6	431.000	439.327	-8.327
7	660.000	666.893	-6.893
8	777.000	774.788	2.212
9	915.000	930.015	-15.015
10	613.000	613.887	-0.887
11	485.000	489.129	-4.129
12	277.000	295.207	-18.207
13	244.000	242.637	1.363
14	296.000	299.224	-3.224
15	319.000	312.200	6.800
16	370.000	366.298	3.702
17	313.000	315.907	-2.907
18	556.000	547.450	8.550
19	831.000	830.440	0.560
20	960.000	962.240	-2.240

PERIOD	OBSERVED	FORECAST	RESIDUAL
21	1152.000	1148.599	3.401
22	759.000	757.095	1.905
23	607.000	600.970	6.030
24	371.000	361.181	9.819
25	298.000	299.458	-1.458
26	378.000	367.472	10.528
27	373.000	384.355	-11.355
28	443.000	447.065	-4.065
29	374.000	383.347	-9.347
30	660.000	662.102	-2.102
31	1004.000	998.891	5.109
32	1153.000	1154.540	-1.540
33	1388.000	1374.865	13.135
34	904.000	904.450	-0.450
35	715.000	716.137	-1.137
36	441.000	429.146	11.854

MEAN ABSOLUTE DEVIATION : MAD = 5.516123
MEAN SQUARED ERROR : MSE = 52.47957

results during months 1 to 24—we estimated the model parameters using this data, and the forecasts really represent the best "fit" of the model to the data. The errors observed during months 25 to 36 are much more characteristic of true model performance.

Table 10.4 summarizes the approximate 95-percent one-period-ahead confidence intervals for the historical data in months 1 to 36.

The last option is to plot the observed values of the time series and the one-period-ahead forecasts. When we enter this plotting option, the program will chain APLOT, which was also used in PLOTTER. The WINTERS program will preset the following variables before chaining APLOT.

Number of files to Plot = 2

(File 1 = observed values; File 2 = forecasted values)

Chart Option = Point for File 1, and Curve for File 2.

TABLE 10.4 Confidence interval estimates

PERIOD	FORECAST	95 %	CONFIDENCE	INTERVAL
1	189.586	189.586	--	189.586
2	235.168	232.160	--	238.176
3	245.879	231.308	--	260.450
4	289.914	275.895	--	303.933
5	250.461	239.125	--	261.797
6	439.327	422.141	--	456.514
7	666.893	649.116	--	684.671
8	774.788	757.903	--	791.672
9	930.015	914.835	--	945.195
10	613.887	598.309	--	629.465
11	489.129	474.938	--	503.321
12	295.207	281.379	--	309.035
13	242.637	223.641	--	261.633
14	299.224	281.151	--	317.297
15	312.200	294.441	--	329.959
16	366.298	347.848	--	384.748
17	315.907	297.778	--	334.036
18	547.450	529.661	--	565.238
19	830.440	812.456	--	848.424
20	962.240	945.153	--	979.327

PERIOD	FORECAST	95 %	CONFIDENCE	INTERVAL
21	1148.599	1132.202	--	1164.996
22	757.095	741.276	--	772.914
23	600.970	585.703	--	616.237
24	361.181	345.931	--	376.431
25	299.458	283.134	--	315.782
26	367.472	351.501	--	383.442
27	384.355	367.281	--	401.430
28	447.065	428.885	--	465.245
29	383.347	365.294	--	401.399
30	662.102	643.302	--	680.902
31	998.891	980.543	--	1017.238
32	1154.540	1136.509	--	1172.571
33	1374.865	1357.326	--	1392.403
34	904.450	886.945	--	921.954
35	716.137	699.121	--	733.152
36	429.146	412.536	--	445.755

When APLOT is loaded into memory, the following prompts are displayed on the screen:

```
PLOT WITH GRID LINES < N FOR NO >? N

HEADING FOR THE PLOT =? SALES OF SOFT DRINK (OBSERVED VS.
                        FORECASTED)
X TITLE FOR THE PLOT =? MONTH
Y TITLE FOR THE PLOT =? SALES
MINIMUM X VALUE = [DEFAULT: 1]? 0
MAXIMUM X VALUE = [DEFAULT: 36 ]?
MINIMUM Y VALUE = [DEFAULT: 189 ]? 150
MAXIMUM Y VALUE = [DEFAULT: 1388 ]? 1650
```

With the plotting parameters as specified above, Fig. 10.4(a) is displayed on the screen. This is a plot of the observed values as a function of time. The observed values of the time series and the one-period-ahead forecasts are then plotted as shown in Figure 10.4(b). Since we are in the APLOT program, we can

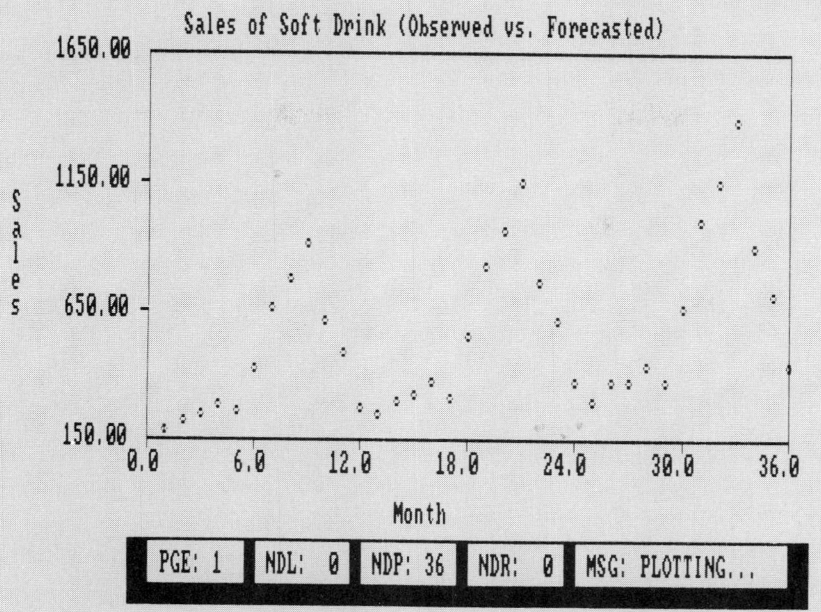

(a)

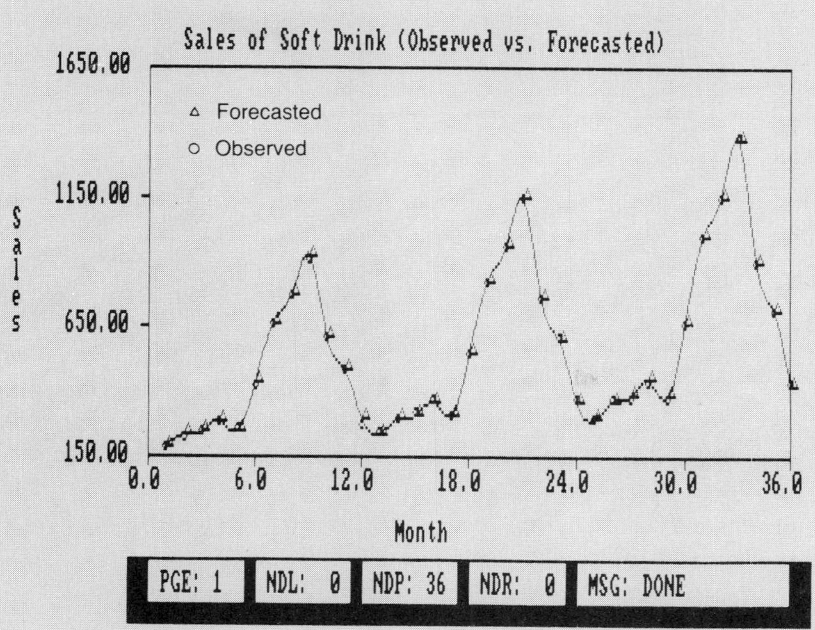

(b)

FIGURE 10.4 Plot of observed vs. forecasted time series

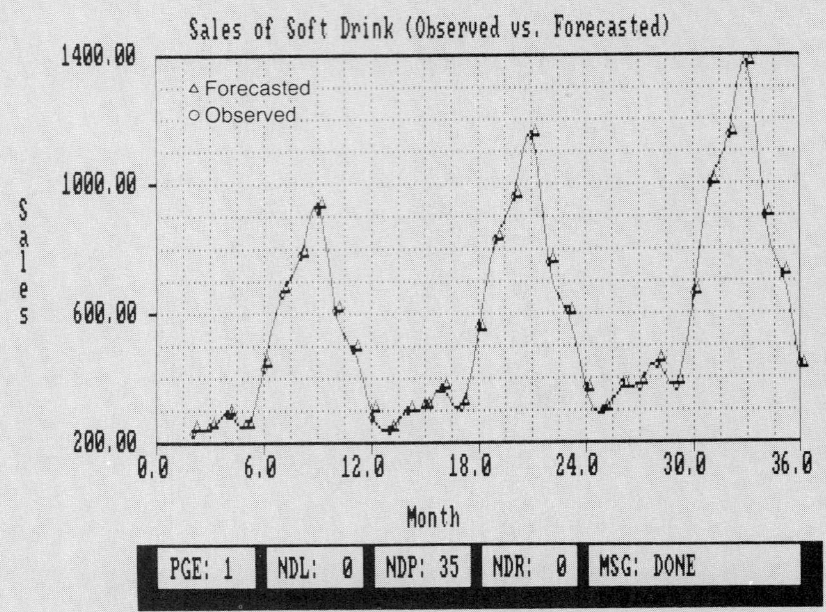

FIGURE 10.5 Variation in plotting option (with grids)

access all of the plotting features discussed in Chapter 7. We show two plotting variations. Figure 10.5 is obtained when we specify grid lines on the chart; Figure 10.6 shows an example of scrolling the graph pages. Figure 10.6(a) plots the first 12 months' sales trend. To obtain Figure 10.6(b), which is page 2 of the WINTER·DAT file (Section 7.6), we simply press the [→] key.

Finally, if we choose the "plot residual vs. time" options, we obtain Fig. 10.7. Analysis of the residual patterns is frequently helpful in checking the assumption that the forecast errors are purely random and not caused by any serious model inadequacies. If a plot of residuals against time has no noticeable pattern, we conclude that the forecasting system is stable and accounts for the trend and seasonal components present in the time series. Figure 10.7 represents this normal situation.

10.3.11 MAKING FORECASTS

Once we find the parameter estimates in a time series model, the next step is to forecast future values, by estimating the expected demand in a time τ periods in the future. Typically, the decision problem at hand requires a forecast over

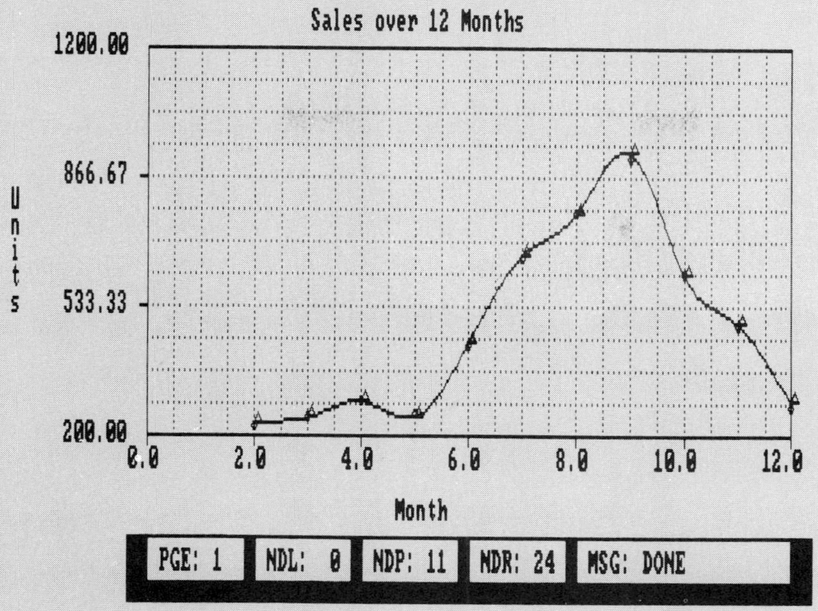

(a)

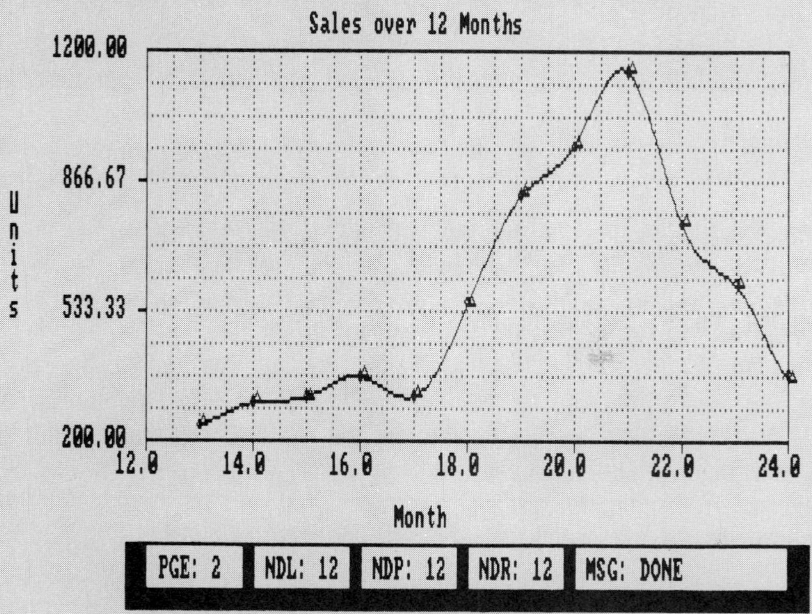

(b)

FIGURE 10.6 Creating multiple graph pages

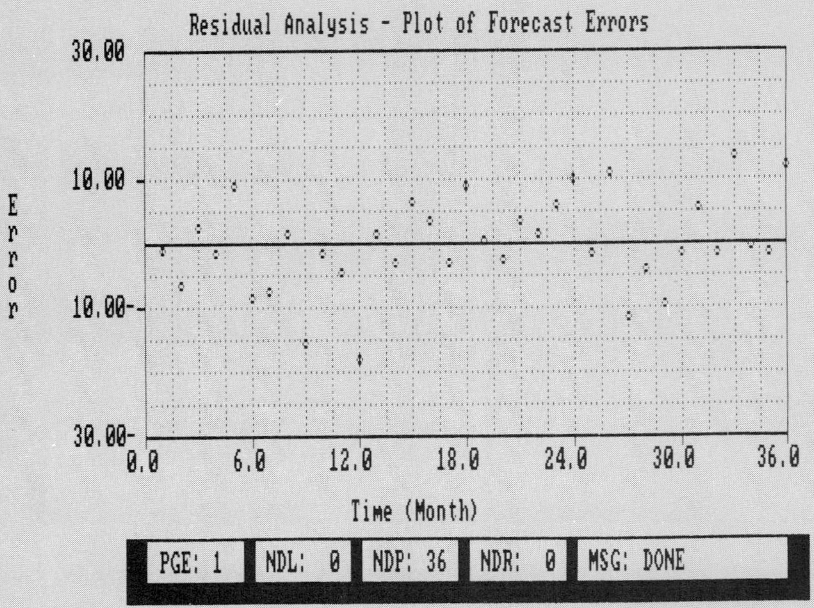

FIGURE 10.7 Residual vs. time

a number of future periods. Thus, when this option is entered, we receive the first prompt message:

```
HOW MANY PERIODS AHEAD FORECASTS? 12
```

TABLE 10.5 Forecasted future values

PERIOD	FORECAST	95 %	CONFIDENCE	INTERVAL
37	354.449	336.927	--	371.971
38	434.795	417.273	--	452.317
39	451.210	433.689	--	468.732
40	525.704	508.182	--	543.226
41	449.919	432.397	--	467.441
42	778.185	760.663	--	795.707
43	1172.579	1155.058	--	1190.102
44	1351.653	1334.131	--	1369.175
45	1607.643	1590.121	--	1625.165
46	1054.171	1036.649	--	1071.693
47	833.204	815.682	--	850.726
48	499.170	481.648	--	516.691

Upon responding to the prompt, we see Table 10.5 appear on the screen, showing point forecast values along with the prediction (confidence) intervals. This completes the run of the model.

10.4 SUMMARY

In this chapter we discussed how we analyze and forecast a time series that has multiplicative seasonal variation. The Winters' method presented herein is an exponential smoothing technique that is best used to forecast a time series with linear trend and multiplicative seasonal variation, but it can also be used to forecast a time series having no trend. In this case, we may set $\beta = 0$ and $b(0) = 0$.

The use of an appropriate forecasting method depends on the user's knowledge of how to analyze the underlying data pattern and monitor the performance of the chosen forecasting technique. No computer software replaces the essence of human judgment in forecasting—it simply helps the user in making a better decision. Before leaving this chapter we would like to recommend the following:

1. Before attempting to run the WINTERS' program, plot past observations using the PLOTTER program developed in Chapter 7. Try to find any noticeable pattern, trend, or abnormality in the data.
2. For an increasing or decreasing trend with a noticeable seasonal pattern, use the WINTERS' program shown in this chapter.
3. If the data are abnormal, investigate the reason for the abnormality. If the abnormality of any specific observation remains unanswered or originates from an unavoidable circumstance (such as a strike), delete these specific observations from the data.
4. If none of the above are true, use an autocorrelations analysis to validate the data. The graphical autocorrelation analysis provides important information about the pattern in time series data and its subcomponents. It also aids in determining whether one has been using the correct forecasting model. A complete discussion of this topic is given in [3].

AEDIT and APLOT files are required to run the WINTERS' program.

```
---------------------- VARIABLE LIST ----------------------

ARRAYS         :
CURVE$         : CHART TYPE TO BE USED.
```

PROGRAM 10.1 Winters' Model

```
D#          : DEMANDS.
DF#         : FORECAST OF DEMAND.
F#          : SEASONALITY FACTOR.
TF#         : TEMPORARY STORAGES FOR SEASONALITY FACTORS.
W           : CONSTANTS USED IN CALCULATING CONFIDENCE INTERVAL.

INTEGERS    :

AHEAD%      : N-PERIOD AHEAD FORECAST.
BGN%        : STARTING PERIOD.
CI%         : CONFIDENCE LEVEL.
COL%        : FLAG INDICATING INVALID "COLUMN" OPTION.
COUNT%      : NUMBER OF LINES PRINTED.
DX%         : NUMBER OF OPTIONS BYPASSED.
DX2%        : NUMBER OF OPTIONS BYPASSED.
FIRST%      : ROW POSITION OF FIRST OPTION.
FLAG%       : FLAG FOR SELECTING OPTIONS.
FLAG1%      : FLAG FOR SELECTING OPTIONS.
I%, J%      : SENTINEL NUMBERS.
LAST%       : ROW POSITION OF LAST OPTION.
LEFT%       : FLAG INDICATING INVALID "SCROLL LEFT" OPTION.
LST%        : ENDING PERIOD.
NEWFILE%    : FLAG INDICATING THE FILE IS NEW.
NOD%        : NUMBER OF DATA AVAILABLE.
ORDER%      : FLAG INDICATING THE ORDER OF INPUT.
PERIOD%     : NUMBER OF PERIODS IN A CYCLE.
RIGHT%      : FLAG% INDICATING INVALID "SCROLL RIGHT" OPTION.
SL%         : STARTING LINE TO CHAIN BACK.
SX%         : ROW POSITION OF MESSAGE.
SY%         : COLUMN POSITION OF MESSAGE.
T1%         : TEMPORARY STORAGE.
T2%         : TEMPORARY STORAGE.
X%          : ROW POSITION OF SCREEN CURSOR.
Y%          : COLUMN POSITION OF SCREEN CURSOR.

REALS       :
A           : SMOOTHING CONSTANT FOR AVERAGE.
B           : SMOOTHING CONSTANT FOR TREND.
C           : SMOOTHING CONSTANT FOR SEASONALITY.
DFI#        : FORECAST OF DEMAND AT ITH PERIOD.
DI#         : DEMAND AT ITH PERIOD.
DIFF        : DIFFERENCE BETWEEN OBSERVED AND FORECAST.
D0#         : CURRENT SMOOTHED AVERAGE.
D1#         : PREVIOUS SMOOTHED AVERAGE.
FJ#         : SEASONALITY FACTOR AT JTH PERIOD.
G#          : TREND.
MAD#        : MEAN ABSOLUTE DEVIATION.
MINI#       : MINIMUM VALUE.
S#          : MEAN SQUARE ERROR.
TD0#        : TEMPORARY STORAGE FOR SMOOTHED AVERAGE.
TEMP        : TEMPORARY STORAGE.
TEMP0       : TEMPORARY STORAGE.
```

PROGRAM 10.1 (continued)

```
TEMP1          : TEMPORARY STORAGE.
TEMP2          : TEMPORARY STORAGE.
TEMP3          : TEMPORARY STORAGE.
TEMP4          : TEMPORARY STORAGE.
TEMP5          : TEMPORARY STORAGE.
TEMP6          : TEMPORARY STORAGE.
TEMP7          : TEMPORARY STORAGE.
TEMP8          : TEMPORARY STORAGE.
TEMP9          : TEMPORARY STORAGE.
TEMP#          : TEMPORARY STORAGE.
TG#            : TEMPORARY STORAGE FOR TREND.
TRYA           : TEMPORARY SMOOTHING CONSTANT FOR AVERAGES.
TRYB           : TEMPORARY SMOOTHING CONSTANT FOR SEASONALITY.
TRYC           : TEMPORARY SMOOTHING CONSTANT FOR TREND.
V1#            : AVERAGE FOR FIRST CYCLE.
V2#            : AVERAGE FOR SECOND CYCLE.
X              : THE LARGEST OF ALL THREE SMOOTHING CONSTANTS.
Y              : 1-X.
Z              : Z VALUE OF NORMAL DISTRIBUTION.

CHARACTERS     :
ANS$           : RESPONSE FROM KEYBOARD.
BLANK$         : BLANK SPACES.
CALLFILE$      : NAME OF THE FILE THAT'S CHAINING EDITOR.
CHAINFILE$     : NAME OF FILE TO BE CHAINED TO.
FD$            : DISK DRIVE USED FOR THE DATA FILES.
FILE$          : INPUT FILE NAME.
FILE2$         : NAME OF FILE TO BE CHAINED TO.
M$             : ''COMMAND :''
PD$            : DISK DRIVE USED FOR THE PACKAGE.
PFILE$         : NAME OF FILE THAT'S CHAINING PLOTTER.
PRD$           : MESSAGE FOR PERIOD USED.
REP$           : RESPONSE FROM USER.
TEMP$          : TEMPORARY STORAGE.
```

PROGRAM 10.1 Winters' Model

```
10    '-------Program 10.1 : ----- WINTERS' MODEL  -------------------------
20    SCREEN 0,1 : CLS : KEY OFF
30    LOCATE 10,1
40    PRINT "Which disk drive does contain WINTERS?"
50    PRINT "DRIVE A IS ON YOUR LEFT,"
60    PRINT "DRIVE B IS ON YOUR RIGHT,"
70    PRINT "DRIVE C IS YOUR HARD (FIXED) DISK DRIVE."
80    INPUT "ENTER [ A, B, or C ]";PD$
90    PD$=PD$+":" : FD$="B:" : DX%=0
100   DIM D#(200), DF#(200), F#(60), TF#(60), W(200)
110   SX%=5 : SY%=56 : CI%=95
120   M$="COMMAND :" : BLANK$="                              "
130   PRD$="MONTH " : PERIOD%=12 : Z=1.96 : NOD%=2
140   GOSUB 250
150   X%=DX%+5 : Y%=15: LOCATE X%,Y%,1,0,7
160   FIRST%=5 : LAST%=13
170   ANS$=INKEY$ : IF ANS$="" THEN 170
180   IF ANS$=CHR$(0)+CHR$(80) THEN IF X%<LAST% THEN X%=X%+1 ELSE X%=FIRST%
```

PROGRAM 10.1 Winters' Model

```
190  IF ANS$=CHR$(0)+CHR$(72) THEN IF X%>FIRST% THEN X%=X%-1 ELSE X%=LAST%
200  LOCATE X%,Y%: IF ANS$<>CHR$(13) THEN 170
210  FLAG1%=CSRLIN : FLAG1%=FLAG1%-4
220  ON FLAG1% GOSUB 2690,2410,2920,2730,2730,460,1320,2150,3940
230  IF FLAG1%<>1 THEN GOTO 140 ELSE GOTO 150
240  '------------------------- PRINT MAIN MENU --------------------------
250  SCREEN 0,1 : CLS : LOCATE 3,1
260  PRINT TAB(10) "******  WINTERS'  MODEL MENU  ******"
270  PRINT
280  PRINT TAB(10) "*    _ CHANGE DEFAULT DISK DRIVE    *"
290  PRINT TAB(10) "*    _ CHANGE CONFIDENCE LEVEL      *"
300  PRINT TAB(10) "*    _ SELECT FORECAST PERIOD       *"
310  PRINT TAB(10) "*    _ CREATE INPUT FILE            *"
320  PRINT TAB(10) "*    _ EDIT(EXAMINE) INPUT DATA     *"
330  PRINT TAB(10) "*    _ EXECUTE                      *"
340  PRINT TAB(10) "*    _ EXAMINE RESULTS              *"
350  PRINT TAB(10) "*    _ DO FORECASTS                 *"
360  PRINT TAB(10) "*    _ EXIT                         *"
370  PRINT
380  PRINT TAB(10) "************************************" : BEEP
390  LOCATE 3,65,1 : PRINT "STATUS"
400  LOCATE 4,SY% : PRINT "------------------------"
410  LOCATE SX%,SY% : PRINT "DEFAULT DRIVE    = "+FD$
420  LOCATE SX%+1,SY% : PRINT "CONFIDENCE LEVEL =";CI%;"%"
430  LOCATE SX%+2,SY% : PRINT "FORECAST PERIOD  = ";PRD$
440  RETURN
450  '------------------------- EXECUTE ----------------------------------
460  CLS : INPUT "INPUT FILE NAME =";TEMP$ : TEMP$=FD$+TEMP$
470  IF FILE$<>TEMP$ THEN FILE$=TEMP$ : GOSUB 2850
480  INPUT "WANT TO PROVIDE YOUR OWN SMOOTHING FACTORS";REP$
490  REP$=LEFT$(REP$,1) : IF REP$="N" OR REP$="n" THEN 550
500  INPUT "SMOOTHING CONSATNT FOR AVERAGE     : ALPHA =";A
510  INPUT "SMOOTHING CONSTANT FOR TREND       : BETA  =";B
520  INPUT "SMOOTHING CONSTANT FOR SESONALITY  : GAMMA =";C
530  GOSUB 620
540  GOTO 570
550  GOSUB 620     'FINDING INITIAL FACTORS
560  GOSUB 790     'FINDING GOOD SMOOTHING CONSTANTS
570  AHEAD%=1 : BGN%=1 : LST%=NOD%
580  GOSUB 1140     'FORECAST HISTORICAL DATA
590  DX%=6
600  RETURN
610  '------------------------- FIND INITIAL FACTORS ---------------------
620  PRINT "FINDING INITIAL FACTORS..."
630  V1#=0 : V2#=0 : TEMP#=0
640  FOR I%=1 TO PERIOD% : V1#=V1#+D#(I%) : NEXT
650  FOR I%=PERIOD%+1 TO 2*PERIOD% : V2#=V2#+D#(I%) : NEXT
660  V1#=V1#/PERIOD% : V2#=V2#/PERIOD%
670  G#=(V2#-V1#)/PERIOD% : D0#=V1#-(PERIOD%*.5)*G#
680  FOR I%=1 TO PERIOD%
690      F#(I%)=D#(I%)/(V1#-(((PERIOD%+1)*.5-I%)*G#))
700      NEXT
710  FOR I%=PERIOD%+1 TO 2*PERIOD%
720      F#(I%)=D#(I%)/(V2#-(((PERIOD%+1)*.5-I%+PERIOD%)*G#))
730      NEXT
740  FOR I%=1 TO PERIOD% : F#(I%)=(F#(I%)+F#(I%+PERIOD%))*.5 : NEXT
750  FOR I%=1 TO PERIOD% : TEMP#=TEMP#+F#(I%) : NEXT
760  FOR I%=1 TO PERIOD% : F#(I%)=F#(I%)*PERIOD%/TEMP# : NEXT
770  RETURN
780  '-------------------- SEARCH FOR SMOOTHING CONSTANTS ----------------
790  PRINT "SEARCHING FOR GOOD SMOOTHING CONSTANTS..."
800  MINI#=100000!
810  TRYA=0! : TRYB=0! : TRYC=0!
820  WHILE (TRYA<=.25)
830       TRYA=TRYA+.05
840       WHILE (TRYC<=.2)
850            TRYC=TRYC+.05
860            WHILE (TRYB<=.2)
870                 TRYB=TRYB+.05
880                 MAD#=0!
890                 J%=1
900                 TD0#=D0# : TG#=G#
910                 FOR I%=1 TO PERIOD% : TF#(I%)=F#(I%) : NEXT
920                 FOR I%=1 TO NOD%
930                      DI#=D#(I%)
940                      IF (J% > PERIOD%) THEN J%=J%-PERIOD% : GOTO 940
950                      FJ#=F#(J%)
960                      DFI#=(TD0#+TG#)*FJ#
970                      D1#=TD0#
980                      TD0#=TRYA*(DI#/FJ#)+(1-TRYA)*(D1#+TG#)
```

PROGRAM 10.1 (continued)

```
990                  FJ#=TRYC*(DI#/TD0#)+(1-TRYC)*FJ#
1000                 F#(J%)=FJ#
1010                 TG#=TRYB*(TD0#-D1#)+(1-TRYB)*TG#
1020                 MAD#=MAD#+ABS(DFI#-DI#)
1030                 J%=J%+1
1040                 NEXT I%
1050          MAD#=MAD#/NOD%
1060          IF (MAD# < MINI#) THEN MINI#=MAD# : A=TRYA : C=TRYC : B=TRYB
                  ELSE TRYB=3!
1070          WEND
1080      TRYB=0!
1090      WEND
1100  TRYC=0!
1110  WEND
1120  RETURN
1130  '------------------ FORECAST HISTORICAL DATA -----------------------
1140  MAD#=0!
1150  TEMP=0 : J%=1
1160  FOR I%=1 TO NOD%
1170       DI#=D#(I%)
1180       IF (J% > PERIOD%) THEN J%=J%-PERIOD% : GOTO 1180
1190       FJ#=F#(J%)
1200       TEMP=(I%-1)*TEMP+ABS(D#(I%)/FJ#-(D0#+G#))
1210       TEMP=TEMP/I% : W(I%)=TEMP
1220       DF#(I%)=(D0#+G#)*FJ#
1230       D1#=D0#
1240       D0#=A*(DI#/FJ#)+(1-A)*(D1#+G#)
1250       FJ#=C*(DI#/D0#)+(1-C)*FJ#
1260       F#(J%)=FJ#
1270       G#=B*(D0#-D1#)+(1-B)*G#
1280       J%=J%+1
1290       NEXT I%
1300  RETURN
1310  '------------------------- RESULTS MENU ----------------------------
1320  SCREEN 0:CLS : LOCATE 6,1
1330  PRINT TAB(10) "*********** WINTERS' RESULTS MENU ***********"
1340  PRINT
1350  PRINT TAB(10) "*   _ TABULATE SMOOTHING FACTORS                *"
1360  PRINT TAB(10) "*   _ TABULATE OBSERVED & FORECAST VALUES       *"
1370  PRINT TAB(10) "*   _ TABULATE FORECAST & CONFIDENCE INTERVAL   *"
1380  PRINT TAB(10) "*   _ PLOT OBSERVED & FORECAST VALUES           *"
1390  PRINT TAB(10) "*   _ PLOT RESIDUAL VS TIME                     *"
1400  PRINT TAB(10) "*   _ EXIT                                      *"
1410  PRINT
1420  PRINT TAB(10) "***********************************************": BEEP
1430  X%=8+DX2% : Y%=14: LOCATE X%,Y%,1,0,7
1440  FIRST%=8 : LAST%=13
1450  ANS$=INKEY$ : IF ANS$="" THEN 1450
1460  IF ANS$=CHR$(0)+CHR$(80) THEN IF X%<LAST% THEN X%=X%+1 ELSE X%=FIRST%
1470  IF ANS$=CHR$(0)+CHR$(72) THEN IF X%>FIRST% THEN X%=X%-1 ELSE X%=LAST%
1480  LOCATE X%,Y%: IF ANS$<>CHR$(13) THEN 1450
1490  FLAG%=CSRLIN : FLAG%=FLAG%-7
1500  PRINT
1510  ON FLAG% GOSUB 3210,1630,1950,3480,3770,1540
1520  IF FLAG% <>6 THEN 1320
1530  DX%=7 : DX2%=0
1540  RETURN
1550  '----------------------- PRINT HEADING ----------------------------
1560  CLS : PRINT TAB(10) "PERIOD";
1570  PRINT TAB(33) "OBSERVED";
1580  PRINT TAB(53) "FORECAST";
1590  PRINT TAB(71) "RESIDUAL"
1600  FOR II%=1 TO 80 : PRINT "-"; : NEXT
1610  RETURN
1620  '----------------------- TABULATE RESULTS ------------------------
1630  LOCATE ,,0
1640  GOSUB 1560
1650  MAD#=0!: S#=0!
1660  FOR I%=1 TO NOD%
1670  PRINT USING "#############";I%;
1680  PRINT TAB(21) USING "################.###";D#(I%);
1690  PRINT USING "################.###";DF#(I%);
1700  DIFF=D#(I%)-DF#(I%)
1710  MAD#=MAD#+ABS(DIFF)
1720  S#=S#+DIFF*DIFF
1730  PRINT USING "##############.###";DIFF
1740  IF (I% MOD 20 <> 0) AND (I% <= NOD%) THEN 1790
1750  BEEP
1760  ANS$=INKEY$ : IF ANS$="" THEN 1760
1770  CLS
```

PROGRAM 10.1 (continued)

```
1780  GOSUB 1560
1790  NEXT I%
1800  S#=S#/(NOD%-1) : MAD#=MAD#/NOD%
1810  PRINT
1820  PRINT "MEAN ABSOLUTE DEVIATION : MAD = ";CSNG(MAD#)
1830  PRINT "MEAN SQUARED ERROR      : MSE = ";CSNG(S#);: BEEP
1840  ANS$=INKEY$ : IF ANS$="" THEN 1840
1850  DX2%=2 : RETURN
1860  '-----------------------  PRINT HEADING  ---------------------------
1870  CLS
1880  PRINT "PERIOD";
1890  PRINT TAB(20) "FORECAST";
1900  PRINT TAB(47) USING "##";CI%;
1910  PRINT " %     CONFIDENCE      INTERVAL"
1920  FOR II%=1 TO 80 : PRINT "-"; : NEXT
1930  RETURN
1940  '--------------------  TABULATE CONFIDENCE INTERVAL  ----------------
1950  LOCATE ,,0 : J%=BGN% : T%=0 : COUNT%=0
1960  GOSUB 1870
1970  FOR I%=BGN% TO LST%
1980       COUNT%=COUNT%+1
1990       PRINT USING "####";I%;
2000       PRINT USING "###################.###";DF#(I%);
2010       IF AHEAD%<>1 THEN T%=T%+1 ELSE T%=1
2020       GOSUB 2290
2030       J%=J%+1
2040       PRINT TAB(35) USING "#################.###";LB;
2050       PRINT "  --";
2060       PRINT USING "#################.###";UB
2070       IF COUNT% MOD 20 <> 0 THEN 2110
2080       BEEP
2090       ANS$=INKEY$ : IF ANS$="" THEN 2090
2100       GOSUB 1870
2110       NEXT I%
2120  BEEP
2130  ANS$=INKEY$ : IF ANS$="" THEN 2130
2140  DX2%=3 : RETURN
2150  '--------------------  DO FORECASTS  --------------------------------
2160  CLS : INPUT "HOW MANY PERIODS AHEAD FORECASTS";AHEAD%
2170 BGN%=NOD%+1 : LST%=NOD%+AHEAD%
2180 J%=NOD%+1
2190 FOR I%=NOD%+1 TO NOD%+AHEAD%
2200        IF (J% > PERIOD%) THEN J%=J%-PERIOD% : GOTO 2200
2210     W(I%)=W(NOD%)
2220     DF#(I%)=(D0#+G#*(I%-NOD%))*F#(J%)
2230     J%=J%+1
2240     NEXT
2250 GOSUB 1950
2260 DX%=8
2270 RETURN
2280 '------------------------  CONFIDENCE INTERVAL  ----------------------
2290 X=A : IF (C > X) THEN X=C
2300 IF (B > X) THEN X=B
2310 Y=1-X
2320 TEMP1=(1+Y)*(1+Y)*(1+Y) : TEMP2=1+4*Y+5*Y*Y
2330 TEMP3=(1+3*Y)*2*X : TEMP4=2*X*X
2340 TEMP5=TEMP4*T*T : TEMP6=X/TEMP1
2350 TEMP7=TEMP2+TEMP3*T+TEMP5 : TEMP8=1+TEMP6*TEMP7
2360 TEMP9=TEMP2+TEMP3+TEMP4 : TEMP0=TEMP8/(1+TEMP6*TEMP9)
2370 D=1.25*SQR(TEMP0) : E=Z*D*W(I%-1)
2380 LB=DF#(I%)-E : UB=DF#(I%)+E
2390 RETURN
2400 '-----------------------  CONFIDENCE LEVEL MENU  --------------------
2410 CLS : SCREEN 0 : LOCATE 6,1
2420 PRINT TAB(20) "***  CONFIDENCE LEVEL MENU ***"
2430 PRINT
2440 PRINT TAB(20) "*           _ 99 %          *"
2450 PRINT TAB(20) "*           _ 98 %          *"
2460 PRINT TAB(20) "*           _ 95 %          *"
2470 PRINT TAB(20) "*           _ 90 %          *"
2480 PRINT TAB(20) "*           _ 80 %          *"
2490 PRINT TAB(20) "*           _ 50 %          *"
2500 PRINT TAB(20) "*           _ EXIT          *"
2510 PRINT
2520 PRINT TAB(20) "******************************" : BEEP
2530 X%=8 : Y%=31: LOCATE X%,Y%,1,0,7
2540 FIRST%=8 : LAST%=14
2550 ANS$=INKEY$ : IF ANS$="" THEN 2550
2560 IF ANS$=CHR$(0)+CHR$(80) THEN IF X%<LAST% THEN X%=X%+1 ELSE X%=FIRST%
2570 IF ANS$=CHR$(0)+CHR$(72) THEN IF X%>FIRST% THEN X%=X%-1 ELSE X%=LAST%
```

PROGRAM 10.1 (continued)

```
2580 LOCATE X%,Y% : IF ANS$<> CHR$(13) THEN 2550
2590 FLAG%=CSRLIN : FLAG%=FLAG%-7
2600 ON FLAG% GOSUB 2670,2660,2650,2640,2630,2620,2610
2610 RETURN
2620 CI%=50 : DX%=2 : Z=0    : RETURN
2630 CI%=80 : DX%=2 : Z=.84  : RETURN
2640 CI%=90 : DX%=2 : Z=1.65 : RETURN
2650 CI%=95 : DX%=2 : Z=1.96 : RETURN
2660 CI%=98 : DX%=2 : Z=2.06 : RETURN
2670 CI%=99 : DX%=2 : Z=2.56 : RETURN
2680 '------------------------ CHANGE DEFAULT DRIVE ---------------------
2690 IF FD$="A:" THEN FD$="B:" ELSE IF FD$="B:" THEN FD$="C:" ELSE FD$="A:"
2700 LOCATE 5,75: PRINT FD$ : BEEP
2710 RETURN
2720 '------------------------- DATA EDITOR ----------------------------
2730 CLS : BEEP
2740 INPUT "INPUT FILE NAME =";FILE$ : FILE$=FD$+FILE$
2750 IF FLAG1%=4 THEN NEWFILE%=1 ELSE NEWFILE%=0
2760 DX%=FLAG1% : SL%=100
2770 ORDER%=1 : ORDER$="ROW    ORDER"
2780 LEFT%=1 : RIGHT%=1 : COL%=1 : CORDER%=1
2790 CHAINFILE$=PD$+"AEDIT.BAS"         ' See Chapter 6 for program listing.
2800 CALLFILE$=PD$+"WINTER.BAS"
2810 COMMON NEWFILE%,FILE$,CALLFILE$,DX%,SL%,FD$,PD$,RIGHT%,
          LEFT%,COL%,CORDER%,ORDER%,ORDER$
2820 CHAIN CHAINFILE$
2830 RETURN
2840 '------------------------- READING FILE ---------------------------
2850 OPEN FILE$ FOR INPUT AS #2
2860 INPUT #2,NOD%,T1%,T2%
2870 FOR J%=1 TO NOD%
2880      INPUT #2,D#(J%)
2890     NEXT
2900 CLOSE #2
2910 RETURN
2920 '-------------------- FORECAST PERIOD MENU ------------------------
2930 SCREEN 0,1 : CLS : LOCATE 6,1
2940 PRINT TAB(20) "******  FORECAST PERIOD MENU  ******"
2950 PRINT
2960 PRINT TAB(20) "*             _ QUARTERLY           *"
2970 PRINT TAB(20) "*             _ MONTHLY             *"
2980 PRINT TAB(20) "*             _ WEEKLY              *"
2990 PRINT TAB(20) "*             _ OTHERS              *"
3000 PRINT TAB(20) "*             _ EXIT                *"
3010 PRINT
3020 PRINT TAB(20) "************************************" : BEEP
3030 X%=8 : Y%=31: LOCATE X%,Y%,1,0,7
3040 FIRST%=8 : LAST%=12
3050 ANS$=INKEY$ : IF ANS$="" THEN 3050
3060 IF ANS$=CHR$(0)+CHR$(80) THEN IF X%<LAST% THEN X%=X%+1 ELSE X%=FIRST%
3070 IF ANS$=CHR$(0)+CHR$(72) THEN IF X%>FIRST% THEN X%=X%-1 ELSE X%=LAST%
3080 LOCATE X%,Y%: IF ANS$<>CHR$(13) THEN 3050
3090 FLAG%=CSRLIN : FLAG%=FLAG%-7
3100 ON FLAG% GOSUB 3140,3150,3160,3170,3110
3110 DX%=3
3120 RETURN
3130 '----------------------- SELECT FORECAST PERIOD --------------------
3140 PRD$="QUART " : PERIOD%=4 : RETURN
3150 PRD$="MONTH " : PERIOD%=12 : RETURN
3160 PRD$="WEEK  " : PERIOD%=52 : RETURN
3170 CLS : INPUT "NUMBER OF PERIODS IN A SEASONAL CYCLE";PERIOD%
3180 PRD$="OTHERS"
3190 RETURN
3200 '--------------------- TABULATE SMOOTHING FACTORS -----------------
3210 CLS : FOR I%=1 TO 75 : PRINT "-";: NEXT
3220 PRINT "SMOOTHING CONSTANTS :"
3230 PRINT "     * SMOOTHING CONSTANT FOR AVERAGE      : ALPHA =";
3240 PRINT USING "##.##";A
3250 PRINT "     * SMOOTHING CONSTANT FOR TREND        : BETA  =";
3260 PRINT USING "##.##";B
3270 PRINT "     * SMOOTHING CONSTANT FOR SEASONALITY  : GAMMA =";
3280 PRINT USING "##.##";C
3290 PRINT
3300 PRINT "SMOOTHED AVERAGE     : (A0) =";
3310 PRINT USING "################.###";D0#
3320 PRINT "TREND FACTOR         : (B0) =";
3330 PRINT USING "################.###";G#
3340 PRINT "SEASONALITY FACTORS :"
3350 FLAG%=0 : COUNT%=9
3360 FOR I%=1 TO PERIOD%
```

PROGRAM 10.1 (continued)

```
3370      COUNT%=COUNT%+1
3380      IF COUNT%>22 THEN FLAG%=1 : ANS$=INKEY$ : IF ANS$="" THEN 3380
3390      IF FLAG%=1 THEN CLS : COUNT%=1 : FLAG%=0
3400      PRINT "    F[";: PRINT USING "##";I%;: PRINT "]= ";
3410      PRINT USING "##.###";F#(I%)
3420      NEXT
3430 FOR I%=1 TO 75 : PRINT "-";: NEXT : LOCATE,,0 : BEEP
3440 ANS$=INKEY$ : IF ANS$="" THEN 3440
3450 DX2%=1
3460 RETURN
3470 '----------------------- PLOT DATA --------------------------------
3480 CLS : FILE2$=FD$+"TEMP.DAT"
3490 INPUT "PLOT WITH GRID LINES < N FOR NO >";ANS$
3500 ANS$=LEFT$(ANS$,1) : IF ANS$="N" OR ANS$="n" THEN GRD$="N" ELSE GRD$="G"
3510 FILESTK$(1)=FILE2$
3520 OPEN FILE2$ FOR OUTPUT AS #2
3530 PRINT #2,NOD%;NOD%;2
3540 FOR J%=1 TO NOD%
3550      PRINT #2,D#(J%)
3560      NEXT
3570 FOR J%=1 TO NOD%
3580      PRINT #2,J%;
3590      NEXT
3600 CLOSE #2
3610 FILE2$=FD$+"TEMP1.DAT"
3620 FILESTK$(2)=FILE2$
3630 OPEN FILE2$ FOR OUTPUT AS #2
3640 PRINT #2, NOD%;;NOD%;2
3650 FOR J%=1 TO NOD%
3660      PRINT #2, DF#(J%);
3670      NEXT
3680 FOR J%=1 TO NOD%
3690      PRINT #2, J%;
3700      NEXT
3710 CLOSE #2
3720 NOF%=2 : CURVE$(1)="P" : CURVE$(2)="C" : FLAG%=7
3730 FILE2$=PD$+"APLOT.BAS" : PFILE$=PD$+"WINTER.BAS" : SL%=140
3740 CHAIN FILE2$,,ALL     ' See Chapter 7 for program listing of APLOT.
3750 RETURN
3760 '----------------------- PLOT RESIDUAL ----------------------------
3770 CLS : FILE2$=FD$+"TEMP.DAT"
3780 INPUT "PLOT WITH GRID LINES < N FOR NO >";ANS$
3790 ANS$=LEFT$(ANS$,1) : IF ANS$="N" OR ANS$="n" THEN GRD$="N" ELSE GRD$="G"
3800 FILESTK$(1)=FILE2$
3810 OPEN FILE2$ FOR OUTPUT AS #2
3820 PRINT #2,NOD%;NOD%;2
3830 FOR J%=1 TO NOD%
3840      PRINT #2,D#(J%)-DF#(J%)
3850      NEXT
3860 FOR J%=1 TO NOD%
3870      PRINT #2,J%;
3880      NEXT
3890 CLOSE #2
3900 NOF%=1 : CURVE$(1)="P" :FLAG%=7
3910 FILE2$=PD$+"APLOT.BAS" : PFILE$=PD$+"WINTER.BAS" : SL%=140
3920 CHAIN FILE2$,,ALL
3930 RETURN
3940 END
```

PROGRAM 10.1 Winters' Model

EXERCISES

10.1 The following data represent monthly wine sales (in millions of bottles) for the past three years.

a) Using the first two years of data, determine appropriate starting parameters for the Winters' model.

b) Forecast the monthly wine sales in year 4 using the parameters in (a).

c) How well does this model seem to perform?

Year	Month											
	Jan.	Feb.	Mar.	Apr.	May	June	July	Aug.	Sept.	Oct.	Nov.	Dec.
1	2.82	2.67	2.76	2.72	3.21	3.40	2.31	2.22	2.93	4.52	5.93	7.35
2	2.54	2.53	3.03	3.27	4.12	3.73	3.15	2.45	2.97	4.76	6.85	8.29
3	3.12	3.04	4.15	3.87	4.25	4.76	4.17	2.36	3.53	5.59	7.87	9.41
4	?											

10.2 The following data represent gas consumption by households in a metropolitan area of Ontario. (The data are adapted from [4]).

Year	Month					
	Jan.	Feb.	Mar.	Apr.	May	June
1	196	196	173	105	75	39
2	227	217	197	110	88	51
3	216	218	193	120	99	59

Year	Month					
	July	Aug.	Sept.	Oct.	Nov.	Dec.
1	13	20	37	73	108	191
2	27	23	41	90	107	172
3	33	37	59	95	128	201

a) Using the Winters' seasonal smoothing model, forecast the consumption in year 4. Use the initialization procedures outlined in the chapter.

b) Plot the demand data along with the forecasted values for the Winters' model. Discuss your results briefly.

REFERENCES

1. Bowerman, B. L., and R. T. O'Connell, *Forecasting and Time Series,* Duxbury Press, North Scituate, Mass., 1979 (Chapter 7).

2. Hines, W. W., and D. C. Montgomery, *Probability and Statistics in Engineering and Management Science,* 2nd ed., John Wiley, 1980 (Chapter 13).

3. Montgomery, D. C., and L. A. Johnson, *Forecasting and Time Series Analysis,* McGraw-Hill, 1976 (Chapter 5).

4. Peterson, R., and E. A. Silver, *Decision Systems for Inventory Management and Production Planning,* Wiley, New York, 1979 (Chapter 4).

5. Winters, P. R., "Forecasting Sales by Exponentially Weighted Moving Averages," *Management Science* **6** (3) 324–342, 1960.

CHAPTER ELEVEN
Multiple Regression Analysis

In many engineering and business problems there are two or more variables that are inherently related, and it is necessary to explore the nature of this relationship. Regression analysis is a statistical technique for modeling and investigating the relationship between two or more variables.

In this chapter, we will discuss regression models that contain multiple independent variables, as well as the constant terms (i.e., multiple regression models). We will begin by describing the format of the classical multiple regressional model and explaining with a simple example how the least squares parameter estimates can be obtained from the model. We will then discuss how one interprets regression coefficients and statistics in the multiple regression model, with particular emphasis on the various plots of regression statistics that can aid in analyzing the model.

11.1 MULTIPLE REGRESSION MODEL

Matrix algebra provides a clear and concise means of describing the techniques of regression analysis. We presume that the reader has a prior knowledge of matrix algebra, and make no attempt to describe or prove its basic theorems. These materials are clearly presented in other textbooks, which should provide an ample review for the interested reader [3].

11.1.1 MODEL REPRESENTATION

Suppose we desire to find a relationship between a dependent variable y and several independent variables, say $x_1, x_2, \ldots, x_k$. An appropriate model might be

$$y = b_0 + b_1x_1 + b_2x_2 + \ldots + b_kx_k + e \quad \textbf{(11.1)}$$

where $b_0, b_1, \ldots, b_k$ are unknown parameters and e is a random error component. If a constant term is used for the ith parameter in the model, $x_i = 1$. Equation (11.1) is often called a multiple linear regression model. There are $k + 1$ unknown parameters to be estimated, $b_0, b_1, b_2, \ldots, b_k$.

Any linear relationship between the unknown parameters can be expressed in the form of Eq. (11.1). For example, if the independent variable is a time series y_t that is a polynomial function of time,

$$y_t = b_0 + b_1 + b_2t + b_3t^2 + b_4t^3 + e_t\,, \quad \textbf{(11.2)}$$

then we may write $x_1 = 1, x_2 = t, x_3 = t^2, x_4 = t^3$. Thus we see that Eq. (11.2) can be expressed in the form of the multiple linear regression model of Eq. (11.1).

Certain time series may require more complex functions of time as independent variables. One such time series is

$$y = \exp(b_0 + b_1x_1 + b_2x_2) \cdot e \quad \textbf{(11.3)}$$

By taking the logarithms of both sides, this exponential model can be transformed to

$$\log y = b_0 + b_1x_1 + b_2x_2 + \log e\,. \quad \textbf{(11.4)}$$

A reciprocal model such as

$$y = \frac{1}{b_0 + b_1x_1 + b_2x_2 + e}\,. \quad \textbf{(11.5)}$$

can be transformed to

$$\frac{1}{y} = b_0 + b_1x_1 + b_2x_2 + e\,. \quad \textbf{(11.6)}$$

In general, any regression model that is linear in the parameters (the b values) is a linear regression model, regardless of the shape of the surface that it generates.

11.1.2 ESTIMATION OF THE MODEL PARAMETERS

We will assume that the general model is of the form of Eq. (11.1) and that there are n observations on the dependent variable. The model, written in terms of the observations, is

$$y_j = b_0 + b_1 x_{1j} + b_2 x_{2j} + \ldots + b_k x_{kj} + e_j \tag{11.7}$$

where $j = 1, 2, \ldots, n$ and x_{ij} denotes the jth level or value taken on by the ith independent variable. The term x_{ij} is frequently called the regressor variable. Note that $n > k + 1$ to estimate the parameter b_i. We may summarize the regression data elements in matrix form. To represent Eq. (11.7) in matrix form, we first define

$$\mathbf{y} = \begin{bmatrix} y_1 \\ \cdot \\ \cdot \\ \cdot \\ y_n \end{bmatrix}, \quad \mathbf{b} = \begin{bmatrix} b_0 \\ \cdot \\ \cdot \\ \cdot \\ b_k \end{bmatrix}, \quad \mathbf{x} = \begin{bmatrix} 1 & x_{11} & \ldots & x_{k1} \\ \cdot & \cdot & & \cdot \\ \cdot & \cdot & & \cdot \\ \cdot & \cdot & & \cdot \\ 1 & x_{1n} & \cdots & x_{kn} \end{bmatrix}, \quad \mathbf{e} = \begin{bmatrix} e_1 \\ \cdot \\ \cdot \\ \cdot \\ e_n \end{bmatrix}$$

With this notation, Eq. (11.7) can be expressed in the compact matrix form

$$\boldsymbol{y} = \boldsymbol{Xb} + \boldsymbol{e}\,. \tag{11.8}$$

An appropriate estimation criterion is to use the method of least squares, which minimizes the sum of the squares of the errors. The sum of the squares of the errors is defined as

$$\text{SSE} = \sum_{j=1}^{n} e_j^2 = \sum_{j=1}^{n} \left(y_j - \sum_{i=0}^{k} b_i x_{ij} \right)^2. \tag{11.9}$$

In terms of our matrix notation this becomes

$$\begin{aligned} \text{SSE} &= (\mathbf{y} - \mathbf{Xb})'(\mathbf{y} - \mathbf{Xb}) \\ &= \mathbf{y}'\mathbf{y} - 2\mathbf{bXy} + \mathbf{b}'\mathbf{X}'\mathbf{Xb} \end{aligned} \tag{11.10}$$

where a prime on a vector or matrix denotes its transpose. To determine the least squares estimators, we minimize SSE by differentiating with respect to **b**, equating to 0, and solving for **b**:

$$\begin{aligned} \frac{\partial\, \text{SSE}}{\partial\, \mathbf{b}} \bigg|\, \hat{\mathbf{b}} &= -2\mathbf{X}'\mathbf{y} + 2\mathbf{X}'\mathbf{X}\hat{\mathbf{b}} = 0 \\ \hat{\mathbf{b}} &= (\mathbf{X}'\mathbf{X}^{-1})\mathbf{X}'\mathbf{y}\,. \end{aligned} \tag{11.11}$$

The estimated regression model is

$$\hat{\mathbf{y}} = \mathbf{X}\hat{\mathbf{b}}, \tag{11.12}$$

and the difference between the observation y_j and the estimated value $\hat{y}_j$ is a residual (error), say $e_j = y_j - \hat{y}_j$. The $(n \times 1)$ vector of residuals is denoted by

$$\mathbf{e} = \mathbf{y} - \hat{\mathbf{y}}\,. \tag{11.13}$$

11.1.3 NUMERICAL EXAMPLE

Consider the problem of finding the least squares estimates of the parameters for the regression function $y = b_0 + b_1x_1 + b_2x_2$ where the variables y, x_1, and x_2 represent the following:

y = car mileage performance,
x_1 = the units of gas treatment product A added to the gasoline,
x_2 = the units of gas treatment product B added to the gasoline.

A series of experiments, which assigned 0, 1, and 2 units of the two different products in all possible combinations, produce the following data.

	1	2	3	4	5	6	7	8	9
y_j	18	23	24	28	30	26	30	32	35
x_{1j}	0	1	2	0	1	2	0	1	2
x_{2j}	0	0	0	1	1	1	2	2	2

We may rewrite our regression equation in the form of Eq. (11.7) by choosing $k = 2$. Then we calculate the matrix $\mathbf{X}'\mathbf{X}$ where

$$\mathbf{X}' = \begin{bmatrix} 1 & 1 & 1 & 1 & 1 & 1 & 1 & 1 & 1 \\ 0 & 1 & 2 & 0 & 1 & 2 & 0 & 1 & 2 \\ 0 & 0 & 0 & 1 & 1 & 1 & 2 & 2 & 2 \end{bmatrix}.$$

The result of such calculations is the matrix

$$\mathbf{X}'\mathbf{X} = \begin{bmatrix} 9 & 9 & 9 \\ 9 & 15 & 9 \\ 9 & 9 & 15 \end{bmatrix}.$$

The inverse is calculated

$$(\mathbf{X}'\mathbf{X})^{-1} = \begin{bmatrix} \frac{4}{9} & -\frac{1}{6} & -\frac{1}{6} \\ -\frac{1}{6} & \frac{1}{6} & 0 \\ -\frac{1}{6} & 0 & \frac{1}{6} \end{bmatrix}.$$

We then calculate $\mathbf{X}'\mathbf{y}$ to find

$$\mathbf{X}'\mathbf{y} = \begin{bmatrix} 246 \\ 255 \\ 278 \end{bmatrix}.$$

Finally we calculate $(\mathbf{X}'\mathbf{X})^{-1}\,\mathbf{X}'\mathbf{y}$ to obtain

$$\hat{\mathbf{b}} = \begin{bmatrix} 20.50 \\ 1.50 \\ 5.33 \end{bmatrix}.$$

The least squares estimate of the regression function is therefore given by the equation

$$\mathbf{y} = 20.5 + 1.5x_1 + 5.33x_2 .$$

11.2 STATISTICAL PROPERTIES OF THE REGRESSION MODEL

11.2.1 IMPORTANT STATISTICAL RESULTS

Deriving the statistical properties of the multiple regression model is a rather lengthy process, so we provide here simply a summary of the important results. Based on these results, we will assess the adequacy of the multiple regression model.

1. The least squares estimator of each coefficient b_i, $i = 0, 1, \ldots, k$ is the best linear unbiased estimator.
2. The error variance $\text{VAR}(e) = \sigma^2$ can be estimated by the mean squares error (MSE):

$$\hat{\sigma}^2 = \frac{\text{SSE}}{n - (k + 1)} \equiv \text{MSE} \qquad \textbf{(11.14)}$$

   where n = number of observations and k = number of independent variables in the model.
3. The estimated regression parameters $\hat{b}_i$, normalized by subtracting the mean and dividing by $\hat{\sigma}$, follow the t-distribution with $n - k - 1$ degrees of freedom:

$$\frac{\hat{b}_i - b_i}{\hat{\sigma}\sqrt{C_{ii}}}, \qquad i = 0, 1, \ldots, k \qquad \textbf{(11.15)}$$

   where C_{ii} is the diagonal element of $(\mathbf{X}'\mathbf{X})$ corresponding to $\hat{b}_i$.

11.2.2 SIGNIFICANCE OF THE MODEL PARAMETERS

Before a multiple regression model is used to predict future observations, we should be certain that all the parameters in the model are statistically significant. A nonsignificant parameter is assumed to be zero and would be eliminated from the model. Several statistical tests can be employed if the errors are normally distributed.

The *F*-test. The overall significance of the regression model may be tested by computing the statistic

$$F = \frac{\sum_{j=1}^{n} \frac{(\hat{y}_j - \bar{y})^2}{k}}{\hat{\sigma}^2}. \tag{11.16}$$

where $\bar{y} = \frac{1}{n}\Sigma y_j$ is the average of the y_js. F is compared to the upper α percentage point of the F-distribution with k and $n - k - 1$ degrees of freedom (denoted by $F_{\alpha,k,n-k-1}$). If $F > F_{\alpha,k,n-k-1}$, at least one parameter in the model is significant. On the other hand, if $F < F_{\alpha,k,n-k-1}$, all parameters in the model are zero and a poor regression model has been constructed.

The *t*-test. The significance of individual regression parameters may be examined by performing t-tests. To test the significance of the model parameter b_i, we use the statistic computed in Eq. (11.15), assuming $b_i = 0$:

$$t = \frac{\hat{b}_i}{\hat{\sigma}\sqrt{C_{ii}}}. \tag{11.17}$$

If $|t| > t_{\alpha/2,n-k-1}$, the parameter b_i would be assumed to be nonzero at the level of $100(1-\alpha)$ percent confidence.

11.2.3 CONFIDENCE INTERVALS

To develop a procedure for obtaining confidence interval estimates of b_i, we must assume the error e_j is normally and independently distributed with mean zero and variance σ^2. From the result shown in Eq. (11.14), a $100(1 - \alpha)$ percent confidence interval for the regression coefficient b_i, $i = 0, \ldots, k$, is defined by

$$\hat{b}_i - t_{\alpha/2,n-k-1}\sqrt{\hat{\sigma}^2 C_{ii}} \le b_i \le \hat{b}_i + t_{\alpha/2,n-k-1}\sqrt{\hat{\sigma}^2 C_{ii}}, \tag{11.18}$$

where $t_{\alpha/2,n-k-1}$ is the upper $\alpha/2$ percentage point of the t-distribution with $n - k - 1$ degrees of freedom.

The confidence interval in Eq. (11.18) might be more properly called a two-sided confidence interval, as it specifies both a lower and upper limit on b_i. The length of the observed confidence interval measures the quality of the information obtained from the sample. The longer the confidence interval, the more confident we are that the interval actually contains the value of b_i. On the other hand, the longer the interval, the less information we have about the true value of b_i. Ideally we want to obtain a relatively short interval with high confidence.

11.2.4 PREDICTION OF NEW OBSERVATIONS

The regression model can be used to predict future observations of y corresponding to particular values of the independent variables, say $\mathbf{x}'_\tau = [x_{1\tau}, x_{2\tau}, \ldots, x_{k\tau}]$. A point estimate of the future observation y_τ at $\mathbf{x}'_\tau$ is calculated by

$$\hat{y}_\tau = \mathbf{x}'_\tau \hat{\mathbf{b}} . \qquad \mathbf{(11.19)}$$

Now consider an interval estimate of this future observation y_τ. The new observation is independent of the observations used to develop the regression model. Thus a $100(1 - \alpha)$ percent *prediction interval* for this future observation is defined by

$$\hat{y}_\tau \pm t_{\alpha/2, n-k-1} S , \qquad \mathbf{(11.20)}$$

where

$$S = \sqrt{\hat{\sigma}^2(1 + \mathbf{x}'_\tau(\mathbf{X}'\mathbf{X})^{-1}\mathbf{x}_\tau} .$$

11.3 MEASURE OF MODEL ADEQUACY

Model validation is an important part of building a multiple regression model. The residuals of a regression help provide a useful measure of the extent to which the estimated regression line fits the sample data points. Roughly speaking, a good regression equation is one that explains a large proportion of the variance of y. In this section, we will explain how the residual information can be used to validate the regression model.

11.3.1 GOODNESS OF FIT BY R^2

It is frequently useful to summarize the breakdown of the variation of y in terms of an *analysis of variance.* To do this, we break down the difference between y_j and its mean $\bar{y}$ as follows:

$$(y_j - \bar{y}) = (y_j - \hat{y}_j) + (\hat{y}_j - \bar{y}) . \qquad \mathbf{(11.21)}$$

Squaring both sides and summing over all observations (1 to n) we obtain

$$\Sigma(y_j - \bar{y})^2 = \Sigma(y_j - \hat{y}_j)^2 + \Sigma(\hat{y}_j - \bar{y})^2 . \qquad \mathbf{(11.22)}$$

Using the standard statistical terminology, Eq. (11.21) is defined as

TSS	=	SSE	+	SSR
Total sum of squares		Residual sum of squares		Regression sum of squares

The two components of TSS measure the amount of variability in the y accounted for by the regression model and the residual variation left unexplained by the regression model. We use the components to calculate R^2 as follows:

$$R^2 = \frac{\text{SSR}}{\text{TSS}} = 1 - \frac{\text{SSE}}{\text{TSS}}. \tag{11.23}$$

R^2 measures the proportion of the variation in y "explained" by the multiple regression model. It ranges in value from 0 to 1. In the context of our discussion, R^2 is only a *descriptive statistic.* Roughly speaking, we associate a high value of R^2 with a good fit of the regression model and a low value with a poor fit. (The statistic R^2 should be used with caution because it is always possible to make R^2 equal to 1 by simply adding enough terms to the model. Also, R^2 will always increase if we add a variable to the model, but this does not necessarily mean the new model is superior to the old model. For more discussion on this subject, see [3]).

11.3.2 RESIDUAL ANALYSIS

Analysis of the residuals, defined by Eq. (11.13), can also provide information helpful in checking the assumption that errors are normally and independently

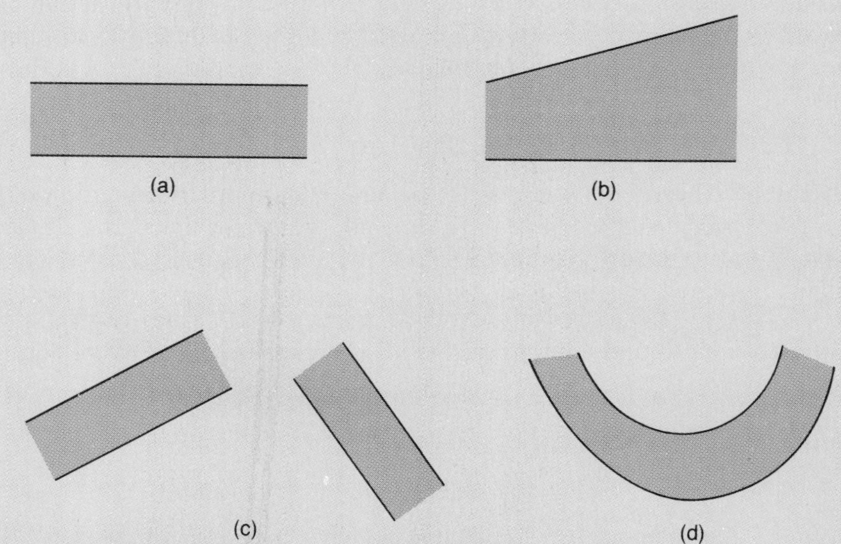

FIGURE 11.1 Patterns for residual plots: (a) is a normal pattern; (b), (c), and (d) are abnormal patterns.

distributed random variables with mean zero and variance σ^2 and in determining if additional terms would be desirable.

To do this, we may plot the residuals (1) in time sequence, (2) against the $\hat{y}_j$, and (3) against the independent variable x. These graphs will usually look like one of the four general patterns in Fig. 11.1. Draper and Smith [2] explain the characteristics of each pattern. Pattern (a) in Fig. 11.1 indicates the normal situation, while patterns (b), (c), and (d) represent anomalies. If a plot of residuals appears as in pattern (b), the variance of the observations may be increasing with time or with the magnitude of the y_j or x_i. If a plot of the residuals looks like pattern (c), the linear term must be added to the model. If a plot of the residuals looks like pattern (d), higher-order terms should be added to the model.

In the next section, we use the concepts discussed thus far in an interactive computer graphics program that performs multiple regression analysis.

11.4 DESCRIPTION OF THE MULTIPLE REGRESSION PROGRAM

11.4.1 PROGRAMMING LOGIC

The general programming logic for the multiple regression program, named REGR, is shown in Fig. 11.2. Program 11.1, which lists the complete code for REGR, appears at the end of this chapter along with definitions of the variable names used in the program. [Due to the IBM PC file specification convention (eight characters or less), we use a short filename REGR instead of REGRESSION.]

As in the WINTERS' program, the REGR program uses both the DATA EDITOR (AEDIT) and APLOT programs, which were developed in Chapter 6 and 7, respectively. A short program is written to create a data file for the t-table entries, which are required in computing the confidence interval estimates for the regression parameters. This program is shown in program 11.2. These three program files must be available before the user can run the REGR program. No additional programming is required of the user to link these files to REGR.

11.4.2 REGRESSION MODELING EXAMPLE

We will explain how to run the REGR program with the following example based on regression data from Bowerman and O'Connell [1].

Consider a problem in which we wish to examine the net sales of a plastic products company. We believe that the net sales of the product are closely

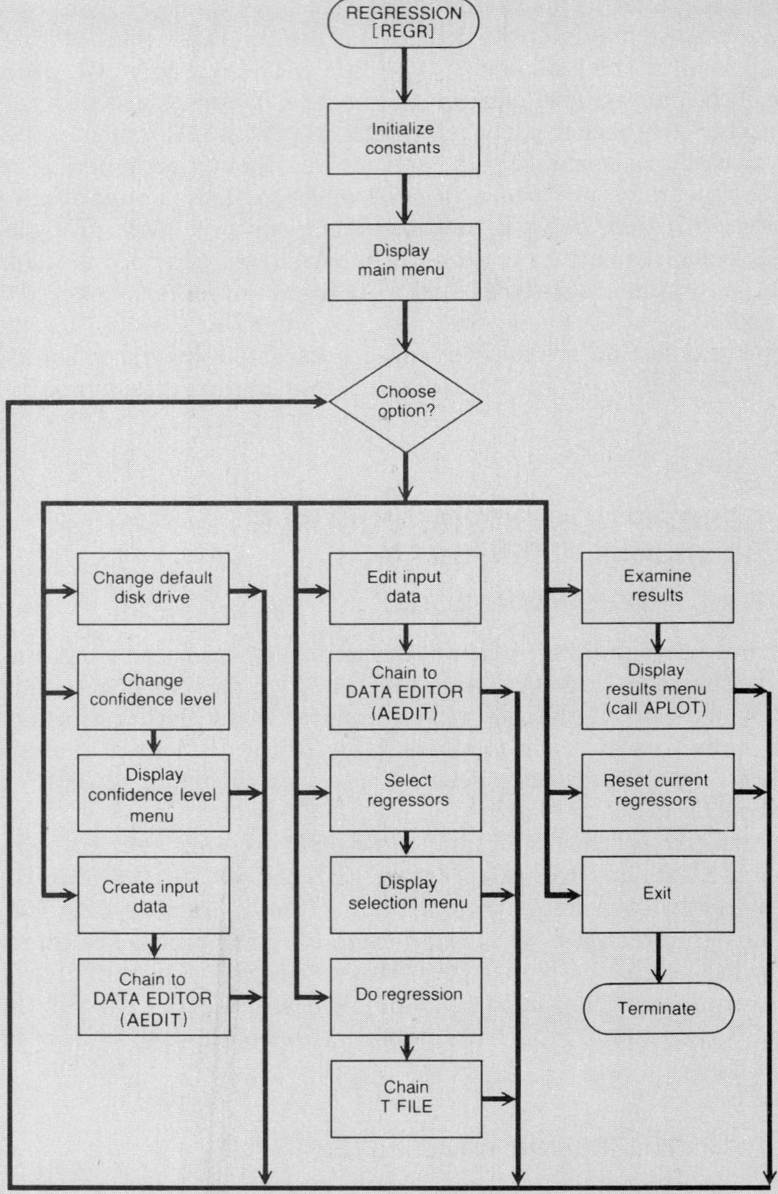

FIGURE 11.2 Programming logic for REGR

related to the price of the product, the automobile production, and the net sales of the cosmetics industry. These two industries are the major users of the company's products. Thus the following regression model is suggested:

$$y_t = b_0 + b_1 x_{1t} + b_2 x_{2t} + b_3 x_{3t} + e_t \tag{11.24}$$

where

y_t = the net sales of the product in week t,

x_{1t} = the price of the product in week t,

x_{2t} = the automobile production in week t,

x_{3t} = the net sales of the cosmetics industry in week t.

Note that x_{1t}, x_{2t}, and x_{3t} are time series; they are summarized in Table 11.1. We wish first to estimate the parameters b_i in order to test the adequacy of the model.

11.4.3 PROGRAM LOADING AND MENU SELECTION

When we load and execute the REGR program, the following prompt appears on the screen:

```
WHICH DISK DRIVE DOES CONTAIN REGR, AEDIT, AND APLOT?
DRIVE A IS ON YOUR LEFT,
DRIVE B IS ON YOUR RIGHT,
DRIVE C IS YOUR HARD DISK DRIVE.
ENTER [ A, B, OR C ]?
```

We then specify the drive where the diskette containing REGR, DATA EDITOR (AEDIT), and APLOT is located. (Be sure to have all the three files on the same diskette.) After we have specified the drive ("B" in our example), the following menu appears on the screen:

```
****** REGRESSION ANALYSIS MENU ******            STATUS
                                            ----------------------
*     _ CHANGE DEFAULT DISK DRIVE          *  DEFAULT DRIVE    = B:
*     _ CHANGE CONFIDENCE LEVEL            *  CONFIDENCE LEVEL= 95 %
*     _ CREATE INPUT FILE                  *  CURRENT REGRESSORS :
*     _ EDIT(EXAMINE) INPUT FILE           *  NONE
*     _ SELECT REGRESSORS                  *
*     _ DO REGRESSION                      *
*     _ EXAMINE RESULTS                    *
*     _ RESET CURRENT REGRESSORS           *
*     _ EXIT                               *
****************************************
```

TABLE 11.1 Input data

Period t	Demand y	Price ($) x_1	Automobile production (Unit = 1000) x_2	Net sales of the cosmetics industry (Unit = million dollars) x_3
1	7.38	3.85	3.80	5.50
2	8.51	3.75	4.00	6.75
3	9.52	3.70	4.30	7.25
4	7.50	3.70	3.70	5.50
5	9.33	3.60	3.85	7.00
6	8.28	3.60	3.80	6.50
7	8.75	3.60	3.75	6.75
8	7.87	3.80	3.85	5.25
9	7.10	3.80	3.65	5.25
10	8.00	3.85	4.00	6.00
11	7.89	3.90	4.10	6.50
12	8.15	3.90	4.00	6.25
13	9.10	3.70	4.10	7.00
14	8.86	3.75	4.20	6.90
15	8.90	3.75	4.10	6.80
16	8.87	3.80	4.10	6.80
17	9.26	3.70	4.20	7.10
18	9.00	3.80	4.30	7.00
19	8.75	3.70	4.10	6.80
20	7.95	3.80	3.75	6.50
21	7.65	3.80	3.75	6.25
22	7.27	3.75	3.65	6.00
23	8.00	3.70	3.90	6.50
24	8.50	3.55	3.65	7.00
25	8.75	3.60	4.10	6.80
26	9.21	3.65	4.25	6.80
27	8.27	3.70	3.65	6.50
28	7.67	3.75	3.75	5.75
29	7.93	3.80	3.85	5.80
30	9.26	3.70	4.25	6.80

The data are adapted from B. L. Bowerman and R. T. O'Connell, *Forecasting and Time Series*, Duxbury Press, North Scituate, Mass., 1979.

The menu display format is similar to that of the WINTERS' program in Chapter 10. Here, we have nine main menu items to pick from. We again use [↑] and [↓] keys to position the cursor and pick the menu item by pressing the [ENTER] key. System default status messages are also displayed on the right-hand side of the screen: default drive in use, confidence level being used in the statistical test, and current regressors—that is, the independent variables we are using to do the multiple regression analysis. The first two menu items (changing default disk drive and changing confidence level) are the same as in the WINTERS' program. (See Sections 10.3.4 and 10.3.5.) In the sections ahead, we will explain each remaining menu option in detail.

11.4.4 CREATING AN INPUT DATA FILE

When we select this option, the program chains the DATA EDITOR (AEDIT) program developed in Chapter 6. The REGR program then transfers control to the DATA EDITOR program and passes all control variables to it from the

```
          ( Y )          ( X1 )        COMMAND
 1 :      7.380          3.850         B BACKWARD
 2 :      8.510          3.750         C COLUMN
 3 :      9.520          3.700         D DOWN
 4 :      7.500          3.700         E EXIT
 5 :      9.330          3.600         F FORWARD
 6 :      8.280          3.600         I INSERT
 7 :      8.750          3.600         K KILL
 8 :      7.870          3.800         O ORDER
 9 :      7.100          3.800         R ROW
10 :      8.000          3.850         S SAVE
11 :      7.890          3.900         U UP
12 :      8.150          3.900
13 :      9.100          3.700
14 :      8.860          3.750
15 :      8.900          3.750
16 :      8.870          3.800
17 :      9.260          3.700
18 :      9.000          3.800

COMMAND :?                             ROW      ORDER
                                       DEFAULT CMD : D
```

```
          ( Y )          ( X1 )        COMMAND
19 :      8.750          3.700         B BACKWARD
20 :      7.950          3.800         C COLUMN
21 :      7.650          3.800         D DOWN
22 :      7.270          3.750         E EXIT
23 :      8.000          3.700         F FORWARD
24 :      8.500          3.550         I INSERT
25 :      8.750          3.600         K KILL
26 :      9.210          3.650         O ORDER
27 :      8.270          3.700         R ROW
28 :      7.670          3.750         S SAVE
29 :      7.930          3.800         U UP
30 :      9.260          3.700
31 :
32 :
33 :
34 :
35 :
36 :

COMMAND :?                             ROW      ORDER
                                       DEFAULT CMD : D
```

FIGURE 11.3 Scrolling data pages

```
                     ( X2 )    |    ( X3 )    |     COMMAND
 1 :                  3.800    |     5.500    |  B BACKWARD
 2 :                  4.000    |     6.750    |  C COLUMN
 3 :                  4.300    |     7.250    |  D DOWN
 4 :                  3.700    |     5.500    |  E EXIT
 5 :                  3.850    |     7.000    |  F FORWARD
 6 :                  3.800    |     6.500    |  I INSERT
 7 :                  3.750    |     6.750    |  K KILL
 8 :                  3.850    |     5.250    |  O ORDER
 9 :                  3.650    |     5.250    |  R ROW
10 :                  4.000    |     6.000    |  S SAVE
11 :                  4.100    |     6.500    |  U UP
12 :                  4.000    |     6.250    |
13 :                  4.100    |     7.000    |
14 :                  4.200    |     6.900    |
15 :                  4.100    |     6.800    |
16 :                  4.100    |     6.800    |
17 :                  4.200    |     7.100    |
18 :                  4.300    |     7.000    |
                                              |  ROW      ORDER
COMMAND  :?                                   |  DEFAULT CMD  :  F
```

```
                     ( X2 )    |    ( X3 )    |     COMMAND
19 :                  4.100    |     6.800    |  B BACKWARD
20 :                  3.750    |     6.500    |  C COLUMN
21 :                  3.750    |     6.250    |  D DOWN
22 :                  3.650    |     6.000    |  E EXIT
23 :                  3.900    |     6.500    |  F FORWARD
24 :                  3.650    |     7.000    |  I INSERT
25 :                  4.100    |     6.800    |  K KILL
26 :                  4.250    |     6.800    |  O ORDER
27 :                  3.650    |     6.500    |  R ROW
28 :                  3.750    |     5.750    |  S SAVE
29 :                  3.850    |     5.800    |  U UP
30 :                  4.250    |     6.800    |
31 :                               |              |
32 :                               |              |
33 :                               |              |
34 :                               |              |
35 :                               |              |
36 :                               |              |
                                              |  ROW      ORDER
COMMAND  :?                                   |  DEFAULT CMD  :  D
```

FIGURE 11.3 (continued)

current program. From this point on, we create an input data file according to the procedure given in Section 6.3. For this example, we name the input data file REGR.DAT. Creating a data file for the regression problem is an easy and quick process. Since there are several independent variables to consider and each independent variable requires its own data entry column, scrolling data pages in both *column* and *row* directions makes the data entry process much easier. The amount of data we can enter on each data page is set to 18 rows and 2 columns, for a total of 36 entry positions. The first data page for our regression example should look like Fig. 11.3(a) when completed by DATA EDITOR. To complete the column entries for y and x_1, we scroll down to the second data page using the "D" command. After completing the data entries, the second data page should look like Fig. 11.3(b).

To enter values for x_2 and x_3, we first use the "U" command to scroll to the top page (the first data page), and the "F" command to scroll to the right. DATA EDITOR will clear the current data page and provide two columns for x_2 and x_3. Then we enter the data elements as we did for columns y and x_1. When the data entry is finished, the data page should look like Fig. 11.3(c). We scroll down to the next data page to complete the remaining data entries. This is shown in Fig. 11.3(d). Whenever we return to the left data page, we use the "B" command. We save the data file that is created by using the "S" command, then exit this option.

11.4.5 EDITING THE INPUT DATA FILE

Any data file created by using DATA EDITOR can be accessed and edited by choosing this option. When this option is entered we see a prompt for the file name:

```
INPUT FILE NAME = ?
```

We then specify the data file name we want to edit (examine) and are automatically put into DATA EDITOR. All the commands remain the same as above. We will demonstrate the use of this option later in this program, when we enter new observations of independent variables for use in predicting the future demand, $\hat{y}$.

11.4.6 SELECTING REGRESSORS

This option allows us to select independent variables to use in the multiple regressor analysis. When we enter this option, we will see the following menu:

```
                                                              MESSAGE
                                                         -----------------
              NOW SELECT DATA FOR C  1   :

*** SELECTION OF INDEPENDENT VARIABLES ***

*              _ NO CHANGE                   *
*              _ SWAP                        *
*              _ POLYNOMIAL                  *
*              _ MULTIPLICATION              *
*              _ RECIPROCAL                  *
*              _ NATURAL LOG                 *
*              _ CONSTANT                    *
*              _ SINE                        *
*              _ COSINE                      *
*              _ CANCEL                      *
*              _ EXIT                        *

******************************************
```

At the top of the menu, there is a prompt "NOW SELECT DATA FOR C n", where n is an integer ranging from 1 through 9. "C n" is the combination of xs that we are going to use for the nth regressor in the regression model. There are 11 subcommands to pick from. We again use the [↑] and [↓] keys to position the cursor and press the [ENTER] key to pick the command. The message area displays the chosen functional format for the regressor.

The data file REGR.DAT contains historical data for one dependent variable y and three independent variables x_1, x_2, and x_3. If we want to estimate the regression coefficients b_i based on just these three independent variables such that $y = b_0 + b_1x_1 + b_2x_2 + b_3x_3$, no changes in regressors are required. The REGRESSION program assumes that the default regressors are in the form of the sum of all independent variables. The REGRESSION program also automatically inserts the dummy variable b_0 in the regression equation. If this selection is acceptable, we can skip this option and go directly to the "DO REGRESSION" option. To observe the use of each subcommand, we consider entering the regressors for the following regression model:

$$y = b_0 + b_1x_1 + b_2x_3 + b_3x_1^2 + b_4x_1x_2 + b_5\frac{1}{x_3} + b_6 \ln x_1 + 1 .$$

Suppose our data file contains the time series for one dependent variable y and three independent variables x_1, x_2, and x_3. The regressor is transformed as follows, prompt by prompt:

Step 1: ``NOW SELECT DATA FOR C 1``
We select the "NO CHANGE" option and see the message "cl = xl" displayed in the message area to the right.

Step 2: ``NOW SELECT DATA FOR C 2``
We select the "SWAP" option and see the prompt "REPLACE by x _?" If we enter "3" here, we will see the message "c2 = x3".

Step 3: ``NOW SELECT DATA FOR C 3``
We select the "SQUARE" option and see the prompt "SQUARE OF x _?". If we enter "1" here, we will see the message "c3 = x1**2".

Step 4: ``NOW SELECT DATA FOR C 4``
We select the "MULTIPLICATION" option and see the prompt "MULTIPLICATION OF WHICH TWO VARIABLES?" If we enter "1, 2" here, we will see the message "c4 = x1*x2".

Step 5: ``NOW SELECT DATA FOR C 5``
We select the "RECIPROCAL" option and see the prompt "RECIPROCAL of x_?". If we enter "3" here, we will see the message "c5 = 1/x3".

Step 6: ``NOW SELECT DATA FOR C 6``
We select the "NATURAL LOG" option and see the prompt "NATURAL LOG OF x_?". If we enter "1" here, we will see the message "c6 = LN(x1)".

Step 7: "NOW SELECT DATA FOR C 7"
We select the "CONSTANT" option and see the prompt "CONSTANT = ?". If we enter "1" here, we will see the message "c7 = 1".

We have now changed the input data according to the new set of regressors. If they are all correct, we can exit the menu and do regression analysis; otherwise, we choose the "CANCEL" option to cancel all the previous selections, and start all over again from c1.

11.4.7 DOING REGRESSION

When we choose this option, we will see the following prompt:

```
INPUT FILE NAME=?
```

We specify the file name REGR.DAT and then press the [ENTER] key. The program loads REGR.DAT into memory and executes. (Recall that we are executing here the default regression model $y = b_0 + b_1x_1 + b_2x_2 + b_3x_3$.) Since it takes time to complete all relevant statistics, the computer displays a status message, telling how close to completion it is.

```
INPUT FILE NAME =? REGR.DAT
EXECUTING...
50 % FINISHED
70 % FINISHED
DONE !
```

11.4.8 EXAMINING RESULTS

When execution is completed, the screen is cleared and the regression results menu is displayed:

```
***********  REGRESSION RESULTS MENU  ***********
*    _ TABULATE STATISTICS                        *
*    _ TABULATE OBSERVED AND FITTED VALUES        *
*    _ PLOT OBSERVED AND FITTED VALUES            *
*    _ PLOT RESIDUAL VS DEPENDENT VARIABLE Y      *
*    _ PLOT RESIDUAL VS REGRESSORS                *
*    _ PREDICT FUTURE VALUES                      *
*    _ EXIT                                       *
***************************************************
```

Six subcommands are available for displaying the regression results. We will select each subcommand in the order listed. Once again we use the [↑] and [↓] keys to select a subcommand.

TABLE 11.2 Regression statistics

**** ANALYSIS OF VARIANCE ***

SOURCE OF VARIATION	SUM OF SQUARES	DEGREE OF FREEDOM	MEAN SQUARES
REGRESSION	12.027	3	4.009
RESIDUAL	1.432	26	0.055
TOTAL	13.459	29	

F-STATISTIC = 72.7972
R-SQUARED = 0.8936
S-SQUARED = 0.0551

Y = 7.589104 -2.357723 X1+ 1.612214 X2+ .5011518 X3

**** REGRESSION COEFFICIENTS ****

N	B[I]	95% C.I.			T-STATISTIC
0	7.589	2.576	--	12.602	3.104
1	-2.358	-3.666	--	-1.050	-3.696
2	1.612	1.007	--	2.218	5.459
3	0.501	0.243	--	0.759	3.981

Tabulate statistics. When this subcommand is entered, Table 11.2 is displayed on the screen. Table 11.2 summarizes the analysis of variance and the statistics for F, R^2, and $\hat{\sigma}^2$ and writes out the estimated regression coefficients and t-statistics.

The F-test statistics in this table indicates that at least one of the three independent variables contributes significantly to the model ($F = 72.7972 > F_{.05,3,26}$). The estimated error variance σ^2 is 0.0551. The value $R^2 = 0.8936$ implies that 89.36 percent of the variability in y has been explained when the three independent variables are used.

Since $|t| > t_{.025,26} = 2.056$ for each regression coefficient considered, we conclude that all independent variables contribute significantly to the model. We should note, however, that this does not necessarily imply that the relationship found is appropriate for predicting future observations. Further tests of model adequacy are required, such as plots of residuals against y and independent variables (supplied by choosing other subcommands).

Tabulate observed and fitted values. When we invoke this option, we obtain Table 11.3, which shows the estimated values of y and the residuals. The

MAD and MSE statistics are also shown in this table. The estimated values and residuals are calculated to the same accuracy as the original data. Table 11.4 shows the 95-percent confidence (prediction) interval estimates for the historical data in period 1 to 30.

Plot observed and fitted values. When we enter this plotting option, the program will chain the APLOT file (program 7.2), which was also used in PLOTTER. When the APLOT program is loaded into memory, the following prompts are displayed on the screen:

```
HEADING FOR THE PLOT =? PLOT OF OBSERVED VS. FITTED VALUES
X TITLE FOR THE PLOT =? TIME (MONTH)
Y TITLE FOR THE PLOT =? DEMAND
MINIMUM X VALUE = [DEFAULT: 1 ]? 0
MAXIMUM X VALUE = [DEFAULT: 30 ]? 36
MINIMUM Y VALUE = [DEFAULT: 7.1 ]? 6
MAXIMUM Y VALUE = [DEFAULT: 9.520001 ]? 12
```

TABLE 11.3 Observed vs. fitted values

PERIOD	OBSERVED	FORECAST	RESIDUAL
1	7.380	7.395	-0.015
2	8.510	8.579	-0.069
3	9.520	9.431	0.089
4	7.500	7.587	-0.087
5	9.330	8.816	0.514
6	8.280	8.485	-0.205
7	8.750	8.530	0.220
8	7.870	7.468	0.402
9	7.100	7.145	-0.045
10	8.000	7.968	0.032
11	7.890	8.262	-0.372
12	8.150	7.975	0.175
13	9.100	8.984	0.116
14	8.860	8.977	-0.117
15	8.900	8.766	0.134
16	8.870	8.648	0.222
17	9.260	9.195	0.065
18	9.000	9.070	-0.070
19	8.750	8.883	-0.133
20	7.950	7.933	0.017

PERIOD	OBSERVED	FORECAST	RESIDUAL
21	7.650	7.808	-0.158
22	7.270	7.639	-0.369
23	8.000	8.411	-0.411
24	8.500	8.612	-0.112
25	8.750	9.119	-0.369
26	9.210	9.243	-0.033
27	8.270	8.008	0.262
28	7.670	7.675	-0.005
29	7.930	7.743	0.187
30	9.260	9.125	0.135

MEAN ABSOLUTE DEVIATION : MAD = .1713708 (2.044347 %)
MEAN SQUARED ERROR : MSE = 5.506974E-02

TABLE 11.4 Confidence intervals

NEED CONFIDENCE INTERVAL :? YES

PERIOD	FORECAST	95 %	PREDICTION	INTERVAL
1	7.395	6.881	--	7.908
2	8.579	8.085	--	9.074
3	9.431	8.919	--	9.944
4	7.587	7.060	--	8.114
5	8.816	8.304	--	9.329
6	8.485	7.974	--	8.996
7	8.530	8.015	--	9.044
8	7.468	6.929	--	8.007
9	7.145	6.621	--	7.670
10	7.968	7.464	--	8.472
11	8.262	7.736	--	8.787
12	7.975	7.455	--	8.495
13	8.984	8.487	--	9.480
14	8.977	8.476	--	9.477
15	8.766	8.271	--	9.260
16	8.648	8.145	--	9.150
17	9.195	8.692	--	9.698
18	9.070	8.556	--	9.585
19	8.883	8.389	--	9.378
20	7.933	7.409	--	8.457
21	7.808	7.299	--	8.317
22	7.639	7.133	--	8.145
23	8.411	7.920	--	8.901
24	8.612	8.066	--	9.158
25	9.119	8.599	--	9.640
26	9.243	8.717	--	9.770
27	8.008	7.490	--	8.525
28	7.675	7.172	--	8.178
29	7.743	7.243	--	8.244
30	9.125	8.613	--	9.637

After we specify the plotting parameters above, Fig. 11.4 is displayed on the screen. Symbol "o" in Fig. 11.4 marks the position of each observed data item; symbol "Δ" marks the position of each value estimated by the model.

Plot residuals. The residuals can also be plotted against y in Fig. 11.5(a) and against x_i in Figs. 11.5(b), 11.5(c), and 11.5(d). The purpose of these plots is to see if they indicate that the model is inadequate. We observe the following:

1. *Residual versus y (Fig. 11.5a):* There is some evidence that the smaller observed values were overpredicted by the model, while the larger observed values were underpredicted. In this case, additional effort would normally be made to find one or more independent variables that might be added to the model.
2. *Residual versus x_i:* The pattern in Fig. 11.5(c) appears to be normal, but the patterns in Figs. 11.5(b) and 11.5(d) indicate that the relationship between y and x_1 (or x_3) is not linear (in our example, the relationship is

in fact quadratic) or that regressor variables not now in the model affect the response.

3. *Residual versus time (Fig. 11.6):* No unusual behavior is indicated by this plot, implying that a long-term time effect is not influencing the data.

Predict future values. Once we obtain a regression model, we can predict the value of a new observation. To do this through the REGR program, we should add the future values of independent variables to the data file before calling this option. When we finish editing data file REGR.DAT, it should look like Fig. 11.7. We then return to the "examine the results" menu to invoke this option. With the sets of independent variables specified in Fig. 11.7, the predicted values shown in Table 11.5 would result.

11.4.9 RESETTING CURRENT REGRESSORS

We select this option when we want to restore the initial set of regressors in the input file. The change in input data is cumulative—that is, whatever changes

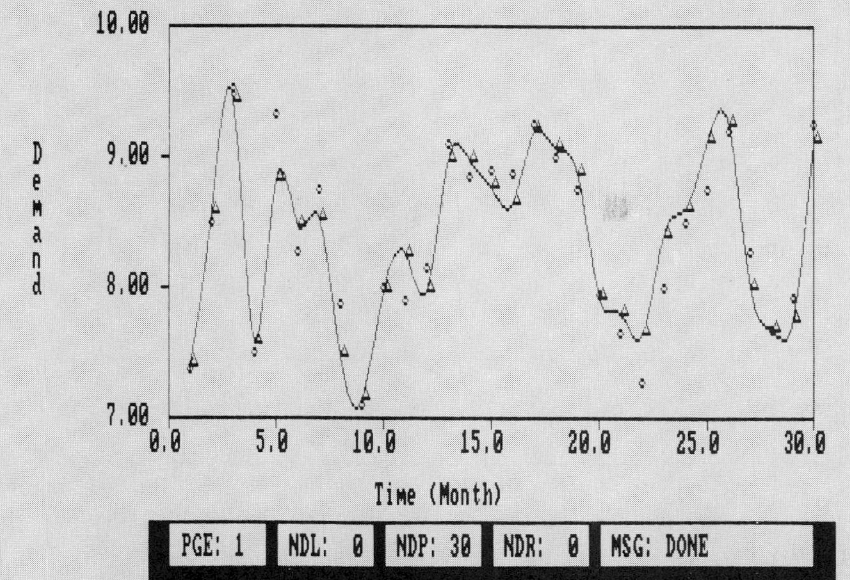

FIGURE 11.4 Plot of observed vs. fitted values

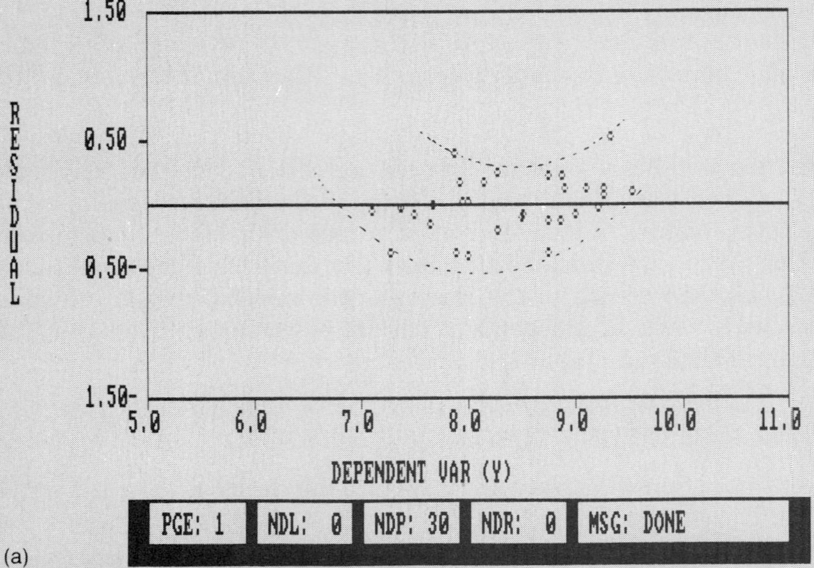

(a)

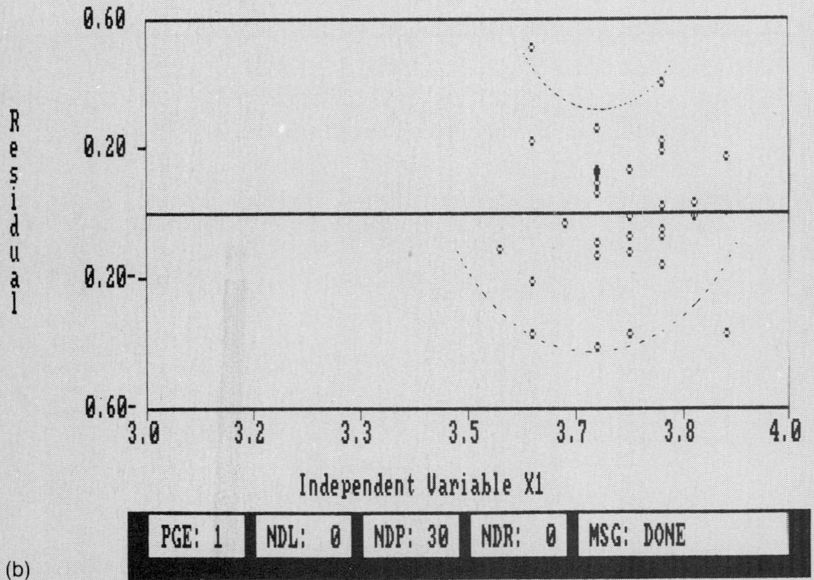

(b)

FIGURE 11.5 (a) Residual vs. dependent variable y, (b) plot of residual against variable X_1, (c) plot of residual against variable X_2, and (d) plot of residual against variable X_3

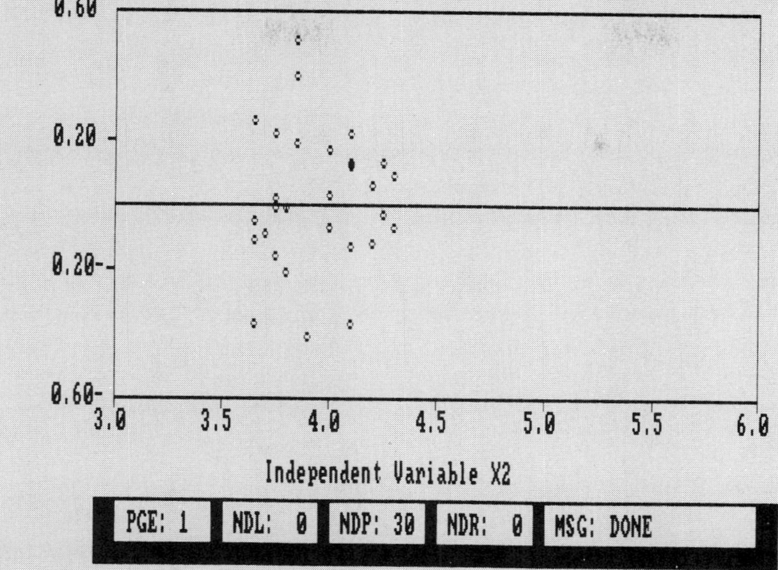
Residual
0.60
0.20
0.20-
0.60-
3.0 3.5 4.0 4.5 5.0 5.5 6.0
Independent Variable X2
PGE: 1
NDL: 0
NDP: 30
NDR: 0
MSG: DONE

(c)

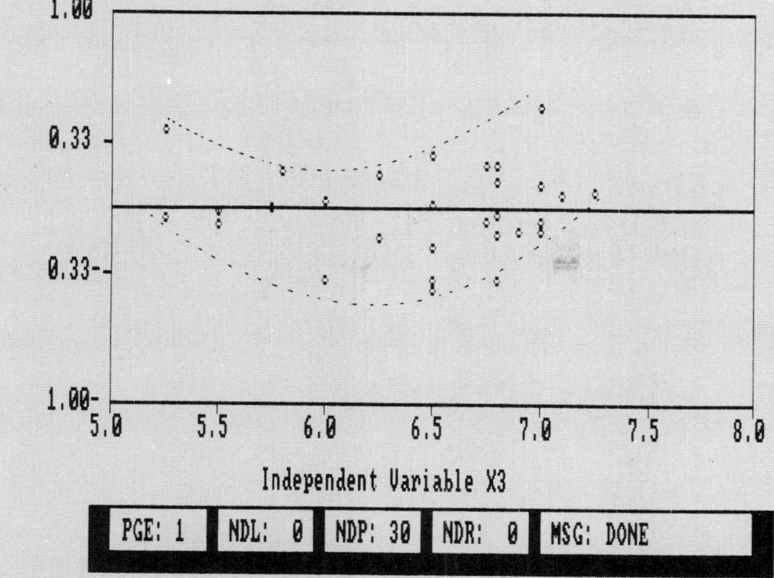
Residual
1.00
0.33
0.33-
1.00-
5.0 5.5 6.0 6.5 7.0 7.5 8.0
Independent Variable X3
PGE: 1
NDL: 0
NDP: 30
NDR: 0
MSG: DONE

(d)

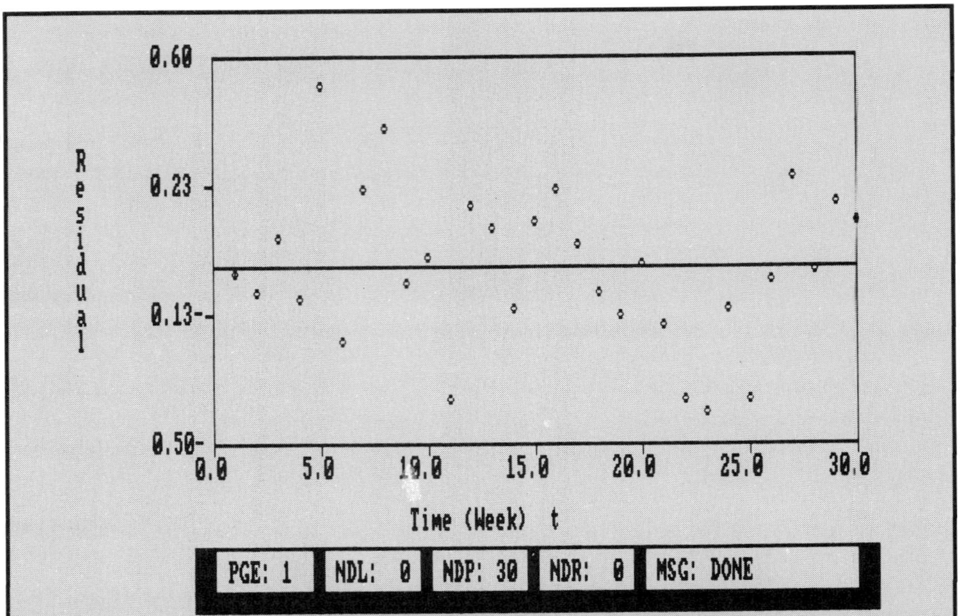

FIGURE 11.6 Residual vs. time

we make will be based on the previous set of regressor data instead of on the original data. Therefore, if we have changed the independent variables from x_1, x_2, x_3 to x_1, x_3, x_1**2, x_1*x_2, $1/x_3$, LN(x_1), and 1, the next selection will be based on the last seven variables instead of on the first three variables. A problem arises if later we want to do regression analysis on x_1, x_2, x_1**2 and x_2**2 because x_2 is no longer available. When this happens, we select the "RESET CURRENT REGRESSORS" option to get back the original input data x_1, x_2, and x_3.

11.4.10 DOING REGRESSION WITH A NEW SET OF REGRESSORS

If we're not satisfied with the estimated model after examining the results, we can try some other model with different set of regressors. By looking at the plot of residual versus dependent variable (y), we see an unexplained quadratic relation between y and the independent variables. We therefore select a new set of regressors containing x_1, x_2, x_3, x_1**2, x_2**2, x_3**2 and do the regression analysis again with a modified model.

```
           ( Y )           ( X1 )          COMMAND
19 :       8.750           3.700           B  BACKWARD
20 :       7.950           3.800           C  COLUMN
21 :       7.650           3.800           D  DOWN
22 :       7.270           3.750           E  EXIT
23 :       8.000           3.700           F  FORWARD
24 :       8.500           3.550           I  INSERT
25 :       8.750           3.600           K  KILL
26 :       9.210           3.650           O  ORDER
27 :       8.270           3.700           R  ROW
28 :       7.670           3.750           S  SAVE
29 :       7.930           3.800           U  UP
30 :       9.260           3.700
31 :                       3.800
32 :                       3.750
33 :                       3.850
34 :
35 :
36 :
                                           ROW     ORDER
COMMAND  :?                                DEFAULT CMD  :  D
```

```
           ( X2 )          ( X3 )          COMMAND
19 :       4.100           6.800           B  BACKWARD
20 :       3.750           6.500           C  COLUMN
21 :       3.750           6.250           D  DOWN
22 :       3.650           6.000           E  EXIT
23 :       3.900           6.500           F  FORWARD
24 :       3.650           7.000           I  INSERT
25 :       4.100           6.800           K  KILL
26 :       4.250           6.800           O  ORDER
27 :       3.650           6.500           R  ROW
28 :       3.750           5.750           S  SAVE
29 :       3.850           5.800           U  UP
30 :       4.250           6.800
31 :       3.900           6.800
32 :       3.850           6.850
33 :       3.900           6.900
34 :
35 :
36 :
                                           ROW     ORDER
COMMAND  :?                                DEFAULT CMD  :  D
```

FIGURE 11.7 Edited data file (REGR,DAT)

$$y = b_0 + b_1x_1 + b_2x_2 + b_3x_3 + b_4x_1^2 + b_5x_2^2 + b_6x_3^2$$

In doing so, we first reset the current regressor and then pick the "SELECT REGRESSORS" option.

TABLE 11.5 Predicted values of *y*

PERIOD	FORECAST	95 %	PREDICTION	INTERVAL
31	8.325	7.804	--	8.846
32	8.388	7.871	--	8.904
33	8.257	7.702	--	8.812

After we have selected all six of the regressors, the screen will look like this:

```
                                                              MESSAGE
                                                        ------------------
          NOW SELECT DATA FOR C  7   :                  C1= X1
                                                        C2= X2
*** SELECTION OF INDEPENDENT VARIABLES ***              C3= X3
                                                        C4= X1**2
*                _ NO CHANGE                    *       C5= X2**2
*                _ SWAP                         *       C6= X3**2
*                _ POLYNOMIAL                   *
*                _ MULTIPLICATION               *
*                _ RECIPROCAL                   *
*                _ NATURAL LOG                  *
*                _ CONSTANT                     *
*                _ SINE                         *
*                _ COSINE                       *
*                _ CANCEL                       *
*                _ EXIT                         *

*************************************************
```

TABLE 11.6 Regression statistics for the new regressors

**** ANALYSIS OF VARIANCE ***

SOURCE OF VARIATION	SUM OF SQUARES	DEGREE OF FREEDOM	MEAN SQUARES
REGRESSION	12.329	6	2.055
RESIDUAL	1.130	23	0.049
TOTAL	13.459	29	

```
F-STATISTIC  =     41.8353
R-SQUARED    =      0.9161
S-SQUARED    =      0.0491

Y = -39.48528 + 15.63426 X1+ 15.65072 X2-4.340606 X3-2.338928 X1**2-1.819535
X2**2+ .4000178 X3**2
```

**** REGRESSION COEFFICIENTS ****

N	B[I]	95% C.I.			T-STATISTIC
0	-39.485	-184.879	--	105.908	-0.559
1	15.634	-55.181	--	86.450	0.454
2	15.651	-4.861	--	36.162	1.569
3	-4.341	-8.551	--	-0.131	-2.120
4	-2.339	-11.815	--	7.137	-0.508
5	-1.820	-4.426	--	0.787	-1.436
6	0.400	0.054	--	0.746	2.377

We now select the "DO REGRESSION" option. The results are listed in Table 11.6.

The values for $\hat{\sigma}^2$ and R^2 in this table indicate that the new model is better than the first model, but t-statistics indicate that only b_3 and b_6 are significant terms. (See Section 11.2.2.) We would probably repeat this modeling process several times until we obtain a more acceptable form.

11.5 SUMMARY

In this chapter we briefly reviewed the widely used statistical technique of multiple regression. We discussed, among other topics, least squares estimation of the parameters, interval estimation, prediction of new observations, and methods for hypothesis testing. We further discussed various tests of model adequacy, with particular emphasis on various plots of regression statistics.

AEDIT, APLOT, and TFILE must be available to run REGRESSION.

```
------------------    VARIABLE LIST    ------------------

ARRAYS      :

B#              : COEFFICIENTS OF REGRESSION MODEL.
CURVE$          : CHART TYPE TO BE USED.
INV#            : INVERSE MATRIX.
K$              : FIELDS FOR RANDOM ACCESS FILE.
STATUS$         : MESSAGES.
T#              : BUFFER FOR REGRESSOR SELECTION.
TEMP#           : TEMPORARY STORAGE.
TEMP1#          : TEMPORARY STORAGE.
X#              : DATA FOR INDEPENDENT VARIABLES.
XX#             : PRODUCT OF A MATRIX WITH ITS INVERSE.
XY#             : PRODUCT OF TWO MATRICES.
Y#              : DATA FOR DEPENDENT VARIABLE.
YHAT#           : ESTIMATES OF DEPENDENT VARIABLE.

INTEGERS    :

C0%             : COLUMN NUMBER.
C1%             : COLUMN NUMBER.
CI%             : CONFIDENCE LEVEL.
CODE%           : CODE USED IN RANDOM FILE.
CODE1%          : CODE USED IN RANDOM FILE.
CODE2%          : CODE USED IN RANDOM FILE.
COLP%           : PAGE NUMBER.
```

PROGRAM 11.1 REGRESSION[†]

[†]Due to the file specification convention (eight characters or less), the REGRESSION program is named REGR. The user must save the program on disk under REGR. Otherwise a DOS error will result.

```
COLUMNX%          : NUMBER OF INDEPENDENT VARIABLES.
COUNT%            : NUMBER OF REGRESSORS SELECTED.
DFE%              : DEGREE OF FREEDOM FOR ERROR TERM.
DFR%              : DEGREE OF FREEDOM FOR REGRESSION.
DFY%              : DEGREE OF FREEDOM FOR TOTAL SUM OF SQUARES.
DONE%             : FLAG INDICATING END OF EXECUTION.
DX%               : NUMBER OF OPTIONS BYPASSED.
DX2%              : NUMBER OF OPTIONS BYPASSED.
FIRST%            : ROW POSITION OF FIRST OPTION.
FLAG%             : FLAG INDICATING OPTION CHOSEN.
FLAG1%            : FLAG INDICATING OPTION CHOSEN.
I%, J%, K%        : SENTINEL NUMBERS.
L%, M%            : SENTINEL NUMBERS.
KEEP%             : FLAG INDICATING THE FILE HAS BEEN SAVED.
LAST%             : ROW POSITION OF LAST OPTION IN THE MENU.
LEAVE%            : FLAG INDICATING EXIT OF FILES.
MODIFIED%         : FLAG INDICATING MODIFICATION OF FILES.
MX%               : ROW POSITION OF MESSAGE.
MY%               : COLUMN POSITION OF MESSAGE.
NEWFILE%          : FLAG INDICATING NEW FILE BEING CREATED.
NOF%              : NUMBER OF FILES TO BE PLOTTED.
ORDER%            : FLAG INDICATING THE INPUT ORDER.
ROW%              : NUMBER OF INDEPENDENT DATA.
ROWP%             : PAGE NUMBER.
ROWX              : NUMBER OF DEPENDENT DATA.
SFLAG%            : FLAG INDICATING SELECTION OF REGRESSORS.
SL%               : STARTING LINE TO CHAIN BACK.
SX%               : ROW POSITION OF MESSAGE.
SY%               : COLUMN POSITION OF MESSAGE.
TINDEX%           : INDEX FOR SEARCHING T-DISTRIBUTION TABLE.
T1%, T2%          : TEMPORARY STORAGE.
X%                : ROW POSITION OF SCREEN CURSOR.
XFULL%            : FLAG INDICATING THE BUFFER IS FULL.
Y%                : COLUMN POSITION OF SCREEN CURSOR.

REALS_________:

BXY#              : TEMPORARY STORAGE.
F0#               : F-STATISTIC FOR THE REGRESSION ANALYSIS.
MAD#              : MEAN ABSOLUTE DEVIATION.
MSE#              : MEAN SQUARE ERROR.
MSR#              : MEAN SQUARE ERROR FOR REGRESSION.
R2#               : COEFFICIENT OF DETERMINATION.
S#                : SUM OF SQUARE OF DIFFERENCE.
SSE#              : SUM OF SQUARES DUE TO ERROR.
SSR#              : SUM OF SQUARE DUE TO REGRESSION.
SUM#              : SUM OF DEPENDENT VARIABLE.
SYY#              : TOTAL SUM OF SQUARES.
TA, T1            : TEMPORARY STORAGE.
T2, T3            : TEMPORARY STORAGE.
T1#, T2#          : TEMPORARY STORAGE.
XXKJ#             : TEMPORARY STORAGE.
```

PROGRAM 11.1 (continued)

```
YBAR#          : AVERAGE OF DEPENDENT VARIABLE.
YY#            : SUM OF SQUARE OF Y.

CHARACTERS :

ANS$           : RESPONSE FROM KEYBOARD.
B$             : BLANKS.
CALLFILE$      : NAME OF THE FILE THAT'S CHAINING EDITOR.
CHAINFILE$     : NAME OF THE FILE TO BE CHAINED TO.
C0$            : COLUMN NUMBER.
C1$            : COLUMN NUMBER.
FD$            : DISK DRIVE USED FOR THE DATA FILES.
FILE$          : INPUT FILE NAME.
FILE2$         : NAME OF THE FILE TO BE CHAINED TO.
M$             : MESSAGE.
ORDER$         : MESSAGE.
PD$            : DISK DRIVE USED FOR THE PACKAGE.
PFILE$         : T-DISTRIBUTION TABLE.
TEMP$          : TEMPORARY STORAGE.
```

PROGRAM 11.1 REGRESSION

```
10    'Program 11.1: REGRESSION  -----------------------------
20    OPTION BASE 1
30    KEY OFF: SCREEN 0,1: WIDTH 80: CLS
40    LOCATE 10,1
50    PRINT "Which disk drive does contain REGR, AEDIT AND APLOT?"
60    PRINT "DRIVE A IS ON YOUR LEFT,"
70    PRINT "DRIVE B IS ON YOUR RIGHT,"
80    PRINT "DRIVE C IS YOUR HARD DISK DRIVE.": BEEP
90    INPUT "ENTER [ A, B, OR C ]";PD$
100   PD$=PD$+":" : FD$="B:": DX%=0
110   DIM X#(200,10), Y#(200), XX#(10,10), INV#(10,10), XY#(10), YHAT#(200)
120   DIM B#(10), K$(6), P$(10), STATUS$(10)
130   XFULL%=0 : DONE%=0 : CI%=95 : TINDEX%=4
140   ROWP%=1: COLP%=1: KEEP%=0: LEAVE%=0: MODIFIED%=0
150   MX%=5 : MY%=59 : SX%=5 : SY%=58
160   M$="COMMAND :"
170   B$="                    "
180   BLANK$="                                              "
190   GOSUB 300
200   X%=DX%+5: Y%=15: LOCATE X%,Y%,1,0,7
210   FIRST%=5 : LAST%=13
220   ANS$=INKEY$ : IF ANS$="" THEN 220
230   IF ANS$=CHR$(0)+CHR$(80) THEN IF X%<LAST% THEN X%=X%+1 ELSE X%=FIRST%
240   IF ANS$=CHR$(0)+CHR$(72) THEN IF X%>FIRST% THEN X%=X%-1 ELSE X%=LAST%
250   LOCATE X%,Y%: IF ANS$<>CHR$(13) THEN 220
260   FLAG1%=CSRLIN : FLAG1%=FLAG1%-4
270   ON FLAG1% GOSUB 6000,5720,540,540,740,2690,2610,2640,6650
280   IF FLAG1%<>1 THEN GOTO 190 ELSE GOTO 200
290   '------------------------- PRINT MAIN MENU --------------------------
300   CLS: SCREEN 0,1 : WIDTH 80: LOCATE 3,1
310   IF STATUS$(1)="" THEN FOR I%=1 TO COLUMNX%-1 : I$=CHR$(I%+48) :
          STATUS$(I%)="C"+I$+"= X"+I$ : NEXT
320   PRINT TAB(10) "****** REGRESSION ANALYSIS MENU ******"
330   PRINT
340   PRINT TAB(10) "*    _ CHANGE DEFAULT DISK DRIVE     *"
350   PRINT TAB(10) "*    _ CHANGE CONFIDENCE LEVEL       *"
360   PRINT TAB(10) "*    _ CREATE INPUT FILE             *"
370   PRINT TAB(10) "*    _ EDIT(EXAMINE) INPUT FILE      *"
380   PRINT TAB(10) "*    _ SELECT REGRESSORS             *"
390   PRINT TAB(10) "*    _ DO REGRESSION                 *"
400   PRINT TAB(10) "*    _ EXAMINE RESULTS               *"
410   PRINT TAB(10) "*    _ RESET CURRENT REGRESSORS      *"
420   PRINT TAB(10) "*    _ EXIT                          *"
430   PRINT
```

PROGRAM 11.1 REGRESSION

```
440  PRINT TAB(10) "****************************************": BEEP
450  LOCATE 3,66,1 : PRINT "STATUS"
460  LOCATE 4,58 : PRINT "----------------------"
470  LOCATE SX%,SY% : PRINT "DEFAULT DRIVE    = "+FD$
480  LOCATE SX%+1,SY% : PRINT "CONFIDENCE LEVEL=";CI%;"%"
490  LOCATE SX%+2,SY% : PRINT "CURRENT REGRESSORS :"
500  IF COLUMNX%=0 THEN LOCATE SX%+3,SY% : PRINT "NONE"
510  FOR I%=1 TO COLUMNX%-1 : LOCATE SX%+I%+2,SY%: PRINT STATUS$(I%) : NEXT
520  RETURN
530  '---------------------- DATA EDITOR --------------------------------
540  CLS: BEEP: INPUT "INPUT FILE NAME =";FILE$ : FILE$= FD$+FILE$
550  IF FLAG1%=3 THEN NEWFILE%=1 ELSE NEWFILE%=0
560  DX%=FLAG1%: SL%=110
570  ORDER%=1: ORDER$="ROW    ORDER"
580  CHAINFILE$=PD$+"AEDIT.BAS"
590  CALLFILE$=PD$+"REGR.BAS"
600  COMMON NEWFILE%,FILE$,CALLFILE$,DX%,SL%,FD$,PD$,ORDER%,ORDER$
610  CHAIN CHAINFILE$
620  RETURN
630  '------------------------ READING FILE -----------------------------
640  OPEN FILE$ FOR INPUT AS #2
650  INPUT #2,ROWX%: INPUT #2,ROW% : INPUT #2,COLUMNX%
660  KEEP%=0
670  FOR J%=1 TO COLUMNX%
680  IF J%<>1 THEN FOR I%=1 TO ROW% : INPUT #2,X#(I%,J%) : NEXT I% ELSE
       FOR I%=1 TO ROWX% : INPUT #2,Y#(I%) : NEXT I%
690  NEXT J%
700  CLOSE #2 : XFULL%=1
710  FOR I%=1 TO ROW% : X#(I%,1)=1! : NEXT I%
720  RETURN
730  '----------------------- SELECT REGRESSORS ------------------------
740  DIM T#(200,9) : LOCATE ,,0
750  DONE%=0 : SFLAG%=0: MX%=5
760  CLS : INPUT "INPUT FILE NAME =";TEMP$: TEMP$=FD$+TEMP$
770  IF TEMP$<>FILE$ THEN FILE$=TEMP$:GOSUB 640
780  FOR J%=2 TO COLUMNX%
790  FOR I%=1 TO ROW%
800  T#(I%,J%-1)=X#(I%,J%)
810  NEXT I%
820  NEXT J%
830  FOR I%=1 TO COLUMNX% : P$(I%)=STATUS$(I%) : NEXT
840  COUNT%=1
850  CLS: SCREEN 0,1: LOCATE 5,11
860  PRINT "NOW SELECT DATA FOR C     :" : COLOR 20,0,0
870  LOCATE 5,33 : PRINT COUNT% : COLOR 15,0,0
880  PRINT
890  PRINT "*** SELECTION OF INDEPENDENT VARIABLES ***"
900  PRINT
910  PRINT "*           _ NO CHANGE                    *"
920  PRINT "*           _ SWAP                         *"
930  PRINT "*           _ POLYNOMIAL                   *"
940  PRINT "*           _ MULTIPLICATION               *"
950  PRINT "*           _ RECIPROCAL                   *"
960  PRINT "*           _ NATURAL LOG                  *"
970  PRINT "*           _ CONSTANT                     *"
980  PRINT "*           _ SINE                         *"
990  PRINT "*           _ COSINE                       *"
1000 PRINT "*           _ CANCEL                       *"
1010 PRINT "*           _ EXIT                         *"
1020 PRINT
1030 PRINT "****************************************" : BEEP
1040 LOCATE 3,65,1 : PRINT "MESSAGE"
1050 LOCATE 4,59 : PRINT "------------------"
1060 X%=9: Y%=12
1070 LOCATE X%,Y%,1,0,7
1080 ANS$=INKEY$
1090 IF ANS$="" THEN 1080
1100 IF ANS$=CHR$(0)+CHR$(80) THEN IF X%<19 THEN X%=X%+1 ELSE X%=9
1110 IF ANS$=CHR$(0)+CHR$(72) THEN IF X%>9 THEN X%=X%-1 ELSE X%=19
1120 LOCATE X%,Y% : IF ANS$<>CHR$(13) THEN 1080
1130 FLAG%=CSRLIN : FLAG%=FLAG%-8
1140 ON FLAG% GOSUB 1220,1280,1410,1550,1700,1830,1980,2110,2250,
       2390,2570
1150 IF FLAG%=11 THEN DX%=5: GOTO 1200
1160 COUNT%=COUNT%+1: LOCATE 5,33
1170 COLOR 20,0,0
1180 PRINT COUNT% : COLOR 15,0,0:LOCATE X%,Y%,1: GOTO 1080
1190 RETURN
1200 RETURN
1210 '----------------------- NO CHANGE ------------------------------
```

PROGRAM 11.1 (continued)

```
1220 T1%= COUNT%+48 : COUNT$=CHR$(T1%)
1230 STATUS$(COUNT%)="C"+COUNT$+"= X"+COUNT$
1240 LOCATE MX%,MY%: PRINT STATUS$(COUNT%)
1250 MX%=MX%+1: SFLAG%=1
1260 RETURN
1270 '------------------------ SWAP -------------------------------------
1280 LOCATE 22,1
1290 INPUT " REPLACE BY X_";C0%
1300 T1%=COUNT%+48 : COUNT$=CHR$(T1%)
1310 T2%=C0%+48 : C0$=CHR$(T2%)
1320 STATUS$(COUNT%)="C"+COUNT$+"= X"+C0$
1330 LOCATE MX%,MY%: PRINT STATUS$(COUNT%)
1340 MX%=MX%+1 : SFLAG%=1
1350 FOR I%=1 TO ROW%
1360 X#(I%,COUNT%+1)=T#(I%,C0%)
1370 NEXT I%
1380 LOCATE 22,1 : PRINT BLANK$ : LOCATE X%,Y%
1390 RETURN
1400 '------------------------ POLYNOMIAL --------------------------------
1410 LOCATE 22,1
1420 INPUT " WHICH X_";C0%
1425 LOCATE 22,1: INPUT " TO WHAT POWER";POWER$
1430 T1%=COUNT%+48 : COUNT$=CHR$(T1%): POWER%=VAL(POWER$)
1440 T2%=C0%+48 : C0$=CHR$(T2%)
1450 STATUS$(COUNT%)="C"+COUNT$+"= X"+C0$+"**"+POWER$
1460 LOCATE MX%,MY%: PRINT STATUS$(COUNT%)
1470 MX%=MX%+1 : SFLAG%=1
1480 FOR I%=1 TO ROW%
1490 TIC#=T#(I%,C0%)
1491 TEMP#=1!
1492     FOR J%=1 TO POWER%
1494         TEMP#=TEMP#*TIC#
1496         NEXT J%
1500 X#(I%,COUNT%+1)=TEMP#
1510 NEXT I%
1520 LOCATE 22,1 : PRINT BLANK$: LOCATE X%,Y%
1530 RETURN
1540 '------------------------ MULTIPLY ---------------------------------
1550 LOCATE 22,1
1560 INPUT " MULTIPLICATION OF WHICH 2 VARIABLES";C0%,C1%
1570 T1%=COUNT%+48 : COUNT$=CHR$(T1%)
1580 T2%=C0%+48 : C0$=CHR$(T2%)
1590 T3%=C1%+48 : C1$=CHR$(T3%)
1600 STATUS$(COUNT%)="C"+COUNT$+"= X"+C0$+"* X"+C1$
1610 LOCATE MX%,MY%
1620 PRINT STATUS$(COUNT%)
1630 MX%=MX%+1 : SFLAG%=1
1640 FOR I%=1 TO ROW%
1650 X#(I%,COUNT%+1)=T#(I%,C0%)*T#(I%,C1%)
1660 NEXT I%
1670 LOCATE 22,1 : PRINT BLANK$: LOCATE X%,Y%
1680 RETURN
1690 '------------------------ RECIPROCAL -------------------------------
1700 LOCATE 22,1
1710 INPUT " RECIPROCAL OF X_";C0%
1720 T1%=COUNT%+48 : COUNT$=CHR$(T1%)
1730 T2%=C0%+48 : C0$=CHR$(T2%)
1740 STATUS$(COUNT%)="C"+COUNT$+"= 1/X"+C0$
1750 LOCATE MX%,MY%: PRINT STATUS$(COUNT%)
1760 MX%=MX%+1 : SFLAG%=1
1770 FOR I%=1 TO ROW%
1780 X#(I%,COUNT%+1)=1!/T#(I%,C0%)
1790 NEXT I%
1800 LOCATE 22,1 : PRINT BLANK$: LOCATE X%,Y%
1810 RETURN
1820 '------------------------ NATURAL LOG ------------------------------
1830 LOCATE 22,1
1840 INPUT " NATURAL LOG OF X_";C0%
1850 T1%=COUNT%+48 : COUNT$=CHR$(T1%)
1860 T2%=C0%+48 : C0$=CHR$(T2%)
1870 STATUS$(COUNT%)="C"+COUNT$+"= LN(X"+C0$+")"
1880 LOCATE MX%,MY%: PRINT B$
1890 LOCATE MX%,MY%
1900 PRINT STATUS$(COUNT%)
1910 MX%=MX%+1 : SFLAG%=1
1920 FOR I%=1 TO ROW%
1930 X#(I%,COUNT%+1)=LOG(T#(I%,C0%))
1940 NEXT I%
1950 LOCATE 22,1: PRINT BLANK$: LOCATE X%,Y%
1960 RETURN
```

PROGRAM 11.1 (continued)

```
1970 '------------------------ CONSTANT --------------------------------
1980 LOCATE 22,1
1990 INPUT " CONSTANT=";C0%
2000 T1%=COUNT%+48 : COUNT$=CHR$(T1%)
2010 T2%=C0%+48 : C0$=CHR$(T2%)
2020 STATUS$(COUNT%)="C"+COUNT$+"= "+C0$
2030 LOCATE MX%,MY%: PRINT STATUS$(COUNT%)
2040 MX%=MX%+1 : SFLAG%=1
2050 FOR I%=1 TO ROW%
2060 X#(I%,COUNT%+1)=C0%
2070 NEXT I%
2080 LOCATE 22,1 : PRINT BLANK$: LOCATE X%,Y%
2090 RETURN
2100 '------------------------ SINE ------------------------------------
2110 LOCATE 22,1
2120 INPUT " SINE OF X_";C0%
2130 T1%=COUNT%+48 : COUNT$=CHR$(T1%)
2140 T2%=C0%+48 : C0$=CHR$(T2%)
2150 STATUS$(COUNT%)="C"+COUNT$+"= SIN(X"+C0$+")"
2160 LOCATE MX%,MY%: PRINT STATUS$(COUNT%)
2170 MX%=MX%+1 : SFLAG%=1
2180 FOR I%=1 TO ROW%
2190 TEMP=T#(I%,C0%)*3.141593/180
2200 X#(I%,COUNT%+1)=SIN(TEMP)
2210 NEXT I%
2220 LOCATE 22,1 : PRINT BLANK$: LOCATE X%,Y%
2230 RETURN
2240 '------------------------ COSINE ----------------------------------
2250 LOCATE 22,1
2260 INPUT " COSINE OF X_";C0%
2270 T1%=COUNT%+48 : COUNT$=CHR$(T1%)
2280 T2%=C0%+48 : C0$=CHR$(T2%)
2290 STATUS$(COUNT%)="C"+COUNT$+"= COS(X"+C0$+")"
2300 LOCATE MX%,MY%: PRINT STATUS$(COUNT%)
2310 MX%=MX%+1 : SFLAG%=1
2320 FOR I%=1 TO ROW%
2330 TEMP=T#(I%,C0%)*3.141593/180
2340 X#(I%,COUNT%+1)=COS(TEMP)
2350 NEXT I%
2360 LOCATE 22,1 : PRINT BLANK$: LOCATE X%,Y%
2370 RETURN
2380 '------------------------ CANCEL ----------------------------------
2390 FOR I%=1 TO COLUMNX% : STATUS$(I%)=P$(I%) : NEXT
2400 MX%=5
2410 FOR I%=1 TO COUNT%
2420 LOCATE MX%,MY% : PRINT B$
2430 MX%=MX%+1
2440 NEXT I%
2450 LOCATE MX%,MY%: PRINT "SELECTIONS CANCELED" : BEEP
2460 FOR J%=2 TO COLUMNX%
2470 FOR I%=1 TO ROW%
2480 X#(I%,J%)=T#(I%,J%-1)
2490 NEXT I%
2500 NEXT J%
2510 LOCATE MX%,MY%: PRINT B$
2520 MX%=5
2530 X%=9 : LOCATE X%,Y%,1,0,7
2540 COUNT%=0 : SFLAG%=0
2550 RETURN
2560 '------------------------ EXIT ------------------------------------
2570 IF SFLAG%=1 THEN COLUMNX%=COUNT%
2580 ERASE T#
2590 RETURN
2600 GOSUB 3040
2610 IF DONE%=1 THEN GOSUB 2800 ELSE GOSUB 2690
2620 RETURN
2630 '---------------------- RESET REGRESSORS --------------------------
2640 GOSUB 640
2650 FOR I%=1 TO COLUMNX%-1 : I$=CHR$(I%+48)
2660      STATUS$(I%)="C"+I$+"= X"+I$ : NEXT
2670 DONE%=0 : RETURN
2680 '------------------------ DO REGRESSION ---------------------------
2690 CLS: INPUT "INPUT FILE NAME =";TEMP$ : TEMP$=FD$+TEMP$
2700 IF FILE$<>TEMP$ THEN FILE$=TEMP$ : GOSUB 640
2710 GOSUB 3040
2720 GOSUB 3320
2730 GOSUB 3440
2740 GOSUB 3740
2750 GOSUB 3810
2760 GOSUB 3860
```

PROGRAM 11.1 (continued)

```
2770 GOSUB 3950
2780 GOSUB 4040
2790 GOSUB 4110
2800 DX2%=0
2805 SCREEN 0:CLS : LOCATE 6,1
2810 PRINT TAB(10) "*********** REGRESSION RESULTS MENU ***********"
2820 PRINT
2830 PRINT TAB(10) "*    _ TABULATE STATISTICS                          *"
2840 PRINT TAB(10) "*    _ TABULATE OBSERVED AND FITTED VALUES          *"
2850 PRINT TAB(10) "*    _ PLOT OBSERVED AND FITTED VALUES              *"
2860 PRINT TAB(10) "*    _ PLOT RESIDUAL VS DEPENDENT VARIABLE Y        *"
2870 PRINT TAB(10) "*    _ PLOT RESIDUAL VS REGRESSORS                  *"
2880 PRINT TAB(10) "*    _ FORECAST FUTURE VALUES                       *"
2890 PRINT TAB(10) "*    _ EXIT                                         *"
2900 PRINT
2910 PRINT TAB(10) "************************************************": BEEP
2920 X%=8+DX2%: Y%=14: LOCATE X%,Y%,1,0,7
2930 FIRST%=8 : LAST%=14
2940 ANS$=INKEY$ : IF ANS$="" THEN 2940
2950 IF ANS$=CHR$(0)+CHR$(80) THEN IF X%<LAST% THEN X%=X%+1 ELSE X%=FIRST%
2960 IF ANS$=CHR$(0)+CHR$(72) THEN IF X%>FIRST% THEN X%=X%-1 ELSE X%=LAST%
2970 LOCATE X%,Y%: IF ANS$<>CHR$(13) THEN 2940
2980 FLAG%=CSRLIN : FLAG%=FLAG%-7
2990 PRINT
3000 ON FLAG% GOSUB 4230,4940,6040,6340,6480,5250,3020
3010 IF FLAG% <>7 THEN 2805
3020 RETURN
3030 '----------------- LOOK UP T-DISTRIBUTION TABLE --------------------
3040 PFILE$=PD$+"TFILE" : OPEN PFILE$ AS #1 LEN=36
3050 FIELD #1, 6 AS K$(1), 6 AS K$(2), 6 AS K$(3)
       , 6 AS K$(4), 6 AS K$(5), 6 AS K$(6)
3060 CODE%=ROWX%-COLUMNX% : IF CODE% > 120 THEN CODE%=200
3070 IF (CODE% >30) AND (CODE% <>40) AND (CODE% <>60) AND (CODE% <>120)
       AND (CODE% <>200) THEN 3100
3080 GET #1, CODE%
3090 TA= CVS(K$(TINDEX%))
3100 IF (CODE% < 40) THEN CODE1%=30 : CODE2%=40 ELSE IF (CODE% < 60) THEN
       CODE1%=40 : CODE2%=60 ELSE CODE1%=60 : CODE2%=120
3110 GET #1,CODE1%
3120 T1=CVS(K$(TINDEX%))
3130 GET #1,CODE2%
3140 T2=CVS(K$(TINDEX%))
3150 T3=(CODE% - CODE1%)*(T1-T2)
3160 T4=(CODE2%-CODE1%)
3170 TA=T1-(T3/T4)
3180 CLOSE #1
3190 PRINT "EXECUTING...": BEEP
3200 FOR I%=1 TO 10
3210 FOR J%=1 TO 10
3220 XX#(I%,J%)=0!
3230 INV#(I%,J%)=0!
3240 NEXT J%
3250 NEXT I%
3260 FOR I%=1 TO 10 : TEMP#(I%)=0! : TEMP1#(I%)=0!
3270 B#(I%)=0! : XY#(I%)=0!
3280 NEXT I%
3290 IF STATUS$(1)="" THEN FOR I%=1 TO COLUMNX%-1 : I$=CHR$(I%+48) :
       STATUS$(I%)="C"+I$+"= X"+I$ : NEXT
3300 RETURN
3310 '------------------------ PRODUCT X'X -----------------------------
3320 FOR K%=1 TO COLUMNX%
3330 FOR J%=1 TO COLUMNX%
3340 XXKJ#=XX#(K%,J%)
3350 FOR I%=1 TO ROWX%
3360 XXKJ#=XXKJ#+X#(I%,K%)*X#(I%,J%)
3370 NEXT I%
3380 XX#(K%,J%)=XXKJ#
3390 NEXT J%
3400 NEXT K%
3410 PRINT "50 % FINISHED"
3420 RETURN
3430 '------------------------ PRODUCT X'X-1 ---------------------------
3440 K%=1
3450 FOR I%=1 TO COLUMNX% : INV#(I%,I%)=1! : NEXT I%
3460 FOR I%=1 TO COLUMNX%
3470 TEMP1#=XX#(K%,K%)
3480 IF (TEMP1#=0!) THEN 3540
3490 FOR J%=1 TO COLUMNX%
3500 INV#(K%,J%)=INV#(K%,J%)/TEMP1#
3510 XX#(K%,J%)=XX#(K%,J%)/TEMP1#
```

PROGRAM 11.1 (continued)

```
3520 NEXT J%
3530 GOTO 3610
3540 L%=1
3550 WHILE (XX#(L%,K%)=0!) AND (L%<COLUMNX%)
3560 L%=L%+1 : WEND
3570 FOR J%=1 TO COLUMNX%
3580 INV#(K%,J%)=INV#(K%,J%)+INV#(L%,J%)/XX#(L%,K%)
3590 XX#(K%,J%)=XX#(K%,J%)+XX#(L%,J%)/XX#(L%,K%)
3600 NEXT J%
3610 FOR M%=1 TO COLUMNX%
3620 IF (M%=K%) THEN 3680
3630 TEMP2#=XX#(M%,K%)
3640 FOR J%=1 TO COLUMNX%
3650 INV#(M%,J%)=INV#(M%,J%)-INV#(K%,J%)*TEMP2#
3660 XX#(M%,J%)=XX#(M%,J%)-XX#(K%,J%)*TEMP2#
3670 NEXT J%
3680 NEXT M%
3690 K%=K%+1
3700 NEXT I%
3710 PRINT "70 % FINISHED"
3720 RETURN
3730 '------------------------ PRODUCT X'Y ------------------------------
3740 FOR J%=1 TO COLUMNX%
3750 FOR I%=1 TO ROWX%
3760 XY#(J%)=X#(I%,J%)*Y#(I%)+XY#(J%)
3770 NEXT I%
3780 NEXT J%
3790 RETURN
3800 '------------------------ PRODUCT B ---------------------------------
3810 FOR I%=1 TO COLUMNX%
3820 FOR J%=1 TO COLUMNX%
3830 B#(I%)=INV#(I%,J%)*XY#(J%)+B#(I%)
3840 NEXT J%
3850 NEXT I%
3860 FOR I%=1 TO ROWX%  'YHAT
3870 YHATI#=0!
3880 FOR J%=1 TO COLUMNX%
3890 YHATI#=YHATI#+X#(I%,J%)*B#(J%)
3900 NEXT J%
3910 YHAT#(I%)=YHATI#
3920 NEXT I%
3930 RETURN
3940 '------------------------ SYY ---------------------------------------
3950 YY#=0!: SUM#=0!
3960 FOR I%=1 TO ROWX%
3970 YY#=YY#+Y#(I%)*Y#(I%)
3980 SUM#=SUM#+Y#(I%)
3390 NEXT I%
4000 YBAR#=SUM#/ROWX%
4010 SYY#=YY#-(SUM#*YBAR#)
4020 RETURN
4030 '------------------------ PRODUCT BX'Y -----------------------------
4040 BXY#=0!
4050 FOR J%=1 TO COLUMNX%
4060 BXY#=BXY#+B#(J%)*XY#(J%)
4070 NEXT J%
4080 PRINT "DONE !" : BEEP
4090 RETURN
4100 '------------------------ CALCULATIONS ----------------------------
4110 SSR#=BXY#-SUM#*YBAR#
4120 SSE#=SYY#-SSR#
4130 DFY%=ROWX%-1
4140 DFE%=ROWX%-COLUMNX%
4150 DFR%=DFY%-DFE%
4160 MSR#=SSR#/DFR%
4170 MSE#=SSE#/DFE%
4180 R2#=SSR#/SYY#
4190 FO#=MSR#/MSE#
4200 DONE%=1
4210 RETURN
4220 '------------------------ TABULATE STATISTICS ----------------------
4230 CLS
4240 LOCATE ,,0
4250 PRINT TAB(23) "****  ANALYSIS OF VARIANCE ***"
4260 PRINT : PRINT
4270 FOR I%= 1 TO 80 : PRINT "-";: NEXT
4280 PRINT "SOURCE OF";
4290 PRINT TAB(53) "DEGREE OF"
4300 PRINT "VARIATION";
4310 PRINT TAB(27) "SUM OF SQUARES";
```

PROGRAM 11.1 (continued)

```
4320 PRINT TAB(53) "FREEDOM";
4330 PRINT TAB(68) "MEAN SQUARES"
4340 FOR I%=1 TO 80: PRINT "-" ;: NEXT
4350 PRINT "REGRESSION";
4360 PRINT TAB(21) USING "#################.###";SSR#;
4370 PRINT USING "##################";DFR%;
4380 PRINT USING "###################.###";MSR#
4390 PRINT "RESIDUAL";
4400 PRINT TAB(21) USING "#################.###";SSE#;
4410 PRINT USING "##################";DFE%;
4420 PRINT USING "###################.###";MSE#
4430 PRINT "TOTAL";
4440 PRINT TAB(21) USING "#################.###";SYY#;
4450 PRINT USING "##################";DFY%
4460 FOR I%=1 TO 80 : PRINT "-" ;: NEXT
4470 PRINT : PRINT
4480 PRINT "F-STATISTIC  = ";: PRINT USING "#########.####";F0#
4490 PRINT "R-SQUARED    = ";: PRINT USING "#########.####";R2#
4500 PRINT "S-SQUARED    = ";: PRINT USING "#########.####";MSE#
4510 PRINT : PRINT
4520 PRINT "Y = ";CSNG(B#(1));
4530 FOR I%=2 TO COLUMNX%
4540 IF B#(I%)>=0 THEN PRINT "+";
4550 PRINT CSNG(B#(I%)); : RC$=MID$(STATUS$(I%-1),5) :PRINT RC$;
4560 NEXT
4570 BEEP
4580 ANS$=INKEY$ : IF ANS$="" THEN 4580
4590 CLS
4600 LOCATE ,,0
4610 PRINT TAB(23) "****  REGRESSION COEFFICIENTS  ****"
4620 PRINT : PRINT
4630 FOR I%=1 TO 80 : PRINT "-"; : NEXT
4640 PRINT " N";
4650 PRINT TAB(13) "B[I]";
4660 PRINT TAB(45) USING "##";CI%; : PRINT "% C.I.";
4670 PRINT TAB(69) "T-STATISTIC"
4680 FOR I%=1 TO 80 : PRINT "-"; : NEXT
4690 FOR I%=1 TO COLUMNX%
4700 O2C#=MSE#*INV#(I%,I%) : O2C#=SQR(O2C#)
4710 T1#=TA*O2C# : T2#=1/O2C#
4720 PRINT I%-1;
4730 PRINT TAB(7) USING "######.###";B#(I%);
4740 PRINT TAB(27) USING "############.###";B#(I%)-T1#;
4750 PRINT "  --";
4760 PRINT USING "############.###";B#(I%)+T1#;
4770 PRINT USING "###############.###";B#(I%)*T2#
4780 NEXT I%
4790 FOR I%=1 TO 80 : PRINT "-";: NEXT
4800 PRINT : PRINT
4810 BEEP
4820 ANS$=INKEY$ : IF ANS$="" THEN 4820
4830 DX2%=1
4840 RETURN
4850 '------------------------  PRINT COLUMN HEADING  ----------------------
4860 CLS
4870 PRINT TAB(10) "PERIOD";
4880 PRINT TAB(33) "OBSERVED";
4890 PRINT TAB(53) "FORECAST";
4900 PRINT TAB(71) "RESIDUAL"
4910 FOR II%=1 TO 80 : PRINT "-"; : NEXT
4920 RETURN
4930 '------------------------  TABULATE OBSERVED & FORECAST  --------------
4940 LOCATE ,,0
4950 GOSUB 4860
4960 MAD#=0! : S#=0!
4970 FOR I%=1 TO ROWX%
4980 PRINT USING "##############";I%;
4990 PRINT TAB(21) USING "#################.###";Y#(I%);
5000 PRINT USING "#################.###";YHAT#(I%);
5010 DIFF=Y#(I%)-YHAT#(I%)
5020 MAD#=MAD#+ABS(DIFF)
5030 S#=S#+DIFF*DIFF
5040 PRINT USING "###############.###";DIFF
5050 IF (I% MOD 20 <> 0) AND (I% <= ROWX%) THEN 5100
5060 BEEP
5070 ANS$=INKEY$ : IF ANS$="" THEN 5070
5080 CLS
5090 GOSUB 4860
5100 NEXT I%
5110 S#=S#/DFE% : MAD#=MAD#/ROWX%
```

PROGRAM 11.1 (continued)

```
5120 PRINT
5130 PRINT "MEAN ABSOLUTE DEVIATION : MAD = ";CSNG(MAD#);
5140 PRINT " (";CSNG(MAD#/YBAR#)*100;" %)"
5150 PRINT "MEAN SQUARED ERROR      : MSE = ";CSNG(S#);: BEEP
5160 ANS$=INKEY$ : IF ANS$="" THEN 5160
5170 CLS : INPUT "NEED CONFIDENCE INTERVAL :";ANS$
5180 IF ANS$="N" OR ANS$="n" THEN 5220
5190 LOCATE ,,0
5200 FST%=1 : LST%=ROWX%
5210 GOSUB 5390
5220 DX2%=2
5230 RETURN
5240 '------------------------ DO PREDICTION ----------------------------
5250 IF ROW%>ROWX% THEN GOSUB 5310 : GOTO 5280
5260 CLS : PRINT "THERE IS NO FUTURE VALUES OF INDEPENDENT "
5270 PRINT "VARIABLES AVAILABLE FOR FORECASTING Y !" : BEEP
5280 DX2%=6
5290 RETURN
5300 '------------------------ TABULATE CONFIDENCE INTERVAL -------------
5310 FST%=ROWX%+1 : LST%=ROW%
5320 FOR I%=FST% TO LST%
5330 YHATI#=0!
5340 FOR J%=1 TO COLUMNX%
5350 YHATI#=YHATI#+X#(I%,J%)*B#(J%)
5360 NEXT J%
5370 YHAT#(I%)=YHATI#
5380 NEXT I%
5390 CLS
5400 PRINT "PERIOD";
5410 PRINT TAB(20) "FORECAST";
5420 PRINT TAB(47) USING "##";CI%;
5430 PRINT " %      PREDICTION       INTERVAL" : COUNT%=0
5440 FOR I%=1 TO 80 : PRINT "-"; : NEXT
5450 FOR I%=FST% TO LST% : COUNT%=COUNT%+1
5460 PRINT USING "####";I%;
5470 PRINT USING "###################.###";YHAT#(I%);
5480 FOR J%=1 TO COLUMNX% : TEMP#(J%)=0! : NEXT
5490 FOR J%=1 TO COLUMNX%
5500 FOR K%=1 TO COLUMNX%
5510 TEMP#(J%)= TEMP#(J%)+X#(I%,K%)*INV#(K%,J%)
5520 NEXT K%
5530 NEXT J%
5540 T1#=0!
5550 FOR J%=1 TO COLUMNX%
5560 T1#=T1#+TEMP#(J%)*X#(I%,J%)
5570 NEXT J%
5580 T2#= (T1#+1)*MSE#
5590 T2#=SQR(T2#)*TA
5600 PRINT TAB(35) USING "################.###";YHAT#(I%)-T2#;
5610 PRINT "  --";
5620 PRINT USING "################.###";YHAT#(I%)+T2#
5630 IF COUNT% MOD 20 <> 0 THEN 5670
5640 BEEP
5650 ANS$=INKEY$ : IF ANS$="" THEN 5650
5660 CLS
5670 NEXT I%
5680 BEEP
5690 ANS$=INKEY$ : IF ANS$="" THEN 5690
5700 RETURN
5710 '------------------------ CONFIDENCE LEVEL MENU --------------------
5720 CLS:SCREEN 0,1: LOCATE 6,1
5730 PRINT TAB(20) "***  CONFIDENCE LEVEL MENU  ***"
5740 PRINT
5750 PRINT TAB(20) "*          _ 99 %              *"
5760 PRINT TAB(20) "*          _ 98 %              *"
5770 PRINT TAB(20) "*          _ 95 %              *"
5780 PRINT TAB(20) "*          _ 90 %              *"
5790 PRINT TAB(20) "*          _ 80 %              *"
5800 PRINT TAB(20) "*          _ 50 %              *"
5810 PRINT TAB(20) "*          _ EXIT              *"
5820 PRINT
5830 PRINT TAB(20) "*******************************"
5840 X%=8 : Y%=31: LOCATE X%,Y%,1,0,7
5850 FIRST%=8 : LAST%=14
5860 ANS$=INKEY$ : IF ANS$="" THEN 5860
5870 IF ANS$=CHR$(0)+CHR$(80) THEN IF X%<LAST% THEN X%=X%+1 ELSE X%=FIRST%
5880 IF ANS$=CHR$(0)+CHR$(72) THEN IF X%>FIRST% THEN X%=X%-1 ELSE X%=LAST%
```

PROGRAM 11.1 (continued)

```
5890 LOCATE X%,Y% : IF ANS$<> CHR$(13) THEN 5860
5900 FLAG%=CSRLIN : FLAG%=FLAG%-7
5910 ON FLAG% GOSUB 5980,5970,5960,5950,5940,5930,5920
5920 RETURN
5930 CI%=50 : TINDEX%=1 : RETURN
5940 CI%=80 : TINDEX%=2 : RETURN
5950 CI%=90 : TINDEX%=3 : RETURN
5960 CI%=95 : TINDEX%=4 : RETURN
5970 CI%=98 : TINDEX%=5 : RETURN
5980 CI%=99 : TINDEX%=6 : RETURN
5990 '------------------- CHANGE DEFAULT DRIVE ---------------------------
6000 IF FD$="A:" THEN FD$="B:" ELSE IF FD$="B:" THEN FD$="C:" ELSE FD$="A:"
6010 LOCATE 5,76: PRINT FD$: BEEP
6020 RETURN
6030 '------------------- PLOT OBSERVED VS FORECAST ----------------------
6040 CLS : FILE2$=FD$+"TEMP.DAT"
6050 INPUT "PLOT WITH GRID LINES < N FOR NO >";ANS$
6060 ANS$=LEFT$(ANS$,1) : IF ANS$="N" OR ANS$="n" THEN GRD$="N" ELSE GRD$="G"
6070 FILESTK$(1)=FILE2$
6080 OPEN FILE2$ FOR OUTPUT AS #2
6090 PRINT #2,ROWX%;ROWX%;2
6100 FOR J%=1 TO ROWX%
6110 PRINT #2,Y#(J%);
6120 NEXT
6130 FOR J%=1 TO ROWX%
6140 PRINT #2,J%;
6150 NEXT
6160 CLOSE #2
6170 CLS : FILE2$=FD$+"TEMP1.DAT"
6180 FILESTK$(2)=FILE2$
6190 OPEN FILE2$ FOR OUTPUT AS #2
6200 PRINT #2,ROWX%;ROWX%;2
6210 FOR J%=1 TO ROWX%
6220 PRINT #2,YHAT#(J%);
6230 NEXT
6240 FOR J%=1 TO ROWX%
6250 PRINT #2,J%;
6260 NEXT
6270 CLOSE #2
6280 NOF%=2 : CURVE$(1)="P" : CURVE$(2)="C" : FLAG1%=7
6290 FILE2$=PD$+"APLOT.BAS" : PFILE$=PD$+"REGR.BAS" : SL%=270
6300 CHAIN FILE2$ ,,ALL
6310 DX2%=3
6320 RETURN
6330 '------------------------ PLOT RESIDUALS VS Y ----------------------
6340 CLS : FILE2$=FD$+"TEMP.DAT"
6350 INPUT "PLOT WITH GRID LINES < N FOR NO >";ANS$
6360 ANS$=LEFT$(ANS$,1) : IF ANS$="N" OR ANS$="n" THEN GRD$="N" ELSE GRD$="G"
6370 FILESTK$(1)=FILE2$
6380 OPEN FILE2$ FOR OUTPUT AS #2
6390 PRINT #2,ROWX%;ROWX%;2
6400 FOR J%=1 TO ROWX%
6410 PRINT #2,Y#(J%)-YHAT#(J%);
6420 NEXT
6430 FOR J%=1 TO ROWX%
6440 PRINT #2,Y#(J%);
6450 NEXT
6460 CLOSE #2 : GOTO 6610
6470 '--------------------- PLOT RESIDUALS VS REGRESSORS -----------------
6480 CLS : INPUT "CHOOSE WHICH REGRESSOR C_";C0% : C0%=C0%+1
6490 INPUT "PLOT WITH GRID LINES < N FOR NO >";ANS$
6500 ANS$=LEFT$(ANS$,1) : IF ANS$="N" OR ANS$="n" THEN GRD$="N" ELSE GRD$="G"
6510 FILE2$=FD$+"TEMP.BAS" : FILESTK$(1)=FILE2$
6520 OPEN FILE2$ FOR OUTPUT AS #2
6530 PRINT #2,ROWX%;ROWX%;2
6540 FOR J%=1 TO ROWX%
6550 PRINT #2,Y#(J%)-YHAT#(J%);
6560 NEXT
6570 FOR J%=1 TO ROWX%
6580 PRINT #2,X#(J%,C0%);
6590 NEXT
6600 CLOSE #2
6610 NOF%=1 : CURVE$(1)="P" : FLAG1%=7
6620 PFILE$=PD$+"REGR.BAS" : SL%=270
6630 FILE2$=PD$+"APLOT.BAS"
6640 CHAIN FILE2$ ,,ALL
6650 END
```

PROGRAM 11.1 REGRESSION

The user must create a t-distribution file using the following program and save this data file under TFILE.

```
10 '   Program 11.2 : Routine to create a t-table (TFILE)
20  CLS : KEY OFF
30  INPUT "FILE NAME =";FILE$    ' suggest to use a name, TFILE
40  INPUT "NUMBER OF ROWS =";ROW%
50  OPEN FILE$ AS #1 LEN=36
60  FIELD #1, 6 AS A$,6 AS B$,6 AS C$,6 AS D$,6 AS E$,6 AS F$
70  FOR I%=1 TO ROW%
80  INPUT "DEGREE OF FREEDOM AND T-STATISTICS =";DOF%,T1,T2,T3,T4,T5,T6
90  LSET A$=MKS$(T1)
100  LSET B$=MKS$(T2)
110  LSET C$=MKS$(T3)
120  LSET D$=MKS$(T4)
130  LSET E$=MKS$(T5)
140  LSET F$=MKS$(T6)
150  PUT #1,DOF%
160  NEXT
170  CLOSE
180  END
```

PROGRAM 11.2 Routine to Create a *t*-Table (TFILE)

For example, to create a partial t-distribution file shown below we respond as follows:

Percentage Points of α of the t-Distribution

df α	0.10	0.05	0.025	0.01	0.005	0.0025
1	3.078	6.314	12.706	31.821	63.657	127.320
2	1.886	2.920	4.303	6.965	9.925	14.089
3	1.638	2.353	3.182	4.541	5.841	7.453

df = degree of freedom

```
FILE NAME =? TFILE
NUMBER OF ROWS =? 3
DEGREE OF FREEDOM AND T-STATISTICS =? 1, 3.078, 6.314, 12.706, 31.821, 63.657, 1
27.320
DEGREE OF FREEDOM AND T-STATISTICS =? 2, 1.886, 2.920, 4.303, 6.965, 9.925, 14.0
89
DEGREE OF FREEDOM AND T-STATISTICS =? 3, 1.638, 2.353, 3.182, 4.541, 5.841, 7.45
3
```

The user must create a t-distribution file with a sufficient number of degrees of freedom (up to 120) by consulting a statistics book. (See [3].) Note that we have only six entries (0.10 through 0.0025) for a given df. If users want to create

TABLE 11.7 Percentage points α of the t-distribution (truncated)

df \ α	0.10	0.05	0.025	0.01	0.005	0.0025
1	3.078	6.314	12.706	31.821	63.657	127.32
2	1.866	2.920	4.303	6.965	9.925	14.089
3	1.638	2.353	3.182	4.541	5.841	7.453
4	1.533	2.132	2.776	3.747	4.604	5.598
5	1.476	2.015	2.571	3.365	4.032	4.773
6	1.440	1.943	2.447	3.143	3.707	4.317
7	1.415	1.895	2.365	2.998	3.499	4.029
8	1.397	1.860	2.306	2.896	3.355	3.833
9	1.383	1.833	2.262	2.821	3.250	3.690
10	1.372	1.812	2.228	2.764	3.169	3.581
11	1.363	1.796	2.201	2.718	3.106	3.497
12	1.356	1.782	2.179	2.681	3.055	3.428
13	1.350	1.771	2.160	2.650	3.012	3.372
14	1.345	1.761	2.145	2.624	2.977	3.326
15	1.341	1.753	2.131	2.602	2.947	3.286
16	1.337	1.746	2.120	2.583	2.921	3.252
17	1.333	1.740	2.110	2.567	2.898	3.222
18	1.330	1.734	2.101	2.552	2.878	3.197
19	1.328	1.729	2.093	2.539	2.861	3.174
20	1.325	1.725	2.086	2.528	2.845	3.153
21	1.323	1.721	2.080	2.518	2.831	3.135
22	1.321	1.717	2.074	2.508	2.819	3.119
23	1.319	1.714	2.069	2.500	2.807	3.104
24	1.318	1.711	2.064	2.492	2.797	3.091
25	1.316	1.708	2.060	2.485	2.787	3.078
26	1.315	1.706	2.056	2.479	2.779	3.067
27	1.314	1.703	2.052	2.473	2.771	3.057
28	1.313	1.701	2.048	2.467	2.763	3.047
29	1.311	1.699	2.045	2.462	2.756	3.038
30	1.310	1.697	2.042	2.457	2.750	3.030
40	1.303	1.684	2.021	2.423	2.704	2.971
60	1.296	1.671	2.000	2.390	2.660	2.915
120	1.289	1.658	1.980	2.358	2.617	2.860

a t-distribution file with more than six entries, they must change lines 50, 60, and 80 in Program 11.2. The t-distribution table shown in Table 11.7 may be sufficient for normal regression analysis.

EXERCISES

11.1 The data in this problem, adapted from Hines and Montgomery [3], represent the electric power (y) consumed each month by a chemical plant. The power consumption is thought to be related to the average ambient temperature (x_1), the number of days in the month (x_2), the average product purity (x_3), and the number of tons of product produced (x_4).

y	x_1	x_2	x_3	x_4
240	25	24	91	100
236	31	21	90	95
290	45	24	88	110
274	60	25	87	88
301	65	25	91	94
316	72	26	94	99
300	80	25	87	97
296	84	25	86	96
267	75	24	88	110
276	60	25	91	105
288	50	25	90	100
261	38	23	89	98

a) Fit a multiple regression model to these data.
b) Using the REGR program, determine the significance of each regression parameter.
c) Compute the residuals from this model and analyze the residuals as was discussed in this chapter.
d) Estimate the power consumption with $x_1 = 62$, $x_2 = 25$, $x_3 = 93$, and $x_4 = 105$.

11.2 Consider the following data.

y	−4.5	−1.45	−1.35	−1.68	−2.75	−3.26	−4.82	−5.15	−6.25	−8.13
x	0.25	0.50	0.75	1.00	1.25	1.50	1.75	2.00	2.25	2.50

a) Fit a second-order polynomial to the data.
b) Test for significance of the regression parameters.
c) Plot the residual patterns and discuss the appropriateness of the model.

11.3 Consider the data shown below, which represent the monthly delivery of a certain model of computer to a dealer.

Month	1	2	3	4	5	6	7	8	9	10	11	12
Units	41	54	74	81	73	62	61	32	50	72	53	42

a) Fit the regression model

$$y_t = b_0 + b_1 \cos(\pi t/3) + b_2 \sin(\pi t/3) + e_t$$

to these data using the REGR program.

b) Plot the residuals as a function of time and determine the appropriateness of the model.

REFERENCES

1. Bowerman, B. L., and R. T. O'Connell, *Forecasting and Time Series,* Duxbury Press, North Scituate, Mass., 1979 (Chapter 2).

2. Draper N. R., and H. Smith, *Applied Regression Analysis,* Wiley, New York, 1966 (Chapter 3).

3. Hines, W. W., and D. C. Montgomery, *Probability and Statistics in Engineering and Management Science,* 2nd ed., Wiley, New York, 1980 (Chapters 12 and 13).

CHAPTER TWELVE
Economic Analysis under Risk

Computer simulations often produce large amounts of output because users want to vary the model's constraints, relationships, or input conditions. This ability to vary conditions is precisely what makes simulation valuable. As models become more complex and users pose more questions, the amount of output can become enormous and the task of interpreting the results overwhelming. At the same time, failure to try enough conditions may leave the analyst without an adequate understanding of the model's behavior. When one must interpret large amounts of output from a simulation, computer graphics is an important tool. In this chapter, we will develop a risk analysis model to demonstrate how interactive computer graphics can facilitate the understanding of simulation results.

12.1 RISK ANALYSIS

12.1.1 PROJECT RISK

The principal determinants of economic worth in engineering projects are the cash flow streams. Cash flows are projected at the time the project is first proposed, and (at least implicitly) are considered to be subject to probabilistic deviation from their expected values. Variations in the outcomes of the future events have been of primary concern to most decision makers in evaluating investment proposals. The variation from the judgmental estimates is often termed "risk."

We often use variance or standard deviation as the principal measure of risk, thereby summarizing the spread of a statistical distribution. We might also compute the probability that the net present value (NPV) of a project will be negative, $P\{\text{NPV} \leq 0\}$. Another way of expressing this is the probability that the present value of cash inflows will be less than the present value of the cost of the project. To derive this probability, we need at least part of the statistical distribution of present values. This is obtained by introducing the concept of risk analysis.

Risk analysis is defined here as the process of developing probability distributions for some measure of the merit of an investment proposal (in this case, net present value). To do this, probability distributions are required for random variables such as cash flow, the planning horizon, and the discount rate. The probability distributions are then aggregated analytically or through simulation to obtain the desired probability distribution for net present value. For simplicity, we will assume that the cash flow elements are the only random variables in our example.

12.1.2 NET PRESENT VALUE CRITERION

Uncertain cash flow streams can be treated as a series of random variables for the purpose of computing project present value. Let F_t be a stream of random net cash flows generated by a particular project at time period $t (t = 0, 1, 2, \ldots, n)$. A particular cash flow, F_t, may be positive in sign (inflow) or negative in sign (outflow). Both inflows and outflows can occur in any period. The net effect in a particular period is the item of consequence. The relationship between the net present value (NPV) of the cash flow stream and its constituent cash flow elements is

$$\text{NPV} = \sum_{t=0}^{n} \frac{F_t}{(1 + i)^t} \tag{12.1}$$

where i is the minimum attractive rate of return.

Since a random process governs the values taken by F_t, the relative frequencies of the random values taken by the cash flow can usually be represented by probability or density functions $[f(F)_t]$. This randomness can be expressed by the mean and variance of the distribution of F_t. Thus the summation of the discounted random cash flows (that is, the project NPV) is also a random variable. We are left with two crucial questions: how do we obtain the probability distribution of NPV, and how do we devise a decision rule for evaluating this distribution? We will first discuss a method for finding the probability distribution of NPV.

12.1.3 METHOD OF OBTAINING THE PROBABILITY DISTRIBUTION OF NPV

The cash flow in a given year F_t is often a function of a number of other critical variables, such as selling prices, size of the market, investment required, inflation rate, operating costs, and so on. A number of these random variables are correlated with each other. Consequently, the probability distribution for the NPV is not easy to develop by analysis in most real-world situations. Computer simulation of possible changes in the critical factors is in general an easier way of combining those distributions—in some cases, the only practical way. This procedure is often referred to as a *risk simulation* [1].

Risk simulation involves repeated chance trials using outcomes from a random number generator adjusted to provide various probability distributions. It is therefore necessary to create a simulation model that provides output concerning the distribution of probable outcomes of a project. Monte Carlo methods (computer-based sampling experiments) are used to select values from probability distributions modeling the critical factors possessing substantial uncertainty. The values selected are then used to compute the NPV for those parameters.

The process is repeated with different sets of selected data. Present value figures fall into a frequency distribution describing the likelihood that a particular NPV might occur. An additional computer program is then used to develop a probability distribution of the differences between any two mutually exclusive alternatives. It is thus possible to ascertain the probability that one alternative will be more attractive than the other. Figure 12.1 shows the process schematically.

12.1.4 DECISION RULES

Single project evaluation. When the probability distribution of NPV has been obtained, the crucial question is how to use this distribution in project analysis. Recall that the probability distribution gives the probability that a random variable will attain some value x. We can use this information, in turn, to define the cumulative distribution, which expresses the probability that the random variable will attain a value smaller or equal to some x, that is $P(X \leq x)$. A common notation for the cumulative distribution is $F(x) = P(X \leq x)$. Thus if the NPV distribution is known, we can compute the probability that the NPV of a project will be negative. We use this probabilistic information to judge how attractive the project is.

Two mutually exclusive projects. We can extend the concept of a cumulative distribution to analyze an investment choice between project A and

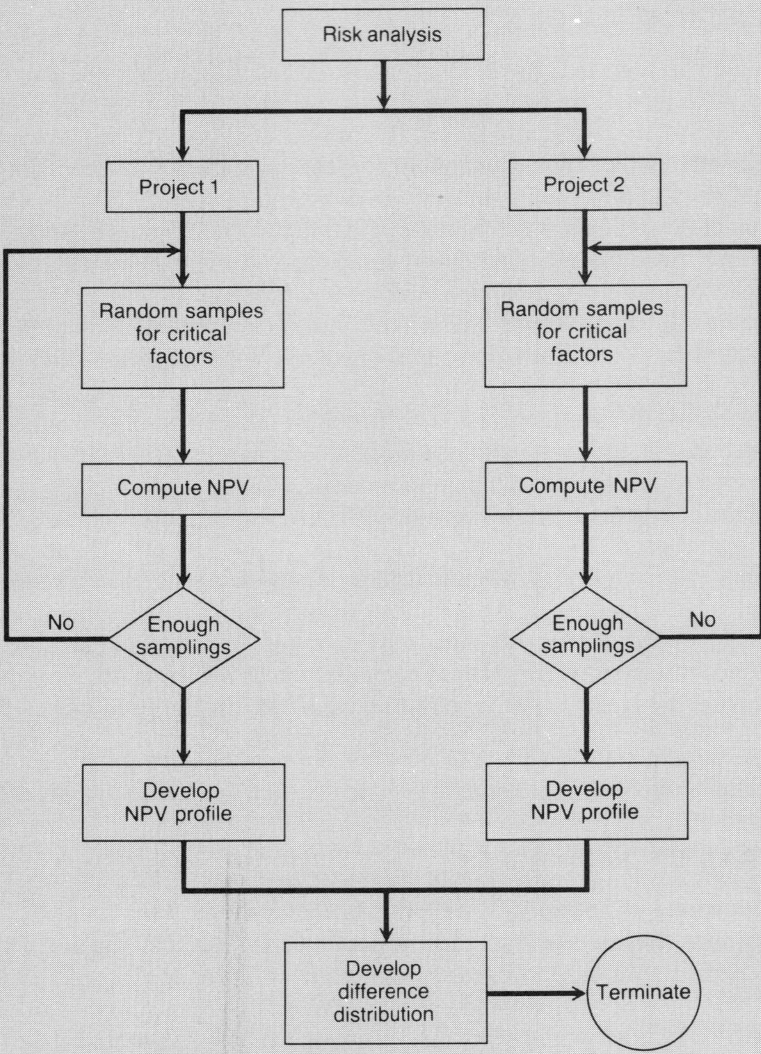

FIGURE 12.1 Simulation process

project B. This requires us to develop a cumulative distribution of the difference in net present value:

$$P\{\Delta \leq NPV_A - NPV_B\}.$$

A Δ of 0 is equivalent to finding the probability that the NPV of project A will exceed project B. If this probability is 1, project A is preferable to project B. If this probability is equal to 0, the reverse is true. This type of information is useful when we have to discriminate between two competing projects.

12.2 SELECTING INPUT PROBABILITY DISTRIBUTIONS

Two heuristic procedures are extensively used to choose a cash flow distribution in the absence of data. The first step in either approach is to identify an interval $[L, H]$ within which random variable X (the cash flow occurring at the end of the period) is contained with a probability close to 1. To obtain subjective estimates of L and H, we must provide our most pessimistic (L) and optimistic (H) estimates of the cash flow occurring at the end of each period. We can also treat the project life, the discount rate, and other project parameters as random variables. If this is done, we should also provide the subjective estimates of the other random variables in a similar manner.

Once an interval $[L, H]$ has been subjectively identified, the next step is to determine the probability distribution of X over that interval. Two probability distributions are used extensively in simulations.

12.2.1 TRIANGULAR DISTRIBUTION

In the triangular approach, we must first identify our subjective estimate of the most likely cash flow value (M_o) at the end of each period. This most likely value is the mode of the distribution of X. Given a certain L, H, and M_o, the random variable X is considered to have a triangular distribution over the interval $[L, H]$ with mode M_o. The triangular distribution is described by a continuous density function that follows the general form given in Fig. 12.2. It is defined with respect to the position of M_o as

$$f(x) = \begin{cases} \dfrac{2(x - L)}{(H - L)(M_o - L)}, & L \le x \le M_o \\[2ex] \dfrac{2(H - x)}{(H - L)(H - M_o)}, & M_o \le x \le H \end{cases} \tag{12.2}$$

The cumulative probability distribution is similarly obtained by

$$F(x) = \begin{cases} \dfrac{(x - L)^2}{(H - L)(M_o - L)}, & L \le x \le M_o \\[2ex] 1 - \dfrac{(H - x)^2}{(H - L)(H - M_o)}, & M_o \le x \le H \end{cases} \tag{12.3}$$

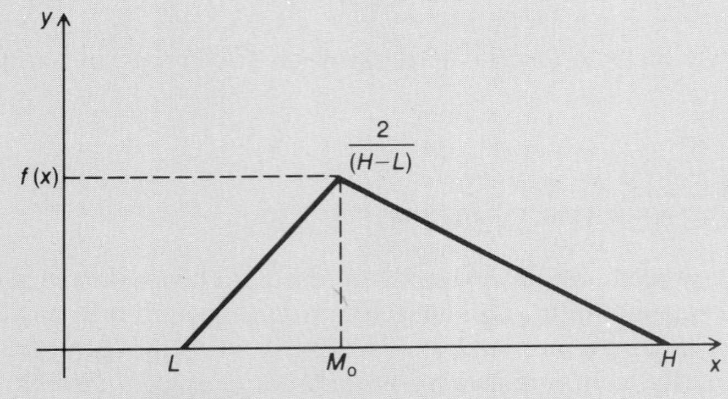

FIGURE 12.2 Triangular distribution

The expected value and variance of the triangular distribution are then expressed by

$$E(X) = \frac{L + M_o + H}{3} \tag{12.4}$$

$$V(X) = \frac{1}{18}[(L^2 + M_o^2 + H^2 - LH - M_oH - M_oL)]. \tag{12.5}$$

12.2.2 BETA DISTRIBUTION

A second approach to determining a density function over $[L, H]$ is to assume that the random variable X has a beta distribution over this interval with shape parameters a and b. The beta distribution offers more modeling flexibility because its properties are closer to those of random cash flows. It has a finite range ($L \leq X \leq H$), continuity, and unimodality (given that a and b are both greater than zero). It can also assume various degrees of skewness and peakedness, a desirable property in this application.

Standard beta distribution. The standard beta distribution for a random variable y is defined as

$$f(y) = \frac{\Gamma(a + b + 2)}{\Gamma(a + 1)\Gamma(b + 1)} y^a(1 - y)^b \qquad 0 \leq y \leq 1 \tag{12.6}$$

where Γ is a gamma function operator. For the standardized beta distribution, we know that the mean, variance, and mode are computed as

$$E(y) = \frac{a + 1}{a + b + 2}, \tag{12.7}$$

$$\text{VAR}(y) = \frac{(a + 1)(b + 1)}{(a + b + 3)(a + b + 2)^2}, \tag{12.8}$$

and

$$M = \frac{a}{a + b}. \tag{12.9}$$

This equation becomes less forbidding once we realize that the first portion is merely a constant used to satisfy the requirement that the area under the curve must be unity if it is to represent a probability distribution. Thus for any selection of the a and b parameters, we may rewrite the equation as

$$f(y) = \frac{1}{c} y^a (1 - y)^b, \qquad 0 \le y \le 1 \tag{12.10}$$

where c is a constant.

For all positive values of a and b, the curve meets the horizontal axis at the points $y=0$ and $y=1$. When $a=b$, the curve will be symmetric with mode at $M = 0.5$. Note that when $a = 0$ and $b > 0$ the distribution assumes a "J" shape with the top of the "J" at $y = 0$, but when $b = 0$ and $a > 0$, the shape is reversed with the top at $y = 1$. It is also seen that when a = b = 0, Eq. (12.10) reduces to

$$f(y) = \frac{1}{c}$$

which is the probability density function for the uniform distribution. We further note that if $a > b$, the beta distribution is skewed to the left (negative skewness). If $a < b$, the distribution is skewed to the right (positive skewness). These relationships are presented in Fig. 12.3. Note that the standard beta distribution is bounded between 0 and 1 and that the shape of the distribution is totally determined by a and b. The scope of the beta distribution can be broadened by allowing the variate to range between any pair of finite limits $[L, H]$. In the following section, we will show how this is done.

Beta distribution with arbitrary limits. To use the beta distribution in our cash flow modeling, we must first extract the values of a and b from the H, M_o, and L values. A transformation of these values to the *standard beta* interval $[0, 1]$ yields

$$y = \frac{x - L}{H - L}$$

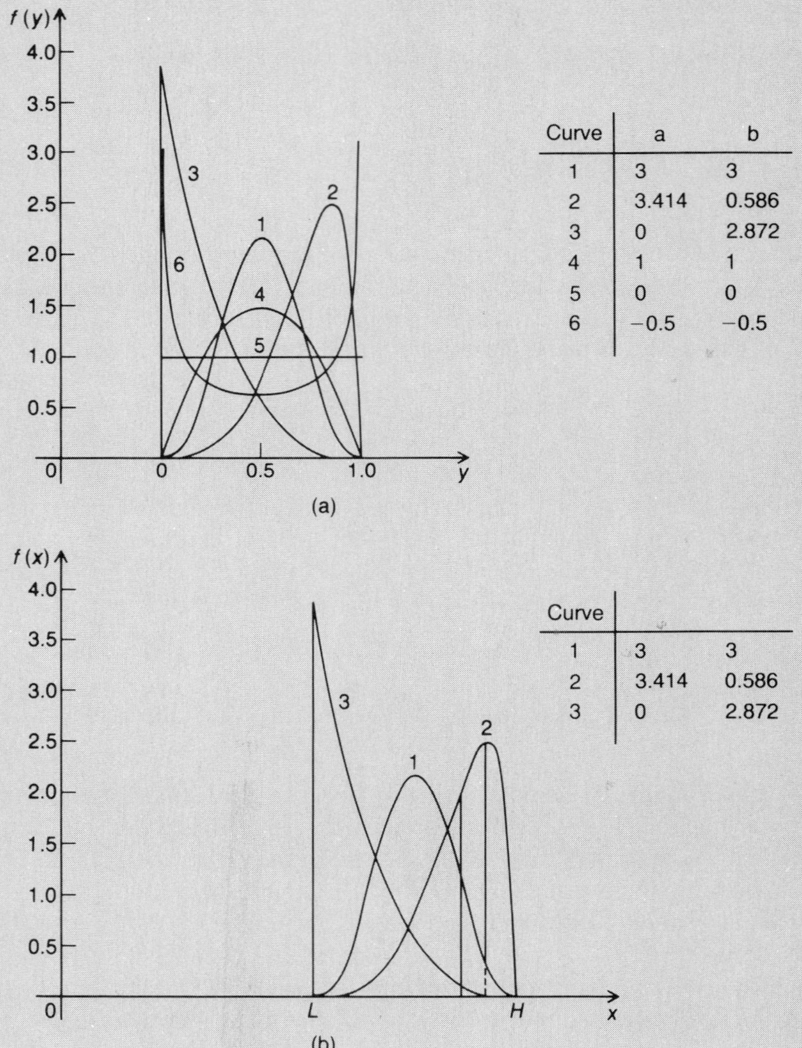

FIGURE 12.3 Shapes of beta distribution: (a) standard beta distribution: (b) transformed beta distribution. Source: W. J. McBride and C. W. McClelland, "PERT and the Beta Distribution," *IEEE Transactions on Engineering Management,* EM 14 (4), 1968

or

$$x = L + (H - L)y\,. \tag{12.11}$$

This linear relation of Eq. (12.16) transforms the standard beta distribution into

$$f(x) = \underbrace{\frac{\Gamma(a + b + 2)}{\Gamma(a + 1)\Gamma(b + 1)(H - L)^{a+b+1}}}_{\text{constant}}(x - L)^a(H - x)^b, \quad \text{for } L \le x \le H \tag{12.12}$$

There is no closed form for the cumulative distribution, but expressions for the mean(μ), variance (σ^2), and mode (M_o), of this distribution are as follows:

$$E[X] = \mu = L + \left[\frac{(H - L)(a + 1)}{(a + b + 2)}\right], \tag{12.13}$$

$$\text{VAR}[X] = \sigma^2 = \left[\frac{(H - L)^2(a + 1)(b + 1)}{(a + b + 2)^2(a + b + 3)}\right], \tag{12.14}$$

$$M_o = \frac{Lb + Ha}{a + b} \quad (\text{for } a, b \ge 0)\,. \tag{12.15}$$

Estimating parameters *a* and *b*. The use of the beta distribution in simulation modeling causes some difficulty because it is not always clear how to choose parameters a and b so as to specify the distribution completely. The usual approach is to set the curve's standard deviation at one-sixth of the range. This is a reasonable approach because one-sixth of the range can be used as a rough estimate of standard deviation for most unimodal distributions. The random variable X in Eq. (12.11) is simply a linear function of the standard beta random variable. Thus it is much easier for us to work with the standard beta function to find the a and b. Once these are found, we can use Eqs. (12.13) through (12.15) to determine μ and σ^2 for the beta distribution with some arbitrary range (L, H).

The first step in estimating a and b is to transform the mode M_o (most likely estimate) to the mode M of the standardized beta random variable:

$$M = \frac{M_o - L}{H - L} = \frac{a}{a + b}\,. \tag{12.16}$$

Rewriting Eq. (12.16) in terms of b gives us

$$b = \frac{a}{M} - a\,. \tag{12.17}$$

From our assumption, we set $\text{VAR}(y) = (1/6)^2$ to obtain

$$\frac{(a + 1)(b + 1)}{(a + b + 3)(a + b + 2)^2} = \frac{1}{6}\,. \tag{12.18}$$

Substituting Eq. (12.17) into Eq. (12.18) and rearranging terms, it follows that

$$a^3 + (7M - 36M^2 + 36M^3)a^2 - 20M^2a - 24M^3 = 0. \qquad \textbf{(12.19)}$$

As seen in Eq. (12.16), computing M from values of L, M_o, and H requires no more than simple arithmetic. Once M is found, a is determined from Eq. (12.19) and we return again to the modal equation Eq. (12.17) to solve for b. [To avoid solving the cubic terms in Eq. (12.19), Greer [2] developed a chart.]

12.3 GENERATING RANDOM VARIABLES

Now that we have specified the distributions for random cash flows, the next step is to generate random variables with these distributions in order to run the simulation model. The basic element required is a source of independent identically distributed uniform random variables between 0 and 1, $U(0,1)$. It is therefore very important that a statistically reliable $U(0,1)$ random number generator be available. The IBM PC provides a random number generator, U = RND(X), where X is a numeric expression that affects the returned value. When X is positive or not specified, RND(X) generates the next random number in the sequence. The same sequence of random numbers is generated each time the program is run unless the random number generator is reseeded. This is done by using the RANDOMIZE N statement, where N is an integer expression ($-32768 < N < 32767$) that will be used as the random number seed.

12.3.1 TRIANGULAR RANDOM DEVIATE

Since the cumulative distribution of the triangular distribution is available (see Eq. (12.3)), we will use the inverse transformation method [3] to generate a triangular random deviate.

Using the expression given in Eq. (12.16), we first find the mode M of the standardized triangular random variable by transforming M_o:

$$M = \frac{(M_o - L)}{(H - L)}.$$

Then the distribution function given in Eq. (12.2) is easily inverted to obtain the relationship

$$X = \begin{cases} L + [F(x)(H - L)(M_o - L)], & 0 \le F(x) \le M \\ H - \{[1 - F(X)](H - L)(H - M_o)\}, & M \le F(x) \le 1. \end{cases} \qquad \textbf{(12.20)}$$

Since we know that $0 \le F(x) \le 1$ and $0 \le U \le 1$, we can obtain the desired triangular random deviate by letting $U = F(x)$ and substituting this into

Eq. (12.20). In summary, we do the following:

Step 1: Compute M.
Step 2: Generate a uniform random deviate, U.
Step 3: If $U \leq M$, compute $X = L + [U \cdot (H - L)(M_o - L)]$. Otherwise, compute $X = H - [(1 - U)(H - L)(H - M_o)]$.

12.3.2 BETA RANDOM DEVIATE

Several alternative algorithms can be used to generate random variables from a beta distribution, most of which are beyond the scope of this text. Many such algorithms are designed for special problem structures and require a high level of statistical sophistication of the user. Here we will discuss a general method developed by Law and Kelton [3] for generating a beta (a, b) random deviate over the interval $[0, 1]$ for any $a > 0$ and $b > 0$.

The Law and Kelton method derives from the fact that if γ_1 and γ_2 are independent random variables with γ_1 gamma $(a, 1)$ and γ_2 gamma $(b, 1)$, the ratio $\gamma_1/(\gamma_1 + \gamma_2)$ is distributed as beta (a, b), where $(a, 1)$ and $(b, 1)$ are the shape parameters for the gamma distribution. More precisely, we may proceed as follows to generate a beta random deviate over the arbitrary interval $[L, H]$:

Step 1: Generate two gamma random deviates, γ_1 gamma $(a, 1)$ and γ_2 gamma $(b, 1)$ independent of γ_1.
Step 2: Set

$$Y = \frac{\gamma_1}{(\gamma_1 + \gamma_2)}.$$

Step 3: Compute $X = L + (H - L)Y$.

To generate a gamma random deviate $\gamma \sim (a, 1)$, we set $d = (e + a)/e$, $e = 2.7327\ldots$, and follow three steps.

Step 1: Generate $U_1 \sim U(0, 1)$ and let $P = dU_1$. If $P > 1$, go to step 3. Otherwise, go to step 2.
Step 2: Let $Z = P^{1/a}$, and generate another uniform random deviate $U_2 \sim U(0, 1)$. If $U_2 \leq e^{-Z}$, set $\gamma = Z$ and stop. Otherwise, go back to step 1.
Step 3: Let $Z = -\ln[(d - P)/a]$ and generate $U_2 \sim U(0, 1)$. If $U_2 \leq Z^{a-1}$, set $\gamma = Z$ and stop. Otherwise, go back to step 1.

Generating a random deviate from a beta distribution will usually take more execution time than generating it from a triangular distribution. Therefore, we will use the triangular approach in estimating the random variables in our case example.

12.4 DESCRIPTION OF RISK SIMULATION PROGRAM

12.4.1 COMPUTER PROGRAMMING LOGIC

Our risk simulation program (program 12.1) is written in IBM BASICA. The complete code is provided at the end of this chapter. The general programming logic is shown in Fig. 12.4.

The computer program is comprised of three subprograms: (1) a program for entering data and simulation parameters (i.e., IN1A for cash flow inputs, IN1B for inputs to the Monte Carlo sampling process, and IN2 for the inputs of the discounting process); (2) a program for performing the Monte Carlo sampling and calculating the resulting statistics; and (3) a program for directing the next step to be performed (i.e., displaying the simulation results).

Five possible options are available to the user in the third subroutine: (1) plot the statistics; (2) make a new run with reseeded random numbers; (3) change the discount rate; (4) change the number of Monte Carlo samplings (replications); and (5) exit the program.

If we select the first option, four additional options are available for displaying the statistics. They are: (1) display the histogram for project 1; (2) display the histogram for project 2; (3) display the superimposed distributions of projects 1 and 2; and (4) display the histogram of difference distribution (project 1 − project 2).

12.4.2 RISK SIMULATION CASE EXAMPLE

Consider the two mutually exclusive investment proposals shown in Table 12.1. Both proposals have an economic life of three years. The size of the initial investment required is known with certainty for both proposals; their

TABLE 12.1 Proposal cash flow profiles (lowest, most likely, highest)

	Cash flow ($1000)	
End of year	**Proposal 1**	**Proposal 2**
0	(−10, −10, −10)*	(−15, −15, −15)*
1	(5, 8, 12)	(5, 10, 13)
2	(10, 15, 20)	(20, 25, 30)
3	(10, 20, 30)	(10, 15, 40)

*When one enters a deterministic cash flow, the lowest, most likely, and highest estimates are identical.

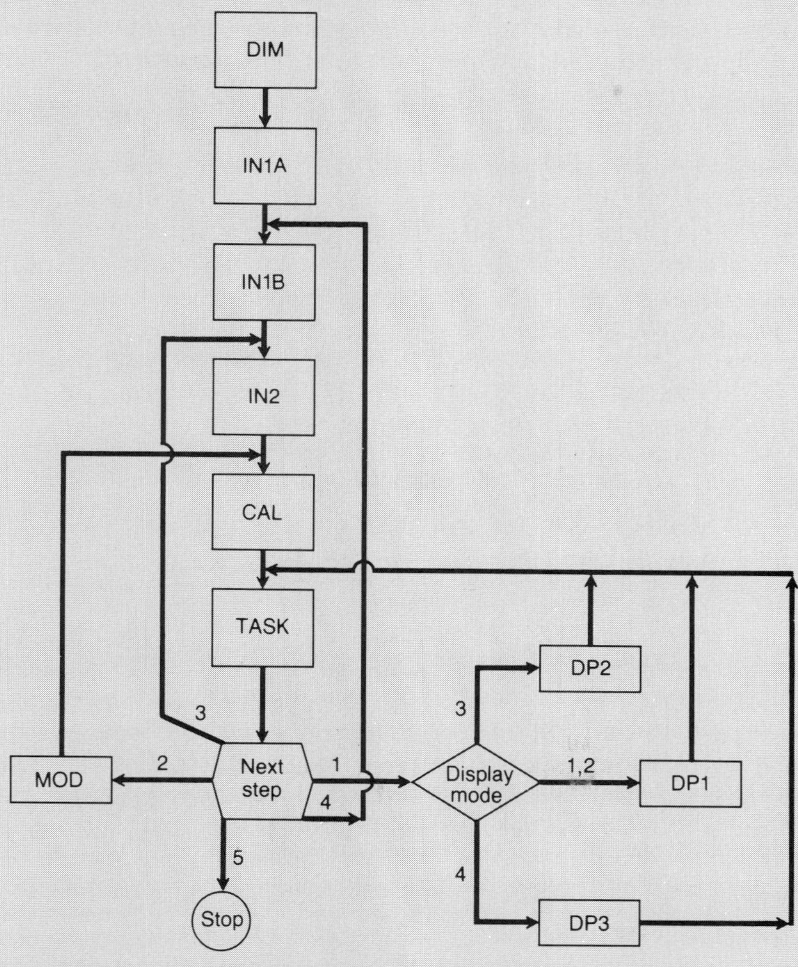

FIGURE 12.4 Programming logic. DIM: Declares arrays. IN1A: Reads in cash flow profiles. IN1B: Reads in simulation parameters. IN2: Reads in discounting parameter. CAL: Calculates present value statistics. TASK: Determines the next task to be performed. MOD: Reseeds the random number. DP1: Displays the distribution for single project. DP2: Displays the superimposed distribution. DP3: Displays the difference distribution.

respective net cash flows over the life of the investment are given in terms of three estimates (lowest possible, most likely, highest possible.) These three estimates are equivalent to the pessimistic, most likely, and optimistic estimates in a triangular distribution. The question is, which alternative is more economically attractive at an interest rate of 20 percent (cost of capital or minimum attractive rate of return). For illustration purposes, the number of repetitions (the number of Monte Carlo samplings) is set at 100.

Once we load the simulation program, the computer signals "ready" on the screen. We are now ready to execute the program. By typing in "RUN" and pressing the [ENTER] key, the program executes. From this point on, the program is self-documenting, so one can enter input data as required.

12.4.3 DATA ENTRY

With the data given in the Table 12.1 as sample inputs, we would have

```
          TYPE OF DECISION PROBLEM
          1. SINGLE PROJECT EVALUATION
          2. COMPARISON OF TWO MUTUALLY EXCLUSIVE PROJECTS

          <ENTER 1 OR 2>? 2

          NUMBER OF MONTE CARLO SAMPLINGS (LESS THAN 300)? 100

          PROJECT LIFE FOR PROJECT 1? 3
          PROJECT LIFE FOR PROJECT 2? 3
          DISCOUNT RATE (%)? 20

          CASH FLOW PROFILE -- PROJECT 1

PERIOD 0 <LOW, MOST LIKELY, HIGH>? -10,-10,-10
PERIOD 1 <LOW, MOST LIKELY, HIGH>? 5,8,12
PERIOD 2 <LOW, MOST LIKELY, HIGH>? 10,15,20
PERIOD 3 <LOW, MOST LIKELY, HIGH>? 10,20,30

          CASH FLOW PROFILE - PROJECT 2

PERIOD 0 <LOW, MOST LIKELY, HIGH>? -15,-15,-15
PERIOD 1 <LOW, MOST LIKELY, HIGH>? 5,10,13
PERIOD 2 <LOW, MOST LIKELY, HIGH>? 20,25,30
PERIOD 3 <LOW, MOST LIKELY, HIGH>? 10,15,40
```

12.4.4 SYSTEM FEEDBACK

Because it takes time to perform the Monte Carlo samplings, the computer prints a status message on the CRT screen. This is done by

```
                    MONTE CARLO SAMPLING

      IN PROCESSING LOOP   54 OF 100   FOR PROJECT- 1
```

This message indicates that the system is busy and gives some idea of how close to completion it is.

12.4.5 STATISTICAL SUMMARY REPORT

The first statistical summary output is as follows:

```
** SUMMARY OF SIMULATION RESULTS **

     PROJECT-1 PROFILE

THE NUMBER OF ITERATIONS        =    100
THE EXPECTED VALUE              = $ 19.09002
THE STANDARD DEVIATION          = $ 3.102889
THE DISCOUNT RATE USED          =    20 %
THE MINIMUM VALUE OBSERVED      = $ 12.26861
THE MAXIMUM VALUE OBSERVED      = $ 26.37404
THE PROBABILITY (PW <= 0)       =    0 %

     PROJECT-2 PROFILE

THE NUMBER OF ITERATIONS        =    100
THE EXPECTED VALUE              = $ 22.65906
THE STANDARD DEVIATION          = $ 4.548998
THE DISCOUNT RATE USED          =    20 %
THE MINIMUM VALUE OBSERVED      = $ 14.09189
THE MAXIMUM VALUE OBSERVED      = $ 33.57834
THE PROBABILITY (PW <= 0)       =    0 %

< PRESS ANY KEY TO CONTINUE ....>
```

(*Note:* The symbol PW (present worth) is used interchangeably with NPV.) After the prompt, the computer will display

```
     DIFFERENCE DISTRIBUTION
     < PROJECT 1 - PROJECT 2>

THE NUMBER OF ITERATIONS        =    100
THE EXPECTED VALUE              = $-3.569035
THE STANDARD DEVIATION          = $ 5.465127
THE DISCOUNT RATE USED          =    20 %
THE MINIMUM VALUE OBSERVED      = $-16.31067
THE MAXIMUM VALUE OBSERVED      = $ 8.788292
THE PROBABILITY (PW1 <= PW2)    =    73 %

< PRESS ANY KEY TO CONTINUE ....>
```

Note that the random number generators used on earlier versions of IBM PC models may be different from the later models (such as XT). In that case, the sampling results would deviate from those presented above.

The summary report shows that the expected NPV of project 1 amounts to \$19.09 with a standard deviation of \$3.10, while that of project 2 is \$22.65 with a standard deviation of \$4.54. All of the NPVs for both projects are greater than zero, indicating that there is no possibility of realizing negative returns. Thus if these two projects were mutually independent, both would be acceptable to the investor. Since these projects are mutually exclusive, the difference distribution provides an additional piece of information in judging the economic choice between the two.

The expected difference in the NPV is −\$3.56 with a standard deviation of \$5.46. The probability that the NPV of project 2 exceeds that of project 1 is calculated as 73 percent. This implies that there is still a 27 percent probability that the reverse situation may hold true. The ultimate decision is up to the investor, but this type of additional information will aid him or her in discerning the best project of a set of projects in a complex decision environment.

12.4.6 PLOTTING STATISTICS

After displaying the present value statistics, the computer will print the following options on the screen.

```
NEXT STEP TO BE PERFORMED

1. PLOT THE STATISTICS
2. MAKE NEW RUN WITH RESEEDED RANDOM NUMBERS
3. CHANGE THE DISCOUNT RATE
4. CHANGE THE # OF MONTE CARLO SAMPLINGS
5. EXIT PROGRAM

< INPUT CHOICE >?
```

With option 1, the computer puts the program in graphics mode and displays the following options:

```
    ** GRAPHICAL DISPLAY OPTIONS **

1. DISPLAY THE HISTOGRAM FOR PROJECT-1
2. DISPLAY THE HISTOGRAM FOR PROJECT-2
3. DISPLAY THE SUPERIMPOSED HISTOGRAM (PROJECTS 1 AND 2)
4. DISPLAY THE DIFFERENCE DIST. (PROJECT 1 - PROJECT 2)

    [ ENTER YOUR CHOICE ] ?
```

Assume that display option 1 is selected. The computer then asks for the number of cells to use in histogram plotting:

```
        THE SUGGESTED NUMBER OF CELLS FOR DISPLAY:

         NO. OF OBSERVATIONS        NO. OF CELLS
                  1 -  20                 5
                 21 -  50                10
                 51 - 200                20
                    > 200                30

   ENTER THE NUMBER OF CELLS FOR HISTOGRAM DISPLAY -->?
```

CELL STATISTICS (WIDTH = 0.99)

CELL NO	OBS FREQ	REL FREQ	CUM FREQ	UPPER BOUND
1	1	0.01	0.01	12.89
2	3	0.03	0.04	13.87
3	3	0.03	0.07	14.86
4	9	0.09	0.16	15.85
5	10	0.10	0.26	16.84
6	8	0.08	0.34	17.82
7	16	0.16	0.50	18.81
8	10	0.10	0.60	19.80
9	11	0.11	0.71	20.78
10	8	0.08	0.79	21.77
11	5	0.05	0.84	22.76
12	7	0.07	0.91	23.75
13	8	0.08	0.99	24.73
14	0	0.00	0.99	25.72
15	1	0.01	1.00	26.71

SAMPLE STATISTICSS:

MEAN	=	19.09
STAND DEV	=	3.10
MIN VALUE	=	12.27
MAX VALUE	=	26.37
PW (<=0)	=	0.00

Press any key to continue...

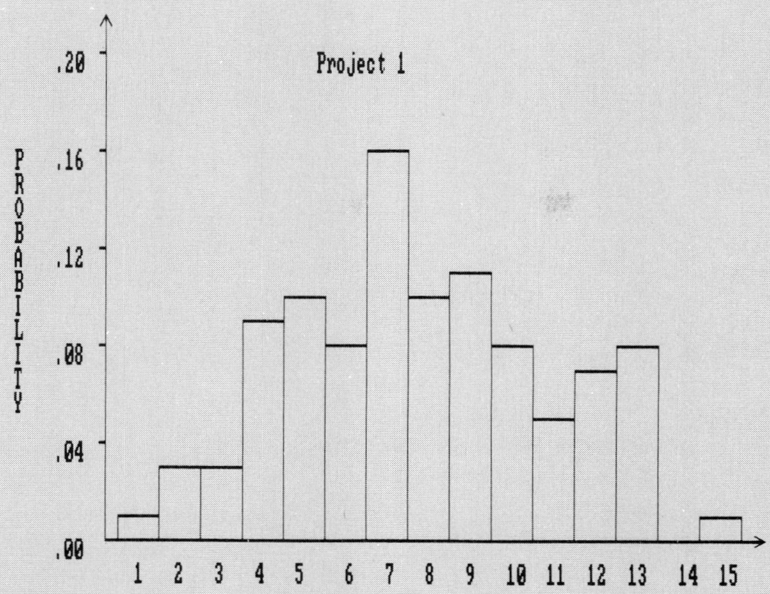

FIGURE 12.5 Project summary—project 1

CELL STATISTICS (WIDTH = 1.36)

CELL NO	OBS FREQ	REL FREQ	CUM FREQ	UPPER BOUND
1	4	0.04	0.04	14.94
2	3	0.03	0.07	16.31
3	9	0.09	0.16	17.67
4	6	0.06	0.22	19.04
5	12	0.12	0.34	20.40
6	13	0.13	0.47	21.76
7	10	0.10	0.57	23.13
8	10	0.10	0.67	24.49
9	7	0.07	0.74	25.86
10	7	0.07	0.81	27.22
11	6	0.06	0.87	28.58
12	7	0.07	0.94	29.95
13	2	0.02	0.96	31.31
14	2	0.02	0.98	32.68
15	2	0.02	1.00	34.04

SAMPLE STATISTICSS:

MEAN	=	22.66
STAND DEV	=	4.55
MIN VALUE	=	14.09
MAX VALUE	=	33.58
PW (<=0)	=	0.00

Press any key to continue...

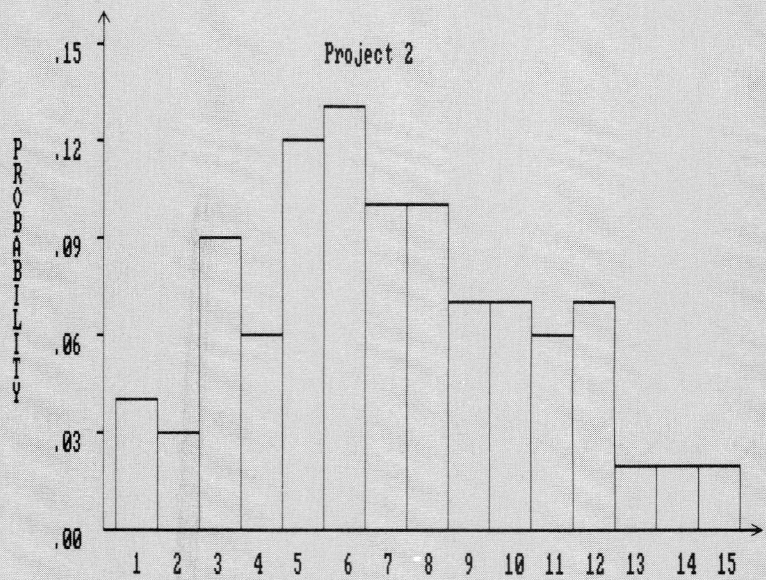

FIGURE 12.6 Project summary—project 2

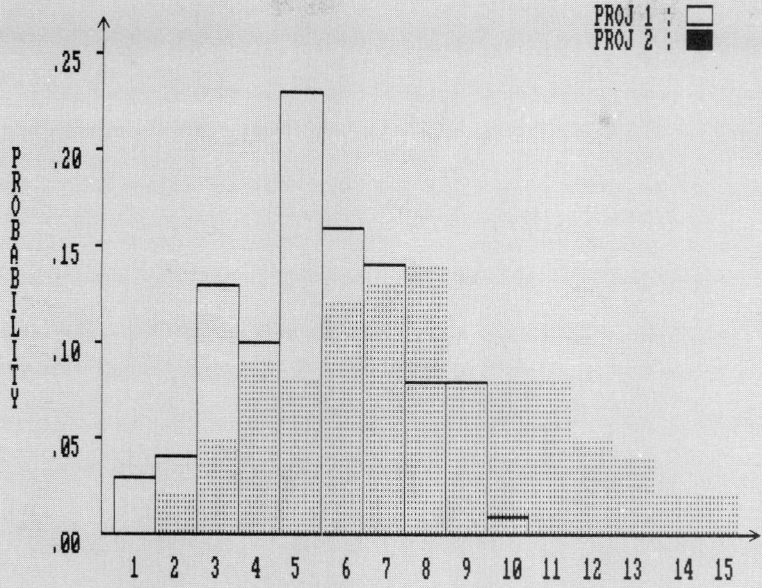

FIGURE 12.7 Combining probability distributions

Assume that we set the number of cells at 15. Figure 12.5 is then obtained as the histogram of present value for project 1, along with the cell statistics. After displaying the histogram, the program returns to the main option menu shown at the beginning of this section. We can manipulate the form of histograms by changing the number of cells: we simply choose the plotting option again, change the number of cells, and replot the statistics. Figure 12.6 can be obtained in a similar fashion.

When we choose plotting option 3, we obtain Fig. 12.7, which combines and plots the two histograms in the same chart. A shade pattern is used on the histogram of project 2 to emphasize the overlapping portions of the statistics.

When we choose option 4, we obtain the histogram plot of the difference distribution (project 1 − project 2). This is shown in Fig. 12.8, from which we can read the probability that the NPV of project 2 will exceed project 1 for any given level.

12.5 REPLICATION AND PRECISION OF RESULTS

As we have seen, the risk simulation model contains random elements (e.g., cash flows) and the outputs from the simulation are only a limited number of

CELL STATISTICS (WIDTH = 1.91)

CELL NO	OBS FREQ	REL FREQ	CUM FREQ	UPPER BOUND
1	2	0.02	0.02	-15.26
2	2	0.02	0.04	-13.35
3	2	0.02	0.06	-11.45
4	7	0.07	0.13	-9.54
5	12	0.12	0.25	-7.63
6	13	0.13	0.38	-5.72
7	10	0.10	0.48	-3.82
8	12	0.12	0.60	-1.91
9	13	0.13	0.73	0.00
10	10	0.10	0.83	1.91
11	7	0.07	0.90	3.82
12	6	0.06	0.96	5.72
13	3	0.03	0.99	7.63
14	1	0.01	1.00	9.54
15	0	0.00	1.00	11.45

SAMPLE STATISTICSS:

MEAN = -3.57
STAND DEV = 5.47
MIN VALUE = -16.31
MAX VALUE = 8.79
PW (<=0) = 73.00

Press any key to continue...

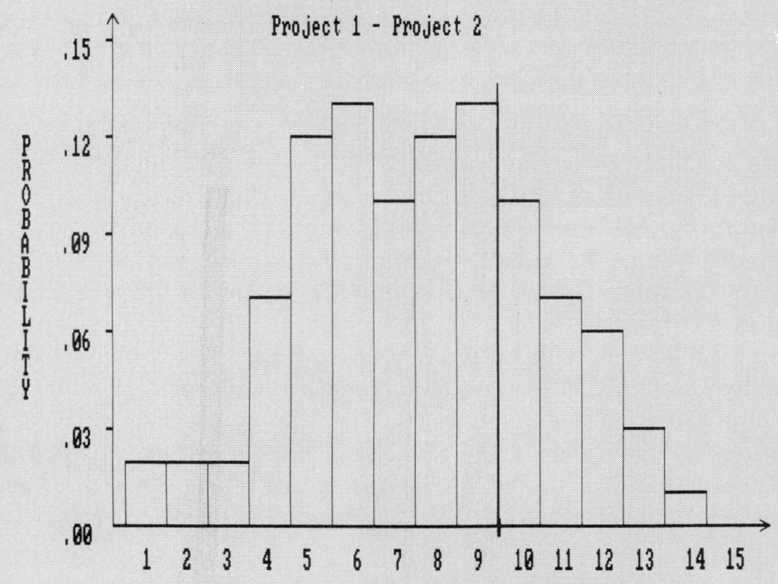

FIGURE 12.8 Difference distribution

observed samples of these random variables. As a consequence, any decisions made on the basis of simulation results should consider the inherent variability of the simulation outputs.

Note that in our example the NPVs range from a minimum of $12.27 to a maximum of $26.37 for project 1. If we print out all 100 observations (NPVs), we find that most of the values are not very close to the expected value ($19.09). We clearly need a method for ascertaining how close an estimator (mean value) is to the true measure. The usual approach to assessing the accuracy of an estimator is to construct a confidence interval for the true measure—that is, we determine an interval about the mean within which the true value may be expected to fall with a certain probability (e.g., 95 percent). Two approaches are possible for constructing a confidence interval.

First, we might fix the replication numbers and then determine the confidence interval for the estimator at the specified level of precision. One disadvantage of this fixed sample size approach is that we have no control over the length of the confidence interval. A second, alternative approach is to determine the number of replications required to obtain a confidence interval with a specified precision. A complete discussion of this subject is beyond the scope of this text but can be found in [3]. Our objective here is to remind the user that a few replications are generally not sufficient to obtain an acceptable estimate of a measure of performance. Table 12.2 summarizes the simulation results obtained by varying the number of replications. It is clear that as we increase

TABLE 12.2 Replication results and 95 percent confidence interval estimates

		Net present value		
Replications		Project 1	Project 2	Difference [Project 1 − Project 2]
100	Mean	19.090	22.659	−3.569
	SD	3.103	4.549	5.465
	CI	[18.474, 19.706]	[21.756, 23.561]	[−4.653, −2.485]
200	Mean	19.106	22.635	−3.528
	SD	2.975	4.225	5.360
	CI	[18.691, 19.521]	[22.046, 23.224]	[−4.275, −2.781]
300	Mean	18.955	22.781	−3.826
	SD	3.176	4.088	4.942
	CI	[18.593, 19.316]	[22.316, 23.245]	[−4.388, −3.264]

SD = Standard deviation
CI = Confidence interval

the number of replications, length of the confidence interval decreases for specified precision. In other words, the relative precision of the estimator increases the larger the number of replicate runs.

12.6 SUMMARY

Risk analysis is a technique for economic evaluation. It provides the analyst a convenient way to support management with reliable information about the uncertainties in alternative investment opportunities, corporate strategies, or operational procedures. Investment risk analysis requires the analyst to estimate the uncertainty associated with each factor affecting the decision. Monte Carlo methods are used to select values from probability distributions describing the likelihood of various values of the critical factors. Computer-based sampling experiments can produce large amounts of output. In this chapter we demonstrated how interactive computer graphics can facilitate the understanding of simulation results.

```
10 ' Program 12.1 : Risk Analysis on IBM PC (DOS 2.00)
20 CLS: KEY OFF :SCREEN 2
30    '----------- Dimension Array Variables ---------------
40 DIM L1(10),M1(10),H1(10),L2(10),M2(10),H2(10)
50 DIM P1(300),P2(300),P3(300),P(300)
60 DIM L(10),M(10),H(10),C(10)
70 DIM A(3),V(3),Z1(3),Z2(3),W(3),UPBD(52),OBS(52),REL(52),CUM(52)
80 DIM OBX(52),OBY(52), A$(11)
90 A$(1)="P": A$(2)="R": A$(3)="O": A$(4)="B": A$(5)="A": A$(6)="B"
100 A$(7)="I": A$(8)="L": A$(9)="I": A$(10)="T": A$(11)="Y"
110    '---------  Main Program ---------------
120 YY=0 : E=0
130 LOCATE 10,15: PRINT "TYPE OF DECISION PROBLEM"
140 LOCATE 11,15: PRINT "1. Single Project Evaluation"
150 LOCATE 12,15: PRINT "2. Comparison of Two Mutually Exclusive Projects"
160 LOCATE 14,15: INPUT "<Enter 1 or 2>";TY
170    '---------  Input Parameters ----------
180 LOCATE 16,15: INPUT "Number of Monte Carlo Samplings (less than 300)";NN
190 IF YY=4 THEN GOTO 430
200 LOCATE 18,15: INPUT "Project Life for Project 1";N1
210 IF TY=1 THEN 230
220 LOCATE 19,15: INPUT "Project Life for Project 2";N2
230 LOCATE 20,15: INPUT "Discount Rate (%)";MARR: MARR=MARR/100
240 IF YY=3 THEN 430
250 CLS
260 LOCATE 2,15: PRINT "CASH FLOW PROFILE -- PROJECT 1"
270 PRINT: N=N1
280 FOR I=0 TO N
290 PRINT "PERIOD"; I; "<LOW, MOST LIKELY, HIGH>";
300 INPUT L1(I),M1(I),H1(I)
310 NEXT I
320 IF TY=1 GOTO 430
330 PRINT: PRINT TAB(15) "CASH FLOW PROFILE - PROJECT 2"
340 PRINT
350 FOR I=0 TO N2
360 PRINT "PERIOD"; I; "<LOW, MOST LIKELY, HIGH>";
370 INPUT L2(I),M2(I),H2(I)
380 NEXT I
390 IF N1=N2 THEN 430
400 FACTOR(2)=(MARR*(1+MARR)^N2)/((1+MARR)^N2-1)
410 FACTOR(1)=(MARR*(1+MARR)^N1)/((1+MARR)^N1-1)
```

PROGRAM 12.1 Risk Analysis on IBM PC (DOS 2.00)

```
420     '------- Monte Carlo Sampling --------------
430 CLS: LOCATE 10,25: PRINT " Monte Carlo Sampling"
440 GOSUB 1410
450 LOCATE 13,13: PRINT "In Processing Loop        of";NN; " for Project-";E
460 FOR II=1 TO NN
470 LOCATE 13,33: PRINT II
480 FOR J=0 TO N
490 IF L(J)=M(J) AND  M(J)=H(J) THEN  C(J)=L(J): GOTO 570
500 R=RND(J)
510 X=(M(J)-L(J))/(H(J)-L(J))
520 U1=(M(J)-L(J))*(H(J)-L(J))*R
530 U2=(H(J)-M(J))*(H(J)-L(J))*(1-R)
540 IF R<=X THEN 560
550 C(J)=H(J)-SQR(U2) :GOTO 570
560 C(J)=L(J)+SQR(U1)
570 NEXT J
580     '-------- Compute Present Value ---------------------
590 SUM=0
600 FOR K=0 TO N
610 PW=C(K)/((1+MARR)^K)
620 SUM=SUM+PW
630 NEXT K
640 P(II)=SUM
650 IF TY=1 OR N1=N2 THEN 690
660     '----------- Compute Annual Equivalent Values --------
670 P(II)=FACTOR(II)*P(II)
680     '------------ Transfer Present Value Arrays   --------
690 ON E GOTO 700, 710
700 P1(II)=P(II): GOTO 730
710 P2(II)=P(II)
720 P3(II)=P1(II)-P2(II)
730 ERASE C
740 NEXT II
750 LOCATE 15,17: PRINT  "[The computer is compiling statistics]"
760 YSUM=0 : XSUM=0
770 FOR JJ=1 TO NN
780 XSUM=XSUM+P(JJ)
790 YSUM=YSUM+P(JJ)^2
800 NEXT JJ
810     '----------- Compute Statistics ---------------------
820 XBAR=XSUM/NN
830 SD=SQR((YSUM-XSUM^2/NN)/(NN-1))
840 GOSUB 1470
850 A(E)=XBAR: V(E)=SD: Z1(E)=MN: Z2(E)=MX: W(E)=Q
860     '---------- Next Task To Be Performed ------------------
870 IF TY=1 THEN GOTO 940
880 IF TY=2 AND E=1 THEN GOTO 430
890 IF TY=2 AND E=3 THEN GOTO 940
900 IF TY=2 AND E=2 THEN E=3
910 FOR I=1 TO NN: P(I)=P3(I): NEXT I
920 GOTO 760
930     '----------- Print Simulation Results ------------------
940 CLS:BEEP:LOCATE 2,15: PRINT "** SUMMARY OF SIMULATION RESULTS **"
950 II=1: PRINT
960 GOSUB 1560
970 PRINT TAB(15) "THE NUMBER OF ITERATIONS       =  ";NN
980 PRINT TAB(15) "THE EXPECTED VALUE             = $";A(II)
990 PRINT TAB(15) "THE STANDARD DEVIATION         = $";V(II)
1000 PRINT TAB(15) "THE DISCOUNT RATE USED         =  ";MARR*100; "%"
1010 PRINT TAB(15) "THE MINIMUM VALUE OBSERVED     = $";Z1(II)
1020 PRINT TAB(15) "THE MAXIMUM VALUE OBSERVED     = $";Z2(II)
1030 ON II GOTO 1040,1040,1060
1040 PRINT TAB(15) "THE PROBABILITY (PW <= 0)      =  ";W(II);"%"
1050 GOTO 1100
1060 IF N1<>N2 THEN 1090
1070 PRINT TAB(15) "THE PROBABILITY (PW1 <= PW2) =  ";W(II);"%"
1080 GOTO 1100
1090 PRINT TAB(15) "THE PROBABILITY (AE1 <= AE2) =  ";W(II);"%"
1100 PRINT: PRINT TAB(15) "< Press any key to continue ....>
1110 IF INKEY$="" THEN 1110
1115 LOCATE 14,15: PRINT "                                            "
1116 LOCATE 14,1
1120 II=II+1
1130 IF TY=2 AND II<4 THEN GOTO 960
1140     '---------------- Print Option Menu ------------------
1150 CLS: LOCATE 4,15
1160 PRINT "NEXT STEP TO BE PERFORMED": PRINT
1170 PRINT TAB(15) "1. PLOT THE STATISTICS"
1180 PRINT TAB(15) "2. MAKE NEW RUN WITH RESEEDED RANDOM NUMBERS"
1190 PRINT TAB(15) "3. CHANGE THE DISCOUNT RATE"
```

PROGRAM 12.1 (continued)

```
1200 PRINT TAB(15) "4. CHANGE THE # OF MONTE CARLO SAMPLINGS"
1210 PRINT TAB(15) "5. EXIT PROGRAM"
1220 PRINT: PRINT TAB(15) "< Input Choice >";: INPUT YY
1230 CLS
1240 ON YY GOTO 1280,1250,230,180,1270
1250 RANDOMIZE : GOTO 430
1260     '--------- Terminate Program --------------
1270 END
1280 IF TY=1 THEN II=1 ELSE 1300
1290 GOSUB 1610 : GOTO 1150
1300 CLS:BEEP: LOCATE 3,20:PRINT "** Graphical Display Options **"
1310 PRINT
1320 PRINT TAB(15) " 1. DISPLAY THE HISTOGRAM FOR PROJECT-1"
1330 PRINT TAB(15) " 2. DISPLAY THE HISTOGRAM FOR PROJECT-2"
1340 PRINT TAB(15) " 3. DISPLAY THE SUPERIMPOSED HISTOGRAM (PROJECTS 1 AND 2)"
1350 PRINT TAB(15) " 4. DISPLAY THE DIFFERENCE DIST. (PROJECT 1 - PROJECT 2)"
1360 PRINT: PRINT TAB(20) "[ Enter Your Choice ] ";: INPUT II
1370 GOSUB 1610 : GOTO 1140
1380     '----------- *** SUBROUTINES *** --------------
1390     '
1400     '------------ Transfer Input Data to Work Area -------------
1410 IF TY=2 AND E=1 THEN 1440
1420 FOR I=0 TO N1: L(I)=L1(I): M(I)=M1(I): H(I)=H1(I): NEXT I
1430 E=1 : RETURN
1440 ERASE L,M,H
1450 FOR I=0 TO N2: L(I)=L2(I): M(I)=M2(I): H(I)=H2(I): NEXT I
1460 E=2 : RETURN
1470     ' ------------ Find Max- and Min PWs -------------
1480 MX=-2E+10: MN=2E+10 : Q=0
1490 FOR I=1 TO NN
1500 IF P(I)>MX THEN MX=P(I)
1510 IF P(I)<MN THEN MN=P(I)
1520 IF P(I) <=0 THEN Q=Q+1
1530 NEXT I
1540 Q=100*(Q/NN)
1550 RETURN
1560     '------------- Print Heading ---------------------
1570 IF TY=1 THEN  LOCATE 5,20: PRINT "PROJECT PROFILE": PRINT: RETURN
1580 IF TY=2 AND II=1 THEN PRINT TAB(20) "PROJECT-1 PROFILE": PRINT: RETURN
1590 IF TY=2 AND II=2 THEN PRINT TAB(20) "PROJECT-2 PROFILE": PRINT: RETURN
1600 IF TY=2 AND II=3 THEN  CLS: LOCATE 5,20: PRINT "DIFFERENCE DISTRIBUTION":
                   PRINT TAB(20) "< PROJECT 1 - PROJECT 2>": PRINT: RETURN
1610     '---------- HISTOGRAM PLOT --------------
1620     '----- Initilization -----
1630 X1%=80: Y1%=176: X2%=600: Y2%=176: X3%=80: Y3%=16
1640 IZ=II
1650 IF II=3 THEN CHECK=1 ELSE CHECK=0
1660 ON II GOTO 1670, 1670, 1760, 1980
1670      FOR I=1 TO NN
1680      IF II=1 THEN P(I)=P1(I) ELSE P(I)=P2(I)
1690      NEXT I
1700      M1=Z1(II): M2=Z2(II): MEAN=A(II): SD=V(II)
1710     GOSUB 2060
1720     GOSUB 2180
1730     GOSUB 2970
1740     RETURN
1750     ,----- SUPERIMPOSED DISTRIBUTION ------
1760 GOSUB 2060
1770      IF Z1(1)<=Z1(2) THEN M1=Z1(1) ELSE M1=Z1(2)
1780      IF Z2(1)>=Z2(2) THEN M2=Z2(1) ELSE M2=Z2(2)
1790      FOR II=1 TO 2
1800          FOR I=1 TO NN
1810              IF II=1 THEN P(I)=P1(I) ELSE P(I)=P2(I)
1820          NEXT I
1830          GOSUB 2180
1840          IF II=1 THEN M4=M3
1850          FOR I=1 TO CELL
1860              IF II=1 THEN OBX(I)=OBS(I) ELSE OBY(I)=OBS(I)
1870          NEXT I
1880      NEXT II
1890      IF M3<M4 THEN M3=M4
1900      FOR II=1 TO 2
1910          FOR I=1 TO CELL
1920              IF II=1 THEN OBS(I)=OBX(I) ELSE OBS(I)=OBY(I)
1930          NEXT I
1940          GOSUB 2970
1950      NEXT II
1960 RETURN
1970     '---- Difference Distribution --------
1980 FOR I=1 TO NN
```

PROGRAM 12.1 (continued)

```
1990     P(I)=P3(I)
2000 NEXT I
2010 M1=Z1(3): M2=Z2(3): MEAN=A(3): SD=V(3)
2020     GOSUB 2060
2030     GOSUB 2180
2040     GOSUB 2970
2050 RETURN
2060     '----- Information (Cell Numbers) -----
2070 CLS: LOCATE 3,8: PRINT "THE SUGGESTED NUMBER OF CELLS FOR DISPLAY:": PRINT
2080 PRINT TAB(10); "NO. OF OBSERVATIONS"; TAB(35); "NO. OF CELLS"
2090 PRINT TAB(20); "1 -  20"; TAB(41); "5"
2100 PRINT TAB(19);"21 -  50"; TAB(40); "10"
2110 PRINT TAB(19);"51 - 200"; TAB(40); "20"
2120 PRINT TAB(19);"   > 200"; TAB(40); "30"
2130 PRINT: PRINT
2140 INPUT "ENTER THE NUMBER OF CELLS FOR HISTOGRAM DISPLAY -->"; CELL : BEEP
2150 CLS
2160 RETURN
2170     '------ Compute Cell Statistics -----------
2180 R=(M2-M1)/CELL: R=R*1.05
2190 M6=0
2200 IF M2<=0 OR M1>=0 THEN 2280
2210 R=(M2-M1+2*R)/CELL
2220 M5=FIX(M1/R)-1
2230 M6=-M5
2240 M5=M5*R
2250 UPBD(0)=M5
2260 UPBD(1)=M5+R
2270 GOTO 2300
2280 UPBD(0)=M1-R*.05*CELL/2
2290 UPBD(1)=UPBD(0)+R
2300 FOR I=2 TO CELL
2310     UPBD(I)=UPBD(I-1)+R
2320 NEXT I
2330     '----- Clear OBS Array -----
2340 FOR I=1 TO CELL
2350     OBS(I)=0
2360 NEXT I
2370 FOR I=1 TO NN
2380 J=P(I)-UPBD(0)
2390 K=J/R
2400 IF K=FIX(K) THEN K=K ELSE K=FIX(K)+1
2410 OBS(K)=OBS(K)+1
2420 NEXT I
2430 M3=0
2440 REL(1)=OBS(1)
2450 CUM(1)=REL(1)
2460 M3=OBS(1)
2470 FOR I=2 TO CELL
2480     REL(I)=OBS(I)
2490     CUM(I)=CUM(I-1)+REL(I)
2500     IF OBS(I)>M3 THEN M3=OBS(I)
2510 NEXT I
2520 IF CUM(CELL)<>NN THEN CUM(CELL)=NN
2530 IF M3=FIX(M3/5)*5 THEN M3=M3 ELSE M3=FIX(M3/5)*5+5
2540 IF CHECK=1 THEN RETURN
2550     '----- Display Cell and Sample Statistics ------
2560 PRINT CHR$(12); TAB(6) "CELL STATISTICS (WIDTH =";
2570 PRINT USING "###.##"; R;
2580 PRINT TAB(37)")" TAB(50) "SAMPLE STATISTICSS:"
2590 PRINT
2600 PRINT TAB(3) "CELL"; TAB(11)"OBS"; TAB(19) "REL"; TAB(27) "CUM"; TAB(36)
     "UPPER";
2610 PRINT TAB(50) "MEAN       = ";
2620 PRINT USING "####.##"; MEAN
2630 PRINT TAB(4) "NO"; TAB(11) "FREQ"; TAB(19) "FREQ"; TAB(27) "FREQ"; TAB(36)
     "BOUND";
2640 PRINT TAB(50) "STAND DEV = ";
2650 PRINT USING "####.##"; SD
2660 PRINT TAB(2) "----------------------------------------"; TAB(50)
     "MIN VALUE = ";
2670 PRINT USING "####.##"; M1
2680 PRINT TAB(50) "MAX VALUE = ";
2690 PRINT USING "####.##"; M2
2700 LOCATE 7,50,0
2710 IF IZ=4 THEN IZ=3
2720 PRINT USING "PW (<=0)  = ####.##";W(IZ)
2730 XYZ=0 : LOCATE 6,1
2740 FOR I= 1 TO CELL
2750 XYZ=XYZ+1
```

PROGRAM 12.1 (continued)

```
2760      PRINT TAB(4);
2770      PRINT USING "##"; I;
2780      PRINT TAB(11);
2790      PRINT USING "###"; OBS(I);
2800      PRINT TAB(19);
2810      PRINT USING "#.##"; REL(I)/NN;
2820      PRINT TAB(27);
2830      PRINT USING "#.##"; CUM(I)/NN;
2840      PRINT TAB(34);
2850      PRINT USING "####.##"; UPBD(I)
2860 IF XYZ < 16 THEN 2910
2870 PRINT
2880 PRINT CHR$(7)TAB(10)"Press any key to continue..."
2890 IF INKEY$="" THEN 2890
2900 XYZ=0 :PRINT
2910 NEXT I
2920 PRINT
2930 PRINT CHR$(7) TAB(5) "Press any key to continue..."
2940 IF INKEY$="" THEN 2940 ELSE CLS
2950 RETURN
2960      '----------- Histogram Plot Routine  Starts Here -------
2970 BEEP
2980 IF CHECK=1 AND II=2 THEN GOTO 3230
2990 IF CHECK=1 THEN GOSUB 3670
3000 LINE (X1%,Y1%)-(X2%,Y2%)
3010 LINE (X1%,Y1%)-(X3%,Y3%)
3020 Y4%=Y3%: D%=32
3030 FOR I=1 TO 5
3040      LINE (75,Y4%)-(80,Y4%)
3050      Y4%=Y4%+D%
3060 NEXT I
3070      '----------- Scale Y axis ----------
3080 J=7
3090 FOR I=1 TO 11
3100      LOCATE J,2,0
3110      PRINT A$(I)
3120      J=J+1
3130 NEXT I
3140 L1%=3: L2%=4: L3%=6
3150 YY=M3
3160 FOR I=1 TO 6
3170      LOCATE L1%,L3%,0
3180      PRINT USING ".##";YY/NN
3190      YY=YY-M3/5
3200      L1%=L1%+L2%
3210 NEXT I
3220      '----------- Plot Histogram --------
3230 B%=(X2%-X1%-20)/CELL
3240 X4%=X1%+10
3250 X5%=X4%+B%
3260 IF CHECK=1 AND II=2 THEN GOTO 3380
3270 IF M6=0 THEN GOTO 3300
3280 M6=M6*B%+X1%+10
3290 LINE (M6-1,Y1%-2)-(M6+1,Y1%+3),,B
3300 FOR I=1 TO CELL
3310      Y4%=Y1%-FIX(OBS(I)/M3*(Y1%-Y3%)+.5)
3320      LINE (X4%,Y1%)-(X5%,Y4%),,B
3330      X4%=X5%
3340      X5%=X4%+B%
3350 NEXT I
3360 GOTO 3480
3370      '----------- Plot  Superimposed Histogram ------
3380 FOR I=1 TO CELL
3390      Y4%=Y1%-FIX(OBS(I)/M3*(Y1%-Y3%)+.5)
3400      PX=X5%-X4%: PY=Y1%-Y4%
3410      FOR JJ=X4% TO X5% STEP 3
3420      FOR J=1 TO PY STEP 2: PSET (JJ,Y1%-J): NEXT J
3430      NEXT JJ
3440      X4%=X5%
3450      X5%=X4%+B%
3460 NEXT I
3470      '----------- Scale X axis ----------
3480 X4%=X1%+10: X4%=X4%+B%/2:
3490 Y4%=Y1%+10: Y4%=FIX(Y4%/8)+1
3500 IF CELL>20 THEN GOTO 3580
3510 FOR I=1 TO CELL
3520      X5%=FIX(X4%/8)
3530      LOCATE Y4%,X5%
3540      PRINT I;
3550      X4%=X4%+B%
```

PROGRAM 12.1 (continued)

```
3560 NEXT I
3570 GOTO 3610
3580 X5%=FIX(X4%/8)+12
3590 LOCATE Y4%,X5%
3600 PRINT "NO. OF CELL=";CELL;" ::  WIDTH=";R;
3610 LOCATE 1,1,0
3620 BEEP
3630 INPUT "HIT THE RETURN KEY TO CONTINUE -->";K$
3640 IF R0=2 THEN RETURN
3650 RETURN
3660     '----------- Print Legend ----------
3670 LOCATE 1,60,0
3680 PRINT "PROJ 1 : ": LINE (545,0)-(565,6),,B
3690 LOCATE 2,60,0
3700 PRINT "PROJ 2 : ":
3710 FOR I=1 TO 7: FOR J=1 TO 21: PSET(544+J,7+I): NEXT J: NEXT I
3720 RETURN
```

PROGRAM 12.1 Risk Analysis on IBM PC (DOS 2.00)

EXERCISES

12.1 Consider the following project, whose projected net cash flows over the next five years are given by the three estimates. A quantity in parentheses represents a negative cash flow.

	Year					
Market projection	0	1	2	3	4	5
Pessimistic	($1,891,610)	($1,254,410)	($326,620)	$227,350	$753,750	$657,300
Optimistic	(562,810)	106,170	707,430	918,290	918,680	980,400
Most likely	(1,161,215)	(499,266)	150,595	607,372	803,229	720,800

a) Find the expected NPV of this project at $i = 12$ percent.
b) Find the variance of the NPV of this project.
c) Determine the probability that the NPV of the project is negative.

12.2 Consider the following mutually exclusive investment proposals.

	Project A			**Project B**		
Year end	Pessimistic	Most likely	Optimistic	Pessimistic	Most likely	Optimistic
0	−15	−10	−7	−30	−20	−15
1	2	4	5	7	8	9
2	3	5	7	12	15	18
3	2	4	8	5	8	10

a) Assuming $i = 10$ percent, determine the probability that project A is profitable.
b) Determine the probability that project B is profitable.
c) Determine the probability that NPV_A exceeds NPV_B.

12.3 Modify the risk analysis program to handle the uncertainty about the project life.

12.4 Suppose we want to estimate the cash flows in terms of a beta distribution. Write a subroutine that generates beta random deviates. With this subroutine, repeat problem 12.2 and compare the NPV statistics. Can you draw any conclusion from these results?

REFERENCES

1. Greer, W. R., "Capital Budgeting Analysis with the Timing of Events Uncertain," *The Accounting Review,* 103–114, January 1970.

2. Hertz, D. B., and H. Thomas, *Risk Analysis and Its Applications,* Wiley, New York, 1983.

3. Law, A. M., and D. Kelton, *Simulation Modeling and Analysis,* McGraw-Hill, New York, 1982 (Chapters 5, 7, and 9).

APPENDIX A
Hexadecimal Conversion Table

The hexadecimal (or hex) notation for a number is the base 16 representation of the number. To avoid confusing the hex number with the decimal number, we add a "&H" prefix to the hex notation. In the hexadecimal numeration system, the number &H215 refers to $2(16)^2 + 1(16)^1 + 5(16)^0 = 533$.

In base 10 (decimal system), ten symbols are used to represent numbers. For work with hexadecimal system, we need 16 symbols. We use the symbols 0 through 9 to represent the decimal numbers 0 through 9, and symbols A, B, C, D, E, and F to represent 10, 11, 12, 13, 14, and 15.

If we were counting in hex, our count would go like this: &H1, &H2, &H3, &H4, &H5, &H6, &H7, &H8, &H9, &HA, &HB, &HC, &HD, &HE, &HF, &H10, &H11, &H12, &H13, &H14, &H15, &H16, &H17, &H18, &H19, &H1A, &H1B . . . .

To convert &H3A2E to decimal, we write

$$\begin{aligned}\&\text{H3A2E} &= 3(16)^3 + 10(16)^2 + 2(16)^1 + 14(16)^0 \\ &= 3(4096) + 10(256) + 2(16) + 14(1) \\ &= 14894\end{aligned}$$

To convert the decimal 533 to hex notation, we first identify the largest multiple of the largest power of 16 that can be subtracted from 533. That number is $2(16)^2 = 512$. Subtracting yields $533 - 512 = 21$. Next, we identify the largest multiple of the largest power of 16 that can be subtracted from 21. That number is $1(16)^1 = 16$. Subtracting yields 5. This number is less than 16, and we stop the process. Thus

$$533 = 2(16)^2 + 1(16)^1 + 5$$
$$= \&H215.$$

Table A.1 can be used to save calculation time. We can also use the HEX$ statement to find the hexadecimal value of the decimal argument on the IBM PC. For example, the following BASIC statements return the hexadecimal equivalent of the decimal value 533:

```
10  X = 533
20  A$ = HEX$(X)
30  PRINT A$
```

Each of the decimal numbers from 0 to 15 can be represented by a four-bit binary (0000 through 1111), or by a one-digit hex (&H0 through &HF). Similarly, the decimal numbers from 0 through 255 have one-byte (eight-bit) binary representation(00000000 through 11111111). These numbers can also be represented by two-digit hex numbers from &H00 through &HFF. As an example, the decimal 195 is represented by binary 11000011, and by hex &HC3.

195 = 11000011 = &HC3

lower nibble = &H3

upper nibble = &HC

Note that the lower nibble 0011 has hex value &H3, while the upper nibble has hex value &HC. This association is not an accidental occurrence, and is consistent. To convert between binary and hex representation of a number, we can associate hex digits with binary nibbles. To write &H5F in binary form we do as follows:

&H5F → &H5 = 5 = 0101 (upper nibble)

&H5F → &HF = 15 = 1111 (lower nibble)

→ 01011111

TABLE A.1 Hexadecimal conversion tables

Largest Multiple of 16

	16^3	16^2	16^1	16^0
1	4096	256	16	1
2	8192	512	32	2
3	12288	768	48	3
4	16384	1024	64	4
5	20480	1280	80	5
6	24576	1536	96	6
7	28672	1792	112	7
8	32768	2048	128	8
9	36864	2304	144	9
A	40960	2560	160	10
B	45056	2816	176	11
C	49152	3072	192	12
D	53248	3328	208	13
E	57344	3584	224	14
F	61440	3840	240	15

Direct Conversion

Hex (&H)	Decimal	Hex (&H)	Decimal
1	1	10	16
2	2	20	32
3	3	30	48
4	4	40	64
5	5	50	80
6	6	60	96
7	7	70	112
8	8	80	128
9	9	90	144
A	10	A0	160
B	11	B0	176
C	12	C0	192
D	13	D0	208
E	14	E0	224
F	15	F0	240
100	256	1000	4096
200	512	2000	8192
300	768	3000	12288
400	1024	4000	16384
500	1280	5000	20480
600	1536	6000	24576
700	1792	7000	28672
800	2048	8000	32768
900	2304	9000	36864
A00	2560	A000	40960
B00	2816	B000	45056
C00	3072	C000	49152
D00	3328	D000	53248
E00	3584	E000	57344
F00	3840	F000	61440

Conversion to Binary

Hex (&H)	Binary
0	0000
1	0001
2	0010
3	0011
4	0100
5	0101
6	0110
7	0111
8	1000
9	1001
A	1010
B	1011
C	1100
D	1101
E	1110
F	1111

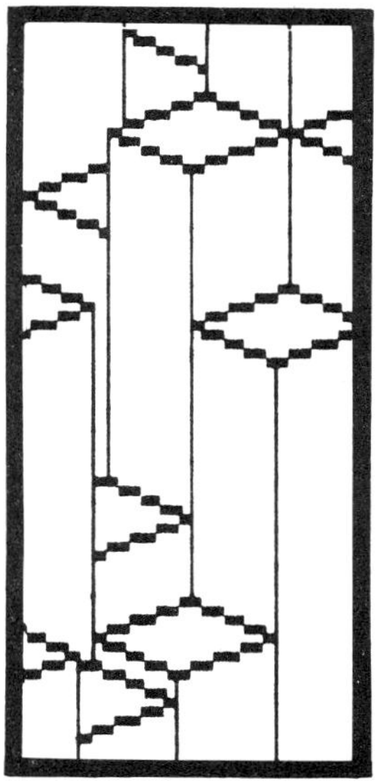

APPENDIX B
Statistical (Business) Graphics

Computer graphics plays an important role in statistical data presentation and analysis. Although automated statistical graphics is usually considered a form of *business graphics,* it is not limited just to business problems. For instance, statistical graphics can help engineers understand complex sets of data and present results more clearly. For this reason it may be more appropriate to use the term "statistical graphics" instead of "business graphics."

Statistical graphics takes a variety of forms, ranging from simple pie charts to complex 3-D bar graphs. Line, bar, and area graphs may be the most commonly applied statistical graphics. We will present two programming examples in this appendix.

B.1 PROGRAM TO PLOT 3-D HISTOGRAMS

In Chapters 4 and 9, we discussed the techniques of drawing 3-D functions. A special case of 3-D functions is the 3-D histogram. Program B.1 draws a 3-D histogram with hidden lines removed. The program uses a blackout technique: hidden portions of each histogram bar were drawn, but were then erased by the drawing of a closer histogram bar. This technique of hidden line elimination is fairly easy to use, and gives nice results in short execution time. It is limited, however; the viewpoint is fixed and planned in advance. This planning is needed so that only the vertices of visible surfaces are provided, and so that the region to be *blacked out* can be identified. Figure B.1 shows the parameters that define each specific portion of the histogram plot.

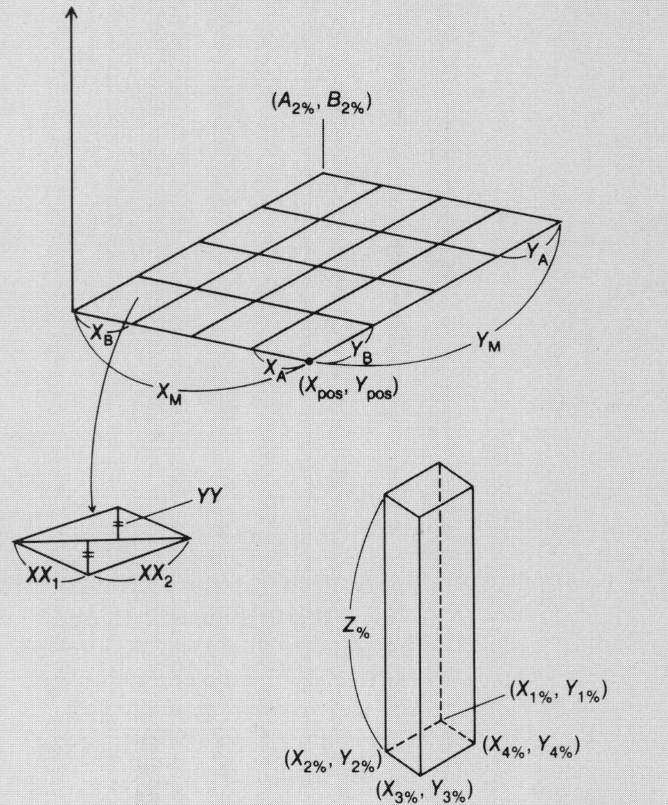

FIGURE B.1 Parameters used in the 3-D histogram program

To illustrate the use of the program, we will consider the data given in Table B.1. These data represent the sales of new cars by a certain dealership

TABLE B.1 Auto sales by each operating division (unit = 10)

Division (Company)	1	2	3	4	5	6
Quarter 1	10	15	6	4	12	15
Quarter 2	20	28	12	8	18	25
Quarter 3	30	32	18	9	22	40
Quarter 4	10	8	5	6	16	22

over the last four quarters. The dealership has six operating divisions (companies) within its sales district area. We assume that each operating division carries only one type of automobile. We are interested in plotting the sales performance of each division over the last four quarters.

We proceed as follows:

```
* TITLE OF HISTOGRAM (MAX 10 CHAR)--->? Auto Sales
* NAME  OF X-AXIS    (MAX  5 CHAR)--->? Quarter
* NAME  OF Y-AXIS    (MAX  5 CHAR)--->? Company
* THE NUMBER OF ITEMS OF X-AXIS (MAX: 10) --->? 4
* THE NUMBER OF ITEMS OF Y-AXIS (MAX: 12) --->? 6

          Input Data for Quarter 1  - Company 1 ? 10
          Input Data for Quarter 1  - Company 2 ? 15
          Input Data for Quarter 1  - Company 3 ? 6
          Input Data for Quarter 1  - Company 4 ? 4
          Input Data for Quarter 1  - Company 5 ? 12
          Input Data for Quarter 1  - Company 6 ? 15
```

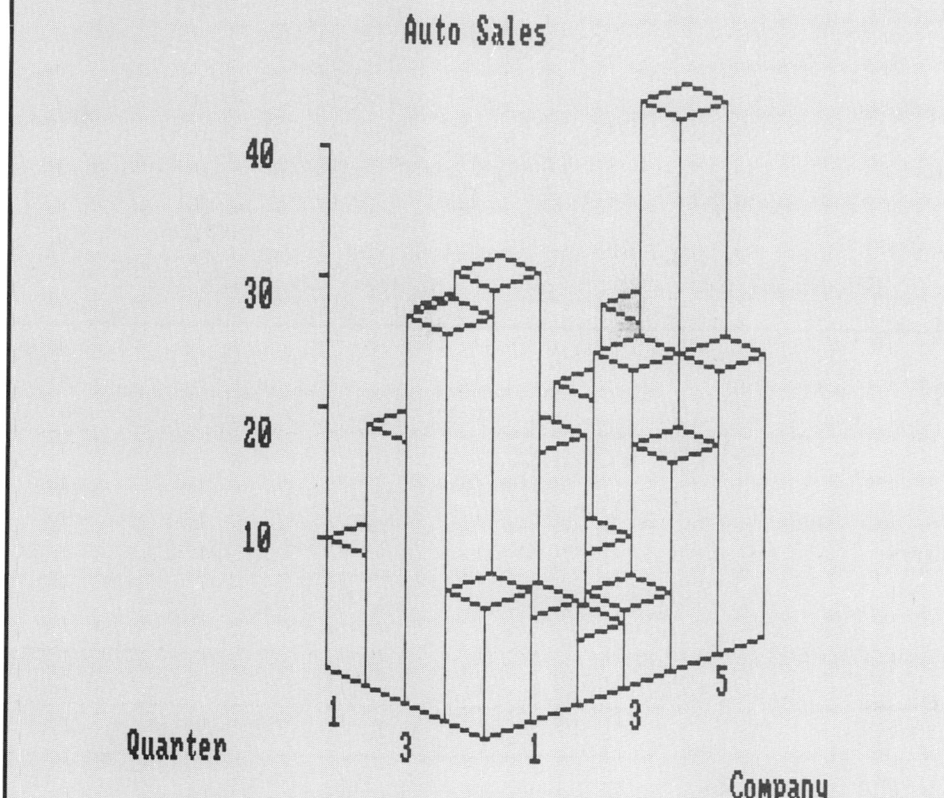

FIGURE B.2 Auto sales by company and quarter

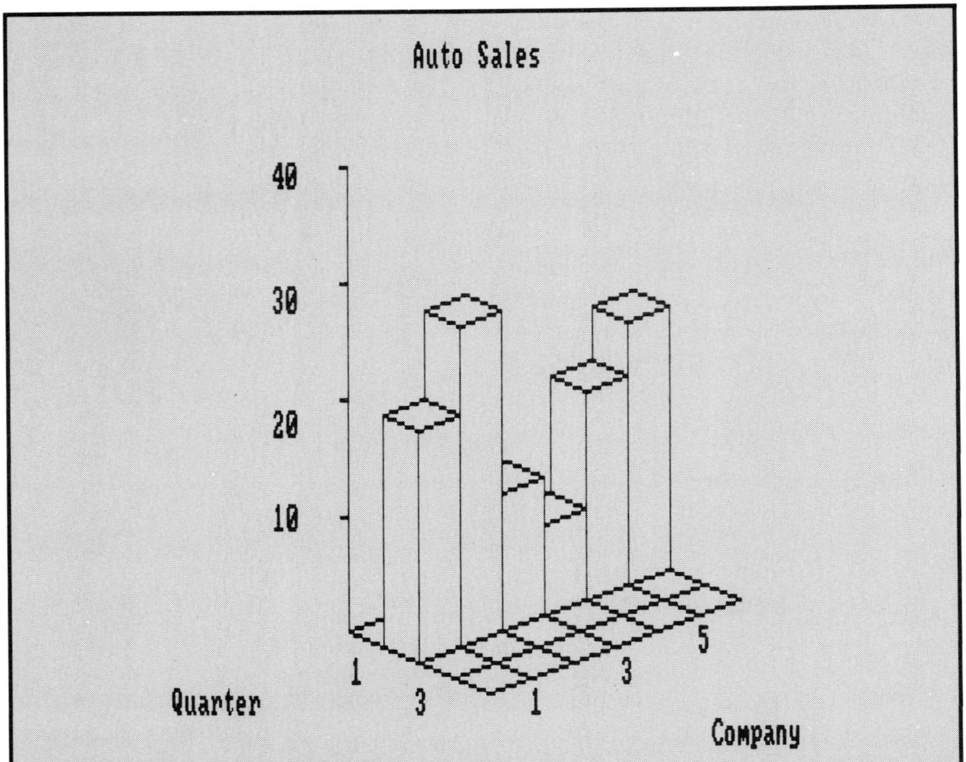

FIGURE B.3 Sales performance of each company during quarter 2

```
Input Data for Quarter 2  - Company 1 ? 20
Input Data for Quarter 2  - Company 2 ? 28
Input Data for Quarter 2  - Company 3 ? 12
Input Data for Quarter 2  - Company 4 ? 8
Input Data for Quarter 2  - Company 5 ? 18
Input Data for Quarter 2  - Company 6 ? 23

Input Data for Quarter 3  - Company 1 ? 30
Input Data for Quarter 3  - Company 2 ? 32

Input Data for Quarter 3  - Company 3 ? 18
Input Data for Quarter 3  - Company 4 ? 9
Input Data for Quarter 3  - Company 5 ? 22
Input Data for Quarter 3  - Company 6 ? 40

Input Data for Quarter 4  - Company 1 ? 10
Input Data for Quarter 4  - Company 2 ? 8
Input Data for Quarter 4  - Company 3 ? 5
Input Data for Quarter 4  - Company 4 ? 6
Input Data for Quarter 4  - Company 5 ? 16
Input Data for Quarter 4  - Company 6 ? 22
```

The first graphical output looks like Fig. B.2. The figure indicates that each operating division experienced the best sales record in the third quarter and that company 6 consistently outperformed the rest over the last four

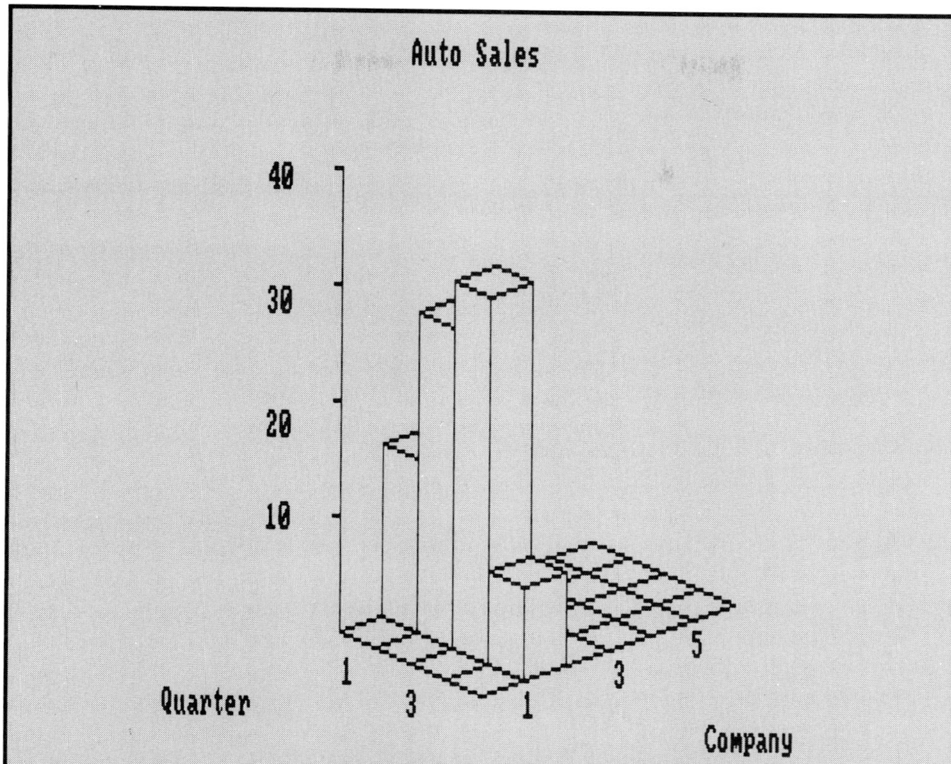

FIGURE B.4 Sales performance of company 2 over the last four quarters

quarters. We can obtain a sectional view of the histogram by specifying the portion of the data we want to look at. In doing so, we respond to prompts as follows:

```
DETAIL PICTURE (YES=1: NO=2) --->? 1
ENTER FIRST AND LAST VALUE OF X-AXIS--->? 2,2
ENTER FIRST AND LAST VALUE OF Y-AXIS--->? 1,6
```

With the parameters above, we obtain Fig. B.3 giving the sales performance of each division during the second quarter. This sectional view provides management with a comparative analysis of each divisions' performance. Figure B.4 is obtained by specifying the parameters as follows:

```
DETAIL PICTURE (YES=1: NO=2) --->? 1
ENTER FIRST AND LAST VALUE OF X-AXIS--->? 1,4
ENTER FIRST AND LAST VALUE OF Y-AXIS--->? 2,2
```

Figure B.4 shows the sales performance of company 2 over the quarters. By varying the input parameters we can obtain a variety of other sectional views of the histogram.

```
100 ' 3-DIMENSIONAL HISTOGRAM ON IBM PC (DOS 2.00 VERSION)
110 DIM SA(10,12)
120 KEY OFF: SCREEN 2  : CLS
130 ' ----- Plot  Parameters -------
140 XX1=22:  XX2=26:  YY=-4: MX=0:
150 XPO=310: YPO=169: ZPO=0: ICHECK=0
160 ICHECK=1
170 ' ----- Titles      -------
180 INPUT "* TITLE OF HISTOGRAM (MAX 10 CHAR)--->";TITLE$
190 INPUT "* NAME  OF X-AXIS    (MAX  5 CHAR)--->";XNAME$
200 INPUT "* NAME  OF Y-AXIS    (MAX  5 CHAR)--->";YNAME$
210 INPUT "* THE NUMBER OF ITEMS OF X-AXIS (MAX: 10) --->";XM
220 INPUT "* THE NUMBER OF ITEMS OF Y-AXIS (MAX: 12) --->";YM
230 PRINT
240 IF XM>10 OR YM>12 THEN END
250 XB=1: YB=1: XA=XM: YA=YM
260 GOSUB 340
270 GOSUB 460
280 GOSUB 650
290 GOSUB 810
300 GOSUB 1160
310 IF ICHECK=0 THEN 320 ELSE GOTO 270
320 END
330 '------- Input Data ------------------
340 FOR I=1 TO XM
350      FOR J=1 TO YM
360      PRINT TAB(10) " Input Data for "XNAME$;
370      PRINT I " - " YNAME$;
380      PRINT J;
390      INPUT SA(I,J)
400      IF MX<SA(I,J) THEN MX=SA(I,J)
410      NEXT J : PRINT
420 NEXT I
430 IF MX=0 THEN PRINT "* INFORMATION MESSAGE *" ELSE RETURN
440 PRINT "MAX VALUE OF YOUR DATA IS ZERO."
450 PRINT "NO PICTURE IS DISPLAYED.": END
460 ' --------- Draw the Base Board -----------
470 CLS
480 FOR J=1 TO 2
490   Y1%=YPO: X1%=XPO
500   IF J=1 THEN Y2%=YPO+YY*YM  ELSE Y2%=YPO+YY*XM
510   IF J=1 THEN X2%=XPO+XX2*YM ELSE X2%=XPO-XX1*XM
520   LINE (X1%,Y1%)-(X2%,Y2%)
530   IF J=1 THEN FOR I=1 TO 1: A=XM: B=1: C=-1: NEXT I
              ELSE FOR I=1 TO 1: A=1:  B=YM:C=1:  NEXT I
540      FOR I=A TO B STEP C
550      IF J=1 THEN X1%=X1%-XX1          ELSE X1%=X1%+XX2
560      IF J=1 THEN X2%=X2%-XX1          ELSE X2%=X2%+XX2
570      Y1%=Y1%+YY: Y2%=Y2%+YY
580      LINE (X1%,Y1%)-(X2%,Y2%)
590      L1%=X1%/8  : L2%=Y1%/8+1.5
600      LOCATE L2%,L1%
610      IF FIX(I/2)<>I/2 THEN PRINT I
620      NEXT I
630 NEXT J
640 RETURN
650 '-------------- Print Titles and Scale Z-axis ---------
530 LOCATE 1,34: PRINT TITLE$
660 LOCATE 1,34: PRINT TITLE$
670 LOCATE 22,15: PRINT XNAME$
680 LOCATE 23,57: PRINT YNAME$
690 IF ICHECK=1 THEN ZPO=Y2%-10
700 Z1=5: Z2=ZPO/4: MZ=MX/4
710 X1%=X2%-XX2*YM: Y1%=Y2%-YY*YM
720 LINE (X1%,Y1%)-(X1%,Y1%-ZPO)
730 FOR I=1 TO 4
740 Y1%=Y1%-Z2
750 LINE (X1%,Y1%)-(X1%-Z1,Y1%)
```

PROGRAM B.1 Program to Plot a 3-D Histogram

```
760 LOCATE Y1%/8+1,(X1%-Z1)/8-5
770 PRINT MZ*I
780 NEXT I
790 RETURN
800 ' ------------ Compute the scales of 3-D Bar -------------
810 A2%=X2%      : B2%=Y2%
820 FOR I=YM TO 1 STEP -1
830 A2%=A2%-XX2 : B2%=B2%-YY
840 X3%=A2%      : Y3%=B2%
850 FOR J=1 TO XM
860 X2%=X3%      : Y2%=Y3%
870 X3%=X2%+XX1 : Y3%=Y2%-YY
880 X4%=X3%+XX2 : Y4%=Y2%
890 X1%=X4%-XX1 : Y1%=Y2%+YY
900 IF SA(J,I)=0 THEN GOTO 950
910 IF I>YA OR I<YB THEN GOTO 950
920 IF J>XA OR J<XB THEN GOTO 950
930 Z%=(SA(J,I)/MX)*ZPO
940 GOSUB 980
950 NEXT J
960 NEXT I
970 RETURN
980 ' --------- Plot the 3-D Bar ---------
990 FOR K=X2% TO X4%
1000 IF K<=X1% THEN K1%=(K-X2%)*YY/XX2  ELSE K1%=(X4%-K)*YY/XX1
1010 LINE (K,Y2%-Z%)-(K,Y2%-Z%+K1%),0
1020 NEXT K
1030 LINE (X2%,Y2%)-(X4%,Y4%-Z%),0,BF
1040 LINE (X3%,Y3%)-(X3%,Y3%+YY+YY),0
1050 LINE (X2%,Y2%)-(X3%,Y3%)
1060 LINE -(X4%,Y4%)
1070 LINE -(X4%,Y4%-Z%)
1080 LINE -(X1%,Y1%-Z%)
1090 LINE -(X2%,Y2%-Z%)
1100 LINE -(X3%,Y3%-Z%)
1110 LINE -(X4%,Y4%-Z%)
1120 LINE (X2%,Y2%)-(X2%,Y2%-Z%)
1130 LINE (X3%,Y3%)-(X3%,Y3%-Z%)
1140 RETURN
1150 ' -------- Draw a Portion of the Picture ---------
1160 LOCATE 24
1170 INPUT "PRESS RETURN TO CONTINUE";Y$
1180 CLS
1190 INPUT "DETAIL PICTURE (YES=1: NO=2) --->";Y
1200 IF Y=1 THEN ICHECK=ICHECK+1 ELSE ICHECK=0
1210 IF ICHECK=0 THEN RETURN
1220 PRINT: INPUT "ENTER FIRST AND LAST VALUE OF X-AXIS--->";XB,XA
1230 PRINT: INPUT "ENTER FIRST AND LAST VALUE OF Y-AXIS--->";YB,YA
1240 RETURN
```

PROGRAM B.1 (continued)

B.2 PROGRAM TO PLOT 3-D STACKED BAR CHARTS

We can plot two or more sets of data within one chart in order to compare relationships between variables, such as sales of products in relation to month. Stacked bar charts can be effective for presenting the multiple relationships. Such charts can take a variety of forms; we will demonstrate a typical form with a 3-D look.

Program B.2 will plot up to three data files in a chart. To demonstrate the use of program B.2, we will consider the data summarized in Table B.2. These data represent the auto sales of three different models over the last 12 months for a typical auto dealership. We want to plot the sales trends of all three

TABLE B.2 Auto sales of three different models in 1985 (unit = 100)

Model	Month											
	Jan	Feb	Mar	Apr	May	June	July	Aug	Sept	Oct	Nov	Dec
Honda	10	12	15	18	20	26	30	24	16	8	6	5
Datsun	6	12	13	15	18	17	20	23	18	15	13	10
Chevy	13	22	25	28	30	33	37	40	38	32	23	18

models on the same chart. When we execute program B.2 and respond to the input queries, we see the following screen output:

```
TITLE OF BAR CHART (MAX 60 CHAR)--->? Auto Sales by Modesl in 1985 (unit = 100)

NO. OF MONTHS (MAX : 12)--->? 12

NO. OF DATA FILES TO PLOT (MAX :  3)--->? 3

FILE NO. 1  - FILE  NAME (MAX : 10)--->? Honda
FILE NO. 2  - FILE  NAME (MAX : 10)--->? Datsun
FILE NO. 3  - FILE  NAME (MAX : 10)--->? Chevy
Input Data for Honda in Month 1 ? 10
Input Data for Datsun in Month 1 ? 6
Input Data for Chevy in Month 1 ? 13

Input Data for Honda in Month 2 ? 12
Input Data for Datsun in Month 2 ? 12
Input Data for Chevy in Month 2 ? 22

Input Data for Honda in Month 3 ? 15
Input Data for Datsun in Month 3 ? 13
Input Data for Chevy in Month 3 ? 25

Input Data for Honda in Month 4 ? 18
Input Data for Datsun in Month 4 ? 15
Input Data for Chevy in Month 4 ? 28

Input Data for Honda in Month 5 ? 20
Input Data for Datsun in Month 5 ? 18
Input Data for Chevy in Month 5 ? 30

Input Data for Honda in Month 6 ? 26
Input Data for Datsun in Month 6 ? 17
Input Data for Chevy in Month 6 ? 33

Input Data for Honda in Month 7 ? 30
Input Data for Datsun in Month 7 ? 20
Input Data for Chevy in Month 7 ? 37

Input Data for Honda in Month 8 ? 24
Input Data for Datsun in Month 8 ? 23
Input Data for Chevy in Month 8 ? 40

Input Data for Honda in Month 9 ? 16
Input Data for Datsun in Month 9 ? 18
Input Data for Chevy in Month 9 ? 38

Input Data for Honda in Month 10 ? 8
Input Data for Datsun in Month 10 ? 15
Input Data for Chevy in Month 10 ? 32

Input Data for Honda in Month 11 ? 6
Input Data for Datsun in Month 11 ? 13
Input Data for Chevy in Month 11 ? 23

Input Data for Honda in Month 12 ? 5
Input Data for Datsun in Month 12 ? 10
Input Data for Chevy in Month 12 ? 18
```

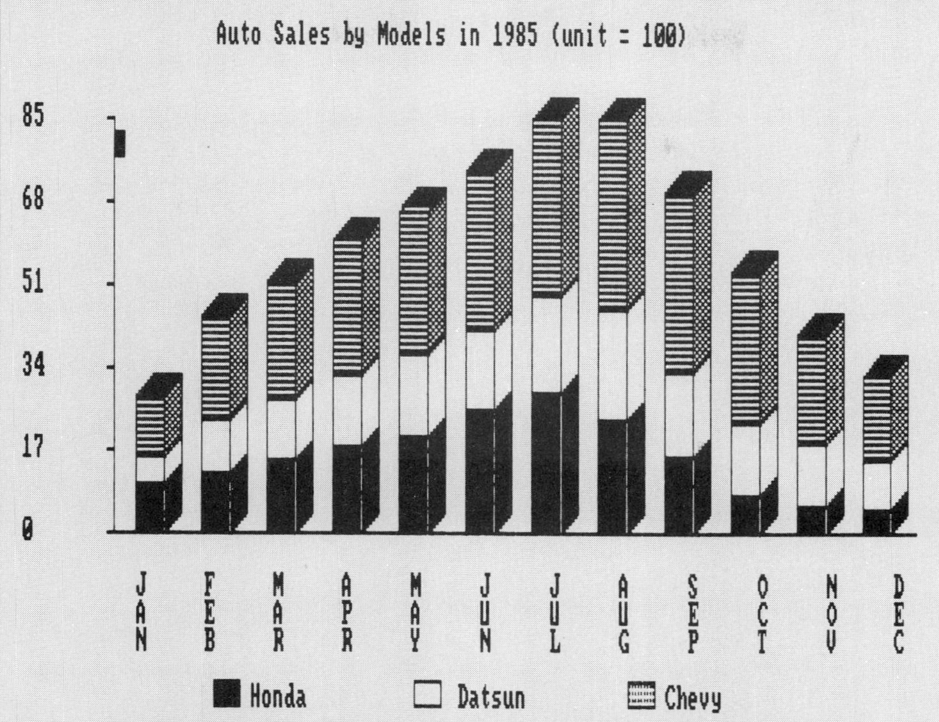

FIGURE B.5 Auto sales by models in 1985 (unit = 100)

With the input data in Table B.2, we obtain Fig. B.5. The figure clearly shows how one data group is differentiated from another by a combination of color and fill patterns. The graph dramatically shows the performance of each model. The 3-D effect gives the facts power. This is one of the most important elements in designing a business graphics package: the facts we need should present themselves.

```
100 ' Program to Draw 3-D Bar Chart
110 KEY OFF: SCREEN 2: CLS
120 DIM SALE(12,3),MO$(3)
130 MO$(1)="J      F      M      A      M      J      J      A      S      O      N      D"

140 MO$(2)="A      E      A      P      A      U      U      U      E      C      O      E"

150 MO$(3)="N      B      R      R      Y      N      L      G      P      T      V      C"
```

PROGRAM B.2 Program to Plot 3-D Stacked Bar Charts

```
160 XX=80: YY=148
170 T0=0:  T=0
180 X1=20: X2=12: X3=14: XL=X1+X2+X3: Y2=X2/2
190 '----------- Titles ----------------
200 CLS
210 LOCATE 5
220 INPUT "TITLE OF BAR CHART (MAX 60 CHAR)--->";T$
230 PRINT: PRINT
240 INPUT "NO. OF MONTHS (MAX : 12)--->"; M
250 PRINT: PRINT
260 INPUT "NO. OF DATA FILES TO PLOT (MAX :  3)--->"; N
270 PRINT
280 FOR I=1 TO N
290       PRINT
300       PRINT "FILE NO.";I;
310       INPUT " - FILE  NAME (MAX : 10)--->";NA$(I)
320 NEXT I
330 ' --------- Input Data -------------
340 FOR I=1 TO M : PRINT
350       FOR J=1 TO N
360       PRINT "Input Data for "NA$(J);: PRINT " in Month"I;: INPUT SALE(I,J)
370       T0=T0+SALE(I,J)
380       NEXT J
390       IF T<T0 THEN T=T0
400       T0=0
410 NEXT I
420 GOSUB 450
430 GOSUB 790
440 END
450 ' --------------- Print Headings and Scales -------------
460 CLS
470 XA=40-LEN(T$)\2
480 LOCATE 1,XA: PRINT T$
490 LOCATE 21,13: PRINT MO$(1)
500 LOCATE 22,13: PRINT MO$(2)
510 LOCATE 23,13: PRINT MO$(3)
520 XA=XX+15+XL*12: YA=YY
530 XB=XX         : YB=28
540 LENGTH=YY-YB
550 LINE (XX,YY)-(XA,YA)
560 LINE (XX,YY)-(XB,YB)
570 YA=198: XA=150: YB=YA-7
580 FOR I=1 TO N
590       XB=XA+18
600       IF I=1 THEN LINE (XA,YA)-(XB,YB),,BF ELSE LINE (XA,YA)-(XB,YB),,B
610       LOCATE 25,XA\8+5: PRINT NA$(I);
620       XA=XA+8*LEN(NA$(I))+100
630 NEXT I
640 IF N=2 OR N=1 THEN GOTO 690
650 FOR I=1 TO 18 STEP 2: FOR J=1 TO 7 STEP 2
660       PSET(XB-I,YB+J)
670       NEXT J
680 NEXT I
690 T0=CINT(T/5): IF T0=0 THEN T0=1: T=T0*5
700 YA=19
710 FOR I=1 TO 6
720       LY=YA-(I-1)*3
730       LOCATE LY,2
740       PRINT T0*(I-1)
750       YB=YY-8*(I-1)*3
760       LINE (XX,YB)-STEP(-5,0)
770 NEXT I
780 RETURN
790 ' --------------- Draw 3-D Bars -----------------
800 FOR I=1 TO M
810       XA=XX+(I-1)*XL+15
820       YB=YY
830       LL=0
840       FOR J=1 TO N
850            IF SALE(I,J)=0 THEN GOTO 1040
860            YB=YB-LL
870            LL=SALE(I,J)*LENGTH/T
880            LINE (XA,YB)-STEP(0,-LL)
890            LINE -STEP(X1,0)
900            LINE -STEP(X2,-Y2)
910            LINE -STEP(0,LL)
```

PROGRAM B.2 (continued)

```
920          LINE -STEP(-X2,Y2)
930          LINE -STEP(-X1,0)
940          IF J=1 THEN PAINT STEP(2,-2)
950         IF J=1 THEN LINE (XA+X1,YB)-STEP(0,-LL),0  ELSE LINE (XA+X1,YB)
               -STEP(0,-LL)
960         IF J=3 THEN GOTO 970 ELSE GOTO 1040
970         IF J=3 THEN FOR K=1 TO X1: FOR KK=1 TO LL STEP 2
980             PSET(XA+K,YB-KK)
990             NEXT KK:        NEXT K
1000         IF J=3 THEN FOR K=1 TO X2: FOR KK=1 TO LL STEP 2
1010              YC=K/2
1020              PSET(XA+X1+K,YB-YC-KK)
1030              NEXT KK:        NEXT K
1040     NEXT J
1050     IF YB=YY AND LL=0 THEN GOTO 1100
1060     LINE (XA,YB)-STEP(0,-LL)
1070     LINE -STEP(X2,-Y2)
1080     LINE -STEP(X1,0)
1090     FOR K=1 TO X2\2: LINE (XA+K*2,YB-LL-K)-STEP(X1,0): NEXT K
1100 NEXT I
1110 RETURN
```

PROGRAM B.2 **Program to Plot 3-D Stacked Bar Charts**

Index

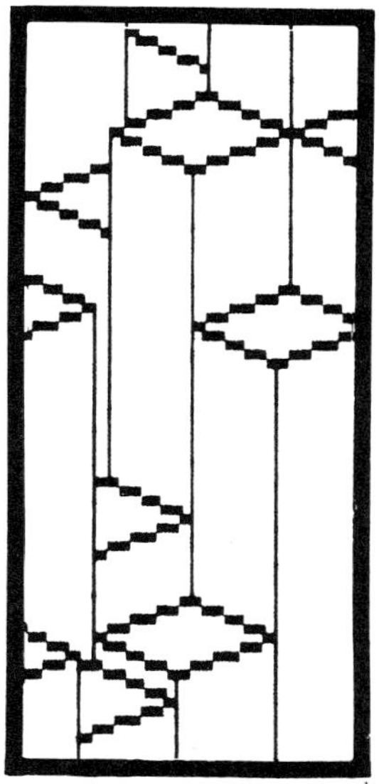

Index

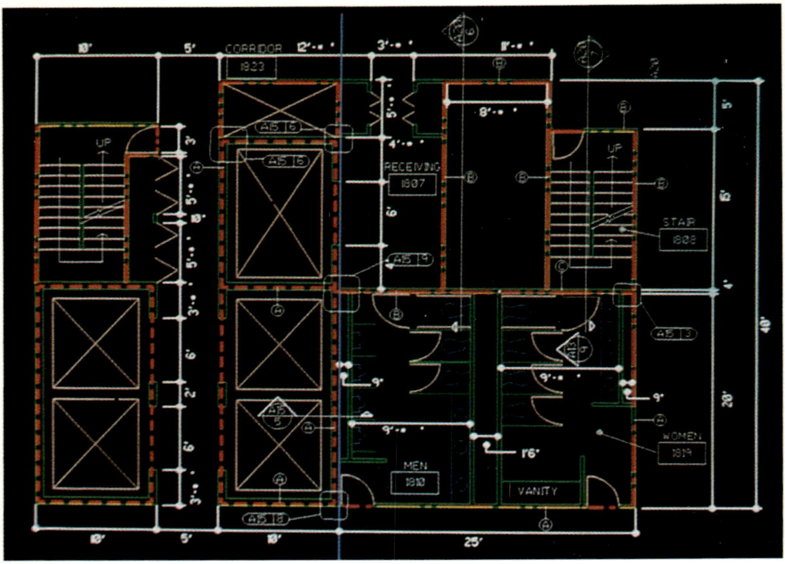

Architectural floor plan with notations, created on Intergraph Corporation computer graphics system.

Three-dimensional architectural model, created on Intergraph Corporation computer graphics system.